MW00474505

WITHOUT HISTORY

Illuminations: Cultural Formations of the Americas

John Beverley and Sara Castro-Klarén, Editors

WITHOUT HISTORY

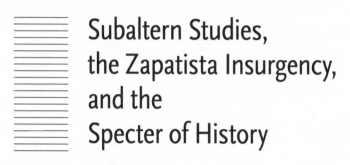

Subaltern Studies,
the Zapatista Insurgency,
and the
Specter of History

JOSÉ RABASA

UNIVERSITY OF PITTSBURGH PRESS

Published by the University of Pittsburgh Press, Pittsburgh, Pa., 15260
Copyright © 2010, University of Pittsburgh Press
All rights reserved
Manufactured in the United States of America
Printed on acid-free paper
10 9 8 7 6 5 4 3 2 1

Library of Congress Cataloging-in-Publication Data

Rabasa, José, 1948–
    Without history : subaltern studies, the Zapatista insurgency, and the specter of history / José
Rabasa.
        p.   cm.
    Includes bibliographical references and index.
    ISBN 978-0-8229-6065-2 (pbk. : alk. paper)
    1. Indians of Mexico—Historiography. 2. Historiography—Political aspects—Mexico.
3. Indians of Mexico—Study and teaching. 4. Ejército Zapatista de Liberación Nacional (Mexico)
5. Acteal Massacre, Acteal, Mexico, 1997—Personal narratives. 6. Acteal Massacre,
Acteal, Mexico, 1997—Historiography. 7. Chiapas (Mexico) —History—Peasant Uprising,
1994—Historiography. 8. Mexico—Ethnic relations—Historiography. 9. Mexico—Politics and
government—1988–2000—Historiography.   I. Title.
    F1219.3.H56R33 2010
    972.08'35—dc22   2010002370

For Magali

CONTENTS

List of Illustrations   *viii*

Acknowledgments   *ix*

1. Introduction   1
2. Pre-Columbian Pasts and Indian Presents in Mexican History   17
3. Of Zapatismo: Reflections on the Folkloric and the Impossible in a Subaltern Insurrection   37
4. Historical and Epistemological Limits in Subaltern Studies   62
5. Beyond Representation? The Impossibility of the Local (Notes on Subaltern Studies in Light of a Rebellion in Tepoztlán, Morelos)   74
6. Negri by Zapata: Constituent Power and the Limits of Autonomy   92
7. The Comparative Frame in Subaltern Studies   124
8. On the History of the History of Peoples *Without* History   138
9. Revolutionary Spiritualities in Chiapas Today: Immanent History and the Comparative Frame in Subaltern Studies   148
10. *Without* History? Apostasy as a Historical Category   172
11. In the Mesoamerican Archive: Speech, Script, and Time in Tezozomoc and Chimalpahin   205
12. On Documentary and Testimony: The Revisionists' History, the Politics of Truth, and the Remembrance of the Massacre at Acteal, Chiapas   230
13. Exception to the Political   251

Notes   *281*

References   *325*

Index   *345*

ILLUSTRATIONS

2.1. Tenochtitlan. The Codex Mendoza. Folio 1v   21

4.1. The Codex Telleriano-Remensis. Folio 46r   63

4.2. The Codex Telleriano-Remensis. Folio 49r   64

4.3. The Codex Telleriano-Remensis. Folio 12v   65

6.1. *Vida y sueños de la cañada Perla, comunidad de Taniperla, Chiapas*   92–93

9.1. The Map of Cholula. Relación geográfica de Cholula   150

9.2. Ancient Cholula. Historia Tolteca-Chichimeca. Folio 26v–27r   150

9.3. Three women from Las Abejas   167

10.1. The Codex of Tlatelolco   188–189

10.2. The Mural at Ixmiquilpan, Hidalgo   191

10.3. The Monument to Francisco Tenamaztle, Nochistlan, Zacatecas   195

10.4. Commemorative plaque, Nochistlan, Zacatecas   195

11.1. Portrait of Fernando Alvarado Tezozomoc   213

12.1. Faustina pointing. *Alonso's Dream*   243

12.2. Paramilitary. *Alonso's Dream*   243

12.3. Vicente anticipating the massacre. *A Massacre Foretold*   244

12.4. Antonio. *A Massacre Foretold*   246

13.1. "Detenciones al por mayor" by El Fisgón   253

ACKNOWLEDGMENTS

It is practically impossible to thank all those who have read, commented, and discussed with me the essays included in this book. Rather than risk forgetting individuals, I have chosen to thank the collectives I have worked with over the years. During the 1990s I benefited greatly from the stimulating debates among the members of the Latin American Subaltern Studies Group (LASSG). Several of the essays included here were first presented at conferences and seminars organized by LASSG. Some of these essays have previously been included in books edited by members of the collective.

LASSG disbanded around 2000, and since then, I have been fortunate to be part of the Subaltern and the Popular Workshop at the University of California at Santa Barbara. The group has included scholars working in a wide range of fields (anthropology, architecture, art history, cultural studies, English, film studies, history, and political science) and geographic areas (Africa, Ireland, Latin America, the Middle East, Oceania, and South Asia). This collective has provided supportive criticism that has led to joint publications. All of the group's gatherings have been held in Santa Barbara, with the exception of one year when the collective traveled to Cairo, Egypt. The meeting in Cairo included the additional input from Middle Eastern scholars who had attended the conference.

In addition to these two collectives, I would like to thank my students (graduate and undergraduates alike) at the University of Michigan, the University of California at Berkeley, and Harvard University, where I have tested my ideas and received invaluable feedback. I must also thank colleagues at these institutions who have engaged my work. This book would not be what it is without the editorial advice I have received from the periodicals and the published volumes in which many of these essays have previously appeared. I remain thankful to these publishers and journals for their permission to reprint my essays in this book. I acknowledge this permission in the notes that accompany each essay. I also want to thank Amy Smith Bell for her thorough editing of the final manuscript.

I would also like to thank curators and administrators at the Bodleian Library of the University of Oxford, the Bibliothèque Nationale de France, Biblioteca del Insitituto Nacional de Antropología e Historia, and the Nettie

Lee Benson Latin American Collection of the University of Texas Libraries for their guidance and the production of images.

Finally, Laurence Cuelenaere has been my strongest critic of the most recent essays included in this book.

1 ≡≡≡≡ Introduction

This book is a collection of essays I have written since the mid-1990s. I have decided to publish previously published pieces as they have appeared in different venues rather than updating them, aside from basic modifications in format and style. These essays share questions, theoretical approaches, and themes; in many ways, they converse with each other. They do not constitute a historical chronology; rather, they expand theoretical and thematic continuities across different temporalities. The pieces follow a chronological order, often reflecting the transformation, perhaps a refinement, of concepts both in my own work and in the literature I have engaged with over the years. My writings also reflect the impact of radical events since the mid-1900s on the (im)possibility of revolutionary thought—namely, the 1994 Zapatista uprising in Chiapas, the 9/11 attack on New York's World Trade Center towers and the ensuing wars (first against Afghanistan and then against Iraq), and the coming to power in Latin America of leftist governments of diverse convictions. As the subtitle of this book indicates, the essays herein are limited to a series of reflections on the meaning of subaltern studies, the significance of the Zapatista insurgency, and the specter of history.

Throughout the pieces the continuation of indigenous life after the Spanish invasion and the historical implications of insurgencies is a common concern. By this, I am referring to the ever-present possibility of breaking from the structures of power and the narratives that have inscribed (and continue to) indigenous life under a series of frames. Over the centuries these frames have included the history of salvation, the "benevolent" civilizing missions, the incorporation into the nation, the promises of development, and the iron-fisted law of the market. These narratives all take for granted a radical break between the pre-Columbian past and the Indian present. Although the criteria and tenor of the breaks differ in specific epochs, one may identify constants. Whereas the pre-Columbian past tends to be idealized as an object of nostalgia, the Indian present tends to be reduced to degraded manifestations of the ancient grandeur.

Viceroys, presidents, and dictators have posed for photographs and paintings next to monumental stones while impoverished Indians have made sense of the monumental past in ways that cannot be confined to nor dismissed by the discourses that missionaries, archaeologists, or Indian intellectuals have elaborated over the centuries. There is an antiquarian vocation as early as the first missionaries who, after burning the ancient records of the past, set out to reconstruct native life before the Spanish invasion. Indian intellectuals of the colonial period complicated these efforts by collecting the voices of the elders and continuing to practice Mesoamerican forms of recording and narrating the past. If in the colonial period the reconstruction of the past was motivated by religious and administrative concerns, in the republican period the study of the ancient civilizations played a central role in the creation of a national identity. Even when the destruction of the ancient world severed communities from the political structures of daily life, indigenous forms of life have endured centuries of systematic destruction. The legacy of conquest and colonization, however, includes the creation of privileged sectors (caciquisms) that have benefited from the exploitation of the Indians. Having said this, it is an imperative that we avoid projecting into Mesoamerican antiquity the concept of the state and class differentiation that characterize the capitalist regime of property. It is not a question of elaborating a rosy or, for that matter, a terrifying picture of ancient Mesoamerica in the manner of those who build the museums of the ancient grandeur. Rather, it is a matter of recognizing the continuum of Indian communalism. Nothing remains the same after the invasion, and yet modes of communalism and their corresponding life forms have survived to the present.

These essays share the conviction that the modern and the nonmodern, capitalism and communalism, are contemporaneous and retain discrete temporalities. I argue that indigenous communalism cannot be reduced to an all-embracing concept of temporal heterogeneity under capitalism and the diversity that multicultural states recognize. The contemporaneity of the modern and the nonmodern entails their independent existence. But then, what is the nature of the shared temporality of independent existences implicit in the contemporaneous? We may tentatively answer this question by defining a range of temporalities that go from the shared calendrical and sidereal time to the shared time of communication. Whereas the calendrical and the sidereal lack a concrete experiential ground (for example, at the time of this writing—June 19, 2009, 5:23 P.M.—both indigenous communities and the IMF coexist), verbal exchanges cannot but be coeval. The contemporaneity of the modern and the nonmodern enables us to conceive of modernity (that is, capital, the state, history) as just one temporality, even when it aspires to absorb all life. The concept of "contemporaneity" also complicates the tendency to confine the premodern to effects of the modern as if all human life on earth could be reduced to variations (alternative or not) of the modern. This definition of contemporaneity avoids essentializing the contemporaneous in terms of modernity—that is, of a history of cosmopolitanism that arguably originates in the West but has attained a global status.

There is also a common thread throughout these essays that questions the assumption that the narratives of salvation, civilization, national formation, development, and the market exhaust all possible forms of existence. Whether under the rule of capital, the state, or history, the prevailing story is that there is no outside to these structures. If this judgment is perhaps true of the scholars who address capital, the state, and history, it remains questionable that all human life is defined and circumscribed by these institutions. I argue that capital, the state, and history can be observed, worked on, manipulated, and avoided from perspectives that cannot be simply translated into Western discourses of the sort we scholars with different degrees of conviction produce in our association with academic institutions, the state, or the now ubiquitous NGOs. As the title of this book implies, there is a "without history" that bears a corresponding "without state." If in the long history of European expansionism the attribution of "without" signified the denial of state and history to the worlds that Europeans encountered, one may fruitfully turn the absence into a productive exteriority, into a practice for containing the teleology implicit in histories of salvation, civilizing missions, national formations, development, and market economy. One of the virtues of subaltern studies—as was first conceptualized by Indian scholars working under the leadership of Ranajit Guha in the early 1980s—consists of the conceptualization of an ethos that attends to the voices, the daily practices, the forms of memory, and the strategies of mobilization that subalterns have devised to keep colonial and nationalist modes of (epistemological, political, and economic) domination at bay.

Subaltern Studies

Exchanges between scholars in Latin American literary and cultural studies and members of the South Asian Subaltern Studies Group date back to the early 1980s. However, it was not until 1990, in the aftermath of the fall of the Berlin wall and the loss of the elections by the Sandinistas in Nicaragua, that the reflection on subaltern studies led to the creation of a collective known as the Latin American Subaltern Studies Group (LASSG). The motivation for the creation of this group was to find ways of responding to what at that time seemed like the unsurpassable hegemony of neoliberal policies and the demise of the left, most particularly of revolutionary politics.[1] This is not the place to assess the positive impact the group had on the field of Latin American literary and cultural studies; nor is it the appropriate venue to respond to the strong criticisms LASSG received for what some in the United States and Latin America have characterized as an importation of theories that are not applicable to Latin America. I mention the group because the majority of the essays in this book were written in conversation with many members of LASSG and in exchanges with scholars interested in subaltern studies working on South Asia, the Middle East, and Ireland.

In assessing the conversations scholars of and in Latin America have had with their counterparts in India, I ought to mention the transformation subaltern studies has undergone in the South Asian context since the South Asian Subaltern Studies Group collective was founded in 1982. Indian scholars date their project in terms of "early" and "later" subaltern studies. This is not central to the essays in this volume, however, and interested readers will find these transformations perhaps nowhere more clearly outlined than in historian Dipesh Chakrabarty's work.[2] Reading the Indian subalternists, I have chosen to ignore this periodization that defines a break with their earlier interest in the study of insurrections and the kinds of stories we may tell about them. In fact, the essays in this book challenge the generalities some of the Indian scholars have assumed about the global historical transformations that underlie their change of emphasis from the study of subaltern insurgencies and subaltern consciousness in Guha's classic text, *Elementary Aspects of Peasant Insurgency in Colonial India*, to the study of the state and subaltern representation in more recent work.

The essay "Can the Subaltern Speak?" by the postcolonial theorist Gayatri Chakravorty Spivak is perhaps the earliest critique of the historiography of insurgency and subaltern consciousness. Spivak's question and answer in the negative have not been exempted of criticism. Even when her essay is generally recognized for its rigorous discussion of the assumptions that subalterns can interact with the state without learning the languages of the state or requiring the mediation of intellectuals, her intervention has often been characterized as imperialistic in spirit. In my essays I contend that Spivak's question is pertinent only when the subaltern is expected to interface with the state. However, her question loses its pertinence in situations in which subalterns choose to remain *outside* the state and history (that is, all the discourses that legitimate the former) either by creating autonomous regions or by reminding the states that the strategies and knowledges that enable mobilizations cannot be comprehended (neither understood nor contained) by the state regardless of how multicultural its aspirations may be.

The question of insurgencies remains central throughout my essays because of specific events in Latin America—namely, the emergence of Ejercito Zapatista de Liberación Nacional (the EZLN, or the Zapatista Army of National Liberation) in 1994, the rebellion of the Asamblea Popular de los Pueblos de Oaxaca (APPO) in 2006, and the indigenous mobilizations in Bolivia that supported the Movimiento al Socialismo (MAS) leading to the 2005 electoral triumph of Evo Morales and Álvaro García Linera in Bolivia. Whereas the Zapatista autonomous regions in Chiapas and the insurgency of the APPO (which has been likened to the 1871 Paris Commune) propose alternative forms of government to the state, the Morales/García Linera's regime constitutes a paradigmatic case for considering the tenuous relationship between a self-declared revolutionary state and indigenous popular mobilizations.

The promise of subaltern studies resides in the possibility of interrupting narratives that end up in single histories. The denial of the existence of an *outside* history, capital, and the state would constitute one such instance of single history regardless of the claims of nonteleology or the proposal of multiple understandings history or, for that matter, the insistence on temporal heterogeneity. Single history is also implied in claims of an all-pervasive modernity of the West on a global scale. Little is to be gained from conceptions of alternative modernities that rescue societies from the dustbin of the premodern—that is, of all those forms of life bound to disappear with the coming into being of modernity. If the "premodern" carries a built-in teleology in the "pre-" that situates forms of life as "not-yet modern," the concept "nonmodern" enables us to conceive of "elsewheres" not delimited in their definition to propositions about what is modern that one inevitably finds in the prefix "pre-" or in the negation "anti-."[3] The nonmodern should be considered as an "elsewhere" unbound by modern conceptions of history that privilege the institutions, historical events, and philosophical concepts that have defined the West. Needless to say, one need not be a "European" to reproduce the privileges of modernity.

Subaltern studies enables us to identify the comparativism—hence, the teleology—implicit in periodizations that claim structural universal effects. In choosing narratives of modernity that privilege 1492, 1789, or the emergence of second-degree observers à la Niklas Luhmann, we end up privileging specific principles of exclusion. By assuming that events entail global structures, periodizations confine evolving worlds to comparisons that erase the particularity of histories that claim a full realization of humanity. Those who make of the modern the only existing world (an undeniable fact when defined as a shared temporality that makes all societies contemporary) tend to ignore how modern thought defines "the correct" and "the erroneous" in terms of more or less advanced forms of life. Modernity, in its march toward progress, is through and through comparativist, consequently teleological in its conceptualization of the not-so-modern. Given that subalternity is a relational concept, there is the danger of being locked into a comparativist frame that could lead to the reiteration of the same violence we expose in practicing subaltern studies.

The Zapatista Insurgency

There is perhaps no legal document that better illustrates the connection between the law and private property than the Leyes Revolucionarias (revolutionary laws) that the EZLN published on December 1, 1993, in the *Despertar Mexicano*, the official information organ of the EZLN. These revolutionary laws should be read in the context of the state of exception the EZLN declares on the basis of Article 39 of the Mexican Constitution. This article establishes that sovereignty resides in the people, who have the right to alter and modify their form of government. The revolutionary laws—insofar as they define the rules for the expropriation of private property, the appropriation of the means of production, and the collective nature of the emergent regime of property— suggest that the revolutionary process would entail a *withering* of the law in the destruction of the state (*el estado*). The document makes no mention of the Leninist concept of "the withering of the state" or, for that matter, of Evgeny Pashukanis's seminal study *The General Theory of Law and Marxism*, which calls for "the withering of the law." However, the internal logic in their proposed regulation of property suggests that the revolutionary laws would govern the transition to a regime where capitalist forms of private property no longer exist. The section on the Ley Agraria Revolucionaria (agrarian law) also suggests that indigenous communalism provides a model for the new society to emerge.

If these laws and the Declaración de la Selva Lacandona, which declared war on the Mexican state in 1993 but was not published until January 2, 1994, do not define in explicit terms the indigenous nature of the insurgency, the first words in the Declaración indicate that the subject of the declaration is indigenous: "Somos producto de 500 años de lucha" [We are the product of five hundred years of struggle]. In the course of the first months of struggle, the EZLN published a series of documents that redefined the struggle from the initial declaration of war and the call to march on Mexico City to a political practice that has become the signature of the Zapatistas, perhaps not better expressed than in the title of John Holloway's *Change the World without Taking Power*. However, we ought to resist the temptation of writing a history of Zapatismo based on different articulations of their calls for *Revolución* (the capital "R" here replicates the Zapatista documents) rather than tactical maneuvers in the long-term strategy for a struggle against neoliberalism on both national and international contexts. As such, rather than historicizing these sources, we ought to read the corpus of declarations, communiqués, and political analyses as contributions to the dismantling of capitalist regimes of private property.

For the ultimate irony, drawing a history of the EZLN would reinforce the counterinsurgent discourses that confine the insurgency to the dustbin of history, thereby denying Zapatismo of all relevance to the present. Take, for instance, how in the context of the recent call for an *encuentro americano contra la impunidad* (American encounter against impunity), a reporter writing on the soap opera *Mi pecado*, located in San Cristobal de las Casas, confines the Zapatista uprising to history: "El levantamiento armado del EZLN en esta región ya es sólo parte de la historia, una leyenda, y los habitantes de esta hermosa población chiapaneca hoy, mejor se sustraen a la grabación de la telenovela *Mi pecado*, producción de Juan Osorio, que acordarse del subcomandante Marcos" [The armed uprising of the EZLN in this region is just part of history, a legend, and the inhabitants of this beautiful city today would rather withdraw from the filming of the soap opera *Mi pecado*, produced by Juan Osorio, than remember Subcomandante Marcos].[4] The reporter confines all talk about the Zapatistas to legend, to ineffectual remnants of a past that has been archived as history. One may nevertheless recognize in this confinement to history the sense that the impact of the Zapatistas has been greatly undermined. The *encuentro americano contra la impunidad* aspires to create a tribunal for the judging of cases of human rights abuse that have not found a hearing in national and international courts. According to the journalist Hermann Belinghuassen, several of the activists participating in the *encuentro*, including the director of the Centro de Derecho Humanos Fray Bartolomé de las Casas (CDHFBC), have been harassed by the police.

The conveners of the *encuentro* cite Article 17 of the Mexican Constitution, which guarantees the right to the expeditious establishment of a tribunal to impart justice for its legitimacy, to validate the creation of an extraordinary tribunal. Thus the appeal to Article 17 for the establishment of an extraordinary tribunal resonates with the invocation of Article 39, which the Zapatistas had drawn from to justify their insurrection in the declaration of January 2, 1994. Both the declaration of war and the call for an extraordinary tribunal have therefore drawn their legitimacy from human rights discourse.

The conveners of the *encuentro* are betting on what anthropologist Paul Rabinow has diagnosed as follows: "Although there are governments who contest and combat 'rights talk,' and the groups who articulate it, on a variety of grounds, including national sovereignty and traditional culture, it is plausible to argue that currently no secular counterdiscourse exists that has anything like the legitimacy, power, and potential for successful expansion that the human rights discourse does."[5] Because of rampant abuse and impunity, Mexico belongs to those states that combat and contest "rights talk." It is as if the Mexican government, and by extension international organizations, were immune to the forces of human rights discourse. The force of the Zapatista "rights talk" does not reside in the application of Articles 39 and 17, but in the call for the destruction of capitalism and the state that looks after the interest of the dominant classes. Whereas the appeal to Article 39 and the Ley Revolucionaria cannot be limited to the mere denunciation of abuse (it offers the rationale for creating a new form of government), the appeal to Article 17 and the creation of an extraordinary tribunal cannot be limited to anomalous Mexico (it offers the platform for a continental mobilization against impunity).

Even when the Zapatistas sought to modify the Mexican constitution in 2001, their proposal to transform Article 4, which defined individual rights to access culture, carried the paradox that the proposed modification of the constitution established the autonomy of indigenous communities and the noninterference of the state in the practice of their normative systems. The modification of the Mexican constitution would lay the ground for further changes. In appealing for the creation of a constituent assembly in the *Sexta Declaración de la Selva Lacandona*, the Zapatistas would define a juridical model that would regulate (not unlike the Ley Revolucionaria) the destruction of the capitalist regime of property: the withering of the state and the law that protects the interests of capital.[6]

To my mind, the Zapatista insurrection is most distinct in the Indian character of their call for *Revolución*. The indigenous spirit of the uprising became increasingly more explicitly defined in the months that followed the uprising on January 1, 1994. The novelty of the Zapatistas became manifest in their systematic appeal and respect for indigenous forms of life. Indigeneity not only pertains to language, dress, and mythology; it also pertains to forms of social organization, communal democratic practices grounded in consensual politics, and techniques of mobilization. At the risk of essentializing indigeneity, I refer to these life forms as millennial practices with deep roots in Mesoamerican antiquity. But we should not be afraid of essentialism as long as we stay away from defining permanent unalterable traits. We may understand Indian essentialism as a strategic move that warns us against conceptualizations of indigenous societies that for the past five hundred years have argued (and planned) their inevitable demise. The millennial communalism of indigenous societies is not manifest in the fixity of museum pieces but in the ever-recurrent innovation that has surprised multiple regimes of power over the centuries.

This is the spirit of the opening statement in the *Declaración*. Given the systematic undermining and call for the destruction of Indian societies (from the conquest to the manipulations of Indians by leftist revolutionary movements in the twentieth century—we hope this no longer occurs), one cannot exaggerate the need for this reminder. Understood as such, the indigenous nature of the Zapatista rebellion has contributed to the redefinition of the *duration* of insurgency. To Marx's assessment of the first workers' government in the Paris Commune ("Working men's Paris, with its Commune, will be for ever [*sic*] celebrated as the glorious harbinger of a new society"), we must add the assessment that the autonomous governments of indigenous peoples of Chiapas have defined a new mode of conducting revolution that, if grounded in a millennial nonmodern memory of insurgency, now forms part of the *duration* of insurgency that expands the accumulated experience of modern workers.[7] The modern and the nonmodern may now coexist without incurring contradiction on a global scale. Beyond the stories we may tell about the Paris Commune and the Zapatista autonomous regions, their promise remains deposited in the immanent temporality of future revolutionary movements.

The Specter of History

The question of the specter of history assumes two modalities: one pertains to repetition, the other pertains to immanence. Whereas the first modality exposes the work of history itself as haunting the present, the second modality carries the promise of liberation in the "life history" of individuals and communities that history cannot access or delimit. The first binds the past to the reasons of the state, the second opens the possibility of eluding the state. The first modality betrays the obligation to historicize, which in turn privileges a particular historical consciousness that enables taking a distance by means of periodization. Even while privileging a particular historical consciousness, the call to historicize presupposes universal applicability and assumes the existence of global structural transformations. In our time, modernity constitutes a specter of history by foreclosing the possibility of nonmodern spaces that even when interacting with capital, may remain untouched by capital, perhaps offering a glimpse of life after capital. Thus the specter of history consists of the iron-fisted logic of historical necessity but also of the anecdotic trivialization of historical contingency. The specter also conveys the sense that only history has access to the truths of the past, which in turn foreshadow the perils of repetition.

The antidote to history's warning against repetition is the eternal recurrence of the immanent possibility of liberation that lies deeply sedimented in the life histories of individuals and communities. Repetition as such manifests the *now* of insurrection, which, in passing, we ought to differentiate from the impatient call for change in the cry for "now" in responding to the question, "When do we want it?" The "now" of insurgency belongs to the category of the eternal, of the flight that severs all ties with both historical contingency and necessity. We may also trace the work of immanence in the continuities of indigenous life that conquest and colonization never managed to access. For if the conquest managed to destroy the governing structures of the ancient world, there is a continuity of communal life that cannot be reduced to the structures of power that we may identify with the hierarchical social organization of the "Aztec" or the "Inca" empires. I would add quotation marks to "empire" as well, but for the brevity of argument I will let this category stand as universally applicable. I would just add that empire talk about social structures in the Americas often carries the same logic of destruction that informed Spanish rationalizations of conquest based on the obligation to destroy the tyranny of native rulers. If we may argue that indigenous communalism may remain untouched by capital, we may equally argue that the social structures of the ancient "empires" did not alter what we may call along with Marx archaic forms of communalism. Indeed, after citing the American anthropologists so much admired by Friedrich Engels in *The Origin of the Family, Private Property, and the State*, Marx added: "We must not let ourselves to be alarmed at the word 'archaic.'"[8]

Beyond addressing recent developments in subaltern studies, the essays in this collection return to Antonio Gramsci, who first coined the concept of the subaltern, as well as to Marx and Lenin. By engaging these theoreticians as contemporaneous, this book seeks to expose the hubris of recent work claiming original genealogies of decolonization that purportedly have overridden the significance of Marx, Lenin, and Gramsci by confining their work to modalities of Eurocentrism—as if one can avoid Eurocentrism by pulling oneself up from the bootstraps. By considering their theoretical contributions as contemporaneous—that is, by refusing to historicize them—we may situate debates in subaltern studies in terms that are often assumed but that remain undertheorized. Questions pertaining to subaltern speech, decolonization, historicism, and the state (indeed, to capital) have a body of literature we cannot afford to ignore. This is not because of the adage "history repeats itself" but rather because of the immanence of repetition that brings forth the ever present (im)possibility of total liberation from capital. Gramsci offers a reflection on counterhegemonic blocks that remains haunted by the vanguardism Lenin put forth in *What Is to Be Done?* to expose the limits of spontaneity and voluntarisms—immanent categories par excellence.

If Gramsci addresses Lenin's vanguardism, we may profitably read Lenin's concepts of the "withering of the state" in *The State and Revolution*, where spontaneity and voluntarism are not readily dismissed. We must also read Lenin's essay "Leftwing Childishness and Petty-Bourgeois Mentality," which draws the limits of "state capitalism" and "dual power," even if just to argue with him. His reflections on the "withering of the state," and I would add the "withering of history," build on Marx's account of the 1871 Paris Commune where he posed the questions: "Must the old state machine be *smashed*? And *what* should be placed in its place?"[9] The communalism that Marx traces in the Paris Commune finds a complementary discussion in Marx's letter to Vera Zasulich on the Russian commune and the concept of the archaic. For Marx and Lenin the experience of the Paris Commune forms part of the *duration* of insurgency in modern societies, but their consideration of Russian communalism and the Soviets can be profitably expanded with the long *duration* of indigenous communalism and insurgency in the Americas. Again, we profitably consider these (modern and indigenous) *durations* as contemporaneous without being forced to reduce one to the other.

The possibility of a state that abolishes itself would appear haunted by the history of capital and the state, and the vicissitudes (indeed, the tragic ends) of those who in promoting the withering of the state during the Russian Revolution were subjected to the trials of the Stalinist purges. In addressing the debates surrounding the Russian Revolution and key texts by Marx, Lenin, and Gramsci, the essays in this book approach their writings as contemporaneous rather than as historically specific. The questions pertaining to insurgency, the commune, the withering of the state, state capitalism, and counterhegemonic blocks remain vital today. Moreover, I argue that these Marxist classics are significant only from a perspective that makes them contemporaneous—hence, that does not confine them to the truths we may ascribe to them by historically circumscribing their significance to the past, which one cannot but construe from the present.

Reading these great thinkers from the "past" should not be reduced to the commonplace that one cannot afford to ignore history if one wants to avoid its repetition. The limits of the injunction on the obligation to read history does not reside in *repetition*, but rather on the trivialization of the past one incurs in historicizing. In critiquing the writings of Lenin or Gramsci, I treat them not as dated expressions that we would have surpassed (pure neoliberal historicism), but as texts that we must engage in imagining our present. The past is not something that happened a long time ago but a presence that *faces* us in its immediacy. Nor should we confine the past to human experience; instead, we must expand the meaning of the past to include the possibility that the universe in its totality is made of objects with life histories, with intentionality that not only exceeds human consciousness but also shapes human consciousness. If mediation and representation may be unavoidable (although posing the conditional "may" already entails the [im]possibility of avoiding mediation and representation) in the experience of the past, history might not be the most desirable mode of inscribing it.

History is often characterized as the study of a temporal other existing in the past, but what then if the past is the only lived temporality we truly experience, even if under the paradoxical *now*? Would this imply that one never quite arrives in good faith at the point in which the past is turned into an object of study, indeed naturalized for our collecting, paradoxically by assuming a position *without* history? Periodization, the moral injunction—perhaps nowhere more aptly captured than in literary critic Frederic Jameson's dictum "we cannot not periodize"—turns into an artifice that should enable us to identify multiple contemporary life histories that in coexisting act on each other without ever finding a resolution in a single history.[10] The contemporaneity between the communes and capitalist production may also be traced in the Andean and Mesoamerican contexts where we find the ancient, the colonial, and the modern coexisting in the interface of the nonmodern and the modern. A recurrent critical gesture in these essays consists in tracing the specters of the pasts in immanent life histories of the present. One may also understand immanence in terms of the contemporaneity of multiple pasts that may be likened to geological formations where different temporal strata lay side by side in simultaneous horizontal layers with singular life histories.[11]

The essays in this collection are exclusively concerned with colonial texts as well as others in which the ancient, the colonial, and the modern coexist. I have already touched on the layers of the past that we may liken to geological strata coexisting in a given moment. The essays that center on colonial texts further illustrate the specter of history in both the ways in which history homogenizes the past (even when claiming temporal heterogeneity) and the ways in which the life histories of communities remain untouched by the colonial discourses that seek to confine their pertinence to the colonial archives. I examine colonial texts that offer examples of how ethnographic inquests reconstructed Mesoamerican antiquity to survey daily life (creating a memory for future generations of Indians), of how accounts of rebellions formulated counterinsurgent strategies (recording subaltern voices and strategies of mobilization), of how indigenous pictorial depictions of colonial institutions manifest instances of returns of the gaze (revealing an *elsewhere* from which Indians observe the missionary observer), and of how sixteenth-century Nahua historians faced the task of incorporating ancient Mesoamerica into the history of salvation (recording the voices of the elders so that future generations can bring them back to life). In the end these essays offer colonial cases for examining how writing of history for the exercise of power produces a "without history": spaces and temporalities with a life of their own.

Without History

The term "without" entails an amphibology: at once it signifies both *absence* and *outside*. The concept of history itself presupposes an absence and an outside in positing an origin or beginning that either assumes a nothing—that is, an outside that cannot be taken as a source and ground of history (out of nothing, its nonfoundation, ex nihilo); or posits an origin in mythical expressions— that is, a prehistory that contains the seeds of history proper (in a progression, a lack to be supplemented, teleology).[12] One may argue that there is a history of the world—indeed, that there has never been a prehistory, as if nonhistorical nature never existed and all cultural forms were historical by necessity, what we may define as *historicality* following a long line of philosophers. But then we have to acknowledge that this premise itself is the product of a particular historical formation of the West. In the case of ancient Mesoamerica and its origin stories, the assumption of a creation ex nihilo or the flight of the gods in metaphysics, whether cosmic or in the realm of humans, would not have made sense. When it did, it was precisely in stories about the gods taking flight, about how the ancient world had been destroyed by the conquest; stories that missionaries and bureaucrats but also recent historians tell about a colonial divide that conceptualizes the conquest in terms of a complete break without continuity. In the end these narratives betray the legacy of the Christian world that was imposed during the conquest.

We may observe with Jean-Luc Nancy that the emergence of metaphysics entails the flight of the gods and is through and through monotheistic. If Nancy dates this flight of the gods at the beginning of the West, with the invention of metaphysics in sixth-century Mediterranean space, he offers the possibility of tracing what he refers to as "an oriental *analogon*, which is given at the *same* time, constituted by Buddhism and Confucianism."[13] Nancy does not explore the analogon; he just mentions it. But as in all comparative work, the translation into Western categories would need to be taken back into an "oriental" space in which the translated categories would be endlessly further elaborated in an infinite progression. The analogon would manifest in its moving back and forth in the translating process an antinomy haunted by endless polemics. The analogon could very well start on the *other side of the street*, with non-Western thinkers reflecting on the West.

However, Nancy privileges a single view of the world. In a gesture reminiscent of the Zapatistas' motto "un mundo en que quepan muchos" [a world in which many fit], he calls for the understanding that "a world is precisely that in which there is room for everyone: but a genuine one in which things can genuinely *take place* (in this world). Otherwise, this is not a 'world': it is a

'globe' or a 'glome,' it is a 'land of exile' and a 'vale of tears.'"[14] As commend-
able as might be Nancy's and the Zapatistas' call for a world in which many,
all, everyone fits—a world that would contain and promote the participation
of the many—we still face the question of the ways in which this world, in its
singularity, might remain blind to the exclusion of forms of conceptualizing
the world that differ. These forms call for the need of a multiplicity of worlds
that can never be enclosed by a single world and in the end perhaps a single
history of the world, even when inclusive. Nevertheless, there is a radical difference between Nancy's and the Zapatistas' call for one world in that for the
latter, the origin of the proposal resides outside Western discourse—that is, in
Tzotzil, Tojolabal, Tzeltal, Mam, and other Maya languages spoken by members of the EZLN and Zapatista support bases. The articulations in Spanish
entail a translation of propositions drawn in a world that cannot be merely
subsumed by the single world as defined by Western categories and history of
metaphysics—hence the constant argument in these essays for plural-world
forms of dwelling in which one may pass from one world to others without
translation or incurring contradiction.

When linked to history, we discover that the terms "lack" and "outside,"
although distinct, may connect. The "lack of history" is the effect of historiographical gestures that define what ought to remain outside meaningful
historical discourse. Gestures indeed involve desires as well as techniques for
incorporating peoples into a common life as defined by stories of national formation, universal histories of salvation, or developmental programs. But indigenous peoples have never been passive subjects of these technologies—that
is, they have never quite wholly internalized their normative discourses. The
effect of history's claims to represent its "whither" thus produces subalterns
whose stories of the past lack the objectifying distance of "proper" history. In
recounting the experience of oppression (and liberation), these stories promise
deliverance in the flight of the *now* of insurrection. In recent years the question of history and its desirability has been at the forefront of disputes among
South Asian scholars over how best to remember and theorize India's past.
Ashis Nandy has put it in unmistakable terms in the opening lines to his essay
"History's Forgotten Doubles": "However odd this might sound to readers of a
collection on world history, millions of people still live outside 'history.' They
do have theories of the past; they *do* believe that the past is important and
shapes the present and the future, but they also recognize, confront, and live
a past different from that constructed by historians and historical consciousness. They even have a different way of arriving at that past."[15]

The "good" history of the objective historian, who appeals to the facts
in his or her investigations of the events, emerges under analysis as a trompe
l'oeil. As such, the battle for the past involves an aporia and invokes an antin-

omy—that is, the infinite polemics of the term "history"—that could very well be resolved by choosing to remain *without* history. The immediate response is to denounce the negation of history as "outside" and "lack," but we may want to proceed a bit slower and not rush to call all forms of remembrance "history." In fact, the call for "good" history defines itself as a guardian of the past for the state's well-being. It defines the criteria of rationality and the acceptable discourses in both the court of public opinion and the court of law. In this regard revisionist history seeks to create a new standard of truth or set of valid documents that would enable the recognition of previously marginalized memory and the inclusion of minority cultures by the (multicultural) state. It also assigns itself the task of writing socially responsible history that would enable subalterns to learn the languages of the state. In this way language, history, and the state draw their legitimacy from each other. Whereas in juridical spaces the police (and there is more than metaphor in this analogue) produce the documents to be archived, the judge rules according to the historical evidence (documents in the archive) supporting the cases. What counts as "evidence" is never static, but the role evidence plays for producing legitimate stories and its vigilance for the welfare of the current or future state remains unaltered.

The official histories of yesterday become incessantly replaced by the new stories and the fresh criteria of evidence that define the historian's aspirations to officialdom. The historian will of course claim a privileged method for the critical evaluation of evidence, but this claim ultimately incurs in a circular argument: what counts as "evidence" in history depends on the epistemological as well as the ethical criteria that define meaningful data. The historian could very well retort that as interpretative social science, history's circular methodology is entirely appropriate.[16] The issue would then be the extent to which the historian is consciously aware of and willing to acknowledge the marginalization of certain kinds of stories on the basis that the evidence put forth lacks appropriate ethical grounds or correct epistemological criteria for establishing truth. The link between history and the state (in reinforcing or in redefining the status quo) produces subalternity (the subaltern cannot speak— that is, his or her discourse lacks legitimacy) but also the "without history" (the possibility of choosing to remain outside history, a fortiori, to foreclose the constitution of a new state). One can rush to demand the recognition of one's history by the state, but one should also ask to what extent one is engaging in a new—perhaps even more nefarious—form of policing the past.

If what I said before regarding the past as the only true experience of temporality holds true, the battle will now be over the ways in which we create the world: the commonalities we bring forth and those we lose when privileging history's definitions of evidence. Rather than lamenting the denial of history, whether in the mode of "outside" (absolute exteriority, nonfoundational origins, creation ex nihilo) or "lack" (protohistories, absences to be amended, forms to be completed), we may turn the exercise of "the without" into a political virtue for forestalling the state and its history. In the mode of "outside"—the stories about the past, the reenactments, and the voices that resonate in a temporal duration that links the listener to a continuum—the "without" cannot be breached without a redefinition of "whither history" that at once calls for the "withering of history and the state." But this gesture entails refraining from pursuing the protohistoricity of a lack to be expropriated by technochronologies that erase the habitus that infused the events of the past with meaning. In reflecting on "the whither" and "the withering" of history, these essays attend to the immanence of the past and the specters that haunt but also enable our imagining of the future in the ever-present now of insurgency.

2 ⟰   Pre-Columbian Pasts
and Indian Presents in
Mexican History

This essay is the first in a series of studies on how the pre-Columbian past
has been collected in different moments in Mexican history and what has
been the relationship between these forms of knowledge and policies toward
Indians. On the one hand, these studies examine forms of ordering the pre-
Columbian past (that is, modes of knowing, organizing, and interpreting
artifacts). On the other, they study forms of containing disorder in the corresponding Indian presents (that is, modes of subordination, control, and
counterinsurgency). Idealized perspectives of the pre-Columbian period have
had contemporaneous views that denigrate and undermine historical Indians
(the many recent pages on the political insufficiency of the Zapatistas is one of
the many instances). Indian resistance includes both passive forms of reject-
ing Westernization as well as armed rebellions. In studying forms of creating
order and containing disorder, we must keep in mind what I call "writing violence in colonialist discourses."

This concept suggests a definition of Latin American Subaltern Studies
that would develop an inventory of the Culture of Conquest that continues to
produce subalternity, while simultaneously defining the terms of a discourse
that could dialogue with other rationalities to those dominant in the "West."[1]
Subaltern studies therefore would retake the histories of uprisings, insurgencies, rebellions, and national identities without subjecting them to the criteria
that privilege moments where elites have organized them according to their
political programs. This perspective would enable us to break away from teleological schemata that situate the meaning of the past in terms of approximation to (a questionably more developed) modern present. We would thus avoid

privileging an elite "third world" intellectual cadre that would have immediate access to subalterns. Quite the contrary, it would register the signs that inscribe "me," the "third world" intellectual (or, for that matter, the "first world" sympathizer) as a collaborator of colonial discourses. As John Beverley has put it: "Subaltern studies begins with a critique of the adequacy of any intellectual construction of the subaltern since, nolens volens, the constitution of the intelligentsia itself and intellectual discourse and its institutions is not unrelated to the production of subalternity itself."[2] Colonialist writing practices, then, do not just pertain to the (early) colonial period; rather, they inform contemporary modernization programs that folklorize forms of life and deplore the loss of old—thereby confining Indian cultures to the museum and the curio shop.

In the span of a decade after the conquest of Mexico, Mesoamerican civilizations came to be conceptualized as a form of antiquity by missionaries and crown officials. War, the burning of books, the persecution of spiritual leaders forced a way of life into clandestinity. Indigenous cultures, in the lingo of the early missionaries, became *antiguallas* (ancient history, old customs)—an array of cultural practices that Indians held in esteem regardless of their proscription by the Catholic Church. Paradoxically, the missionary's impulse to eradicate (to extirpate idolatries and superstitions) was intimately bound to a will to preserve (to resurrect the grandeur and moral order of old). Mexican historiography of the pre-Columbian period has been from its inception Janus-like: it at once has preserved a memory of old and severed contemporary Indian "presents" from history. (This exclusion from history should be understood as constituting a mode of "living history" rather than as verifying a recalcitrance to modernity). Ancient Mexico is conceptualized as *dead*—which does not exclude a ghostlike continuity that forevermore threatens the social order or progress—and becomes a patrimony of the *patria* (the fatherland) as early as Fray Diego de Durán's *Historia de las Indias de la Nueva España e islas de Tierra Firme* (ca. 1580) and of the *nación* (the nation) since the Independence from Spain in 1821. It is not so much a question of Indians having historical significance only insofar as they could be integrated into the Church or the nation, but of using *their* history against them. Colonialist discourses first proscribe Mesoamerican cultures and then reduce the effects of the destruction—the Indian "presents"—to shadows of the ancient grandeur.[3]

Mexico's *Clio*, from the reconstruction of the pre-Columbian world in the Codex Mendoza (ca. 1540) to the collection of past and present indigenous artifacts in the Museo Nacional de Antropología e Historia in Mexico City (1964), has tended to privilege antiquarian historiography. Antiquarianism, I must add, does not preclude building monuments to better preserve the meaning of its findings. Those familiar with Friedrich Nietzsche's *The Use and Abuse of History* will not fail to recall his preference for the term "polypsest" over "palimpsest" in his discussion of antiquarian history. Antiquarian historians would not only read the scribbles of the past but also reconstruct the past from its multiple rubbings (erasures). The antiquarian identifies the history of his town, the nation, with the history of the self: "He greets the soul of his people from afar as his own, across the dim and troubled centuries." But the antiquarian also brings about one more erasure as it "undervalues the present growth."[4]

Consequently, collections of the pre-Columbian pasts have had corresponding subaltern Indian presents. The story of the collection of past and present indigenous artifacts tends to be told in progressivist terms that privilege the emergence of the social sciences.[5] Against a monumental history that reads the past to find a kernel of the present and projects a present mentality into the past, I seek to elaborate an archaeology of the historiography of pre-Columbian Mesoamerica and its effects on the indigenous population. This archaeology does not pretend to have access to a more objectivist view of the past, however, but it is fully motivated by a desire to understand how indigenous people have been and continue to be marginalized through the expropriation of their cultures and history. These are the tasks of a book-length project that goes beyond the scope of a single essay.

Here I illustrate my project with two instances of writing violence in Mexican history: (1) the production of the Codex Mendoza in the mid-sixteenth century and (2) Carlos Sigüenza y Góngora's account of the 1692 riots in Mexico City and Tlaxcala in *Alboroto y motín de los indios de México*. Examining the Codex Mendoza enables us to trace how the *tlacuiloque* as writers of history were subordinated to Spanish historiography by a Spanish interpreter. Looking at *Alboroto y motín de los indios de México* enables us to isolate forms of subaltern insurgency in spite of, perhaps because of, Sigüenza y Góngora's racist phantasms.[6] Choosing these unique texts enables me to address two related and distinct modalities of collecting and recollecting the past. Their readings here are intended as examples of the type of work my research envisions, rather than finished studies of either text or historical moment. They exemplify two archaeological tasks implicit in the definition of subaltern studies on which I elaborate: (a) drawing an inventory of the systems of thought that have informed the collecting of the pre-Columbian past; and (b) identifying life forms and rationalities in documents whose purposes were not to record them as such but to provide information for their eradication or neutralization.[7] By conceptualizing "pre-Columbian pasts and Indian presents," I seek to define a terrain for reading Mexican history against the grain. It is no longer a question of opposing the masses (Indian presents and their representation) to the great men (pre-Columbian pasts and their collectors), nor simply of writing history from the bottom up, but of avoiding—indeed, destroying—the grounds that privilege *up* in interpretation.

Although this work bears similarities to that of Enrique Florescano's *Memoria mexicana* and Serge Gruzinski's *Conquest of Mexico*, it differs from theirs in that I do not aim to document degrees of acculturation or describe processes of occidentalization as consequences of literacy. Rather, I seek to examine forms of life that are often seen as undeveloped or historically ineffective. If one fetishizes the letter of the alphabet by positing it as the most evolved system of writing, for example, one also fetishizes the alphabet by defining the meanings that it produces as univocal—for there might be several pictographic versions of an event in any given community, strictly defined rules of what can be said about a pictograph, alphabetical inscriptions of oral texts that do not erase their own logic, and writers and painters who know not what they write and paint. But who would lack some form of acculturation or hybridity after contact? Subalternity cannot be thought outside colonialism or capitalism. As Dipesh Chakravarty has argued, "Stories about how this or that group in Asia, Africa or Latin America resisted the 'penetration' of capitalism do not constitute 'subaltern' history, for subaltern histories do not refer to a resistance prior and exterior to capital."[8]

The Codex Mendoza and the *Encomienda*

The Codex Mendoza (figure 2.1) consists of three parts, providing a pictographic account of (1) the history of Mexico-Tenochtitlan, (2) Mexico-Tenochtitlan's tributaries, and (3) the life cycle of the average Aztec at the time of the conquest. It is important to note that the third part also contains information regarding personal services and labor tribute. Scholars have generally agreed that the Codex Mendoza was produced by several *tlacuilos* (painter-writers) and that it is representative of the best colonial school of painters. Prototypes for the historical and tribute components have been identified by Elizabeth Hill Boone and Frances Berdan.[9] Gordon Brotherston, however, has pointed out that the "[Codex] Féjérváry exactly anticipates the Mendoza Codex, which deals first with the conquest and levying of tribute items and then with birth, growth, and the duties of the citizen of Tenochtitlan."[10]

The different components abide in different degrees to pre-Columbian writing conventions. It is generally agreed that the historical components do not contain formal deviations from similar pre-Columbian texts. Berdan, following the research of Donald Robertson, has pointed out that the scribe of the Matrícula de Tributos, a pre-Columbian prototype of the tributary section, composed the sequence of town glyphs and the corresponding tributes "'against the direction of reading,' while the Mendoza scribe wrote them with or toward the direction of the reading."[11] Brotherston's observation that the Codex Féjérváry anticipates the third section of the Codex Mendoza, the so-called ethnographic part, is not self-evident from a perusal of the pictographic

FIGURE 2.1. Tenochtitlan. Codex Mendoza. Folio 1v. MS. Arch. Selden. A1. Courtesy of the Bodleian Library.

conventions in the Féjérváry. But even if there were no pre-Columbian prototypes for this section, the use of (what would at least be interpreted as) an
indigenous form of writing would authenticate the information regarding
personal service and labor tribute. Rather than isolating this section as ethnographic, we ought to see the whole Codex Mendoza as the result of an ethnographic project and as an example of the rhetorical use (in this case by the
Spaniards) of pictographic writing.[12]

The Codex Mendoza testifies to the continuation of a pictographic tradition as well as to the epistemological need to fill in the gap created by the
burning of books in the early missionary campaigns of the 1520s and 1530s.
The Mendoza is an imaginary elaboration that at once provides historical information *about the past* and reproduces, as it were, a document *from the past*.
It marks a turning point in colonial history when ethnography fulfilled an an-
cillary function to define governmental policies, to aid judges, and to inform
missionaries. The Codex Mendoza, however, was produced for a European audience rather than to solve legal disputes among Amerindians or to identify
superstition and idolatry.

After the conquest *tlacuiloque* became indispensable to the information-
retrieval project of reconstructing the pre-Columbian past in such documents
as the pictorial section of Bernardino de Sahagúns's Florentine Codex, the
tribute records in the Codex Osuna, and the account of the Tlaxacalan participation in the conquest in the Lienzo de Tlaxcala. Iconic script, moreover,
recorded information from within the indigenous cultures that a purely alphabetical text could not contain. Spanish missionaries and authorities were
concerned with creating a code to understand the Indian mind from within
and thus further its occidentalization. Beyond this will to objectify and extirpate indigenous cultures, indigenous people used alphabetical writing and
"European-style" painting in forms that were not directly and explicitly part
of the colonial order meant to repress them. Contemporary scholars, however,
tend to emphasize degrees of purity in their classification of indigenous pictographic documents. In this regard, studies of the strokes of the main *tlacuilo*
of the Codex Mendoza indicate an adoption of cursive line that manifest acculturation.[13] But rather than seeing the Mendoza as a more or less authentic example of pre-Columbian writing or evaluating the "correctness" of the
information it contains, here we observe how the production of texts in the
native tradition fulfills the rhetorical function of authenticating data—pictographic texts would seem to contain more reliable data about the pre-Columbian social order.

We lack detailed information regarding the production of the Codex Mendoza. We also ignore the interests that informed its production as well as the
identity of the interpreter who wrote glosses, supplemented the pictographic

text with an alphabetical narrative, and provided descriptions and explanations of the nature of iconic script. At the end of the alphabetical narrative, the interpreter complains that the *tlacuiloque* have taken too long to produce the text: "diez dias antes de la partida de la flota se dio al ynterpretador esta ystoria para que la ynterpretase el qual descuydo fue de los yndios que acordaron tarde y como cosa de corrida no se tuvo punto en el estilo que convenia ynterpretarse" [the interpreter was given this history ten days prior to the departure of the fleet, and he interpreted it carelessly because the Indians came to agreement late; and so it was done in haste and he did not improve the style suitable for an interpretation.][14]

These remarks are extraordinary for the light they shed on the seriousness of interpretation in colonialist discourses. The interpreter underscores the accuracy of his translation into Spanish: "Y aunque las ynterpretaçiones ban toscas no se a de tener nota sino a la sustançia de las aclaraciones lo que significan las figuras / las quales ban byen declaradas por ser como es el ynterpretador dellas buen lengua mexicana" [and although the interpretations are crude, one should only take into account the substance of the explanations that explain the drawings; these are correctly presented, because the interpreter of them is well versed in the Mexican language].[15] The interpreter implies that the substance of his comments—the facts, as it were—are correctly documented in his glosses and alphabetical narrative. It is a question of style, of the appropriate historical genre, that is at stake in this commentary.

The interpreter confesses that his use of Moorish terms like *alfaqui* and *mezquitas* rather than *sacerdote* and *templo* was a mistake: "fue ynadevertancia del ynterpretador poner tales nombre que son moriscos" [it was a mistake for the interpreter to use the Moorish words]. But more problematic than these misnomers is the style he was forced to adopt because of the rush: "porque no se dio lugar al ynterpretador de nyngun vaga / y como cosa no acordaba ny pensaba se interpreto a uso de proçceso" [because the interpreter did not take time or work at all slowly; and because it was a matter neither agreed upon nor thought about, it was interpreted according to legal conventions].[16] Legal accounts or *relaciones* as a genre would approximate a zero degree of emplotment insofar as the writer limited himself or herself to stating the particulars and abstained from drawing their universal significance—that is, from historical interpretation. Furthermore, the "uso de proçceso" points to the legal framework in which pictographic documents were used.

But the passage also insinuates that the interpreter did not know why the text was solicited in the first place: "como cosa no acordada ny pensada." Clearly he was a latecomer in the chain of production. Given the structural similarity with the Codex Féjérvváry, we need not assume an active Spanish agency organizing the content of the text according to a set of questions.

From a legal perspective, the information regarding who paid tribute is relevant; however, the specific kind (such as warrior suits made of feathers) lacks relevance given Spanish needs. But from a political perspective, the record of labor tribute in the third section was crucial. The value of this data for the Spaniards would reside in its form rather than its contents: who paid tribute to whom and in what kinds? The interpreter complains of not having had enough time to reflect on the contents of the pictorial text, but also, perhaps more important, not enough time to provide a proper narrative because he ignored the purpose of the text.

We are asked to supplement the limitations: "El estilo grosero e ynterpretaçion de lo figurado supla el letor" [The reader must excuse the rough style in the interpretation of the drawings in this history].[17] (The English translators have chosen "to excuse" (that is, to dissimulate, to pretend that it is not there) as the meaning of the Spanish word *suplir*. But this verb also means "to integrate what is missing" as well as "to put oneself in the place of other." (The definition is, according to the *Diccionario de la Real Academia*: "Cumplir o integrar lo que falta en una cosa, o remediar la carencia de ella. // 2. Ponerse en lugar de uno para hacer sus veces.") The reader is called to take the place of the interpreter and thus supplement his faulty interpretation. In the horizon of interpretation, an oral test (that is, the deliberations by those who know or will make sense of why the text was produced) will supplement writing, will add material, and will take the place of the interpreter. The differentiation of pictographic from alphabetical writings as requiring an oral interpretation, as not containing a univocal content, would seem to be breached (in spite of the interpreter's views on the question) in this appeal to the reader to supplement.

Although the style of the Spanish commentary resembles legal conventions, the intent and nature of the interpreter's alphabetic text is to draw out the significance of the contents. The generic constraint of the *relación* to an account of particulars does not mean that the genre did not lend itself to *allegoresis* (stating one thing and meaning another); in this case its "rough style" was circumstantial. The interpreter calls for more interpretation rather than a zero degree of emplotment. Given that the text contains a history, he suggests an implicit narrative resolution with universal significance. One wonders, however, whether the historical nature of the text resides in the pictographic account or in the alphabetical section that needs to be supplemented by the readers. If the pictographic text is *a* history, the interpreter's deficiency would merely consist of a weak *reading*.

But then what was the purpose of glossing and translating? To simply facilitate a reading for King Charles V? But what was the urgency, if the purpose of the text was simply to interpret iconic script for the king? Why produce a text that approximates the writing convention of pre-Columbian traditions? Was this a mere rhetorical effect to reinforce a political argument? My guess is that the Codex Mendoza was part of a series of documents produced to legitimate the *encomienda* in New Spain either on the eve of, or in the immediate years after, the promulgation of the New Laws of 1542 that outlawed the institution of Indian tribute to Spaniards. The New Laws abolished the *encomienda*, but they were not accepted passively. Viceroy Blasco Núñez de Vela was killed when he attempted to enforce the New Laws in Peru. In New Spain there was a series of protests and a vast number of letters were written by members of the religious orders to defend the legality and economic value of individual *encomienda* as well as of the system as a whole. Since the Codex Mendoza was lost to a French corsair on its way to Spain (eventually becoming part of André Thevet's collection of American artifacts), we ignore what effect it would have had either before or after the promulgation of the New Laws. By 1546, however, the New Laws had undergone a series of amendments that revoked laws that had prohibited the inheritance of *encomiendas* and dissolved the disposition that took Indians away from *encomenderos* who mistreated them.

The Codex Mendoza's description and account of the tribute paid to Tenochtitlan establishes a tradition where the *encomienda* would be a continuation of and not an alien structure to the Amerindian world. By documenting rigorous order in the third section, the reader may supplement both iconic and alphabetical texts with a reflection on how the exercise of colonial domination and exploitation were not alien to the pre-Columbian order. Clearly, the Codex Mendoza validates tribute paid to *encomenderos* in the form of labor and personal service. The history of Mexico-Tenochtitlan gives us a clue to its ideological elaboration. As the narrative moves into the last Mexican ruler, Moctezuma (there is no mention of Cuahutemoc, whom Cortés hanged after the fall of Tenochtitlan in 1521), the history of Mexico-Tenochtitlan surreptitiously turns into the history of New Spain. The validity of New Spain as a political institution is grounded in a past that it destroyed: "y estando en el dicho señorio amplio mas en todo estremo el ynperio mexicano / dominando sobre todos los pueblos de desta Nueva España en que le dauan y pagavan grandes tributes y de balor de mucha Riqueza" [and during his reign he greatly extended the Mexican empire, ruling over all the towns of this New Spain, so they gave and paid large and richly valuable tributes].[18] Rather than merely seeing the capitalization of *Riqueza* as an isolated calligraphic anomaly, we ought to observe that it recurs with other "R"-words such as in "muchos estremos y Respetos," "majestad que les Representaua," and "Reconoçimiento de vasallaje."[19] Thus the history of Mexico-Tenochtitlan becomes the antiquity of New Spain and legitimates the new political order while subordinating the indigenous population to the new Spanish lords. The colonial order must impose the discipline that gave Moctezuma *Respeto* (respect), *majestad que Rep-*

resentaua (sovereignty that he represented), and *Reconoçimiento de vasallaje* (recognition of vassalage).

The subordination of the Indians can best be grasped in the summary mention that the interpreter makes of the *tlacuilos*: "el qual descuydo fue de los indios que acordaron tarde" [because the Indians came to agreement late].[20] We must avoid the temptation of reducing the *tlacuilos* to mere artisans that knew not what they wrote; this position would reiterate the interpreter's undermining of the *tlacuilos*. In doings this, we collaborate with the culture of conquest that informed the production of this text. Rather than pressing the *tlacuiloque*—that is, their text—to deliver the goods, to read it as a source of data, we ought to put its silences into play with the power dynamics that inscribed the *tlacuiloque* as incompetent. This statement ultimately foregrounds the new intellectual elite that claims authority "por ser como es el ynterpretador dellas buena lengua mexicana" [because the interpreter of them is well versed in the Mexican language].[21] We can read in the *tlacuiloque*'s disagreements a lack of stable information (that is, the old books had been burned), but more interesting—at least to me—is a cautious reserve (for example, clandestine cultural practices).

Sixteenth-century efforts to reconstruct life before contact not only had the administrative and ideological implications of the Codex Mendoza, regarding the *encomienda* and the payment of tribute, but also responded to a lack of knowledge regarding the everyday life of the Indian present. Franciscan missionaries such as Andrés de Olmos, Toribio de Benavente Motolinía, and Bernardino de Sahagún, the Dominican Diago Durán, and the Jesuit Juan de Tovar justified collection information about the pre-Columbian period on the void of knowledge caused by the systematic burning of books and censorship of religious practices that drove native leaders into clandestinity. Durán's *Historia de las Indias de la Nueva España e islas de Tierra Firme* is a particularly good source to analyze historical antiquation as a will to eradicate Nahua culture (that is, subjecting indigenous knowledge as superstition and idolatry) and to appropriate the institution of history (constituting the Nahuas as incapable of writing their own history). A "reading in reverse" of Durán and other missionary ethnographies, however, would allow us to observe forms of resistance to processes of occidentalization. *Alboroto y motín de los indios de México* establishes connections between passive resistance and insurrection. The antiquarianism of the Codex Mendoza resides in the production of a document *from the past* that legitimates the Spanish colonial order and its oppression of Indians. In the case of *Alboroto y motín*, histories of the pre-Columbian past and the conquest locate places of memory in the city and provide a code for interpreting an Indian present. *Alboroto y motín* is a long, detailed letter to the admiral Don Andrés Pez that described the heavy rains that destroyed the crops, the food shortages that followed, and the eventual uprisings.

Of Books and Rage

A classic site where a pre-Colombian past and an Indian present are juxtaposed is the scene, on a July afternoon in 1692, in which Don Carlos de Sigüenza y Góngora abandoned his desk and books to look out the window at a multitude of rebellious Indians in the streets of Mexico City.[22]

> A nada de cuanto he dicho que pasó esta tarde me hallé presente, porque me estaba en casa sobre mis libros. Y aunque yo había oído en la calle parte del ruido, siendo ordinario los que por las continuas borracheras de los indios nos enfadan siempre, ni aun se me ofrecío abrir las vidrieras de la ventana de mi estudio para ver lo que era hasta que, entrando un criado casi ahogando, se me dijo a grandes voces:—¡Señor, tumulto! Abrí las ventanas a toda prisa y, viendo que corría hacia la plaza infinita gente a medio vestir y casi corriendo entre, los que iban gritando: ¡Muera el Virrey y el Corregidor que tienem atravesado el maíz y nos matan de hambre!, me fui a ella.[23]

> [I was not present at any of the events of this afternoon because I was at home over my books. Although I had heard part of the noise on the street, it did not occur to me, since ordinarily on account of the habitual drunkenness of the Indians we are continually disturbed by uproars, to open the glass partitions of the window of my study to see what it was about until a man servant came in almost choking with excitement and shouted to me: "Sir, a riot!" I opened the windows in all haste and seeing that an infinite number of people were running toward the Plaza, I also went half-dressed and almost running amidst those who kept shouting, "Down with the Viceroy and the Corregidor who have stopped our corn and who are killing us with hunger!"][24]

Here we have the tranquility of the Creole savant, the collector of pre-Columbian artifacts and precious histories from the sixteenth century being disturbed by a "mob" of subalterns who were assaulting the deposits of corn and setting the city in flames. Our consummate antiquarian rushes to the palace to rescue the archives of the nation from the fires. He describes himself in heroic terms: "ya con una barrata, ya con una hacha, cortando vigas, apalancando puertas por mi industria, se le quitaron al fuego de entre las manos no solo algunos cuartos del palacio sino tribunales enteros y de la ciudad su major archivo"[25] [with a bar and with an ax I cut beams and pried open doors by my own efforts and not only some apartments of the Palace but whole halls and the best archives of the city were rescued from the fires.][26] This passage has given place to readings of Sigüenza y Góngora that tend to either highlight his love for the nation (Zarate) or denounce his lack of solidarity with the Indians

(Iglesia). Others have seen in the *Alboroto y motín* a brand of *criollismo* (Paz), a pro-Spanish defense of privilege (Cogdell), and even a resistant carnivalesque text (Moraña).[27]

The task of subaltern studies, however, would consist of recuperating the strategies of mobilization, the interracial allegiances, the role of women, the anticolonial positionings, and the tactics of rumor that remain sedimented in Sigüenza y Góngora's text. But in doing this sort of reading, we should remain careful not to forget that we are dealing with an ideological elaboration; we should therefore avoid claiming access to reality itself. For we witness Sigüenza y Góngora's phantasms, not the uprising itself. It is not a love of Indian things that Sigüenza y Góngora loses in the rebellion of 1692. We should trace instead his fear of insurgency by people of color (along with marginal Spaniards) and racial hatred. And in this respect Sigüenza y Góngora's denunciations of the unruliness of the "Indians"—as well as denunciations in the other versions of the story that blamed the uprising on the Spanish authorities—would manifest typical/tropical modes of containment and semantic control. Ranajit Guha's essay "The Prose of Counter-Insurgency" has isolated the rhetorical strategies used not only by colonial officials but also by nationalist historians to delimit the meaning and significance of subaltern insurgency. These range from condemnations of their tactics to negations of their political nature. Dismissals of the political character of the 1692 uprising can be traced in the work of such conservative critics as Octavio Paz, but it is also endemic to Gramscian readings that would highlight the limitations of peasant revolts.

Although the book *Elementary Aspects of Peasant Insurgency*—Guha borrowed the title from a passage by Gramsci—tends to attribute a lack of sufficient political development to subalterns (without defining peasant rebellions, however, as prepolitical), this book lays out the practice of "writing in reverse" as a mode of reading the specific rationales that inform peasant insurgency.[28] Thus Guha's book traces rebellion in the use of language; differentiates insurgency from crime; maps out forms of struggle in burning, eating, wrecking, and looting; analyzes the language used to understand transmission; and critiques the territorial constructs of the local, the ethnic, the nation, and so forth. These conceptual rearrangements prove invaluable for a reading of Sigüenza y Góngora's account and other documents pertaining to the 1692 riots in Mexico City and Tlaxcala.

The populace (the *plebe*) was composed of "indios, negros criollos y bosales de diferentes naciones, de chinos, de mulatos, de moriscos, de mestizos, de sambaigos, de lobos y también de españoles que en declarandose zaramulos (que es lo mismo que pícaros, chulos y arrebatacapas) y degenerando de sus obligaciones, son los peores entre tan ruin canalla."[29] [Indians, Creoles, *bozales* from various nations, Chinese, mulattoes, moriscos, mestizos, *zambaigos*, *lobos*, and Spaniards as well who, in declaring themselves *zaramullos* (which is the same as knaves, rascals, and cape-snatchers) and in falling away from their allegiance, are the worst of them all in such a vile rabble.[30]] Along with the mestizos and mulattoes, Sigüenza y Góngora identifies *zambaigos* (Indian and Chinese) and *lobos* (Indian and African). In this impulse to classify races and their miscegenation, the Spaniards are the worst lot because they do not assume the responsibilities of their race to the colonial order.

If all the castes were yelling, "¡Muera el virrey y quantos lo defendieren!" [Death to the Viceroy and all those who defend him!], it is the Indians who yell, "¡Mueran los españoles y los gachupines (son los venidos de España) que nos comen nuestro maíz!" [Death to the Spaniards and the Gachupines (applied to those who have come from Spain) who are eating our corn!]. But it is the Indian women, however, who play a particular role in the circulation of rumor and the definition of an anticolonial agenda: "¡Ea señoras!—se decían las indias en su lengua unas a otras—¡vamos con alegría a esta guerra, y como quiera Dios que se acaben en ella los españoles, no importa que muramos sin confesión! ¿No es nuestra tierra? Pues ¿qué quieren en ella los españoles?"[31] [Ah, señoras!—the Indian women kept saying to each other in their own language—let us go joyfully into this war. If God wills that the Spaniards be wiped out in it, it does not matter if we die without confession! Isn't this our land? Then what are the Spaniards doing in it.[32]] The Indian women denounce the colonial situation and defy any threat of punishment in the afterworld, "no importa que muramos sin confesión" [it does not matter if we die without confession].[33]

Sigüenza y Góngora does not comment on this anticolonial shout, which records the uprising as a godless act. And, of course, he does not see himself as a colonized subject, but he does concede that as far as the Indians are concerned, the Spanish occupation of the New World is a colonial situation.[34] By singling out the Indian women as emitting this cry in their tongue, he would seem to suggest that the castes and the marginal Spaniards could not identify themselves with this specific articulation of anticolonial sentiment. Their plight and source of unrest resulted from socioeconomic injustices and obviously, as far as the castes were concerned, from the racism of the dominant peninsular and Creole Spaniards. As such, the castes' rioting must be understood in terms of racial differentials prevalent in what Mary Louise Pratt has called contact zones.[35] Sigüenza y Góngora seems to make a distinction between white Spaniards and people of color: "reconocí con sobrado espacio (pues andaba entre ellos) no ser solos indios los que allí estaban sino de todos colores sin excepción alguna." [I readily recognized (for I walked right among them) that not only Indians were present but all the colors without exception whatsoever.][36]

Although the term *todos colores* could include Spaniards, the emphasis on color highlights the gravity of the events in that the castes solidarized with the Indians. Sigüenza y Góngora goes on to add that the Indians gained the following of the other castes (of all those who frequented the *pulquerías*) by carrying around an Indian woman who pretended to be dead. The display of the "corpse" served to mobilize the masses in the market. Looting ensued and the main governmental buildings were set in flames. The rioters targeted buildings that were locations of power or residences of officials as the viceroy and the *corregidor*. Although the stands at the marketplace were ransacked, there was no indiscriminate burning of private residences.

Let us now look into the role of rumor in mobilizing the crowd and the phantasms it generates in Sigüenza y Góngora's text. He wonders about the discourses that circulated among the Indians during the night: "¿Quién podrá decir con toda verdad los discursos en que gastarían los indios toda la noche?" The rumor prompts the phantasm of Indian women calling a drunken mob to kill the viceroy, to loot, and to take over the city: "Creo que, instigándolos las indias y calentándolos el pulque, sería el primero quitarle la vida luego el día siguiente al señor virrey; quemarle el palacio sería el segundo, hacerse señores de la cuidad y robarlo todo."[37]

Whether this is exactly what the Indians said in the midst of the night should not concern us; what is important here is that Sigüenza y Góngora conveys the efficacy of rumor by wondering about other worse inequities: "otras peores iniquidades." Rumor suggests the phantasm of an irrational mob: "y esto, sin tener otras armas para conseguir tan disparatada y monstruosa empresa sino las del desprecio de su propia vida que les da el pulque y la advertencia del culpabilísimo descuido con que vivimos entre tanta plebe, al mismo tiempo que presumimos de formidables" [and they had no other weapons to succeed in such a foolish and monstrous undertaking than those of the indifference to their own lives, which *pulque* gives them, and the consciousness of the exceedingly culpable carelessness with which we live among a great populace which, at the same time, we suspect of being dangerous].[38]

Rumor circulates information that terrifies the Spaniards with the prospect of a city ruled by Indians. But by signaling the efficacy of rumors, my analysis borders with a justification of the worst fears regarding the "irrationality" of the Indians. My point, however, is to evoke a cry that says, "Enough!"—a threatening "órale!" as exemplified by Subcomandante Marcos in a September 22, 1994, communiqué: "El México de abajo tiene vocación de lucha, es solidario, es banda, es barrio, es palomilla, es raza, es cuate, es huelga, es marcha y mitin, es toma tierras, es cierre de carreteras, es 'no les creo!,' es 'no me dejo,' es 'órale!'"[39] This popular language cannot be translated without distortion. For instance, *banda* or *palomilla* would call for "gang," but Marcos emphasizes a vocation for solidarity. The "no les creo" [I don't believe you], "no me dejo" [I will not take it] sums up the "órale!," which something like "enough!" would hardly do justice.[40]

Sigüenza y Góngora's account seems to dismiss the feasibility of taking over the city, but it expresses the determination of the Indians to engage the Spaniards. *Pulque*, writes Sigüenza y Góngora, is to be blamed for arousing the Indians. The difference between the efficacy of rumor and its phantasm is that the hysteria of Sigüenza y Góngora leads him to imagine a generalized and indiscriminate violence. But there is no evidence of an indiscriminate murder of Spaniards in his text. On the contrary, Spaniards do murder Indians to take away stolen merchandise. Sigüenza y Góngora partially blames the uprising on the vulnerability and ostentatiousness of the Spaniards, who live in a city without walls separating them from the Indian quarters. In the aftermath of the rebellion, Sigüenza y Góngora recommended that Indians should be forbidden from living in the center of Mexico City and be confined to several barrios on the periphery. The viceroy ordered on July 11, 1692, that within twenty days all Indians should move to their barrios.[41]

Murmur was also a preferred mode of communication. At Mass a few days before the uprising, "al entrar [el virrey] por la iglesia se levantó un murmullo no muy confuso entre las mujeres (pues lo oyeron los gentileshombres y pajes que le asistían, ¿cómo pudo su exelencia dejar de oirlo?) en que feamente le execraban y maldecían, atribuyendo a sus omisiones y mal gobierno la falta de maíz y la carestía de pan" [a not very indistinct murmur arose among the women (if the gentlemen-in-waiting and the pages who were in attendance heard it, how could His excellency fail to do so?) as he entered the church; they were execrating and cursing him in an ugly fashion, attributing the shortage of corn and the high price of bread to neglect and poor management on his part].[42]

For Sigüenza y Góngora the viceroy did nothing more than pretend not having heard the grumble, the "órale!" Women had been murmuring and circulating rumors since the seventh of April. This "secret" (hence, illegitimate) communication eventually developed into a public outcry. Sigüenza y Góngora gives us a version of the riot's origins in which he accuses the Indian women of monopolizing corn for tortillas and then buying *pulque* with the money. The men, seeing that their women were favored over Spanish women (Sigüenza y Góngora specifies that Indian women were the only ones who knew how to make tortillas), attributed the preferential treatment to Spanish fear of Indian wrath. Thus a strategic frightening of the Spaniards preceded the rebellion: "se determinaba [la plebe] a espantar (como dicen en su lengua) a los españoles" [(the populace) made up its mind to scare off the Spaniards (as they say in their own language)].[43]

There are several issues to sort out in this passage. Why did Sigüenza y Góngora emphasize that the Indians say "espantar en su lengua"? One wonders whether he was translating or simply documenting the use of the Spanish word in Nahuatl. He also underscored that the Indian women used their language when they contested the Spanish colonial claims over their lands. These specifications on the use of (most likely) Nahuatl implies that Spanish might not have been the common language to communicate across racial and ethnic lines, or at least that Nahuatl was generally understood. Anthropologists and linguists have documented that Indians in both the Andes and Mexico tend to speak Spanish when drunk. Indeed, drunkenness goes hand in hand with the use of Spanish to condemn colonial regimes, as can be witnessed in a passage from Reginaldo de Lizarraga's *Descripción breve del Perú*:

> y cuando están borrachos entonces hablan nuestra lengua, y se preguntan cuando los cristianos nos hemos de volver a nuestra patria, y porque no nos echan de la tierra, pues son más que nosotros, y cuando se ha de acabar el ave maría, que es decir cuando no les hemos de compeler a la doctrina.

> [and it is when they are drunk that they speak our tongue, and they ask each other when are we the Christians going to go back to our fatherland, and why don't they throw us out of their land, since they are more than us, and when will the Hail Mary end, which means when will we not compel them to hear the doctrine.][44]

This is the same colonial situation and anti-Christian sentiment that we find in Sigüenza y Góngora, but the use of Spanish has a specific political motivation: to make sure that the Spaniards know how they feel about their oppression. The difference might reside in that in this instance violence remains exclusively on an imaginary plane, whereas in Sigüenza y Góngora's account the Indians are already rioting. Although riots are both an actualization and an imaginary of violence, as a "place of rage" they are not limited to verbal attacks but also include burning buildings, looting, drinking *pulque*, and *espantar* the Spaniards with the threat of racial warfare.

In their observations on the consumption of alcoholic beverages, colonial officials and missionaries usually juxtaposed statements about a democratization of drunkenness after the colonization. From the very early colonial period, drunkenness, moreover, was associated with idolatrous practices. These commonplaces also recur in Sigüenza y Góngora. For instance, he describes the consumption of *pulque* in one day as greater than the amount that was consumed in one year in the pre-Columbian past: "abunda más el pulque en México solo en un día que en un año entero quando la gobernaban idólatras" [*pulque* is more plentiful in a single day in Mexico City than in a whole year when the capital was governed by idolaters].[45] More souls, according to

Sigüenza y Góngora, were sacrificed to the devil in the *pulquerias* of colonial Mexico than bodies in the temples of old. Thus ancient Mexico remained a paragon of morality, if not an object of desire in relation to the degeneracy of the contemporary Indians. There were, nevertheless, some Indians that retained the nobility of the past in their support of the prohibition of *pulque*: "y aun de los propios indios los pocos que conseruaban algo de nobleza Antigua" [and even by a few of the Indians themselves who had kept something of their former nobility].[46] Here he seems to privilege an Indian elite that tended to look after its own interests rather than feel solidarity with Indian subalterns. It is an elite concerned with retaining privileges that would keep them from labor drafts.[47]

Given that this nobility was subservient to the Spanish order, it is hard to understand Sigüenza y Góngora's remarks about an Indian conspiracy. His account is only a brief version: "Las armas falsas, los miedos, las turbaciones de todo México . . . pedía para su expresión relación muy larga" [The false alarms, apprehensions and excitement in all Mexico . . . would require a very long account for adequate expression].[48] Other Spaniards trusted that the Tlaxcaltecas would come to their aid, but Sigüenza y Góngora discounted an assumed continuous fidelity to the crown since the Tlaxcaltecas rebelled the week after. The letter by an anonymous witness documents the exclusively subaltern nature of the Tlaxcala riots: "fué sola la plebe é indios *masaguales* los que hicieron la hostilidad, estando de parte de su Alcalde Mayor los caciques y nobles" [it was only the populace and the *masaguale* Indians who created the hostilities, for the caciques and the nobility were on the side of the Alcalde Mayor].[49] This letter also confirms Guha's observation on how the specter of a conspiracy "has its source in the psychosis of the dominant groups."[50] For example: "y esto que fue sola sospecha, llegó a cobrar fuerza, diciendo estaban convocados muchos pueblos y que tenían determinado el incendio de la ciudad" [and this that was only a suspicion, grew in force, saying that many towns had gathered and had the determination of burning the city].[51] The momentum did build up; however, the organizing principle should not be understood as a secret confabulation but as resulting from the same conditions of exploitation and oppression.

An aspect of this oppression was the subjection of native religions and knowledges. Idolatry and magic played an important role in the imaginary of violence, at least Sigüenza y Góngora's phantasms. In this account Sigüenza y Góngora describes effigies of Spaniards in clay that were pierced with knives and lances also made of clay, bearing signs of blood on their necks as if their throats had been cut, which would manifest the anticolonial feelings that preceded the riots. These figures were found, according to Sigüenza y Góngora, in the same place where Hernán Cortés's forces had been destroyed on the night he fled Tenochtitlan in 1520. Here Sigüenza y Góngora alludes to Indian histories that recorded this event and dedicated it to their major god, Huitzilopochtli, the god of war. This recollection of the defeat of Cortés's forces as they fled the siege of Tenochtitlan manifests a memory continuum in the Indian's historical consciousness.[52] This site of historical remembrance, if ominous to the Spaniards, was a source of joy for the Indians: "como ominoso para nosotros y para ellos feliz."[53] Indians retained a memory of old in present practices of their beliefs.

And here Sigüenza y Góngora reconnects the scene of reading the books of old with the current events and an ethnography of the present: "no habiéndoseles oluidado aún en estos tiempos sus supersticiones antiguas, arrojan allí en su retrato a quien aborrecen para que, como pereció en aquella acequia y en aquel tiempo tanto español, le suceda también a los que allí maldicen. Esto discurrí que significaban aquellos trastes por lo que he leído de sus historias y por lo que ellos mismos me han dicho de ellas cuando los he agregado."[54] This has been translated as "since they had not forgotten their ancient superstitions even in these days, they throw there in effigy those whom they hate in order that the Spaniards, whom they now curse, may suffer the same fate as those of the earlier date who perished in the canal. I inferred that this was the significance of those objects, judging by what I have read of their histories and by what they themselves told me about them when I have gathered them up."[55] Sigüenza y Góngora underscores the authority of his interpretation by alluding to his historical readings ("he leído de sus historias") and ethnographic research ("lo que ellos mismos me han dicho").

To Sigüenza y Góngora's credit, he preferred the version—actually he testifies as an eyewitness—that traces the beginnings of the uprising to the Indians themselves and not the castes or the poor Spaniards. The mobilization of the multitude presupposed an accurate analysis of the lack of corn: "No discurrían estos sin fundamento" [The latter were not without some basis]—moreover, a strategic use of "palabras devergonsadas" [lewd words], "pleitecillos que entre si trataban sin lastimarse" [petty quarrels among themselves in which they did not hurt each other], and "grandes corrillos" [large groups of loungers] were like "premisas de algún tumulto" [portents of a mob].[56] This letter testifies to the strategic deployment of noise (*Ruido*) in building an uprising. Obviously, Sigüenza y Góngora did not sympathize in the least with the insurgency initiated by the Indians, but despite his disapproval, perhaps because he intended to record its logic for counterinsurgency, his version of the events exemplifies and complements the rebellions studied by Guha in *Elementary Aspects of Peasant Insurgency*. Traditional readings of insurgency in Latin America have tended to emphasize a lack of a political program and have raised the political acumen that the leaders of independence movements displayed in the nineteenth century when they were able to regulate the mobilization of subalterns who by then had a long history of insurgency. One of the tasks of subaltern studies, however, is to retake these histories of uprisings, insurgencies, rebellions, and national identities without subjecting them to criteria that privilege moments where elites have organized them according to their own political programs.

In the Manner of a Short Conclusion

The Codex Mendoza has enabled us to trace the production of a document that not only represented the pre-Columbian past but also reproduced a text that would be taken for an authentic native document. If the *tlacuiloque* were copying from pre-Columbian prototypes, why did the viceroyal authorities bother to produce a "copy" rather than send a pre-Columbian text? My guess has been that the production of the text by postconquest subjects would have a greater impact, since the subjects affected by the *encomienda* would seem to ratify its compatibility with ancient structures. In the end it did not matter what the Mendoza said about the kinds of tribute; what mattered was the fact that the system existed—especially in the form of labor tribute and personal services. The *tlacuiloque* in not agreeing among themselves suggest a form of silence of eschewing inquiry by missionaries, of "resisting the heat"—as Doris Sommer would put it.[57]

As an ethnographic document, however, the Codex Mendoza is not concerned with documenting idolatries and superstitions for their eradication—or, for that matter, resistance—but with establishing a socioeconomic precedent that would legitimize the *encomienda*. This collection of the pre-Columbian past therefore bears an immediate relationship to policies toward Indians. But the Indian present is not only subordinated to Spanish rule politically and economically but also intellectually. The interpreter casts the *tlacuilos* as inept and thus appropriates the institution of history. The key to recollecting the past—the task of interpreting the collection itself—now pertains to the Spanish specialist who presumes to understand pictographic writing and to be fluent in Nahuatl. In this text we witness how the constitution of an intellectual elite is inseparable from the production of subalternity.

Sigüenza y Góngora belongs to a later, fully consolidated intellectual elite that takes as a given—as a natural order—the subalternity of the Indian population; his commendation of the remains of an indigenous nobility strikes me as paternalistic. Sigüenza y Góngora collects pre-Columbian artifacts and early histories as an end in itself. He is an antiquarian in the strictest sense of the term; the preservation of old documents informs his will to collect the past. It is the pre-Columbian past as the antiquity of New Spain that fascinates Sigüenza y Góngora, and not its significance to his contemporary Indians, who are perceived as an unruly mass with no (positive) resemblance to the ancient grandeur. But recollecting the past also enables him to decipher idolatrous and magical practices as well as the significance Indians gave to specific locations within the city. Beyond the archival Spanish written sources, these places of memory testify to living indigenous oral histories. Both the Codex Mendoza and *Alboroto y motín* provide materials for an inventory of the Culture of Conquest that produces subalternity, but *Alboroto y motín* also documents other rationalities to those dominant in the "West." Sigüenza y Góngora's text suggests how forms of passive resistance became fully articulated in the numerous rebellions that broke out in different parts of New Spain during the seventeenth century.

Scholars have tended to see these acts of insurgency not as political, as eruptions of violence without rationality, as sources of energy that had to wait for the political leadership of the Creole elites of the independence movements. If the meaning of history always comes from the future, the emergence of the nation in the nineteenth century privileged these readings of insurgent movements as undeveloped. The Zapatistas today function as a return of the repressed that reminds us that other rationalities could have very well informed other insurgencies in other times.

3 ≡≡≡ Of Zapatismo
Reflections on the Folkloric and the Impossible
in a Subaltern Insurrection

Usted se está equivocando demasiado con la decisión que ha tomado en contra de nosotros, usted cree que matando los Zapatistas de Chiapas o matando al subcomandante Marcos puede acabar con esta lucha. No señor Zedillo, la lucha Zapatista está en todo México, Zapata no ha muerto, vive y vivirá siempre.

[You are equivocating too much with the decision you have taken against us. You believe that killing the Zapatistas of Chiapas or killing Subcomanadante Marco can end this struggle. No, Mr. Zedillo, the Zapatista struggle is in all of Mexico. Zapata is not dead; he is alive and will live for ever.]

—COMITÉ CLANDESTINO REVOLUCIONARIO INDÍGENA,
  COMANDANCIA GENERAL OF THE EZLN

In seeking to learn to speak to (rather than listen to or speak for) the historically muted subject of the subaltern woman, the postcolonial intellectual *systematically* "unlearns" privilege.

—GAYATRI CHAKRAVORTY SPIVAK

"Todos somos indios." La consigna es inobjetable en la medida en que asume el orgullo (novedad histórica) por un componente básico de la nacionalidad. Pero ¿qué decir de "Todos somos Marcos"? La frase parece en exceso retórica, fruto de la pasión militarista, del frenesí romántico o de la escenografía mesiánica.

["We are all Indians." The slogan of the demonstrations is unobjectionable insofar as it expresses pride (a historical novelty) for a basic component of nationality. But what can we say about "We are all Marcos"? This phrase seems too rhetorical, the fruit of militaristic passion, of a romantic frenzy or of a messianic scenography.]

—CARLOS MONSIVÁIS

One of the urgent tasks in the study of subaltern insurrections is to find ways of understanding the compatibility of modern and nonmodern cultural and political practices.[1] Although the "Carta a Zedillo" by the Comité Clandestino Revolucionario Indígena, Comandancia General (CCRI-CG, the Clandestine Indigenous Revolutionary Committee, General Command) reached me, in Ann Arbor, through the Internet (that most modern—perhaps, postmodern—form of communication), it manifests a *folkloric* understanding of revolutionary agency ("Zapata no ha muerto, vive y vivirá para siempre" [Zapata is not dead; he is alive and will live for ever]) and a willingness to taunt the *impos-*

sible by asserting a communicable Indian discourse beyond its immediate, local situation (an effort to internationalize the Zapatista call for democracy, liberty, and justice).[2]

Another communiqué from the CCRI-CG further illustrates a folkloric Zapatismo with a millenarian evocation of Votán Zapata: "Votán-Zapata es el uno que camina en el corazón de todos y cada uno de los hombres y mujeres verdaderos. Todos nosotros somos uno en Votán-Zapata y el es uno en todos nosotros" [Votán-Zapata is the one that walks in the heart of all and each of the true men and women. We are all one in Votán-Zapata and he is one in all of us].[3] Votán—"guardian y corazón del pueblo" [guardian and heart of the people], a pre-Columbian Tzeltal and Tzotzil god, which also names the third day of the twenty-day period and is the night lord of the third *trecena* (thirteen twenty-day periods) of the Tonalamatl ("book of the days," the Mesomaerican divinatory calendar)—merges with Emiliano Zapata, within a poignant view of the power inherent in the multitude as one and the one as the multitude. This communiqué commemorates the betrayal and death of Zapata on April 10, 1919.

A communiqué from 1994, also commemorating Zapata's death, places Votán Zapata within a 501-year period of resistance—"Votán Zapata, tímido fuego que en nuestra muerte vivió 501 años" [Votán Zapata, timid fire that in our death has lived 501 years]—and elaborates in more detail the one/multitude nature of Votán-Zapata: "Es y no es todo en nosotros. . . . Caminado está. . . . Votán Zapata, guardian y corazón del pueblo. Amo de la noche . . . Señor de la montaña . . . Nosotros . . . Votán Zapata, guardian y corazón del pueblo. Uno y muchos es. Ninguno y todos. Estando viene. Votán Zapata, guardian y corazón del pueblo." [It is and is not everything in us. . . . He is walking. . . . Votán Zapata, guardian and heart of the people. Lord of the night . . . Lord of the mountain . . . Us . . . Votán Zapata, guardian and heart of the people. None and all. As being is coming. Votán Zapata, guardian and heart of the people.][4] According to Eduard Seler, Votán may very well correspond not only to Tepeyollotl of the Nahuas and Pitao-Xoo of the Zapotecs, but also to the bat-god of the Cakchiqueles.[5]

Of all the communiqués, this is the one that appears to have struck a most vital chord among the radicalized youth, whose preference for rock and roll has very little in common with the oral traditions and music choices of the young Indians comprising the Ejército Zapatista de Liberación Nacional (EZLN, the Zapatista Army of National Liberation). The impact of this communiqué can perhaps be attested by the prominence given to Votán and the archetypal resonance of the ubiquitous ski masks in articles published in *La Guillotina*, a student publication from Universidad Nacional Autónoma de México (UNAM).[6] By the way, the motto of *La Guillotina* is "¡Exigid lo imposible!" [Demand the impossible!]. In reflecting on Zapatismo, we ought to avoid reductive readings of folklore and retain the impossible as a utopian horizon of alternative rationalities to those dominant in the West. This reflection informs our critique of the ideological constraints that have kept intellectual discourse from giving serious consideration to hybrid cultural and political practices that combine modern and nonmodern forms.

The Zapatista rebellion in Chiapas makes full use of the new technologies that circulate local news in global contexts—their political and physical survival depends on this flow of information. The Zapatistas, furthermore, deploy the novel modes of communication along with consensus politics based on ancestral communalism, just as the indigenous peoples of Chiapas use Western medicine along with *naguales* (animal soul companions) and shamans. Gary Gossen has argued that shamans and *naguales* have as much to do with the spiritual health of the self as of the community: "Once afflicted [by a disequilibrium of the causal forces that determine fate], the only traditional way to remedy one's condition is to hire a shaman to intervene on one's behalf by performing rituals whose primary goal is to restore equilibrium to the several individual spirits that influence the body's well being [*sic*]. In practice, however, the shaman also addresses the matter of restoring harmony and equilibrium to one's social relations."[7]

The factors that determine individual destinies are "predetermined but also, secondarily, subject to the agency of and will of others, both human and supernatural." Indian beliefs in "co-essences," according to Gossen, should be understood as "a fluid language of social analysis and social integration."[8] They complement Western medicine: whereas antibiotics cure the individual, shamans also have the task of situating the individual in the cosmos and guiding him or her through the surrounding social reality. These possibilities of using modern science and technology without being forced to disavow one's knowledge is a new historical configuration. It can be argued that the three Ladinos who immersed themselves in the *Declaración de la Selva Lacandona* in the early eighties were able to tap into Indians' long history of rebellion only as a result of *learning to talk to* the communities and subjecting themselves to their authority.[9] With a few modifications (not only women subalterns or female privilege), the quotation at the opening of the chapter from the literary theorist Gayatri Spivak applies to the three anonymous Ladinos (for all the speaking Marcos does) who "unlearned" privilege in the formation of the EZLN.

Carlos Monsiváis's comments on the slogans shouted in *yesterday*'s march in Mexico City would seem to reiterate the uniqueness of this new historical configuration. Monsiváis goes on to make the distinction between those who might very well have conflicting vocation and those who identify themselves with Marcos in the sense of "if you condemn Marcos for wanting a better world, a more just Mexico, you might as well condemn me and all us who want the same."[10] Given the circumstances of the offensive by the army (the witch hunts, the tortures), it is understandable (strategically correct) to call for peace, but to place all the emphasis on sharing the condemnation (and ultimately the martyrdom) is to ignore the military nature of the EZLN. In the "Todos somos Marcos," we ought to also hear a will to resist and fight back. For there is if not a messianic an eschatological note in the Zapatista call for justice that goes well beyond a "more just Mexico." Monsiváis's remarks, though clearly sympathetic with the cause, manifest the impossibility of the EZLN's subaltern narrative: impossibility in the sense of their incompatibility with "modern" narratives. If this issue of the impossibility of subaltern narratives clearly removes us from the urgency of the immediate events in Chiapas, it also helps us focus on the philosophical significance of the indigenous discursive modalities of the EZLN.

To clear the ground for a serious consideration of the subaltern discourse of the Zapatistas, this essay draws a critique of Antonio Gramsci's blindness to the folkloric and addresses recent scholarship that has begun to supersede this interpretative limitation.[11] This theoretical reexamination seeks to understand how the EZLN can constitute itself as a vanguard that is precisely grounded in its self-conscious subalternity—that is, as an instance of the counterhegemony of the diverse. On the basis of a new ethics, politics, and epistemology of subaltern studies, the second part of this essay moves on to examine the discourse on subalternity that Marcos and the CCRI-CG have elaborated since their revolt on January 1, 1994. I examine how their communiqués have been interpreted from several perspectives, ranging from condemnations of the violence and illegality of the Zapatistas to understandings of the EZLN in terms of a history of guerrilla warfare in Mexico since the 1960s.[12]

These articles and books have tended to be written either as a privileging of Marcos over the indigenous communities (it was Marcos's ethnographic acumen that enabled the mobilization of the Indians) or as an unmasking of the Zapatistas that reveals their links to Archbishop Samuel Ruiz, Marcos's appropriation of the Indian "voices" in the communiqués from the CCRI-CG, and the absence of a "real" army. The critique of these readings enables us to elucidate the subaltern nature of the EZLN and a narrative of the impossible in the communiqués. The apparent impossibility of the project has as much to do with the denial of a credible Indian-led insurgency as with a hegemonic consensus among Mexican intellectuals that revolution was not an option anymore in Latin America, leaving reform as the only viable political process. As for the government's delegation in the negotiations, Mayor Rolando has put it succinctly: "Es imposible que el gobierno comprenda lo que estamos pidiendo"

[It is impossible that the government understands what we are asking].[13] The Zapatistas attribute the incapacity of the government—as well as of intellectuals—to address their demands to a mixture of moral ineptness (the government cannot understand what dignity means), racism (it cannot dialogue with Indians on an equal basis), and intellectual torpidity (it cannot understand the terms of a new communist revolution). The peace talks are proving to be hard lessons for the government on how to speak to subalterns.

It is generally accepted that 1989 marked a radical break in the history of the Left. The fall of the Berlin wall is often taken as the "demise" of socialism.[14] The sight of jubilant East Germans gawking at the commodities of the West made manifest the failure to institute a socialist ethic within socialist societies of Eastern Europe. Indeed, these masses soon became a dangerous "Other" as Western intellectuals and the press perceived them as lacking a democratic worldview. Rather than celebrating a "triumph" of democracy or passing judgment, we ought to read the events of 1989 as manifesting a distance between the ends of the socialist state and the desires of civil society. The most parallel event in the Americas was the Sandinistas' defeat in the 1990 elections in Nicaragua. What we witness in these events is a failure of the Left to *represent* the interests of the people.[15] This crisis in political representation had an aesthetic antecedent in socialist realism as early as the 1930s in the Soviet Union. Instead of posing the will to represent as a generally misguided project of the West, subaltern studies would ultimately foreground, as John Beverley has put it, "the inadequacy of the models of intellectual and political protagonists that correspond to the period of liberation struggle in the sixties in which many of us were formed."[16]

As we reflect on Zapatismo, we must go beyond representation or even performance (ultimately, a modality of the former). There is much to gain if we view the insurrection in terms of Antonio Negri's concept of constituent subjectivities: "Constituent power against constituted power, constituent power as singular subjectivity, as productivity and cooperation, that asks how to be situated in society—how to develop its own creativity."[17] In one of his most recent communiqués, Subcomandante Marcos establishes a connection with labor movements in Italy that suggests a connection with Negri. Under the figure of his literary interlocutor Durito ("the Little Hard One"), a scarab, Marcos conveys his solidarity with the workers of Fiat in Turin by giving to their cause the pay he received for a contribution to a collection of essays. I would like to give as an example of Negri's concept of emergent subjectivities, in addition to the "Todos somos Marcos" slogan in Monsiváis's letter, the massive demonstration on May 1, 1995, where the unemployed, street children, housewives, alternative unions, small businessmen, and radicalized high school students marched together.

Chiapas turns out to be a metonym for the nation: beyond the Zapatista's local struggle, the EZLN demands a national debate over the meaning and future of democracy in Mexico. A recent communiqué from the CCRI-CG suggests the basis for a new internationalism: "Llamamos a todos, a legales y a clandestinos, armados y pacíficos, civiles y militares, a todos los que luchan, en todas las formas, en todos los niveles y en todas partes por la democracia, la libertad y la justicia en el mundo" [We call on all, legal and clandestine, armed and pacifists, civilians and military, on all who struggle, by all means, on all levels and everywhere for democracy, liberty and justice in the world].[18] The political program of the Zapatistas calls for the multiple engagement of democratic groups, for the creation of a political space where different positions may confront each other, rather than a pluralistic centrist position.

There is no doubt that the discourse of power has devised forms of representation with a capacity to objectify, know, and control sociocultural and geopolitical domains on a global scale.[19] A Foucauldian perspective would map sites of power as well as of resistance. The task of a specifically Latin American Subaltern Studies project, confronted with phenomena like the Zapatistas, would not limit itself, however, to an affirmation of resistance, a documentation of fluid identities and social fragmentation, or a study of emergent citizenships and new political movements.[20] The study of new social movements and patterns of resistant subalternity must devise an epistemology that curtails the appropriation of its findings by dominant discourse. Although subaltern studies has much to learn from (in fact, has built on) postmodern theories, the project cannot limit itself to understandings of power that ignore oppositions such as dominant classes relative to dominated subjects or the colonizer relative to the colonized. These oppositions tend to be dismissed as instances of Western binary thinking. These oppositions—as in the case of subalternity—are not stable but relational. For if subalternity partakes of hegemony and consensus, it is perhaps equally or even more urgent to examine how subaltern subjects are constituted through dominance and coercion. War, in this regard, would not be an exceptional state of affairs but the course of the world. Consensus would then be the result of a discursive violence that has been interiorized.

Less concerned with identifying and studying "subalterns" as positive entities, the project, as I envision it, would call for an analysis of the mechanisms that produce subalternity as well as the formulation of political and cultural practices that would end it. But before dwelling on issues pertaining to ethics, politics, and epistemologies of subaltern studies, I draw a critique of Gramsci's blindness to the folkloric. Gramsci first used the term "subaltern," beyond military referents, in his *Notes on Italian History*. His writings also inaugurated the concept of hegemony as a new mode of understanding ideology. Although readings of Gramsci have a long history in Latin America (including Ernesto

Laclau's early work, *Politics and Ideology in Marxist Theory*), they have tended not to be critical of his understandings of Culture or his conception of the corresponding counterhegemonic blocs.[21] Gramsci's notion of the folkloric, which he opposes to the modernist conception of the historical emergence of national Culture, needs to be critiqued to make space to comprehend the dynamics of subaltern movements. What is at stake in this critique is the compatibility of modern and nonmodern forms of culture and politics and not the celebration of some sort of pristine indigenous community. We must keep in mind, nonetheless, that the possibility of critiquing the ideology of progress is a recent phenomenon not readily available to Gramsci.

For Gramsci, notions of popular culture and indigenous knowledge were incompatible with his understanding of a Culture that could be established as a counterhegemony. As Gramsci put it in "The Modern Prince," one must study elements of popular psychology "in order to transform them, by educating them, into a modern mentality."[22] His understanding of cultural politics unavoidably privileged Western conceptions of knowledge, art, and ethics— evidently, of History. The elaboration of a counterhegemonic culture signified an alternative modernity that would transform premodern subjects. In "On education," Gramsci wrote: "The first, primary grade should not last longer than three or four years, and in addition to imparting the first 'instrumental' notions of schooling—reading, writing, sums, geography, history—ought in particular to deal with an aspect of education which is now neglected—i.e., with 'rights' and 'duties,' with the first notions of the State and society as primordial elements of a new conception of the world which challenges the conceptions that are imparted by the various traditional social environments, i.e., the conceptions which can be termed folkloristic."[23]

The "folkloristic" would reduce all forms of knowledge not bound by Western criteria of truth to superstition at worst and to unexamined "common sense" at best. "Common sense," in this regard, would parallel what semioticians call "natural signs"—that is, an uncritical understanding of the world where the signifier bypasses the signified and is thus identified with referents. The history of philosophy, in itself, would be a chronicle of the institutionalization of "common sense": "Every philosophical current leaves behind a sedimentation of 'common sense': this is the document of its historical effectiveness."[24] For Gramsci, "common sense" continually transforms itself as it incorporates scientific ideas and philosophical opinions into everyday life: "'Common sense' is the folklore of philosophy, and is always half way between folklore properly speaking and the philosophy, science, and economics of the specialists."[25] This understanding of "common sense" as the folklore of philosophy enables us to turn this concept against Gramsci by pointing out that the reduction of what he terms "traditional social environments" to folklore is in itself a manifestation of philosophical folklore. I call this critical gesture a form of "enlightened de-enlightenment."

Although "common sense" and folklore were clearly inferior forms of knowledge in Gramsci's assessment, their role in rebellions and insurrections—especially of the peasant—cannot be ignored. If he was critical of voluntarism, of instinct (and called for a transformation of peasants' mentality by modernity), subaltern insurgencies would call for a theoretical reflection rather than a dismissal on grounds of insufficient consciousness—lacking plans in advance or not following a theoretical line. Theory, then, should hold a dialectical relation with movements of revolt that fall out of the schema of historico-philosophical outlooks. The task of subaltern studies, as defined in this essay, would seek to conceptualize multiple possibilities of creative political action rather than defining a more "mature" political type of formation. Subaltern studies therefore would not pretend to have a privileged access to subalterns; rather, it would define intellectual work as one more intervention in insurgent movements. In developing practices, the intellectual would grow parallel to the emergent social actors and their interventions in everyday life.

We may now consider Gramsci's position and the prominence subaltern studies gives to negation in the context of Gautam Bhadra's analysis of the 1857 rebellion in India.[26] Bhadra concludes his study with a brief allusion to fragmentary leadership in peasant insurrections: "Yet this episodic and fragmentary narrative points to the existence in 1857 of what Gramsci has called 'multiple elements of conscious leadership' at the popular level."[27] Badhra's account works against dismissals of the indigenous leaders' role in the insurrection as "minor incidents" by academic historians like S. N. Sen in *Eighteen Fifty-Seven*, or mockeries as "mushroom dignities" by soldier historians like R.H.W. Dunlop in *Service and Adventure with the Khakee Ressalah or, Meerut Volunteer Horse, during the Mutinies of 1857–58*. In Badhra's account the indigenous leaders played an integral role in the popular insurrection. The four leaders shared ordinariness and had learned to use the logic of insurrection in the practice of everyday life: "The consciousness with which they all fought had been 'formed through everyday experience'; it was an 'elementary historical acquisition.'"[28]

Badhra's analysis of this rebellion differs in the tone and the details of the insurrection from Gramsci's historical examples: "It was the perception and day-to-day experience of the authority of the alien state in his immediate surroundings that determined the rebel's action."[29] Although one could argue that the situation of Sardinia and the Italian South in general was one of internal colonialism, Gramsci's counterhegemonic state and project of modernity would reinscribe the South within a narrative that posits historical continuity. In the case of the British empire the colonial situation foreclosed a connection, and the consciousness of the rebels was one of insurgency against a colonial power—not against a landed aristocracy, as in the case of what Gramsci conceptualizes as a progressive peasantry (that is, one that does not align itself with the local landlords against the urban leadership of both south and north). In this regard the work of the Indian subalternists falls within a postcolonial subject position that is fully aware of the colonial impulses that accompany the project of modernity.

This transformation of historiography, however, still believes that the task of tertiary discourse is to recover the place in history *for* subalterns. Its task is to prove that the insurgent can rely on a historian's performance, not that the performance of the insurgent itself can recover his or her place in history. This faith in the historian has less felicitous consequences. It is not just that positivistic knowledge of subalterns as objects of study runs the risk of providing information to the same institutions that have as an end to control and thus perpetuate subalternity. Beyond the misuse of empirical knowledge, we must question the epistemology that first emerges in the modern period and we readily identify with the emergence of objectivity and subjectivity in the work of Descartes. This split of the subject and object of knowledge implies a series of forms of disciplining subjectivity. From this perspective the issue would no longer be one of misuse of knowledge but of the power embedded in the epistemological apparatus itself. The problem would now reside in the production of the subaltern as an object of knowledge, rather than in claiming that subaltern studies will produce a more accurate representation. Subaltern studies cannot continue to practice a Cartesian epistemology in which the subject refines his cognitive apparatuses to gain a more objective perspective. This modern project would aim to formulate a form of life, a horizon of communication where knowledge would no longer distort its object. But this epistemological end takes for granted a commensurable position that the gaps in resistance-texts call into question.[30] It presumes that the form of life of the subaltern can be contained within the objectification of the intellectual. Moreover, it obviates the conflict between Western epistemology (as theory of what we can know and what counts as knowledge) and forms of life with different truth values.

We should instead elaborate inventories of forms of discourse/power that produce subalternity. In this regard, theories of colonial discourse would provide a way to gain access to forms of writing violence in colonialist discourses that informed and gained consolidation in the modernist projects to subject the world to European powers. It is crucial that we retain modernity(ies), European power(s), colonialist discourse(s) in the plural to avoid reifying Reason. The compatibility of the modern and the nonmodern of a subaltern politics would call for an understanding of reason that does not presuppose a reduction of nonmodern forms of life to the irrational (to locate them in an anterior historical moment—hence, as ineffectual practices). Reason, as devised by Kant and Hegel, is but one of the possible understandings of modernity. It is only by inventing alternatives to Reason that subaltern studies will devise a counterhegemony that will not generate subalternity in turn. Gramsci's understanding of Culture cannot avoid the need to constitute an intellectual vanguard. If the critique of vanguardism figures prominently in the historiography of the Southeast Asian Subaltern Group, it is a political principle for the Zapatistas. I see this possibility of nonvanguardist meshings of autonomous political movements as the utopian (nevertheless real) horizon of subaltern studies. If Gramscian counterhegemony aspires to state control of truth criteria, the circulation of knowledge, and the consumption of cultural capital, the task of subaltern studies, as I understand its utopian impulse, would not consist of a new administration of capital (cultural or otherwise) but a dissolution of capital's hegemony—not reform, but revolution.

In a key moment in her critique of the Southeast Asian Subaltern Group, Gayatri Spivak has suggested an internationalization of historiography that would include "the political economy of the independent peasant movement in Mexico."[31] Her recommendation entails a political economy of the Zapatistas that would avoid (neo)colonialist impulses to situate contemporary communal societies within a developmentalist narrative and thus to constitute them as incompatible with other forms of property—in fact, as irremediably bound to disappear. This is not the place to elaborate this project in any detail, however.[32] John Womack has documented the astuteness of the Zapatistas in forming an independent movement during the Mexican Revolution of 1910 that was sufficiently powerful to define agrarian policy up to Salinas's recent reforms of Article 27 of the Mexican Constitution. And it is not a coincidence that in the armed insurrection of January 1, 1994, the EZLN identified itself with the political theory as well as the military strategies of Zapata without excluding the whole pantheon of national heroes as forebears.

One of the last communiqué by the CCRI-CG mocks the identification— unmasking—of EZLN with the Fuerzas de Liberación Nacional (the National Liberation Forces):

> Al nombre de "Fuerzas de Liberacion Nacional" entre los antecedentes del EZLN, el gobierno debe agregar el de todas las organizaciones guerrilleras de los años 70s y 80s, a Arturo Gámiz, a Lucio Cabañas, a Genaro Vázquez Rojas, a Emiliano Zapata, a Francisco Villa, a Vicente Guerrero, a José María Morelos y Pavón, a Miguel Hidalgo y Costilla, a Benito Juárez y a muchos otros que ya borraron de los libros de historia porque un pueblo con memoria es un pueblo rebelde.
>
> [To the name of the "National Liberation Forces" as an antecedent of the EZLN, the government should add the names of the guerrillas from the 1970s and

1980s—Arturo Gámiz, Lucio Cabañas, Genaro Vázquez Rojas, Emiliano Zapata, Francisco Villa, Vicente Guerrero, José María Morelos y Pavón, Miguel Hidalgo y Costilla, Benito Juárez, and many others—that have been erased from history books because a people with a memory is a rebel people.][33]

Womack's and the Zapatistas' narratives are tragic, but certainly not because they mark an end of history; rather, they mark a continuation in struggle. Francis Barker has recently argued (against the *bovine* history of the New Historicists) that all history is tragic, but "in contrast to the fetishized memorialization of a dead past, it will certainly have to be a history of the present, shot through with the knowledge and the poetry of that critical part of the present which is the dangerous past."[34] The Zapatista's injunction—"un pueblo con memoria es un pueblo rebelde" [a people with a memory is a rebel people]— suggests an open-ended tragic understanding of Indian insurgency's histories. Womack's concluding comment in his "Epilogue" also suggests a historical narrative without closure: "A foreign visitor winced at seeing them. In this village, he thought, children still learn respect for elders, duty to kin, honor in work and play, curious lessons to carry into a world about to fly a man to the moon, deliberately capable of nuclear war, already guilty of genocide. But being Anenecuilcans, he decided, they would probably stand the strain."[35]

The EZLN stands as a testimony of the endurance of the Anenecuilcans, of indigenous Mexico in general, and in particular of Emiliano Zapata's legacy. In the epigraph from the CCRI-CG, the Zapatistas remind Zedillo that this endurance, which should not be seen as a form of essentialism, depends on a living history: "No Señor Zedillo, la lucha Zapatista está en todo México, Zapata no ha muerto, vive y vivirá siempre" [No Mr. Zedillo, Zapata is in all Mexico. Zapata is not dead; he is alive and will live forever].[36] Zapata did not revolt against the leaders of the Mexican revolution for a better grant of land, but for what already belonged to the Anenecuilcans. Central to the Zapatistas of Anenecuilco were titles that the community had preserved since the colonial period, titles for land that was legally theirs. In this respect their claims are like those of all Native Americans, for whom land redistribution would imply legitimating the usurpation of what was theirs from the start. As Womack has pointed out: "The land titles Zapata's uncle passed on to him in September 1909 were almost sacred documents. It was no mere bundle of legal claims that Zapata took charge of, but the collected testimony to the honor of all Anenecuilco chiefs before him, the accumulated trust of all past generations in the pueblo. This was his responsibility. And when a year and a half later he decided to commit the village to revolution, he buried the titles under the floor of its church."[37]

Contrary to Gramsci's claim that subalterns in their struggles "have left no reliable document," the Anenecuilcans have passed from generation to generation a record of their historical rights. If the Anenecuilcans contradict the lack of documents, Gramsci would be partially right when he asserts that subalterns "have not achieved any consciousness of the class 'for itself.'"[38] But this judgment would imply that Indian insurgency would embody a legitimate political consciousness only when inscribed in terms of Western history. There was a utopian element in Zapata's revolt precisely in that it did not understand itself in terms of a Western telos but as an ever-present possibility of reclaiming its communal lands. Moreover, Zapata saw very clearly the need to intervene in—and certainly not be absorbed by—national politics to achieve local ends. The Plan de Ayala testifies to his lucidity.[39]

Although Zapata and the EZLN exemplify indigenous insurgency, the subaltern, as the "Founding Statement" of the Latin American Subaltern Studies Group put it, should be understood as a migrating subject that includes "an array of the masses—peasants, proletarians, the informal and formal sectors, the sub- and underemployed, vendors, those outside or at the margin of the money economy, lumpens and ex-lumpens of all sorts, children, the growing numbers of the homeless."[40] Colonial documents on indigenous rebellions without fail give prominence to the leadership of women and make mention of blacks, mulattos, and mestizos joining ranks with Indians; in the case of the Zapatistas, they find support among urban lumpen proletarians who wear the ubiquitous ski mask at rock concerts or in the recent demonstrations as a symbol of solidarity. Marcos's characterization of the *México de abajo*—that is, "from below" (referring to the Mexico of the penthouse, the middle floor, and the basement) —vividly portrays subaltern rage: "El México de abajo tiene vocación de lucha, es solidario, es banda, es barrio, es palomilla, es raza, es cuate, es huelga, es marcha y mitín, es toma tierras, es cierre de carreteras, es 'no les creo!' es 'no me dejo,' es '¡órale!'" This popular language cannot be translated without distortion.[41] For instance *banda* or *palomilla* would call for "gang," but Marcos emphasizes a vocation for solidarity. The "no les creo" [I don't believe you], "no me dejo" [I will not take it] sums up the "¡órale!" which something like "enough" would hardly do justice. In chapter 2, I have traced this same *México de abajo* in the context of a 1692 rebellion in Mexico City. There, as in the case of the demonstrators, there is a solidarity with the Indians: "Todos somos indios," "Todos somos Marcos." One can hear the "¡órale!"

The state-sponsored ideology of *mestizaje* after the 1910 Revolution theoretically should have extended bonds of solidarity with Indians, but its historical effect was to promote a systematic denial of Indian roots—though the pre-Columbian past was idealized—and a program of acculturation that aimed to destroy indigenous languages and cultures. Only "mestizos" were deemed by the state to be "authentic" Mexicans. In this regard the "Todos somos Indios" would seem to augur (at least on a symbolic plane) the possibility of a radical change in the structures of feeling where the plurality of the Indian peoples of Mexico would be recognized and respected. This emergent sensibility would ultimately depend on the indigenous leadership and its capacity to negotiate on its own with the government. The porosity among Indian groups in rural Mexico and the corresponding responses from urban subalterns would differ from subalterns in India, who seem to be less mobile, communicative, and communicable. This difference, however, has as much to do with a long history of insurrections in Mexico where Indians occupied the same urban and rural spaces with the *castas* (racial mixtures that colonial documents laboriously break up ad infinitum—namely, beyond mestizos and mulattos, documents identify *zambaigos* [Indian and Chinese], *lobos* [Indian and African], *pardos* [mestizo and African], *castizos* [mestizo and Spaniard], and so on). These classifications clearly have a very different meaning than the caste system in India, and a different history. Not only is there a memory continuum (obviously with different interpretations in time, as in any other culture) in the remembrance of past Indian insurrections, but also of the *México de abajo*.

Nevertheless, we should heed the CCRI-CG's constant insistence on the Indian leadership of the EZLN in the face of the government's and the press's accusations of manipulation by "profesionales de la violencia" [professionals of violence], as illustrated in a 1995 communiqué: "Lo reiteramos, el EZLN es una organización de mexicanos, mayoritariamente indígena, dirigida por un co-mité colegiado de las distintas etnias de Chiapas y no tiene, en su composición absolutamente a ningún miembro no indígena" [We reiterate it, the EZLN is an organization of Mexicans, with an Indian majority, directed by a commit-tee that gathers all the different ethnic groups of Chiapas and does not have, in its composition, one single member that is not an Indian].[42] This statement suggests that nationalism as a mode of relating communities without erasing their linguistic and cultural specificities should be taken seriously as a sub-altern political program that should not be "folklorized." If the specificity of the Zapatistas and the history of Mexico should not be erased through a read-ing that draws parallelisms with rebellions in India and elsewhere in South-east Asia, the rhetorics of counterinsurgency that Ranajit Guha has identified are nonetheless germane to the Mexican government's policies that have at-tempted to contain Marcos and infantilize the Zapatistas.[43] For instance, some sectors of the press in the days that followed the rebellion dismissed the first communiqués that listed NAFTA as one of the motivations for the rebellion. How could Indians understand NAFTA without foreign advisers? This same press has regularly condemned the insurgency as illegal violence.[44]

A recent collection of articles published under the title *Chiapas: La guerra de las ideas* [Chiapas: The war of ideas] condemns the violence; proscribes the utopian impulse; suggests that international drug dealers financed the EZLN;

blames liberation theology and the Bishop of San Cristobal de Las Casas, Samuel Ruiz, for the violence; and unmasks the manipulation of the Indians by Marcos.[45] The title of this collection gives the impression that its contributors are the only ones who carry out a legitimate "war of ideas." The question is against whom, for at least some of the articles—even though they do not fully sympathize with the taking of arms by the EZLN—suggest that they are also waging a "war of ideas" against the government. But the book's editor never seems to consider the violent nature and implications of the moral superiority he ascribes to the contributors of the volume. What do you do to outlaws? What about the communiqués of Marcos and the CCRI-CG that call for dialogue and carry out war by other means, as the military theorist Carl von Clausewitz would put it? Despite the mastery of media shown by the communiqués, some quarters of the press still disparage their *literary* quality. Most of the contributors chose to ignore that NAFTA was the culmination—the icing on the cake—of neoliberal policies that Salinas had been implementing during his *sexenio* (six-year term).

Of particular relevance to Chiapas was Salinas's reform of Article 27 of the constitution, which "guaranteed that villages had the right to hold property as corporations, that the pueblo was a legitimate institution in the new order [of the 1910 Mexican revolution]."[46] Marcos underscored this point several times in the interviews held with reporters Blanche Petrich and Elio Henríquez for *La Jornada* in 1994:

> Esas reformas cancelaron toda posibilidad legal de tener tierra, que era lo que finalmente los mantenía como grupo paramilitar de autodefensa. Luego llegó el fraude electoral del '88 y ahí los compañeros vieron que tampoco el voto servía porque no se respetaba lo que era evidente. Estos dos fueron los detonantes, pero a mi se me hace que lo que más radicalizó a los compañeros fue la reforma al artículo 27, esa fue la puerta que se les cerró a los indígenas para sobrevivir de manera legal y pacífica. Por eso se alzaron en armas, para que se les oyera, porque ya estaban cansados de pagar una cuota de sangre tan alta.

> [Those reforms canceled all legal possibilities of their holding land. And that possibility is what had kept them functioning as paramilitary self-defense groups. Then came the electoral fraud of 1988. The compañeros saw that voting didn't matter either because there was no respect for basic things. These were the two detonators, but in my view it was the reform of Article 27 that most radicalized the compañeros. That reform closed the door on the indigenous people's strategies for surviving legally and peacefully. That's why they rose up in arms, so that they would be heard.][47]

The Zapatista uprising in January presented itself as a response to the selling of the country to transnational corporations. As El Sup (the nickname often given to Marcos, mocking Superman as in "*superclinton*") has put it, the Indians in Chiapas are among the last few patriots that are willing to fight for the country. In an interview Marcos cited the CCRI-CG's motivation for taking arms: "Porque nosotros, lo que no estamos de acuerdo es que nuestro país se venda al extranjero. Como quiera, morir de hambre pasa, pero lo que no pasa es que en este país mande otro que no sea mexicano" [We disagree with selling our country to foreigners. Although we can live with starvation, we cannot accept that this country be ruled by someone that is not a Mexican].[48] This nationalist statement has very little to do with the state-sponsored nationalism of the Partido Revolucionario Institucional (PRI)—a nationalism that, by the way, also informs the tourist industry that has confined indigenous cultures to curio shops, museums, and archaeological sites.

As in the case of Badhra's rebels, the Zapatista leadership has a clear understanding of the national situation based on a historical experience. Unlike Badhra's individualized rebels, the Zapatista contingent includes, besides Marcos, a number of *sin cara* (faceless) and *sin nombre* (nameless) leaders—with the noms de guerre of Comandantes Tacho, David, and Trinidad, and Mayor Rolando—who have nevertheless gained visibility and a voice in interviews they have held with the press. It is important to note that the CCRI-CG has kept Marcos from participating in the recent peace negotiations with the government. This subordination of Marcos has as much to do with safeguarding him as with keeping in check his protagonist tendencies. The representatives in the round of talks in April and May 1995 were once more infantilized, and in the discussions in July 1995 there seems to have been a breakdown regarding the Zapatistas' demands for a respect for their dignity.

Comandante Tacho deplored but also mocked the ineptness of the representatives from the government: "También nos dijeron que están estudiando mucho que es la dignidad, que están consultando y haciendo estudios de la dignidad. Que lo que más podían entender era que la dignidad era el servicio a los demás. Y nos pidieron que nosotros les dijéramos que entendemos por dignidad. Les respondimos que sigan con la investigación. A nosotros nos da risa y nos reímos frente a ellos" [They also told us that they were studying very much what is dignity, that they are doing research and studies on dignity. What they could understand more was that dignity was service to others. And they asked us to tell them what dignity means to us. We answered them that they should go on with their research. It makes us laugh, and we laughed in their faces].[49] The collective memory of five hundred years of oppression enabled the Zapatista leadership to link local demands to a national agenda. When blamed for wasting time in the negotiations with such issues as respect for dignity, the Zapatista delegation, according to Tacho, responded that "nosotros no somos los culpables, todos los indígenas de México llevamos cinco siglos con la pobreza, el desprecio y con la marginación" [we told them that we were not to be blamed because all the Indians of Mexico have lived for the last five hundred years in poverty, disdain, and marginalization].[50]

The emergence of the Zapatista movement with an Indian feminine leadership also signals a recentering of rationality and the nation in and on Indian terms. As expressed in a CCRI-CG interview on February 3–4, 1994, Marcos is subordinate to the CCRI-CG, which had arrived at the decision of going to war after the committee of each community consulted its members: "Los Comités pasaron a preguntar a cada hombre, a cada mujer, a cada niño si ya era tiempo de hacer la guerra o no" [the Committees went on to ask each man, each woman, each child if it was time to go to war or not].[51] When queried why women and children participated in the revolutionary organization, Ramona, who is described as a small comandante, responded: "Porque las mujeres también están viviendo en una situación más difícil, porque las mujeres son ellas que están más explotadas, oprimidas fuertemente todavía. ¿Por qué? Porque las mujeres desde hace tantos años, pos desde hace 500 años, no tiene sus derechos de hablar, de participar en una asamblea" [Because women are also living in a difficult situation, because women are the most exploited ones, still strongly oppressed. Why? Because women for many years, indeed for the past five hundred years, have not had the freedom to speak, to participate in an assembly].[52]

Because of a severe illness, Ramona has been replaced in the table of negotiations by Comandante Trinidad, who is in her sixties and has been described "con el rostro parcialmente cubierto por un paliacate rojo y una larga cabellera entrecana y lacia" [with her face partially covered with a red bandanna and long graying and straight hair].[53] Trinidad has demanded a special table to discuss women issues and denounced the response of the government that mocked her by asking why not also have "a mesa de jóvenes, de niños o de ancianos" [a table of youth, of children, or of the elderly].[54] If the indigenous leadership has gained prominence in the past few months, the indigenous leaders since the earliest interviews have underscored the subordinate role of Marcos. For instance, in an early interview a member of the CCRI-CG stated that Marcos is a spokesperson and a military strategist but not the political theorist: "Pues Marcos es como subcomandante. Marcos tiene la facilidad del castilla. Nosotros todavía fallan un chingo. . . . [El manda en lo militar.] Nosotros, pues, más la cuestión política, organizativa" [Well, Marcos is like a subcomandante. Marcos has the facility of the *castilla*. We still make a "chingo" of mistakes. . . . (He leads the military aspect.) We are in charge of the political and organizational questions].[55] Because of their flawed Spanish, Marcos functions as a spokesperson and at least in this interview the *chingo* of mistakes of the Indians' *castilla* are not corrected. Undoubtedly, Marcos at first was indispensable for placing the Zapatistas on a national and international front.

In one set of texts or statements, Marcos and the CCRI-CG developed a lively rhetoric, often irreverent and mocking of the government, and a critique of the political economy as well as the ideological warfare conducted by the government. In another set they underscored how the political positions and decisions to go to war were made after consensus was reached in every indigenous community. Marcos's pen might very well be involved in some of the CCRI-CG texts, but it is only in bad faith that some members of the national and the international press have ascribed authorship to him. So much ink has flowed trying to unmask Marcos—that is, to peg an identity and a proper name on El Sup. At a time when most Mexican intellectuals were willing to believe that revolution, Marxism, and guerrillas were dead, and that the Left in Latin America could only be reformist, the emergence of the Zapatistas had to be explained away. The theories that informed these views were either wrong or the EZLN was an anomaly if not a historical aberration that tried to exhume Marx and the rest. Thus Jorge Castañeda has reduced the Zapatistas to an "armed reformism."[56]

It does not occur to Castañeda that the EZLN might at once be reformist (seek specific democratic transformations) and revolutionary (express a sense of injustice that calls for a radical new time). In a letter responding to Zedillo's inaugural speech, Marcos underscored the revolutionary character of the Zapatistas: "Usted ya no es usted. Es ahora la personificación de un sistema injusto, anti-democrático y criminal. Nosotros, los 'ilegales,' los 'transgresores de la ley,' los 'profesionales de la violencia,' los 'sin nombre,' somos ahora y desde siempre la esperanza de todos. No es nada personal, señor Zedillo. Simplemente ocurre que nosotros nos hemos propuesto cambiar el mundo, y el sistema político que usted representa es el principal estorbo para lograrlo" [You are not yourself anymore. You are now the personification of an unjust system, antidemocratic, and criminal. We, the "illegal," the "transgressors of the law," the "professionals of violence," the "nameless," are now and have always been the hope of all. It is nothing personal, Mr. Zedillo. It is simply that we have proposed ourselves to change the world, and the political system that you represent is the main obstacle to achieve it].[57] The end of changing the world presupposes the destruction of the PRI and the state apparatuses that support it. It does not mean, however, that the EZLN aspires to take over the state. It remains a revolutionary movement, but the strategy that informs it is not any longer inspired by the Cuban Revolution.

When the press reduces the EZLN to the personal history of Marcos-the-militant from previous armed movements in Mexico, it ends up reinscribing the Zapatistas as a variation and advancement of the guerrillas in Guatemala, the FSLN in Nicaragua, and the last instance in a series of armed movements in Mexico. Marcos inevitably assumes the image of a caudillo, a role he has contested, but the press insists on it: "Marcos es el caudillo—aunque él lo niega—de un levantamiento armado en el país del surrealismo [Marcos is the caudillo—even if he denies it—of an uprising in the country of surrealism]."[58] This is seemingly an empathetic version of the unmasking—with an exoticizing turn: "el país del surrealismo." But the rhetoric of counterinsurgency can be traced in the reference to Marcos as a caudillo.

In the ranks of those who seek to unmask Marcos to discredit him prominently figures Alma Guillermoprieto's recent article in the *New York Review of Books*. Her article (although it was signed on February 2) appeared in a suspicious moment that inevitably (regardless of her intentions) would come into play with a "Political Update" from the Chase Bank. It called for the extermination of the Zapatistas ("The national government will need to eliminate the Zapatista to demonstrate their effective control of the national territory and of security policy") and the apparent compliance to this demand by the Mexican government that revealed the "true" identity of Marcos, printed "his" photograph, and placed an order for his arrest and that of the other leaders of the EZLN.[59] Marcos emerges as a professional of violence who manipulates the Indians and (perhaps more in tune with the Chase Bank memorandum) the EZLN as hardly a military force. The government justified its decision to send the army into Zapatista territories because arms caches had been found in the states of Veracruz and Mexico.

Critics of Marcos who attempt to identify him manifest a will to control the meaning of texts by means of the construction of their authors. Poststructuralist concepts of the "author function" as developed by Foucault offer another way of reading the "author*ity*" in the communiqués by Marcos and the CCRI-CG.[60] Instead of insisting on who the real Marcos is, one should understand the particular author-function he as well as the CCRI-CG occupy and produce. The communiqués by the CCRI-CG are ascribed to a collective body and as such manifest the values and position of the indigenous community. They derive their authority and legitimacy inasmuch as they are the expression of a collective body that by definition is subaltern. For dominant discourse, Indians, as long as they speak and think "as Indians," cannot write or formulate a coherent political program. Beyond the obvious racism, this dismissal of indigenous intellectuality entails structural determinants that date back to the early colonization of the Americas—the subjection of native knowledges as superstitious or idolatrous. Indians had to abandon indigenous forms of life in order to make sense. In this regard, the CCRI-CG manifest an instance of writing the impossible in its affirmation that the EZLN is an Indian-led insurgency.

Their call for justice has ancestral roots that cannot be reduced to an immediate program of reforms. The Zapatistas' call for justice is in the realm of the incalculable, as defined by Derrida: "the law is the element of calculation and it is just that there be law. But justice is incalculable. It requires us to calculate with the incalculable."[61] Tacho's demand for respect of dignity conveys this call for justice as incalculable. What could make amends for the oppression of indigenous peoples over the past five hundred years? But equally radical are CCRI-CG's call for a broad national and international front to struggle for the transition to a radical democracy, which perhaps is nowhere better defined than in Durito's text—the one whose pay went to the Fiat workers in Turin.

Marcos refutes the characterization of the EZLN as an armed reformist movement: "cualquier intento de 'reforma' o de 'equilibrio' de esta deformación es imposible DESDE DENTRO DEL SISTEMA DE PARTIDO DE ESTADO. . . . ES NECESARIA UNA REVOLUCIÓN, una nueva revolución" [any attempt of "reform" or "equilibrium" of this deformation is impossible FROM WITHIN THE STATE PARTY SYSTEM. . . . A REVOLUTION IS NECESSARY, a new revolution].[62] Durito reminds us that this call for revolution actually went back to a communiqué from January 20, 1994, where Marcos had first spoken of "un espacio democrático de resolución de la confrontación entre diversas propuestas políticas" [a democratic space for the confrontation of diverse political proposals]. Durito criticizes Marcos's obscure and indigestible style and goes on to clarify what should be understood by revolution. It is "una concepción incluyente, antivanguardista y colectiva" [an inclusive, antivanguardist, and collective conception] that is no longer a problem "de LA organización, EL método, y de EL caudillo (ojo con las mayúsculas)" [of THE organization, THE method, and THE caudillo (beware the caps)]" but a task that pertains to all those who see the revolution as necessary and possible and for its realization everyone is important.[63]

The end of the revolution would not be anymore "la conquista del Poder o la implantación (por vías pacíficas o violentas) de un nuevo sistema social, sino de algo anterior a una y otra cosa. Se trata de construir la antesala del mundo nuevo, un espacio donde, con igualdad de derechos y obligaciones, las distintas fuerzas políticas se 'disputen' el apoyo de la mayoría de la sociedad" [the conquest of Power or the implantation (by means of peaceful or violent means) of a new social system, but of something anterior to one and the other thing. It is a question of building the antechamber of a new world, a space where, with equal rights and obligations, the different political forces would "dispute" the support of society's majority].[64]

This proposition bears striking parallelisms with Negri's understanding of communism and the constituent power of the multitude: "We may conceive the multitude as minoritarian or subaltern, or more accurately as exploited, but the multitude is always already central to the dynamics of social production; it is always already in a position of power. The power it is endowed with, however, is a power qualitatively different from the power of the State."[65] These calls for revolution do not have in common an alternative socialist state but a political space that is not bound by the logic of capitalism and socialism as alternative administrations of capital.[66] Both Negri and the Zapatistas call for the formation of strong subjectivities that would resist any transfer of power to a transcendental institution—that is, to any form of political mediation that resides outside the processes of the masses. It could be argued that this commonalty could be traced back to a shared affinity with the Zapatismo of the Plan de Ayala. Nevertheless, the connections between the EZLN and the Italian labor movement bear the auspices of a new internationalism that would not be grounded any longer in a party or follow the program of a socialist model.

Within the long memory of the indigenous oppression, grief, mourning, and rebellion, socialism is but one particular political form, one of the many regimes of laws that have been available from the West. Marcos is but one of the many Western interlocutors that have advocated justice for the Indians. We must here recall Bartolomé de Las Casas, the bishop after whom the town of San Cristobal is named, who, at the end of his long life of struggle against the injustices committed against the Indians, called for a restoration of all sovereignty to the indigenous leaders and condemned the colonial enterprise in its entirety. Las Casas's radicalism went to the extent that he threatened Philip II with excommunication and called for a restitution of all stolen goods and sovereignty to the Indians.[67] Because the colonial enterprise was wrong, the Indians had the right to make war against the Spaniards and uproot them from their territories: "La octava [conclusión] que las gentes naturales de todas partes y de qualquiera dellas donde havemos entrado en las Indias tienen derecho adquirido de hazernos guerra justissima y raernos de la haz de la tierra y este derecho les durara hasta el dia del juyzio" [The eight (states) that the native people of these parts and of every one where we have entered in the Indies have the right to make a most just war against us and to erase us from the face of the earth, and they hold this right until doomsday].[68]

One might very well wonder if this position is even within the realm of the impossible today. Indian histories have kept a record of both those institutions of the West that have sought to restore justice as well as those that have oppressed them. This is not the first indigenous rebellion in Mexican history, and one of the tasks of subaltern studies would call for a recuperation of the communities' memories of earlier Indian insurgencies and an understanding of how they were subjected to dominant forms of the nation-state. This *knowledge* (not of positivistic data but of the discursive devices that subject Indian cultures and a parallel indigenous awareness that their histories are figures of the impossible) would spare us the banal characterization of the Zapatistas as the first postmodern, or for that matter postcommunist, revolutionary move-ment. It is precisely in terms of this long history that one can define the subal-tern subject position of the CCRI-CG, of the Zapatista insurgency in general, and of Marcos himself as exterior to the logic of capitalism or socialism.

One of the tasks of subaltern studies would consist of writing histories of Indian insurgencies in Mexico that would not be interpreted according to supposedly more advanced or developed political movements. These histories would practice what Guha has called writing in reverse—that is, against the grain of the documents that first recorded rebellions but also against the coun-terinsurgent histories that sought to explain and contain insurrection. This would include tertiary histories that would privilege the wars of independence, the revolution, or Marxist theory as providing categories to evaluate earlier movements as ineffectual. The Zapatistas respond to the specific conditions of postmodernity (globalization, transnationalism, the "demise" of socialism, neoliberalism, and so on). And if their response is determined by these politi-cal and economic conditions, the EZLN should not be reduced to a postmod-ern phenomenon: Zapatismo is and is not (post)modern. As I pointed out at the beginning of this chapter, subaltern movements should be seen as cultural forms where the modern and nonmodern are compatible. Indeed, the EZLN manifests, in its interpretation of the sources of their oppression and counter-insurgent modes of containment, a lucidity that has been from the start a part of Indian resistance to colonialism. It also entails, at least implicit to the Zap-atista denunciation of paternalism, a critique of Gramsci's "folklorization" of popular culture. Subaltern studies would therefore also make it its business to draw an inventory of modes of colonial discourse, of forms of writing violence, that have sedimented in "commonsense" developmentalist tropes.[69]

In addressing the subject positions of Marcos (and the CCRI-CG by exten-sion), we must keep in mind that "he" is a series of communiqués, interviews, and speeches that have been recorded in video, and not some sort of coher-ent and consistent self behind the statements he utters. Also, let's not forget that these multiple subject positions have little to do with a celebration of a postmodern fragmented self. Furthermore, Marcos's and the CCRI-CG's un-derstanding of history, and their role within it, is profoundly tragic and escha-tological (though not teleological). It is worth recalling here Walter Benjamin's distinction between progress and *jetztzein*, "the 'time of the now' which is shot through with the chips of Messianic time."[70] The Zapatistas, like Benjamin, would confront "mythical violence," the violence of the storm (progress) that keeps the angel from redeeming the past ("awaken the dead, and make whole what has been smashed"), with "divine violence," a revolutionary violence conceived as "the highest manifestation of unalloyed violence."[71]

The communiqués of Marcos and the CCRI-CG evoke a history where the enemy has always been victorious, but they also formulate a discourse on violence that grounds its purity in the impossibility (paradoxically, also the condition of possibility) of its demands. Although the Zapatistas are a military force, the power of their violence resides in the new world they call forth—a sense of justice, democracy, and liberty that the government *cannot* understand because it calls for its demise. Marcos's multiple subject positions fulfill tactical and strategic functions within his discourse. Within one communiqué he might very well open his text with a poem by Paul Eluard (a gesture that situates his voice within a long-standing Marxist aesthetic), move on to evoke millenarian indigenous narratives (thus asserting that the EZLN struggle for justice has ancestral roots), elaborate a critique of the political economy of Mexico in terms of the four main social classes (the social scientist here complements the intellectual and the "anthropologist"), include multiple voices in the critique where the "social scientist" gains force from popular speech (IMF data are made palatable by satire, humor, evocations of the populace—the "¡órale!" mentioned earlier). I could go on and on and draw an exhaustive map of the author-functions in Marcos's communiqués, but there is a danger that in doing so, we might reiterate the same closures that author-criticism imposes on texts. An inventory of Marcos's subject positions, hence author functions, runs the risk of neutralizing his discourse.

There are other ways of reading these subject positions. Foucault in his "What Is an Author?" poses the question, "What difference does it make who is speaking?"[72] I would answer that in the case of Marcos, the question is neither rhetorical nor academic. If one conceives of Marcos as a *revolutionary* in the context of a consensus that Marxism, revolution, communism, and so on are dead, where guerrilla warfare or utopian thinking cannot be *imagined* outside the Cuban model, and revolution is considered unthinkable in a situation that supposedly enables other forms of expression, then it does matter who is speaking. Hence the urgency to elaborate an ethics of reading subalternity. Cheryll Walker's critique of the generally accepted notion among poststructuralist critics of the "death of the author" is pertinent to Marcos, the author of revolutionary discourse.[73] Walker has pointed out that questioning the death of the author would not necessarily mean returning to some sort of (patriarchal) author criticism that would posit an individual as the origin of a text; yet, Walker argues, "writing is not [as Barthes and, to a lesser extent, Foucault would have us believe] 'the destruction of every voice' but *the proliferation of possibilities of hearing*."[74] Marcos's subaltern position resides in an exteriority to the logic of socialism and capitalism that haunts his articulation of an Indian-led insurgency. The positive response by the demonstrators in Mexico City manifests not only the efficacy of the subject positions he deploys in his communiqués, but "a proliferation of possibilities of hearing."

As an intellectual, Marcos no longer defines his task as one of representation. He does not speak for the Zapatistas (he is one more Zapatista and, as an intellectual, a subordinate) nor does he portray them.[75] This does not mean that Marcos has not functioned as a spokesperson nor that he has not literarily recreated guerrilla life in the *Selva Lacandona,* or provided explanations of how power operates today. But these "mirrors," as he calls them (we must keep in mind that the numerous communiqués from the CCRI-CG as well as the interviews of the indigenous leadership have also produced mirrors), of who the Zapatistas are, what they want, and who oppresses them must give way to a "crystal ball." He understands this as the production of revolutionary spaces that systematically would undermine the constitution of a vanguard.

Marcos's understanding of the role of the intellectual from within an illegal army can be extended to others working through legal channels. Intellectual work would run parallel to emergent social movements rather than articulate for them a political program. Intellectual work would thereby operate on one of the multiple spaces of intervention. If as an intellectual Marcos might define the ends of the Zapatista insurrection, its realization would ultimately depend on the constituent power of the multitude: "En suma no estamos proponiendo una revolución ortodoxa, sino algo mucho más difícil: una revolución que haga posible la revolución . . ." [To sum up, we are not proposing an orthodox revolution but something much more difficult: a revolution that will make the revolution possible. . .].[76] The ellipsis are his, suggesting that this open-ended closing of the section on revolution in the communiqué must be completed with the political creativity of the different groups struggling for democracy, liberty, and justice—to repeat once more the Zapatistas' main three demands. Demands that define the need to retain the impossible alive in the face of forms of "writing violence" that have systematically infantilized subalterns.

The notion of writing violence points to the constitution of forms of life that follow a different logic as violent—that is, as devoid of Reason. It also refers to objects of representation—that is, massacres, tortures, rapes, and other forms of material terror. There is an aesthetic, an epistemology, and an ethics of colonial violence. The aesthetic of colonial violence has at hand a whole series of epic topoi that have circulated in Western literature at least since Homer and still are used in denigratory representations of Third World peoples.[77] A colonialist ethics informs the laws and regulations that different colonial and neocolonial enterprises have formulated to control voyages of exploration, to justify wars of aggression, and to rationalize permanent occupations of territories. Clear instances of epistemic violence have been the colonialists' subjections of indigenous knowledges as irrational, superstitious, and idolatrous. In the Zapatista communiqués we have seen how Marcos and indigenous leaders like Tacho, Trinidad, and David have responded to colonialist forms of writing violence by seeing through them, by laughing at counterinsurgent rhetorical moves, and by denouncing the cynical duplicity of the state.

Such is the predicament of postcolonial intellectuals practicing subaltern studies. The specific categories of aesthetic, ethical, and epistemological forms of colonial violence comprise a culture of conquest that still informs the history of the present, of what Foucault has defined as the ontohistory of what makes us subjects.[78] In our case it is the history of what makes intellectuals oppressive subjects. This ontohistory would consist of an "enlightened de-enlightenment." Subaltern studies would thus first have the task of elaborating an inventory of the colonial legacy of modernity, before even beginning to conceptualize "elsewheres" to dominant Western rationalities (to borrow Donna Haraway's utopian phrase).[79] Historical narratives are hardly "insignificant" events in the cultural identities of people. As the Zapatistas put it, "un pueblo con memoria es un pueblo rebelde" [a people with a memory is a rebel people]. Also consider Rigoberta Menchú's Quiche community's refusal to accept a Ladino version of the conquest and colonization.[80] Clearly, it is not *inconsequential* for her community to "turn the clocks back" and claim a clear understanding of colonialism—a subalternist reading of the ruses of developmentalist ideologies. Both Menchú's *testimonio* and the communiqués of the EZLN are forms of subaltern discourse that should not be confused with what subaltern studies produces in elite intellectual centers.

Subaltern politics and revolutionary interventions are obviously not dependent on nor inspired by academic theory. In the case of Marcos, however, there is a likelihood that he has read Gramsci and perhaps elaborated a critique of Gramsci's blindness toward the folkloric. Furthermore, in his interview with Blanche Petrich and Elio Henríquez, Marcos evokes Zapatismo as he critiques the vanguardism of the Cuban inspired *foquismo* prevalent in the 1970s guerrillas: "nuestra tutoría militar viene de Villa, principalmente Zapata, y de lo que no debió hacerse de las guerrillas de los setenta, es decir, empezar con un movimiento militar localizado y esperar a que las bases se fueran sumando paulatinamente o iluminadas por ese foco guerrillero" [our military instruction comes from Villa, principally from Zapata. It also comes by way of negative example from what was done by the guerrillas of the 1970s. They started with a local military movement and expected that the base would slowly join in or that they would be enlightened by this guerrilla *foco*].[81]

In the manner of a coda, I would like to underscore that my approach to issues pertaining to the *folkloric* and the *impossible* clearly does not presume the transparency that Spivak criticizes Foucault and Deleuze in their claim that subalterns "know far better than [the intellectual] and they certainly say it very well."[82] The impossibility of speaking and the eminent folklorization that has haunted the discourse of Zapatistas at every stage of their dialogue with the government—exchanges that could very well be understood as colonial encounters caught in a struggle to the death—do not manifest subalterns who "know far better" and "say it very well." Rather, it allows for a clear understanding that the possibility of their call for justice, liberty, and democracy resides paradoxically in the impossibility of being understood. The point of departure is not that "subalterns speak very well," but that they "cannot speak" and "choose not to learn how"—indeed, they demand that the discourse of power "learn how to speak to them."

This position is perhaps nowhere better exemplified than in Comandante Trinidad, who at a session with the government chose to address the official representatives in Tojolobal and then ask them in Spanish if it all was clear.[83] Rather than seeing Trinidad's intervention as a symbolic statement about the difficulties of negotiating in another language, we ought to see it as an allegory of the inevitable subalternization of Indian discourse. Obviously, her denunciation of the oppressive situation of women and children living under the military occupation of the *Selva* cannot be a mere question of translation, but at a more elemental level, it must be seen as criticism of deep-seated colonialist attitudes that cannot accept that an old Indian woman could have anything to say and would be able to say it. This allegory of the impossibility of communication implies that the subject of the West is not only dying but that its demise will come only as a result of specific struggles that make manifest its colonialist (read sexist, classist, racist) worldview that remains concealed in its claims to universality. In discussing Zapatismo, I have brought into play and critiqued theoretical points derived from Gramsci, Foucault, and Spivak. My point has not been to understand Zapatismo in the light of these thinkers but to sustain a dialogue where Zapatismo ultimately provides a critique of the discourses we produce as privileged intellectuals.

Historical and Epistemological Limits in Subaltern Studies

Mira que los frayles y clérigos cada uno tienen su manera de penitencia; mira que los frayles de San Francisco tienen una manera de doctrina y una manera de vida y una manera de vestido y una manera de oración; y los de Sant Agustín tienen otra; y los de Santo Domingo tienen otra; y los clérigos otra . . . y así mismo era entre los que goardaban a los dioses nuestros, que los de México tenían una manera de vestido y una manera de orar . . . y otros pueblos de otra; en cada pueblo tenían una manera de sacrificios.

[Consider that the friars and the secular clergy each has its own form of penance; consider that the Franciscan friars have one manner of doctrine and one way of life and one dress and one way of prayer; and the Augustinians another; and the Dominicans another; and the secular clergy another . . . and it was also like this among those who kept our gods, so that the ones from Mexico had one way of dress and prayer . . . and other towns had another; each town had its own way of sacrificing.]

—DON CARLOS DE OMETOCHTZIN

According to one of the witnesses in the inquisitional trial of Don Carlos Ometochtzin, this cacique of Tezcoco exposed a plural worldview in speeches to his town. If a variety of Catholic perspectives exist, Ometochtzin asked, why shouldn't they coexist with the multiple Mexican variants of the pre-Columbian period? This epistemological boldness led the Holy Office to judge and execute Ometochtzin for being a heretical dogmatizer. In the pages of the Codex Telleriano-Remensis (figure 4.1) corresponding to the years 1541–1543, a *tlacuilo* (Indian painter and writer trained in a pre-Columbian pictorial tradition) manifests a similar perspective to Ometochtzin's. Two friars are depicted, a Dominican and a Franciscan, who are identified by postures, dress, and symbols representative of their orders. In the section on the colonial period the *tlacuilo* invented a pictorial vocabulary, which she derived from the ancient tradition, to capture the new realities of horse, the colonial institutions, historical figures of the conquest, and, as in this particular page, differences among the missionaries.[1]

As in Ometochtzin's speech, the *tlacuilo* not only encodes the different worlds of the Franciscans and the Dominicans but also includes on the same page an indigenous view of the world in the painting of the Mixton War in

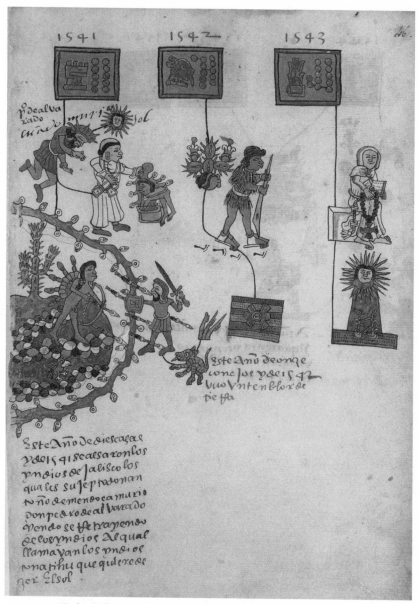

FIGURE 4.1. Codex Telleriano-Remensis. Folio 46r. Courtesy of the Bibliothèque Nationale de France.

1541. We know that this uprising in northern Mexico created a great source of apprehension for colonial authorities. The *tlacuilo*'s depiction of these events must have created anxiety among the supervising missionaries of Telleriano-Remensis. Three pages later the Dominican friar Pedro de los Rios takes over

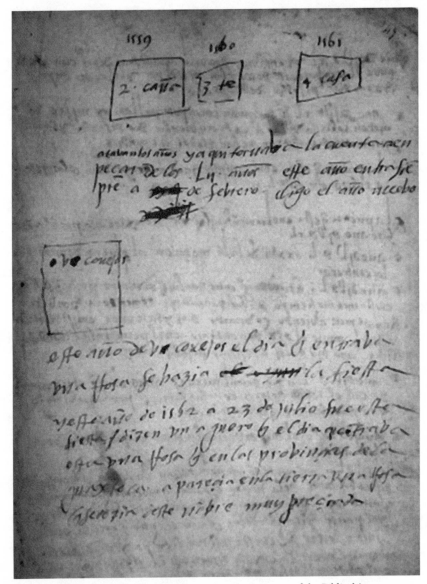

FIGURE 4.2. Codex Telleriano-Remensis. Folio 49r. Courtesy of the Bibliothèque Nationale de France.

the production of the codex. He stops using color and the inscription of the dates lacks the care of the *tlacuilo* (figure 4.2). Also annoying are the shoddy calligraphies, full of scratches, of the Spanish commentators, whose negative observations destroy the physical and epistemological integrity of the manuscript. In a page from the *tonalamatl* (the divinatory calendar) we can observe

FIGURE 4.3. Codex Telleriano-Remensis. Folio 12v. Courtesy of the Bibliothèque Nationale de France.

how aesthetically repugnant calligraphies and scratches invade the pictorial text and stand in stark contrast to the alphabetical script of the Indian and mestizo scribes who imitate print and limit themselves to merely identifying the figures and other information contained in the pictorial text (figure 4.3).

A recent Zapatista communiqué exemplifies the capacity to dwell in multiple worlds as a constant in subaltern discourses from the conquest to the present. I am thinking of that moment of lucidity in which Comandante Trinidad, during a session in dialogues with the government, addressed the representatives of the Mexican government in the Tojolabal language and then asked them if they had understood. More than an affirmation of Tojolabal, Trinidad's speech act invokes a conception of the world that cannot simply reduce the force of her statement to an issue of translation. The well-known question of the literary theorist Gayatri Chakravorty Spivak—"Can the subaltern speak?"—assumes an unexpected turn as it is the government who is incapable of speaking: a racist subject, epistemologically inept, morally dense, and unable to understand the historical present of a now, of a messianic present, the *jetztzeit* of Walter Benjamin, which has nothing to do with the historical concept of progress.[2]

On the basis of these *desencuentros culturales* (cultural disencounters), to borrow Julio Ramos's expression, I would like to explore three historical and epistemological limits in subaltern studies.[3]

1. The necessity to dwell in a plurality of worlds is a characteristic of subalterns, spaces, and discourses.

2. The coexistence of different worlds in subaltern discourses implies a form of *enlightened de-enlightenment*.

3. All assumptions of dominant systems or ideologies ultimately amount to a hoax, a sort of self-induced trompe l'oeil.

What are the connections and implications of these limits to the questions raised by Robert Young in his essay "Ideologies of the Postcolonial"?[4] In addressing present and past subaltern speech acts in Mexican history, I first want to evoke the lost possibility of a coexistence of a plurality of worlds in Ometochtzin's and the *tlacuilo*'s expressions. I also want to call attention to the impending danger of falling prey to Western hubris once again in the dialogues between the Mexican government and the Zapatistas. If Trinidad complicates the location of the postcolonial in metropolitan centers and the concept of "migrancy," Ometochtzin and the *tlacuilo* serve as a reminder that the postcolonial has multiple pasts that should make us wary of accepting single stories of modernity.[5]

We must question the contradictory tendency to assert that "everything" started in the nineteenth century, while flattening the past by indiscriminately applying to earlier periods in Western history categories that were not operative before the end of the eighteenth century. We must avoid making the equally flattening gesture of reducing earlier colonial enterprises to the rape and subsequent abandonment of the lands. Clearly, this statement is not intended as an apologetic of Spanish colonialism but a corrective of historical homogenization. The speech acts of Trinidad, Ometochtzin, and the *tlacuilo* also raise questions regarding the effectiveness of resistance models, of a politics of recognition, and of a return to humanism after the poststructuralist critique of the subject. In this essay I do not address these questions directly but tangentially—by doing *something else.*

By "limits" I understand both the separation of two things or cultural spaces as well as the limits of knowledge that would correspond to the limits of an object. Following the theories of Kierkegaard and Heidegger, Ranajit Guha has drawn the distinction between fear of sedition due to a lack of knowledge of the world beyond the confines of the English Club (the home away from home) and anxiety that results from indefiniteness, the impossibility of knowing the limits of the ruled, and the realization of colonial failure.[6] Although Guha writes about the crisis of nineteenth-century liberal thought in India, his observations on a will to hegemony, imperial failure, and the implementation of dominance are applicable to the consensus required in imparting baptism and the emphasis on love in the Spanish body of laws that sought to regulate exploration, pacification, and settlement. The Mixton War clearly evokes the fear of Indian uprisings, but the glance of the *tlacuilo* who could not only conceive but also codify a plurality of worlds within a single space of representation entailed the kind of anxiety we associate with the uncanny. Trinidad's address in Tojolabal also threads the limits of knowledge and control—beyond fear of rebellion, the realization by the government that its assumed monopoly on rationality is bankrupt.

Subalternity and the Plurality of Worlds

If the subaltern studies scholar can inhabit several worlds within a Western tradition, she can only intuit the coexistence and compatibility of modern and nonmodern worlds in subaltern subjects. Of course, I do not exclude the possibility of the subaltern intellectual who works at ease both in the Western discourses of subaltern studies and in nonmodern forms of expression and communication. Nor do I discard the unlearning of historical and epistemological privilege in everyday practices, as manifest in the actions of Subcomandante Marcos who immersed himself with three other Ladinos in Chiapas in the early 1980s to form the Zapatista movement in conjunction with the indigenous communities.[7] Subaltern studies, insofar as they are "studies," are limited to an unlearning of theoretical privilege. I leave to the good or bad consciousness of the anthropologist and the translator to decide whether she dwells in a plurality of worlds comprising modern and nonmodern forms of life. One must qualify that the conception of a plurality of worlds does not imply a hybrid complex but rather the coexistence of different hybrid spaces. The Tojolabal world of Comandante Trinidad is as hybrid as the Spanish she used to address the government, but they are not the same world. Moreover, one must underscore a porosity between these worlds, a communicative space in which the world of the Tojolabal enriches Western categories, while the latter would interrogate suspicious claims of authenticity that reify Tojolabal culture. As such, the coexistence of plural worlds gives place to an antiessentialist thought that spares us the need to establish so-called strategic essentialisms—that is, identities grounded in a binary opposition to a hegemonic essentialism.[8]

The notion of plural noncontradictory worlds allows us to think of subjects that are at once mestizo, hybrid, and nomadic without incurring the celebration of a cultural synthesis or limiting oneself to a conflict between two or more cultures. Cognitives differences in languages give place to the notion of relatively incommensurable worlds with discursive spaces of their own.[9] To speak of incommensurability entails drawing the limits of translation— questioning the transparency and accessibility of other languages—as well as drawing the limits of all attempts to logically subordinate one language to another.[10] Under this perspective Trinidad's intervention suggests that to think the Zapatista demands in Tojolabal lacks an equivalent in Spanish. To think in Spanish, however, means having access to a whole series of anthropological, legal, and performative discourses that obviously cannot be reduced to the discourses of the government nor to some sort of dominant logic of the West that we tend to identify with that metaphysical entity we call "writing," as if writing consisted of a homogeneous space and time. Whereas the lucidity of Ometochtzin comes to us through inquisitorial writing, the painting of the *tlacuilo* reminds us that painting or pictographic script, rather than the Latin alphabet, constituted the main channel of communication in the sixteenth century.[11]

As early as the middle of the sixteenth century, the Franciscan friar Bernardino de Sahagún conceived the centrality of pictographic writing for understanding the world of the Nahuas, the so-called Aztecs of central Mexico. His ethnographic investigations included three moments that went from a first pictographic record, to an oral expression of the contents of the paintings that his Indian assistants wrote in Nahuatl, to a third moment in which this information enabled the identification of cultural forms in everyday life or in the confession. These knowledges also had the finality of accessing Nahua metaphysics and the cartographies of the body. In terms reminiscent of William of Ockham's logic of concepts, Sahagún saw his inquiries on writing and speech as keys to understanding the mental world of the Nahuas. Ockham postulated the arbitrary nature of speech and writing with respect to what he called "mental concepts," for example, the terms *flor* in Spanish and *xóchitl* in Nahuatl differ, but the mental concept would be the same. Also implicit in

Ockham's thought is the assumption that different languages carry different logics with different degrees of rationality, and by extension different forms of organizing and conceiving the world.[12] For Ockham, Latin was the most adequate language for science, logic, and grammar. Hence it is not surprising that Sahagún and other Franciscans taught Latin to trilingual Indian collegians, since it was assumed that the "secrets" of Nahuatl would be made manifest by means of a discussion of Nahuatl grammar in Latin. It is worthwhile remembering that the term "grammar" in the sixteenth century meant more than the mere rules of proper speech and writing.

Sahagún saw the possibility of naming, organizing, and conceiving the world from multiple perspectives, but in contrast to Ometochtzin and the *tlacuilo*, it was impossible for him to understand without incurring a contradiction that a plurality of worlds could coexist in one cultural space, let alone in an individual conscience. Expressions of plural-world dwelling like those of Ometochtzin and the *tlacuilo* were proof that Indians lied when they converted to Catholicism at the beginning of the evangelization of Mexico. If the language of fear informs his definition of his work as developing an arsenal to forestall the return of the devil, anxiety is manifest in the irresolvable dilemma missionaries faced between the destruction of social mores that hispanization brought about among the Nahuas and the unfathomable secrets of Nahuatl that haunted the translation of Christianity. Ometochtzin seemed perplexed by the impasse but retained a lofty distance that certainly annoyed the missionaries. Trinidad confirms what these Indians from the sixteenth century saw very clearly: to survive in a colonial regime, one must know how to dwell in at least two worlds. The degree of visibility of this subaltern knowledge is proportional to the tolerance of the society. Ometochtzin lost his life for historical and epistemological lucidity; we ignore the fate of the *tlacuilo*. As for Trinidad, she faces the danger that her discourse could become meaningless precisely to the extent that the dialogues delineate the historical and epistemological limitations of the representatives of the government.

Enlightened De-enlightenment

Comandante Trinidad's intervention manifests a view where a plurality of worlds are compatible and there is an ethical obligation to recognize the possibility of inhabiting them without incurring contradiction. But this very recent *enlightenment* in Western discourse had already formed part of Indian discourse since the beginning of the colonization of America. Consequently, the discourses of the Zapatistas can be read as the light to finish with all enlightenments. The coexistence of multiple worlds had its corresponding modality in colonial discourses. In fact, the constitution of a separate world with its own categories is structural to colonial power. The Spanish Crown insisted not only in the knowledge of Indian languages for the evangelical as well as administrative purposes, but also on the codification of indigenous law, the *usos y costumbres* (uses and customs), for ruling on cases involving Indians.[13] Both the "grammars" of Indian languages and the codification of Indian law are European inventions. If in principle the ends of grammars and Indian laws was to protect indigenous communities from the destructive effects of hispanization, in practice they were key to the governability of the colonies. Colonial authorities had the last word on the correct use of language and the authenticity of the *usos y costumbres*. Because of their purported incapacity to understand Spanish laws and their inability to speak their own languages correctly, Indians were confined to the status of minors.

This form of colonial enlightenment anticipates the emergence of ethnography in the eighteenth century, when this discipline defined itself as the science that writes the truth of oral peoples. However, it would be incorrect to project to the sixteenth century the categories that promoted the classification of inferior languages and cultures under the binary "peoples with States" versus "peoples in a state of nature"—that is, peoples "with" and "without" history.[14] It becomes evident in texts like the Telleriano-Remensis that the Spanish authorities saw the necessity of knowing the historical past of the peoples they sought to rule and (unless for rhetorical and ideological effects) were disinclined to claim historical exclusivity. It is one thing is to believe in universal history and another to willfully ignore the historical specificities of the peoples they sought to incorporate into the telos of Roman Catholicism.[15] Whether out of respect or for political immediacy, knowing the *usos y costumbres* (hence the local histories) was deemed indispensable to the administration of the colonies.

The binary that surfaces with the enlightenment led most of Latin America after the wars of independence to undermine, if not invalidate and destroy, indigenous legal and linguistic spaces. Under the same stroke of the pen, Indians were excluded from full citizenship in the new states, thereby instituting a form of internal colonialism.[16] The angel of history, the concept of progress, reduced Indian languages and cultures to folklore, to premodern forms of life condemned to disappear. The *tlacuilo* of the Telleriano-Remensis already exposed the relativity of the modern by identifying the differences between the Dominican and the Franciscan modalities (missionaries use the terms "modern" and "ancient" to define the rupture of the conquest).

The pictorial language used to depict the Mixton War manifests a "messianic present," the *now* of a moment of contestation foreign to the iron-fisted logic of historical progress. Opposite to the codification and destruction of languages and the *usos y costumbres*, we find "magical" spaces, with their own logics (if you wish, folkloric expressions) that follow rules Western discourses cannot codify. One thing is to live, think, speak, debate *usos y costumbres* in Tojolabal, whether to conduct everyday life or to organize the Zapatista uprising, and quite another to understand, discuss, debate in Spanish the adequacy of *usos y costumbres* to define cultural rights and the autonomy of Indian peoples. The massacre of Acteal in December 1997 unfortunately evidences the lack of reason, the lack of arguments in both Western and indigenous terms, of the Indians associated with the Partido Revolucionario Institucional (PRI), the official party of the state.[17] From a technical use of the concept of folklore in the work of Antonio Gramsci—according to which philosophical doctrines take the status of folklore as they lose their force (that is, become "common sense" in Gramsci's terms)—we can argue that Trinidad's gesture is an instance of an *enlightened de-enlightenment* inasmuch as it undermines (reduces to folklore) the rationality of all forms of enlightenment that would pretend to establish that the contending forms of modernity are the only valid and possible spaces of history.

All assumptions of dominant systems or ideologies ultimately amount to a hoax, a sort of self-induced trompe l'oeil. If the texts of Ometochtzin, the *tlacuilo*, and Comandante Trinidad partake of a fabric of rebellion, resistance, and subversion, the concept of plural worlds liberates us of the moral that exclusively values cultural artifacts in which one can find acts of resistance. These Indian subjects enable us to break from that deceptive, if not fastidious, variant of the cogito "I resist, therefore I am." From them we learn that resistance pertains more to the materials, in the fashion of the glass blower. All presuppositions and framings of a dominant system constitute historical and epistemological limitations. Of course, this formulation does not exclude, nor does it ignore, modes of oppression that constitute binaries; however, the existence of two worlds need not entail a binary relation as the only mode of dwelling.

Nothing prevents us from viewing—with the *tlacuilo* and Ometochtzin— the Dominicans, the Franciscans, and the rebels from the Mixton as discrete, independent worlds. Nevertheless, one can also read a denunciation of Spanish intolerance in the *tlacuilo*'s affirmation of plurality. Accordingly, baptisms would establish the limits of participation in the colonial Christian world, confession the spaces unknown to the rulers, and the river in the painting of the Mixton the symbolic separation between the magico-religious world of the Indian rebels and the Christian world of the Requerimiento. (The *Requerimiento* is the infamous document that informed Indians of the Pope's authority to grant sovereignty over their lands to the Spanish Crown and then gave them the choice to either subject themselves peacefully or endure war and slavery.) Thus on a temporal plane this page moves from the required catechization before baptism, to the refusal of the interpellation of the Requerimiento, to the surveillance and punishment of the confession—from a triumphal evangelization to the realization of colonial failure.

Guha would argue that this page testifies to the passage from a hegemonic will to the inevitability of ruling by "dominance without hegemony."[18] Indeed, we can also read an act of subversion in the *tlacuilo*'s analytical lucidity implied in his capacity to identify the relativity of a world that conceives itself as universal and totalizing, and thereby reduce to the absurd the interpellation of the Requerimiento: "Hey you, either subject yourself to the Spanish Crown or I'll kill you." We have no reason, however, to assume that the *tlacuilo* would think of himself in terms of a sort of Hegelian master/slave dialectic. The assumed recognition of Spanish sovereignty or of a single god in baptism amounts to fantasies on the part of those in power. Under the structure of "dominance without hegemony," Indians dwell in the world of the horse, of alphabetical writing, of musical instruments, of narratives of conquest—a world not necessarily inconsistent with nor conceived in opposition to forms of life preceding the conquest. Hence Indians ride horses, play guitars, write histories, inscribe themselves in the narrative of conquest differently but not necessarily in terms of a binary—as it were, they have more urgent and interesting things to do than defining themselves in opposition to a dominant mode. Instead of rushing to celebrate the ascendancy of the slave to mastery, we ought to recall that Hegel had already mocked such a dialectical resolution when he conceived it as "stubbornness, a type of freedom which does not get beyond the attitude of bondage."[19]

The last laugh of what Hegel called the "cunning of history" would correspond to that modulation of the cogito that demands recognition, the assertion: "Me too, I am also a subject." One formulation would be: "I resist, therefore I am." Another would be the notion of recognition through translation. Whereas the former places the process of identity formation in a binary relation that postulates a dominant ideology, the latter grants a language the capacity of accessing another language by means of an equivalence. As in the case of Sahagún, translation as equivalence partakes of a will to control and measure the colonial world. The capacity to translate the language of the enemy is a fundamental principle in the discourse of war. It is also clear that resistance is hardly the only mode of warring. Resistance is not just reactive but depends on a stable construction of the enemy as a dominant discourse or ideology. Why should one define oneself in opposition to the languages of the rulers when one can dwell—that is, act in and on its worlds, without abandoning one's own?

The Telleriano-Remensis exemplifies this capacity to create a discursive space that does not react to but instead adopts elements from Western codes to communicate the specificity of a plurality of worlds. We never find the *tlacuilo* situating herself in opposition to alphabetical writing or Renaissance pictorial perspective. The frontal image of the Franciscan captures the individualism promoted by the confession, but beyond the inquisitorial vigilance, we ought to imagine the *tlacuilo* looking at us from the past with an ironic smile that brags of her ability to codify in her own pictorial language a Western cultural modality by means of a symbolic use of perspective. We witness the delineation of borders but not a transitional existence.[20]

Colonial discourse, however, aspires to create intermediary subjects, states of *nepantla* (according to the Nahuatl expression), and persecutes those who, like Ometochtzin, refused to think of themselves within a master/slave dialectic. The concept of *nepantla*—neither here nor there, neither in the ancient order nor in the Christian—can be understood in terms of not being really convinced of the necessity of dwelling in only one world. Trinidad's intervention reminds the government representatives that there is a Tojolabal world that cannot be subjected by translation. The exteriority and incommensurability of the subaltern world engenders fear of insurrection (evidenced by the Mixton War, the Zapatista uprising), as well as anxiety in the face of the epistemological lucidity and the historical "now" that capture the relativity of Western forms of life and make manifest spaces that elude the "cunning" of Hegelian reason.

5

Beyond Representation?
The Impossibility of the Local (Notes on Subaltern Studies in Light of a Rebellion in Tepoztlán, Morelos)

To the old women of Tepoztlán who faced down the riot police with wooden sticks

This essay emphasizes the *now* of the rebellion in Tepoztlán—a small village a forty-five minutes' drive from Mexico City—with an update on the situation at the end. I wrote the essay in 1995 while in Tepoztlán, on leave from my U.S. academic institution. The rebellion in Tepoztlán began the morning of August 24, 1995, which I witnessed as I was getting on a bus to go to San Andrés Sacamch'en de los Pobres, Chiapas (officially named San Andrés Larráinzar) for the conversations that have become known as "Larráinzar VI" between the government and the Ejercito Zapatista de Liberación Nacional (EZLN). The EZLN, an army mostly composed of Indians, had surprised the world on January 1, 1994, with an assault on several cities in Chiapas.[1]

As I read this essay today, back in Ann Arbor, I cannot help but feel a distance from the intensity I experienced that morning when I left my wife, Catherine, and two children, Magali and Pablo, in an extreme political situation. The residents of Tepoztlán had barricaded the town and armed themselves with wooden sticks. Catherine eventually lent her solidarity by making the rounds of the barricades with large containers of coffee. Magali, thirteen at the time, had the fortune of having a social science teacher who not only supported the rebellion but discussed it in class to impart invaluable lessons on citizenship. To date, I wonder about how this experience helped shape my politically committed now fifteen-year-old who attends school board meetings, cooks for Food Not Bombs, and has participated in the organization of a student political action group in her high school. I also wonder about Pablo's experience. He played with his friends in the plaza during the nightly town meetings when new guards of the Municipal Palace assumed their post, leaders summarized the day's events, and the people of Tepoztlán expressed their views on the rebellion and the appropriate politics to follow.

Given that this sort of personal note is commonplace in recent self-reflex-ive modes of writing ethnography, I should dispel the illusion that what I am doing in this essay is ethnographic. I am not an anthropologist by training, nor do I want to be one. I am writing on this rebellion because of my interests in subaltern studies and, more particularly, on the Zapatismo of the EZLN. Tepoztlán, in this respect, is an exemplary instance of a subaltern struggle and assertion of a new politics of citizenship that tries the government's com-mitment to democracy. For both the Zapatistas in Chiapas and Tepoztlán, the Mexican state—as identified with the Partido Revolucionario Institucional (PRI)—is an *outlaw state* whose credibility depends on living up to its prom-ises of democratic reform. Thus ungovernability is a category that speaks less about "others" living outside or resisting the national project than about a breakdown of state institutions.

One of the most amusing benchmarks of the beginnings of modern philos-ophy—in particular, of philosophies concerned with current events, *la phi-losophie de l'actualité* (as the French like to call it)—is Hegel's statement that "reading the morning paper is a kind of realistic prayer."[2] Newspapers, how-ever, situate our prayers in local interests, whether these might be school board decisions, the latest rapist in the community, or, from an international point of view, the collapse of the Mexican peso and its impact on the U.S. economy. Hegel's observation assumes that one must read the news (the compulsion to *see* the morning news on TV is today's equivalent) to fully function in our im-mediate context, which might very well mean making decisions about invest-ments in today's highly volatile "emergent" economics. Newspapers (especially those located in metropolitan centers of power) reify the local as universal inasmuch as they make sense of the world selectively, according to particular interests. If it is in the nature of things to be "localocentric," only the metropo-lis can afford to fetishize a particular perspective.

Other news, in other circuits of information, until very recently were the realm of area studies specialists—one cannot pray with last week's papers. One could always call friends and get a briefing on events, but the call is motivated by an awareness of being limited to read partial truths and lacks the religios-ity that accompanies our morning consumption of the *real*. The circulation of newspapers today on the Internet has opened new sites of "prayer" and also has made it possible to dismantle the control of information by press agencies. It is worthwhile to remember that only a few years ago the United States pulled out of UNESCO for its insistence (because of what was perceived as overtly political: maintaining a Third World bias) on creating an international bank of information (the New International Order). This circulation of information, however, does not exclude forms of control that do or may yet come to exist over e-mail and the World Wide Web.

The Internet was thus conceived by the Zapatistas in Chiapas as one of the channels to convey their communiqués to an international community. Since the early days of the uprising in 1994, cyberspace has become the means to disseminate information but also a place where members of the international community can contribute to their cause. The effectiveness of the Zapatistas— as a subaltern group—in building solidarity in Europe, the United States, Latin America, Australia, and other parts of the world is a unique phenomenon. They have managed to internationalize their local struggle. It is also worthwhile to remember that this most modern form of communication does not contradict ancestral, Indian communal forms of social organization that emphasize consensus and the participation of the whole community—men, women, and children alike. If the Zapatistas' use of the Internet globalizes the local, the insurrection in Tepoztlán localizes the global. In both instances Hegel's highly individualized prayer-metaphor gives place to collective forms of action and reading.

In chapter 3 of this book I have examined the nature of the *impossible* and the *folkloric* inherent to the subaltern character of the Zapatista insurrection. The impossible and the folkloric refer respectively to (1) a *complete liberation*—that is, to redress five hundred years of injustice against Indians (in Antonio Negri's terms, of constituting communism as a critique of capitalist and socialist state-forms); and to (2) the *compatibility of modern and nonmodern political and cultural forms*—that is, to build international solidarity by means of the Internet while evoking the pre-Columbian Votán, the heart of the people (in Reynaldo Ileto's terms, of accepting the reality of other conceptual systems). That chapter was conceived and written, as it were, in cyberspace, in Ann Arbor, reading local news in the Internet. I am currently writing in Tepoztlán, Morelos.

The people of Tepoztlán—an old bastion of Zapatismo during the 1910 Mexican Revolution—have overthrown their elected government for not consulting the town in their dealings with a transnational enterprise that sought to build a golf course, eight hundred luxury homes, and a GTE communications center in communal lands (which were, according to the Tepoztecos, illicitly sold thirty years ago) and a protected natural refuge.[3] The village has been barricaded, and its youth guard the town with big wooden sticks. More recently, the town has called for the election of a new major and city council, defining itself as a free municipality (*municipio libre*)—that is, not bound to the authorities of the state of Morelos. The old Zapatista motto *mandar obedeciendo* (to rule obeying) led to the destitution of the mayor and city council, but also, perhaps more important, to an election of a new government following the ancestral democratic traditions and customs of the town. There is a tightened vigilance of the new officers.

Although I am now located in the field, my local connection to the Internet still remains central—no longer as a space to gain information but as a tool to reach hundreds of networks in case of an emergency, in the eventuality of a repression by the army or the riot police. My "immersion" in the local, however, has made manifest to me that the local, like the subaltern, is an elusive concept that becomes meaningful only as a relational term. "Local" or "subaltern" relative to what? I still read the newspapers religiously to learn about the events of Tepoztlán; in fact, I read the relevant articles published in different newspapers and magazines in the bulletin boards that display them in the main plaza of Tepoztlán. One might assume that these *representations* (articles "describing" the events and "speaking" for the people) function as mirrors, as if the self-consciousness and identity of the people of Tepoztlán would depend on them. This eerie feeling disappears, however, once we view this display of representations not as informative of what is occurring in the town but as mirrors of the outside world.

Beyond representing the Tepoztecos (a function of dubious value to the citizens of Tepoztlán), these news items manifest cracks in the seamless narrative of neoliberalism and the inevitability of globalism. For the Tepoztecos, and for the purposes of this essay, representations of the events are significant in what they convey about changes in the *structures of feeling* of those who make it their business to report and interpret the events surrounding the emergence of the Tepoztecos as the subject of their own history. Rather than providing one more account of the events (although to some extent this is inevitable), I reflect here on the intertwining of the local and the global. Beyond representation, the local manifests its impossibility in its bond to the global. Ultimately, the local must be seen as a catachresis for the national and the global in all their contradictions. Local and regional identities, as well as nationalisms not subsumed under the nation-state, have evolved in Tepoztlán, like in the case of Chiapas, as points of contention for bending the humdrum of globalism. The global might very well be a determinant of local communities and contribute to their deterioration, but it lacks the symbolic elements to institutionalize an alternative community.[4]

I would like to relate this uprising in Tepoztlán to the Zapatistas of Chiapas and dwell on the need to move beyond representation and explore the impossibility of the local in subaltern movements. These tasks, however, call for a critique of subaltern studies as well as for the need to trace the transformations the concept of the subaltern has undergone as it has traveled from the Italy of Antonio Gramsci in the 1930s to the South Asian Subaltern Studies

Group in the 1980s to the emergent Latin American Subaltern Studies Group (LASSG) in the 1990s. Tepoztlán and Chiapas force us to make the concept of the subaltern travel from the metropolitan centers of power in the U.S. academy to the local/regional sites of struggle and to resist the temptation of reading these insurrections through Gramsci, the Indian group, or even the Latin American proposals. We must, on the contrary, outline the insufficiencies of these metropolitan-based theoretical formulations from the point of view of Tepoztlán and Chiapas.

The first part of this essay traces the transformations the concept of the subaltern has undergone as it has traveled (geographically and historically) from Italy to India to Latin America. Our discussion places special attention on how Gramsci's blindness to the "folkloric" has been superseded in both the Indian and the Latin American subaltern studies groups. There is, however, a need to critique signs of a creeping vanguardism in both the Latin American and Southeast Asian discourses. This discussion of Gramsci (and to a lesser extent, the Southeast Asian group) further elaborates some of the points addressed in chapter 3 of this volume. As I have pointed out, there is a continuity between this essay and the earlier piece, where changes in the location of writing as well as the emergence of new events accent the differences. These changes correspond to a physical and an intellectual movement from the global to the local, to invert the title of a recent conference in Mexico.[5] The gist of my critique of subaltern studies aims precisely to trace in the evolution of the concept a transition from understanding subalterns as objects of study in global contexts to subjects of history in local practices. The second part of the essay consists of a series of notes that suggest the possibility of giving serious consideration to the indigenous discourse of Chiapas and Tepoztlán. These notes underscore how Zapatismo, as manifest in these regions of Mexico, constitutes a new vanguard that is precisely grounded in its self-conscious subalternity—that is, as an instance of the hegemony of the diverse.

I would like to identify what is usable in the evolution of the concept of the subaltern. Clearly I am more interested in the transformations the concept has undergone than in assessing how Gramscian or, for that matter, un-Gramscian are the expansions of thematics, the elaborations of the category, and the emergent sensibilities in the Indian group in the 1980s and the Latin American in the 1990s. These instances of traveling cultures and theories have less to do with the circulation of a specific theory than with the formation of a discourse on subalternity.

Italy, India, and Latin America: From the 1930s to 1995

Antonio Gramsci first used the term "subaltern," beyond military referents, in his "Notes on Italian History" in *Selections from the Prison Notebooks*. His

writings also inaugurated the concept of hegemony as a new mode of understanding ideology. Although readings of Gramsci have a long history in Latin
America (including Ernesto Laclau's early work, *Politics and Ideology in Marxist Theory*), they have tended not to be critical of his understandings of Culture
(the capital "C" marks an elitist conception) and the corresponding counterhegemonic blocs.[6] To understand subaltern movements, Gramsci's notion of
the folkloric, which he opposes to the modernist conception of the historical
emergence of national Culture in particular, needs to be critiqued. What is at
stake in this critique is the compatibility of modern and nonmodern forms of
culture and politics and not the celebration of some sort of pristine indigenous
community. We must keep in mind that the possibility of critiquing the ideology of progress is a recent phenomenon not readily available to Gramsci.

For Gramsci, notions of popular culture and indigenous knowledge were
incompatible with his understanding of a Culture that could be established as
a counterhegemony. As he put it in "The Modern Prince," one must study elements of popular psychology "in order to transform them, by educating them,
into a modern mentality."[7] His understanding of cultural politics unavoidably
privileged Western conceptions of knowledge, art, and ethics—evidently, of
History. The elaboration of a counterhegemonic culture signified an alternative modernity that would transform premodern subjects. In his essay "On
Education," Gramsci wrote: "The first, primary grade should not last longer
than three or four years, and in addition to imparting the first 'instrumental'
notions of schooling—reading, writing, sums, geography, history—ought in
particular to deal with an aspect of education which is now neglected—i.e.,
with 'rights' and 'duties,' with the first notions of the State and society as primordial elements of a new conception of the world which challenges the conceptions that are imparted by the various traditional social environments, i.e.,
the conceptions which can be termed folkloristic."[8]

The "folkloristic" would reduce all forms of knowledge not bound by
Western criteria of truth to superstition at worst and to unexamined "common sense" at best. "Common sense," in this regard, would parallel what
semioticians call natural signs—that is, an uncritical understanding of the
world where the signifier bypasses the signified and is thus identified with referents. The history of philosophy in itself would be a chronicle of the institutionalization of "common sense": "Every philosophical current leaves behind
a sedimentation of 'common sense': this is the document of its historical effectiveness."[9] For Gramsci, "common sense" continually transforms itself as
it incorporates scientific ideas and philosophical opinions into everyday life:
"'Common sense' is the folklore of philosophy, and is always half way between
folklore properly speaking and the philosophy, science, and economics of the
specialists."[10] This understanding of "common sense" as the folklore of phi-

losophy enables us to turn this concept against Gramsci by pointing out that the reduction of what he terms "traditional social environments" to folklore is in itself a manifestation of philosophical folklore. I call this critical gesture a form of *enlightened de-enlightenment*.

Although common sense and folklore were clearly inferior forms of knowledge in Gramsci's assessment, their role in rebellions and insurrections—especially of peasants—cannot be ignored. If he was critical of voluntarism, of instinct (and called for a transformation of peasants' mentality by modernity), subaltern insurgencies would call for a theoretical reflection rather than a dismissal on grounds of insufficient consciousness—lacking plans in advance or not following a theoretical line. Theory then should hold a dialectical relation with movements of revolt that fall out of the schema of historico-philosophical outlooks. The task of subaltern studies, as defined in this essay, would seek to conceptualize multiple possibilities of creative political action rather than defining a more mature political formation. Subaltern studies therefore would not pretend to have a privileged access to subalterns—rather, it would define intellectual work as one more intervention in insurgent movements. In developing practices, the intellectual would grow parallel to the emergent social actors and their interventions in everyday life. *Protagonism* would thus be subjected to infinite deconstruction.

We may now consider this last observation by Gramsci in the context of Gautam Bhadra's analysis of the 1857 rebellion in India. Bhadra draws the conclusion of his study with a brief allusion to fragmentary leadership in peasant insurrections: "Yet this episodic and fragmentary narrative points to the existence in 1857 of what Gramsci has called 'multiple elements of conscious leadership' at the popular level."[11] Gramsci would use this historical event as a means to further prove his theory. For Gramsci, the task would consist of translating life into theoretical language. Our question would now be: What changes does subaltern theory undergo as Gramsci travels from Fascist Italy in the 1930s to postcolonial India in the 1980s? Guha's preface to the first volume of *Subaltern Studies* suggests a difference between Gramsci's project and that of the Indian subaltern studies group: "It will be idle of us, of course, to hope that the range of contributions to this series may even remotely match the six-point project envisaged by Antonio Gramsci in his 'Notes on Italian History.'"[12]

It is fair to say that the main difference and the modesty of Guha is less academic than political. The political urgency and concreteness of Gramsci's historiography, which never left out the immediate significance of his examples to praxis, are impossible to match given the different historical moments and loci of writing. The historiography of the Indian group in exchange supplies a richness of detail and methodology that were not available to Gramsci, who might still surprise us in "The Modern Prince" with such statements as "it never occurs to them [subalterns] that their history might have some possible importance, that there might be some value in leaving documentary evidence of it."[13] We have learned in the aftermath of deconstruction to distrust the preeminence given to the written letter. We must pay special attention to the (post)colonial element at play in the Indian group. We must also attend to theoretical changes as well as to emergent structures of feeling. Now to Bhadra's concluding thoughts.

Badhra's account works against dismissals of the indigenous leaders' role in the insurrection as "minor incidents" by academic historians like S. N. Sen in *Eighteen Fifty-seven* or mockeries as "mushroom dignities" by soldier historians like R.H.W. Dunlop in *Service and Adventure with the Khakee Ressalah or, Meerut Volunteer Horse, during the Mutinies of 1857–58*. In Badhra's account the indigenous leaders played an integral role in the popular insurrection. The four leaders shared ordinariness and had learned to use the logic of insurrection in the practice of everyday life: "The consciousness with which they all fought had been 'formed through everyday experience'; it was an 'elementary historical acquisition.'" Badhra's analysis of this rebellion differs in the tone and the details of the insurrection from Gramsci's historical examples: "It was the perception and day-to-day experience of the authority of the alien state in his immediate surroundings that determined the rebel's action."[14]

Although one could argue that the situation of Sardinia and the Italian South in general was one of internal colonialism, Gramsci's counterhegemonic state and project of modernity would reinscribe them within a narrative that posits historical continuity. In the case of the British empire, the colonial situation foreclosed a connection and the consciousness of the rebels was one of insurgency against a colonial power—not against a landed aristocracy as in the case of what Gramsci conceptualizes as a progressive peasantry (that is, one that does not align itself with the local landlords against the urban leadership of both south and north). In this regard, the work of the Southeast Asian subalternists falls within a postcolonial subject position that is fully aware of the colonial impulses that accompany the modernist project.

This call for a radical transformation of historiography, however, still believes that the task of tertiary discourse is to recover the place in history *for* subalterns. Its task is to prove that the insurgent can rely on the historian's performance and not that the performance of the insurgent itself can recover his or her place in history. This faith in the historian has less felicitous moments among other members of the Indian group. Given this sort of conclusion regarding tertiary discourse, we need not wonder why Gayatri Spivak raised the question, "Can the subaltern speak?" For better or worse, the Latin American Subaltern Studies project bears the imprint of Spivak's critique of Guha and the Indian historiographical project in general.[15] I point to the shortcomings of the Indian group to foreground the critical process that has led them to address insurgent formations that Gramsci would reduce to "folklore" or undeveloped consciousness.

In a key moment in her critique of the subaltern group, Spivak suggests an internationalization of historiography that would include "the political economy of the independent peasant movement in Mexico [the Zapatistas of the 1910 revolution!]."[16] She has in mind Partha Chatterjee's comparative studies of Indian communal power with European *history* and African *anthropology*. Spivak makes a parenthetical remark ("an interesting disciplinary breakdown)" that should be pursued more closely. I would like to underscore that the disciplinary breakdown is a commonplace in Western constructions of Otherness. Implied in Chatterjee's examples, in what he has called the evidence, drawn from studies of European feudalism and African "tribal" societies (I retain his quotation marks over tribal), is a *universal* narrative of the transition from feudalism to capitalism.[17] Whereas anthropology would study the "Other" of capitalism in contemporary Africa, and by implication India, medieval and early modern European history would provide the categories to understand *communalism* as existing in an earlier temporality.

Not only is Chatterjee repeating, as Spivak has pointed out by way of Guha, "that tendency within Western Marxism which would refuse class-consciousness to the pre-capitalist subaltern, especially in the theaters of imperialism." He is also repeating the denial of coevalness in the production of anthropology's object of study. Thus Chatterjee repeats a series of commonplaces regarding Marxist definitions of communalism that tend to see it "as 'the negation of capital.' Communalism was thus defined as 'what capital is not,' and was assumed to have 'an antithetical relation' to capital, so that the establishment of capitalist commodity relations required the destruction of community relations."[18] I cite this passage from an essay by Terence Ranger to underscore the critical impulse that informs the subaltern group and the fruitfulness of their debates, rather than to further document the conventionality of Chatterjee's essay. The passage also foregrounds the continuation of imperialism and neocolonialism in nonsuspect quarters of Western Marxism and poststructuralism. By moving "back" into a colonial situation, into a moment in the production of African communalism as "Other"—not by Marxist but by colonial experts such as "missionaries, native commissioners, mining compound and municipal medics, and employers"—Ranger further establishes the ways in which Western Marxism repeats forms of subjection characteristic of colonialist discourses.

One of the defining positions of the Latin American Subaltern Studies Group (perhaps under debate but nevertheless new vis-à-vis the starting motivations of the Indian group) is the questioning of the adequacy of intellectuals to represent subalterns. As John Beverley has put it: "What is at stake in the move to subaltern studies, we believe, is a growing sense of the inadequacy of the models of intellectual and political protagonist that correspond to the period of liberation struggle in the sixties in which many of us were formed."[19] I suggest that this radical questioning of the adequacy of intellectuals is a logical consequence of the Indian groups' critique of bourgeois, as well as of some forms of Marxist historiography. The implications of a poststructuralist critique of humanism are overdetermined in the case of the Latin American group by a post-1989 "situatedness." Only from that locus of enunciation could the "Founding Statement" address the following epistemological as well as ethico-political issues of subaltern studies: "Clearly, it is a question not only of new ways of looking at the subaltern, new and more powerful forms of information retrieval, but also of building new relations between ourselves and those human contemporaries whom we posit as objects of study."[20]

This statement suggests that epistemology, the positing of new ways of looking and constituting objects of study, must be tempered by an ethos that knows how to respect silences in subaltern discourses. It is not a coincidence that the "Founding Statement" concludes by citing Rigoberta Menchú's final words in her testimony: "I am still keeping secret what I think no-one should know. Not even anthropologists or intellectuals, no matter how many books they have, can find out all our secrets."[21] Doris Sommer's identification of silence as ethico-aesthetic is obviously pertinent to subaltern studies: "Announcing limited access is the point, not whether or not some information is really withheld. Resistance does not necessarily signal a genuine epistemological impasse; it is enough that the impasse is claimed in this ethico-aesthetic strategy to position the reader within limits."[22] Sommer advocates a new sensibility, an awareness of the restrictions that texts of resistance place on readers. Readers must first learn to recognize figures that mark gaps before an ethic of respect could be implanted. Equally dangerous to missing the gaps is the tendency by professional readers, who because of a shared space, hastily fill in the gaps. Subaltern discourse, as exemplified by Rigoberta Menchú's denial of complete access to her culture, aims, as Sommer has pointed out, to create conflictive or incommensurable positions. Thus this incommensurability blocks assimilationist impulses in Western discourses while paradoxically underscoring the compatibility of modern and nonmodern forms of life in subaltern texts and insurrections.

As it has traveled from Italy in the 1930s to Latin America in the 1990s, the concept of the subaltern has undergone transformations entailing radical revisions of the place of the intellectual. Four major positions can be singled out: (1) the organic intellectual in Gramsci functioned as the consciousness and theory of what subalterns did instinctively in the process of acquiring a modern mentality; (2) the intellectual in tertiary history makes allowances for the specific practices of subalterns but still retains the task of furnishing a mirror for the subaltern (that is, to recover the place in history for subalterns); (3) Beverley has expounded the inadequacy of the models of intellectual and political protagonist; (4) and Sommer and the "Founding Statement" have called for a new ethics and sensibility. These theoretical transformations in subaltern studies have had a felicitous correspondence in the insurrections of Chiapas and Tepoztlán. The new ethics of respect for silence and gaps in what Sommer has called "resistance texts" now faces a new subaltern practice that strategically deploys silence—the subaltern-*cannot*-speak syndrome—to make manifest the racism and parochialism of dominant discourses: dialogue as a learning process in which the government representatives must learn how to speak to subalterns, and the Tepoztecos and Zapatistas in Chiapas, who gain consciousness of their power to assert their demands in peace negotiations.

From the Global to the Local

The communiqués by Subcomandante Marcos, the Comité Clandestino Revolucionario Indígena, Comandancia General (the Clandestine Indigenous Revolutionary Committee, General Command) of the EZLN, and the Indian *comandantes* David, Tacho, Trini, and Ramona, among others, address the prejudices that have hindered the reception of calls for justice, democracy, and liberty. The representatives of the government and certain sectors of the Mexican intelligentsia were forced to learn about the prevailing racism in Mexico from these subalterns who emerged from the Selva Lacandona on January 1, 1994. As of writing this essay, the attitudes of the government and some members of oppositional parties (from both the right and the left) continue to endanger the peace negotiations and dialogue with EZLN in which members of numerous Indian ethnic groups participate as advisers.[23] If one wonders at times about the sincerity of the learned lessons regarding respect for Indian proposals, the new politics based on civil society have gained a momentum and theoretical sophistication that brings shame on those who balk at the dialogues.[24]

The sketchy notion of an emergent hegemony of the diverse with the recent developments in Latin American Subaltern Studies gains a full articulation in the discourse of the Zapatistas and other resistance movements that have emerged in Mexico during the past year—among them, the rebellion in Tepoztlán, the strike by the independent union of the public bus system Ruta 100, the association of small and mid-size businesses called El Barzón whose members refuse to pay banks outrageous changes of interest rates, and the movement of students who were not admitted to the Universidad Nacional Autónoma de México (UNAM, the National Autonomous University of Mexico) and have denounced a flagrant corruption in the administration of admission exams. Luis Javier Garrido, in a *La Jornada* article, has written that if globalism and neoliberalism "have proven to be a challenge for intellectuals, who up to the present have not been able to address the issues with clarity, because they fail to grasp the significance of the events, broad cross-sections of society are fully mobilized because they live in their flesh the effects of these politics."[25]

This new politics calls for a full participation of all sectors of the nation in an alternative social and economic project. This project, as Pablo González Casanovas has put it, "would change the system of a State Party, and the State, for a system of national organization of civil society."[26] We must recall that González Casanovas's tentative theorizations on a new system of national organization depend on and draw their inspiration from the subaltern politics of the EZLN.[27] Central to the novel politics of the Zapatistas is an autonomy from political parties and a struggle that does not aspire to take over the state. The learning processes involved in the dialogue the Zapatistas have promoted between different sectors of civil society has a deeper modality in the emphasis on consensus and communalism that underlies all the decisions of the EZLN. This is exemplified in the Consulta Nacional e Internacional (the National and International Consultation) of August 1995, where more than one million participated in the discussion of six points that would define the kinds of politics and issues that should guide their struggle. The Zapatistas' emphasis on building "a hegemony of the diverse" implies the formation of strong subjectivities as a constituent power (the impossible as the condition of the possible) and the exercise of cultural and political practices that up until very recently were seen as in conflict with modernity (the folkloric as the space for the articulation of local struggles). Let us now examine the role of the folkloric and the impossible in the Tepoztlán rebellion.

The tendency to dismiss forms of popular culture as folklore (used as a pejorative term that obviously ignores the notion of Gramsci's technical use) bars an understanding of how Indian communities organize and perpetuate themselves. Folklore is a key component of the Tepoztlán uprising and the stories we tell about it. In telling these stories, however, there is a danger of making caricatures of local struggles and their folklore for a capitalist, metropolitan consumption.[28] Indeed, a good-willed lament over the disappearance of traditional forms of life, which in the same breath confirms an iron-fisted logic of the invincibility of transnational power often accompanies this tendency to turn local struggles into caricature. Stories from all over the world have been profiled on cohosts Linda Wertheimer and Robert Siegel's National Public Radio program "All Things Considered." These stories provide a place to examine how local folklore and struggles can turn into caricature and lost causes.

On September 7, 1995, for example, NPR's David Welna reported on the rebellion in Tepoztlán for "All Things Considered," which included a sound track for ambience. He said: "In the Mexican town of Tepoztlán nothing of any importance ever begins without a curtain-raiser of noisy firecrackers and nothing ever develops without a brass band to move it along." Welna goes on to mention that the particular occasion is the seizure of the Presidencia Municipal (town hall) and ousting of the city council and mayor. Welna has recorded speeches and interviewed several important people in the town, ranging from a fiery speech by one of "the most respected elders" (this is Welna's term; he fails to provide a name) to an interview in English of German Almazán, a multilingual (French, German, English) fruit vendor in the plaza.

Welna complements this local perspective with the opinion of Juan Kladt Sobrino, who leads the development project of Grupo KS, and Homero Aridjis, a poet and environmentalist from Mexico City. He concludes with a brief interview of Tomás Cajiga, an architect who lives in Tepoztlán. Cajiga, who once supported the project, is now critical because it will destroy the tranquil lifestyle he enjoys with his family. But Cajiga also predicts that the project will come through because "they have enough support from government agencies, they have enough permits to really justify the use of force in the construction of this golf course, if need be." This assessment of the situation repeats Kladt Sobrino's potent and self-assured assertion, revealed earlier on in Welna's piece, that he is not worried about Tepoztecos invading "his" lands because "anyone entering private property can be punished." Cajiga deplores the inevitability of globalism and the incapacity to resist transnational interests supported by the government. By closing the story with Cajiga's pessimistic assessment, Welna seems to confirm Cajiga's view of an inevitable defeat of the Tepozteco rebellion. The radio piece therefore opens with a caricature (clearly sympathetic) of folklore and closes with a lamentation over a world that is doomed to vanish.

The folklorism of brass bands, firecrackers, and effigies hanging from the roof of the town hall has its match in a, perhaps equally folkloric, view of a Mexico ruled by corrupt officials willing to be bought by transnational enterprises. But more annoying than the folkloric opening and closing, remarks that frame the story between caricature and lament, are host Robert Siegel's introductory comments to Welna's story: "In Mexico, the construction of a golf course is causing a rebellion in the rural town that borders the project. Residents of Tepoztlán say they do not want the golf course because it will change their traditional way of life and put too great a demand on their scarce water supplies. Over the weekend, there were violent demonstrations and the mayor quit. The standoff has pitted international developers backed by the government against Mexicans who are deeply suspicious of change." Seigel's categories define the town as bordering the project, the defense of the town's sovereignty as a violent demonstration, and the reverence for ancestral traditions as a suspicion of change. These categories are, to say the least, offensive to the people of Tepoztlán. Seigel's objective tone obviates the town's perspective: The project plans to build on communal lands that were illegally sold thirty years ago, the riot police invaded the town, and the government's and the developer's "modernism" destroys traditional communal forms of organization and consensus politics. In Seigel's introduction and Welna's piece, the culture and dignity of Tepoztlán becomes a caricature in the global context of NPR. The struggle to avoid the death of a people amounts to little more than quaint cultural practices that are hopelessly bound to disappear with the onslaught of modernity.

Even when critics of folklore are correct in condemning the curiosity that outsiders have for Indian art and cultural practices—a fascination that (as in the case of the NPR story) conveniently brackets a complicity with the oppression of Indians—these same cultural practices must be understood as forms of cultural endurance and social reproduction. Rosa Rojas, in her book *Chiapas: La paz violenta*, quite correctly sees the press's fascination with the mask of the Zapatistas as one more folkloric item that exemplifies how reporters systematically exclude news regarding the oppression of Indians (as it were, only armed Indians deserve the attention of journalists). But we should not overlook that the masks, like the traditional costumes, fulfill other functions than satisfying a craving for the exotic or the outlaw.[29] Needless to say, while masks protect individual identities, costumes assert cultural patterns; there is a felicitous coexistence of the two in the Zapatistas from Chiapas. Likewise, beyond "condiments" of social occasions, firecrackers are forms of communication (calls to action, signals of alert), and brass bands are forms of social reproduction (every barrio of Tepoztlán has its particular kind of musical ensemble). There is more than an entertainment value when, for instance, the contingent from the Barrio de la Santísima appears at the evening change of guard at the Presidencia Municipal with a drum and a *chirimía* (a flageolet) that accompanies the chanting of slogans. Music functions as an intensifier of solidarity and a definer of a particular barrio identity.

In the main room of the Presidencia Municipal hang images of the Virgin of Guadalupe, Emiliano Zapata, and an icon, which follows pre-Colombian pictorial conventions, of El Tepozteco, El Señor de los Vientos (The Tepozteco, the Lord of the Winds). Whereas the first two figures are ubiquitous to the whole state of Morelos, El Tepozteco is particular to Tepoztlán. Every September 8, as part of the feast the Virgin of the Nativity (Virgen de la Natividad), the patroness of Tepoztlán, the town stages a play that reenacts the conversion of the ruler of Tepoztlán at the time of the conquest. It is a play that at once reinforces the Christian identity of the Tepoztecos and asserts continuity with the pre-Columbian beliefs so that the god of Christianity is accommodated within the old pantheon. On this feast of the Virgin of the Nativity the people traditionally ascend the mountain to render offerings to El Tepozteco, on the remains of a pre-Columbian temple.

In a popular assembly on October 1, when Lazaro Rodríguez Castañeda was sworn in as the first mayor of the "municipio libre, constitucional y popular de Tepoztlán" [the free, constitutional and popular municipality of Tepoztlán], a personification of El Señor de los Vientos, El Tepozteco handed down in a symbolic act the *bastón de mando* (the staff of command) to the new mayor. El Tepozteco spoke the following: "You shall not attempt to undo our region by allowing yourself to be deceived by light that are not stars, because they are moons, nor will you allow the imposition of something that is alien to the will of the people, because if you allow it the people itself will demand your heart for sacrifice to soothe the wrath of the gods." This symbolic act, which perhaps could be easily dismissed as an atavistic and quaint resurgence of pre-Columbian rituals, institutes a popular vigilance over the new mayor and council under the threat of being sacrificed to the gods. Traitors will be sacrificed, if not by extirpating their hearts, perhaps by hanging in the manner of the effigies hanging from the roof of the Presidencia.

El Tepozteco and his speech forms part of what Antonio García de León has described as a permanent carnival in rebellious Tepoztlán, "where the children, the youth and the women constitute the most combative sectors, the most decided to defend at whatever cost a territoriality that in Tepoztlán is not a written law, but a millenarian tradition."[30] These clearly nonmodern political practices and claims of territoriality define the impossibility of the local in the Tepoztlán uprising. This is not to say that they are incompatible with modern practices, such as appealing to Articles 39 and 115 of the Mexican Constitution to legitimate the legality of their municipio libre—that is, its constitutionality. For the Tepoztecos nonmodern forms of territoriality are perfectly compatible to claims based on the constitution; however, the state can only recognize their claims at the expense of its authority. In this regard, the rebellion in Tepoztlán forms part of an emergent new politics defined by González Casanovas as a call to "change the system of a State party, and the State, for a system of national organization of civil society."

González Casanovas's proposal defines the "local" as the site of resistance to transnational interests and processes of globalization. Beyond representation, the impossibility of the local resides in the emergence of strong subjectivities and a hegemony of the diverse. The EZLN's politics of dialogue—as a learning process in which the Indian communities define and debate concepts of autonomy, demand a respect of their traditional cultures, and give prominence to women's issues—has gained an unexpected (by the government) momentum that increasingly brings into play multiple, diverse sectors of civil society. In the process the locale named Chiapas has become a catachresis for a national, if not an international, struggle against neoliberalism.

The transformations that the concept of the subaltern has undergone warn us against reading the new insurgencies through the lenses of Gramsci or even of the more recent Southeast Asian and Latin American subaltern groups. The evolution of subaltern studies traced in this essay concluded with the dissolution of the intellectual as a privileged agent in the articulation and definition of social change. Furthermore, this line of analysis would reveal how intellectuals tend to play integral roles in processes of subalternization. Intellectual work would now be a practice that runs parallel to insurrections but does not dictate their meaning or define their direction; rather, it would make manifest how these processes of appropriation erase the diverse. Ultimately, the impossibility of the local faces the likelihood of repression as the state might refuse to give place to a new system of national (and international) organization of civil society. If the citizens of Tepoztlán listened to the David Welna's NPR piece discussed earlier, they would not find a mirror of their struggle but of an opinion that considers as inevitable the eminent danger that the state could lose (that is, be willing to wage losing) its commitment to peace. The willingness of the people to sustain a struggle to death is, paradoxically, the only deterrent of violence.

Tepoztlán, November 1995

Although Tepoztlán has warded off an invasion of the town, the struggle to assert its sovereignty unfortunately has had its toll. Two Tepoztecos have died since I wrote this essay, and members of Consejo de Unidad Tepozteca (CUT) have been systematically accosted, harassed, and kidnapped by the police when doing their business outside the village. There have been many other incidents: On December 3, 1995, Pedro Margarito Barragán Gutiérrez, a supporter of the development project, was accidentally murdered, shot in the back, by fellow supporters who had fired their guns at a multitude of Tepoztecans. Three opponents of the project, including one named Gerardo Demesa Padilla—a founding member of CUT and a leading thinker of civil defense strategies in Tepoztlán—were arrested and charged with the homicide. Witnesses and forensic reports failed to establish a connection between them and the crime, but nearly three years after the event, on September 19, 1997, Demesa Padilla was sentenced to eight years in prison for *homicidio simple*; the judge found that even though Demesa Padilla did not shoot Barragán Gutiérrez, he had provoked the incident that led to the homicide. Demesa Padilla has appealed the verdict.

The Morelos police ambushed a caravan of eight hundred Tepoztecans on April 10, 1996, when they were traveling to the town of Tlaltizapan to present a petition to President Ernesto Zedillo Ponce de León, who was presiding over a commemoration of the seventy-seventh anniversary of Emiliano Zapata's assassination. Under the orders of Governor Jorge Carrillo Olea, several police units attacked the Tepoztecan caravan, which included children, women, and elders; several Tepoztecos were wounded by gunshots and sixty-four-year-old Marcos Olmedo Gutiérrez was found dead a few hours later with clear signs of torture and a bullet in his neck. Two foreign journalists (from France and Spain) and an amateur video camera from Tepoztlán witnessed and recorded the events, contradicting Carrillo Olea's version of armed Tepoztecos attacking the police. Zedillo was thus forced to fault the police and as a result of wide press coverage of the massacre, Grupo KS, unable to justify the murder and violence against the Tepoztecos, canceled the megaproject on April 13, 1996. KS continues to claim its right to the plots, and in the word of one of their vice presidents, José de los Ríos, they cancelled the project because "no hay gente interesada en invertir donde no hay gobernabilidad" [nobody is interested in investing where there is no governability].[31] Obviously, de los Ríos has in mind the people of Tepoztlán as the ungovernable and not Carillo Olea, the governor of the state of Morelos, who instructed his police to assault the caravan. Ironically, two years after the rebellion, the Tepoztecos claim a 60 percent reduction of crime in spite of, or more likely as a result of, the absence of a police force.

On a happier note, on September 11, 1997, Tepoztlán received with fire-crackers and music the caravan of 1,111 Zapatistas from Chiapas, in this last stop before marching into Mexico City. Three thousand Indians from the area joined the caravan from Chiapas. Tepoztlán remains barricaded and continues its struggle in solidarity with other Indians in Mexico.

Ann Arbor, October 1997

In June 1999, I visited Tepoztlán and interviewed Asciano Cedillo Méndez, the education regent of Tepoztlán, who informed me that the town had agreed to hold elections in March 1997. In order to receive federal funds from the state, however, the Tepoztecos had to renounce its status of Municipio Libre. The CUT agreed to hold elections and abide by state requirements that only members of officially recognized political parties could run for office. The CUT made an agreement with the Partido Revolucionario Democratico (PRD) to use this party to present a *planilla* (voting ballot) of officers who were elected according to the community-based juridical norms, the so-called *usos y cos-*

tumbres in a public assembly of the town. Thus they retained the right to use their own legal traditions and comply with the state's requirements to receive federal funds.

I returned to Tepoztlán in the summer of 2000 and found the town immersed in a celebration. When I inquired about the reason for celebrating, an old man in the plaza told me that the PRI had been defeated. At first I thought he was speaking of Fox's recent election, but no, the reason was the election of the new mayor, Lázaro Rodríguez Castañeda (who had already served as mayor during the uprising), and the *planilla* the town had elected according to their juridical norms. Tepoztlán citizens have dismantled the barricades and given up their status as Municipio Libre, but they also have invented a way to circumvent the state's requirements to gain access to federal funds without giving up their own legal and political forms. In a word, their autonomy is a fact even if the state does not recognize it.

Berkeley, October 2000

6 Negri by Zapata

Constituent Power and the Limits of Autonomy

The mural *Vida y sueños de la cañada Perla* (figure 6.1) in the community of Taniperla, Chiapas, was destroyed by the army on April 11, 1998, in an effort that sought to neutralize the constituent power that had materialized in the Municipio Autónomo Ricardo Flores Magón.[1] Next to Emiliano Zapata (the leader of the southern armies during the Mexican Revolution of 1910) stands an armed Ricardo Flores Magón, the anarcho-communist leader and theoretician of revolution, who represented the most radical wing of the insurrection of 1910. The words "Para la lucha actividad actividad actividad es lo que de-

FIGURE 6.1. *Vida y sueños de la cañada Perla, comunidad de Taniperla, Chiapas.* Courtesy of the Junta de Buen Gobierno el Camino del Futuro. Caracol de Resistencia hacia un Nuevo Amanecer. La Garrucha, Chiapas.

manda el momento" [For the struggle activity activity activity is what the moment demands] were extracted from Flores Magón's last essay in *Regeneración*, the organ of the radical Partido Liberal Mexicano, which advocated armed insurrection as the only way to destroy capitalism.[2]

His *morral*, hung over his shoulder, bears the name of *Regeneración*, along with the name of another revolutionary publication, *El Ahuizote*; the seeds of rebellion, the letters of the word *libertad*, spin on his left hand. Flores Magón's last manifesto directed at "La Junta Organizadora del Partido Liberal Mexicano a los miembros del partido, a los anarquistas de todo el mundo y a los trabajadores en general" [To the Organizing Junta of the Liberal Mexican Party, to the anarchists of all the world and to workers in general] was written in Los Angeles, California, and published in *Regeneración* on March 16, 1918. *Regeneración* was closed down for good on March 21, 1918. This manifesto led to the imprisonment of Flores Magón and his associate Librado Rivera, who were condemned to twenty and fifteen years in prison respectively. Flores Magón died four years later, on November 20, 1922, in the U.S. federal penitentiary of Leavenworth, Kansas. Flores Magón and Zapata preside as ghosts whose ideals have prevailed beyond their deaths.

The Zapatista repossessions of haciendas and factories in the southern state of Morelos during the 1910 insurrection, as well as their dictum "la tierra es de quien la trabaja" [the land belongs to those who work it], embodied the clearest example of Flores Magón's theory of direct action, the immediate takeover of the means of production. Indeed, Zapata implemented the takeovers independently of Flores Magón's writings and the programs of the Partido Liberal. But it was after the Zapatista takeovers that Flores Magón came in contact with Zapata's forces, leading the Zapatistas to change their motto from the reformist "justice, liberty, and law" to the revolutionary call for "tierra y libertad," a position consistent with Flores Magón's anarcho-communist aph-

orisms on revolution. Some of these include: "El verdadero revolucionario es un ilegal por excelencia" [The true revolutionary is an illegal par excellence]; "La ley conserva, la revolución renueva" [Law conserves, revolution renews]; and "Los revolucionarios tenemos que ser forzosamente ilegales. Tenemos que salirnos del camino trillado de los convencionalismos y abrir nuevas vías" [As revolutionaries we must be illegals. We must divert from the beaten path of conventionalisms and open new ways].[3] These aphorisms are reiterated today in the communiqués of Subcomandante Marcos. However, we must underscore the differences in that Marcos and the Zapatistas in Chiapas find themselves in the predicament of advocating revolution, of inventing new paths and sensibilities, while developing political arguments for a transformation of the Mexican Constitution that would recognize the right of the indigenous peoples of Chiapas and Mexico to autonomy—that is, the recognition of the right to be ruled by their normative systems, to develop their cultures and languages, and to control the natural resources within their territories.

The Acuerdos de San Andrés, signed by the Zapatistas and the federal government in February 1996, committed the federal government to a recognition of the right to self-determination and the creation of autonomous Indian communities, regions, and peoples, no longer limited to individual communities. The definition of "Indians as Peoples" is central to Convention 169 of Indigenous and Tribal Peoples (1989) of the International Labor Organization, an agreement signed by the Mexican government.[4] Autonomous indigenous regions and peoples would remain part of the Mexican nation, but would be able to determine the use of natural resources located in the regions, the commitment of the government to provide communication infrastructures, the transfer of state-run radio stations, and the promotion of the knowledge of Indian cultures and languages on a national level—all schools in the federation would include Indian languages and cultures in their curricula.

This transformation of the Mexican nation in Article 4 of the constitution would paradoxically establish an autonomy from the structures of the state. I say "paradoxically" because, beyond the effective access to the jurisdiction of the state ("efectivo acceso a la juridicción del Estado") as specified in Article 4, the accords would recognize the noninterference of the state in the practices of their normative systems. The EZLN walked out of the dialogues on August 29, 1996, and made public the reasons for the interruption and the conditions for resuming the dialogue in a communiqué of September 3, 1996.[5] Among the conditions listed were (1) the liberation of all the imprisoned Zapatistas; (2) a governmental interlocutor with a capacity to decide, a political willingness to negotiate, and a respect for the delegation of the EZLN; (3) the installation of a commission that would follow and verify the fulfillment of Acuerdos de San Andrés; (4) serious propositions for reaching agreements in the discussions on the "Mesa Dos: Democracia y Justicia" ("Table Two: Democracy and Justice")[6]; and (5) an end to the military and political harassment of Indians in Chiapas and the disbanding of paramilitary groups sponsored by the state.

These have been reduced to three signals for a return to the dialogue: (1) the implementation of the accords; (2) the liberation of prisoners; (3) the withdrawal of the army. These demands were in place during President Vicente Fox's presidential campaign, who at that time stated that he would resolve the situation in Chiapas in five minutes. The signals remain pending. The situation has only worsened since he took power.[7] Not one week goes by in which representatives from different communities from the Municipio Autónomo Ricardo Flores Magón, just to mention one entity in the state of Chiapas, do not denounce abuses by federal authorities or members of the state's Seguridad Pública (public security, a euphemism for the army). Parallel denunciations are presented daily in other states.

In February and March of 2001 the EZLN held a "Zapatour" in which Marcos and handful of the Zapatista *comandantes* visited several towns on their way to Mexico City, sharing with the people their ideals, their demands to the government, and their willingness to arrive at a peaceful solution of the conflict. The Zapatour was such a success that it clouded the fame in which the recently elected Fox was basking. The peak of the Zapatour was Comandante Esther's address to the Congreso de la Unión, after representatives from the PRI and the PRD understood the political capital they would derive from allowing the EZLN to address Congress. Esther did not limit herself to exposing the demands of the Zapatistas, specifically of the women; rather, her speech also underscored the symbolic fact of an indigenous woman addressing Congress: "Esta tribuna es un símbolo. Por eso convocó tanta polémica. Por eso queríamos hablar en ella y por eso algunos no querían que aquí estuviéramos. Y es un símbolo también que sea yo, una mujer pobre, indígena y zapatista, quien tome la palabra y sea el mío el mensaje central de nuestra palabra como zapatistas" [This tribune is a symbol. This is why it summoned up so much polemic. That is why we wanted to speak here and why some did not want us here. And it is also a symbol that it is me, a poor woman, an Indian and a Zapatista, who addresses you and that the central message of our word as Zapatistas is mine].[8]

Once the Zapatistas returned to Chiapas, Congress approved a version of the accords that was unacceptable to them as well as to the Congreso Nacional Indígena (National Indigenous Congress), whose representatives had also addressed Congress. The approved version was even more restrictive than the one proposed by the former president, Ernesto Zedillo. The law modifying Article 4 was approved by the required two-thirds of the states' legislatures. Not one day passes in which indigenous peoples do not denounce the law on regional, state, and federal levels. Let this very brief narrative on the Zapatour, the presence of the Zapatistas in Congress, and the approval of the law fulfill the function of a backdrop to my discussion of the parallelisms between Zapatismo and Negri, in particular with respect to the limits of autonomist projects. If it remains necessary to continue to indict and denounce the actions of Congress and President Fox, who could very well have vetoed the law, the objective of this chapter is to create a crisis within the discourse of autonomy. My intent is not to undermine the indigenous struggles for autonomy, but to emphasize the need to think in terms of a process of autonomization and to make manifest the philosophical background that overdetermines the debates with the state—to sharpen the arms of critique for a critique of arms.

There is a tension, perhaps a paradox, an aporia, in the Zapatista revolutionary ideals and the call for a transformation of the state, a tension that according to Antonio Negri has haunted revolutionary political theory and praxis in the West since Machiavelli—a tension between constituent power, which by definition exists outside the law, and the will to control and domesticate the democratic passion of the multitude into a coherent concept of a people. The most common form of control advocates the institutionalization of a constitution and the surrender of the power of the multitude to a representative form of government: for example, a constitutional republic, the Soviet state, a parliamentary democracy. This project of transforming the Mexican Constitution as part of a revolutionary process entails an aporia between the transformation of the constitution in such terms that would enable the exercise of constituent power and the institutionalization of the constitutional changes that would demand the surrender of the multitude to a state of law.

Theoreticians of constitutional law have faced a paradox, as manifest in Emile Boutmy's statement cited by Negri: "Constituent power is an imperative act of nation, rising from nowhere and organizing the hierarchies of law."[9] Boutmy's phrase—"rising from nowhere and organizing the hierarchies of law"—sums up the contradiction of affirming the autonomy of the foundation of law and sovereignty. But sovereignty itself, as Negri has pointed out, stands in opposition to constituent power: "constitutive strength never ends up as [constituted] power, nor does the multitude tend to become a totality but, rather, a set of singularities, an open multiplicity."[10] It is precisely constitutive strength that sets apart the "constitutionalist paradigm [which] always refers to the 'mixed constitution,' the mediation of inequality, and therefore . . . is a non-democratic paradigm" from "the paradigm of constituent power [which] is that of a force that bursts apart, breaks, interrupts, unhinges any preexisting equilibrium and possible continuity."[11] Indeed, for Negri, "revolution is necessary, as necessary as the human need to be moral, to constitute oneself ethically, to free body and mind from slavery, and constituent power is the means toward this end."[12] Here I am summing up, or rather eliding, Negri's critique of a number of theoreticians ranging from Max Weber and Carl Schmitt to Hannah Arendt and Jürgen Habermas.

Negri's penchant for aphorism lends itself to citation independently of his critique of constitutionalism. *Insurgencies* consists of a series of studies of constituent power in Machiavelli's "people in arms," Harrington's "discovery of material determinations of the relations of power," "the American renovation of classical constitutionalism and the French ideology of social emancipation," and "the egalitarian impulse of communism and the enterprising spirit of the Bolsheviks." Negri notes that his is neither a genealogy nor an archaeology of constituent power, but the hermeneutic of a faculty of humankind: "It is clear that each of these enterprises [Machiavelli, Harrington, and so on] will discover its meaning within the set of events that shapes them individually. But it is also true that the meaning of these events is inscribed in the consciousness of us all and etched in our being because it has somehow determined it."[13] By "us" let us understand all subjectivities that participate in political processes that bear the imprint of these events in Euro-American history, of which history I dare to say that it affects the totality of subjects engaged in one form or another of the political discourses of the West. This generalized presence of the West makes paradoxical any distinction with a non-West grounded on a binary opposition. Indeed, we must understand this "forced" biculturalism (West and non-West coexisting in one culture and subjectivity) as a liberatory dwelling in multiple worlds and thereby resist reducing the non-West to varieties of European "elsewheres," however productive this category might be.[14]

Negri's particular studies of Euro-American political theory are at once individual cases that bear universal implications. Its universality travels and incorporates other latitudes, but it never gives itself as such. In principle, the concept of constituent power would have a history only if understood in the materiality of concrete historical and social configurations. As such, its manifestations will always be specific to singular subjects and situations that cannot be exhausted by Euro-American political history. The "America" in the term "Euro-America" does not refer to the United States but to the hybrid discourses that have been produced since the European colonization of the Americas in the sixteenth century; arguably all forms of political discourse are infected by an "American" determination.

Even if determined by the events pertaining to the history of Euro-American political theory, the multiplicity of constituent strength entails the singularity of the experience and the strength of concrete struggles. Specific histories of constituent power may very well, as in the case of indigenous struggles in Chiapas, also articulate discourses other than those of Euro-American political theory and history. This "otherness"—which should not be reified as "the

Other," but posited as "an otherness," as in revolution, the impossible, and the unnameable—demands that we not only account for Indians speaking in the terms and languages of the West but speaking *about* "the West, its revolutions, and its discourses" in indigenous languages and discursive traditions.[15] In reading Negri by Zapata, we will need to account for the colonial past and present of Indians, for the limits of the concept of autonomy, and for the need to think in terms of autonomization as process rather than autonomy as an accomplished state.[16]

Before moving on, let me premise the discussion with a caveat: The title of this essay, "Negri by Zapata," inevitably invokes the rhetorical strategy of reading north by south as a subversion of the dominance European thought has had over the rest of the world—the so-called Occidentalism.[17] The reduction of Euro-American thought to a homogeneous, static Culture—the capitalized "C" translates those in Occidentalism—not only erases all differences within the West but reduces the dynamics of cultural identity of the West to a relationship to the non-West, if this clear-cut distinction still holds in geopolitical terms. This model inevitably harnesses the identity of the non-West to the subversion, transculturation, and appropriation of the West. As it is well-known and hardly needs repetition, but a clarification might still be in order, Hegel's dialectic of the master and the slaves has provided a language for understanding colonial dominance and its transgression. Even if this has been an enabling mode of resisting Western hegemonies, there is no reason why we should limit the identities of West and non-West alike to conceptual frames in which each defines itself in opposition to the other—as in the politics of identity and difference. Hegel conceived the dialectic of the master/slave in terms of European thought, the history of which amounts to a series of "professorial" supersessions.[18]

Its application to the history of colonialism, then, constitutes an extrapolation not originally intended that we could further develop by imagining the dialectic in terms of an indigenous culture in which disciple overcomes master. By this, I want to suggest an indigenous subject undergoing initiation rites and gaining knowledge that has nothing to do with the West. Moreover, we can imagine this indigenous subject sitting in a seminar on Hegel's *Phenomenology of Mind*, following the unfolding of the figures without internalizing the categories as a colonized subject, rather than understanding the dialectic in its European terms. She may find in the Hegelian corpus certain references to non-European cultures offensive, and perhaps she may simply dismiss them as limitations in Hegel without having the urge to contradict him. Furthermore, she may laugh at the superficiality of those who, having been formed in the West, reduce their philosophers to Eurocentric statements. This indigenous subject could very well love and practice Euro-American thought and find absurd the self-depreciation of those Euro-Americans who seek to invent alternative (read: nativistic) ways of thought. However, we can also imagine a Euro-American having thoughts, preoccupations, and horizons of meaning and freedom other than those in which she would be bound to differentiate herself by establishing an opposition to non-European cultures. Different horizons of meaning and revolution may meet, dialogue, and enrich each other, without establishing hierarchical relations. Even if this ideal situation would not in itself erase the hierarchies of value that we are "all" aware of, the articulation of its (im)possibility would counter the determinacy of current hierarchical structures.

Thus we may be free to think with Negri without having the moral obligation of subverting, appropriating, or transculturating his thought—that is, an obligation to transculturate that would go beyond the fact that making Negri travel to other latitudes and social realities already implies a transformation of his thought, a transformation that we should nevertheless see as integral to his thought. The immanence of struggles constitutes their singularity and necessary specificity. One may thus think the West with Negri, agreeing or not, without feeling bound and limited by his thought, hence pressed to declare one's autonomy. To think Negri without applying him remains a possibility (to my mind, the application of theory equals unarmed, defenseless thought), but beyond thinking within his tradition lies the possibility of thinking Negri and the West in non-Western categories. I will return to this; for now let me point out that thinking Empire, colonial power, and the West in general has been a figure of thought in colonial situations in the Americas since the European invasion in the sixteenth century. In fact, missionaries demanded that Indians represent the colonial order and the history of their oppression in their own indigenous categories and systems of writing.[19]

In running Negri by Zapata, my aim is to outline the connections and interrelations between Euro-American thought and the project of establishing the autonomy of Indian peoples (*pueblos indígenas*). The "by" would thus suggest a "Zapata" reading and writing about Negri. Ideally, neither Negri nor Zapata would be privileged. Zapata in the context of the Zapatista insurrection in Chiapas, as Subcomandante Marcos has repeatedly asserted in his communiqués, stands for an entire array of revolutionary practices.[20] Evocations of Zapata encompass ethico-political maxims, a folklore, a metaphysics, elements for a theory of cross-cultural communication, and an affirmation of constituent power. As I have pointed out, the concept of constituent power is one of Negri's salient signatures; Negri's *Insurgencies* is a history of a particular, but nevertheless crucial, series of Western debates and answers to the crisis posed by constituent power in political theory. Indeed, Negri equates the political with constituent power. The history of constituent power provides an instance of an exception to the commonplace that the West self-fashions itself relative to the non-West, the Other, the Orient, and what not. There is an element of truth to Occidentalism, but it bears the elements of an ideology, of a fetish that by linking the identity of the West in a binary opposition ends up limiting the understanding of the cultural and material fields that inform the creative imaginings of non-Western cultures. Both the West and the non-West have preoccupations, interests, and traditions that do not relate one to the other. In the history of constituent power outlined in Negri's *Insurgencies*, the Other is not the non-West, but revolution, the multitude, the democratic absolute, the impossible.

One of the findings of the Zapatistas consists precisely in defining the existence of Indian and Western forms in nonhierarchical spaces that are nevertheless linguistically, culturally, juridically, and politically distinct. In this regard, the Zapatistas should be inscribed as an instance of the "beyond modern rationalism" that Negri calls forth in his history of constituent power.[21] The Indians participating in the debates with the government and in the drafting of the Acuerdos de San Andrés were, or at least found no inherent contradiction in desiring to be, as well versed in Euro-American traditions as in their specific Indian cultures.[22] If the critiques of indigenous fascination with First World intellectuals fulfilled a necessary ideological function parallel to the constitution of blocs of Third World countries, the paradigms of the modern nation and the national-popular underlying the political viability of these positions up to the 1970s have for all practical purposes disappeared with the weakening of the nation-state and the emergence of Empire, as has been defined by coauthors Michael Hardt and Antonio Negri in *Empire*.[23] The struggle for Indian autonomy, an offshoot of the rebellion in Chiapas, aims at the heart of Empire beyond the local.

In the title of this essay, Negri's name stands for a current of thought compatible with Flores Magón's anarcho-communist revolutionary program. As it were, behind Flores Magón's image in the mural at Taniperla we may read Negri, Paolo Virno, Michael Hardt, and other representatives of recent radical Italian thought.[24] Zapata, in turn, can be read as a condensation of a long line of revolutionaries that includes such figures as Rubén Jaramillo in the 1950s and 1960s, the guerrillas Genaro Vázquez and Lucio Cabañas in the 1960s and 1970s, and obviously Marcos and the Zapatistas of today.[25] The images of Flores Magón and Zapata lack the stasis of metaphor. Their position and posture in the mural suggests a metonymic flow into a historical horizon punctuated with little Zapatistas on the mountains and the rising sun.[26]

Historical temporality flows from the future to the past in the mode of future anterior. To go beyond an allegorical reading of the woman in the left-hand corner as a nourishing Mother Earth, further reinforced by the two breastlike mountains next to her, is to see her placing the liberation of women as the beginning and the end of the revolution. Thus the movement of Flores Magón and Zapata lacks the fixity of ideological posts as in the typical use of portraits of Marx, Lenin, Mao, and others in socialist cults of personality. In the likeness of specters, Flores Magón and Zapata inspire the *new* movement, one that aspires to the impossible. Marcos does not figure in the mural but his "presence," also in the manner of a ghost, presides over the armed men and women Zapatistas guarding Taniperla from the mountains. Marcos and the Zapatistas further elaborate the theoretical writings of Flores Magón and the indigenous discourse of Zapata. As such, the mural does not partake of an Apollonian impulse to fix meaning, but to communicate the strength of living labor.

Armando Bartra has pointed out apropos of Flores Magón that the most original political thought in Mexico has been written in the press, facing the need to theorize the concrete.[27] Marcos's clandestine writings and publications in Mexican newspapers, in particular in *La Jornada*, are without a doubt the most brilliant contemporary articulation of Bartra's assessment of theorizing from the concrete. In his introduction to a selection of pieces from *Regeneración*, Bartra singles out the originality of Flores Magón by underscoring the parallelism with Lenin's thought in *What Is to Be Done?* (1902), in particular, with the role of the press in a revolutionary process. Eventually Flores Magón became familiar with and wrote about Lenin and the Bolshevik revolution. We should underscore that Lenin's April Theses (1917) are without doubt the most congenial to Flores Magón's anarcho-communist thought. Bartra has characterized the writings in *Regeneración* as "textos en los que en un soplo se dice bolsheviques y zapatistas" [texts in which one says Bolshevik and Zapatista in one breath].[28]

We also find similarities between Marcos's and Negri's thought that as far as we can ascertain were independently thought. When Hardt and Negri define "communism," we can imagine Flores Magón and Marcos agreeing with their response in *Empire* to the label of anarchists: "You are a bunch of anarchists, the new Plato on the block will finally yell at us. That is not true. We would be anarchists if we were not to speak (as did Thrasymachus and Callicles, Plato's immortal interlocutors) from the standpoint of a materiality constituted in the networks of productive cooperation, in other words, from the perspective of a humanity that is constructed productively, that is constituted through the 'common name' of freedom. No, we are not anarchists but communists who have seen how much repression and destruction of humanity have been wrought by liberal and socialist big governments."[29] Note that upholding the necessity of the state does not figure as a distinctive characteristic of Hardt and Negri's communism; on the contrary, they dismiss liberal and socialist big governments along with any argument for a theory in which socialism would serve as a stage in the dissolution of the state under communism. Elsewhere in *Empire*, Hardt and Negri specifically override the necessity of a transitional phase, of a purgatory: "We are not proposing the umpteenth version of the inevitable passage through purgatory. . . . We are not repeating the schema of an ideal teleology that justifies any passage in the name of a promised land."[30] One can also imagine the people of Taniperla as well as Marcos and the Zapatistas fully subscribing to this definition of communism without purgatory.

If Flores Magón and Lenin opened the twentieth century with an identification of revolution with armed struggle, the invention of other forms of revolutionary praxis defines both the Zapatistas' and Negri's manifestos for the twenty-first century. (Nothing is more alien to the Zapatistas and Negri than the terrorist act on the World Trade Center on September 11, 2001.) For the Zapatistas this need for new forms of revolution implies never again having the need for a January 1, 1994, the date of the initial uprising, which had a high cost in lives. For Negri and a host of radical political Italian thinkers, as expressed in "Do You Remember Revolution?," reinventing revolution entails a demystification of violence: "There is no 'good' version of armed struggle, no alternative to the elitist practice of the Red Brigades; armed struggle is in itself incompatible with and antithetical to the new movements."[31]

For the record, the Mexican army has carried on a low-intensity war against Indian communities in violation of the suspension of hostilities on January 12, 1994, that many Zapatistas, including some from Taniperla and including Professor Valdez Ruvalcaba who coordinated the painting of the mural, were imprisoned in the penitentiary of Cerro Hueco, and that Negri and other Italian intellectuals were jailed in Italian prisons on trumped-up charges of terrorism; Negri is currently under house arrest.[32] It is not arbitrary to juxtapose the Zapatistas and radical Italian theorists. After all, Marcos has alluded to the workers' committees known as COBAS (*comitati di base*), and one of the social centers bore the name "Ya Basta" in solidarity with the Chiapas uprising. The *centri sociali*, autonomous youth organizations for political action, have served as a model for the COBAS in lieu of forming a "new union."[33] The social center has evolved into the Associazione Ya Basta, which in December 2000, after assuming the initiative to collect funds in Italy, took the materials for building an electric turbine to the community of La Realidad, the headquarters of the Zapatistas in the Selva Lacandona.[34]

Even if the mural can be read as an idealization of life in an autonomous community, the *sueños* of Taniperla are not a utopia in the sense of a model of a world to be realized; they are dreams already materialized in the community's creative energy and everyday life represented in the mural. The idea of

the mural was from the start a collective effort between Sergio Valdez Ruvalcaba, better known as Checo, and the people of Taniperla. Although Checo is
a talented draftsman, he merely guided the community's efforts, telling them
to paint whatever they wanted: "cada quien dibuje lo que quiera." The community dialogued and decided on the following topics: "el agua es vida" [water
is life], "la cooperativa por la unidad" [the cooperative for unity], "la asamblea
para decidir" [the assembly to make decisions], "los zapatistas nos cuidan"
[the Zapatistas look after us], "Zapata por heroe y chingón" [Zapata for being a
hero and a *chingón*], "el cafetal por la ganancita" [the coffee plantation for the
little earnings], "la palabra de la mujer" [the word of women], "la radio para
comunicar" [radio for communication], and "los principales por su palabra"
[the *principales* for their word].[35]

Thus the mural itself is the result of collective dialogue, an instance of
communal government represented in the mural by the woman bringing the
proposals in her *morral* (which not only contains *pozol* but also documents
pertaining to the meeting's agenda, according to one of the Tzeltal painters)
and the man reading a document at the entrance of the Casa Municipal. These
two figures bring to the assembly the issues discussed in the separate groups
of men and women. If the two circles separate the community along gender
lines, the participation of men and women at the meeting will be on an equal
footing. The mention that the *morral* contains *pozol* in addition to documents
should not be read as merely stating that women now have proposals to make,
not just food to prepare. *Pozol* is a Maya discovery, a fermented beverage made
out of corn with nutritional and medicinal properties. The transnational food
enterprise Quest International and the University of Minnesota obtained a
patent in the United States (#5919695) for the use of a bacteria they isolated
from the beverage, thereby making the medicinal properties of *pozol* private
property of Quest International and the University of Minnesota.[36] This case is
a vivid example of how transnational enterprises appropriate (or rather, steal)
the knowledge of indigenous peoples. Jacques Lacan has corrected Hegel's
dialectic by arguing that the master extracts the knowledge (*savoir*) from the
slaves, and that work (or rather, spoliation) produces no knowledge, contrary
to what the Hegelian dialectic, or at least some of its interpreters, would lead
us to believe: "Philosophy [in this case, science] in its historical function is this
extraction, this treason, I would say, of the knowledge of the slave, to obtain a
transmutation as knowledge of the master."[37]

The mural is the product of living labor representing itself. Clearly, the
subsequent destruction of the mural by the army represents an obstacle to
the creativity of the community of Taniperla, thus exemplifying Negri's point
(after Deleuze's correction of Foucault) that resistance precedes power: "One
might say in this sense that resistance is actually prior to power. When impe-

rial government intervenes, it selects the liberatory impulses of the multitude in order to destroy them, and in return it is driven forward by resistance. . . . Each imperial action is a rebound of the resistance of the multitude that poses a new obstacle for the multitude to overcome."[38] If the mural at Taniperla was destroyed, the liberatory impulses expressed in the mural recur in other *municipios* that declared themselves autonomous self-governments. These forms of self-government do not react to the power of the army as the traditional understanding of resistance would have it, but operate under the concept of communities in resistance as a space for the construction of a new world.[39] As such, the army and power in general lag behind the creative effort of rebellion—they react and devise new forms of oppression and control that seek to curtail constituent power.

In this equation "Zapata" stands for the long-standing history of indigenous rebellions. Zapata also stands for the demand to recognize the *usos y costumbres*, the indigenous normative systems that can be traced back to the colonial period and perhaps in some instances to *before* the European invasion. The first use of the term *usos y costumbres* in Spanish colonial law, as far as I know, goes back to Law XIX of the New Laws of 1542 that called for a dissolution of the *encomiendas* (grants given to *conquistadores* in which Indians paid tribute in kind and labor) and the liberation of slaves, and prescribed love as the only acceptable treatment of Indians: "no den lugar que en los pleitos de entre yndios o con ellos se hagan proçessos ordinarios ni aya alargas como suele acontecer por la maliçia de algunos abogados y procuradores, sino que sumariamente sean determinados, guardando sus usos y costumbres" [make sure that in litigation between Indians and with them there are no ordinary processes nor continuances as they are commonly due to the evildoing of some lawyers and prosecutors, rather that cases are summarily determined, following their uses and customs].[40] The implementation of the *usos y costumbres* at once protects Indian communities from Spaniards, criollos, and mestizos, and alienates Indians in a separate republic, in a structure not unlike apartheid. Indians today prefer the term "indigenous normative systems" over *usos y costumbres* (the chosen term of the Mexican government), but the colonial legacy of these separate legal apparatuses will continue to haunt them, especially if the communities choose to ignore their colonial origins.[41]

In tracing the history of colonization, we must heed the recommendation that Gayatri Chakravorty Spivak has made regarding the need to avoid the equally pernicious acts of either locating colonialism in a distant or not so distant past, or asserting a continuous colonial form of dominance to the present.[42] The first can be readily proven as false given neocolonial articulations of dominance, but more important than locating colonialism in easily identifiable practices is the mapping of forms of colonial discourse that we continue to reproduce in spite of our most honorable intentions. As for the tracing of continuous colonial forms, the danger resides in losing track of the historical nature of the different modes and categories of exercising colonial power. In this respect, we must differentiate the practices of the Enlightenment from those of the early modern period. Whereas the opposition in the context of sixteenth-century Spain is between Christians and non-Christians (pagans, Muslims, and Jews), in eighteenth-century Northern Europe the opposition is between peoples with and without history, with and without writing, and/or with and without a state. I will come back to this distinction later. Even though we can trace the categories and epistemologies pertaining to both periods in Mexico and Latin America (the second in the variant of internal colonialism), the sediments of the Spanish colonization constitute historical realities very different from those in African and Asian countries whose colonial pasts date back to the late eighteenth century.

Paradoxically, Spivak's question "Can the Subaltern Speak?" builds on a binary that sets an absolute distance between Europe and its Others, a binary that has a history dating back to the eighteenth century. Spivak's question and negative answer reproduce the terms of this absolute binary in a circular argument: dominant discourses define the colonized as incapable of reasoning, hence subalterns are incapable of reasoning and need the mediation and representation of what Spivak calls First World intellectuals, a category that would include intellectuals like herself who, in spite of their colonial pasts, can fully operate in metropolitan circles.[43] The "subaltern cannot speak" construct thus betrays a metalepsis, the substitution of effect for cause, a figure that Spivak knows very well as can be seen in her discussion of *hysteron proteron* in *Death of a Discipline*. Indeed, my point has less to do with exposing her fallacious reasoning than with documenting the historical background in which the metalepsis makes sense. Her rhetorical sophistication and the long series of critiques and responses to the denial of speech to subalterns should warn us about the ruses imbedded in the phrasing of the question.[44]

Offhand, she would seem to dismiss subalterns who learn the languages of the West while continuing to dwell in their native worlds: one either is a First World intellectual who speaks or a subaltern bound to silence. Colonizers might very well be, and most often are, incapable of understanding indigenous discourses, but there is nothing *other* than the internalization of the will of the colonizer, which pits Western discourses against indigenous life forms, that should keep subalterns from mastering the languages of the West while retaining their own. The notion that "the subaltern can't speak" carries as its ultimate irony the corollary that if a subaltern speaks she (it is clearly a she for Spivak) would no longer be a subaltern. Under this formulation subaltern studies assumes the form of the absurd proposition, of a fetish, inasmuch as the liberatory project of recuperating subaltern histories as articulated by Ranajit Guha (who has taught us how to read the political motivations in subaltern insurrections, otherwise dismissed as irrational outbursts of violence) has transformed itself into a metaphysics of denegation and a statement of privilege.[45] Even if we were to accept that this binary between intellectuals and subalterns reflects the binaries imposed by imperial powers in the eighteenth and nineteenth centuries, we should not generalize the impossibility of subalterns speaking to other regions with different colonial histories.

Take as paradigmatic the Enlightenment's distinction between peoples with and without history, with and without a state, and the error of attributing these binaries to the form of imperialism practiced by Spain in the sixteenth and seventeenth centuries, or even before, in the so-called *reconquista* of Muslim territories in southern Spain. If there is a binary in early modern Spanish expansionism, it is between Christians and non-Christians (alternately—with their own histories, writing systems, and political states—pagans, Muslims, and Jews). These specifications have little to do with a squabble over historical facts, rather with the social, economic, and cultural sedimentations that underlie the present. In the case of those regions colonized by Spain in the early modern period, we often find a second (if not a third and fourth) wave of colonization bearing the imprint of the Enlightenment. These posterior colonizations in places like Chiapas were implemented both by native elites as well as by foreign "investors-settlers."[46]

Colonizations following the "ideals" of the Enlightenment were superimposed on sociopolitical structures that were the result of three hundred years of Spanish rule. It is not a matter of comparing the two models of imperialism but of tracing the effects. When at the turn of the twentieth century Zapata claims communal lands of his town of Atenecuilco that had been privatized by liberal legislation inspired in the Enlightenment, he does so on the basis of legal documents that dated back to the colonial period. Spanish colonial laws included legislation that protected the communities from the kinds of expropriation that became prevalent after the wars of independence. These laws cannot be seen as merely preserving the status of Indian communities before the conquest, but also as creating traditions reflecting the influence of Christianity and the impact of the socioeconomic-technological transformation introduced by the colonial order. It is important to note that indigenous communities reinvent themselves under colonial and republican rule, wherein tradition is subject to debate.

If history played a fundamental role in defining the legitimacy of the communities, the past also bears a legacy of rebellion. The most notable figure in present-day Chiapas is the hybrid Votán Zapata, a mixture of the nonmodern embedded in Votán, the pre-Columbian numen signified as "the guardian and heart of the people," and the modern embedded in Zapata and the Revolution of 1910. As it were, the spirit of Votán assumes an epochal instantiation in Zapata.[47] We can trace a tradition of invoking the leaders of the past spanning the very beginning of the colonial period to the present-day rebellion in Chiapas. Spanish authorities were concerned not only with learning the past to preserve the normative systems in the indigenous communities, but also with gaining knowledge regarding other uses of history in which Indians invoked the spirits of the ancient leaders in a spirit of rebellion.

Let me dwell on this last point by citing a passage from one of the *Cantares Mexicanos*, a series of songs first collected by Bernardino de Sahagún and his indigenous assistants in 1550 through 1585:

> The ruler Atl Popoca comes to do a shield dance here in Mexico. It seems this lord lays hold of dried up egret-plume flower shields, lays hold of withered stripers, here before your eyes, Tlaxcallans. Hey! Huexotzincas, hey!
>
> It seems he's come to take a lance from the Spaniards. It seems this lord lays hold of dried-up egret-plume flower shields, lays hold of withered stripers, here before your eyes, Tlaxcallans. Hey! Huexotzincans, hey!
>
> Motelchiuh is the one who thrusts his shield, and it's the time of lords! Yes even so he sallies forth, having appeared. And when they've captured the conquistadores' guns, then Rabbit says, "Let there be dancing!" Tlaxcallans, hey! Huexotzincas, hey![48]

The text invokes the arrival of armed ghost warriors who are not only a threat to the Spaniards but also to their Indian allies, the Tlaxcallans and the Huexotzincas. According to John Bierhorst, this song belongs to the ghost-dance genre associated with the Plains Indians; ghost dances generally invoke the warriors of old to join them in a rebellion against the colonial order. Here, the warriors of old are taking possession of the Spaniards' lances and their guns. Whatever the motivation for keeping a record of these songs, the missionaries can hardly be seen as conceiving the Nahuas as a people without history; quite the contrary, beyond writing and painting histories, the Nahuas invoked the past to bring it to life in song and dance. They are people with intense histories that haunted the Spaniards with the revival of the old, with the return of ghosts. The songs spoke a language that evaded the missionaries' comprehension.

It is never a question of a lack of history but of history in a different key. And I say "beyond writing" to underscore the performance of history in pre-Columbian and colonial Mexico, and certainly not because the Spaniards of the early modern period thought the Amerindians as a whole lacked writing; otherwise how would we explain the ubiquitous reference to writing systems and the missionary projects of reconstructing the burned codices by producing replicas of pre-Columbian writing systems? Even when these histories were written using the Latin alphabet, their production as well as their reading must be understood in terms of an oral performance, and certainly not in the privacy of the individual world of the bourgeois writer and reader: the writing was (and continues to be) collective and the reading public.[49]

There are, of course, those who denigrate and deny the status of writing to the iconic script used by Amerindians or for that matter those who cast insults, who denigrate Indians with racist remarks. But there is, in my opinion, a much more interesting and enduring aspect to the colonial process in those texts and projects that seek to appropriate indigenous history, often a collaborative effort of Spaniards, mestizos, and Indians. For instance, the ghost song and dance quoted earlier would be arrested by someone like the Dominican Diego Durán, who conceived history in terms of a resurrection of the Ancient Mexican grandeur in his *Historia de las Indias de la Nueva España e islas de Tierra Firme* (c. 1581): "Ha sido mi deseo de darle vida y resucitarle de la muerte y olvido en que estaba, a cabo de tanto tiempo" [My desire has been to give it life and resurrect it from the death and oblivion in which it has rested for such a long time].[50] Later on in the *Historia de las Indias de la Nueva España*, Durán is even more emphatic in his praise of Nahua pre-Columbian historians and his will to resurrect the dead:

> Pero los historiadores y pintores pintaban con historias vivas y matices, con el pincel de su curiosidad, con vivos colores, las vidas y hazañas de estos valerosos caballeros y señores, para que su fama volase, con la claridad del sol, por todas las naciones. Cuya fama y memoria quise yo referir en esta historia, para que, conservada aquí, dure todo el tiempo que durare, para que los amadores de la virtud se aficionen a la seguir.

> [But the Mexican historians and painters painted with vivid histories and tints, with the brush of their curiosity, with vivid colors, the lives and feats of these courageous knights and lords, so that their fame would fly with the clarity of the sun over all nations. To their fame and glory I wish to refer in this my history, so that conserved here, it will last for the time it may last, so that the lovers of virtue may become fond of following it.][51]

We must read this text as counterinsurgent inasmuch as it claims resurrection as a trope for writing a history that will bring to life the ancient grandeur so that the "lovers of virtue" find a model for their actions. Durán not only alludes to Indian histories using iconic script as sources of his information, but also praises their pictorial beauty and the force of their corresponding verbal discourses. Just as he emulates the rhetorical colors of old and the inscription of history in stone, we cannot ignore that Duran's history seeks to bury the past for good.

In this regard, we may associate Durán's *Historia* with what Michel de Certeau has said about the metaphor of resurrection in Michelet's unpublished preface to the *Histoire de France*: "It aims at calming the dead who still haunt the present, and offering them scriptural tombs."[52] Nothing, however, guarantees the quieting down of the spirits of old. We can indeed imagine the pictorial component in Durán's *Historia* decorating bureaucratic buildings if not *pulquerías* (those public spaces in which the uprising of 1692 in Mexico City was gestated, chronicled by Carlos de Sigüenza y Góngora) and inspiring a whole tradition of Mexican muralists up to Diego Rivera and the *Vida y sueños de la cañada Perla*.[53] There is, however, an ambivalence in his call for virtue inasmuch as the association of political virtue suggests Machiavelli's use of this term in *The Prince* and the historical style of his commentary on Titus Livius in *The Discourses*. Durán intends his call for virtue to the mestizo and criollos and perhaps the indigenous elites collaborating with the Spaniards, hardly the same subjects that invoked the ghosts of old in song and dance—in an open call for rebellion!

Not unlike the ghost songs of the *Cantares Mexicanos*, the spirit of Flores Magón and especially Zapata belong to an imaginary of insurrection among the indigenous peoples of Chiapas, as evidenced in Marcos's reminiscence of Lord Ik': "O si, como ahora se dice en las montañas, el señor Ik' no murió, sino que vive como una luz que aparece, de tanto en tanto, por entre cerros y cañadas, con el sombrero y el caballo de Zapata" [Or perhaps, as it is told today in the mountains, lord Ik' did not die, but rather lives like a light that appears off and on, between the hills and the ravines, with the hat and the horse of Zapata].[54] Lord Ik' (Black Lord) was Comandante Hugo's nom de guerre. Hugo, an elder who, according to Marcos, was key to the January 1, 1994, uprising died in the assault of San Cristóbal de las Casas. Ik' was also one of the founders of the EZLN and a mentor to a whole generation of Zapatistas. In the manner of a latter-day Mackandal, the famed leader of the Haitian revolution who after his death would reappear in different animal and human forms, Zapata as Ik' or Ik' as Zapata testifies to the agency of the "gods," to the power of Votán (the guardian and heart of the people), to the compatibility of the modern and the nonmodern in the Zapatista insurrection, to the hybrid figure of Votán Zapata.[55]

Note the reference to the *one* and the *multitude* in the following communiqué of April, 10, 1994: "Es y no es todo en nosotros . . . Caminado está. . . Votán Zapata, guardian y corazón del pueblo. Amo de la noche . . . Señor de la montaña . . . Nosotros . . . Votán, guardian y corazón del pueblo. Uno y muchos es. Ninguno y todos. Estando viene. Votán, guardian y corazón del pueblo" [Is and is not everything in us. . . He is walking . . . Votán Zapata, guardian and heart of the people. Lord of the night. . . Lord of the mountain . . . Us . . .

Votán Zapata, guardian and heart of the people. None and all . . . As being is coming . . . Votán Zapata, guardian and heart of the people].[56] Votán Zapata, as one and many, attests to the singular in the multitude, to the singular subjectivity of constituent power, to the "many" comprising the multitude that refuses to be reduced to a "much." According to Hardt and Negri: "Democracy thus appears as constituent power. It is a power expressed in the multitude of singular subjects that excludes every transfer of powers. Constituent power excludes there being any type of foundation that resides outside the process of the multitude."[57]

For in Negri the "gods" also seem to live but in the figure of Dionysus, or at least he and Hardt write in *Labor of Dionysus*: "Our work is dedicated to the creative, Dionysian powers of the netherworld." They identify the Dionysian creator with communism: "Communism is the only Dionysian creator."[58] Elsewhere, in his discussion of Spinoza's contributions to the theory of constituent power in *Insurgencies*, Negri speaks of "a democratic living god," of "Democracy, a real democracy of right and appropriation, equal distribution of wealth, and equal participation in production [that] becomes the living god," of "Democracy [that] is the project of the multitude, a creative force, a living god." Negri goes on to outline the need "to emphasize and study the relation that ties the development of constituent thought to three ideological dimensions of Western thought: the Judeo-Christian tradition of creativity, the natural right concerning the social foundation, and the transcendental theory of the foundation. Now, the development of the concept of constituent power, even in its radically critical figures, is somewhat limited by these three ideal conditions—and no matter how much it works to unhinge them, it remains partially tied to them." Negri adopts the radical atheism of Machiavelli's, Spinoza's, and Marx's constituent theories, by which he means that "the concept of creativity is tied essentially to man."[59]

All this suggests that Negri can establish at once his commitment to radical atheism while at the same time partake of "a metaphysics of democracy and creativity," the living god of democracy and the Dionysian spirit of communism. The secular and the atheistic have their limits, paradoxically, in the same impulse that leads Negri to critique the religious conception of creativity in Machiavelli, Spinoza, and Marx. Negri identifies this remnant of Judeo-Christian conceptions of creativity in the tendency to conceive the strength of the multitude in terms of unity: "To claim this, however, means forgetting that the strength of the multitude is not only in the strength of the 'much' but also the strength of the 'many,' that is, the strength of singularities and differences."[60] This statement would make suspect any attempt to establish a unity on the principle of atheism and secularity, and even less desirable if, as Negri asserts, the crisis of constituent power, brought about by the three ideologies of the West, will never be totally unhinged. It seems more pertinent to explore the ways in which the agency of the "gods" may very well coexist with the will to a radical atheism. After all, given these ideologies haunting modern rationality, who is to deny, in the name of secularism, that it is not true that "el señor Ik' no murió, sino que vive como una luz que aparece, de tanto en tanto, por entre cerros y cañadas, con el sombrero y el caballo de Zapata" [lord Ik' did not die; rather he lives like a light that appears off and on, between the hills and the ravines, with the hat and the horse of Zapata)?[61] Moreover, on what grounds can one invoke the autonomy of individual consciousness to de-nounce the heteronomy of the "agency of the gods"? Who is to say that Votán, "the guardian and heart of the people," does not reside within the singularities comprising the multitude?

Negri has written the following apropos of Derrida's *Specters of Marx*, a statement that could have been uttered by Flores Magón and captures well the spirit of the ghosts in the mural of Taniperla: "It seems to me that if the specter of capitalism is substantially present in Derrida's book (and with that the more recent developments of capitalist dominion), the 'specter of communism,' on the other hand, is harder to identify, if not undetectable. If Derrida sharpens the 'arms of criticism' with great zeal and intelligence, the other spectrology nevertheless goes by the wayside, the one organized through a 'criticism of arms.' Communism's ghost is not only the product of critique; it is also, and above all, a passion, destructive of the world of capital and constructive of freedom, 'the real movement that destroys the present state of things.'"[62]

After reading this passage one is left wondering, what are arms? Negri sug-gests, beyond the conventional meaning of arms—that is, *armed struggle*—that we must invent other forms of materializing the passion of communism, the destruction of the world of capital, in the constitutive strength of the mul-titude. The abandonment of armed struggle apparently poses a contradiction in Negri's distinction between the "arms of criticism" and the "criticism of arms." It seems that the solution to this aporia would reside in the passage from the arms of criticism as critique of capital and the state to the criticism of arms as the formation of new subjectivities. Negri takes care to distinguish these new subjects from the "new man," always a finished product, of various socialist states modeled on Stalinism. In spite of their radically different loca-tions and socioeconomic conditions of subjects in metropolitan centers and the Selva Lacandona, the autonomization of subjectivities and communities carries in both locations the shared task of a "criticism of arms" that no longer advocates armed struggle.

In *The Politics of Subversion*, Negri speaks of the socialized worker, of a new proletariat consisting of the highly-educated workforce of the information age, an intellectual labor force. The student struggles in Paris in 1986 manifested for Negri the *"emergence of a new social subject*: an intellectual subject which is nonetheless proletarian, polychrome, a collective plot of the need for equality; a political subject that rejects the political and immediately gives rise to an ethical determination for existence and struggle."[63] Ethics informs the new practices and thus replaces politics, as in political parties. Here again we find great commonalties with the Zapatistas' refusal to accommodate their struggle to the line of a particular party. The intellectual proletarian of the metropolitan centers differs greatly from the Indian peasants comprising the insurrection in Chiapas, but nothing keeps the multiplicity of Indian struggles from being thought as "polychrome, a collective need for equality." The task for Negri and the Zapatistas would now consist not in establishing a new state (as in the old model of taking over the state) but of destroying the state, "this monstrous bourgeois and capitalist fetish and succeeding, as a consequence, in devolving all its various functions to the community."[64]

The notion of devolving functions to the community presupposes a process of autonomization in self-government. Ideally, these would be subjects that cannot be expropriated—that is, insurgent subjects giving rise to the power of subversion: "Subversion is the destruction of violence that is inherent in exploitation and runs through society, indistinctly, massively and terribly: subversion is *countervailing power.* . . . Subversion is the radical nature of the truth. It is an applied form of this radicalism. *Subversion is the calm and implacable countervailing of the masses.*" Negri goes on to state as one of the truths the norm against killing, whereby the task is to invent a violence to destroy the monopoly of violence by the state and exploitation that "because it is creative, destroys without killing."[65]

Negri defines the emergence of the new subjects within Marx's conceptual framework of a transition from "formal subsumption" to "real subsumption" of labor to Capital. Under the real subsumption the whole society would be subjected to the capitalist mode of production.[66] Clearly, Negri is thinking of a post-Fordist proletariat that would apparently have little to do with the indigenous peoples of Chiapas, who cannot be classified as a proletariat even though they exist under the formal subsumption of Capital. The "people in arms" would consist of a mass intellectuality that now controls the entrepreneurial power of productive labor, a condition that enables Negri to envision Soviets of mass intellectuality: "The soviets of mass intellectuality can pose themselves this task by constructing, outside of the state, a mechanism within which a democracy of the everyday can organize active communication, the interactivity of citizens, and at the same time produce increasingly free and complex subjectivities."[67]

Negri's language can be transposed to the life represented in the mural at Taniperla wherein mass intellectuality would lose its First World association with new technologies and encompass any collective effort to construct a democracy of the everyday. The arms of the socialized worker (that is, the control of the means of production) are in the hands of the post-Fordist proletariat, a condition that lends itself to political, entrepreneurial, and economic autonomies. But even though the material conditions of Indians in Chiapas are at the opposite pole from a post-Fordist proletarian, we can trace similarities in the projects for the autonomization of Indian peoples. Moreover, among the demands of Zapatistas are the conditions for creating an infrastructure that would enable Indians to participate (to some extent they are already participating) in the mass intellectuality characteristic of post-Fordist societies: access to education for both men and women, communication infrastructures, control of means of production and the natural resources within their territories. The beginnings of these are mapped out in the mural of Taniperla, where we see the communal school, the introduction of electricity, and the antenna emblematic of a full participation in the new communication technologies. It is important that we insist again on speaking in terms of autonomization rather than of sanctioned autonomies, for reasons not unlike the difference between *new subjectivities* of constituent power and the *new man* of constituted socialist regimes.[68]

Life in Taniperla manifests the ways in which autonomous self-government destroys capital and constructs freedom, from within an understanding of resistance that does not react but precedes power itself. The Zapatista insurrection and the political resolution of the conflict in the accords of San Andrés is perhaps the recent political event that best exemplifies the limits of constituent power laid out by Negri. The project of indigenous autonomy and its constituent power are haunted by the three limits outlined by Negri: "the Judeo-Christian tradition of creativity, the natural right concerning the social foundation, and the transcendental theory of the foundation."[69] At both ends of the spectrum of "development," of the quantitative differences of the nonmodern, the modern, and the postmodern, we find in Negri and the Zapatistas a common effort to go beyond modern rationality. Both Negri's and the Zapatistas' project of autonomization, however, can never be completely free from these limits. Beyond a discussion of the extent and nature of indigenous autonomy, which has centered on geographic definitions (autonomy at the level of municipios, regions, peoples) with major implications, we must attend to the aporias the discourse of autonomy that comes from a philosophical tradition that, beginning with Kant, sought to ground moral and political thought on the individual subject.

I limit my remarks on Kant to drawing key concepts pertaining to any project of autonomy. If Negri singles out Kant with respect to the "transcendental theory of foundation," we can also trace the other two ideals in Kant. Because of its immediate concern with politics, peace, and human rights, I center my discussion on Kant's *Toward Perpetual Peace: A Philosophical Project*. Of these three ideal conditions, the one central to the discourse of autonomy is the transcendental theory of the foundation of morals because of its immediate connection to the autonomy of individual freedom, to what Kant calls the *formal* principle—that is, the *categorical imperative*: "So act that you can will your maxim should become a universal law (whatever the end may be)."[70] From this formulation of the categorical imperative in *Toward Perpetual Peace*, Kant derives the "principle of moral politics that a people is to unite itself into a state in accordance with freedom and equality as the sole concepts of right, and this principle is not based on prudence but upon duty."[71]

These two principles bind the freedom of the individual to the natural foundation of the state. A state organized according to the pure principles of right would in turn expect other states to organize themselves in accordance with those principles, which would also serve as a model for the union of this state with others and the lawful relationship between states. The natural right concerning the social foundation in Kant entails the discourse of human rights that grounds the demands for the recognition of rights to culture, language, and self-determination. Kant's formulation of human rights presupposes a union of politics and morals: "The right of human beings must be held sacred, however great a sacrifice this may cost the ruling power."[72]

If this right of human beings limits the ruling power to an ethics binding ends and means, it also creates an aporia for the principle of revolution: inasmuch as the means in revolution are by definition illegal, they cannot justify the ends. Clearly, an accomplished revolution can establish the legality of the new state on ethico-political grounds. There is, as it were, a period of struggle that by definition is illegal and unethical. This judgment is based on public right: "all actions relating to the rights of others are wrong if their maxim is incompatible with publicity."[73] Kant reminds us that by definition rebellion cannot be public.

Flores Magón, Marcos and the Zapatistas, and perhaps Negri himself, when he characterizes constituent power as existing outside the law, express this sense of illegality as a condition that paradoxically is ethical not only as to its ends, but also as to its potential critique of the present. For Flores Magón (as for Lenin and the ideology of armed struggle in general), the end would be synonymous with the overthrow of the state. In Negri (as with the Zapatistas) the critique of arms would aspire to transform existing constitutions in ways that would enable constituent strength by opening new possibilities of autonomous self-government. As such, beyond reform, the transformation of the constitution grounds the establishment of spaces for revolutionary practices aiming at the destruction of the state. One may fulfill the principle of publicity by affirming that the end of the struggle is the destruction of the state without having the obligation, in an agonistic context, of making one's strategies public. One may be public without being transparent: creativity, cunning, and surprise are unalienable rights—not because the state guarantees them, but rather because they are integral components of ethico-political practices.

As for the limits of the Judeo-Christian tradition of creativity, Kant's philosophy entails a teleological concept of nature that privileges unity as the end of all processes; for Kant, the state is the natural form of organizing society and the autonomy of the will occasions a sovereign unified subject. The moral principle and its articulation in laws and culture presuppose an evolution of reason and morality in history: "Providence is thus justified in the course of the world; for the moral principle in the human being never dies out, and reason, which is capable pragmatically of carrying out rightful ideas in accordance with that principle, grows steadily with advancing culture, but so too does the guilt for those transgressions." Kant has a moment of doubt in the possibility that humans cannot be bettered, which he dispels by insisting that we must "assume that the principles of right have objective reality, that is, that they can be carried out."[74] This amounts to an act of faith in the objectivity of the moral maxims to avoid falling into despair. As such, the troubling thought that humans are frail and the need to believe the contrary corrupts the autonomy of the freedom of the will and the categorical imperative. The historicity itself of the evolution of morals and reasons would make suspect the formal nature of the maxims and would bind them to particular cultural expressions. Otherwise, what is to keep us from assuming that all humans in all societies and moments in history have followed the principles of pure reason in the development of their governments and social institutions, if not the belief in the superiority of the institutions that Kant defines as more evolved—specifically, a constitutional republic?

With Kant we inevitably face a tension between the multiplicity of peoples with rights and their belonging to a single state. Kant identifies this process of unification in constitutional terms, that is, a civil constitution or "the act of the general will by means of which a multitude becomes a people."[75] Kant favors republicanism over democracy in the taming of the multitude, what he refers to as the disorderly multitude that has to be ruled by a representative government. In Negri's terms, constituent strength must be subordinated to constituted power. If one of the salient characteristics of constituent power resides in its existence outside the law, one wonders whether a dialogue is possible between the affirmation of constituent power and the force of the multitude and the will to resolve a conflict by the rule of law, by a constitutional resolution.

This tension between the disorderly multitude and its domestication as a people has a parallelism, actually surfaces as a corollary to the tension between the liberty of individual peoples and the Kantian definition of civilization as those states in which all members would "subject themselves to a lawful coercion to be instituted by themselves."[76] This distinction entails a philosophical anthropology. We need to consider whether there is in Kant a structural difference between what the German philosopher calls "European savages" and their American counterparts. Whereas the first incorporates the defeated into the body of subjects (note the language of ingestion), the American tribes literally incorporate—that is, cannibalistically ingest—the enemy. Is this a bad joke or a difference that enables him to define the superiority of Europe? We have to proceed cautiously and perhaps go beyond a simple dismissal of Kant and look for deeper limits and unsolvable aporias not defined by a structural binary European/non-European peoples. My point is not to expose Kant's racism or imperialism but to circumscribe our own discourse from within his categories and aporias.[77]

Consider the following anticolonial statements: "If one compares with this [the publicly lawful relation between nations] the *inhospitable* behavior of civilized, especially commercial states, the injustice they show in visiting foreign lands and peoples (which with them is tantamount to *conquering* them) goes to horrifying lengths. When America, the negro countries, the Spice islands, the Cape, and so forth were discovered, they were to them, countries belonging to no one, since they counted the inhabitants as nothing." Further down Kant derives pleasure from the bankruptcy of the trading companies: "The worst of this (or, considered from the standpoint of a moral judge, the best) is that the commercial states do not even profit from this violence, that all the trading companies are on the verge of collapse; that the Sugar Islands, that place of the cruelest and most calculated slavery, yield no true profit but serve only a mediate and indeed not very laudable purpose, namely trading sailors for warships and so in Europe, and this for powers that make much ado of their piety."[78] These unintended global impacts, that "a violation of right on *one* place of the earth is felt in *all*," illustrates and justifies Kant's article: "Cosmopolitan right shall be limited to conditions of universal *hospitality*."[79]

Now, reconcile these statements with the following formulation of the right to impose war on societies "in a state of nature"—that is, without a state: "But a human being (or a nation) in a mere state of nature denies me this assurance and already wrongs me just by being near me in this condition even if not actively (*facto*) yet by the lawlessness of his condition (*statu iniustu*), by which he constantly threatens me; and I can coerce him either to enter with me into a condition of being under civil laws or to leave my neighborhood."[80] One wonders if the condition of lawlessness will be judged on empirical principles or if this statement constitutes a mere instance of a formal distinction between civilization as societies with states and barbarism as societies without states. These statements can only be reconciled in terms of the "good way" of coercing relative to "bad conquest."

Is Kant thereby inventing the very same characteristics of what Hardt and Negri have identified as the peaceful vocation of "Empire"?[81] In Hardt and Negri's schema, human rights organizations fulfill an analogous function to the missionaries of old inasmuch as they lend moral credence to military intervention. Thus, "empire" surfaces as the ultimate arbiter of the right to one's culture, language, and self-determination—to one's sacrosanct autonomy as an individual and as a member of a nation.

In the case of the Acuerdos de San Andrés and the mural of Taniperla, we can distinguish at least two forms of life, defining debates over and formulations of the meaning of autonomy. In fact, the life world of Taniperla, as coded in the mural, is an instance of the right to self-determination as outlined in the Acuerdos de San Andrés—the promotion of indigenous cultures and languages, the right to follow indigenous normative systems, and the definition of development from within the community. This list does not exhaust the points of the agreements but touches on some of the most sensitive issues of the signed document. After all, indigenous languages, normative systems, and models of development affect the administration, use, and benefits to be derived from the natural resources in Chiapas. In the end the debate comes down to a struggle between (at least) two economic models for the nation that primarily affect indigenous peoples; however, it is worthwhile remembering that the uprising of the EZLN was not for the particular rights of indigenous communities in Chiapas; rather, from the start it invoked Indian peoples as a whole and called for a transformation of the state.

The call for autonomy includes not only indigenous peoples, but the right of any municipio, regardless of its ethnic composition and moreover the right of any sector of civil society, to constitute itself as autonomous. We must also underscore that the EZLN rebellion primarily does not propose a politics for the protection of indigenous forms of life, as in an ecological model of the right of particular cultures to survive: the rebellion in itself articulates indigenous life forms.[82] As such, it exemplifies the always-singular nature of constituent power and the *many* comprising the multitude. This obviously does not mean that the Mexican state has not subjected indigenous peoples to war against its life forms, but that biopower defines the terms of the struggle itself. Flores Magón stands for the languages of the West deployed in the struggle with the state over the right to self-determination and autonomy, but indigenous forms of life articulate the Zapatista communitarian ethos, its critique of modern rationality and developmentalism, and the organization of insurrection itself based on the democratic processes of consensus within the Indian communities.

Under Flores Magón, we must also imagine Negri's contribution to the critique of arms (alternatives to armed struggle), and why not Derrida's sharpening of the arms of critique. Deconstruction, as defined by Derrida in the *Politics of Friendship*, is inseparable from democracy—"no deconstruction without democracy, no democracy without deconstruction"—and as such this formula binds the two projects into an endless self-delimitation: "Democracy is the *autos* of deconstructive self-delimitation. Delimitation not only in the name of a regulative idea and an indefinite perfectibility, but every time in the singular urgency of a *here and now.*"[83]

The debates over the meaning of democracy in the *Politics of Friendship* have *everything* and have *nothing* to do with the debates over democracy in the Acuerdos de San Andrés. They have *nothing to do* with indigenous autonomy insofar as the questions pertaining to soil and blood in Derrida's deconstruction of democracy refer to discourse inherited from Greece, as manifest in the distinction between *polemos* (as in war between nations, peoples) and *stasis* (as in civil war, internal dissent). The risk of homogenization in speaking of self-delimitation and perfectibility resides in the privilege granted to Euro-American discourses on democracy: indigenous peoples have their own history and discourses on blood and soil, which should not be reduced to nor translated into Greek categories informing Western discourses on democracy. They have *everything to do* because deconstruction's indefinite perfectibility would promise the deliverance of the West from a discourse that can only think in terms of a single universality: whether to declare its existence, its transformative nature, or its impossibility. Nothing should keep us from imagining Indians inventing a language to discourse on these Greek terms and the meaning of deconstruction. We would thus postulate two horizons of universality that might interact with each other but at no point could one reduce the other to its categories.

As such, the debates over the recognition of Indian rights to their normative systems would not entail recognition of these rights from within a singular universality, but a transformation of a hegemonic discourse. In fact, this transformation would ultimately question the desires for a new hegemonic discourse that in this case would validate indigenous normative systems under the principles of universality—that is, a theory of natural rights obviously grounded in the modernity of Western discourses. This would involve a recognition, as in *re*-cognition, a knowing again of these normative systems and accepting them as legitimate, but also a recognition of the right to have one's own normative systems and the right to refuse others access to them. A people may choose to make them *public* to outsiders, but the demand for recognition would have nothing to do with gaining the acceptance from outsiders in a position of power and dominance, as in the dialectic of the master and the slave in Hegel's *Phenomenology*.

A tension inevitably arises in the language of the accords, which defends the right of indigenous peoples to self-determination and the implied (often explicitly stated) assumption that indigenous people practice their languages, cultures, and normative systems regardless of the recognition of this right by the state. I must underscore that my interrogation does pertain to the Indians' pursuit of autonomy, but to the discourse that haunts the arguments that out of necessity autonomy must be framed in legal discourse grounded in a Western philosophical tradition and the state's desire to fix the meaning and delimit the space of autonomy. The danger here is that the language of law that seeks to promote, defend, and institutionalize indigenous life forms will subordinate the strength of the multitude and of constituent power to a constitutional resolution of the "conflict" that will assign the proper administration of autonomy to specialists well versed in the "correct procedures." These specialists will range from university-trained experts in development (human or otherwise) to anthropologists who will mediate disputes on the history of the communities and the meaning of tradition.

One can also expect a bureaucratic structure entrusted with the administration of funds and the capacity of judicial oversight. A whole array of human rights, presently used for the defense of indigenous peoples, could turn against the communities in the name of feminist agendas or religious tolerance. I am not saying that issues pertaining to gender or the expulsion of religious groups from communities are not already relevant in the indigenous communities—the place of women and the nondenominational temple in the mural of Taniperla prove the contrary—but that the constitutionalization of the autonomies would redefine the struggle in terms of cultural survival and particular rights. As in the ecological model, only those forms considered beautiful (read: pure) would be worthy of preservation, thereby taking away the same right to self-determination the law would seek to recognize. The liberation of women and the tolerance of differences must emerge from within the indigenous life forms in order to be meaningful and creative of new possibilities of gender relations and cultural diversity not contemplated, perhaps unimaginable, by the law and its bureaucrats.[84] Thus the institutionalization of autonomy—the adoption of a constituted form at the expense of constituent power—would actually hinder the process of autonomization already in place. In setting out procedures for the autonomous regions, the language of the laws diminishes the role that bicultural indigenous intellectuals would eventually play in the definition of the autonomous processes in their communities: "serán los indígenas quienes dentro del marco constitucional y en el ejercicio pleno de sus derechos decidan los medios y formas en que habrán de conducir sus propios procesos de transformación" [it will be the Indians who, within the constitutional frame and the full exercise of their right, will decide the means and the forms in which they will conduct their own processes of transformation].[85]

I limit myself to citing one instance in which language, apparently empowering to Indians, ends up subordinating them to "a constitutional frame" that overrides the authority of their own normative systems. The constitutional frame calls for a new pact with the state that would assume new responsibilities with respect to Indian peoples. If the pact states that "no serán ni la unilateralidad ni la subestimación sobre las capacidades indígenas para construir su futuro las que definan las políticas del Estado" [neither unilaterality nor underestimation of the Indians' capacities to construct their future will define the politics of the state], Indians lack a voice in this phrase, they remain a marginalized third person, rather than a subject exercising his or her constituent power. Was it unavoidable given the legal framework that the accords were articulated *in the name of* the Indians rather than *with* the Indians as interlocutors? My objective is not to undermine the importance of the accords or the necessity of creating a new juridical frame, but to isolate the elements of a crisis from within the discourse of autonomy.

This crisis is nowhere better expressed than in one of the *whereas* stated in a communiqué "a los hermanos indígenas de todo México" [to all the Indian brothers in all of Mexico] by the CCRI-CG of the EZLN, signed by Comandantes Tacho, David, and Zabedo and Subcomandante Marcos: "Los problemas que existen en torno a la autonomía, justicia, representación política, mujeres, medios de comunicación y cultura, en el entendimiento de que el asunto de la libre determinación y la autonomía implica también y muy centralmente la relación de dependencia que se impone vía programas, proyectos y presupuestos, la posible remunicipalización, la forma de elección de autoridades y en general las muchas maneras de asociación y organización" [The problems that exist concerning autonomy, justice, political representation, women, means of communication and culture also imply in a very central mode a relation of dependency that is imposed by means of programs, projects and budgets, the possible remunicipalization, the form of electing authorities and in general the multiple ways of association and organization].[86]

This aporia is the consequence of an inherent disparity between the language of autonomy practiced in the communities and the language of autonomy practiced in the debates giving form to the Acuerdos de San Andrés. The language of law gives place to procedures in the administration of the autonomous regions that do not give enough importance to the bicultural indigenous intellectuals who will assume the responsibility of defining the autonomization of their communities. The aporias of feminist discourses, of human rights, of multiple agencies ("the times of the gods and the time of history" in Dipesh Chakrabarty's terms), of coexisting pluralities of life forms, and so on can be traced in the mural of Taniperla.[87] The concept of autonomy in itself carries an aporia with respect to the concept of heteronomy that might very well be an integral component of an indigenous normative system. Indians would thus be demanding autonomy for the right to self-determination based on heteronomous principles. And what is to say that Votán, "the heart of the people," is less universal than the categorical imperative?

Hegel's critique of Kant in the *Phenomenology of Mind* provides the terms for a critique of Kantian formalism, but by reading Hegel against the grain we may derive categories that enable us to speak of a plurality of coexisting universalities. In one breath Hegel summarily dismisses Kant's formalism and any appeal to empiricism: "For universality devoid of content is formal; and an absolute content amounts to a distinction which is no distinction, i.e., means absence of content." Further down Hegel adds: "Reason as law-giver is reduced to being reason as criterion; instead of laying down laws reason now only tests *what is* laid down."[88] Is this a mere statement of fact that we always dwell and begin in a body of law, and consequently we are limited to testing "what is"? Hegel suggests that the concept of autonomy, as defined by Kant, never completely sheds its heteronomous origins in a state of law that necessarily precedes or at least is coterminous with the formulation of pure rational concepts.[89]

But even if we granted Kant the formal and transcendental character of his maxims, inherent to Kant is a an evolutionary model of the laws and institutions. There is nothing that can prevent that one materialization of law would entail a repudiation of a former ethos; take as an example Kant's references, more or less systematic, to race or gender. Is it that *man* out of his autonomous free will arrived a the conclusion that *women* are not inferior, or was it a transformation that came about as a result of demands placed by *women*, who in the first place did not participate in the autonomy of free will? Wouldn't definitions of who is a rational being inevitably vitiate the autonomy of the freedom of the will? Or, in accordance with the terms in his essay on the question "What Is Enlightenment?," wouldn't the answer reside in the historical moment when humanity achieves freedom to determine itself?[90] From here the process of relativization of freedom, truth, and the law is inevitable once we trace the limits of the ever-evolving process of Enlightenment as also comprising forms of "de-enlightenment" that would confine earlier forms of thought to particular modes of relating to the universal.

As I have pointed out in light of Derrida's view of deconstruction's indefinite perfectibility, it would include within its horizon (unless we are willing to "impose homogenizing calculability while exalting land and blood") the understanding that indigenous cultures and normative systems partake of a universality *defined by* and *definitive of* their form of life.[91] Clearly, this moment in deconstruction's indefinite perfectibility would abandon its pretense to a universal applicability by opening to the possibility that deconstruction can be subject to debate and clarification in terms other than those that gave rise to it from within the discourses and categories of the West. Not all of us think in *Greek*, which does not mean that *Greek* does not affect us all. Furthermore, the legacy of Greek cannot be completely unhinged by a willful gesture of stepping out of Eurocentrism.

In reflecting on the mural of Taniperla and the Zapatista insurrection in general, we find that a porosity of the inside/outside of life forms entails a communication plagued by aporias, by a crisis that must not be resolved but creatively deployed in an inexhaustible affirmation of freedom. Flores Magón's seeds of freedom coexist with Zapata's maxim, "la tierra es de quien la trabaja" [land belongs to those who work it] in two discourses that, without contradicting each other, partake of an aporia: the two life forms must be explained in the terms of the other. We know that Flores Magón played a part in the formulation of Zapata's maxim "tierra y libertad" (land and freedom), and that the revolutionary insurrection from the south fed into the agrarianism of the anarcho-communism of the Partido Liberal.[92] Flores Magón and the intellectual tradition of the West—obviously including Kant's conception of autonomy and constitutionalism, Negri's concept of constituent power, and Derridean deconstruction—would have to be explained, clarified, interpreted in Tzeltal categories, and not just the other way, as in the one-way street in which the anthropological discourses of the West assume the privileged position of explaining the life forms of the rest of the world, a concept of the world as the rest of their own creation.

The title of this chapter proposes reading Negri by Zapata, which would mean both "with" Zapata, as in participating in parallel revolutionary processes that may inform each other, but also as "by" in the sense of Negri being read by Zapata, as in the process in which Negri and the philosophical and political tradition of the West would be thought in indigenous terms. We may thus imagine Indians reading and discoursing on revolution, the impossible, and communism as formulated by Derrida, Negri, and other projects grounded in the West—under the category of the West, I would include discourses that appropriate Indian (and non-Western) categories but remain within the languages and debates defined from within the West—without facing the need to have them impinge upon or pose a threat to their native discursive traditions.[93]

The many of the multitude and the strength of constituent power cannot but formulate singular projects of autonomous self-government that by definition create their own *sense* (as in meaning and direction) of universality, of revolution—beyond a will to hegemony. The danger is not the implementation of the Acuerdos de San Andrés nor that there should be laws recognizing Indian autonomies, but the reduction of the accords to a constitutional resolution of the conflict that would domesticate the constituent power of the multitude. For the crisis of constituent power to be productive, it must retain the will not to be resolved. This of course requires a multitude ready to assert its force, its practice of autonomization.

7 ≡ The Comparative Frame
in Subaltern Studies

One can open just about any page in the work of Antonio Gramsci and find a vocabulary of progress and historical development that establishes teleology for comparative purposes. Gramsci's terms include "historical places," "emergence," "conditions of transformations," "levels of development," "degrees of homogeneity," "levels of political consciousness," "historical maturity," and so on. There is a vanguardism in his call for subaltern studies, if this is what Gramsci would have called his studies of dominance and subordination. Note that the terms of the teleology have more to do with the complexity of political organizations than with the stagist models characteristic of transition to capitalism narratives. If the passages I cite from Gramsci could be read as limited to his time, my argument concerning the comparative framework of subaltern studies traces the teleological reasoning in more recent articulations of the past twenty years.

Implicit in the very concept of the subaltern is a notion of the subaltern's lack of political agency by comparison with more evolved political forms. But I wonder if the use of the term "subaltern" does not constitute a socius or a collectivity by attributing the deficiencies of subalternity. To my mind, subaltern studies should address the processes of subordination, rather than assume subalterns exist in some unproblematic fashion. The subaltern as a relational term always entails a comparative frame with respect to other subjects or groups manifesting a more or less degree of subalternity. In this regard, already in Gramsci, the concepts of the people, popular culture, and the national popular give form and agency to subalterns. Moreover, the concept of the subaltern, at least in the initial formulation in Ranajit Guha's call for a subaltern studies project, is synonymous with the people.[1]

In recent debates in political theory and cultural studies, the concept of "the people" has been opposed to that of "the multitude."[2] The rationale for the unitary power of the people to subordinate the force of the multitude can be traced back at least to the English philosopher Thomas Hobbes. Now, do the concepts of "the popular" and "national popular" conflict with the multitude? Does the multitude carry the elements for imagining a way out of the epistemic violence that underlies the category of the subaltern and the domesticating function of the people? Does the plurality of the multitude correspond to forms of subalternity inasmuch as it resists being reduced to the people and a vanguard ideology? Does the standard Marxian differentiation, between forming a class as determined by socioeconomic determinations and forming a class as a political organization, entail the need to reduce the former to a unitary identity defined by the intellectual and political vanguard? Is there an aporia between the *spontaneity* of the Paris Commune of 1871 in *The Civil War in France* and the strict definition of class in the *Eighteenth Brumaire*? Is this a subtext in current debates in subaltern studies? Is this aporia also manifest in Lenin's theories of the Soviets in the April Theses and the theory of the vanguard in *What Is to Be Done?*[3]

Is the critique of spontaneity circumscribed by the model of phases and of history as emerging from a capitalist society? Does Marx suggests that the Paris Commune exemplifies historical immanence when he writes: "*It was only the working class* that could formulate the word 'Commune'—and initiate by the fighting Commune of Paris—this new aspiration"?[4] Does Marx avoid Lenin's concept of the "withering away" of the state when he specifies that "the working class cannot simply lay hold of the ready-made state machinery, and wield it for its own purposes"?[5] These complex questions cannot be suitably addressed, let alone answered in the space of this chapter. Here I examine the aporia of spontaneity and vanguardism in the context of Gramsci, the South Asian Subaltern Studies Group, and the Zapatista project in Chiapas.[6]

My point is not to compare different historical moments or geopolitical formations but to elaborate a critique of the comparative frame in subaltern studies and to propose a form of conducting subaltern studies that avoids teleological subordination and subsumption of political expressions and movements.[7] This essay forms part of series I have written since 1994 in which I explore the relationship between theoretical academic work and the Zapatista insurrection in Chiapas. The objective has had more to do with elaborating parallel practices and sites of struggle than with doing solidarity work, however necessary the latter is. It is clearly not a question of a detached academic principle of "wait and see" what will be . . . what? . . . the end? I rather practice a "do more of it now" in different spaces and wage my commitment to the past five hundred years of indigenous resistance in the Americas.

Vanguardism in Gramsci is perhaps nowhere more clearly articulated than when he appraises Lenin and Henri de Man indirectly in a note on Machiavelli from 1930: "Nonetheless, De Man has an incidental merit: demonstrated the need to study and work out the elements of popular psychology, historically and sociologically, actively (that is, in order to transform them by means of education into a modern mentality [cioè per transformarli, educandoli, in una mentalità moderna]) and not descriptively as he does—a necessity that was at least implicit (and perhaps also explicitly stated) in Ilytch's doctrine, of which De Man is totally ignorant." The "nonetheless" refers to what he considers De Man's "intellectual teratology," a concept that lumps together "admirers of folklore," "occultists," and subaltern movements: "In these movements, then, there exists a 'multiplicity' of elements of 'conscious leadership,' but none of them predominates or goes beyond the level of 'popular science'—'common sense,' that is, the [traditional] conception of the world—of a given stratum." They lack the inscription of a permanent record: "The elements of 'conscious leadership' in the 'most spontaneous' of movements cannot be ascertained, simply because they have left no verifiable record." Gramsci outlines practical and methodological problems in "scholars who argue that spontaneity is the immanent and objective 'method' of the historical process, and political adventurers who argue for it as a 'political' method."[8]

Whereas the former betrays a mistaken conception, the latter entails the desire to replace a given leadership with a different one. Spontaneity would be a mistaken conception because it would obviate the role of the Party in the definition and organization of struggles. In fact, given a conception of history in which capitalism and bourgeois ideology are dominant forms, it would seem obvious that historical immanence would reproduce the limitations of a historical phase. In the case of the Zapatistas, the historical immanence conveys backgrounds and life forms that exist outside a single historical trajectory. In their case, spontaneity would clearly curtail the hegemonic vocation of the intellectual and political vanguard. Who needs the intellectuals and the Party, if the people instinctively, historically, know their oppression by the mere fact of their subjugation?

In the Zapatista struggles the intellectual is limited to play the role of advocate, assessor, and spokesperson perhaps to struggle side-by-side but always under the indigenous leadership. But this is not too distant from the Marx that addresses the question of spontaneity in the "First Draft of the 'Civil War in France'": "They know at the same time that great strides may be [made] at once through the Communal form of political organization and that the time has come to begin the movement for themselves and mankind."⁹ This statement is clearly enunciated from an organicist conception of history; my point, however, is to locate a signpost in Marxism that allows for the notion of historical immanence and spontaneity not bound to a single historical trajectory. Wouldn't the articulations in *direct democracy* be conducted in languages and life forms autonomous from the dictates of the Party? Wouldn't the education of subjectivity into a modern mentality be perceived as a manipulation? Gramsci quite candidly answers in the affirmative: the people must be manipulated.

Gramsci reminds us that spontaneity lends itself to the manipulation of political adventurers and the ever-present cry against movements that frame projects and insurrections outside the directives of the Party. Among the most recent event, I cite the Zapatista uprising of 1994, when a majority of intellectuals in Mexico, both of a Marxist and bourgeois conviction, invoked the figure of the-white-man-manipulating-ignorant-Indians. I will speak of the Zapatistas later. For now, let us recall the isolation of Che Guevara's *foco* guerrilla on the grounds that *foquismo* assumed that Bolivian peasants would immediately recognize Che's guerrilla as a means to end their oppression. Domitila Barrios de Chúngara's 1971 *testimonio*, "*Si me permiten hablar...*" (*Let Me Speak*) provides a lucid critique of Che's guerrilla along these lines: "I am not a *foquista*. I think that nothing should be improvised.... One does not make a revolutionary movement from night to day [un movimiento revolucionario no se hace de la noche a la mañana]. Isolated movements are worthless. I think that it is the people who have to liberate themselves [es el pueblo que tiene que liberarse]. And if there is a group that carries forth a stronger action, what is most important is that it has the support of the people."¹⁰

In this passage we hear the official Communist Party line that condemned Che's guerrilla, and the phrase that it is the people who will liberate themselves echoes Marx and Lenin, but Barrios de Chúngara's *testimonio* was criticized for apparently dismissing theoretical language and, more explicitly, intellectuals who, according to her expression, do not know how to *speak to* the people. Thus in her interview with the Brazilian educator Moena Viezzers for the second Spanish edition, in 1978, of "*Si me permiten hablar...*," Barrios de Chúngara specifies that Marxist-Leninist intellectuals must complement her *testimonio*: "Yo creo que es necesario integrar a los intelectuales con nosotros. Porque nosotros no queremos hacer nuestra lucha apartada de los obreros y campesinos nomás, sino que tiene que estar la gente intelectual. Pero siempre tienen que estar ellos acomodados a nuestra realidad, aplicando correctamente la teoría marxista-leninista a la realidad del pais" [I belief that it is necessary to integrate intellectuals with us. Because we don't want to struggle just removed from worker and peasants; rather, intellectual people must be part of it. But they must always accommodate themselves to our reality, applying correctly Marxist-Leninist theory to the reality of the country].[11]

Her *testimonio* can therefore be read as an instance of popular-national literature produced by a proletarian for a proletarian audience, even if *la sabiduría del pueblo*, the "wisdom of the people" that it collects, is mediated by an intellectual. Barrios de Chúngara's intent is to document, to "create a verifiable record" of what Gramsci called "the elements of 'conscious leadership' in the 'most spontaneous' of movements," as expressed in her own words: "Y debe haber testimonio. Y eso fue lo malo, que nosotros no dejamos anotado todo lo que pasa. Muy poco se ha anotado" [And there must be *testimonio*. And that was what was wrong, that we didn't leave anything written. Very little has been written].[12]

Gramsci's reference to "Ilytch's doctrine" alludes to Lenin's *What Is to Be Done?*—in particular, to those passages where Lenin discusses the leadership of intellectuals, where he writes: "This [Social-Democratic] consciousness could only be brought to them from without." Lenin does not explicitly, at least here, say that one must "study and work out the elements of popular psychology," as Gramsci would put it, but nonetheless there is in Lenin an organicist view of riots and strikes: "The 'spontaneous element' in essence, represents nothing more nor less than consciousness in an embryonic form."[13] Lenin explains in a footnote that workers should be educated in the great books and not limited to propaganda literature: "This does not mean, of course that workers have no part in creating such an ideology. But they take part not as workers, but as socialist theoreticians . . . ; care must be taken that the workers do not confine themselves to the artificially restricted limit of '*literature for the workers*' but that they study *general literature* to an increasing degree."[14]

One is left wondering what would be the place of Barrios de Chúngara's *testimonio*, which by her own judgment lacks the sophistication of theory, but nevertheless contains the experience and wisdom of the workers in and on their own terms; note that Moema Viezzer asked for her approval before publication. It is clearly an "instrument for reflection" that was produced by a miner woman as a miner woman, with knowledge that cannot be but spontaneous. Again, the aporia between the spontaneity (linguistic, imaginative, cognitive, and so on) of those who build movements and constitute autonomous political spaces—such as the Paris Commune of 1871, the Zapatista insurrection, and the constitution of a political class defined by criteria introduced externally—would appear to be bound by a comparative frame.

Gramsci seems to endorse De Man's call for an appropriate psychology "in order to transform them, by educating them, into a modern mentality."

Gramsci's cultural politics subordinates the production of a popular culture to Culture, to the production of high literature. Ideally, literature would reflect historically and sociologically the state of the nation, hence the concept of the national popular and Gramsci's comparisons between French literature and what he characterizes as the deplorable backwardness of Italian literature. One cannot but agree that workers as workers cannot produce theoretical contributions that would enrich the intellectual tradition of Marxian thought, given the specialized language of philosophy and the Western tradition it builds on. At least in part, this education corresponds to the modern mentality Gramsci seeks to implant. But the modern mentality Gramsci speaks about also entails the Enlightenment ideals that would undo the hold of magic and folklore (to avoid the more charged term "superstition") on subalterns (for Gramsci, magic and folklore constitute definitional traits of subalterns).

Given the fact that one might be educated in philosophy and write theory, and also write songs, make films, and participate in other less intellectualized everyday cultural practices, we may assume that they would all share, for Gramsci, the most modern mentality. What then can we say about cultural forms still under the hold of not-most-modern-ideas, which may indeed coincide with spontaneity and the historical immanent? Gramsci is quite unambiguous about the status of folklore: "For the teacher, then, to know 'folklore' means to know what other conceptions of the world and of life are actually active in the intellectual and moral formation of young people, in order to uproot them and replace them with conceptions which are deemed to be superior [per estirparli e sostituirle con concezioni ritenute superiori]."[15] One might want to explain away this sort of manipulation as representative of his time, but my point in citing this passage and others is to argue that they constitute integral components of the comparative frame in subaltern studies, even if expressed in more attenuated terms today.[16]

Gramsci would seem to say that there is no such thing as a popular culture produced by subalterns as subalterns that is worth considering, unless it were to reflect the most advanced modern ideas. In some passages Gramsci *does* seem to make allowances for historical immanence—that is, for languages, expressions, and conceptualizations of the world outside the parameters of modern ideas; but if the production of Culture entails a consciousness that by definition is not subaltern, then what will be the place of cultural artifacts elaborated outside the vanguard? This cultural production by subalterns, who have not been subjected to the tutelage of the vanguard or have invented forms that the intellectual vanguard could not begin to envision, might very well not be concerned with the national component that preoccupied Gramsci. However, subaltern cultural production (that is, culture not-conceived-in-terms-of-the-most-advanced-modern-ideas) should not necessarily be in conflict with the national popular or with the formulations of intellectuals working side-by-side with subaltern movements.

Before elaborating this point, let me briefly point out that I retain the concept of the nonmodern despite a tendency today to speak of all social formations as modern. This gesture that brings all societies unto the fold of the modern builds on the assumption that what is commonly defined as nonmodern cannot coexist with the modern. This is a possibility that colonialist discourses systematically excluded. As Partha Chatterjee has put it: "Much recent ethnographic work has established that these 'other' times are not survivors from a pre-modern past: they are new products of the encounter with modernity itself."[17] This statement would seem absolutely transparent if we were to say that all societies after the encounter with modernity (or in the case of the Americas, after the European invasion in the sixteenth century) were forced to respond and invent life forms that inevitably placed them in the "time" of modernity; however, this does not necessarily imply that non-European societies and their life forms abandoned the "times" that were nonmodern, even when modernity demanded that these "times" be left behind. We must remain suspicious of the built-in teleology implicit in the "pre-" of premodern. Chatterjee could not be more correct in underscoring that the "other" times should not be seen as remnants: this view entails an inevitably teleological framework.

My point is to underscore the (not-modern) immanent that might converse with the modern ideas without being subordinated to them. Did the Lenin of the April Theses contemplate the necessity that the socialist world of the Soviets would have to be articulated in their own idioms? In fact, the language and the components of a revolutionary imaginary could very well be antithetical (although not contradictory) to Gramsci's (that is, the vanguard intellectual's) understanding of the modern. If we go by the name of the armed wing of the Zapatistas in Chiapas, the Ejercito Zapatista de Liberación Nacional (EZLN, the Zapatista Army of National Liberation), the national popular would seem to continue to be part of the Zapatistas of the twenty-first century. The inflection of the national by local idioms, however, would now be circumscribed by a plurinational project.

I now outline a series of ideas that one may generally recognize as Gramsci's, which were present at the origin of the South Asian Subaltern Studies Collective. Under Gramsci's formulation subalterns may know spontaneously the causes of their oppression and the need to organize politically (that is, subalternity contains the rudimentary elements of conscious leadership, of discipline), but only modern theory will give them a full understanding and guarantee that their force is not misdirected by reactionary groups. Gramsci makes room for knowledge through a popular conception of the world, for "what is very tritely [pedestremente] called 'instinct,' which is itself a rudimentary and basic historical acquisition [e non é ancheso che un'acquisizione storica primitiva ed elementare]," and then goes on to advocate that "it should be possible to have reciprocal 'reduction,' so to speak, a passage from one to the other and vice versa [un passaggio di uni all'altra e viceversa]."[18]

This comparative frame of subaltern studies ultimately defines the project as one in which subordinated groups must be educated in order that they overcome their subalternity. Elsewhere, Gramsci does make allowance for processes that seem to be understood by the subaltern classes directly, but then he adds that this understanding implies that it is no longer a subaltern class "or at least is demonstrably on the way to emerging from its subordinate position."[19] The premise is that elementary (primitiva ed elementare) forms of consciousness must be translated into a theoretical language and that, in the process of putting it into practice, theory would override the elementary forms.

One can trace these lines from Gramsci's in the title of Ranajit Guha's *Elementary Aspects of Peasant Insurgency in Colonial India*, and perhaps even more directly in Gautam Bhadra's assessment of the 1857 rebellion in India: "Yet this episodic and fragmentary narrative points to the existence in 1857 of what Gramsci has called 'multiple elements of conscious leadership' at the popular level."[20] In his introduction to *Elementary Aspects*, Guha posits the underdeveloped politics of subaltern insurgencies in historical terms, but one wonders what he would say about "primitive" movements today: "As such, it was perhaps less primitive than it is often presumed to be. More often than not it lacked neither in leadership nor aim nor even in some rudiments of a program, although none of the attributes could compare in maturity or sophistication with those of the historically more advanced movements of the twentieth century."[21] If Guha should be read as a historian, the language of progress—"advanced," "maturity," "sophistication," and so on—betrays a developmental model of what a truly politically sophisticated insurgency would look like. For all his critique of subordinating the history of subaltern insurgencies to the history of Britain, the nationalist movement, or socialist historiography, he circumscribes the peasant insurgency from within a frame that privileges certain criteria defined in terms of the "more advanced movements." He rounds up his observations in the following categorical terms: "It would be wrong of course to overestimate the maturity of this politics and read into it the qualities of a subsequent phase of more refined class conflict, widespread anti-imperialist struggle and generally a higher level of militancy among the masses."[22]

As subaltern studies travels from fascist Italy to postcolonial India, the question of colonialism is brought to the foreground. Subalternity is the result of political, economic, and social subordination but also the consequence of epistemic violence that undermined and sought to destroy indigenous knowledges. I am thinking, in particular of Gayatri Spivak's definition of epistemic violence: "The clearest available example of such epistemic violence is the remotely orchestrated, far-flung, and heterogeneous project to constitute the colonial subject as Other. This project is also the asymmetrical obliteration of the trace of that Other in its precarious Subject-ivity."[23] In rewriting this essay for *A Critique of Postcolonial Reason*, Spivak softens the negative answer she gave to the question concerning the speech of the subaltern: "I was so unnerved by this failure of communication that, in the first version of this text, I wrote, in the accents of passionate lament: the subaltern cannot speak! It was an inadvisable remark."[24]

To my mind, the question of the historically muted subaltern is but one instance of the constitution of subalternity. The apparent inevitability of accessing speech, however, need not imply a one-way street to hegemonic discourse: "When a line of communication is established between a member of subaltern groups and the circuits of citizenship or institutionality, the subaltern has been inserted into the long road to hegemony."[25] Subaltern groups are here posited as an empirically verifiable entity rather than the consequences of epistemic violence; indeed, wouldn't this "long road" entail a constitution of life forms incompatible with institutionality and citizenship, hence as inevitably bound to disappear "into the long road to hegemony"? But why can't indigenous knowledges coexist with the most modern?

Spivak's first version of her essay on the impossibility of subaltern speech was mainly concerned with addressing the question of power, desire, and interest in a critique of Michel Foucault and Gilles Deleuze's demise of the pertinence of ideology. It is only after establishing contact with the South Asian Subaltern Studies group that Spivak introduced the language of subalternity in the revised version of the essay.[26] Even if first conceived without Gramsci in mind, her critique of Foucault and Deleuze is circumscribed by debates in Marxism over spontaneity, class instinct, and vanguardism. Her elaboration of Marx's distinction between belonging to a class and being organized as a class necessarily resonates with Lenin and Gramsci, even if she was not "thinking" of them when she wrote the first version. My argument does not reside in establishing her direct filiation to Gramsci, but in outlining a commonality with debates in Marxism that circumscribe statements on spontaneity.

Thus in Spivak's *Death of a Discipline* we can trace the issue Gramsci raises about "the need to study and develop the elements of popular psychology, historically and sociologically, actively (i.e., in order to transform them, by educating them, into a modern mentality)" when she proposes "learning to learn from below": "Primary health care groups . . . if they are to remain uncoercive, must learn or be at home in the cultural idiom of the place. Otherwise the change does not stick. At this point I am clearly displacing the analogy further, wishing to add to the role of the interpreter the role of the primary health care group, at home in the idiom of the culture, patiently engaging in uncoercive change in the habit of normality."[27] The art of making-changes-stick suggests that one learns from below to better transform cultures deemed not-yet-modern.

If Gramsci posed the question of colonialism in *The Southern Question*, the privilege given to the intellectual vanguard from the proletarian north would subscribe the education of the south according to the most advanced modern ideas, rather than make allowance for what Gramsci perceived as backward— that is, "folklore" and "magic." Note these two words are codes for nonmodern ideas. Gramsci does underscore an intellectual tradition from the south when he states: "all cultural initiatives by medium intellectuals [tutte le iniziative culturalidocute agli intelelectuali medi] that have taken place in the twentieth century in Central and Northern Italy have been characterized by 'southern-ism' [furono caratterizzate dal meridionalismo]."[28] But let us also observe that for Gramsci, these are "men of immense culture and intelligence [uomini di grandissima cultura e inteligentza], who emerged from the traditional soil of the south but were tied to European and hence world culture [legati alla cul-tura europea e quindi mondiale]."[29]

As it were, the energy of the south is canalized through universal culture. In his claim for the southern intellectual, there seems to be no positive assess-ment of popular culture. Gramsci is particularly lucid with respect to issues of spontaneity in his call to attend to the particular forms of thought that inform social movements and revolutionary processes. These forms often clash with modern knowledge, but nevertheless he thinks that they must be translated to theoretical language. If there is a dialectic between these two forms of life, the telos undoubtedly points to the homogenization of thought in modern sci-ence and the Party, "to change the political direction of certain forces which have to be absorbed if a new, homogeneous politico-economic historical bloc, without internal contradictions is to be successfully formed" [per mutare cioè la direzione politica de certe forze che è necessario assorbire per realizare un nuovo, omogeneo, senza contradiddizione interne, blocco storico economico-politico]."[30]

In its most refined form, the teleological impulse in the comparative frame of subaltern studies constitutes its model of interpretation and evaluation. It is true that the present from which we write—the hindsight of how history evolved—cannot but be privileged in comparative studies. But the issue here is whether history reads in the singular. Inevitably we will compare singular vis-à-vis multiple historical horizons. Note that this is not a mere postmodern gesture that would deny the existence of universal history, but the affirmation of a plurality of historical horizons with singular flows of immanence. The comparative frame in subaltern studies would seem to assume a singular history defined in terms of more or less advanced movements, political institutions, and ideas. The challenge I have cited comes from the indigenous insurrection of the Zapatistas and resides in the interruption of this discourse of progress. The Zapatistas do not represent themselves as embodying a most advanced political model of insurrection, but rather place the emphasis on a historical immanence that situates and articulates the insurrection in terms of the creation of autonomous regions in local idioms. Even if it can be argued that all I am doing here is translating their practice into the language of theory, the fact remains that the Zapatistas would read through claims of vanguardism and pedagogical manipulations. The Juntas de Buen Gobierno [Juntas of Good Government], the Caracoles, resonates with Marx's speculations on the experience of the Paris Commune of 1871.[31]

We might even think of a connection with the Soviets of the April Theses and *The State and the Revolution*. But we should avoid comparing these cases, especially if the objective is to validate the Zapatista insurrection with reference to Marx and Lenin. The historical immanence of the Zapatista communities is indigenous. They articulate the insurrection with a nativistic imaginary that points to a background and history that has nothing to do with modern science, with the exception, of course, of the discourses modernity has built to negate and destroy indigenous life forms. But this is not new. Indigenous peoples in the Americas have accommodated Western discourses to their life forms since the European invasion in the sixteenth century. They have been modern and not modern all along.

From a Gramscian perspective, the ability to understand and articulate historico-political conditions of oppression is already a sign that one is no longer a subaltern. The question, however, is whether the language one uses to articulate these conditions must correspond to Euro-American theory, whereby all nativistic discourses would signal a condition of subalternity. In order to articulate and resist its oppression, must a social group abandon nativistic discourses? But wouldn't this logic imply a colonialist impulse that subordinates forms of discourse? Wouldn't it be an instance of epistemic violence? These seem to be dead ends in the comparative frame of subaltern studies.

Among the members of the South Asian subaltern Studies group, Dipesh Chakrabarty has addressed these issues in a most systematic form in *Provincializing Europe*, and more recently in *Habitations of Modernity*. Chakrabarty differentiates two modalities of history that he defines as "History 1" and "History 2s." Whereas History 1 pertains to "the universal and necessary history posited by the logic of capital" and is Marxist in its inspiration, History 2s acknowledges the "futures that already *are* there, the futurity that humans cannot avoid aligning themselves with" and is Heideggerian.[32] I cannot do justice to Chakrabarty's argument here, but merely lay out his understanding of these terms and raise some questions concerning the comparative frame of subaltern studies and its implicit teleology. Chakrabarty has elaborated a thorough critique of all stagist narratives of a transition to capital, but there is a built-in teleology in the concept of the subaltern that Chakrabarty seems to reiterate, perhaps consciously and willingly, not unlike Gramsci.

In Chakrabarty's conceptualization History 1 and History 2s interact and affect each other but also mark a contradiction in his thinking: "Marx and Heidegger represent for me two contradictory but profoundly connected tendencies that coexist within modern European social thought." A few sentences later, in the closing statement of the book, Chakrabarty offers the following disclaimer: "As I hope is obvious from what has been said, provincializing Europe cannot ever be a project of shunning European thought. For at the end of European imperialism, European thought is a gift to us all. We can talk of provincializing it only in an anticolonial spirit of gratitude."[33] Do we have a choice to shun Europe while practicing academic forms of writing? Should we be thankful for the intellectual formation we have received in Western (-style) institutions? Can we speak of "at the end of European imperialism" today? These are, indeed, generous gestures for reconciliation and for ending any semblance of resentment. But can one be anticolonial while privileging European thought? Or is it that we should limit our claims to countercolonial moves from within a philosophical tradition that with a bit of work would manifest its complicities with Euro-American imperial projects? It would seem to me that as a Marxist and Heideggerian intellectual (in the terms he has conceived these traditions), Chakrabarty can only approximate nativist discourses from the outside. There is for Chakrabarty an interaction between History 1 and History 2s (in both understandings as social formations and as academic practices), although not without a contradiction in his mind. The paths between these two histories is porous and involves a two-way process, but there is no sense that what inevitably ends up defined as "subaltern" might interact with the academic practitioner of Marxist analysis and Heideggerian hermeneutics.

The dialogue remains abstract (that is, it occurs only in the mind of the academic) or else is simply subject to manipulation, in a pedagogy of the oppressed in which nonmodern subjects will ultimately be receptive to the teachings by the intellectuals on the nature of the state. The deck is stacked, for "this dialogue takes place within a field of possibilities that is already structured from the very beginning in favor of a certain outcome."[34] For the subaltern, by definition, could not begin to conceptualize the Marx and Heidegger invoked on his behalf. But is this so? Does this mean that by definition all nonmodern subjects lack the capacity to observe the Marxist and Heideggerian observer and make sense of the statements he produces, from a background that cannot be subsumed by European-derived philosophy? Or is it that the Heideggerian interpreter can access these worlds and in the process appropriate them under the modality of a "nonmodern" self harbored within the modern subject, one that might be discovered in the process of an imagined dialogue with the nonmodern? After all, subaltern studies is bound by an intellectual trajectory: "I was only pointing to a utopian line that may well designate the limit of how we are trained to think."[35]

This is a most candid expression of the limits of subaltern studies. We have the option of imagining a hermeneutics that would eventually make the nonmodern manifest in increasingly better translations, or rather, in "much-needed, yet inevitably poor translations."[36] The other options would further our understanding of the limit by gaining an understanding that the background from which and against which nonmodern subjects make sense of our world inevitably remains inaccessible to modern European thought, provincialized or not. Now, these nonmodern subjects might actually learn the ways of European thinking without necessarily abandoning their capacity to dwell in their own worlds. This has traditionally been the role of the native informant, who by the hubris of the anthropologist or the missionary was expected to render all the goods of his culture. The nonmodern subject conversant with the modern would bring up questions that challenge the modern but would refrain from serving as translator. Our option here would be to further the distance by insisting that all translation would travel back to the source for verification and thus be caught within an infinite progression.

I close with an instance of revolutionary spirituality in Chiapas, in which we can trace the work of immanent history.[37] My example belongs to the warrior mysticism in the murals one finds at Zapatista bases that lend support to the EZLN. I can only briefly dwell on a mural from the community of Taniperla.[38] This mural includes Zapata and Ricardo Flores Magón, the anarcho-communist theoretician of the Mexican revolution of 1910. We find multiple backgrounds for interpreting the mural. One can at once provide a reading that places the emphasis on the interactions between the anarcho-communist tradition and the program of the rural peasantry led by Zapata. The reference to Zapata makes manifest an immanent history of indigenous claims to their rights to land and to sovereignty over their territories.

The communitarian maxim of *mandar obedeciendo* (to govern obeying), which we tend to identify with Zapata, has a long tradition that predates Marx's description of the accountability of the leaders of the Paris Commune. Again, the point is not to validate the Zapatistas with Marx, but to signal parallelisms between these two *communist* projects, parallels already manifest in Flores Magón's anarchist call for direct action and the Zapatista takeover of the haciendas in the Mexican southern state of Morelos. Zapata also merges with the pre-Columbian figure of Votán, the "heart of the people." The Zapatista spirituality is informed by a nativistic tradition that often juxtaposes Zapata and the pre-Columbian deity Quetzalcoatl in murals in the Zapatista bases. Here we find a reference to the two Quetzalcoatl that correspond to the diurnal and nocturnal passage of Venus.[39] We find the legendary figure dressed in white that often appears in the horizon riding his horse and holding his rifle, according to native testimony, and the multiple Zapatistas on the mountains that guard Taniperla. Other nativistic motifs are the figure of Mother Earth as embodied in the large woman on the left side of the mural, and the birds. A new-age reading might interpret the birds as a sign of a native colorful view of the world, but a more historically informed reading would identify as *quautli*, as ancient eagle warriors descending to the earth to become incarnate in the Zapatista forces.

At the other end of the ideological spectrum, the telecommunications tower conveys the use and mastery of Western technology. Even though the dominant spirituality is nativistic, the mural includes a temple committed to ecumenism that seeks to counter the violence of native communities that banish non-Catholic members, and the violence of the paramilitary groups that terrorize the communities often with the support of members from the Presbyterian Church. The ecumenical mission consists of avoiding religious warfare and the explanation of massacres in terms of religious conflicts. In Taniperla there is room for Protestants, Catholics, nativists, and atheists, if we were to take seriously the figure of Ricardo Flores Magón as an ancestor.

As for the question of popular culture, the mural combines the popular and the nativistic in that it at once invokes precolonial spirituality and figures from the national pantheon: it recuperates Zapata from the state's appropriation and rehabilitates Flores Magón, the bête noire of the Revolution of 1910. There are also elements of popular culture in the EZLN, more particularly in Subcomandante Marcos's texts that call the nation into "arms," into multiple struggles that do not aspire to a homogeneous concept of the national popular, but rather to a broad spectrum of spaces of resistance. To an extent, his populism crosses borders and converses with an international community. It is at once nativistic and international. It inserts itself in the planetary but retains a multiplicity of histories as sites of the immanent in insurrections.

On the History of the History of Peoples *Without* History

In this account, both the people who claim history as their own and the people to whom history has been denied emerge as participants in the same historical trajectory.

—ERIC WOLF

Nowhere does one find the singularity of the Zapatista insurrection better expressed than in their consideration of Indians as ends in themselves. The Zapatistas articulate a process of social transformation in which indigenous languages and cultures ground the communities' processes of autonomization. Indigenous knowledges and linguistic practices coexist and dialogue with life forms with radically different philosophical backgrounds that for reasons of expediency I refer to as "Western." By "background" I mean the absolute presupposition *against which* and *from which* the members of a given culture make sense of each other and the world.[1] If inspired by the Zapatistas, I only pretend to provide a reflection that may dialogue with the multiple expressions of Zapatismo. In the process I discuss some of the proposals of coauthors Michael Hardt and Antonio Negri's *Multitude*. The objective is not to compare these two projects, rather to juxtapose them while resisting the impulse to subsume one to the other.

To my mind, the singularity of the Zapatista insurrection could not be more striking than when we juxtapose it with Antonio Gramsci's and Mao Zedong's call for the use and transformation of peasant mentality. Hardt and Negri have captured this move in Mao by saying: "the Chinese revolution was really a revolution conducted *with* the peasantry, not a revolution *by* the peasantry." Further down they add, "*the final victory of the peasant revolution is the end of peasantry.*"[2] As for Gramsci, consider the following passage from the *Prison Notebooks*: "For the teacher, then, to know 'folklore' means to know what other conceptions of the world and of life are actually active in the intellectual and moral formation of young people, in order to uproot them and replace them with conceptions which are deemed to be superior" [per estirparli e sostituirle con concezioniritenute superiori].[3]

If in the *Southern Question* Gramsci denounced the North's colonialist discourse on the South, for Gramsci the peasantry of the South would be hegemonized by the proletarian North. Even if, as Hardt and Negri have reminded us, the small landholdings of the peasantry and its corresponding mode of production are bound to disappear, the denigration of and the use of folklore for the transformation of peasants into a modern mentality is manipulative and elitist. Indian life forms cannot be reduced to the economic structures of small land-holding farmers characteristic of the European peasantry. Liberal projects in the nineteenth century sought to turn communal forms of property into individually owned holdings. This process reduced Indians to peons working in large *haciendas*, given that very few Indians partook of the new structure of property. The Revolution of 1910 and Mexico's constitution of 1917 partially redressed this expropriation of communal lands with the creation of the *ejido* and the restitution of communal holdings.

Strictly speaking, Indians are not peasants, nor should Indians be exclusively identified with rural areas. This is not the place to discuss the long-lasting prejudice against peasants that one can trace from Marx's *Eighteenth Brumaire of Louis Bonaparte* to Hardt and Negri's *Multitude*, but we can note the equally long tradition that views peasant communes as having the capacity to proceed directly toward communism.[4] Hardt and Negri, for their part, also appeal to Pierre Clastres's analysis of Amerindian "primitive" cultures as "societies against the state": "The history of peoples with a history is, as they say, the history of class struggle; the history of peoples without history is, we should say at least with equal conviction, the history of their struggle against the state. We need to grasp the kind of struggles that Clastres sees and recognize the adequate form in our present age."[5] Let's examine this paradox: "the history of peoples without history."

Peoples with and *without* History

The binary that constitutes peoples with and without history, writing, and the state dates back to the Enlightenment. As such, the binary manifests a particular form of the "Europe and its others" syndrome. This cultural malaise infects peoples who are constituted as lacking history and, by extension, the state with an internalization of the terms that leads to a desire to prove the contrary. Ranajit Guha's work on Indian historiography, in particular his essay "An Indian Historiography of India," offers a most lucid articulation of how history in its post-Enlightenment disciplinary form posed a challenge to Bengali historians that led them to prove to the imperial historians that Bangla was an appropriate language for history. Guha traces a series of moments in the writing of Indian history in the nineteenth century that go from the initial desire to prove the appropriateness of Bangla, which included a recognition of the gift of history by the English, to the denunciation of the British Empire and the circulation of pamphlets associated with terrorist groups in the 1920s that sought to destroy the Raj.

In doing this, Bengali historians worked out the internalization of the colonialist denial of history and state to India. Notwithstanding this process of countering the reduction of India to a people without history and the supposed deficiencies of Bangla for the articulation of Western discourses, the practice of history as discipline continues undisturbed among Indian historians well into our days. From the early *Elementary Aspects of Peasant Insurgency* to *History at the Limits of World-History*, Guha has exposed the ways in which historiography subordinates and subsumes subaltern peoples in narratives of Empire, Nation, and Socialism. The exercise of power and state formation is inherent to the practice of history. Thus Guha's *History at the Limits of World-History* provides an analysis of Hegel's philosophy of history at the root of the negation of history in India. Guha also underscores the formation of a discipline and its exclusion of Indian texts as the Mahabharata as history. Guha has no qualms in accepting a narrow definition of history but also traces the colonialist impulse in historical writing.

Following Rabindranath Tagore, Guha calls for reimagining forms of memory that would capture historicality. When Guha presented this idea at Columbia University, he was attacked by many in the audience, including Gayatri Chakravorty Spivak and Partha Chaterjee, but as far as I know, the only published statement is a translation into Spanish of the Persian historian Hamid Dabashi's intervention: "No soy un suabalternista" [I am not a subalternist]. Dabashi criticized Guha for his ignorance of Persian sources (a subject that I am completely ignorant, hence will abstain from discussing) and for launching a frontal attack on Hegel instead of pursuing a guerrilla tactic that would target Hegel, Modernity, Eurocentrism, and Globalization from plurivocal and plurifocal perspectives. This turn from frontal attack to guerrilla provides elements for the critique of meta-narratives. Dabashi, however, finds a transparency of terms when he invokes "history or *itihasa*" in one breath.[6] One should wonder if this gesture subsumes *itihasa* under history, thereby privileging the latter term as a universal concept.

I ignore the nature of the Persian libraries Dabashi mentions, but the universality and self-evidence of the term "history" remains problematic. The rebuttal of Guha's frontal attack on Hegel entails a statement in the line that "we" Indians and Persians have always read the Mahabarata as history. I cannot assess the full meanings of *itihasa*, often translated as "thus verily happened" or as "so it was." Nor can I evaluate the equivalence one can draw with errors incurred when one defines the Old Testament as mythology, but it seems to me that the specifics of *itihasa* are lost when paired with history. As if history (and, for that matter, mythology) were a transparent category and a transhistorical reading/writing practice. To my mind, one should attend to the fact that history is a Western invention that dates back to the Greeks of the fifth century B.C., in particular to Herodotus, and the self-conscious differentiation from myth, which was in fact constituted in the process. The ambivalence surrounding the status of *itihasa* as combining myth and history suggests that we should proceed more cautiously in approximating the meanings of this Sanskrit term. Otherwise, the rescue of the Mahabarhata will assume the universality of Greco-Abrahamic life forms in particular, rather than understanding the process as the *globalatinization* of all natural and cultural phenomena.[7]

Even if the Persian libraries contained many texts that one could consider history (and, for that matter, philosophy and literature) because of an importation of these literary practices from Greek culture, the disciplinary of history entails a break from pre-Enlightenment historical writings, which I gather was Guha's main point in speaking of Ramram Basu as the first Indian historian in the disciplinary mode. If Dabashi at first agreed in principle with Guha's positioning of *marvel* against *experience*, of *civil society* against the *state*, and the *poetics* of resistance against the *prose* of power, he ends up chastising Guha for pairing the *marvel* of the Mahabarhata, with the *experience* of Hegel. But Dabashi chooses to ignore that Guha was targeting the practice of history among Indians today (not really Hegel), as it becomes evident when Guha introduces Tagore's critique of the poverty of historiography. It all seems to come down to a disciplinary squabble—with implications beyond the academy. Dabashi's insistence on the guerrilla warfare remains purely academic as long as "good" history—Dipesh Chakrabarty has insisted on this in his critiques of Guha—contributes to the formation of responsible citizens for representative democracies.[8] The world of subaltern insurrections is a world ruled by the imagination, marvel, civil society, and poetics, which the prose of counterinsurgency—that is, history—has sought to neutralize in its pursuit of the causes and effects of rebellions.

In addressing the denial of history and state, I have emphasized the Enlightenment because the descriptions of Amerindian peoples without states during the sixteenth century limited themselves to societies that in fact did not have states. The complex urban structures of the Andes and Mexico were always understood as societies with states—indeed, with states to conquer and expropriate. These urban civilizations were also conceived as laden with layers of history that had to be understood (indeed, invented as historical) in order to administer them. As such, the binary "peoples with history" versus "peoples without history" as formulated by the Enlightenment constitutes a particular form of the "Europe and its others" syndrome. Clastres has no qualms in using the term "Savage" or "Primitive" as a descriptive category for societies without states.[9] In fact, his objective is to understand the singular spatial and temporal forms of peoples without state and history. If they are coeval with modernity (to borrow Johannes Fabian's term in *Time and the Other*), with the time of anthropologists and other observers who communicate with them in a shared present (even if they do not understand each other), the fact remains that their sense of space and time often radically differs from those of modernity. Clastres specifies that the definition of society without a state does not apply to the Andes and Mexico, but we may ask if after the destruction of Andean and Mesoamerican states we do not find societies who, having been stripped of their indigenous states, have resisted the colonial and the national states of the past five hundred years.[10]

If it strikes as dissonant to pair "Savage" dwellers of the tropical forests with settled peoples from the highlands, indigenous organizations today have taken significant steps in overcoming the internal disparaging of the "Primitive."[11] The destruction of the indigenous states led to forms of collaboration that proved indispensable for the efficacy of colonial and national rule (from the *jueces* and *gobernadores* of the colonial period to the *caciques* of today). Despite these privileged sectors, Indians have been systematically excluded from the state and history. Exclusionary practices carry an ambivalence that we should not rush to erase by calling for the full integration of Indians into the nation. The "without" may be interpreted as peoples who exist *without* (outside) history and the state, and consequently who define themselves against the state and history.

In this regard, the Zapatistas maxim of *mandar obedeciendo* (command obeying) and the constant alternation of representatives in the Juntas de Buen Gobierno manifests the conviction not only that their struggles no longer aspire to take over the state, but also that the state must be avoided from within.[12] The paradox of speaking of "the history of peoples without history" would convey the existence of histories of oppression and revolt, of forms of resistance, and of the strategies of survival of the past five hundred years. The objective would not be to have the state recognize these histories and include them into its account of the nation and its pasts, rather to teach these histories to future generations of autonomous peoples who have and will continue to exist *without* history and the state. But this clearly has little to do with the history of peoples with state, with the history of class struggle, as Hardt and Negri characterized it. Here again we find a paradox in that the oppression of Indians is none other than their oppression as a class even if defined along ethnic and racial terms, but ambivalence surfaces when we posit their struggle not from within the state and the desire for recognition, but as a struggle for autonomization from the desires that seek the recognition of the state. The only recognition sought would correspond to the right to keep the (European) standards of the state from defining the worth of their own life forms. The "Europe and its others" syndrome manifests a cultural malaise that infects those peoples *without* history and the state by an internalization of the negation that leads to a desire to prove the contrary rather than to assert their singularity.

Singularity

In one of his recent communiqués, "En (auto) defensa de las jirafas," Marcos draws on the giraffe as a trope to speak of those forms of life, of difference, of singularity that the market targets for extinction.[13] It is no longer a question of the individual being threatened by the communal but of those singular forms that challenge the constitution of homogenous individual(istic) subjects of neoliberalism. The communiqué extends the struggles of the Zapatistas beyond Chiapas to the rural and urban dwellers in Mexico and the world. This is the kind of cultural politics that enables us to link the Zapatista struggle, as Manuel Callaghan has asked us to consider, with the "serial protests that gained prominence since Seattle." In his call for contributions to the journal, Callaghan speaks of "broader movements struggling with direct or radical democracy applied towards liberatory politics," also a staple in the Zapatista communiqués since 1994.[14] My insistence on suspending the outrage of the denial of history, on interrogating the desire to prove "Europe's others" as historical societies, is predicated on the invocation of singular life forms that may challenge the hegemony of *globalatinization*.

For if it is true that neoliberalism only supports forms of artistic expression that subject themselves to the hegemony of the market, as Marcos underscored in his praise of giraffes (read: singular forms of life that are targeted by economic and military war), it uses a language of love and benevolence that expropriates discourses of freedom. For it is part of the logic of neoliberalism to recognize only forms of life that conform to the parameters of the West. In this regard, efforts to prove that "Europe's others" have writing, history, science, and state reiterate the globalatinization that only recognizes forms that it can subsume under its categories. The "history of the history of peoples *without* history" would then correspond to the singularity of struggles that the state and its history cannot *recognize* because the discourses that resistance articulates remain unintelligible to those who presume that their categories are universal. The articulation of singularity would resonate with Dabashi's call for plurivocal and plurifocal guerrilla warfare against Hegel, Modernity, Eurocentrism, Globalization—but we should add to this list History and the

State. But in order that this guerrilla not be contained within academic discourse (regardless of how important it might seem to us academics), it must trace connections and articulations that inform protests, strategies for the expropriation of means of production, direct action, and the autonomization of life.

Thus this guerrilla will create space for knowledge production that invents practices for confronting the state and furthering the *without* history. Autonomization would now be understood as process rather than as claims that privilege institutionalized spaces—namely, the political, the aesthetic, the ethical, the universities, and whatnot. As such, the singular partakes of a process and manifests a site of struggle. It is not enough—and in fact, it is contrary to the emphasis on the singular to unveil—to expose the hegemony of postmodernism and post-Fordism, of globalization as the new hegemonic historical moment as if there is no *without* history and the state.

Modern, Postmodern, and Nonmodern

In our efforts to upturn the hegemony of the West, we have recently insisted on the fact that modernity is not exclusively a Euro-American invention. As such, modernity is diluted into any claim to newness in history. The effort to undermine the West's exclusive claims to science or democracy leads to a subsumption of all singular forms—such as the process of desiring the recognition of history and the state. This entails a logic that excludes practices and knowledges that do not meet the standards of science by confining them to magic, superstition, or obscurantism. Thus our ancestors end up embodying the values of the Enlightenment and our contemporaries readied—by means of stereotype—for persecution, minimally, for epistemological violence.

In anthropology, Hardt and Negri have reminded us, the old categories of the savage and the primitive were first displaced by the peasant and more recently by global anthropology: "The task of global anthropology, as many contemporary anthropologists formulate it, is to abandon the traditional structure of otherness altogether and discover instead a concept of cultural difference based on singularity." This abandonment of otherness, of the primitive and the savage, as object of study, leads to a generalized state of modernity that bears what to my ears rings as a slogan: "equally as modern as, yet different, from Europe."[15] This generalized state of modernity conveys the notion that all peoples today, in the singularity of their societies, are contemporaneous. This gesture cannot but be welcomed in that it breaks from the "Europe and its others" cluster and the syndromes that accompany the internalization of its binaries.

Yet it might turn out to be disingenuous in that the values of modernity—the desires to be recognized as modern—remain hegemonic, not unlike the desire for history. Note their definition of the limits of the modern: "Some of the phenomena that pose the strongest challenge for this conception of African modernity and cosmopolitanism are the forms of ritual and magic that continue to be integral elements of contemporary life."[16] So "magic and ritual" remain "other," in fact, a challenge within the new anthropologist's desire to trace modernity globally. Thus certain forms of life would be excluded as premodern, as backward, as life forms that are incompatible with modernity. Subjects would under this logic be expected to police themselves and expel the premodern from their soul. Wouldn't the new anthropologist end up reinventing the applied anthropology of postrevolutionary Mexico that devised policies for the integration of Indians into the state?[17] It does not occur to Hardt and Negri that multiple singular life forms may coexist within one subject and society without incurring in a contradiction as has been the case in Amerindian societies from first contact with Europe up to the Zapatistas today.[18]

Why do Hardt and Negri fail to be consistent in their call for a multitude made of singularities? There might be modes of the occult that are not of their liking, as they might not be of mine, but to pose a generalization about "magic and ritual" as challenges to the anthropological enterprise, if not of the state, threatens the diversity of Indian forms of life. This positioning entails enlightened epistemological privilege that inevitably smacks of vanguardism, of a top-down assessment of backwardness rather than a contribution to a horizontal assessment of strategies, debates, and struggles over the meaning of obscurantism that play out within the communities themselves. If Hardt and Negri's critique of the nostalgia for rural life that often accompanies discourses on the peasantry, and if their diagnosis of the eventual disappearance of the peasant forms of property seem inevitable, the transition from peasant to Indians (now rural and urban) entails a passage to communal forms of property and social organization, of which the Zapatistas insurgency remains representative. If their efforts to step out of Eurocentrism are noteworthy, the historical trajectory privileges changes in the European North: "Contemporary capitalist production is characterized by a series of passages that name different faces of the same shift: from the hegemony of industrial labor to that of immaterial labor, from Fordism to post-Fordism, and from the modern to the postmodern. Periodization frames the movement of history in terms of the passage from one relatively stable paradigm to another."[19]

The Multitude *without* History

If the utterance "there is no longer an outside to capital" rings true, it calls for the qualification: *except for all life forms that are constituted as backward, hence condemned to disappear.*[20] In this regard, Capitalism always constitutes its *withouts*. The Zapatistas defined the processes of exclusion as integral to what they call the "'IV Guerra mundial,' que se libra por el neoliberalismo contra la humanidad" ['IV World War' exerted by neoliberalism against humanity].[21] Capitalism affects all societies globally, but this does not mean that the history and periodization of the evolving tendencies in Western societies should be understood as an all-encompassing single history. Hardt and Negri, but also Paolo Virno, situate the emergence of the multitude as a most recent configuration of the future subject of "political action aimed at transformation and liberation."[22] They oppose the diversity and plurality of singularities that make up the multitude to the people, which, they argue, always aims at the constitution of the one, of the state.

But let's turn to Virno's *A Grammar for the Multitude* for a description of the multitude as a redefinition of "the One": "It remains clear that the multitude does not rid itself of the *One*, of the universal, of the common/shared; rather, it redefines the One. The One of the multitude no longer has anything to do with the One constituted by the State, with the One towards which the people converge."[23] Virno's reasoning on what he calls the "*general intellect* or public intellect" defines the One as a "*sharing*" of linguistic and cognitive [that] is the constituent element of the post-Fordist process of labor. All the workers enter into production in as much as they are speaking-thinking."[24] This offers an impeccable assessment of the new hegemony of immaterial labor, one that would affect all Western societies (including the metropolitan centers in the Third World). But post-Fordism does not subsume the history nor the condition of all the singularities that comprise the multitude. Unless we want to turn the multitude into a synecdoche that stands for the whole, we ought to understand how this trope would erase the singularities of societies and cultures that never were part of Fordism. These singularities that comprise this minority, which actually corresponds to a majority numerically, would not be disposed to articulate their processes of autonomization in post-Fordist terms, even if the general intellect remains a possibility. In short, the post-Fordism trope does not travel well when taken outside the hegemony of immaterial labor, which in fact constitutes a very limited hegemony outside Western societies. In the context of indigenous struggles, the primacy of post-Fordism hardly qualifies as a form of consent, as hegemonic, rather as a violent coercion into submission when not a war for the extermination of all those others that are considered an error of humanity.[25]

The iron-clad logic of historical tendencies that define the new historical epoch of Empire as the most advanced historical moment reiterates the hegemony of exclusion it seeks to expose. It runs the risk of constituting a vertical imposition that unwittingly may conspire against insurgencies of peoples that for centuries have existed *without* history and the state—in the words of the Zapatistas, "los muertos de siempre" [the dead of always], whose history of oppression and resistance informs the creation of processes of autonomization.[26] Our writings as intellectuals should remain vigilant of the epistemic violence we inflict with our slogans, generalizations, and desires to constitute a master model for interpreting the globalization that haunts us all but with different degrees of virulence. If the Zapatista definition of the multitude, of all those who are persecuted by neoliberalism for their singularity, travels well into the metropolitan centers of Europe, the United States, Latin America, and elsewhere in the world, we should keep in mind the following assessment of the Zapatistas in Chiapas:

> Este es un territorio rebelde, en resistencia, invadido por decenas de miles de soldados federales, policias, servicios de inteligencia, espías de las diversas naciones "desarrolladas," funcionarios en función de contrainsurgencia, y oportunistas de todo tipo. Un territorio compuesto por decenas de miles de indígenas mexicanos acosados, perseguidos, hostigados, atacados por negarse a dejar de ser indígenas, mexicanos y seres humanos, es decir, ciudadanos del mundo.

> [This is a rebel territory, in resistance, invaded by tens of thousands of federal soldiers, police, intelligence services, spies from the various "developed" nations, counterintelligence officials and opportunists of all types. A territory composed of tens of thousands of Mexican indigenous, harassed, persecuted, attacked for refusing to stop being indigenous, Mexican and human beings— that is, citizens of the world.][27]

9

Revolutionary Spiritualities in Chiapas Today
Immanent History and the Comparative Frame in Subaltern Studies

This chapter traces some of the signature concepts of the Zapatista insurrection of 1994 and the pacifism of Las Abejas back to native colonial pictorial articulations of the possibility of dwelling in a plurality of worlds, of the possibility of being modern and nonmodern without incurring contradiction. I prefer the notion of the "nonmodern" to the "pre-Modern" in that the latter carries a built-in teleology that posits modernity as a historical necessity. It has been argued that the Spanish invasion of the Americas in the sixteenth century should be considered as the beginning of modernity; we should take care not to define indigenous forms of life under colonial power as one more instance of the modern but as life forms with their own periodicity.

In this regard, the juxtaposition of Mesoamerican, colonial, and modern texts in this essay seeks to reproduce the sense of a multitemporal present that characterizes the native colonial pictorial maps and histories, the Zapatista communiqués, and even Antonio Gramsci's understanding of historical immanence. I first draw from the map of Cholula in the Relación Geográfica of 1581 an example and a definition of immanent history. I close with the question of revolutionary spiritualities in Chiapas today. If native hybrid pictorial and alphabetical texts from central Mexico lend themselves for an initial articulation of historical immanence and plural-world dwelling, these colonial texts also give historical depth to the mural *Vida y sueño de la cañada Perla* and the photographic *testimonio* of the pacifist Catholic organization Las Abejas (The Bees) examined in this essay.[1] My critique of Gramsci's concept of subaltern studies enables me not only to document further what I mean by immanent history, but also to lay out strategies for curtailing the constitution of a transcendental concept or institution that would subordinate immanence to an exterior source of meaning.

Cartographic Specters or the Immanence of Memory

In the map of Cholula from 1581 (figure 9.1), we can trace the indigenous production of artifacts for Spanish bureaucrats that comprised at least two codes. If we know the identity of the *corregidor*, Gabriel Rojas, who provided the verbal responses to the questionnaire of the Relaciones Geográficas, which included a question requesting a pictorial representation of the locations, the *tlacuilo* (the native painter), who drew the map of Cholula remains unknown. For the most part the painting of maps was delegated to the *tlacuilo*, but Rojas's written information proves invaluable for tracing the double register the *tlacuilo* deploys in the map of Cholula. On the one hand, the townscape of Cholula would satisfy the Relaciones Geográficas's request of pictorial representations. On the other hand, the *tlacuilo* inscribed the signs that would enable readers to recognize precolonial structures and meanings beyond the colonial order signified by the gridiron pattern of streets, the use of alphabetical writing, and the massive buildings occupying the center of the town.[2]

The *tlacuilo* displays an ability to use European cartographic systems of representation, but the map also contains indigenous pictographic forms. Under a close examination the map manifests that the Spanish pictorial vocabulary is used as signifiers rather than the signifieds usually associated with the meanings conveyed by grids, perspective, and landscape in chorographic maps and townscapes. These forms do not convey the corresponding realities of street patterns, the realistic depictions of cities, and the topography of the surroundings, but rather the system of representation itself. That is not to say that buildings and temples represented in the map did not have a corresponding reality but that beyond these structures we find an immanent historical layer that becomes manifest when we juxtapose a map of precolonial Cholula (figure 9.2) from the Historia Tolteca-Chichimeca (ca. 1545–1565).[3] As in the case of the *tlacuilo* who drafted the map of Cholula, the "authors" of the Historia Tolteca-Chichimeca remain anonymous; it was produced independently of Spanish authorities mainly intended for use within the community of Quautinchan.

In both cases we must assume a collective "author" rather than an individual *tlacuilo* working independently. Even when the map of Cholula was produced at the request of the *corregidor* Rojas, we can imagine the *tlacuilo* consulting the elders of Cholula and, as such, tracing the past under the ruins that remain legible despite the erasure inflicted by the colonial city. The juxtaposition of the two maps, which constitute places of memory for the collective remembrance of the ancient past, reveals a palimpsest in which under the new

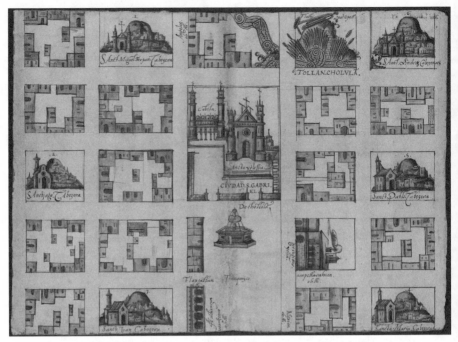

FIGURE 9.1. Map of Cholula. Relación geográfica de Cholula. Courtesy of the University of Texas Libraries.

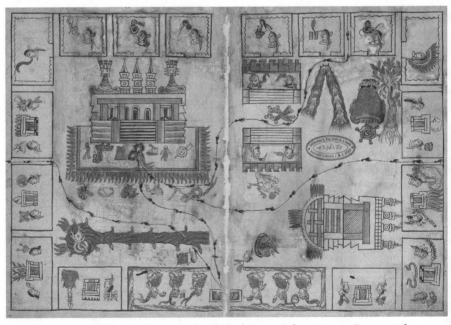

FIGURE 9.2. Ancient Cholula. Historia Tolteca-Chichimeca. Folios 26v–27r. Courtesy of the Bibliothèque Nationale de France.

Cholula one can trace the continuation of the ancient Mesoamerican past in the Indian colonial present. Thus the map of Cholula provides a frontispiece for the question of immanent history.

The first thing one notices is the conjunction of at least two codes operating on the surface of the map. We find a body of water represented by a traditional glyph in the central square on the top and the inclusion of glyphs that write the name of Tollan, a combination of *tolin* ("rush," "reed") and *-tlan* (a relational word that means "next to," "among"). The juxtaposition of the sign of water (*atl*) and a hill (*tepetl*) is a conventional form of writing *altepetl*, the term for the precolonial polity that included a conglomerate of *calpulli* (from *calli* ["house"] and *-pul*, a suffix that denotes "large"), the most basic social unit often translated as "big house" or "neighborhood." In this case it names Tollan Cholula and thereby establishes the connection of the city with the ancient civilization of the Toltecs, who abandoned Tollan in the ninth century. Separated by the trumpet we read the term *tlachiualtepetl*, which combines *tlachiualli* ("something made," "artificial") and *tepetl* ("mountain"), the name of the main precolonial temple in Cholula. The pyramid consists of a series of layers that correspond to different historical moments and form a hill in their superimposition. The trumpet, which in Nahuatl is called *tepuzquilistli*, a combination of *tepuztli* ("metal") and *quiquiztli* ("conch"), invokes the blowing of the conch in precolonial times to congregate the community around the temple.

According to Rojas—a bureaucrat charged with administering tributaries of the Crown—the missionaries found "muchos caracoles marinos con que los indios antiguamente tañían en lugar de trompetas" [many snails that Indians played instead of trumpets], when the missionaries inquired about the two occasions on which lightning destroyed the large cross that was constructed on top of *tlachiualtepetl* to neutralize the forces of Chiconauh Quiahuitl (*chiconauh* ["seven"] *quiahuitl* ["rain"]), the deity to whom the ancient temple was dedicated.[4] The trumpet fulfills this function now under Christianity. The Franciscan Monastery of Saint Gabriel and the chapel to the side in the central part of the map have replaced a precolonial temple, but also note that there are six churches next to hills in the squares surrounding the map. These churches correspond to the sites of six *calpulli* that the map identifies as *cabeceras*. Each of these *calpulli* had a temple that is now symbolized by a hill, but Cholula was flat with the exception of two smaller mounts next to the *tlachiualtepetl*, the artificial hill.

Serge Gruzinski sees in this recurrent hill different perspectives from which the *tlachiualtepetl* could be perceived from the different neighborhood.[5] If this is the case, the representation of the hill, always on the right-hand side, is not very realistic. The painter obviously could have placed the hill in locations that would correspond to the positions of the churches with respect to the *tlachiualtepetl*. In the same fashion that the *tlachiualtepetl* has been reduced to a mount, the hills on the different neighborhoods could be seen as conveying the political autonomy of the *calpulli*, which in precolonial times had a particular temple. We can read behind the churches the presence of the old temples, a continuation of the past in the present that the citizens of Cholula could not have failed to recognize. Indeed, Rojas confirms this when he writes: "Y estos ídolos tenían, también, unos cerrillos menores hechos a mano a modo del sobredicho, con su ermita en lo alto, llamada *teucalli*, que quiere decir 'casa de dios'" [And these idols also had hand-made small hills according to the mode explained above, with its hermitage on top, called *teucalli*, which means "house of god"]. Further down, Rojas adds: "y aun hay hoy, por toda la ciudad, reliquias de otros muchos menores que, con los edificios de las casas, [se] han ido gastando, como lo hace hoy de los que hay" [and even today, there are relics all over the city of other less important ones, that with the structures of the houses, they have been decaying, as it occurs today with those still standing].[6]

The temples and their hills have been destroyed and the debris has been used for the construction of the new city. Note that for Rojas the debris is not just material remains, but relics that haunt the city with a memory of old. Moreover, the debris from the old temples and houses coexists with the ruins of the chapel's dome, which collapsed on the night that followed the celebration of its completion: "Que fue milagro que Dios obró en que cayese de noche, que, de ser asi el día antes, hiciera un estrago notable, por haber más de mil personas dentro. Estas ruinas se han quedado así porque, como los indios van en disminución, no la tornan a edificar" [That it was a miracle by God that it collapsed at night, that, if it had been the day before, it would have a notable devastation, since there were more than one thousand people inside. These ruins remain as such, because the Indians become increasingly fewer, they do not rebuild it].[7] In the map of Cholula the elaborate dome of the chapel, on the left of the convent of San Gabriel, figures intact. The map simulates an organized town built on a geometric grid, but archaeological digs have demonstrated that the depiction of the grid stands for the new Spanish order rather than for an accurate representation of the city blocks. The scenographic realistic representation of the hills and the churches of the neighborhood, a highly symbolic gesture, alternate with orthographic schematic depictions of buildings within the blocks. Thus the *tlacuilo* displays his mastery of Spanish codes in his juxtaposition, in his citing of orthographic and scenographic systems of representation.

For Gruzinski the map resembles a Necker cube that shifts backgrounds alternating between a hollow cube and a solid one. He also speaks of a mestizo mind to characterize the genius of the *tlacuilo*'s production of cultural artifacts that deploy elements from different cultures for an end not contemplated by the supervising authorities. As such, the mixture of the precolonial and the colonial alternate in the dominance of one of the components that ultimately makes it very hard to distinguish the Indianization of Christianity from the Christianization of the precolonial.[8] Thus the discreteness of the European and the Indian life forms would disappear into a mestizo mind. For Barbara Mundy, this is an instance of double consciousness, a term she derives from W.E.B. Du Bois, although she fails to mention the African-American scholar: "In this respect they [Indian maps] show us the double-consciousness of the colonized artist: working to satisfy an immediate local audience and laboring with a set of expectations about the colonizers; this artistic double-consciousness marks a much larger set of images from the New World."[9]

If the mere fact of using European systems of representation and categories makes the artist colonized, then the fact that I am writing here in English and within a U.S. academic context would also make me and you who reads this "colonized." I am contaminating you, if you were not already, by the mere fact that you are following me. There may certainly be a conflict between the two demands of speaking to the community and responding to the colonial instructions, but there is no reason why the *tlacuilo* could not have perceived himself as mastering the codes of European cartography, while at the same time knowing that there is more to the townscape than mere European institutions. He may have experienced a conflict between Christian and Indian spirituality, but this would be a result of the imposition by missionaries and lay officials, not one that the *tlacuilo* would have necessarily internalized. The internalization of the conflict is in fact the end of the ideological warfare conducted by the colonial order, which should not imply that the internalization of incompatibility would need to be a natural consequence of the evangelization.

Indians expressing perplexity over the need to abandon their gods in order to embrace Christianity is at least as notorious in missionary literature as the friars' lamentations that for the Indians the Christian God was one more god that could coexist with the rest. To my mind, the coexistence of multiple systems of representation conveys a capacity to dwell in a plurality of worlds without incurring contradiction. Plural-world dwelling would not necessarily imply a struggle between two consciousnesses as manifest in Mundy's definition of double-consciousness or the blending of two life forms into one, as in Gruzinski's notion of *mestizaje*. Rather, it would imply the ability to participate in at least two discrete worlds without incurring contradiction. The *tlacuilo* displays knowledge of Western forms but also of local practices; as in the case of the Necker cube, in the blink of an eye one finds a Nahuatl world signified.

Subalternized indigenous subjects developed the ability to dwell in more than one world because colonial orders demanded that Indians recognize the authority of and subject themselves to Spanish institutions. The colonial order constituted itself as the only true world whether under the axis of Christianity or of modern science. To protect the integrity of their worlds, indigenous subjects systematically excluded others from learning about and dwelling in their culture. The *tlacuilo* who drafted the map of Cholula was expected to produce a townscape that would follow the principles of European mapmaking. One finds a double coding on the surface of the map that did not seem to have posed a threat to the *corregidor* Rojas. Although Rojas consulted Indians, he does not give us their names. To all appearances, Rojas was a *nahuatlato* (speaker and interpreter of Nahuatl) who translated all the information provided by the Indian informants.

Let's now juxtapose a map from the Historia Tolteca-Chichimeca, a hybrid text that uses both the alphabet and pictorial representation and was produced outside the supervision of Spanish authorities. The fact that the *tlacuilo* used both the alphabet and pictography does not make this text less indigenous, as if one would lose one's "Indianness" by the mere fact of riding horses, weaving with wool, or using the pen to write letters. Nothing remains pure in the aftermath of the European invasion. The Historia Tolteca-Chichimeca provides a pictographic history and an alphabetical transcription of an oral performance of the stories associated with the paintings. This map underlies the map of Cholula of 1581 as in a palimpsest that manifests the ghostly continuity of the precolonial order in the colonial map. It provides a key for understanding the background of the map of Cholula as indigenous. I understand by "background" the philosophical concept that stands for the *absolute presupposition from which and against which one make sense of life forms*.[10] Here I argue for multiple absolute presuppositions that remain discrete though never pure in plural-world dwelling.

The existence of discrete worlds does not imply that one cannot make sense, *exappropriate*, and transform life forms belonging to another world with its own absolute presuppositions. I derive the term "exappropriation" from the French philosopher Jacques Derrida: "What is at stake here, and it obeys another 'logic,' is rather a 'choice' between multiple configurations of mastery without mastery (what I have proposed to call 'exappropriation'). But it also takes the phenomenal form of a war, a conflictual tension between multiple forces of appropriation, between multiple strategies of control."[11] This process of deploying and making sense with life forms belonging to another culture would not exclude the possibility of also understanding those forms in terms of their own background. The ability to switch backgrounds might enable someone to describe the rules of or the contradictions in the social and cultural practices of another culture. The example of the anthropologist who isolates the rules of a culture comes to mind, but we must also observe colonial spaces in which Indians saw through the social, cultural, and religious forms practiced by Spaniards. In fact, indigenous people under colonial regimes have an advantage over the anthropologist in that Indians are required to understand and make themselves familiar with European institutions. Spanish lay officials and missionaries often expressed dismay and persecuted and repressed Indians who showed them contradictions in their most valued doctrinal beliefs and evangelical practices.[12]

In the 1581 map of Cholula the indigenous background coexists with a Spanish background that defines space in terms of European forms of representation and urban landscape. The European life forms function not only as signifieds but also as signifiers that now constitute a vocabulary that the *tlacuilo* has invented to represent European objects from within an indigenous conception of the world. The correspondence of the map of Cholula with the structure that supposedly existed centuries before the arrival of the Spaniards reveals that the new map constitutes a palimpsest for those who could trace the old in the terms of an indigenous background. In addition to the *tlachiualtepetl* (the artificial hill), the map invites the reader to locate the institutions that made up "yn uel ytzontecon mochiuhtica yn toltecayolt" [the true head of the essentially Tolteca]: "Tlachihualtepetl ycatcan, Atlyayauhcan, Xochatlauhtli ypilcayan, Quetzaltotl ycacan, Iztaquautli ytlaquayan, Iztaczollin ynemomoxouayan, Calmecac, Ecoztlan, Temmatlac, Apechtli yyonocan y Couatl ypilhuacan." With the exception of the *tlachiualtepetl* (the artificial mountain) and the *calmecac* (the school) the other institutions listed defy translation.

The *tlacuilo*, or at least the recorded verbal performance of the map, speaks in the present tense: "uel nican monezcaycuiloua yn imaltepeuh yn iuh yyollo quimatico yn tachtouan yn tocolhuan auh tel yn axcan zan iuh catqui yn imauh yn intepeuh yn tolteca calmecactlaca" [here is painted the figure of the town; thus it is; thus our great-grandfathers and grandfathers came to know it; and notwithstanding today also as such it is the town of the Tolteca, the Calmecactlaca]." Observe that the Historia Tolteca-Chichimeca speaks of the coming to be of Cholula in exclusively Indian spiritual terms: "yn zan ipaltzinco yn ipalnemoani, yn tlalticpaque" [only with the power of that by means of which we live, the possessor of the earth].[13] There is no mention of a Christian deity or attempt to demonize these manifestations of the creative force. By underscoring the present, the world witnessed by the ancient great-grandparents remains accessible even after the havoc brought about by the Spanish invasion.

The *tlacuilo* of the map of Cholula conceived at least in part an audience that participated in the indigenous background of the Historia Tolteca-Chichimeca. Those native informants that provided the *corregidor* Rojas with information about precolonial Cholula would have unfailingly recognized the indigenous past on the surface of the depicted colonial present. Rojas quite laconically states: "Y aun hay hoy, por toda la ciudad, reliquias" [and even today, there are relics all over the city].[14] In the map of Cholula, the *tlacuilo* conveys mastery of several codes and the ability to include at least two radically different readings. Beyond comparison and translation, the map of Cholula invites us to shift backgrounds. Thus the *tlacuilo* manifests his capacity to dwell in multiple worlds. Moreover, the mastery of Spanish forms then and modern discourses today need not entail getting caught on the rails of the dialectic bound to hegemonizing and homogenizing discourses.

The Historia Tolteca-Chichimeca also illustrates the fascination native scribes had with the alphabet as a technology for the recording of voice. The recording of voice by means of the alphabet obviously embalms (some would say kills) orality, but by the same token it gives place to a site for the resurrection of the dead. Indian alphabetical texts, at least those recording speech and song, like the Historia Tolteca-Chichimeca, were not intended to be read in private but rather to be subjected to an oral performance, much like in the pictorial codices of the precolonial period. Note the opening remarks that invite the elders to sit and listen to the performance of the alphabetical and pictorial text:

> chacui — chini tanquehue xihuiqui notlatzin ximotlali ypan ycpalli — chitao
> chacui qieaha tanquehe xihualmohuica ximotlali
> chacui tachi — tanquehue — xihuiqui nocoltzin ximotlali
> chontana dios tachi — ma Dios mitzmohuquili nocoltzin
> chini yn chay — tihimaxoconmit notlatzin tepitzin
> chontana chana Dios ma Dios mitzmohuiquili tlatouane

> [*chacui — chini tanquehue* — come my uncle sit down on the chair — *chitao*
> *chacui qieaha tanquehe* — come sit down
> *chacui tachi — tanquehue* — my grandfather, come sit down
> *chontana dios tachi* — my grandfather, may God take you
> *chini yn chay* — may you drink my uncle a little bit
> *chontana chana Dios* — Oh ruler, may God take you][15]

This is a bilingual text that juxtaposes Popoloca and Nahuatl. I have italicized the Popoloca in the translation. This opening statement most likely dates from the early eighteenth century. By invoking the elders to sit and drink, this brief text testifies to a performance almost two hundred years after its production.

Several interpretations have been given for the inclusion of a Popoloca version of the Nahuatl. Michael Swanton has argued that this is a ritual text, although he does not fully explain the function bilingualism would have played in the ritual.[16] A simpler explanation would be that Popoloca speakers attended, and that it merely reflects an invitation. What remains beyond doubt is that it signals the collective participation in the ritual that reminisces the origins and foundation of Quautinchan. We know the document remained in the community up to 1718, when it became part of the Lorenzo Boturini collection. Today it is housed in the Bibliothèque Nationale de France. Since it remained in the community for two hundred years, we may argue that the Historia Tolteca-Chichimeca was produced for internal consumption rather than for arguing a case in Spanish courts. We must also assume that the production of the verbal and the pictorial document involved the whole community and that alphabetical writing was soon to be understood as a record of voice, of a particular voicing of a pictorial text that could be brought back, enhanced, relived in future generations. Ghosts particularly haunt writing as a record of voice.

These two maps are products of immanent history that is constituted in the speech of the communities. This space of immanence makes worlds through native languages and backgrounds that often coexist with Euro-American backgrounds. The community may master the Western codes, stop being subalterns according to a Gramscian definition, but without necessarily subjecting the meaning and significance of their discursive practices to a transcendental principle or institution.

The Comparative Frame of Subaltern Studies

One can open just about any page in Gramsci and find a vocabulary of progress and historical development that establishes a teleology for comparative purposes.[17] Gramsci's terms include "historical places," "emergence," "conditions of transformations," "levels of development," "degrees of homogeneity," "forms of political consciousness," "historical maturity," and so on. There is a vanguardism in his call for subaltern studies, if this is what Gramsci would have called his studies of dominance and subordination. Vanguardism is perhaps nowhere more clearly articulated than when he appraises Henri de Man and Lenin indirectly in a note on Machiavelli from 1930: "He (De Man) demonstrated the need to study and develop [elaborate] the elements of popular psychology, historically and not sociologically, actively (i.e., in order to transform them, by educating them, into a modern mentality) and descriptively as he [Maurice Maeterlinck] does. But this need was at least implicit (perhaps even explicitly stated) in the doctrine of Ilitch [Lenin]—something of which De Man is entirely ignorant."[18]

Gramsci goes on to distinguish "scholars who argue that spontaneity is the immanent and objective 'method' of the historical process, and political adventurers who argue for it as a 'political' method."[19] Whereas the former be-

trays a mistaken conception, the latter entails the desire to replace a given leadership by a different one. I do not quite understand what Gramsci means by
the mistaken conception of "the immanent and objective method" (although
I suspect he is alluding to Lenin's negative conception of spontaneity in *What
Is to Be Done?*); nevertheless, I derive from these passages a concept of historical immanence that should shed further light on the colonial texts examined
above and the discussion of insurgency in Chiapas today. Under Gramsci's
formulation, subalterns may know spontaneously the causes of their oppression and the need to organize politically (that is, they contain the rudimentary
elements of conscious leadership, of discipline). But only modern theory will
give them a full understanding and guarantee that their force is not misdirected by reactionary groups. Gramsci makes room for knowledge through
a popular conception of the world, "what is unimaginatively called 'instinct,'
although it too is in fact a primitive and elementary historical acquisition." But
he advocates for "a reciprocal 'reduction' so to speak," claiming that "a passage
from one to the other and vice versa, must be possible."[20]

Gramsci here lays out the indispensable unity between "spontaneity" and
"conscious leadership," which constitutes "the real political action of subaltern
classes, in so far as this is mass politics and not merely an adventure by groups
claiming to represent the masses."[21] But the comparative frame of subaltern
studies ultimately defines the project as one in which subordinated groups
must be educated so that they may overcome their subalternity. Elsewhere, he
does make allowance for processes that seem to be understood by the subaltern classes directly, but then he adds that this understanding implies that it is
no longer a subaltern class, "or at least is demonstrably on the way to emerging
from its subordinate position."[22] Has there ever been an absolute state of subalternity—that is, one that ignores its subordinate condition and lacks any form
of significant resistance? In other words, aren't all subalterns always already
"on the way to emerging from their subordinate position"? Gramsci's premise is that elementary forms of consciousness must be translated into a theoretical language and that in the process of putting it into practice, theory will
override the elementary forms. In fact, even if modern theory builds from the
spontaneous knowledge of subalterns, it will in the end constitute itself as the
source of truth and the parameters for defining errors, such as the "mistake"
of the immanent method. The new principle in its embodiment in the party
transcends the everyday practices, languages, and articulations of alternate
worlds. But the party and modern theory in general must also translate their
articulations into a language that would make sense in terms of the forces of
immanent history.

Gramsci remains exceptionally lucid with respect to issues of spontaneity
and his call to attend the particular forms of thought that inform social move-

ments and revolutionary process. These forms most often clash with modern knowledge; nevertheless, he considers that they must be translated into theoretical language. If there is a dialectic between these two forms of life, the telos undoubtedly points to the homogenization of thought in modern science and the Party, to the "homogeneous politico-economic historical bloc, without internal contradictions."[23]

The concept of the subaltern as conceived by Gramsci bears a comparative frame that defines the dissolution of subalternity in forms of consciousness that make possible the organization of political blocs that can bring about a revolution, even if he makes allowances for spontaneity or immanent forces. In its most refined form, the teleological impulse in the comparative frame of subaltern studies constitutes its model of interpretation and evaluation as an end. The present from which we write, the hindsight of how history evolved, cannot but be privileged in comparative studies. If comparisons are unavoidable, I would recommend limiting them to artifacts and forms of thought that share a background. The issue here is whether history reads in the singular. Inevitably we will compare singular vis-à-vis multiple historical horizons.

Questions of beginnings also come into play in comparative historical processes: for example, the dating of modernity in the Enlightenment relative to the dating in 1492. What is at stake in building a narrative using these two moments? Lest we forget that the constitution of a beginning, of a zero point constitutive of historical narrative, is a choice the historian makes to tell a story, rather than an onto-historical claim. The stories we tell should make sense in terms of the immanent forces manifest at any given moment. World historical narratives that locate key moments in world history around European-global moments (whether these moments may involve 1492, the French Revolution, or the Industrial Revolution does not make a difference) subordinate the significance of immanent history by positing a transcendental narrative. Thus world-system models undermine the periodization of indigenous histories that cannot be reduced to mere reactions to global formations even when conceived as resistance. These models make Eurocentric conceptions of history and the world all but inevitable. We may seek to debunk the European hubris by documenting how non-Europeans contributed, anticipated, and inaugurated life forms that tend to be identified as solely products of Europe. This is a just project and must be done, but we may end up with an even more hegemonic system of thought in that the dominant would now include as the natural way of seeing and understanding the world, the true knowledge that all humankind has contributed to the making of modernity, rather than a predominantly Western epistemological regime that historically has and continues to subordinate all not-modern forms of life.

The irony of those who make the modern the only existing world (an undeniable fact if defined as the shared temporality that makes all cultures contemporary) resides in the inherent practice of modern thought to define correctness and error in terms of advanced and backward life forms. For instance, a culture that believes in the agency of the "gods" might be as modern as any other coeval cultural formation, but it could nevertheless be relegated to a mistaken conception of history by the most "advanced" modern ideas. Modernity, in its race toward progress, is comparativist through and through, hence teleological in its characterization of the not-so-modern. Given that the comparative frame of subaltern studies also entails the notion that subalternity is a relational concept, we could very well end up speaking of subalterns as comprising a marginalized middle class, slighted intellectuals, ineffectual political activists, political prisoners, and a broad panoply of modern types. Rather than speaking of the modern and the premodern, I have been using the concept of the nonmodern to understand a whole series of life forms that are impermeable to the teleology that constitutes the *pre-* of the modern.

The definition of indigenous knowledges as premodern is primarily the result of exclusionary practices that confine indigenous epistemes to the realm of superstitions, folklore, magic, and so on, which keep us from understanding indigenous life forms in their positivity. Given the inherent logic of subordination in discourses of modernity that constitute the premodern and structurally determine the antimodern, the nonmodern offers the possibility that one may practice the most modern without letting it encroach on the not-modern. Nativist and revivalist movements may conceive of themselves as nonmodern but not necessarily as antimodern. A most common rebuttal to nonmodern is that subalterns also want to be modern and desire modern technology and so forth. Of course they do, but there are subalterns who do not find a contradiction between desiring, acquiring, and mastering modern life forms and continuing to practice forms of life that have nothing to do with modernity, that in fact modernity often finds incompatible. But this epistemic violence that defines modernity in exclusionary terms need not be internalized.

From a Gramscian perspective, the ability to understand and articulate historico-political conditions of oppression is already a sign that one no longer is a subaltern. The question, however, is whether the language one uses to articulate these conditions must correspond to Euro-American theory, hence all nativistic discourses would signal a condition of subalternity. This makes sense in terms of the practicality of nativistic forms in circles such as the IMF or the World Bank, in that these institutions will dismiss any claims that do not meet the standards of their discourse. Does that mean that a social group must abandon nativistic and revivalist discourses or that they must understand these discourses as subaltern forms given the privileged position of science? Wouldn't this logic imply a colonialist impulse that in subordinating forms of discourse inflicts epistemic violence? These questions signal the dead ends of the comparative frame in subaltern studies.[24]

Now the comparative frame of subaltern studies may lose its grip if we consider the possibility that subalterns, say Amerindians under colonial rule—a colonial condition that by the way does not end with the Wars of Independence in the nineteenth century but continues up to the present—may dwell in more than one world without comparing them and thereby without enduring the internalization of modernist hubris.

Revolutionary Spirituality in Las Abejas and the Zapatistas

I examine two instances of revolutionary spirituality in Chiapas today in which one can trace the work of immanent history. The first example is the mural *Vida y sueños de la cañada Perla* (see figure 6.1), which exemplifies the warrior mysticism expressed in the murals of the Zapatista bases that lend support to the Zapatista Army of National Liberation (Ejercito Zapatista de Liberación Nacional, the EZLN).[25] This mural includes Emiliano Zapata, the leader of the Revolution of 1910 southern armies, riding his horse and holding a rifle, and Ricardo Flores Magón, the anarcho-communist theoretician of the Mexican revolution of 1910, who is also armed with a cartridge belt. Both figures are identified with slogans. A passage from Flores Magón's last article in *Regeneración*, the organ of the Partido Liberal, illustrates his call to action: "para lucha actividad, actividad, actividad es lo que reclama el momento" [for the struggle, activity, activity, activity, is what the moment demands]. Observe the word "libertad" spinning on his left hand. Zapata's *paliacate* (his scarf) bears the inscription: "La tierra es de quien la trabaja." His takeovers of the haciendas in the state of Morelos, a brilliant instance of Gramsci's immanent history, have their match in Flores Magón's theorization of direct action.

As in the case of the map of Cholula, we find multiple backgrounds for interpreting the mural. One can at once provide a reading that places the emphasis on a long anarcho-communist tradition and the program of the rural peasantry led by Zapata. The reference to Zapata, I argue, makes manifest an immanent history of indigenous people's demands of land and of sovereignty over their territories. Zapata also merges with the precolonial figure of Votán, the "the guardian and heart of the people." Zapatista spirituality invokes a nativistic tradition that often juxtaposes Zapata and Quetzalcoatl in murals in the Zapatista bases. Here we find a reference to the two Quetzalcoatl that correspond to the diurnal and nocturnal passage of Venus: the legendary Zapata dressed in white that appears on the horizon riding his horse, and the clandestine Zapatistas on the mountains that guard Taniperla. Jan De Vos has traced this two Quetzalcoatl to a communiqué by Subcomandante Marcos from December 1994. In response to Marcos's question about the relationship between Zapata and the gods Votán and Ik'al, Old Man Antonio responds:

> El tal Zapata se apareció acá en las montañas. No se nació, dicen. Se apareció así nomás. Dicen que es el Ik'al y el Votán que hasta acá vinieron a parar en su largo camino y que, para no espantar a las gentes, se hicieron uno sólo. Porque ya de mucho andar juntos el Ik'al y el Votán aprendieron que era lo mismo y que podían hacerse uno sólo en el día y en la noche y cuando se llegaron hasta acá se hicieron uno y se pusieron de nombre Zapata y dijo el Zapata que hasta aquí había llegado y acá iba a encontrar la respuesta de a dónde lleva el largo camino y dijo que en veces sería luz y en veces oscuridad, pero que era el mismo, el Votán Zapata y el Ik'al Zapata, el Zapata blanco y el Zapata negro, y que eran los dos el mismo camino para los hombres y las mujeres verdaderos.

> [That Zapata appeared here in the mountains. He wasn't born, they say. He just appeared just like that. They say he is Ik'al and Votán who came all the way over here in their long journey, and so as not to frighten good people, they became one. Because after being together for so long, Ik'al and Votán learned that they were the same and could become Zapata. And Zapata said he had finally learned where the long road went and that at times it would be light and times darkness but that he was the same, Votán Zapata and Ik'al Zapata, the white Zapata and the black Zapata. They were both the same road for the true men and women.][26]

Note that in the Codex Borgia and in the Codex Vaticanus B, two precolonial religious codices, we find representations of a black Quetzalcoatl linked at the waist to a white Mictlantecutli, "the lord of death." These opposites, as well as the white and black Ik'al and Votán, need not have the positive and negative meanings commonly associated with these colors in the West. Actually, one can read elements of one god in the other.[27] This is, in fact, the gist of Old Man Antonio's story. As Ik'al and Votán merge into one in Zapata, Old Man Antonio in his conversation with Marcos brings together a millenarian memory for the articulation of a revolutionary conception of history and the world, one grounded in the precolonial and espousing a multitemporal sense of the present.

Other nativistic motifs in the mural include the figure of Mother Earth as embodied in the large woman on the left side, and the birds, which a new-age reading might interpret as a sign of a native colorful view of the world. However, a more historically informed reading would identify these with *quautli*, with eagle warriors descending to the earth as Zapatista forces. Mother Earth stands as the beginning, as a point of departure, as emblematic of the place women should have in Mayan communities and the important role they play in the Zapatista insurrection. At the other end of the ideological spectrum, the telecommunications tower conveys the use and mastery of Western technology. Even though the dominant spirituality is nativistic, the mural includes a temple committed to ecumenism, to countering the violence that banishes non-Catholic members from their communities and the terrorism of paramilitary groups associated with the Presbyterian Church that murders Zapatista sympathizers. The mission of ecumenical dialogue neutralizes religious warfare and condemns the explanation of massacres in terms of religious conflicts. In Taniperla there is room for Protestants, Catholics, nativists, and atheists if we are to take seriously the figure of Ricardo Flores Magón as an ancestor, as a revenant that together with Zapata infuses life into the community.

One of the most distinctive traits of the Zapatista insurrection has been the respect mestizo leadership has shown for the life forms of indigenous communities. Indeed, there has been a concerted effort to avoid all forms of vanguardism. Subcomandante Marcos has played an important role as a spokesperson of the EZLN, but his position has been of *sub*comandante at the service and orders of the Indian-led Comité Clandestino Revolucionario Indígena, Comandancia General (the CCRI-CG), which, in turn, always acts on the consensus of the communities. There is an undeniable theorization on the part of Marcos and other comandantes such as Tacho, David, and Azevedo, and even more importantly by the women Zapatistas such as Comandantes Esther, Ramona, and Trinidad, to mention just a few. It is beyond the scope of this essay to go in any detail regarding the question of gender in the Zapatista insurrection, the organization of the movement, the articulation of programs, and the definition of autonomies that have been informed by indigenous thought.[28]

In the mural a man and woman carry proposals worked out in the separate assemblies and meet at the door of the Casa Municipal, which the sign on top in Tzeltal identifies as: Sna yu'un ateletic yu'un comonaletic [House of the authorities of the communities]. The woman wears traditional Tzeltal dress. The decisions at the meeting will define the practices of the everyday life of the communities, will be articulated in Tzeltal, and will retain their roots in millennial communal practices. Marcos has brilliantly articulated the link between historical immanence and constituent power in "Chiapas: La Treceava Estela (primera parte)," the series of seven communiqués that announced the creation of the Juntas de Buen Gobierno, the *caracoles*:

> Durante varias horas, estos seres de corazón moreno han trazado, con sus ideas, un gran caracol. Partiendo de lo internacional, su mirada y su pensamiento ha ido, adentrando, pasando sucesivamente por lo nacional, lo regional y lo local, hasta llegar a lo que ellos llaman "El Votán." "El guardian y corazón del pueblo," los pueblos zapatistas. Así desde la curva más externa del caracol se piensan palabras como "globalización," "guerra de dominación," "resistencia,"

"economía," "ciudad," "campo," "situación política," y otras que el borrador va eliminando después de la pregunta de rigor "¿Está claro o hay pregunta?" Al final del camino de fuera hacia dentro, en el centro del caracol, sólo quedan unas siglas: "EZLN." Después hay propuestas y se dibujan, en el pensamiento y el corazón ventanas y puertas que sólo ellos ven (entre otras cosas, porque aún no existen). La palabra dispar y dispersa empieza a hacer camino común y colectivo. Alguien pregunta "¿Hay acuerdo?" "Hay," responde afirmando la voz colectiva. De nuevo se traza el caracol, pero ahora en camino inverso, de dentro hacia fuera. El borrador sigue también el camino inverso hasta que solo queda, llenando el viejo pizarrón, una frase que para muchos es delirio, pero que para estos hombres y mujeres es una razón de lucha: "un mundo donde quepan muchos mundos." Más despuesito, una decisión se toma.

[During several hours, these beings with a brown heart have traced, with their ideas, a gigantic snail. Starting from the international, their sight and thought has gone deeper, successively passing by the national, the regional and local, until reaching what they call "El Votán." "El Guardián y corazón del pueblo," the Zapatista peoples. Thus from the most external curve of the snail they think such words as "globalization," "war of domination," "resistance," "economy," "city," "country," "political situation," and others that the eraser eliminates after the essential question: "Is it clear or is there another question?" At the end of the path from the outside to the inside, in the center of the snail, only remains the abbreviation: "EZLN." Propositions are made afterwards and windows and doors are drawn that only they see (among other things, because they don't exist yet). The unequal and disparate word begins to make its common and collective path. Someone asks, "Is there an agreement?" "There is," responds in the affirmative the collective voice. Again, the snail is traced, but now in the inverse direction, from within to without. The eraser also follows the inverse path until there only remains, filling the old blackboard, a phrase that for many is delirium, but that for these men and women is a reason to struggle: "a world in which many worlds fit." A bit later, a decision is taken].[29]

The movement inward and outward within the *caracol* establishes that the reflection on categories and social projects will be in indigenous terms. I read in the call for "un mundo donde quepan muchos mundos" a felicitous expression of the plural-world dwelling that I have identified in the map of Cholula and other colonial pictorial codices. This sense of a plurality of worlds has little to do with the liberal multiculturalism that global corporations espouse in their promotion of a homogenous, albeit multiracial, profile of the employees and the world to which they cater. The call for "un mundo donde quepan muchos mundos" constitutes a statement about globalization that underscores the possibility of multiple socioeconomic, political, and cultural worlds. In the world of the "multicultural" corporations, there is no room for autonomous Indian peoples debating and arriving at consensus on the use and benefits to be derived from the natural resources in their territories.[30] Nor is there room for spiritual revolutions that neutralize the exappropriation and commercialization of indigenous life forms. Marcos reminds us that the *caracol* represented the ancients' understanding of knowledge as entering the heart. And as in the case of the *caracoles* of Cholula that convoked the people, the *caracol* now fulfills the promise of bringing the community together so that "la palabra fuera de uno a otro y naciera el acuerdo" [the word would go from one to another and gave birth to agreement]. This politics of consensus underlies the gathering of men and women at the Casa Municipal, at the Sna yu'un ateletic yu'un comonaletic, represented in the mural of Taniperla.

This takes me to the second example of revolutionary spirituality: the Tzotzil pacifist organization Las Abejas and its commitment to Christianity. I find particularly interesting the group's use of writing and photography in the production of a *testimonio* of the massacre of Acteal on December 22, 1997, when several dozen armed paramilitaries organized by the army and the state police murdered forty-five members of Las Abejas—the majority of them women, elders, and children—while they prayed. The *testimonio*, known as . . . *esta es nuestra palabra . . .* , includes photographs by Jutta Meier-Wiedenbach and Claudia Ituarte, an (unsigned) introduction by Pablo Romo, then the director of the Centro de Derecho Humanos "Fray Bartolomé de las Casas," and a short text by Elena Poniatowska. In this case, immanent history corresponds to an indigenous Christianity that informed the emergence of this association, which committed to pacifism in 1992, two years before the Zapatista uprising.

As in the case of the Zapatistas, with whom Las Abejas sympathize, although it does not share their call to arms, Las Abejas organized to fight the corruption of native officials associated with the Partido Revolucionario Institucional (PRI), then the official state party. More generally, they organized to fight the forces of globalization that are destroying native communities in Chiapas. It is beyond the scope of this essay to provide a history of the organization.[31] The group is committed to radical pacifism, perhaps nowhere better expressed than in Pedro Valtierra's photograph of a Tzotzil woman physically resisting the army's entrance to the refugee camp of Xoyep. This image has circulated all over the world, drawing the attention of pacifist organizations such as the Christian Peacemaker Teams. Members of Las Abejas know the power of photography but also the logic of exappropriation that haunts the circulation of images. Thus they converse with the most radical pacifists for the invention of new forms of action.

The production of the verbal testimony involved a process in which human rights workers from the Centro de Derechos Humanos "Fray Bartolomé de las Casas" recorded *testimonios* in Tzotzil and the simultaneous translation into Spanish by a bilingual community member. The *frayba* (as sympathizers know the center) then transcribed the translation into a computer file. Having read *testimonios* before spending time in Acteal, I had the impression that they were by speakers who had difficulties expressing their ideas in Spanish. The *frayba* made the concerted effort to remain faithful to the language of the translator to the extent that the expressions of the translators were intelligible. The translations were edited not only with an eye for intelligibility but also for producing short statements often punctuated by ellipses. This editing further fragments the flow of speech implicit in the alphabetical transcription and even in the audio recording of voice. During my visit in the summer of 2003, the community of Las Abejas was involved in producing a series of *testimonios* to be presented at the Interamerican Commission on Human Rights. For this dossier Las Abejas first recorded the *testimonios* in Tzotzil, then transcribed them into an alphabetical text, and finally translated and typed the Spanish version into a computer file.

On this occasion, they were assisted by a group of students from a Jesuit high school (Instituto Lux from León, Guanajuato) who were doing their social service in Acteal. Members from the community met and discussed how much to alter the Spanish version. Under the advice of the *frayba*, they decided that the transcriptions should remain faithful to the literal translations of the bilingual Tzotzil. The *frayba* warned the high school students against polishing the language because the text could be subjected to a "peritaje antropológico" (to an anthropological evaluation). At first I thought the issue of producing a text that "sounded" Tzotzil was an odd way of proving authenticity. My immediate suggestion was to submit the tapes and written transcription to the anthropologist doing the arbitration. I have come to realize that the presentation of a document that even in Spanish carries the force of Tzotzil rhetoric and poetics not only testifies to authenticity and to an indigenous production, but also forces those involved in the court to recognize Tzotzil signifiers as legitimate. Here we find an instance in which the expropriation of Spanish in the process of translation—a step that really didn't need the high school students, since the bilingual translators were proficient in Spanish—would have rendered the document proper at the expense of Tzotzil life forms.

If the verbal testimonies describe the massacre in detail, the photography never documents the physical effects. As a technology, photography has the capability of producing incontrovertible evidence of torture and murder. The photographers working with the community chose to capture the people in mourning and the abjection poverty and displacement had brought to their lives. We find instances in which the subjects interact with the photographer with the intent of addressing "us," the observers. There is a clear understanding of what photography does and how it is consumed. In some instances the

FIGURE 9.3. Three women from Las Abejas. Courtesy of Jutta Meier-Wiedenbach.

subjects note the presence of the photographer but choose not to acknowledge her presence. I am particularly impressed by Meier-Wiedenbach's photograph that captures an old woman holding a dry piece of tortilla and staring at the photographer and us (figure 9.3). The other two women ignore the presence of Meier-Wiedenbach rather than interact with her. The old woman conveys the suffering due to the lack of food. The piece of tortilla could stand for the centrality of maize in Mayan civilization, but also for the sacred host that brings grace and solidifies the commitment of Las Abejas to pacifism.

In colonial times the use of tortillas as wafers was so common, that was the term used when speaking of the sacrament. Take, for example, the following passage from an *Exercicio quotidiano* found among the papers of the Nahua historian from Chalco, Don Domingo de San Antón Muñón Chimalpahin Quauhtlehuanitzin (1593–1621): "Auh in ihquac yuh quimihtalhui yn totecuiyo Jesu Christo: niman oconmocuilli yn tlaxcalli, auh quinmomaquillitzino yn Apostolome. quimihtalhui, Jnin namechmaca ca nonatcayotzin yn amopampa temac tlaçaloz" [And when our Lord Jesus Christ had thus spoken, then He took tortillas and gave them to the apostles. He said: This that I give you is My body, which because of you is to be betrayed into other's hands].[32] *Tlaxcalli* (tortilla) stands as the most obvious "bread" that Jesus would have broken among the Apostles and the most natural signifier for the host, the Eucharistic wafer. When speaking of the host, contemporary Tzotzil uses *cuxul waj* (bread or tortilla viva) or *sh'ul waj* (santa tortilla).

It is a common practice among the Abejas to end a fast by passing around a dry piece of tortilla with a sprinkle of salt. Meier-Wiedenbach, however, has reminded me that the three women could only have been fasting out of extreme hunger. We should not read too much into this image. But the symbolism that exceeds the immediate intentions of the photographer would in this case lead us to relate the dry tostada with the host, and the practice of breaking a fast as an act of communion. Moreover, we could extend the metaphor of the tostada and the host to the photograph itself inasmuch as it constitutes a vehicle for the spirits. One cannot but associate these three women belonging to different generations with the three Marys of the passion. In tracing this Indianization of the host, we should avoid a facile celebration of how Indians appropriate Christianity to meet their non-Christian spiritual needs and beliefs. I say "facile" because such tracings tend to underestimate how essential to Christianity is the appropriation of Christian truth as one's own.

Appropriation also plays into a logic in which property and propriety inflect each other. As it were, one becomes "proper" in participating in a regime of property. Derrida's concept of "exappropriation" reminds us that the logic of appropriation involves a two-way street, which is fraught with struggles over truth and symbolism. The old woman of the photograph knows that her image will be consumed and exappropriated in spaces out of her control. These could include a human rights discourse that would pity her condition without recognizing the force of her pacifist convictions or, by the same token, the theoretical dismissal of the testimonial power of her image on the grounds that human rights discourses undermine the agency of Las Abejas by emphasizing their victimization. Moreover, she knows that the aesthetic power of photography could depoliticize her image. By these comments I would not want to take away the immediacy and truthfulness of her immediate interaction with the photographer in which, as Meier-Weidenbach conveyed to me, "she was 'saying' something like 'look at me and tell my story.'"[33] In facing the photographer, in looking back at us, and in holding the dry tortilla, she seems to ask us to acknowledge her awareness of how her image will inevitably be exappropriated.

Observe how proper is her attire, considering that she is living in a muddy refugee camp under a shelter made of plastic sheets set up to protect herself from the torrential rains of the season. She understands well the power of photography to transform her image into an icon of Christian pacifist resistance. She seems to be aware of the fact that the photographic image anticipates her death but also that spectrality indwells the photographic experience. The notion that Indians fear photography turns into a cliché once we understand that photography *does hold the power* to fragment life and thus to remind us of our mortality. After the work of Benjamin, Barthes, Cadava, and Derrida, it has become a commonplace in the West to associate photography with death and phantoms. It should not surprise us that Indians would perceive the power of photography to capture death as "time-passed" but also as hosting revenants. The tomb of those murdered in Acteal displays the photographs of all the victims. It is a space for recollecting the semblance of the dead but also a reminder that their deaths were not in vain. On the celebration of the massacre every month on the twenty-second, they are brought back to dwell once more among the living. The revenant of all revenants, the sacrifice of Christ and his return in the Eucharist, which now includes those massacred as witnesses to the truth, is embodied in the dry tortilla held by the old woman.

Not unlike writing, which embalms voice, photography embalms life and temporality. Thus photography also becomes the site for the return of ghosts. In this regard, we can speak of photography and writing as technologies for countering colonialism. The photographs produce signifiers of mourning rather than records of fact. In this respect they are closer to pictographic writing that did not represent objects realistically but prompted verbal performances that told stories not bound to a mere description of the pictographs. The spoken word bore the responsibility of communicating the horrors in their very detail. Consider the following words of terror:

> Las balas cruzaban las cabezas de los niños y los agresores decían *eso sí, eso sí*! Se sentían aliviados; ellos pensaron que todos habíamos muertos. [The bullets crossed the heads of the children and the aggressors said, *do that, do that*! They felt relieved because they thought we were all dead.]
>
> —Catalina Jiménez Luna, Acteal

> Bueno, cuando pasó dos o tres días de la matanza de allá de Acteal, entonces ahí contó mi papá y dice que esta viendo qué está pasando, "yo les eché cuchillo y machete a las que están embarazadas," dijo. Le dijo a mi mamá. Yo lo escuché, lo que dijo mi papá. [Three days after the massacre in Acteal, then my father told the story and said that he was seeing what happened, "I used my machete against those who were pregnant," he said. He told my mother. I heard what my father said.]
>
> —Juan Javier Ruíz Perez, thirteen years old, Canolal[34]

Let me now juxtapose a passage from the Historia de Tlatelolco (1528), arguably the first alphabetically scripted history in Nahuatl: "auh yn otlica omitl xaxamantoc tzontli momoyauhtoc calli tzontlapouhtoc calli chichiliuhtoc / Ocuilti moyatlaminaotlica Auh yn caltech hahalacatoc quatlextli" [And on the roads lay shattered bones and scattered hair; the houses were unroofed, red (with blood); worms crawled in and out the noses; and the walls of the houses were slippery with brains].[35] We do not have the pictorial version, but we can ascertain from extant pictographic codices that the details were not represented in as realistic a form as the verbal account. One may say that the reason the photographic component of . . . *esta es nuestra palabra* . . . does not include images of the mutilated corpses is because photographers were not allowed in Acteal until the bodies had already been sent to Tuxtla Gutierrez, the capital of Chiapas, in an attempt to cover up the massacre. But the contrast could not be more striking between Meier-Wiedenbach's and Ituarte's photographs in . . . *esta es nuestra palabra* . . . , and José Angel Rodríguez's (brilliant) photograph of a group of people holding handkerchiefs on their faces to avoid breathing the stench of the cadavers and observing a putrefied partial leg on a coffin bearing a tag on one of the toes.[36] Meier-Wiedenbach and Ituarte avoid capturing this sort of image out of respect but perhaps also because of their understanding of photography as a place for mourning rather than as a record of morbid curiosity.

In the case of Las Abejas, we find an indigenous organization that has learned to use the codes of human rights organizations and international courts while retaining a sense of its community and its project in terms of an immanent history. Competency in Western forms of discourse and their ability to produce documents for international courts does not entail an abandonment of the group's forms of life. The members of Las Abejas are no longer subalterns—or at least they are on their way toward ending their sub-alternity—according to Gramsci's definition, but they prove resistant to the forces of comparison that would lead to the subordination of their language and culture within a teleology that privileges the West as an unsurpassable background.

In reading colonial and contemporary pictorial and verbal texts, I have traced elements of a long memory that entails modes of historical immanence and diverse backgrounds that define the *absolute presuppositions from and against which* Indians made and continue to make sense of the world. The map of Cholula suggests that the *tlacuilo* who painted it used a map from the Historia Tolteca-Chichimeca as a prototype. But we also saw that the verbal component of the Historia conveyed a history in which the ancient past of the elders was told as part of an evanescent present of the performance despite the havoc brought about by the Spanish invasion. This temporality suggests that the essence of the Toltecs, the *toltecayotl*, retained its actuality, even if under clandestinity. This long memory, this immanent history, constitutes the background of the *tlacuilo* charged with painting the map of Cholula. In the case of the Zapatistas and Las Abejas, we found the coexistence of the precolonial past and the most modern forms of communication. Ancient dual representations of the ancient gods come into play with Zapata, and a piece of tortilla could at once signify millenarian associations of maize with life-giving forces and the Christian host. If I defined two forms of spirituality, it was not to oppose them but to signal two forms of revolutionary activity that in the end might not turn out to be that different: there is a pacifist element to the Zapatistas and a radical militancy to Las Abejas.

But why Gramsci? I would simply say that Gramsci enabled me to conceive of historical immanence precisely by elaborating a critique of the need he found for a transcendental principle or institution—that is, modern theory and the party. By refusing to lend credence to such a demand, I have created one more palimpsest, one more juxtaposition of texts in which the past and the present coexist immanently without any appeal to transcendence. It is not a question of opposing immanence and transcendence but of refusing to subordinate meaning and history to an external principle. Already in Gramsci historical immanence and modern theory feed into each other. Notwithstanding the privilege he gives to the "most modern theory," one could recognize in Gramsci an effort to reflect on the popular and the subaltern in ways that would not dismiss the place of historical immanence in revolutionary processes. We should not expect him to have articulated what has only very recently, in the past ten years or so, become the signature of the Zapatista movement and the EZLN. Marcos's description of the *caracol* suggests a process in which "theory" (as well as all those other terms Marcos mentions in his communiqués: "globalization," "war of domination," "resistance," "economy," "city," "country," "political situation") becomes meaningful only as a result of the process that leads to the heart of the *caracol*, to the EZLN, to the innermost core in which theoretical terms are expropriated for the creation of new spaces. In turn, the process outward culminates with the proposal for "un mundo donde quepan muchos mundos" [a world in which many fit].

This proposal for a world in which many worlds coexist without incurring contradiction, if my analysis is correct, corresponds to the articulations of plural-world dwelling in the map of Cholula and other native pictorial maps and histories in which one can trace not only the coexistence of many worlds but also the expression of perplexity with respect to the enforcement of one world, one history, and one creed by missionaries and lay officials. Spanish imperialism and universal evangelization summoned all peoples on earth into a single universal history wherein an iron-fisted logic defined the spectral past and its immanence as "without history," at once a "lack" and an "outside" in which apostasy threatened the colonial order.[37] Today, insurgency opens spaces—creates an outside of the state and its institutions—for the invention of new political practices.

10 ≡≡≡

Without History?
Apostasy as a Historical Category

In folio 46r of the Codex Telleriano-Remensis (ca. 1545–1563) we find a topology of conquest that illustrates what we may call a *without* history (see figure 4.1).[1] As I have pointed out in chapter 1, "the term 'without' entails an amphibology: at once signifies *absence* and *outside*. The concept of history itself presupposes an absence and an outside in positing an origin or beginning that either assumes a nothing—that is, an outside that cannot be taken as a source and ground of history (out of nothing, its nonfoundation, ex nihilo); or posits an origin in mythical expressions—that is, a prehistory that contains the seeds of history proper (in a progression, a lack to be supplemented, teleology)."[2] As an amphibology, which only works in English and not in Spanish or Latin, the concept of "without" lends itself to constructive equivocation.

In the scenes depicted in this folio, we find the dual sense of "without." First there is the baptismal event, where the stream of water signifies the entry of a willing subject to the Roman Catholic Church and thus a passage from an absence of history to history. Below this scene of baptism we find the same precolonial pictographic glyph for water marking the boundary between the spheres of those who accept their historical status and those who wish to escape from it, to bolt out of the political, religious, and economic structures of the Spanish spiritual and secular dominion, to place themselves *without* history, outside it, as apostates. Whereas the apostate (from Greek *apostates*, literally "rebel," from *aphistanai*, "cause to revolt," apo-, "away from," + *histanai*, "to cause to stand") takes flight from history, the apostle (from the Greek *apostolos*, literally "messenger," from *apostellein*, "to send away," apo- + *stellien*, "to send") is one whose calling is to incorporate new peoples into the sweep of history: in this instance the friar administering baptism who has traveled to the New World in pursuit of an ever-expanding historical mission.

This topology of conquest should make us wary of apologetics (another *apo*-word, this time one that links to *logos*, "word" or "reason," denoting a *defense from*) that underscore the historicity of indigenous peoples, whether in the mode that describes precolonial history as partaking of the Judeo-Christian teleology (a mode much favored by Mesoamerican and Andean historians like Guaman Poma, Garcilaso de la Vega, Tezozomoc, Chimalpahin, or Ixtlixochitl), or in the mode that defines historicality as a trait of humanity (a mode much favored by modern historians). If Indian colonial historians could only make sense of their past from within the universal history prescribed by the Church, modern historians naturalize history by assuming that all it takes is a willingness to apply historical tools to any given past.

There is nevertheless a paradox in the latter assumption that all humans have history, in that one cannot write a history, as distinct from a prehistory without an archive, without written documents, hence the classic differentiation between anthropology and history. Isn't the category of the prehistoric inescapably bound to the teleology of archive-formation? Or is it a question of scholars learning to read texts encoded by unknown grammars? Can the apostate elaborate an apologetic from a location that entails an abandonment of legitimating discourses, indeed that systematically undoes the "grammaticity" of dominant discourses? Is the *tlacuilo*, who painted folio 46r mapping out an exteriority that places the apostate beyond the limits of meaning in a form of *bare life* that escapes sovereign power, to borrow Georgio Agamben's expression in *Homo Sacer*? Can we tell a story that does justice to apostasy? Or are we bound to reinscribe apostasy from within a moral economy that we recognize as credible? Wouldn't such a gesture merely project our desires? What is to be gained by telling stories of apostasy? These are merely guiding questions, hardly answerable in any definite form. The implied "we" in these questions includes you, my reader, who I assume is not the apostate telling his or her own story but a subject reflecting on the event of apostasy.

This chapter draws from a wide variety of documents, including Spanish histories, indigenous narratives and pictorial texts, opinions on the legality and justness of wars of extermination, letters drafted by Tenamaztle in collaboration with Bartolomé de Las Casas, and monuments in the central plaza of Nochistlan, Zacatecas. I dedicate the last section to Alonso de la Vera Cruz's treatise *Relectio de dominio infidelium & justo bello*. My use of sources falls short of exhausting all the documentation on the wars against the Chichimec in the sixteenth century, while expanding the places of memory beyond collections of artifacts held in one or more locations.

Glossing History

As we survey folio 46r vertically, a gloss in Spanish informs us that the Indians from the region of Jalisco rebelled in 1541 and that Viceroy Antonio de Mendoza went north to suppress the insurrection. It also informs us that the floating body above the baptismal font depicts the corpse of Pedro de Alvarado, also known as Tonatiuh ("sun" in Nahuatl), a name given to him because of his blond hair. Alvarado is mainly remembered for the massacre of the Mexica elite at the beginning of Hernán Cortés's invasion of Mexico. Alvarado decided to join the forces of Mendoza when he heard about the effort to suppress the rebellion, while provisioning, on his way to the Philippines, in the Pacific port known today as Barra de Navidad. Histories tell us that Alvarado fell from his horse in the Peñol of Nochistlan after bragging that he would take care of the rebels in no time, dismissing them as "cuatro indios gatillos" (four Indian punks).[3]

The glosses on folio 46r also signal a transition to history in translating Mesoamerican dates to their European equivalent. In the absence of this translation, the Mesoamerican past lacks history, not because the Spaniards were intellectually torpid and could not recognize native calendrical dates, but because the invasion of the Americas had as its ultimate objective the introduction, as in *presenting to* and *placing within*, of the peoples there to what they assumed was universal history. This was a process in which indigenous people come to recognize memorializing of the past as history, a process that would presently lead to a comparison of dating systems. The extent to which we believe this effort was successful depends on how much credence we want to give to the incorporation of Mesoamerican life forms to European culture and how much we want to ignore the fact that the background that inscribes these colonial events remains Mesoamerican. After all, it was the erratic glossator who identified the Mesoamerican inscriptions with European dates. I say "erratic" because there are numerous places in the codex in which the glossator scratches out dates and then corrects them. Unless we are willing to assume that Mesoamericans shared a homogenous sense of time with Europeans, we must assume a Mesoamerican sense of time that remains irreducible to European time, if only because Europeans themselves hardly thought of history in terms of a homogenous temporality. Otherwise, how could we explain the project of fulfilling universal history and the sending of apostles to bring all peoples into the fold?

Missionaries and lay officials were more than able to recognize the historical nature, or better the translatability into their own historical format, of precolonial and colonial pictographic depictions of wars that subjected towns as tributaries of the Aztec state, of geographic itineraries that memorialized territorial claims, and of genealogies that recorded the res gestae associated with specific individual rulers. These records have been characterized as histories in the modes of annals, cartography, and genealogy.[4] We may be generous and define these documents as histories, but I wonder the extent to which our charity erases the nature of memorializing the past in Mesoamerica. Are our efforts complicit with the missionaries' and lay officials' translation of the past to homogeneous temporal frames?

Scholars find themselves in a quandary when they face the need to account for the fact that in Mesoamerican pictographic texts the gods have as much as, if not more, agency than humans—an agency that in passing should be noted as not coincident with that of Greco-Abrahamic divine figures intervening in the world's affairs. But there seems to be an erasure, a lack of boundaries between gods and humans in Mesoamerican life forms that led them to be categorized as idolatry in Judeo-Christian discourses; alas, Greek and Roman pantheons did not play a significant role in histories. As the discrete borders between the sacred and the secular, between myth and history, break down, they give rise to flaccid terms like "myth-history" and the uncritical use of the category "mythohistorical." Whether we celebrate the mythical component or dismiss it as fabulous, we readily sort out and disentangle the Real from the Imaginary. The languages we may use to sort out these realms (my capitalization of Real and Imaginary betray my affinities with Lacan's definition of the three orders, the Real, the Imaginary, and the Symbolic as always coexisting in our attempt at making sense of the world) may differ from those practiced by sixteenth-century Spaniards, but the reductionism might be analogous, even if we recognize and praise the fables for their beauty today.[5]

I have made use of a comparative method that necessarily leads to the erasure of historical difference and privileges our "enlightened" view on myth and history. To what extent do we introduce teleology when we posit the resolution of debates in new forms of thinking? Doesn't this imply that we proceed as if ourselves were *without* history, as if we are free from the constraints of the present from which we write? Much has been written deploring the enlightened binary of peoples with history versus peoples without history. Scholars have been mainly concerned with the denial of history as if the practice of history were inherent to what makes us human. Revisionist histories produce narratives that assess the contributions of non-Western peoples to modernity without giving much thought to the paradoxical integration of the onetime nonhistorical peoples into what ends up constituting by definition a universal single history.[6]

Recent calls for recognition of alternative modernities of non–Euro-American societies betray an anxiety over those societies being denied the status of modernity. If this recognition merely underscores the contemporaneity—that is, the coevalness of all societies existing in a given time—its benefits should perhaps be self-evident. However, the anxiety might easily lead (whatever one might consider desirable or undesirable about the nonmodern) to marginalizing indigenous peoples who choose not to incorporate all things modern or feel that accepting the modern need not exclude nonmodern practices and beliefs that modern ideologies systematically stigmatize. Note my use of the term "nonmodern" and not "premodern," as the latter carries a built-in teleology. Also note that the "modern" and the historical scheme into which it fits depend partly on conceptions of the state. After all, the Enlightenment binary opposes peoples *with* state versus peoples *without* state. Again, the benefits of being included in a state are not self-evident.

Retrocedere and the Will to Apostatize

If the term "apostasy" denotes in its Greek form a standing apart, the often preferred Latin term *retrocedere* ("to regress") conveys an unequivocal historical sense. But in medieval Christian texts like Iohannes Wyclif's *Tractatus de apostasia*, the term apostasy itself carries a historical dimension: "Et concordat nomen *apostasie*, que apostatare procurat; quod fit, quandocunque persona a lege domini recedit. Et dicitur secundum grammaticos ab *apos*, quod est *retro*, et, *stolos, missio*; inde apostata, perversus refuga retro missus. Unde Augustinus vocat antichristum refugam" [And the name *apostasy* agrees, so also does *to apostatize*; this is the case whenever a person recedes from the legal domain. And second grammarians say of *apos* (away from), that it is *retro* (backward), and *stolos* (messenger), *missio* (to send); thence apostate, the spiteful recedes backward whence Augustine called the antichrist a throwback].[7] The reference to Augustine and the Antichrist conveys the place of the apostate as Antichrist in the apocalypse (another *apo-* word, now connected to *kalyptein*, "to cover," "conceal," that is to say, the uncovering of the end of the world, the ultimate standing away from, but also fulfillment of history). Wyclif draws from Proverbs VI, 12–14, a semblance of the apostate: "Homo apostata, vir inutilis, graditur ore perverso, annuit oculis, terit pede, digito loquitur; pravo corde machinatur malum et omni tempore iurgia seminat" (readers can refer to Proverbs).[8]

This portrait of the apostate is then fleshed out in chapter 2 of Wyclif's *Tractatus de apostasia*, with a systematic attribution of uselessness, flattery, dissemblance, perversion, corruption, intrigue, and sowing division to the friars. This is ironic given that by the standards of most of the fourteenth-century establishment, Wyclif himself was something of an apostate. Here he further defines the temporal dimension of the apostate as backsliding: "suppono quod apostasia comittitur, quandocunque quis in mortali peccato ceciderit; quia tunc dirumpens religionem domini retrocedit" [I add that those who have committed apostasy, at whatever time, all fell into mortal sins; because just then they break the religious domain, they regress].⁹ In spite of tracing the characteristics of the apostate to the friars, Wyclif does not identify the Antichrist with a Pope or institution. His attack on Church property and critique of sovereignty were taken by the Lollards and the organizers of the Peasant Revolt of 1381.¹⁰ As used by Wyclif and the Lollards, the concept of apostasy would seem to be at once a religious, political, and ideological concept that would relate to the *flight from history* I have been tracing in the indigenous insurgent in the Telleriano-Remensis.

Wyclif at one point expands his critique of earthly *dominium*, comprising both property and sovereignty, to that of temporal lords as well as the Church. *Dominium* belongs to God only. Hence his argument can be understood as communistic or socialistic, as Michael Henry Dziewicki has put it in his introduction to the 1889 edition of *Tractatus de apostasia*: "To the possible objection that his argument goes so far as to prove that even temporal lords ought to have all things in common, he answers boldly: *So they ought* (p. 91). It is clear that he neither overlooked nor shrank from the Socialistic consequences of his doctrine."¹¹ It is not my intent to argue about the "real Wyclif," although one could envisage a genealogy in which he would figure prominently, if Dziewicki's diagnosis proves right. Note that the status of apostate, even of the Antichrist, does not indicate to a deliberate *standing away* on the part of the individual concerned but is imposed on the individual by observers from without. Wyclif, the Lollards, and the insurgents of the 1381 rebellion did not think of themselves as apostates, but rather as legitimately opposing deviations from original Christianity. Returning to the Codex Telleriano-Remensis, we can see that the *tlacuilo* on folio 46r depicts apostasy as a willful and conscious effort to move outside history, to go backward, according to Christian teleology.

History and the Extermination of the Naked

Documents in the archive enable us to identify the figure of the naked rebel, garbed in feathers, as the Caszcan Francisco Tenamaztle. The flowering-cactus glyph behind him locates the events in Nochistlan. His nudity and feathered attire mark his rebellion as nativistic. They mark a return to old ways, to a self-conscious adoption of nakedness, a condition that scandalized the Spaniards in the first place and prompted them to provide the Indians with dress, culture, life forms beyond mere survival, mere animal life. It was then, and perhaps today, incomprehensible for a people to choose nakedness.

Writing on apostates generates the kind of paradoxes that Jacques Derrida outlined in his critique of Foucault's *Madness and Civilization*, in that telling stories of the mad and the apostate (the latter might very well just be a variation of the former if we take Alfonso X's characterization of the heretic as a form of *locura* in the *Siete partidas*) amount to the impossible project of telling the story of silence.[12] The difference, however, is that as Derrida's title for his article on Foucault reveals ("Cogito and the History of Madness"), the constitution of madness during the seventeenth century is inseparable from the formulation of the Cartesian cogito. Foucault's is ultimately an exercise in periodization that is bound to a single history. The story line is as follows: Once upon a time, the mad wandered freely in the medieval cities without restraint, but starting in the seventeenth century they were confined in asylums. We may thus dream of a medieval time, a premodern epoch, free of the impositions of the state and capital. Robert I. Moore has insisted, in *The Formation of a Persecuting Society*, that persecutory practices in the West should be dated much earlier, between 950 and 1250.

In either case the historical break is internal to the society in question—that is to say, the society of Western Europe. In colonial situations the figure of the apostate appears in the course of a process of incorporation into (Western, universal) history, rather than one in which certain individuals, already members of Western society whose behavior had not before then been stigmatized, were persecuted and confined. The colonial apostate operates within the topology identified earlier in which baptism by the apostle incorporates the Indian subject into the Church and yet retains traces of the old subjectivity in a palimpsest implicit in the superimposition of the name Francisco to Tenamaztle, while the insurrection by the apostate severs ties with the theologico-political order and yet retains the traces of his previous conversion in the circumscribed naked body. This topology may be likened to a glove that as it is turned inside out restructures containment in its inversion. The neophyte and the apostate are separated by waters that discursively seek to encircle them in terms of the friar who baptizes him and Viceroy Mendoza who demands the recognition of Spanish sovereignty.

In this regard the apostle and the apostate are bound to each other. The imagination of missionaries represents the indigenous apostate engaged in the profanation of cadavers and antiliturgical practices:

> los nuestros en las dichas peleas se acouardan y desmayan con la memoria que jamás perdonaron la vida a nadie los dichos tyranos, desolleandolos biuos y asserrándoles las cabeças por medio del celebro, para celebrar sus areitos y mitottes y para tenerlas por tropheo y blazon de triumpho y Victoria alcançada, y les sacan los nervios de las piernas y braços para cuerdas de sus arcos y para ligaturas de sus flechas y saetas, haziendo otras tiranías y crueldades de bestias fieras, profanando los templos, y maltratando las sagradas ymágenes, vsando las sagradas y benditas vestiduras, matando los sacerdotes, aun en el mismo punto que estavan para dezir missa, y mucho dellos apostatando de nuestra religion,

que con ningún género de castigo se pueden restaurar ni recompensar, aunque sea con perpetua esclauonía.

[Ours in those battles would remember and dismay when recollecting that the said tyrant would never forgive nobody's life but would skin them alive and would cut their heads in the middle of their skull, to celebrate their dances and rituals and to have them as trophies and coats of arms of their achieved victories. And they would extract nerves from legs and arms to use as strings of arches and to tie arrows and darts. They would do other tyrannies and cruelties proper of savage beasts, profaning temples and destroying sacred images, killing priests, even at the moment in which they would celebrate mass. Many of them would apostasize from our religion. These are damages that no punishment can restore nor restitute, even with eternal slavery.][13]

The passage assimilates acts of war and rituals that arguably could be mere continuations of old, with the profaning of churches and images and liturgical garments (such as folio 46r depicted as used in the act of baptism), which are obviously new. The rebel on top of the *peñol* would convey the return to nativistic practices that would now include the profaning of Christian rites.

Let me cite one long passage from the *Cronica miscelanea de la Sancta Provincia de Xalisco* (1653) by the seventeenth-century Franciscan friar Antonio Tello. This passage further documents how the Spaniards conceived the nativistic nature of the insurrection:

De aquí tomo el motivo de alzarse toda la sierra hasta Culiacán y hasta Guadalajara, que fue cosa de espanto por un abuso que tomaron de un bayle de un pueblo que se llama Tlaxicoringa, en el cual bayle ponían un calabazo y baylaban al rededor y el calabazo entre ellos, y viniendo un viento recio se llevó el calabazo por los ayres, y unas viejas hechizeras le dixeron que se alzassen, porque así como el viento había levantado aquel calabazo, con el mesmo impetus echarían de la tierra a los españoles, y que no dudasen de ello. Porque sería cierto y entrasen en batalla con los españoles, que estando en ella, vendría un viento y los llevaría de la tierra con gran polvareda, y que no había de quedar español a vida, y esto [lo] celebraban con grandes bayles.

[This was the motif that led to the uprising of the whole sierra from Culiacan to Guadalajara, which was terrifying because of the use of a dance from a town called Tlaxicoringa, in which they would place a gourd and would dance around it and the gourd among them. A powerful wind raised the gourd in the air, and some old witches told them to take arms, because just as the wind raised the gourd, by the same impetus they would throw the Spaniards out of the land; she told them that they shouldn't doubt this. Because it was true and they should battle against Spaniards, and once in it, a wind would come and take them from the earth in a cloud of dust, and that not a single Spaniard would remain alive, and this they celebrated with great dances.][14]

In his *Historia de la Nueva Galicia* (ca. 1650), Tello describes the rebels at Nochistlan as "embijados y desnudos, que parecían al diablo, de quien traían la guisa y forma, tanto que ponian espanto" [painted in red and naked, resembling the devil of whom they had appearance and the form, so much that they caused fear].[15] Tello identifies the rebel depicted in folio 46r as Tenamaztle, but only to celebrate the defeat of his forces and the successful reduction of the Cazcanes—and other Indian nations generically referred to as Chichimecs—into settlements modeled on Spanish towns. In folio 46r we find Viceroy Mendoza just on the other side of a river that symbolically, perhaps materially as well, separated the world of the Cazcan rebels from the Spaniards. Tello represents this scene in no less vivid terms:

> Yendo caminando D. Antonio de Mendoza con su campo, llegó á vista del peñol de Nochistlan por la parte mas fuerte de peña tajada altísima, y se asomaron en lo alto los empeñolados, los cuales parecían adornados con tantas plumas de diferentes colores, que parecía un florido campo de flores, y comenzaron los enemigos á hacer grande algaraza dando grandes voces y gritería, y a arrojar muchas flechas, tocando muchas bocinas y atabales que retumbaba por aquellos collados y valles que causaba espanto y grima, y que se juntaba el cielo con la tierra; y esto sería como á las tres de la tarde, y nuestros amigos mexicanos hicieron lo propio.

> [As d. Antonio de Mendoza was walking with his army, the *peñol* of Nochistlan appeared; on the side of the sharp crag, on top of it, appeared many armed Indians, wearing so many feathers of different colors that it seemed to be a flowery field. And they started to make great noise with great voices and cries, and to throw arrows, playing horns and drums that would resonate all over the hills and valleys, causing fright and uneasiness; it seemed like the sky and the earth would come together; and this ocurred around three in the afternoon, and our Mexican friends did alike.][16]

Tenamaztle, said to have been baptized with the name Diego, figures as a Zacatec who rejected Mendoza's summon to surrender in peace. Later Tello speaks of a Don Francisco, a Cazcan, who surrendered in tears to his *encomendero* Miguel Ibarra. Tello sets an opposition between the willingness to surrender of the sedentary Cazcanes and the indomitable spirit of the nomadic Zacatecs.

In tracing these differences we have to keep an eye for a tendency to create a generic Chichimec of the northern frontier. We have to be alert to such distinctions in interpreting documents that argue that the rebellion was justified because the Spaniards first attacked and enslaved indigenous tribes from the north. Are they speaking of sedentary populations or of all the so-called Chichimecs, regardless of whether they are nomads or settled peoples? One also wonders whether the "Diego" is a mistake or whether Francisco is a different leader. Or is Tello presenting Francisco Tenamaztle as showing signs of docility, a willingness to surrender to the Spaniards? After all, he did surrender to the bishop of Jalisco in 1551. In this slippery naming, one wonders if Tenamaztle's story could ever be told without circumscribing him in the language of law. Tello goes on to explain how Mendoza read the Requerimiento again, "otras dos veces" [two more times], to no avail. The viceroy insists that the Zacatecs would be forgiven if they surrender, otherwise he would exterminate them: "que los acabaria y mataria á sangre y fuego." They laughed at the threat: "y de oir esto se rieron."[17]

The Requerimiento had been systematically read to Indians since Pedrarias Davila first implemented it in the Darien in 1514. This legal instrument establishes the historical necessity of accepting Spanish sovereignty by informing Indians that God created the world, that all men were descendants of Adam and Eve, that God had chosen Saint Peter to represent him on earth and rule over all men, and finally that Saint Peter's authority had been passed down a line of popes until a recent one who granted the kings of Spain sovereignty over their lands. The Requerimiento goes on to give Indians the choice of recognizing the Spanish Crown as their legitimate ruler or facing war and slavery. Technically, the Cazcanes had already accepted Spanish sovereignty and been baptized, and in rebelling defined themselves as apostates. Mendoza's language of love pleads for their submission, using the formulaic "tres veces" [three times]: "envió a requerir con la paz, diciendo que bajasen, que él los perdonaba; a que respondieron no querían paz, que el y los españoles eran unos bellacos, que se fuesen, y dijeron otros desacatos: con todo eso mandó requerir con la paz tres veces, y viendo no querían mandó a los soldados que les acometiesen" [he sent to require them with the offer of peace, telling them to descend, that he was forgiving them; to this they responded that they did not want peace, that he and the Spaniards were despicable, that they should leave, and said other disrespectful things: even considering all this he ordered that they should be required with peace three times, and upon seeing that they refused, he sent the soldiers to attack them].[18]

Mendoza's artillery caused extensive damage, and Tello tells the anecdote of a young Juan del Camino who, while feeding water to his horse, saw "un hombre en un caballo blanco con una banderilla en la mano y cruz roja, el cual dijo: 'Por ahí es la entrada, soldados'" [saw a man on a white horse with a flag in his hand and a red cross, who said: "the entrance is there"].[19] The apostle Santiago riding on his white horse points the way to assault the Cazcan stronghold and participates in the battle against the apostates. The next chapter tells of how more than five thousand Cazcanes, "chicos y grandes" [children and adults] were enslaved.[20] The language of pacification now dominates, describing one Indian leader after another surrendering to the Spanish forces.

Tello's history speaks of a near collapse of the city of Guadalajara, perhaps exaggerating how close the rebellion was to driving the Spaniards out of New Spain. Guadalajara must have consisted of a few houses and was actually at a different location from the current site. The story of how Guadalajara was safeguarded has comic moments as well as gory details. It tells of a woman who, on hearing *indios ladinos,* tells women to stop crying since they were not going to harm them but only kill "á esos barbudos de vuestros maridos y nos casaremos con vosotras" [those bearded husbands of yours and we will marry you] and responded by lifting her skirt and flashing her ass out the window and asking them to kiss it: "de pura rabia volvio la trasera y aún las faldas, diciendo, 'Perros besadme aqui, que no os vereis en ese espejo, sino en este'" [out of pure rage she turned her behind and even the skirt, saying, "Dogs kiss me here, that you will not see yourselves in that mirror but in this one"].[21]

The term *indios ladinos* marks a commonplace in the documents that underscores the danger from apostates who not only regress in history but also carry back knowledge that enables them to challenge Spanish authorities both materially and ideologically. They stand for no mere return to an anterior state but a refusal of the historical incorporation to the Church and the Crown. They feel free to carry back a material and ideological savoir faire. In the already cited opinion, the doctor Ortiz de Hinojosa speaks of the *ladinos* as *españolados* who after having been temporally enslaved, "se bueluen a su rrancherías y se hazen caudillos y capitanes de otros" [return to the ranches and turn into caudillos and captains of others].[22] The nature of the *indio ladino* is perhaps nowhere better represented than in the "Relación del doctor Hernando de Robles sobre la Guerra de los chichimecas," before the Concilio Tercero Provincial Mexicano (1585): "Y han prevalecido de manera que andan ya armados a cauallo y traen consigo mestizos y mulatos que los acudillan y persuaden a los naturales que se alçacen con ellos" [And they have prevailed, so they are already armed with horses and have among them mestizos and mulattoes that they lead and they persuade the natives to take arms with them].[23]

Further down, Hernando de Robles underscores that subjecting Chichimecs to temporal servitude "no solo no es castigo y escarmiento, pero maior inconveniente porque se vienen a huir después que cumplen el servicio y se vuelven entre los suyos y les sirven de espías y guías ciertas para hazer sus saltos y daños en los nuestros, y los capitanean como diestros y sabidores de la tierra, y con esto se hazen más poderosos" [not only it is not a punishment and a lesson, but an even greater inconvenience because later on they flee once they have paid the service and return among their own; serve them as true spies and guides for carrying forth their asaults and damages of our own; and lead them in their skill and knowledge of the land, thereby becoming more powerful]. Hernado de Robles goes on to express a limit case that finds no other resolution to the conflict than war of extermination and slavery of all survivors: "Y se rresuelven todos que no abrá rremedio en tan desordenada barbarie si no es mandándoles hazer Guerra a fuego y sangre y dando facultad a los que los siguieren y uvieren a las manos viuos que los tengan por esclavos perpectuos" [And all agree that there will not be remedy to this disordered barbarism other than ordering them to make war of extermination and granting the license to those who followed this order and held living survivors to hold in perpetual slavery].[24]

During the Concilio of 1585, missionaries from the different orders recommended that before conducting a war of extermination, the viceroy should try to create Indian and Spanish settlements that might induce them to adopt Spanish forms of life: "aunque la experiencia enseña . . . que los medios puestos hasta agora no an bastado . . . ay otros que no se han puesto antes de llegar al último de hazer la Guerra a fuego y sangre y lo demas que se propone, y uno de ellos es hazer algunas poblazones de españoles y naturales . . . entrarán algunos religiosos y los irán trayendo de paz y estorbando los robos que hazen, con su doctrina" [although experience teaches . . . that the means used until now have not sufficed . . . there are other means that have not been implemented before arriving at the point of making war of extermination and the rest of the recommendations, and one of them is to create Spanish and Indian settlements. . . . Some missionaries will enter and will incorporate them peacefully and obstruct the stealing they do with their doctrine].[25] Regardless of the recommendation to try settlement before returning to the war of extermination, the council faced the task of knowing whether the Chichimecs were justified in making war against the Crown on the basis that Spaniards first injured them by taking over their land. It is not clear whether the attacks referred to came from settled tribes or from Chichimecs in general. There is a sense that the nomadic Chichimecs could not have incurred any great loss.

In one of his responses to whether it is just to exterminate the Chichimecs, Ortiz de Hinojosa states: "Y primero a la primera parte, quod hujusmodi chichimecae non laborant neque nent [sic] sed uiuunt de uenatione y de his quae nascuntur ultro, nudi incedentes montiagui, y no tienen cierta habitación, luego tampoco se les hizo injuria en tomarles las dichas tierras desiertas y habitatarlas, y dado que fueran suyas, por las injuries hechas y daños causados, se las pudieran tomar jure belli" [And first the first part, quod hujusmodi chichimecae non laborant neque nent [sic] sed uiuunt de uenatione y de his quae nascuntur ultro, nudi incedentes montiagui, and they have no certain settlements, then no damage was caused to them in taking the said deserted lands and inhabiting them, and if they were theirs, because of the damages they have caused, we could take them by *jure belli*].[26] The Latin provides fodder for arguing the legitimacy of Spanish possession: the Chichimecs do not cultivate the land, do not constitute a nation, and go about naked, Indians have no justification for making war against New Spain, and the Crown for the damages were by private individuals.

Ortiz de Hinojosa, like all those who participated in the Concilio, never questions the justness of a war of extermination. At issue is merely whether one may be waged against the Chichimecs. In the end he explains that the legality of wars of extermination depends on the nature of the Chichimecs—that is, on whether their barbarity could be redeemed: "Y creo que el rremedio que ay para entender el origen de este negocio, es saber si esta gente es de su naturaleza feroz y atrevida y que siempre en todo tiempo lo a sido" [And I believe that the remedy for understanding the origin of this business is to know if they are by nature ferocious and fearless, and that they have always been so].[27] If they are by nature ferocious and fearless (*atrevida*), the final solution would apply. We may wonder if Spanish missionaries and secular authorities could ever colonize the indigenous *habitus* or *background* to the extent that the Chichimecs would be fully incorporated into the universal history of the Church and the Spanish state.[28]

For Tello the extreme danger of apostasy, of contaminating other Indians with the spirit of rebellion, justifies extermination campaigns "a sangre y fuego," and the necessity to create horror stories to keep other Indians from following their course, "con que hasta el dia de hoy no se han atrevido á alzar."[29] Tello describes the customary practices of mutilating, torturing, and murdering the rebels: "Cortaron a unos las narices, á otros las orejas, y manos, y un pie, y luego les curban con aceite hirviendo las heridas; ahorcaron é hicieron esclavos á otros, y á los que salieron ciegos y mancos de haber visto la santa vision de Santiago, muy hostigados enviaron a sus tierras; y fue tal castigo, que hasta el dia de hoy jamas volvieron á al ciudad" [They cut the noses of some, the ears of others, and the hands and one foot, and afterwards they poured burning oil on their wounds. And those who came out one-handed and blind from seeing the holy vision of Saint James, very much harassed, they were sent back to their lands and the punishment was such that up to our day they have not returned to the city].[30] Tello further documents in no less vivid terms, in a celebratory tone, the atrocities related in Bartolomé de Las Casas's *Brevísima relación de la destrucción de Indias* (1552). For those thinking about the wars against the Chichimecs, the question of extermination and perpetual slavery amounts to an issue of acting in good faith.

Writing more than a hundred years after the events in the province of Jalisco, Tello quite laconically assesses the population of Cuina in a parenthetical remark: "(quando esto se escribe, que es el año de mill syscientos cinqüenta y dos, no hay ocho yndios en Cuyna)" [(at the time of writing this, which is the year six hundred fifty two, there are no more than eight Indians in Cuyna)].[31]

A few pages later he adds another parenthesis: "Los de Xalpa . . . eran más de dos mill indios (hoy no hay cinqüenta)" [Those from Xalpa . . . were more than two thousand Indians (today there are not even fifty)].[32] The assessment of the death toll after the battle at the Mixton speaks for itself:

Murieron en lo alto más de diez mill indios y se despeñaron casi otros tantos, entre chicos y grandes y mujeres, y cautivarón más de tres mill y se pusieron a la huida más de diez mil, y estos fueron los que habitaban por aquellas barrancas, que habían ido más a robar que á pelear, si acaso alcanzasen victoria contra los españoles.

[More than ten thousand died on the highest part and almost as many threw themselves from the cliffs; between children and adults and women more than three thousand were enslaved; more than ten thousand fled; and these were those who dwelled in these ravines, who had gone to steal rather than fight, if they would have defeated the Spaniards.][33]

Tello adds that the allies from central Mexico finished killing those who wailed wounded, and blood flowed down the *peñol*: "otro día de mañana fueron los yndios mexicanos y tlaxcaltecas, y los acabaron; quedaron aquellas peñas y riscos corriendo sangre."[34] Among those who took flight and continued to battle the rebellion was Tenamaztle, who did not surrender until 1551. The voices of those exterminated would never be heard again. As far as I know, there are no descendants of the Cazcanes today in the state of Zacatecas.

Indian Conquistadores

This war against settled and nomadic peoples in the northern frontier is a limit case in a story that cannot be generalized to all Indians in New Spain. The history of rebellion as willful apostasy is a history of silence that might be interrupted here and there by Indians negotiating a return to the fold of the Crown's dominions, hence telling an intelligible story. For the most part Indians in sixteenth-century Mexico are on record as negotiating a place under the colonial authorities, in both native and Spanish colonial structures of power, I might add.

As an example of negotiating power, we may cite the account by Don Francisco de Sandoval Acazitli—a cacique from the town of Tlalmanalco, Chalco, in the basin of what is today Mexico City—that records his deeds in the suppression of the rebellion of 1541 depicted in folio 46r. The account was originally written in Nahuatl, although the Nahuatl text is now lost, by Gabriel de Castañeda, a principal from the *barrio* of Colomocho. Acazitli presents himself as a faithful partner of Viceroy Mendoza and requests compensation for his collaboration. Toward the end of the account he cites Mendoza: "Yo os estimo y quiero mucho, por cuanto ha sido aqui el fin de la batalla, y todo lo que quisieredes yo os lo he de conceder, y de honrar y favorecer mucho á este pueblo; y así, Sr. D. Francisco, habeis de ser gobernador, y el alguacil, corregidor" [I esteem and love you very much, for what has been here the end of the battle and I will grant you everything you request; and thus, Mr. D. Francisco, you will be governor, and the constable, corregidor].[35] The term "collaboration" should not be charged with moral judgment but merely understood to mean a joint effort. There were no compelling reasons for Acazitli to side with the Cazcan and Zacatec insurgents other than an anachronistic (or colonialist) reduction of all indigenous peoples to the category of Indian.

Acazitli underscores the language of love that we found in Tello's account of how the rebels were summoned in peace. He cites a priest's calling the Chichimecs into submission: "Venid aca, hijos: ¿es possible que no teneis lástima de vosotros miserables, pues sabeis que os queremos mucho, y lo mismo el sennor virrey os quiere mucho? Venid acá á verle" [Come hither my children: is it possible that you do not pity your miserable selves, because you know how much we love you, and so does the señor viceroy love you].[36] Acazitli informs us that the native participants in the effort to suppress the rebellion were responsible for carrying the artillery. He also offers graphic details of its power to dismember: "les tiraron una pieza grande de artillería, que de ellos murieron llevándoles la cabezas, y á otros por mitad del cuerpo, y á otros el un brazo con la cabeza, haciendose pedazos sus cuerpos, que parecía un remolino, y fueron a caer sus manos y sus carnes sobre la gente, y de ello sobre los árboles" [they shot a large piece of artillery that killed some by blowing their heads off, and others half of their body, and others an arm with the head, breaking them into pieces, that like a whirlwind, their hands and flesh ended up falling on top of the people, and some on the trees].[37]

Acazitli vividly represents his participation in the enslavements of the rebels: "y luego comenzaron a envestir los chichimecas, y á ellos el Sr. D. Francisco con su divisa de quetzalpatzactli de plumería verde, con que les ganaron la cerca, y se la rompieron y quemaron sus jacales, y comenzaron á embatir con ellos . . . ; y subió arriba con el estandarte real, con que fueron vencido y se gano el pueblo, y comenzaron á cautivarlos . . . ; y aquí fué donde tuvieron mucho cautivos todos los de las provincias" [and then the Chichimecs started to attack, and among them Sr. d. Francisco who was wearing his *quetzalpatzactli* ensign made of green feathers. They won the barrier and destroyed it and burned their huts and began to fight against them . . . ; and he went up with the royal banner, with which they were defeated and the town was won, and they began to enslave them . . .; and here is where they gained many slaves those from the provinces].[38] Before the battle he describes the formation of the native contingents from central Mexico, of those from the provinces mentioned in the passage: "Y el orden que se tuvo para la batalla fué que se puso en medio la artillerya, y en una banda iban los tlaxcaltecas, huexotzincas, quauhquechultecas, y luego se seguían los mexicanos y xilotepecas, y luego los aculhuas, y en otro lado los de Michoacan, mextitlan, y los chalcas" [the order followed for the battle was that the artillery was placed in the middle, and on one side went the Tlaxcalteca, Huexozinca, Quauhquechulteca, and then followed Mexicans and Xilotepeca, and then the Aculhua, and on the other side those from Michoacan, Mextitlan, and the Chalca].[39]

Acazitli is obviously particularly proud of his fellow Chalcas, and provides a self-portrait that gives us a feeling of life in the Indian camps: "el día de la festividad de la natividad de nuestro Señor Jesucristo tuvieron danza los de Amaquemecan; y al tercer día de pascua, que fue martes, día de S. Juan, danzó el Sr. D. Francisco, y se cantó en él el canto chichimeca: hubo flores y pebetes, comida y bebida de cacao que dió a los señores; y todas las naciones de diversas provincias danzaron puestas sus armas, sus rodelas y macanas; todos bailaron, sin de que parte ninguna quedase por bailar" [on the feast of the nativity of our Lord Jesus Christ the Amecamecans danced. Sr. D. Francisco danced, and there was singing in it of the Chichimec song; there were flowers and incense, food and cacao drink that was given to the lords; and all the nations danced wearing their arms, their shields and macanas; all danced and not one single part kept from dancing].[40]

From another Nahuatl document, known as *Memorial de los indios de nombre de dios, Durango, acerca de sus servicios al rey, c. 1563*, we learn that Indians originally from central Mexico were forced to participate in the wars against the Chichimecs: "When the Zacatecs rebelled, then the Alcalde mayor called the Mexicans and said, 'Come now, Mexicans, help the King; put down the Chichimecs everywhere.' And then he said, 'If you do not wish to go, I shall fine you forty pesos that you will have to pay because you are the King's subjects.' And then the Mexicans assembled and consulted among themselves and said, 'Let us do and obey the will of God and the King.'"[41] This lukewarm acceptance to participate in the war contrasts with the opening description of the garb worn by a proud Acazitli:

> Don Francisco Acazitli llevó por divisas y armas cuando fué á la guerra de los chichimecas, una calavera de plumería con sus penachos verdes, una rodela de lo mismo, y en ella un bezote de oro retorcido, con su espada y su ichcahuipil, y vestido con un jubon Colorado, y sus zaragüelles, zapatos y borceguíes, y un sombrero blanco, y un pañuelo grande con que se amarraba la cabeza, y un collar de pedrería con dos cadenas.
>
> [When Don Francisco Acazitli went to the war against the Chichimecs, he carried for insignia and heraldic devices a feathered skull with its green crest, a

shield made of the same, and on it a twisted golden ring, with his sword and his *ichcahuipil* [a native defensive armor made of cotton], and wore a red doublet, and his breeches, shoes and buskins, a white hat, and a large handkerchief wrapped around his head, and a necklace of stones with two chains.][42]

Painting the Conquered Conquistadores

We also have two indigenous pictorial sources that further document the participations of indigenous groups from central Mexico in the suppression of Tenamaztle's forces and the long war against the Chichimecs. In the Codex Tlatelolco we find the portraits of two indigenous leaders on their way from central Mexico to Nochistlan (figure 10.1). I am here reproducing the first of six panels that corresponds to the years 1541 through 1554; the line after the series of eight Spanish missionaries and lay officials marks the beginning of a new panel that represents events pertaining to 1556 through 1557. (If I limit myself to the Western dates, it is because the temporal frame of the Codex Tlate-

lolco seems to be exclusively intended for the Spanish addressee.) R. H. Barlow has praised the realism of the portraits as approximating bas relief.[43] We may even wonder if the painter sought to reproduce the semblance of D. Martín Quauhtzin of Tlatelolco, who leads, followed by D. Diego de Teuetzquiti of Tenochtitlan, and that of D. Diego de Mendoza Huitznahuatlailotlac Imauyantzin, who was the cacique of Tlatelolco in 1554 and is depicted presenting a narrative of the deeds of D. Martín Quauhtzin and D. Diego de Teuetzquiti to a group of Spaniards, apparently led by the Viceroy D. Luis de Velasco.[44]

The panel combines Western realist conventions of portraiture with pictographic writings that name the participants and locations, signal discourse, and date the events. The artist throughout the panels displays a mastery of Western pictorial techniques and a desire to depict individual facial features, even if using conventional postures, dress, and signs of authority. Whereas writing records the voices of the ancestors, portraiture captures the resemblance for future generations. These mimetic technologies and their capac-

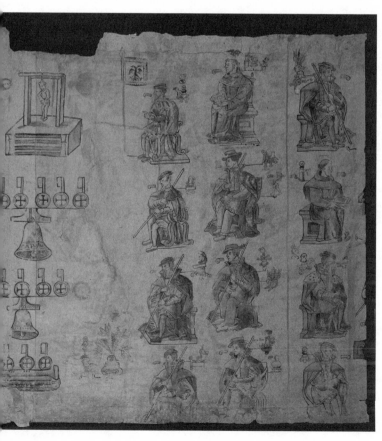

FIGURE 10.1. Codex of Tlatelolco. Courtesy of the Biblioteca del Instituto Nacional de Antropología e Historia.

ity to invoke ghostly apparitions could not but have fascinated indigenous people who learned to use the alphabet and European pictorial conventions early on in the colonization of Mesoamerica, most often by deploying these technologies for ends not contemplated by the supervising missionaries and bureaucrats.

In the case of the two Indian leaders, the artist took care to depict the differences in the dress they wore on their way to Nochistlan. The combination of indigenous and Spanish clothes bears a striking similarity to the costume Acazitli wore. It is not a coincidence that in both Acazitli's account and the depiction in the Codex Tlatelolco there is an attention to detail that traces the material of the clothing. In the case of the cacique from Tlatelolco, he wears a jaguar-skin *jubon* (doublet) made as *ichcahuipil* (an indigenous padded coat), white breeches, socks in his *cactli* (sandals), and he bears a European-style sword but an indigenous shield; on his head rests a *xihutzolli* (diadem) and a *tlalpiloni*, a quetzal feather attire, and his lower lip carries a *tentle* (an insertion made of bone). The cacique from Tenochtitlan also wears a hybrid dress, although less elaborate.

The prominence of the native figures is less pronounced in the other panels. Observe the size of the Indians with respect to the Spaniards riding below them. Also note the glyph for Nochistlan and the depiction of a corpse that indicates military victory. Tenamaztle does not figure as an individual. This memorializing enables the Tlatelolca governor, sitting on a Spanish chair resting on top of the glyph of Tlatelolco, to request privileges within the colonial order. The box decorated with quetzal feathers contains an image of the host that leaves no doubt as to the inscription of the events within Christian universal history. Here we find a clear instance of the ever-present negotiations of power by Indian subjects. Thus the Codex Tlatelolco testifies to the ability to articulate a position of privilege within the colonial order and provides a history from within the parameters of the state. The defeated Chichimecs have no place in this narrative.

The second pictorial document is a mural in the Augustinian church in Ixmiquilpan, Hidalgo (figure 10.2), a town bordering Chichimec territories. Here we find Christianized Indians battling and defeating pagan Indians. At first it might seem liberating to see that the walls of a Catholic church had been given to Indian painters to depict themselves; however, the strangeness of such a concession soon dissipates when we realize that it provides a mirror in which the indigenous community of Ixmiquilpan can imagine themselves as a Christian community of warriors making war against Chichimecs who have either refused incorporation into the Church or have apostatized.[45] As we perceive the citation of Ovid's *Metamorphosis* in the depiction of Medusa on the bottom left, our Christian warrior emerges as another Perseus. The bare,

FIGURE 10.2. Mural at Ixmiquilpan, Hidalgo. Courtesy of Marco Antonio Pacheco.

luscious buttocks of the Chichimec warrior suggest an unbounded sexuality that Church officials would reduce to an ordered family structure by means of the sacrament of marriage.

Saved by Human Rights

The last document I would like to analyze corresponds to the case the Cazcan Francisco Tenamaztle presented to the Council of the Indies with the aid of the Dominican friar Bartolomé de Las Casas. The dossier collected by Miguel León Portilla includes two letters in which Tenamaztle denounces the atrocities committed against his people and explains that he had been arrested and exiled to Spain by Viceroy Luis de Velasco after he surrendered to the bishop of Guadalajara, who died shortly after.[46] Through the mediation (and translation) of Las Casas, Tenamaztle narrates the crimes committed against his person and peoples, and requests the restitution of his sovereignty. The documents are prepared in the language of law expected by the Council of the Indies. The legal discourse that structures these documents makes it practically impossible to identify a voice that would correspond to Tenamaztle's. Even if these documents present his case, Tenamaztle disappears, leaving no paper trace of what happened to him after presenting his case to the Council of the Indies in Valladolid in 1556.

Even if Tenamaztle's dossier articulates a position from within Spanish law, he (in collaboration with Las Casas) develops a language that questions the semantics of conquest. Thus Tenamaztle writes: "Este huir, y esta natural defensa, muy poderosos señores, llaman y han llamado siempre los españoles, usando mal de la propiedad de los vocablos, en todas las Indias, contra el Rey levantarse" [This taking flight, and this natural defense, most powerful lords, is called and has always been called by the Spaniards, making bad use of the propreity of words, in all of the Indies, to arise against the King].[47] Tenamaztle makes this statement right after giving an account of the oppression of Nuño de Guzmán, Juan de Oñate, and Miguel Ibarra. These Spaniards had subjected the Cazcanes to torture, persecution, murder, rape, and hanging of their leaders, atrocities that forced them to flee to the sierras of Xuchipila and make strongholds in the *peñoles* (the crags) of Nochistlan and El Mizton. Tenamaztle underscores that these abuses countered all principles of natural law and the law of nations (*ius gentium*): "El principio y medio de estos daños y agravios recibidos fue un Nuño de Guzmán que primero vino a mis tierras, siendo yo señor dellas, no recognociendo a otro señor en mundo alguno por superior, como hoste público de mi señorío y república, violento opresor mío y de mis súbditos contra derecho natural y de las gentes" [The beginning and middle of all these received damages and offenses was the so-called Nuño de Guzmán, who first came to this lands, while I was lord over them, not recognizing any other lord as superior, as public enemy of my dominion and republic, violent oppressor of me and of my subjects against natural law and law of peoples].[48]

Tenamaztle goes on to underscore that they were living in peace and were attacked as if they were enemies of the Spanish people or king, or as if they had offended the Church, *la universal iglesia*. Abuses, Tenamaztle argues, that entitle him to "justamente [impugnar] a mano armada y resistille" [justly (challenge) with arms and resist him].[49] Given that fleeing and resisting was a question of survival, Tenamaztle puts the king in a situation in which he would have to examine his conscience: "Juzgue vuestra Alteza, como espero que juzgará justa y cathólicamente, como jueces rectíssimos, quién de las naciones aunque carezcan de Fe de Christo, ni de otra ley divina ni humana, sino entendida por sola razón natural y qué especie de bestias hobiera entre las creaturas irracionales a quien no fuera lícito y justíssimo el tal huir, y la tal defensa, y el levantamiento como ellos lo quieren llamar" [May your Highness pass judgment, since I expect that you will judge justly and in a Catholic manner, in the manner of most just judges, of nations even if lacking the Faith of Christ, nor of any other human or divine law, but by means of natural reason alone and what species of beast among irrational creatures, to whom it would not be licit and just to flee, and such a defense, and the uprising as they like to call it].[50] This statement reflects not only Las Casas's thought but also anticipates the arguments that members of the religious orders, most emphatically the Dominicans, will make during the Concilio Tercero.

Tenamaztle's discourse builds a position from within the Spanish legal codes that avoids being characterized as apostate. Tenamaztle emerges as a peaceful leader of a people whose sovereignty has been usurped. He thus reproduces the figure of the noble savage that Las Casas deploys in his pamphlet *Brevísima relación de la destrucción de las Indias* and his anthropological tract *Apologética historia sumaria*. Tenamaztle naturally appropriates all the ideals of Christian civilization and elaborates a form of utopian discourse that makes manifest the semantic matrix that constitutes the binary civilization versus barbarism.[51] Insofar as it includes both components—the civilized (noble) and the barbarian (savage) in a paradoxical concept—the figure of the noble savage embodies and provides the grounds for discarding the binary.

Tenamaztle's letter manifests a sophisticated understanding of law that would not have been expected from an Indian most commonly represented in contemporary documents as naked and immersed in savagery. Consider his reasoning on the question of reparations for damages and the restitution of sovereignty. Tenamaztle first expresses the impossibility of reparations: "si hago o los acuso civilmente a que me paguen y satisfagan los dichos males y daños, no bastarán ellos ni todos sus linajes, aunque tuviesen grandes rentas y grandes estados, a los satisfacer a mí y a los otros caciques y señores y a todo aquel reino y veczinos dél que son los damnificados y agraviados" [if I put forth or make a civil case so that they pay me and repair the wrongs and damages, not them nor their descendants, even if they had great rents and great estates, there would not be enough to satisfy me and the other caciques and lords and that whole kingdom and neighbors that have been damaged and wronged].[52]

If the damages have been so extensive and atrocious that reparations prove impossible, Tenamaztle moves on to request the restitution of freedom and sovereignty: "Vuestra alteza tenga por bien de mandar poner en libertad los vecinos y moradores de Nuchistlán y Xuchipilla y sus subjetos, mandando que yo sea restituido en el señorío dellos, como cosa propia mía y que me dejaron mis padres del qual e sido despojado" [Your highness must have a good reason to free all the inhabitants and dwellers of Nuchiztlán and Xuchipilla and their subjects mandating that I am restituted to their sovereignty, as if it were a thing of my own and that my parents left to me and from which I have been robbed].[53] In exchange, Tenamaztle commits himself to bring *naciones que están bravas* into the fold and service of the Crown. He commits to conduct this service by peaceful means only, *sin lanzas ni espadas*, on the condition that they will never be removed from the protection of the Crown nor given in *encomienda*: "jamás seran de ella sacados, ni encomendados a españoles ni particulares, ni dados en feudo, ni por otra vía alguna que pueda ser pensada."[54]

The consideration that he would attract the rebels by peaceful means only resonates with one of Las Casas's major tracts, *De unico vocationis modo omnium gentium ad veram religionem*, although we should also consider that after the *Nuevas Leyes* of 1542, the Crown stipulates that only love and peaceful means should be used in the pacification of Indians. *Pacificación* replaces *conquista* in this legal tract that responded to Las Casas's denunciations and exposure of the illegality of the slavery and the *encomiendas*. Here we find Las Casas, through the voice of Tenamaztle, articulating a limit case for Spain's claims to dominion. Obviously no form of slavery would be justified, nor war for that matter, but neither would there be *encomiendas*, nor fiefs, nor any form of subordination to Spaniards. Other conditions include: "Y que los caciques y señores queden y sean en sus estados y señoríos sustentados y confirmados, y sucedan en ellos sus herederos conformemente a sus leyes y costumbres Justas que tuvieren, recognosciendo siempre por supremos y soberanos señores y reyes a los reyes Castilla universales" [And that the caciques and lords be sustained and confirmed in their estates and dominions, and be succeeded by their inheritors according to their Just laws and customs always recognizing as supreme and sovereign lords and kings the universal lords and kings of Castile]. This proposal entails the existence of autonomous states within the Crown. He adds that in recognition of this universal rule, they will give "cierto tributo ellos y los que les sucedieren en los dichos estados" [a certain tribute, they and those who succeed them in the aforementioned estates].[55]

The Archival Fog

I would like to characterize this sequence of documents, of memories, of memory-traces, if you will, as a cloud, as a fog that covers the real—that is, the experience of Tenamaztle and, beyond the individuation of the Cazcan leader's struggle, of the multitude of Indian rebels, of apostates, that resisted then and continue to resist today the European invasion of their territories. Even the statement I have just made attributing territorial claims would be lost in a fog of legal tracts on just wars. Observe how a statue of Tenamaztle monumentalizes his memory in the town of Nochistlan today (figure 10.3). When I asked two elders who were sitting on a bench in the plaza about the identity of the Indian represented in the sculpture, their response was an emphatic: "el indio más chingón que ha existido" [the biggest fucking Indian that has ever existed]. Given that one finds at the other end of the plaza a monumental plaque (figure 10.4) that reminds us that the first location of the city of Guadalajara was Nochistlan and that it was founded in 1532 by Juan de Oñate under

FIGURE 10.3. *(left)*
Monument to Francisco Tena-
maztle, Nochistlan, Zacatecas.
José Rabasa personal archive.

FIGURE 10.4. *(below)*
Commemorative plaque,
Nochistlan, Zacatecas. José
Rabasa personal archive.

the orders of Nuño de Guzmán, one can surmise that the same elders who praised Tenamaztle would respond to a query regarding the plaque with an equally emphatic "todos somos descendientes de los primeros españoles" [we are all descendants of the first Spaniards].

The settlement, the plaque reminds us, had only lasted one year, when in 1533 Guadalajara was relocated in what is today Tonala. After the initial subjection of the rebels, which actually meant their taking refuge in the mountains from which they have continued to resist imperial and national states up to the present, the city moved to its current location. The monumentalization of Tenamaztle's insurrection shares a space with a historical landmark that memorializes the same people who subjected Tenamaztle's people to wars of extermination and slavery. Tenamaztle, as his first name Francisco implies, had been baptized when his territory was first invaded by Nuño de Guzmán, as a young child, perhaps without the authorization of his parents. Here we find the traces of a *without* history that the modern state, in complicity with the colonial past, obliterates while domesticating the spirit of apostasy by means of monument.

To paraphrase Michel de Certeau, Tenamaztle's monument resurrects the Cazcan leader only to bury him for good: "The ghosts find access through *writing* on the condition they remain *forever silent*."[56] To these silencings in monumental memoralization, we may add Miguel León Portilla's assessment that if Tenamaztle was defeated in the war, he remains a victor in a history that vindicates his name by turning the Cazcan rebel's case at the Council of the Indies into an early formulation of the declaration of the rights of the citizen at the National Convention of the French revolution, as well as of the declaration of universal human rights at the United Nations in 1948. León Portilla in a recent edition of his *La flecha en el blanco* (now bearing now the title *Francisco Tenamaztle, primer guerrillero de América, defensor de los derechos humanos*) seeks to situate Tenamaztle's dossier in the context of the Zapatista uprising in Chiapas in 1994. It is not clear why he would be the first *guerrillero*, but even less to what extent the dossier that León Portilla collects and how his reading of the letters would exemplify a *guerrillero*, rather than subordinate him from within a discourse that seeks accommodation to the Spanish Crown. Wouldn't it be more appropriate to say that Tenamaztle's letters express Las Casas's thoughts on creating autonomous indigenous states? This is not to deny that Tenamaztle practiced guerrilla warfare, but that the dossier ends up silencing the discourse of apostasy.

The Zapatistas like Tenamaztle, or Tenamaztle like the Zapatistas, are struggles, for León Portilla, concerned with the recognition of rights by the state. But we must wonder to what extent the call for recognition as expressed by León Portilla entails subordination by historical inclusion to the state and its discourse. An alternative reading could ask whether the use of the legal discourses demanded by the imperial or national states might not entail a transformation of the juridical structure that would allow for political and cultural spaces *without* history. In this regard one might speak of autonomy, perhaps of the sovereignty invoked by Tenamaztle in collaboration with Las Casas, as demanding the recognition of the right to have one's own normative systems and the right to determine the use of natural resources, although this latter right to natural resources would have hardly made sense in such sixteenth-century legal tracts as those formulated by Francisco Vitoria and Alonso de la Vera Cruz. The call is not to recognize alternative juridical systems as compatible with or equivalent to those prevalent in Western life forms, but rather of the rights to keep the state from intervening or evaluating indigenous normative systems. Tenamaztle and the Zapatista use the language of the state to claim sovereignty, which would entail the rights to life forms that cannot be translated or subsumed by Western claims to universality. Even the expectation of adopting Christianity would be an ideal end for Las Casas, rather than an actualized state, if we were to take seriously Las Casas's *De unico modo*.

Tenamaztle's Spanish account documents the atrocities that were committed by the first Spanish invaders. Because of his atrocities, Nuño de Guzmán was banished from the region. But other unsavory characters retain their privileges. Tenamaztle's narrative from the victim's point of view recounts the same kind of atrocities that the central Mexican cacique Acazitli proudly attributes to the troops under his command: mutilation, enslavement, and murder were systematically practiced by Spaniards and their Indian partners. There is nothing exaggerated or under dispute about the events of the war against the people of Nochistlan, El Mixton, and Xuchipila, just to mention the three main enclaves. Tenamaztle hardly needs Las Casas to help him tell this story, even if the documents deploy rhetoric reminiscent of the *Brevísima relación de la destrucción de Indias* and demonstrate deep understanding of the legal framework for claiming the restitution of sovereignty.

Tenamaztle's documents also reflect a series of writings in which Las Casas argued that love and reason were the only valid methods to attract infidels to the true religion. In advocating reason and love, Las Casas denounced in *De unico modo* the idea that the political subjection of Indians as a preliminary to conversion would only lead to war and destruction. This is the logic of the Requerimiento that Las Casas systematically exposed as corrupt. In *De unico modo* the psychological and material destruction, he argues in chapter 7, must be repaired to do justice to Indians. We have seen that for Tenamaztle, the damages have been so extensive that reparations were impossible, but he does argue for the restitution of sovereignty.

Tenamaztle's letter takes an interesting turn when he states that in exchange for having his sovereignty restored, he commits himself to bringing all rebels into the fold of empire by peaceful means. Tenamaztle is also willing to pay tribute to the emperor, but does not mention what is to be gained by remaining within the empire other than preventing the fury of the Spaniards. Is the Crown seen as a protector from Spanish conquistadores? This is a case of claiming history as a form of empowerment by means of gaining recognition. Tenamaztle's understanding of sovereignty approximates an autonomous status within the universality of the Spanish empire. As such, it reflects Las Casas's utopian project of nonviolent incorporation of indigenous peoples into the Church. Under this formulation there would be a minimal imposition of dogma but a long-term process of communication, of reasoning, that would eventually lead indigenous peoples to accept baptism willingly, fully conscious of its implications. Observe that this process could in theory take many generations and ultimately wind up in a counterargument to the reasons for the desirability of accepting the tenets of revealed religion. Given that the truths of revealed religion cannot be demonstrated by reason, the conversion efforts remain haunted by logical impasses and differences.

If Tenamaztle figures in the narrative as a willing subject, the insurgents who remain anonymous even today—the Zapatista *comandantes* in Chiapas continue this anonymous struggle—remain covered by the fog of the historical archive. As such, their struggles remain *without* history. These struggles no longer (if they ever did) call for recognition by and within the state. Again, if there is a demand for recognition, it is of the right to keep the state from interfering in their political life. We may trace in this call for the recognition of sovereignty a political concept that situates sovereignty not in the state but in the people. Ideally these would be subjects who have listened to Las Casas and who, remaining unconvinced by the Dominican friar's arguments, choose to remain outside history. Las Casas would have recognized this right, but the Crown or the modern state would most likely define these subjects as insurgents or apostates. In fact, they define themselves as insurgents, as apostates (*pace* the Tenamaztle of the letters), as subjects *without* history, both in the sense of standing outside and lacking the determination of historical discourse.

Alonso de la Vera Cruz on Dominion

Next to Las Casas, I would like to cite the Augustinian friar Alonso de la Vera Cruz. In these two missionaries we can distinguish two modalities of inscribing (or self-inscribing, as in the Las Casas–Tenamaztle collaborative effort) subalterns by using the language of the state. Vera Cruz considers that Spanish dominion over the Indies—even if its original foundation in conquest was illegal—must be recognized as not only legitimate but then required to embody a just administration that promotes the common good. One may even trace a communistic or at least communitarian ethos in what he considers the common good when he argues for the distribution of excessive wealth: "If therefore, it happens that individuals in a commonwealth are in possession of superfluity and cling too avariciously to it, they commit an injustice in not giving it to the indigent; and this evil should be done away with by the ruler of the nation [*praeest in republica tolli*]. . . . Therefore, he may take away even against the will of the citizens, what was superfluous as belonging to those who suffered want."[57]

These propositions would have been enough of a threat to the status quo of the *encomenderos*, the owners of *obrajes*, and certain members of the ecclesiastical hierarchy. The Crown's possession of the Indies, even if lawful, would have to be transformed into a just regime. Las Casas is, in a way, more radical in his denunciation of the conquest and calls for the restitution of sovereignty in what would amount to autonomous territories within Spanish dominion. To my mind, both his proposal and that of Vera Cruz remain operational today in the ways historians continue to articulate the relationship between subalterns and the state. The lucidity of Las Casas and Vera Cruz stand out when read against the background of the opinions on the legality and justice of conducting wars of extermination against the Chichimecs discussed earlier.

Las Casas's anthropology makes room for understanding nomadic forms of life, which he attributes to a voluntary poverty: "no quieren tener ni poseer más cuanto tengan para pasar y sustentar la vida lo necesario."[58] For Vera Cruz, they constitute a limit case: "From this it follows that those who have grazing lands among the Indians called *Chichimeca*, either because such lands were never held in possession or were abandoned [*vel non fuerunt possessae vel fuerunt derelictae*] since they have no inhabitants or tribes with clear boundaries; I say those who have such lands are in licit possession because, especially since these nomadic Indians live after the fashion of animals [*vagantes degerent more brutorum*] and do not till the land, for no harm is done them by pasturing the herds of cattle or beasts of burden belonging to the Spaniards."[59]

It is a limit case in that Vera Cruz, like the majority of his contemporaries, could claim *ignorantiam invincibilem* of what from our vantage point may seem obvious regarding territorial claims by nomads. Note that in his recommendations to future confessors, *ignorantiam invincibilem* would be assessed before requiring restitution of goods or illegally seized lands. Despite this, one cannot but be surprised by the anthropological acumen in the following statement: "We deny that the natives of the New World are so dull and witless as some imagine; in fact, although primitive, they have their own form of government and customs by which they live; they also have oral traditions from their forefathers' laws by which they judge and plan rationally; they carry on enquiries, they consult each other; all of which are actions not of fools and insane but of sagacious persons."[60] In the case of Las Casas's attribution of willingness to live with the most basic material goods and without settled communities, we find the elements of what could be construed as approximating Pierre Clastres's theses on the Guarani's systematic struggle against the state (and history) in *Society against the State*.

It is noteworthy that Vera Cruz frames the question of the Chichimecs in terms of their nomadic life and absence of recognizable territorial claims, rather than on attributes that deny their full humanity, as argued in some of the opinions listed earlier. The issue here has to do with the damage that Spanish holdings of lands for grazing would cause to the Chichimecs "nulla enim fit iniura quia herbas despascant armenta vel iumenta Hispanorum" [no harm is done them by pasturing the herds of cattle or beasts of burden belonging to the Spaniards].[61] It is also a limit case in that the response opens the road for justifying war on the grounds that the Chichimecs obstructed the traffic of goods and damaged lawful possessions. As in the case of Francisco Vitoria, war would be justified when a nation impedes free travel in their territories or denies claims of uncultivated lands. So would it be when missionaries were kept from preaching the gospel. The "would" is not accidental given that neither Vera Cruz nor Vitoria pass judgment, but merely lay out the conditions that would justify war and imposing Spanish dominion. He could not be clearer about this than when he abstains from passing judgment on the first conquistadors and delimits the scope of his investigation: "Nos de iure disputamos" [We are discussing law].[62]

Vera Cruz does have moments, however, in which he pleads with his readers to consider the fairness and accuracy of conquistador narratives that represent Indians as willingly subjecting themselves to Spanish rule: "I beg you, good reader, to put aside all prejudice and reflect by what law, by what right did the Spaniards who came to this region, and armed to their teeth, attack these peoples subduing them as though they were enemies and occupying their lands not their own, seeking out arbitrarily with force and violence all their valuable possessions and robbing people? I do not see by what law or right; perhaps I am just beating the air."[63] "Fortassis in medio sole decutio!," exclaims Vera Cruz at the end of this call on the reader to meditate on the legality of possessions and tribute—indeed, to examine his or her conscience (there were *encomenderas*, indigenous for that matter). In calling on the reader, Vera Cruz describes his treatise as intended for the training of confessors who would lead New Spain's elite (arguably both indigenous and Spanish) into the dark corners of their conscience and the limits of *ignorantiam invicibilem* within a tradition that would include Saint Teresa de Avila's *Cuentas de conciencia* (ca. 1560s) and her *Moradas* (1577), and Thomas de Kempis's *Of the Imitation of Christ* (1418), to mention just two most brilliant parallel examinations of the self.

Vera Cruz's treatise, *Relectio de dominio infidelium & justo bello*, consists of series of lectures he delivered in 1554 and 1555 in Mexico City for the inauguration of the Universidad de México. The treatise, in addressing the sovereignty of infidels and the legality of war, inevitably must respond to the question of the lawfulness of the wars of conquest and the dominion the Pope or the Spanish Crown may claim in the New World. These lectures address eleven doubts or questions pertaining to the Pope's right to spiritual dominion over infidels, the emperor's authority to claim sovereignty over the entire world, the legality and justness of the wars of conquest. They also address aspects pertaining the payment of tribute, the appropriation of land, and forced conversions. Vera Cruz's lectures were directed to future confessors of Spaniards, who would thus lead the Spanish elite to examine their conscience and evaluate the justness of their property, the fairness of tribute exacted from Indians, and the legitimacy of Spanish territorial claims. If guilty, the Spanish elite was expected to restore property and sovereignty and repair damages inflicted as a precondition for the absolution of their sins.

This is a very complex and intricate treatise. At the risk of being reductive, Vera Cruz's position can be summed up as stating that even if the Spaniards conducted an unjust war, the colonial order that followed was to be preserved and perfected: "And since this is morally certain [the Spanish dominion is needed to prevent apostasy, *ita quod retrocederent facile*], no person of sound mind would maintain—even were it evident that in the beginning the emperor's title was founded in injustice—that the emperor is bound to renounce his claim and restore the kingdom to Montezuma and his successors."[64] There seems to be here less of a concern with the creation of *indios ladinos* than with a historical backsliding that the concept of *retrocedere* captures well. To avoid apostasy, Indians had to be held in check by the troops of *nostri imperatoris*. Elsewhere, Vera Cruz puts it in these terms: "Thus, it is possible that those who began the war acted unjustly; but that later, with victory secured, the retention of territory is just."[65] (In passing, let's observe that current efforts to deny the existence of a Spanish empire would face in Vera Cruz's text the task of explaining the existence of an emperor without an empire. The euphemism of speaking of "el Virreinato" rather than of colonial order, a dominion if you will, also manifests a desire to do revisionist history by semantic squabbles. If Tenamaztle complained that the colonial authorities spoke of *levantamiento*, revisionist historians today complain that critiques of colonial discourse use the terms imperialism and colonialism.)

Let's return to the question of giving up dominion in the Indies. One is left wondering if a certain Las Casas would be the kind of unsound person Vera

Cruz is arguing against. For Vera Cruz, the objective now would be to make the Spanish dominion fair and just. Hence tribute should be less burdensome than the one Indians paid before the conquest, the excessive wealth of the colonists should be distributed, and the restitution of seized lands enforced. This would be a most just reformed empire. Following Thomas Aquinas, Vera Cruz proposes that only those policies, laws, and practices that promote the common good would justify imperial rule. He also argues with Aquinas about the right a commonwealth has to dispose of tyrants, but stops short of justifying rebellion against the emperor in the New World. But the possibility of arguing for the removal of corrupt officials remains.

Another approach to the question of tyranny would envisage indigenous groups or members of a commonwealth who would ask the emperor to dispose of their tyrants: "Consequently, supposing that their rulers were tyrants, the Spanish dominion could have been just. Whether the commonwealth made such a transference of dominion, I am at a loss to say."[66] This speculative tone should keep us from reducing Vera Cruz to a specific position. The brilliance of his speculative mode borders on a relativist position respecting the nature of tyranny: "Perhaps what seems tyrannical to another nation [*alterius nationis*] was appropriate and beneficial for this savage people [*gentis barbarae*], so that it was better for them to be governed by their lords with fear and supreme power [*ut si timore et imperio gubernabantur*] than with a display of affection."[67] This leads to the following corollary: if they lived under tyrannical rule, it would make it even less lawful to exact more tribute than their former rulers. Moreover, Vera Cruz specifies that the legality of transferring the dominion and expulsing a tyrant "would not render oppression lawful nor the taking over the accumulated treasures of the commonwealth."[68] One of Vera Cruz's main concerns throughout the tract is the need to avoid exploitative situations that lead to apostasy: forced conversions, baptisms of children without the authorization of parents, or any policy that might compel Indians to feign faith. In a phrase reminiscent of the fear of *indios ladinos* or *españolados*, Vera Cruz warns about those who may pretend to have received the faith and cites Mathew 7: "'this last deceit would be more dangerous than the old'; in such cases, it would be better to desist from converting them."[69]

Evanescence and the Archive

Implicit in a theory of just war is that only one combatant can be just. With respect to Tenamaztle, there was a general consensus that his people had been oppressed and enslaved by the first conquistador in the region, Nuño de Guzmán. But given that the war against the Chichimecs could be construed as a war of self-defense on the part of the Spaniards, Tenamaztle in the end disappears from the archives, leaving no trace of what happened to him after presenting his case in Valladolid. This, despite Tenamaztle's argument that he was a Christian with the right to defend himself, not an apostate. The possible distinction between the Cazcanes, who lived sedentary lives, and their allies the Zacatecs, who were primarily nomadic, disappears in the debates over the legality of conducting wars of extermination on the northern frontier. The Chichimecs and nomadic peoples in general could not claim territories. They are perceived as a burden to be exterminated according to rights Spaniards could claim in natural law. Opinions vary: there are those who argued that the Chichimecs were first attacked without justification, hence had a right to self-defense, but the language of the opinions also grows in its radical determination to exterminate. Sadly, extermination was the end result.

According to natural law as presented by Vera Cruz, who in this regard follows Francisco Vitoria, all nations have the right to travel through the territories of others, to extract metals from unclaimed mines, to appropriate wastelands, to participate in commercial exchanges, and to preach Christianity. This implies that the Chichimecs had the obligation to adopt Spanish forms of settlement, participate in commercial ventures, accept preachers—in sum, the obligation to incorporate themselves into the empire and universal history. The state, in order to be just, was under the obligation of promoting the common good. The task of the missionaries would be to teach Indians the most effective means of acting within history. In the end there is only one choice, because even if Vera Cruz insists that one cannot force Indians to convert and underscores that missionaries were to instruct them by the best means, there is a point when in good faith one could say that they have been preached to sufficiently and that their delaying conversion would be in bad faith. Vera Cruz specifies that syllogisms won't do, perhaps an aside on Las Casas's insistence on the use of reason as the only valid means of converting, "with reasons and adequate information, not arranged in syllogistic form since such could not be done."[70]

But even then, Vera Cruz leaves room for those who have heard the word, have understood it, and choose not to abide by it: "If unbelievers of the New World received the missionaries and allowed them to evangelize freely, and then did not wish to believe [*et si credere nolint*], they should not for that reason be deprived of their dominion." In case this was not clear enough, Vera Cruz underscores the intended meaning: "What I want to say in this conclusion is that, supposing that these unbelievers admitted the first missionaries and allowed them to preach the faith publicly and privately, but then did not wish to accept the belief in the true God, they should not for this reason be attacked nor should they be deprived of their otherwise just dominion."[71]

In following Vera Cruz's train of thought, one wonders what would be the difference between *indios ladinos, españolizados* (who in apostatizing would be worse than in their original state), and these Indians who would be exposed to Spanish and Christian mores, arguably, sufficiently in depth for them to reason their choice for not accepting Christianity. I gather that the difference would reside in that the apostate rebels against the Crown, whereas the latter would live in peace in conversation with the Spaniards. One may choose to remain *without* history in Vera Cruz's tract. Vera Cruz and those responsible for drafting policies regarding peaceful settlements wage on the incorporation of Indians into history and the state inasmuch as Indians in their exchanges with Spaniards will have to live by Spanish mores. The avoidance of apostasy would depend on a form of exemplary patience. Vera Cruz expresses this principle thusly: "it is no less a calamity to apostatize from the faith than not to accept it; in fact, it is a more enormous sin."[72] Antonio Tello records that the policy of peaceful settlements failed in the mid-seventeenth century, and how it led to the extermination of peoples who dwelled on the northern frontier. In the end Vera Cruz's discourse on apostasy and his inability to understand nomadic peoples creates one more shroud of silence.

In the Mesoamerican Archive
Speech, Script, and Time in Tezozomoc and Chimalpahin

We can easily imagine a culture where discourses would circulate without any need of an author. Discourses, whatever their status, form or value, and regardless of our manner of handling them, would unfold in the anonymity of a murmur.

—MICHEL FOUCAULT

In opposition to the *archive*, which designates the system of relations between the unsaid and the said, we give the name *testimony* to the system of relations between the inside and the outside of *langue*, between the sayable and unsayable in every language—that is, between the potentiality of speech and its existence, between the possibility and impossibility of speech.

—GIORGIO AGAMBEN

One may rightly wonder if it is permissible to speak of a single Mesoamerican institution of historical writing given that the practice of history partakes of institutional rules that could very well exclude certain forms of remembering the past and telling stories. Paradoxically, the recognition of certain forms of memory by missionaries and lay officials could signal one more mode of appropriating and transforming Mesoamerican institutions. These historical accounts manifest a will to extract practical knowledge for administrative purposes but also the need to bury the pagan past for good by deploying the trope of resurrection to create a final tomb. We may thus read the work of Hernando Alvarado Tezozomoc and Domingo de San Antón Muñón Chimalpahin Quahtlehuanitzin as responses to the expropriation of the past by missionary historians like the Dominican Diego Durán. If Durán's *Historia de las Indias de la Nueva España e islas de Tierra Firme* adopts the metaphor of resurrection and tells the foundational stories of Mexico-Tenochtitlan in the generic mode of romance, Tezozomoc and Chimalpahin retain the Mesoamerican annalist tradition, the *xiuhamatl* (count of the years), and they express the accounts in a most elegant and refined Nahuatl speech, often citing verbatim the elders whose voices they collect.[1]

One may also question the existence of a singular institution of Meso-american historical writing. This opens another set of questions that lead us to observe that Chimalpahin and Tezozomoc write at the intersection of at least two institutions: one that dates back to Mesoamerican antiquity, the other that partakes of Greco-Abrahamic forms of life.[2] The second institution also calls forth the semblance of a Christianized Mesoamerica, or for that matter of Na-huatlized Christianity—in short of Christian authors practicing hybrid forms of history. Our postcolonial sensibilities partake of institutional constraints and an ethos that demand that we interrogate self-ascriptions of Tezozomoc's and Chimalpahin's Christian identity in favor of a duplicitous (ambivalent) subject who, as if deploying an ironic trope, would say, "I am a Christian" to mean "not really." We must nevertheless retain the notion that the Christian archive, what is actually sayable and unsayable according to its rules, dictates that Nahua subjects constitute themselves as Christians and that these same subjects constitute Mesoamerican antiquity under the influence of the devil. I propose that we give way to an understanding of these subjects in terms of a field of forces constituted by the multiple archival rules, the cultural locations, and the possibility and impossibility of giving testimony of the civilization that was destroyed by the conquest. We may then consider whether Tezozo-moc and Chimalpahin conceptualized their historical vocation as representa-tives of a language community whose art of storytelling was on the brink of disappearing.

One may thus question the ethos and the desires that lead us today to ques-tion the Christianity of such illustrious writers as Tezozomoc and Chimalpa-hin, to name the more self-conscious practitioners of history. This refusal most often calls forth the decolonizing agenda of our time. If the postcolonial ethos demands that we decolonize our present, which needless to say includes the past, we may want to acknowledge that this is an impossible task to ac-complish, even if desirable. In decolonizing, we may want to invoke the art of doing things with inherited colonial structures that colonialism could never anticipate rather than conceiving the task of undoing colonial legacies as if the Nahua historians would engage in an anticolonial practice.

In societies with colonial pasts, it is worthwhile repeating Michel de Cer-teau's dictum, "memory does its work in a locus which is not its own."[3] But rather than rushing to isolate (and celebrate) oppositional practices, we may want to consider that this work of memory is in fact a two-way street. We can trace the insertion of the Mesoamerican voices in the institutions of the Latin alphabet and the use of European pictorial perspective as one more compo-nent in the pictographic system of signifiers. If the Latin alphabet and pictorial perspective were two major Western technologies that were deployed for the normalization of Christian subjects, we find Nahuas expropriating them by making them signify differently within Mesoamerican institutions of histori-cal writing. But we must also consider in what way these same Nahuas insert the qualifying terms of idolatry and the devil that may deplete Mesoamerican spiritual expressions of life. These include calendrical equivalences that erase the lived temporality of everyday life under the semblance of a transparent homogeneity of time and circumscribe Mesoamerican history to messianic time.

As we consider the question of messianic time, we can draw a distinction between eschatology, which anticipates the end of the world, and the Pauline messianic *now,* which partakes of the experience of grace. The possibility of salvation and its loss defines both instances of the messianic that underlie the Christian identities of Tezozomoc and Chimalpahin as well as their styles of giving testimony. Whereas one religious experience of salvation entails preparing the soul under the eminent last judgment, the other conveys the sickness unto death that haunts the state of grace in the duration of each instant in which the flow of time binds the eternal. We may identify these two understandings of the messianic with the Franciscan and the Dominican orders and the training Tezozomoc and Chimalpahin received from them.

De Certeau's dictum that "memory does its work in a locus that is not its own" as well as the cultural practice he defines as "*poaching* in countless ways on the *property* of others" may be fruitfully complicated by linking the concepts of *locus* and *property* to Jacques Derrida's analysis of the notion of archiving. This refers to the formation and transformation of sites of memory that one may trace in the etymology of the word "archive," which includes both *commencement* and *commandment.*[4] Archive as *locus* conveys a memory site that includes speech and body as well as narratives and other forms of remembrance. But in a more literal sense the archive as *locus* conveys location in which writings are kept and preserved for posterity, whether in the *amoxcalli,* the *amoxpialoyan* of a given community, the deposits in the *cabildos* and the Consejo de Indias, or private collections in the domiciles of Tezozomoc and Chimalpahin. Memory in Tezozomoc and Chimalpahin does its work in a private space for a future Nahua collective identity that will find the possibility of remembering the past in an archival configuration organized by these individual authors who claim property as archons that provide the keys for interpreting the collected accounts but who also claim property as ownership and custody of pictographic and alphabetical records of Mesoamerican antiquities.

If Foucault's passage cited at the beginning of this chapter offers a poetic phrase (clearly not a method) for tracing the anonymous voices in testimonies collected by Tezozomoc and Chimalpahin, we may draw from Agamben a formulation of author as witness that he derives from the Latin *auctor.* This formulation "originally designated the person who intervenes in the case of a minor . . . in order to grant him the valid title it requires." Agamben goes on to connect the *auctor* with the concept of witnessing: "The act of the *auctor* completes the act of the incapable person, giving strength of proof to what in itself lacks it and granting life to what could not live alone. It can conversely be said that the imperfect act or incapacity precedes the *auctor*'s act and that the imperfect act completes and gives meaning to the word of the *auctor*-witness."[5] My point is not to fold anachronistically the destruction of Mesoamerican life with Agamben's reflection on Auschwitz, but to extend the meaning "*auctor*-witness" to the writing down of the *voices* of those whose speech would have disappeared in the murmur of everyday life had Tezozomoc and Chimalpahin not recorded their performance of what was commonly said when consulting pictographic renditions of the Mesoamerican past.[6]

Voices within Voices

The connection between Tezozomoc and Chimalpahin is hardly arbitrary or merely due to the fact that these are the two most brilliant Nahua historians of the late sixteenth and early seventeenth centuries. Until recently in the twentieth century, the work of Tezozomoc was attributed to Chimalpahin. The only copies we have of Tezozomoc's *Chronica Mexicayotl*, the chronicle of things Mexica, has come down to us in the hand of Chimalpahin.[7] Tezozomoc figures as one more voice, even if exceptional, in the record of Nahua testimonies collected by Chimalpahin, that in telling stories of the ancient civilization also testified to the power of Nahuatl speech. It is as much a record of events for an accurate reconstruction of the past, as it is of the styles and kinds of stories the elders told about antiquity but also about the Spanish invasion. The multiplicity of the voices conveys a fragmented narrative. Tezozomoc's main source are the elders who were the last witnesses of Tenochtitlan's grandeur and its debacle at the hands of the Spaniards; for the most part they remain anonymous, but Tezozomoc does mention members of his family by name and at least in one instance intercalates the narrative, perhaps already in written form, of an individual he identifies as Alonso Franco: "oncan tlami yn in itlahtol huehue yn Alonso franco catca nican ychan ypan altepetl ciudad mexico tenochtitlan auh yn omomiquillico ypan xihuitl de 1602. años. ynin Mestiço catca" [Here ends the account of the elder Alonso Franco, whose home was here in the altepetl and city of Mexico Tenochtitlan and who died in the year 1602. He was a mestizo].[8]

The containment and enabling of voices in Tezozomoc and Chimalpahin lends multiple depths to the stories, to the murmur bound to disappear in an immemorial past when the accounts were passed on from generation to generation. It is unknown who was the mestizo Alonso Franco, but the account of this *huehue* certainly carried sufficient weight to be included and for his name to be associated with a particular section of the *Chronica Mexicayotl*. We cannot but wonder who was this mestizo with sufficient authority in the Tenochca community to tell the account of Mexitin Azteca Chichimeca's stay in Aztlan until they emerged to wander widely in *chichimecaltlalpan* (all over Chichimec land). Right after Franco's account, Tezozomoc tells the story of Huitzilopochtli, of his sister Malinaxoch, of her abandonment, of her pregnancy with Copil and eventual sacrifice of Copil, and of the defeat of the *Centzonhuitznahua* at the ball court—events that antecede the first settlement of the Mexica in Tenochtitlan. In these stories the mythical and the historical, if we can separate them without incurring discursive violence, inflect each other's truths. I can only suggest here the potential in these Nahuatl narratives for reflecting on foundational stories, on the meaning of sacrifice, and on the nature of historical memory in terms other than those that the Greco-Abrahamic tradition provides. Tezozomoc tells these later foundational stories without mentioning specific sources.

What is in Franco's story that might have revealed a singular point of view and the need to preserve his individualized voice? It is as if Tezozomoc wanted to testify to the power of alphabetical writing to retain the breath of speech that can be brought back to life by endless performances of Franco's words, but Tezozomoc also invokes the voice of his close relatives in a collective authorship, which even if lost in the anonymity of murmur remains no less memorable in the possibility of its reenactment:

> ca huel yntlahtoltzin huel yncamacpatzinco niccac oyuh quimitalhuitiaque yn tlaçotlahtoque yn tlaçopipiltin. yn omonemiltico in ye quin nican mohuica yn oquinmopolhui tt.o Dios. yc mononotzinohuaya quimolhuitzinohuaya nepanol yn iuhqui matticatca yn iyollotzin yn inhuehuenenonotzaltzin yn tlacatlahtoque Don diego de aluarado huanitzin niccauhtzin. Don P.º tlacahuepantzin notlatzin. Don diego de S. Fran.ᶜᵒ tehuetzquititzin. yhuan oc cequintin tlaçopipiltin yn oniquincaquilli yn huel mellahuac quimatia yn huehuenenonotzaliztli. yn nican niccuic yn intlatoltzin.

> [I have indeed heard their account from their very mouths as the loved rulers and the loved noblemen told them, they who came here to live, (who) later departed, they whom Our Lord effaced. Thus they consulted each other and told it among themselves, as they understood their loved ancient one's accounts. I listened to the rulers Don Diego de Alvarado Huanitzin, my dear father, Don Pedro Tlacahuepan, my dear uncle, Don Pedro Tlacahuepan, my dear uncle, Don diego de San Francisco Tehuetzquititzin, and other loved noblemen who indeed rightly understood the ancient ones' accounts. Here I took their words.][9]

Was Franco one of these highborn noblemen despite his mestizo status? Tezozomoc expresses in unequivocal terms the collective authorship in which we can picture the elders looking at pictographic *amoxtli* and voicing their narrative together, jointly, by building on each other's words.

This collective, anonymous testimony contrasts with Tezozomoc and Chimalpahin's definition of their tasks. We have the voice of Chimalpahin intercalated in Tezozomoc's *Chronica Mexicayotl*: "Auh yece y nehuatl nican ninotocatenehua Domingo de S. Anton Muñon chimalpahin. onictepotztocac inicnemilli yn chalcaxiuhtlapolhuallamatl yn iquac ypan in yaoyahualloloque mexica yn oncan chapoltepec yn ipan ome acatl xihuitl 1299 años" [But I who here tell my name, Domingo de San Antón Muñón Chimalpahin, have investigated and considered the year-count book of the Chalca as to the time when the Mexica were besieged in Chapultepec. It was in the year Two Reed, 1299].[10] Susan Schroeder has noted that the Chalca historian first arrived in Mexico City as Domingo Francisco, where the absence of a Spanish surname indicates his humble status. Baptized Domingo Francisco, he claims in his writings the right to use "don" and incorporates the name of the church of San Antonio Abad, where he worked upon arriving in Mexico City, as well as the indigenous names "Chimalpahin" and "Quatlehuanitzin," belonging to distant ancestors.[11] But what is central to our argument concerning his status of author and historian is the consultation with other sources and subsequent correction of Tezozomoc's account. Here and elsewhere, Chimalpahin exposes a method of inquiry that enables him to write annals (in the *xiuhpohualli* tradition of "count of the days") that provide information on events that took place in multiple *altepetl* rather than the traditional practice of writing the *xiuhpohualli* of his *altepetl*, in his case Chalco.

Tezozomoc also conceives his task as a historian of Tenochtitlan in a comparative vein: "Ynic axcan ye nitlaneltilia nicnamictia yn intlahtol yn oc cequintin yn aquique yn tleyn totoca yn achto christianosme momachtianime yn tlacpac omoteneuhque yn huel cenca quimatia yn iuh ye onneciz yn iuh oquitecpantiaque y nehuatl axcan niquinneltilia niquinchicahuilia yn intlahtol" [In order that now I thus certify it, I compare the accounts of others who follow the first Christian neophytes mentioned above—who indeed knew well how the accounts will appear, how they would go about ordering them—I now certify and affirm their accounts].[12] The comparison would now involve pairing the accounts that he had collected with those of others who had also heard and recorded the voices of those who belonged to the generation of the first Christians. This suggests that others had collected the same stories told on different occasions. Tezozomoc underscores the voicing of the account by using the future tense, *onneciz* ("it will appear," "it will come forth"), in the speech event that would make it manifest. But it also signals the process of how the accounts were collectively put together by using the imperfect *oquitecpantiaque* (they went about ordering them).

Let's leave aside for now the reference to the first Christians, and just examine Tezozomoc's method and criteria for the authentication of sources. If it is less systematic than Chimalpahin, who clearly poses himself in the Herodotean understanding of history as inquiry, Tezozomoc, who defines himself as a descendant and survivor, does function as *auctor*-witness by collecting narratives and testifying to their authenticity: "yehuantzitzin onechmochihuilique. huel ninpiltzin. yn nican ye ninotocatenehua. ça nocel y nihuehuetlacahualli y nihuehuenenonotzalle yn oc nechonmochicahuilia tt.° Dios" [They begot me; I am indeed their child, I who declare my name. I myself am the ancient ones' survivor, I who possess the accounts of the ancient ones who were Mexica noblemen, whom lord God has effaced and taken away].[13] In his capacity as survivor and custodian of the ancient accounts, Tezozomoc constitutes the new archive that will be passed on to future generations: "yn huel topial ynin tlahtolli ynic no tehuantin oc ceppa yn topilhuan yn toxhuihuan yn teçohuan yn totlapallohuan yn totechcopa quiçazque ynic mochipa no yehuantin quip-iezque" [These accounts are indeed in our keeping. Therefore we too, but es-pecially our sons, our grandsons, our offspring, those who will issue from us, they too will always guard them].[14] Tezozomoc conceives his authorial func-tion in the production of an archive that will eternalize the memory of antiq-uity for the descendants of Tenochtitlan.

Tezozomoc's *Chronica Mexicayotl* comes down to us in the hand of Chimalpahin, whose collection of documents was indeed part of Carlos de Sigüenza y Góngora's papers. Sigüenza y Góngora in turn had inherited them from Fernando de Alva Ixtlixochitl. The custodians of Tezozomoc's collection of voices could hardly be more illustrious. This is not the place to examine the complex relationship between Ixtlixochitl and Sigüenza y Góngora, but the record suggests that the latter expropriated the collection of documents from the Texcocan historian. It is through this *criollo* that the ancient annals of Tenochtitlan become part of the Mexican national identity. Note that Sigüenza y Góngora's papers further traveled outside Mexico and are now in possession of the Bible Society Library at Cambridge University Library.

Tezozomoc's gift to the descendants of Tenochtitlan is filled with hope for a future whose auguries looked dim at the time he produced the *Chronica Mexicayotl* in 1609, when he listed Don Juan Bautista as the last Indian judge-governor of Tenochtitlan. The last of the Tenochca judge-governors of Teno-chtitlan had been Don Luis de Santa Maria, who passed in 1565: "oncan ipan in tlamico yn intlapacholliz yn tenochca tlaçotlatocatepilhuan yn mexico Teno-chtitlan atlitic" [With him the administration of Mexico Tenochtitlan in the midst of the waters by the highborn heirs of Tenochca rulers came to an end].[15] Tezozomoc conceives of the task of *auctor* in terms that suggest a eucharistic understanding of alphabetical writing, one in which reading aloud and per-formance will bring back, resurrect the voices of the elders that lay dormant in the letter: "quitotihui quiteneuatihui yhuan yn oc yollizque yn tlacatizque yn mexica tepilhuan yn tenochca tepilhuan" [and those children of the Mexica, those children of the Tenochca yet to live, yet to be born, will go on telling them, will go on celebrating them].[16]

It is as if Tezozomoc had in mind Saint Paul's dictum that the new law cancels yet retains the old law, that the integration of the Nahuas into universal history did not exclude the memory of the ancients. Is it that Tezozomoc, to borrow Agamben's terms, called forth to continue Nahua forms of life in the mode of *as not*, "as the revocation of every worldly condition, released from itself to allow for its use."[17] From the tension between the old beliefs and the new Christian demands, Tezozomoc produces the memory of old—that is, a version of the foundational stories of Tenochtitlan as a remnant. The memorable past of Tenochtitlan and the speech of the elders will remain for all time in the universal history of Christianity and yet retain the possibility of a performance that would erase all the traces of the Christian.

Inscribing Mesoamerican Antiquity in the History of Salvation

Tezozomoc grounds the authority of the elders that provided reliable information in the fact that the Tenochca elite from which he descends were the first Christian neophytes. Their credibility has as much to do with their memorable status as nobles as with their credible status as the first Christians. Tezozomoc is a grandson of Moteucçoma on his mother's side, Doña Francisca de Moteucçoma, and lists his father Don Diego de Alvarado Huanitzin as ruler of Tenochtitlan in 1536. Indian judge-governors played an indispensable role in the colonial administration of Tenochtitlan, at least during the first century. These figures could not have fulfilled this role unless they openly accepted their status of Christians. This does not necessarily imply that their Christianity was thoroughly ingrained—a question that hardly concerns Tezozomoc, who proudly posed for a portrait bearing the signs of high status: Spanish dress, dagger, and sword. The contrast could not be more striking than the miniature *macehualli* (commoner) at the bottom of the painting. The painter nevertheless captures a deep sadness in Tezozomoc's eyes (figure 11.1).

One would assume the right to ride a white horse as was given to Don Juan Velasquez Tlacotzin, the first *cihuacoatl*, after the hanging of Quauhtemoc in Huey Mollan: "umpa quimomaquilli yn intlaquemitl españoles yhuan espada daga yhuan ce cauallo yztac" [There (in Huey Mollan) the Spaniards gave him their clothing and a sword, a dagger, and a white horse].[18] In telling the story of his ancestors and nobles of Tenochtitlan as credible neophytes, he inscribes their account within the economy of salvation. This inscription suggests the structure of conversion in which Indian subjects were put in the position of accepting the missionaries' description of their deities as filthy, bloody, deceiving devils. Needless to say for Tezozomoc as well as for the Spanish missionaries, these devils (or, better yet, manifestations of the devil) had agency, even when qualified as false gods. But telling their story as manifestations of the devil, as false gods, as deceivers, saps their power. After all, who wants to believe

FIGURE 11.1. Portrait of Fernando Alvarado Tezozomoc. Courtesy of the Biblioteca del Instituto Nacional de Antropología e Historia.

in false gods, to live under deception? As such, Tezozomoc not only collects stories and writings for an archive of the ancient grandeur of Tenochtitlan—which will retain the memory for future generations—but defines the rules for telling and retelling the stories from within a new institution of Mesoamerican writing. The qualification of their deities as devils could be traced back to the speech of the elders who, having being exposed to Christianity at the beginning of the Spanish invasion, were forced to abhor their ancient rites and beliefs while retaining a memory of them.

This was the particular format enforced by Franciscan missionaries as exemplified by that "ur-catechism" known as *Coloquios y doctrina cristiana* that Bernardino de Sahagún produced 1564 in collaboration with Nahua collegians from the Colegio de Santa Cruz de Tlateloloco. This extraordinary text consists of three main sections that cover: (1) an exposition by the first twelve friars of the mandate by the Pope to evangelize in the true religion and only God; (2) the response by the governing elite and the spiritual leaders to the demand to recognize that the Christian God was the only divinity; (3) the friars lambasting their interlocutors, denouncing their gods and rites as filthy inventions by the devil. The strength of Nahua response has led scholars to read their words as direct citations of what they said in the purported dialogue of 1524. There was certainly a gathering of the elite and a performance of the Requerimiento.

The speech of the missionaries in *Coloquios* actually recasts the Requerimiento's narrative of how the Pope had granted sovereignty over the Indies to the Spaniards; while Cortes repeatedly mentions performing the Requerimiento in his Second Letter, which vividly resonates in his rendition of Moteucçoma's submission. But the demand to recognize the missionaries as envoys, the Nahua response, and what must have been a most rudimentary exposition of Christianity in Nahuatl, would not have made use of the neologisms that were constructed in the decades before the production of *Coloquios* in 1564. The force of the response as crafted by the Sahagún in collaboration with Nahua collegians suggests the need to expose a credible extreme limit case of doubt and interrogation of the advisability of abandoning their deity and rites.

Those witnessing the conversion moment represented in *Coloquios* had to find the opposition by the Nahua elite credible so that the missionaries' refutation and exposition of the catechism would be effective. This passage from native objection to missionary refutation suggests a cathartic function. But even the Nahua speech mourns a loss that could not have been conceptualized in 1524 and expresses subordination in acknowledging the death of their civilization: "ma topan xicnochiuilica in tlein anquimonequiltizque" [may you do to us what you will desire]. The counterargument could not be more vehement: "amo ceme nelli teteu, in ixquich yn anquimmoteutia, in anquintlatlauhtinemi" [none of your gods are true, all which you venerate, whom you go about imploring], nor more terrifying than when the missionaries threaten them: "Auh in axcan ixtlacamo anquicaquiznequi yn ihiyotzin in itlatoltzin dios (in huel iehoatzin amechmomaquilia) cenca amouitizque. auh in dios in oquimopevaltili in amopopoloca, quimotzonquixtiliz ancempoliuizque" [But now if you do not want to listen to his revered breath his revered word (he who truly gives himself to you), you will be in great danger. And god who has initiated your ruin, he will complete it; you will perish for ever].[19] Sahagún translates this as follows: "de aqui en adelante vuestros errores no tienen escusa alguna y nuestro señor dios que os comenzado a destruir por los grandes pecados os acabara" [from now on your errors cannot be excused and our lord who has begun to destroy you for your great sins will finish you].[20]

This formula that conveys the truth and then expects acceptance as if the dogma were transparent can be observed in such major evangelical instruments as Juan de Zumárraga's *Doctrina mas cierta y verdadera para gente sin erudicion*, Alonso de Molina's two confessional manuals, the *Confesionario breve en lengua mexicana y castellana* (1565) and the *Confesionario mayor en lengua mexicana y castellana* (1569), and Juan Bautista's *Confesionario en lengua mexicana y castellana* (1599). The emphasis in the Franciscan confessional manuals and the doctrines resides in the memorization of articles of the faith. Thus we find in Juan Bautista's *confesionario* the question: "cuix huel motenco ticmati in doctrina christiana? [Do you know by heart the Christian Doctrine?].[21] The manual also calls forth a narrative of salvation and pursues the signs of contrition for having incurred in sin. Contrition is thus indispensable to attaining the state of grace, but the actual confession involves going through the Commandments and revealing their transgression. Faith is nothing more than a willingness to accept the truth of Christianity. As in *Coloquios*, the *doctrinas* and *confesionarios* take for granted that the articles of faith are revealed truths and call forth a willingness to accept them. In Zumárraga's *Doctrina*, which theorizes the best way to catechize people without erudition, the ideal is to lead Indians to stutter the articles of faith: "y los indios que se enseñen en ella en los monasterios comienzen a tartamudear en ella."[22] He claims his *Doctrina* contains the essence of the Christian faith.

Zumárraga writes it in the midst of acrimonious debates in the late 1530s over the implementation of baptism in which Dominicans (headed by Bartolomé de Las Casas) expounded the need for a thorough indoctrination and understanding of the mysteries of the faith before baptism, and Franciscans (headed by Motolinía) advocated the baptism of multitudes on demand without prior catechization. The difference between the two orders is nowhere more extremely expressed than in Motolinía's summoning of Charles V to assume his responsibility as emperor of the end of times: "porque dice el Señor: 'sera predicado este Evangelio por todo el universo antes de la cosumación del mundo'. Pues a vuestra merced conviene de oficio darse prisa que se predique el santo Evangelio por todas estas tierras, y los que no quisieren oír de grado el santo Evangelio de Jesucristo, sea por fuerza" [Because the Lord says: "the Gospel will be preached throughout the universe before the world ends." So Your Grace, in your capacity, should hurry that the holy Gospel is preached throughout these lands, and that those who do not willfully listen to the holy Gospel of Jesus Christ, they must be forced]. Motolinía partakes of Duns Scotus's view of God's revelation of himself in history, indeed, to the extent that God changes in time: "Mas es de notar que el profeta Daniel dice en el mismo capitulo; que Dios muda los tiempos y edades, y pasa los reinos de un señorio en otro" [For we must note that the prophet Daniel says in the same chapter: God changes the times and the ages, and passes kingdoms from one lordship to the other].[23]

Zumárraga's *Doctrina* seeks to resolve the dispute claiming to hold the most basic truths and directs his invective toward the "variedad de doctrinas que vemos y avemos visto: las sectas y titulos de theologos: las diferencias de ellos" [the variety of doctrines that we see and have seen: the sects and titles of theologians: the differences among them].[24] One cannot but hear the bitter disputes between Motolinía and Las Casas in the background of this desire to simplify the most basic tenets that Indians must know before baptism. In the context of Chimalpahin, I discuss Las Casas's view that the only acceptable form of baptism presupposed a thorough understanding of the Christian mysteries and the development of a habitus that would enable the experience of faith as a state of grace.

In the Franciscan schema, becoming a Christian turns out to be a question of accepting the catechism, often after baptism, and learning to tell the story of one's life in terms of the before and after conversion. There is a historicist perspective (as well as a relativism) in the Franciscan conceptualization of God as becoming manifest in history and the place of the conquest in a millenarian vocation they ascribe to Charles V. In his accounts of the foundation of Tenochtitlan, Tezozomoc includes both the dates according to the Mesoamerican system and their corresponding notations in the Gregorian calendar. We may approach these equivalences from at least two perspectives. First, the Judeo-Christian dates fulfill the role of circumscribing the events from within a homogenous conception of historical time that suggests that it is a mere exercise in accurate dating based on a universal system ruled by anno domini, a system first instituted by the Venerable Bede in the eighth century. It is somewhat outstanding the ease with which Tezozomoc juxtaposes dates, such as "2. calli xihuitl 1325. años," without elaborating on how the two notations belong to different institutions. He takes care to indicate years in which the fifty-two-year cycles were completed, but he signals these calendrical events without addressing the implications of these cycles from within the Christian linear history of salvation.

Second, if for the most part he limits himself to inscribing dates, on occasions he specifies "motlacatillitzino yn totemaquixticatzin Jesu christo" [after our Savior Jesus Christ was born]. Beyond a secular homogeneous time, Tezozomoc explicitly draws out millenarian implications when he circumscribes to messianic time the Mexica's emergence from Aztlan and their adoption of Huitzilopochtli as tutelar god:

> auh yn ipampa yn ynic ynpallehuilloca yez. quimonequiltitzino yn cen quizcahueyhuecapan yn atlancatzintlin yn atzonquizqui. yn iteoyotzin Dios. ynic moxexellozque yn inyeyan yn innetlaliayan ynic ye huallazque in ye nican omotecaco omoçecenmanaco y nepapan nohuiampa tlallipan. ynic ynpan yez. ynpan huallaz ynpan motlalliquiuh y mellahuac tlanextli. yhuan ynic quinhualmatizque in yehuantin españolesme. ynic quinnemilizcuepaquihui. yhuan ynic huel momaquixtizque yn inyollia yn imanimashuan. yn iuh quichiuhque ye huecauh in yehuantin rroma tlaca. yhuan yn ompa tlaca españa yn españolesme yn huel ixquich yc omocenmanque in ipan cemanahuatl.

> [And because it would help them, the most perfectly sublime, infinite, eternal divinity of God willed that they should be dispersed (from) their abode, their home, so that they might come hither, spread, expand everywhere over various lands; so that in their time there would exist, come, and establish the true light; and so that the Spaniards would go to them and change their way of life, and so that their hearts and souls would be saved; as in other times the people of Rome did it, and so the people of Spain, the Spaniards, who then expanded over all the world.][25]

We should resist reading this passage as mere instance of *preparatio evangelica*, but instead trace the specific teleological impulse we found in Motolinía's letter. There is nothing redeemable to Huitzilopochtli's doctrines or for that matter in the Mexica rulers, something Tezozomoc presents in unequivocal terms when he exposes the cruelty and sacrifices in Moteucçoma's reign in the Spanish version of the *Historia o Chronica mexicana*: "quiso Dios nuestro señor castigarle . . . y derrocar el imperio del demonio que tanto se estendia en este nuevo Mundo" [it was the will of our Lord God that he be punished . . . and that the empire of the devil that was so extensive in this New World be demolished].[26]

For Tezozomoc, God brings about a complete erasure and hardly offers an evaluation of the ways in which the ancients approximated Christian ideals. He offers no instances of rulers prefiguring Christianity, as for example in Ixtlixochitl's comparison of Nezahualcoyotl to the prophet David, but rather offers a perspective closer to Motolinía's views cited earlier on the historical transformation of the paths of God: "Dios muda los tiempos y edades, y pasa los reinos de un señorio en otro" [God changes the times and the ages, and passes kingdoms of one lordship to another].[27] His rendition of the foundational stories of Tenochtitlan, the beauty of the gests of Malinalxochitl, Huitzilopochtli, Copil, and the Centzonhuitznahua, have a closer affinity to the aesthetic role that the Roman pantheon plays in Christendom, where it hardly poses a threat to the established secular and religious institutions. There is certainly a will to remember the ancient rulers, as well as those who continued to rule after the Spaniards arrived, but he binds this remembrance to personal history, to a sense that the Tenochca elite was disappearing.

And yet the *Chronica Mexicayotl* did not survive the vicissitudes of time, at least in his own writing, but only in Chimalpahin's more ambitious and complex project. This is in part because Chimalpahin was a generation younger and could take a distance from his immediate genealogy given his status as a commoner with no immediate claim to royal ancestry.

Simultaneous Historical Times

One of the most striking features of Chimalpahin's history is the simultaneous recording of events in a given year. This practice distances him from the traditional recording of events in Mesoamerican local histories. In this regard he could not be farther from Tezozomoc's history centered on Tenochtitlan, which provides information on other locations only when relevant to the rise of the Mexica. We can picture Chimalpahin following several pictorial texts, consulting alphabetical records from different sources and locations, and drawing from interviews of elders to provide a complete history of central Mexico and significant events in European history, even while privileging Chalco. On occasions he does provide the names of informants, most often connected to his relatives, but for the most part he speaks of female and male elders who narrated the stories.

In addition to the simultaneous citation of sources and events in a given year, Chimalpahin also draws from biblical sources to better situate the events in universal history. These mentions of Judeo-Christian history range from the recurrent generic placement within anno domini, "Nican ypan in ye etzontli xihuitl yn omotlacatillitzino yn totecuiyo *Dios*" [On this one thousand two hundred years have passed since the precious birth of our lord God], to the correction of dates for such events as the Tower of Babel, "Auh ynin tlahtolli yn oquimotlahtoltique huehuetque tlacochcalca cenca ohuititica ynic momatiz; ca mellahuac yn mocuehcuep tlahtolli, yece yn oncan ipan in xihuitl tlahtohua huehuetque yn oquicuepaco yntlahtol, ca ye nepa cenca miectzonxihuitl yn omocuecuep tlahtolli, yn iuh neztoc ycuiliuhtoc ipan christiano teoamoxtli" [This account that was given by the ancient Tlacochalca is very hard to believe; for it is true that tongues were confused, but by the year the ancients say their tongue was confused many years had gone by since the confusion of the tongues as it appears and is written in the Christian book of god].[28] Chimalpahin intercalates a brief account of Babel, Nemrod, and Noah to illuminate the account of how the Nonohualcas Teopixcas Tlacochalcas first emerged in the place named Tlapallan Nonohualco, which according to the *yn iuh ymamatlacuilolpan in tliltica tlapaltica quicuilotehuaque* [as they left it painted on their writings in red and black ink] from which he derived the account, it was there where the ancient became mute: "Auh yehuatl yntoca omochiuh ynic nonohualca, ynic nontiaco yn iquin quemman inpan mociuh" [They were given the name of Nonohualca because they became mute when this occurred].[29]

If the chronology is doubtful and difficult to believe, "cenca ohuititica momatiz" (Molina gives for *mati*: "pensar dudando si sera assi o no"), the story remains fascinating not only because it goes back to a time before the arrival of the Tlacochalca at Chicomoztoc, a time before their migration, perhaps their historical time, but also because Chimalpahin goes on to mention Josefus and the pagan poets, whom he characterizes as the pagan tricksters of words (the *tlahtolchichiuque, enlabiadores* according to Molina, *motenehua*, those called *poetas*), in particular Ovid's story of how the giants, the *tlacahueyaque*, constructed towers to reach the heavens and destroy the gods. Chimalpahin concludes with the laconic statement that Ovid expressed himself in different terms "ca noco tlateotocani amo quimiximachilli yn iceltzin teutl" [because he was an idolater and did not know the one sole God].[30]

In the end Chimalpahin casts doubt on the ancient accounts that would have placed Tlapallan near Babylon by alluding to evidence provided by the ancient count of the years, the *huhuexiuhtlapohualli*, which gives a much more recent date, and to the fact that it does not agree with the Christian count of the years: "amo quinamiqui yn christiano xiuhpouhualli."[31] After questioning the correspondence between the loss of a common language in Mesoamerica with the biblical account of the Tower of Babel, it is as if the mention of Ovid would give him poetic license to tell the fantastic story of Tlacochalca's crossing the sea. They crossed on top of turtles and gigantic sea snails from which they saw the water women who are half fish ("yn acihuatl michintlaco"), the sirens who drew them to their music and lament in the middle of the water ("oquinhuallapichilitiquizque oquinhuallatzotzonilitiquizque yn ayhtic").[32]

Once they have crossed, Chimalpahin proceeds to enumerate the years, the historically verifiable records that enable him to produce a total history of Mesoamerica. He compares and teases out the most reliable count of the years from multiple sources belonging to different locations. Thus under one year Chimalpahin might cite events pertaining to Texcoco, Tenochtitlan, and Amecamecan. This simultaneous mention of events provides a picture of the interactions between the *altepemeh*, even when more attention is given to the story of the Chalcas. In the *Séptima relación*, from which I have drawn the passages on the confusion of languages, the story of the Chalca is unavoidably connected to the rise of Tenochtitlan, first in the flower wars and then as subordinate tributaries, a condition Chimalpahin expresses as a form of death: "Yn ihcuac yn ye iuh nepa onpohualloncaxtolli ypan ome xihuitl opoliuhque yn chalca" [By then it had been fifty-seven years since the Chalca had died]. After Cortés's entrance into Tenochtitlan, the Tenochca lost all their lands when it was determined that they had taken possession by means of war. Chimalpahin provides a most gruesome picture of the Tenochca *cihuatl* returning to their houses in Tenochtitlan: "ça onca omitl tepeuhtoc ça yuh mamani calli" [they found them with bones scattered all over the ground].[33]

In addition to the simultaneous events in Mesoamerica, Chimalpahin records events in Europe such as the crowning of Charles V as emperor of the Holy Roman Empire and the birth of Philip II.[34] It hardly matters that Chimalpahin cites 1528 when in fact Charles V did not receive the crown until 1530. We can thus situate a temporality that encompasses all events in universal history. Not only does he situate the events in their anno domini, but also in terms of biblical history of the world and major events in Europe. Chimalpahin's global history is conceptualized from the perspective of Chalco and other locations in the valley of Mexico City. It is clear to him that Mesoamerica has been incorporated into the universal history of the Catholic Church, but it is also important to understand that he uses native documentation for telling the major events in the incorporation of the Nahuas into Christianity. One may even conceive that events pertaining to European history, such as Charles V's assumption of the Holy Roman Empire, were drawn from native sources that had recorded these events decades earlier.

This obviously does not mean that Chimalpahin did not have access to European sources but that his story of the foundation of the colonial order is grounded in native experiences and records. His references to the *huehuetque* (the ancients) include pictorial sources that established a wide range of colonial events: "2 Calli xihuitl, 1533 años. Ypan in yn amaquemeque chalca quihtohua yhuan quimachiyotia yn ipan ynxiuhtlapolhuallamauh y yecahuico yn teopantli San Luis obispo Tlalmanalco" [2 Calli 1533. The Amaquemeca Chalca say, and left painted in their book of the years, that the church of San Luis Obispo was finished on this year].[35] Reading Chimalpahin, we get the sense that the time of Christianity has been incorporated into Mesoamerican time. Christianity has certainly transformed the everyday life of the Nahua; however, we do not get the impression that the use of calendrical equivalences only works in the direction of a homogeneous time, but that Christian dates now form part of Mesoamerican counts of the years.

One must furthermore underscore that this is a practice that Chimalpahin derives from the pictorial sources and verbal performances that he has collected. The testimonies of the *huehuetque* include the remembrance of both before and after the conquest. Belonging to a generation younger than Tezozo-moc, Chimalpahin no longer recorded (or at least we get this sense) the speech of the elders who witness Mesoamerican life before the Spanish invasion. In this regard this past needs to be reconstructed solely on the basis of picto-rial records, verbal testimonies written down in Latin alphabetical script, such as Tezozomoc's or Alonso Franco's accounts, and the narrations he collected from people who had known survivors of the wars of conquest and the epi-demics. Chimalpahin assumes the author function of a historian who pursues systematic inquiries into a past no longer accessible without the mediation of writing. Even if the *huehuetque* he consults could have repeated the stories they had heard, these remain indirect testimonies. This explains the method of gathering information from several sources belonging to different locations for recording multiple events on a given year.

One never gets the sense that the Mesoamerican past forms part of teleo-logical design as in Tezozomoc's understanding of Hutizilopochtli's guidance of the Mexica in the mode of *preparatio evangelica*, which I would argue re-flects Tezozomoc's Franciscan training at the Colegio de Santa Cruz de Tla-telolco and, more particularly, Motolinía's messianic summoning of Charles V. Chimalpahin's difference with Tezozomoc points to an evangelization by Dominican friars who were not given to apocalyptic accounts of the devasta-tions of the conquest as God's designs to bring Mesoamerica into the fold of the Church. To illustrate this point, I limit myself to Las Casas's theoretical treatise *De unico vocationis modo omnium gentium ad veram religionem*. There are no traces of Chimalpahin's attendance at the Colegio de Taltelolco, and from him we learn of the dislike and hardship of the Franciscans in Chalco: "Oyhui yn yn moquixtique amaquemecan yn San Francisco teopixque, ayac yncatzinco mochihuaya, motolinitzinohuaya; cuix yehuatl ipampa yn moquixtique" [Thus it was that the fathers from San Francisco left Amaquemecan, because no one was doing something in their name, they were suffering; perhaps they left].[36]

Chimalpahin must have learned to read and write under the guidance of Dominicans. The plurivocal nature of his accounts suggests a dialogical method of evangelization favored by the Dominicans. Beyond Las Casas we may trace the Dominican preference for dialogue in Domingo de la Anun-ciación, *Doctrina cristiana breve y compendiosa por vía del diálogo entre un maestro y un discípulo sacada en lengua mexicana y castellana* (1565). If in the case of Sahagún's *Colloquios* we found a credible voice contradicting the friars, they lambasted their beliefs to terrorize the native interlocutors. In Domingo de la Anunciación we find no traces of spiritual terrorism or of the denigration of Nahua deities and their rites, rather an amorous discourse that seeks to pro-mote a Christian *habitus* for the reception of baptism and the state of grace.

The promotion of dialogue for evangelical purposes evokes Las Casas's argument in *De unico modo* that establishes the understanding as the only acceptable mode of summoning pagans. We must resist downplaying the advocacy of dialogue and the understanding by reducing it to manipulation. Unless Las Casas were to contradict himself, his point of departure would lack a conception of the understanding defined exclusively by Greco-Abrahamic categories and modes of argumentation. Such an imposition would entail the teaching of the understanding before the actual practice of catechizing by means of the understanding—in other words, it would entail exerting violence on the rationality of the Indians by imposing a single proper way of reasoning. In order to be consistent, the ideal would have missionaries in true dialogical exchanges in which the missionary would remain open to forms of thought not yet codified by Western discourse.

In the *De unico modo* we find one of the multiple formulations of the "noble savage" figure in Las Casas's work. This figure undermines all forms of historicism that would place the Nahua within a transition narrative by asserting that all Amerindians partake of the best of possible intellects; he leaves no room for a developmentalist model of conversion that would assume being Christian as a more evolved form of humanity. Let us observe the fiction of the noble savage: "Quamquam scundum sanctos, predsertim S. Thomam, certissime est tenendum quod si quispiam nutriretur in silvis vel inter animalia bruta et sequeretur ductum rationis naturalis in appetitu boni et fuga mali, quod est non ponere obicem seu facere quod in se est, quodDeus ei vel per internam inspirationem revelatet ea, quae sunt ad credendum necessaria, vel aliquem fidei praedicatorem ad eum diriggeret" [According to the saints, and most particular Saint Thomas, if an individual matured in the forest and among savage animals, and just followed natural reason with regard to the desire for the good and the repulsion of evil, and did what was to be done on his part, God would reveal by means of an interior inspiration the knowledge needed to believe or would send him a preacher of the faith].[37]

Let us now trace this thought in a passage from the *Tercera relación*: "Oncan peuhtica yn yn huehuetque yn innetlapolloltiliz . . . ynic ompa hualquizque yn Aztlan yn azteca ayamoh ompa quihualmamatiaque yn *diablo* Huitzillopochtli ye quin, huell otlipan, quihuallantiquizque, ynic quihualmomamatique ynic, yehuatl oquihualmoteotitiaque yn Azteca mexitin" [There is where their madness began . . . when they came out of Aztlan the Aztecs not yet carrying the *devil* Huitzilopochtli since it was later well on the road that he started to grow, that the Azteca Mexitin became his carriers that they took him for a god].[38]

Clearly the madness they incurred was idolatry of the devil himself. But let's follow Chimalpahin's reasoning: "Ypampa yn ynic omeyollohua cequintin huehuetque yn iuh momati yn achto ca quimoneltoquitiaya y nelli *Dios*, cemixquichyhuellitzin, yn topampa momiquillitzino" [Because of this some of the ancients doubt when they think that in the beginning they believed in the true God, the all powerful, who died for us].[39] The logic of why they doubted that they were believers in the true God does not quite follow from the previous statement concerning the beginning of the cult of Huitzilopochtli, but maybe what Chimalpahin wants to convey is that in becoming idolaters they did not know the true God. But he goes on to further clarify his thoughts: "Auh aço yuhqui, acanoçomo camo huel mellahuac momati yn aço tlaneltocaya yn iquac huallolinque yn ompa Aztlan" [and perhaps it cannot be like this, never truly true to think that maybe they were believers when they moved from Aztlan]. Chimalpahin concludes his meditation stating: "Auh ca çan in iuh mellahuac momati, yeppa tlateotocani ynic motenehua *gentilesme*" [But if what they think is correct, the idolater of former times is what is called "gentiles"].[40]

Chimalpahin's interrogative phrasing leads us to consider that it is incorrect to think that idolatry always existed by establishing that, before the spell of Huitzilopochtli, the Mexitin Azteca (and by extension all Mesoamericans) were pagans, indeed with sufficient reason to have known the true God in this condition. As in the case of Las Casas, Chimalpahin does not bind knowledge of the redeemer to a historical stage, as Motolinía and Tezozomoc would want us to believe. If it is only on the basis of the understanding that Las Casas would accept the administration of baptism, in principle, Amerindians could remain unconvinced for centuries or, in fact, refuse to accept baptism after all arguments had been exhausted, perhaps by arguing that they have always known the true God and that the Christian version might actually amount to a form of idolatry. This is clearly a bold position that Chimalpahin would not offer without qualification, but one that he actually could have anchored in readings of Las Casas. Let's examine the recording of daily life, the history of his times, in the so-called *Diario*.

Writing the History of the Present

The *Diario*'s first entry for "7 House" year, 1577, has an annotation indicating that "ypan in yn xihuitl oquimihcuilhui yamoxtzin libro in itca d las moradas yn la madre Teresa de Jesus" [in this year mother Teresa de Jesús (. . .) wrote her book named *Las moradas*].[41] This entry corresponds to two years before Chimalpahin was born. It is not until the entry of July 25, 1594, that we have an allusion to writing in the present: "nican motenehua yn ipan axcan xihuitl ticate yhuan huehue xihuitl xi. tochtli. yquac cenca huey. netoliniliztli topan" [here it is mentioned that in the year we are in now, the ancient year of 11 Tochtli, was when a great misery came to us].[42] This first entry would have been written when Chimalpahin was only fifteen. Although the note on *Las moradas* is a marginal later addition, it is in the hand of Chimalpahin. It is as if, in the process of reflecting on and revisiting his own entries, he had realized the correspondence to Santa Teresa's writing of *Las moradas*. We know that Santa Teresa, fearing the extinction of all memory of her work, wrote this book two years after the Inquisition had confiscated the manuscript of the *Libro de la vida*. Even though the *Diario* lacks the self-examination we find in *Las moradas*, one could argue that we find a critical consciousness in Chimalpahin's accounts of contemporary events.

We should remember, however, that among Chimalpahin's papers at the Biblical Society in Cambridge, we find a copy of an *Exercicio quotidiano* in Nahuatl that offers a series of meditations geared to the creation of a spiritual habitus for the reception of the Eucharist. This *Exercicio quotidiano* suggests that rigorous examinations of conscience were not alien to the spiritual life of the Nahuas. In Chimalpahin's copy of this text we find an annotation by Bernardino de Sahagún: "Este exercicio halle entre los yndios, no se quien lo hizo ni quien se le dio tenia muchas fallas E incongruidades mas con verdad se puede decir que se hizo de nuevo que no se enmendo. Este año de 1574 fray Bernardino de Sahagun" [I found this exercise among the Indians. I do not know who produced it, nor who gave it to them. It had many errors and incongruities. But in truth it may be said that it was done anew rather than that it was corrected. In this year of 1574. Fray Bernardino de Sahagún].[43]

Sahagún's comment points in at least two directions. On the one hand, the note suggests an autonomous production of Nahuatl Christian literature by Nahua writers outside the supervision of the missionaries. On the other hand, the note suggests that it could have been given to them by someone from another order. Considering the emphasis is placed on the development of an intellectual and spiritual habitus, rather than the emphasis Franciscans placed on the will and the acceptance of the Christian creed, the *Exercicio* points to a Dominican source. Chimalpahin's attention to time and the recording of daily events in the *Diario*, in some cases of the flow of the hours, often accompanied with acerbic criticism toward the colonial religious and secular authorities, partakes of the habitus of introspection that the *Exercicio quotidiano* and *Las moradas* sought to instill in their readers. The criticism of the colonial authorities includes the exposure of paranoia that led to the hanging of thirty-five Blacks who had been accused of inciting an uprising in 1612, the complete disregard by the viceroy and archbishop who chose to attend a bullfight instead of tending to the suffering of victims from the 1611 earthquake, and the exercise in what may be termed "autochthonous enlightenment criticism" of the conflicting epistemologies for understanding the eclipse of 1611. Chimalpahin inscribes these events from within a Mesoamerican institution of historical writing, more specifically the *xiuhpohualli* (count of the years) tradition, however, not without radically altering Nahua historiography in the process.

This hybrid collection of texts includes years and events that occurred before his birth or before he had sufficient maturity to write; the record of daily
events whose entries become longer and more detailed as the accounts progress in time (hence the tendency to call it a *Diario*); and a brief *xiuhpohualli* in
the old style that covers the years spanning from the biblical beginning of time
(passing through the foundation of Rome, and then moving on to the Mexica
migration from Aztlan and the founding of Tenochtitlan, which includes information regarding Chalco) up to 1608, the actual year in which he writes
this brief account. The copresence of these mixed genres explains the disparity
in naming the text a *Diario* or, as the most recent editors and translators into
English have preferred, *Annals of His Time*. It can be understood as a history
of the present in that some instances mark the passage of the hours and the experience of a "now" defined by the temporality of lived instants. I concentrate
on this aspect of the entry for the eclipse on June 10, 1611.

Chimalpahin juxtaposes two metaphors for the phenomenon of the eclipse,
the Nahuatl *tonatiuh quallo* ("the sun is eaten") and the analogy to a shelter
that creates shade only for those standing under it. He draws the latter simile
from *Sermonario* by Juan Bautista, who derived the passage from an astrology
book and translated it to Nahuatl. Chimalpahin refers to Juan Bautista's simile
as *tlahtolmachiyotl*, which Molina lists as "parabola, semejanza, o figura." Rafael Tena's translation renders *tlahtolmachiyotl* as "comparación," which does
capture Molina's preference for a trope, but the English translators preferred
"statement," which lends it a scientific weight that the Nahuatl term does not
carry. The sequence of metaphors and the insistence on referring to the eclipse
as *tonaituh quallo* throughout the entry suggests an allegorization of the limits
of empirical knowledge. It is not inconceivable that Chimalpahin was aware
of Copernicus, for his writings circulated widely in New Spain. Moreover, he
suggests that the ignorance of the ancients was due to their being pagans—
consequently that Juan Bautista's knowledge of the sky amounts to an article
of faith: "auh yn tachcocolhuan. yn huhuetque. yn oc tlateotocanime yn motenehua Gentilesme catca atle huel quimattiaque. yn itechpa in. yc ypampa yn
omotlapololtitiaque" [and our forefathers, the ancients who were still idolaters,
called gentiles, were not able to find out anything about this, because of this
they were confused].[44]

Chimalpahin underscores that colonial authorities promoted fear by asking people to abstain from eating and drinking, and from leaving their houses
because of a malignant air (given that the astrologers were off by several hours
and people went out into the streets, these cautions proved unfounded). The
entry concludes by mentioning that many people died from stabbings in a generalized state of anomie that affected Spanish and Nahuas alike. In one passage, where Chimalpahin mentions that astrologers interpret eclipses as signs

that a kingdom or a ruler would perish, he exposes their reasoning as indulging in a *post hoc ergo propter hoc* fallacy: "yn campa tlalli ypam momiquiliz. yhuann aqui. amo no huel momati yn campa mochihuatiuh ye quin ihquac necitiuh yn campa ye omochiuh. yece ye onez. ytech yn tonatiuh. ynic omixtlapachoca ca oquinezcayoti, yn iuh mochihuaz" [in what land he will die and who he is cannot be known either, nor where it will happen. That will appear later, at the place where it happened. But it already appeared in the fact that the surface of the sun was darkened, for that was a sign that it would happen].[45] But Chimalpahin's brilliant phenomenological description of the eclipse and the temporality of its experience figure more prominently than his critique of the presumed superiority of Spanish knowledge.

Even when God appears to clear the sky so that all the citizens of New Spain could perceive the marvels of the world by clearing the sky from clouds that were covering the sun, Chimalpahin's language carries a descriptive force: "ca yn ihquac. yc ye pehua. ye tlacoçahuia. in ye mixtlapachoz. yca metztli tonatiuh. yn motenehua ye qualoz. yn ilhuicatl ca nohuiampa mixtli yc tzauhctimanca. acan huel hualnecia. auh çan iyocan. çan ixquich yn oncan yetiuh tonatiuh. çan mixcanactli yn oncan huel yxpan yxco quiquiçaya" [because when the light began to fade, when the surface of the sun began to be covered by the moon, which is called "being eaten," the sky was closed everywhere by clouds, only in the place where the sun was going a few thin clouds flowed by in front of the face of the sun].[46] The juxtaposition of God making visible the eclipse and the description of the experience complement each other in that the description of every detail using all his senses conveys a sense of wonder in the contemplation of the world. The clouds move slowly, the sky clears, the sun figures alone in the center and gradually disappears with a gradation of dark hues: "yn ixcuichehuaca. yn ixpoyahualiz. yn ixmatlallehuaca" [blackness, darkness, dark blueness].[47] The duration passes very slowly until the sky suddenly becomes dark, as if it were eight o'clock at night.

Chimalpahin writes *chicuey tzillini*, literally "eight soundings of metal," suggesting the church bells that first introduced the Nahuas to the Christian keeping of the hours. Here the concept of night is paired with an hour of the day, but the description of the eclipse follows the hours of the early afternoon. It is not only days but hours that make of this recording of daily life a most unconventional form of annals, if that is what we should call this testimony of lived experience. Chimalpahin conveys a stoppage of time, a prolonged instant during the time the sun was eaten: "çan niman aoctle ypan hualla, aoctle ypan oquiz" [in that instant nothing came, nothing passed by].[48] The sun might not die or be eaten, but the metaphor of *tonatiuh quallo* is an apt expression for the experience of a stoppage of time, clearly much more accurate than the simile of Juan Bautista's "shady shelter." Chimalpahin records a *now*, a prolonged instant, not a blink of the eye; it is the temporality of the world that stops in the instant, not a *now* that would pertain to the experience of internal time-consciousness.[49]

As the entry progresses the discourse of science, of what cannot be known by direct observation gives place to the experience of colors, sensations, duration, and minute details. The experience of the phenomenon partakes of the wonders of God who works marvels so that we can appreciate his creation, and in this respect the ancestors in their gentility might have ignored what seems to be a dogma with respect to the geocentric structure of the heavens, but their experience of the world was accurately captured by their metaphors.

In the *Diario* we once more find an instance of the rewriting of European knowledge, indeed of the genre of the *diario*, in terms of the Mesoamerican institution of historical writing, which Chimalpahin summarizes in a phrase that defines his project of writing for future readers and listeners, not unlike Tezozomoc's archive for the generations to come: "O yhuin mochihuin ynic mihtohua oqualoc tonatiuh. yn ipan in omoteneuh cemilhuitl viernes, nican o mochi motecpan yn itlahtollo. yn iuh omochiuh. ynic nican quittazque. yhuan quimatizque yn ixquichtin in quin ye tlacatizque in quin çatepan yc nemiquihui nican tlalticpac" [Regarding this that occurred, what is called the sun was eaten, on the said day Friday a full account of it was put in order here so that all those are born later and will live here on earth afterward, those who will not ever see the like, will see and find out about it here].[50]

Let's complement this anticipation of future readers with another invocation from *La Octava relación*, the expressiveness of which cannot but touch us many centuries later:

> Ayc polihuiz ayc ylcahuiz, mochipa pialoz, ticpiazque yn titepilhuan in titeixhu-ihuan in titeyccahuan in titemintonhuan in titepiptonhuan in titechichicahuan, in tetentzonhuan in titeyxquamolhuan in titeteyztihuan, in titetlapallohuan in titehezçohuan, intitlayllotlacatepilhuan, in ipan otiyolque otitlacatque in icce tlaxillacalyacatl moteneuhua Tlayllotlacan Tecpan, y huel oncan catca y huel oncan omotlahtocatillico yn izquintin in tlaçohuehuetque in tlaçotlahtoque chichimeca, in tlayllotlacatlahtoque in tlayllotlacateteuhctin, ynic mitohua inin tlahtolli "Tlayllotlacan Tecpan pielli."

> [Never will it be lost or forgotten. It will always be kept, because we will keep it. We who are the younger brothers, the children, the grandchildren, the great-grandchildren, the great-great-grandchildren, the very elders. We who are their beard, their eyebrow, their color and blood. We who are the descendants of the Tlailotlaca, who have been born and live in the first *tlaxillacalyacatl*, called Tlailotlacan Tecpan, where the rulers, the loved ancients and loved *tlatoque* Chichimeca, the *tlatoque* and *teuctin tlailotlaca*. Hence it is called "Tlailotlacan Tecpan archive."][51]

Reading Tezozomoc and Chimalpahin in the Mesoamerican institution of historical writing entails paying attention to the author function these writers assume to collect testimonies, to transmit them to posterity, and to negotiate the intersection of Christian and Mesoamerican temporality. On the basis of Agamben's definition of the *auctor*-witness, I have argued that these Nahua historians assume the role of collecting voices that otherwise would disappear in the murmur of everyday speech. These are voices that phrase speech forms that attest to the richness of Nahuatl traditional accounts of the past. It is not just what the ancestors said, the foundational stories they told when consulting the pictographic *amoxtli*, but preserving the actual "voicings" for posterity. In fact, one could say that histories written by missionaries like Durán, Motolinía, Tovar, and Acosta—to just name those intimately related to Tezozomoc's *Chronica Mexicayotl*—recorded the substance of the foundational stories of Tenochtitlan, but what is unique to the Nahua historians is that they preserve the speech forms as well as the historiographical genre one may trace in pictographic accounts. Much has to be done on the diverse speech genres and multiple voice modulations in Tezozomoc and Chimalpahin writings.

Rather than rushing to isolate (and celebrate) oppositional practices, I have underscored that the work of memory is a two-way street. I have traced the insertion of Mesoamerican voices in the institutions of Latin alphabetical script. Reading Tezozomoc and Chimalpahin, we have observed how these Nahua historians insert the qualifying terms of idolatry and the devil, running the risk of depleting Mesoamerican spiritual expressions of life. As they record what we may call the theogonic gests of the main supernatural protagonists in the foundational stories of Tenochtitlan, the effect is one in which the stories of old survive as remains resulting from the negation yet preservation of ancient spirituality from within the Christian institutions of historical writing. The universal history of Christianity now includes, along with the Roman past, traces of Mesoamerican civilization. As Tezozomoc and Chimalpahin knew all too well, there is a secular dimension to Christianity that has as its vocation the subsumption of all history under its temporality. In passing, we may suggest the opposite argument and ask ourselves (along with Gil Anidjar) about the secret history of secularism as grounded in Christian roots: "And is it not *this* secularized religion—Christianity—that has elaborated and deployed a peculiar discourse *about itself* and *as it understood itself and its history* . . . , a discourse that consisted in the critique of religion, that articulated itself as secular criticism?"[52]

The most evident of these practices are the calendrical equivalences between the Mesoamerican and the Gregorian calendars. This practice of simply juxtaposing dates—for example, *ce acatl* (one cane), and 1519—erases the temporality of everyday life under the semblance of a transparent homogeneity of time. Another secular modality, though completely wrapped up in religious language, becomes manifest in the circumscription of Mesoamerican history to messianic time. Beyond the specifically Christian teleology of salvation, the Bible offers a universal history for understanding the significance of events in Mesoamerica but also for enveloping them from within a single world. But having placed the emphasis on the Christian work of memory in the Meso-american institutions of writing, we may return the traffic of ideas and consider that Tezozomoc and Chimalpahin transform these historical forms by making them signify in a locus that is not their own. The significance of their Nahuatl archive remains in a future in which one can only know for certain that there will be readers and listeners who may derive meanings that cannot be anticipated from the perspective of the Christian institution of historical writing.

In the work of Chimalpahin, in particular in the entry on the solar eclipse of July 11, 1611, we find a description of the eclipse that offers an experience of time as duration. His insistence on using the term *tonatiuh quallo* ("the sun is eaten") implicitly questions the accuracy of astrologer's comparison to a "shelter that provides shade." If we may relate Chimalpahin's experience of temporality with the Dominican emphasis on the development of spiritual habitus, we may also retrieve from Dominicans like Las Casas the understanding that the essence of Christianity, the experience of the messianic *now*, does not depend on a historical narrative nor on a particular set of dogmas.

On Documentary and Testimony

The Revisionists' History, the Politics of Truth, and the Remembrance of the Massacre at Acteal, Chiapas

Nevertheless, the ideologues are at work. You can be confident of that. Certain ideologues conjure away the facts, in somewhat the same fashion that the Hitler genocide (to which I am in no way comparing the crimes of Sabra and Shatila) is made to vanish under the pens of the "revisionists." It wasn't a matter of massacres, you see, but of battles.

—PIERRE VIDAL-NAQUET

On December 22, 2007, the community of Acteal, Chiapas, celebrated the tenth anniversary of the massacre of forty-five defenseless, unarmed members of the pacifist civil organization Las Abejas (The Bees). For this occasion Las Abejas sponsored an Encuentro Nacional Contra la Impunidad (National Encounter Against Impunity), in which two documentaries were screened: *A Massacre Foretold* (2007), by the Scottish filmmaker Nick Higgins, and *Acteal: 10 Años de impunidad, ¿y cuantos más . . . ?* (Acteal: 10 years of impunity. And how many more?) (2007), by the Tzotzil member of Las Abejas José Alfredo Jiménez. More than two thousand people participated in this encounter and celebration calling for a national mobilization against impunity and thus seeking to bring to justice the highest authorities responsible for rampant human rights abuses in Mexico, including, importantly, the case of the massacre of Acteal. The call for justice entails, beyond the trial of isolated individuals, an interrogation of the Mexican juridical-legal structures: the objective of the mobilization is to question the model of the nation, hence to dismantle state institutions that monopolize violence while claiming to be democratic. The victims of the massacre included one infant, fourteen children, twenty-one women, and nine men. Five women were pregnant, and one had the fetus pulled out of her womb with a machete. The attack was conducted by paramilitaries trained and armed by the Mexican army and the police force known as Seguridad Pública (Public Security). The monthly celebration of martyrdom recreates a community committed to popular democracy: first by engaging in the Mesoamerican practice of consensus politics, and second by exposing the impunity of those in power.[1]

The tenth anniversary, however, has been haunted by a series of articles that have sought to undermine the community's remembrance of the massacre. My aim has less to do with disputing alternative claims than with offering a poetics of testimony that illuminates the force of the documentaries. These videos provide powerful pedagogical tools for complicating the revisionist appeal to so-called facts and for undoing the attempt to manufacture a historical framework that would generalize all discussions of the event in conformity with the revisionists' perspective.

Higgins's and Jimenez's documentaries have had ample circulation within the Tzotzil communities of Las Abejas and thus exemplify a noncommercial modality of producing popular history—that is, history that effectively counters the hegemony of state historiography. In Higgins's filming of the testimonies we can identify, in those giving testimony (in particular, the Tzotzil witnesses and victims of the massacre), an understanding of video technology—an awareness not only of the visual rhetoric of documentaries, but also of the haptic dimension of being touched by the camera as well as of touching the technology that makes the films possible. In Jimenez's documentary practice we find a young filmmaker who manifests the ability of a community member to produce a cinematic archive. To rephrase Gayatri Chakravorty Spivak, the subaltern can film.

In addition to these two retrospective documentaries that were screened at the Encuentro, three other documentaries were produced in the months following the massacre: *Acteal. Estrategia de muerte* (Acteal, Death Strategy [1998]), by the Mexican filmmaker Carlos Mendoza; *"Towards the Mountain": Chiapas: Prayer for the Weavers* (1999), by the anthropologist Judith Gleason; and *Alonso's Dream* (2000), by the French-Canadian filmmakers Danièle Lacourse and Yvan Patry. Mendoza is part of a team known as Canal 6 de julio, which organized after the fraudulent elections in 1988 with the objective of providing direct accounts of events that would otherwise be subjected to censorship by the official television channels. Mendoza started filming only hours after the massacre became known. He was there when the paramilitaries riding on military trucks were identified, pulled down, and arrested. He also recorded the return of the bodies in caskets to the community of Acteal for a collective burial. Carlos Martínez's *Tierra Sagrada en Zona de conflicto* (Sacred Land in the Zone of Conflict [2000]) is also important to mention. Although it addresses the massacre at Acteal only in passing, Martínez's archive provides footage to the other documentarians for creating a political context as well as a memory that enables them (particularly Higgins's) to trace the origins of violence into a past time when the massacred could not foresee their fate and yet anticipated their own death. Thus the clips themselves take on a new life, become "actors" in the narration of the future.

A discussion of the revisionists' history provides a background for understanding the political and aesthetic challenges the documentarists face. A theoretical discussion of the politics of truth covers three questions: (a) the epistemological limits of testimony; (b) the fabricated and nonfabricated nature of truth; (c) the phenomenology of the violation of the face and the assassination of memory. The respect accorded to the testimonial face offers a key element for examining the remembrance of the massacre of Acteal. In what ways do the documentaries deploy sound and image to resist the imposition of a historical framework that seeks to destroy the face of testimony and the iconicity of Las Abejas who, since the massacre, have reconstituted themselves as a community of martyrs whose land was made sacred by the shedding of innocent blood? In what ways do the documentaries participate in the creation and reproduction of the memory of "los mártires de Acteal" (the martyrs of Acteal) and "la tierra sagrada de Acteal" (the sacred land of Acteal)? There is no hope of appealing to the state, even when there might be honorable persons working within its institutions, if structurally it is fraught with corrupt interests. Recourse resides, therefore, in bringing to light abuses by the state that may be cloaked by impunity but still recognized by most Mexicans who will find their experiences captured by the films on the massacre of Acteal. Beyond the certainties of science, the documentaries' appeal to the subjects' affect (made manifest through both expression and reception) instantiates such work as the ultimate arbiter of truth in testimony.

The Revisionists' History

Revisionist histories, as exemplified by Hector Aguilar Camín's series of articles, "Regreso a Acteal," may also claim truth in testimony, in this case by validating the testimonies of police officers and those who protest imprisonment on false charges.[2] On the basis of Priístas' testimonies to the effect that a group of Abejas ambushed members of the police, Aguilar Camín discredits the Abejas' pacifist vocation.[3] He wrote: "hubo en Pechiquil un choque armado entre agentes de seguridad estatal y miembros no tan pacíficos del grupo Las Abejas" [there was in Pechiquil an armed confrontation between agents of the state's security forces and not-so-pacifist members of the group Las Abejas].[4] This statement strikes at the core of the Abejas' identity as a pacifist Roman Catholic organization.

The state and federal governments denied and continue to deny all responsibility for the paramilitaries and characterize them as spontaneous groups for self-defense that sprang up to resist the threats of the Ejercito Zapatista de Liberación Nacional (EZLN, the Zapatista Army of National Liberation). They have proposed the scenario that the deaths were the result of a legitimate battle between equals—insurgents and self-defense groups—thereby undermining the testimony given by survivors and witnesses that the paramilitaries plotted and executed a massacre. Initially, the federal and state governments had tried to conceal the bodies, but after the event became public, those in power had only the consolation, indeed, the expectation of collective amnesia, or what Pierre Vidal-Naquet has observed as the logic of massacres, citing the examples of Sabra and Shatila: "For a few weeks, the massacre, followed by the Israeli reactions, the establishment of a commission of inquiry, and the first meetings of this commission were front-page news, before disappearing into the common grave of forgetfulness, where massacres are buried."[5] But the Mexican government's wager on forgetting backfired as the international press divulged the massacre and influential foreign states expressed outrage, embarrassing the government of Ernesto Zedillo Ponce de León.

The recent revisionist efforts have adopted to a great extent the perspective of federal and state authorities in which the official version of the events and those of the survivors are given equal weight. Thus Aguilar Camín characterizes the Acteal massacre as the collateral violence of a battle—forty-five people were killed, but this was the consequence of getting caught in the crossfire between Zapatistas and Priístas—and so undoes the claim of a perpetration of a crime against humanity. As such, Aguilar Camín's is a textbook case of what Victoria Sandford has characterized as "the conflicting truths of those with power and those marginalized by it."[6] The work of Aguilar Camín and those following his "police" procedures, like the governmental denials, also matches Vidal-Naquet's exposé of the revisionist commonplace cited at the outset of this chapter. Where Vidal-Naquet writes, "It wasn't a matter of massacres, you see, but of battles," Aguilar Camín coincides: "El tiempo ha sumado testimonio y evidencia que obligan a añadir trazos al cuadro. Uno de ellos es que la matanza de Acteal no fue sólo una matanza sino una batalla" [Time has added testimony and evidence that obligate us to add traces to the picture. One of them is that the massacre of Acteal was not only a massacre but a battle.][7] If the massacre cannot be denied—after all, the police could not make the corpses disappear—the "evidence" now suggests that the victims got caught in the middle of a battle between Zapatistas and the so-called *grupos de autodefensa*. Aguilar Camín wages his bet on "time" as a historical actor against the remembrance and celebration of Las Abejas who, having undergone a transformation into the community of martyrs in a sacred land, vow to reproduce their commitment to pacifism by celebrating the massacre every month on the twenty-second.[8]

The revisionists' history also seeks to augment the official version with the pretense of objectivity and new factual evidence. Revisionists proceed as if they were just listing the facts. At one point in his revisionist account Aguilar Camín questions the credibility of the testimonies in the following terms: "O mintieron los testimonios o mienten las autopsias" [Either the testimonies lie or the autopsies lie].[9] However, confronting survivor testimonies with police evidence in fact commits one to a revisionist attempt to silence the survivors. This cannot be done in all innocence. Nor is there room for emotion in this hammering away at the iconicity of Las Abejas' martyrdom and the conceptualization of Acteal as a sacred land. Aguilar Camín's ultimate objective is to muddle all the evidence that could link the massacre to ex-president Zedillo but also to the current administration that continues to arm and train paramilitaries. Since the massacre of Acteal, federal and state institutions have continued to fund paramilitary groups, paying no heed to the call for the disarmament of paramilitaries.

Thesis

Testimonial documentaries, like all forms of collecting testimony, are by definition forms of engaged dissemination of truth. If testimony necessarily offers the account of a particular individual, its inclusion in a documentary necessarily involves recognition of its veracity. If one were to include a false testimony, one would mark it as such: as untrue. Given this definition, testimonial documentaries call forth an engaged observer: that is, an observer who is willing to believe. The testimonial documentaries are therefore political interventions in the context of disputed truth. In analyzing the work of testimonial documentaries or, for that matter any collection, any argument based on testimony must be suspect of manipulation when claiming no other motivation than providing objective truth. This thesis holds as much for reports by human rights organizations that respond and document atrocities in the immediate aftermath of events as for documentaries and other studies produced after some time has lapsed. One cannot but lend credence to the accounts of those one calls forth to give testimony. In analyzing the work of a testimonial documentary, or for that matter, any testimonial collection, we must acknowledge that the search for wider truths on the basis of testimonial evidence must be leavened by a critical attitude toward the strongly seductive claims of individual testimonies purporting to be objective. There is one more modality of collecting testimonies that does not include the observer form (that is, external mediation) that would consist of witnesses creating their own documentaries. In this case the politics of truth stands in its most open nakedness.

The Politics of Truth

If I address the revisionist texts, it is not to debunk their versions of the events and thus contribute to the detailed responses that have already exposed these manipulations of truth. The goal is rather to shift to the level of the politics of truth, also veiled over in the revisionists' claims to be solely concerned with setting the record straight. Claiming the evidential status of their sources necessarily if unwittingly commits revisionists to a biased approximation to the events—not only because the biases of the sources go unacknowledged but also because the political motivation of safeguarding, for instance, the culpability of former president Ernesto Zedillo Ponce de León, currently a professor of globalization at Yale University, is obviated. For their part the community of the Abejas, human rights organizations, engaged documentary filmmakers, and activists seek not only to expose and denounce Zedillo's culpability and the state's criminality, but also to expose the impunity of the rich and powerful in Mexico. At least among some groups, this amounts to a call to dismantle the Mexican juridico-legal system as a whole.

In writing and reflecting on these documentaries as testimonies of truth, we face the situation that revisionist historians will simply call these testimonies partisan and characterize the tears of the testimonials as sham. They cite the falsity of Benjamin Wilkomirski's narrative of his childhood experience in a German concentration camp, as exposed by Stefan Mächler in *The Wilkomirski Affair: A Study in Autobiographical Truths*, to shore up their reminder to us that history should not be subjected to emotional arguments and that the task of the historian is to tear through appearances in the pursuit of objective truth. One can easily imagine a montage that would produce a comparable revisionist effect.

Here we might benefit from Beatriz Sarlo's interrogation of the epistemological limits of knowing the past in the context of the uses of testimony in the commissions for truth in Argentina. By systematically inquiring into the limits of experience, memory, and the transformation of "testimony into an icon of Truth or into the most important resource for the reconstruction of the past," Sarlo offers an iconoclastic undoing of the primacy of testimony.[10] But hers is not a revisionist text, nor do her political motivations have anything to do with the exculpation of military responsible for the regime of terror during the dictatorship. Rather, she aims to expose the incapacity of testimony to do away with the theory of the two demons—that is, the narrative that proposes that both the left and the right were responsible for the violence. Sarlo's project elicited the indignation of those who experienced torture and the loss of family members. But her iconoclasm offends not only because she shows the testimonials to be subjective and constructed, but also because she defies the possibility of appealing to a historical logic in which testimony holds an unquestionable epistemological privilege. Her critique applies both to revisionist historians who question the evidence and to those who claim truth on the basis of testimony.

Notwithstanding the value of Sarlo's intervention, we may still question the iron-fisted critical stance that underlies her dismantling of testimony—

that is, her appreciative acceptance that "Paul De Man's critique of autobiog-raphy is perhaps the highest point in literary deconstructivism, which today still is a hegemonic current."[11] Sarlo's is one of many possible takes on decon-structivism, and we need not accede to her demand to respond to its "radical critique" of the certainty of knowledge, at least not here. Instead, we may limit ourselves to the observation that testimony partakes of other forms of knowl-edge besides those based on fact and falsification, or even on experience. I refer to Janet Walker's discussion of deconstruction and history, which I take as an antidote to Sarlo's hegemonic deconstructivism (whatever that is) and in particular her location of problems of testimony under the deconstructivist umbrella. Walker adopts the concept of disremembering or remembering that does not bear an obviously indexical relationship to past events from novelist Toni Morrison's *Beloved* and José Muñoz's description of a performance piece by Marga Gómez: "As both Morrison's story of slavery and Muñoz's examples of gay subjectivity suggest, disremembering is not a whimsical practice but a survival strategy for minoritarian subjects. Disremembering can become ur-gent when events are personally unfathomable or socially unacceptable."[12] In Walker's terms: "Disremembering is not the same as not remembering. It is re-membering with a difference," and in fact one could argue that all remember-ing entails a form of disremembering.[13] In any case, the point is that mistaken memories, amnesias, and other such aporia should not entail the dismissal of testimony, but rather a redefinition of epistemological terms that would no longer call forth factuality as the ultimate criterion.

The testimonial film can sidestep the framework revisionists attempt to impose, not by an immediate, innocent, and iconoclastic expression of truth, but by taking full advantage of the fabric of the testimonial film. From Bruno Latour we learn how belief is bound to the iconoclastic destruction of the icon: "'Fetish' and 'fact' can be traced to the same root. The *fact* is that which is fab-ricated and not fabricated. . . . But the *fetish* too is that which is fabricated and not fabricated. There is nothing secret about this joint etymology. Everyone says it constantly, explicitly, obsessively: the scientists in their laboratory prac-tice, the adepts of fetish cults in their rites. But we use these words *after* the hammer has broken them in two: The fetish has become nothing but empty stone onto which meaning is mistakenly projected; the fact has become abso-lute certainty which can be used as a hammer to break away all the delusions of belief."[14]

Bringing fact and fetish back together, Latour calls for an understand-ing that both are fabrications, historical artifacts that at once gain and lose the power of their claims in coming to be known as (artifactual) *factishes*. Therefore, although Latour has Pasteur's fabrication of bacteria in mind ("the scientists in their laboratory practice"), we may extend his notion of fabrication to the cinematographic act of recording moving images and sounds. We may cite Latour again: "I never act; I am slightly surprised by what I do. That which acts through me is also surprised by what I do. . . . Action is not about mastery. It is not a question of a hammer and shards, but one of bifurcations, events, circumstances."[15] Indeed, this applies to the filmmaker, the witness, the viewer, and also to the apparatus. The *artifactuality* of testimonial films will thus include both the human actors (the interaction of witness, filmmaker, cinematographer, and so on) and the agency of the technological innovations of video and film in general.

Rather than seeing these audio-visual texts as truthful representations of the community of martyrs (which they are), we ought to underscore that these documentaries, as Latour would put it, *fabricate* and *not fabricate* the truth of Acteal, by strategically juxtaposing verbal testimony and visual information, providing close-ups of the faces of survivors and witnesses, inserting strident concrete music to the slow-motion images of tanks or of arrogant paramilitaries parading through towns, recording and profiling musicians playing traditional instruments and elders chanting prayers, and capturing the beauty of the highland's landscape with views of immense mountain ranges and deep canyons. The truths produced in the documentaries should be understood as *factishes*, rather than just the facts.[16]

Ultimately, we must ask ourselves in what consists the offense of revisionist histories, of their iconoclasm, of their destruction of the testimonial face? In drawing a phenomenological reflection on the injunction "thou shall not kill," which implies a "me" (the most immediate subject in the injunction against murder), but also the "face" of another person, Jean-Luc Marion has extended the meaning of "to kill" beyond the act of putting to death: "To kill," writes Marion, "thus indicates the destruction of the other person or thing, its objectivization into an insignificant term, entirely annulled, henceforth without force or value."[17] The assassination of memory in revisionist histories furthers the initial objectivization that led to murder. But in the end the assassination of memory depends on, or more precisely, responds to the capacity of the face always to be caught up in an epistemological chain: "The possibility that this face lies to me or, as happens more often, first lies to itself, as one of its possible consequences, in the irreducible gap between expression starting from infinite lived experience and conceptualizable, sayable, and always inadequate expression."[18] In giving us the testimonies, filmmakers ask viewers to respect the injunction "thou shall not kill," and to understand that group of those giving testimonials includes the "me," the face of my testimony, persistent beyond death. With full awareness that the face remains vulnerable, those giving testimony entrust themselves to the filmmakers' commitment to the veracity of their testimony. While remaining conscious of the impossibility of preventing

their violation by viewers, they opt for forcefully acting on the potential objectification by camera.

The Remembrance of the Massacre at Acteal

The documentaries I examine here approach Las Abejas and the massacre
from different perspectives that include anthropological methodologies, political analysis, and the creation of audiovisual archives for countering official
accounts that have distorted and continue to distort the nature of massacre.
These latter archival practices were begun only days after the president of
Mexico, Ernesto Zedillo Ponce de León (1994–2000), addressed the nation
on television to lament the events, calling on the nation to mourn the dead.
The creation of a visual archive of testimonies, incrementally over the years,
has been undertaken to reveal the responsibility of Zedillo by underscoring
that the massacre must be understood in the frame of a state crime. The more
recent documentaries counter revisionist histories that have been written to
safeguard Zedillo and the other officers from accountability in anticipation of
the tenth anniversary of the mass murders.

If Mendoza's 1998 video offers vibrant immediate documentation of the
events, fully conscious of deploying the aesthetics of "imperfect cinema," Higgins's film offers an aesthetically accomplished yet politically forceful addition
to earlier accounts. "To this day, the full story of the massacre of Acteal has
never been told," Higgins tell us in his deep Scottish accent at the beginning
of the film. Jiménez's video responds to the most recent revisionist efforts with
testimonials by survivors of the massacre and by witnesses of the paramilitaries' plans to attack Acteal, but also with testimonials by the well-known
journalist Carlos Rocha, the director of Agencia Detrás de la Noticia (Agency
Behind the News), and General José Francisco Gallardo, who was incarcer-
ated for more than a decade on false charges of corruption aimed at silencing his accusations of terrorism by the military. Rocha and Gallardo testify
authoritatively that the massacre was indeed a state crime. Gallardo's testimony documents the training of the Mexican military and the constitution
of paramilitary forces with the aid of Mexican training films on the subject of
low-intensity warfare.

These films, although produced by the Mexican army, were adapted from
similar training films produced at Fort Bragg, North Carolina, a military base
that bills itself on its Web site as "one of the United States's most combat ready
and active military installations." Moreover, in Mendoza's video we learn that
Israeli experts in counterinsurgency have also participated in the training of
the Mexican army on Mexican soil. In the footage compiled from the Mexican
counterinsurgency films, we see and hear soldiers screaming slogans calling
for death to the Zapatistas and claiming to be crazy and demented ("somos locos

y dementes"). In contrast to these more overtly political films, the documentaries by Lacourse and Patry and Gleason offer ethnographic documentation of Las Abejas' spirituality, which lies at the root of their definition as a pacifist indigenous organization committed to the exposure of state terrorism.

Both early and recent documentaries repeatedly project Zedillo's presidential address in montages that juxtapose his sorrowful expression with images of tanks, heavily armed police, and paramilitaries forcing thousands into refugee camps. His high-pitched voice and stiff posturing on television, calling on the nation collectively to mourn the tragedy, has a false ring when editorially confronted with the state-sponsored military and police violence. These latter images are punctuated with avant-garde music, further exposing and intensifying the sordidness of the presidential address. Given the limitations of the written form, I can only suggest the intensity of the soundtrack in these works by mentioning how in Higgins's film the vibrant strings of Nils Økland's experimental Norwegian folk sound alternate with the Montreal-based Set the Fire on Flames's post-rock/math/noise sound to accentuate the menace already recorded in the slow-motion replay of film stock of tanks. The foreboding of terror one feels while "riding" in the passenger seat on dark roads is palpable. We hear the avant-garde sound of Set the Fire on Flames's "Shitheap-gloria of the new town planning," syncopating the march of the Zapatistas at the start of their travel across the nation to disseminate the ideals of the "other campaign," the *otra campaña* (the promotion of a popular democracy as an alternative to electoral politics during the 2006 presidential elections), flowing seamlessly into the traditional music played by Tzotzil Abejas at the end of a pilgrimage that had carried the virgin to several Abeja communities (for the promotion of Catholic-inspired radical pacifism).

Thus the sequence opens with a speech by Comandante Tacho announcing the beginning of the *nueva campaña* in the context of the Zapatista uprising in 1994, moves to the Zapatistas marching accompanied by Set the Fire on Flames, and then cuts to the Abeja pilgrimage to end with an exposition of the history of the Abejas by a Tzotzil witness named Antonio. In this way Higgins's brilliant montage conveys the shared nature of the struggle for democracy in Mexico. Not unlike the Abejas, who move with ease from traditional music to tropical *cumbia*, Higgins's play with the avant-garde Zapatista march and the Abeja traditional instruments conveys the Tzotzil ability to dwell in a plurality of worlds in which the multiple temporality of the modern and the nonmodern coexist without contradiction. As such, the nonmodern does not refer to a premodern antechamber, rather to an *elsewhere* from which the most modern technologies are observed and deployed.[19]

Across the documentary films, we find a broad range of approaches that include immediate documentation right after the massacre that counter the claims by revisionists: Mendoza's *Acteal. Estrategia de muerte*; two documentaries that offer windows into Tzotzil life forms and practices of remembrance, Gleason's *"Towards the Mountain"* and Lacourse and Patry's *Alonso's Dream*; and two recent documentaries produced on the eve of the tenth anniversary, Higgins's *A Massacre Foretold* and Jiménez's *Acteal. 10 Años de impunidad, ¿y cuantos más . . . ?*. But in every case we must attend not only to the forceful testimony to the reality of the massacre but also to the cinematic rendition of the reenactment of martyrdom in ritual, the welcoming of the gift of death, and the grounding of the community in faith (reenactments that encompass testimony but are not limited to it).

Faith here is not based on abidance to a creed but understood as inseparable from a state of grace. Gleason's *A Prayer for the Weavers* conveys the community of the faithful by organizing the narrative around the prayer chanted by an elder. As the prayer is chanted in Tzotzil, Gleason provides a translation but also interrupts the chant to give information on the Abejas and the massacre. Gleason requests what seems obvious, but what we often forget: "We ask you to listen closely to the people. They are the experts here." Going beyond the intellectual hubris that insists on demonstrating the incompatibility of Mesoamerican life forms and Christianity, a position shared by both anthropologists and postcolonial critics eager to find a proof of their theories of resistance, Gleason remains true to her subjects' spiritual expressions. (Nowhere does the interrogation, by our modern inquisitors, manifest a more insulting form than when revisionist historians denigrate the community of the faithful of Acteal by suggesting that Tzotzil modes of Christianity are flawed, as if the revisionists themselves could claim propriety on what it means to be a Christian, indeed, a *católico*).

The prayer invokes the Holy Mother and the Holy Father and calls for the care of hearts, minds, and bodies. It calls for a gathering of the community, of the community of believers, of *creyentes de la religión católica*, as the Abejas refer to themselves. The remembrance of the dead is likened to a festival—it is indeed a marvelous day, in which they come to dwell among the living; in which the community of believers celebrates the massacre as giving place to the sacred land of martyrs of Acteal. The Abejas see their speech as fighting words that, by manifesting their faith, sting those bent on destroying them. It is an apt metaphor for a militant pacifist organization willing to join forces with the Zapatistas and yet remain independent—the recurrent theme in all the Abejas documentaries. In the background of Gleason's film one hears the cries of the community of weavers who day and night weave in sorrow and sadness. The song ends by calling on the Creator, in the singular, who comes to resonate with the Holy Father, the Holy Mother, the plural "Oh Creators," of the opening lines. One mystery now resides within the other. The singer asks those present to excuse him for ending the oration.

Also in an ethnographic vein, Lacourse and Patry's *Alonso's Dream* organizes the account of the massacre around Tzotzil life forms, which in their case includes the significance of dreams in Tzotzil communities, the centrality of corn and the reverence of Mother Earth, and the tradition of weavers in which the women use waist looms and embroidery in the production of their clothing while the men work with large looms to produce the ubiquitous blue cloth used for skirts. The film punctuates the narrative of the massacre with scenes that document all the stages in the production of the cloth (the fabrication of cotton, spinning, dying, and weaving; traditions passing from fathers to sons) and different moments in the planting and sowing of corn. These latter practices are linked together by an elderly woman who chants a prayer to Mother Earth in scenes of tilling the earth and planting the corn, a chant that recurs and is only completed at the end of the documentary.

This last scene follows the refugee Alonso's narration of the dream by the murdered catechist Alonso—whom the Abejas remember and constitute as an icon of martyrdom in their chants and prayers—a dream in which the land had become extremely fertile. Alonso the narrator also had a dream in which the land was on fire and he ran from the flames; after analysis within the community, it was concluded that dream meant that he and the Abejas were being accused of causing the conflict and that they would have to pay for it. Alonso's refusal to join the paramilitaries and his eventual naming of paramilitaries forced him and his family to abandon the village of Los Chorros and seek refuge in the city of San Cristobal de las Casas. Another reason Alonso cannot return to his community of Los Chorros is that some of the responsible paramilitaries that he named, instead of having been charged and jailed like the others, continue to this day to roam the highlands threatening to kill those who do not join their efforts to combat and destroy Zapatista sympathizers and EZLN bases of support.

In one of the most memorable moments in the film, we find Alonso sitting in his house in San Cristobal with his wife and children, watching edited footage of the town of Los Chorros by the filmmakers Lacourse and Patry. What they (and we) are seeing is originally recorded archival evidence of paramilitaries patrolling the town and imposing their authority, replayed in slow motion and silence (the only sound we hear is the barely audible voice of a man questioning a woman, dialogue that was not completely filtered out in the editing process) so as to accentuate the force of what transpires: Alonso's sudden identification of the paramilitaries by name and his description of their sordid activities terrorizing the municipality of Chenalho. This sequence of a film within a film draws attention to the filmmaking process as it unfolds, since Lacourse and Patry—having shared their footage with Faustina, Alonso, and their children—went on to create this powerful, self-reflexive montage to propel their narrative.

Just before the sequence with Alonso and his family, we had already been introduced to the same images of the paramilitaries Antonio Santis Vázquez and his brother, interrupted by a close-up of Vázquez. The close-up would seem properly to belong to another series of frames, except that it is this very shot that enables Alonso, while he himself is on camera, to recognize and identify Vázquez. One wonders if the redundant inclusion of this whole first sequence of the brothers is a mistake. But the redundancy does, after all, have the doubly reflexive effect of reproducing the process through which the filmmakers shot and edited the video footage to create an archive, screened it for the family, and included the results in the film itself. We become witness, in this way, to the winding and rewinding of the identification process. The play between Alonso the catechist martyr, Alonso the witness, and Alonso the displaced subject living in the city, sums up the collective experience of the Abejas. The segment certainly conveys the *factish* nature of the truth about the paramilitaries— here a handsome, smiling man walking down the streets of his village turns into a paramilitary by means of Faustina's pointing finger and the eeriness of the slow-motion footage (figures 12.1 and 12.2)—and the segment's status as both *fabrication* and *not fabrication*, as Latour would put it.

Now, a detailed discussion of Higgins's *A Massacre Foretold*. Beyond the proffered information (all those elements he might claim "have never been told before), we must attend to the aesthetic form that lends force to the film. This should enable us to sidestep the revisionist framework that seeks to destroy the face of the Abejas, to hammer the iconicity of the testimonials to ruins. *A Massacre Foretold* is a documentary film by Nick Higgins, but what does it mean to attribute authorship when the film is as much a product of the witnesses giving testimony, of anthropologists lending their expert opinion, of human rights activists documenting the events, of religious authorities laying down their moral authority, and of film stock from previous documentaries— most particularly from Carlos Martínez's archives, but also from news briefs taken from NBC and CNN? The stock in Martínéz's archive goes well beyond the materials Martínez used in his own documentary, *Tierra sagrada en zona de conflicto*. Higgins draws from Martínez's archive for his opening scene in which a member of Las Abejas, in his sixties, testifies to the oppression from the paramilitaries and the restrictions they face for carrying out their most basic everyday activities of tending the fields, collecting coffee beans, even traveling to other communities (figure 12.3). In a brilliant instance of in medias

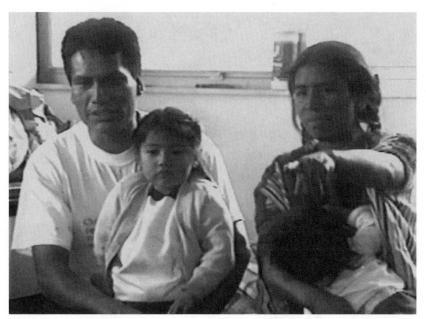

FIGURE 12.1. Faustina pointing. *Alonso's Dream*. Courtesy of Danièle Lacourse and Alter-Ciné.

FIGURE 12.2. Paramilitary. *Alonso's Dream*. Courtesy of Danièle Lacourse and Alter-Ciné.

FIGURE 12.3. Vicente anticipating the massacre. *A Massacre Foretold*. Courtesy of Nick Higgins and Landsdowne Productions.

res a witness named Vicente speaks in voiceover the words "ayer empezó," it started yesterday that the paramilitaries were shooting their arms, "estaban sonando sus armas," before appearing in the frame, with just the mountains in the background. It is November 1997.

We see Alonso, who led the community in prayer on the day of his death in the massacre, and who has become an icon of martyrdom, standing quietly next to Vicente. This is the only image of Alonso, other than the family photographs. Soon after this scene from the past, recurrent throughout the film, Higgins informs us that most of the people depicted were dead twenty-eight days later. The film immediately cuts to Antonio, who reappears at strategic moments, providing the main narrative thread of the events. Later in the film, this opening scene recurs as a reminder of the victims of the massacre. We see children, young boys and girls grouped by gender, for the most part very young, just kids. One boy, no older than six, is particularly moving as he makes his way into the frame, with a toothless smile.

In Higgins's documentary, Martínez's film stock from November 1997 thus functions as an "actor" whose meaning exceeds the immediacy of the events, revealing the nature of temporality in film. It is not just a passage quoted but a voice and sequence of shots that bring the dead back to life and periodically anticipate the massacre. It is a fragment from the past, from a time in which the participants ignored their destiny, even when Vicente's speech conveys an uncanny prescience of death: hence the title of the documentary, *A Massacre Foretold*. Martínez has captured a time that becomes integral to the duration of the remembrance of massacre in Higgins's work. It is a time past, a time that ignored the future but that now functions as testimony of the group's vulnerability. But the sequence itself is invulnerable to revisionist iconoclasm that would seek to smash its iconicity by insisting that maybe Vicente is lying—because Vicente merely states, "ayer empezó." It is an *ayer* "a yesterday," laying deep in the collective unconscious: a continuum of discrete moments that evoke a nearing present. Rather than a sense of time in which the present makes sense of the past, we have here a past that never fully arrives, but comes nevertheless to define our present. Viewers now experience the world with a transformed habitus immersed in a fluidity of unrepresentable time that defines and seats in our memories the experience of self and world. The repetition of scenes and actors ground the significance of immediate and past frames. The recurrence of Antonio, of Bishop Samuel Ruiz, of anthropologist Andres Aubrey, of human rights activist Blanca Martínez Busto, of Maria, and of others pushes the narrative forward. But the interrupted and recurring testimonies also remind us that the documentary itself has a history of its production from clips that create a continuum of a past becoming and defining a never reached present. The film's time frame ends, as does its time of viewing, but viewers now carry its images, noises, music, voices, colors, gestures, and above all the gestures of those who gave testimony. We see gestures by those who can no longer see themselves.

We never see the eyes of the witnesses, with the possible exception of Antonio, who looks at us from behind a visor, a shaded face that allows us to intuit that he is looking at us and yet we never fully see his eyes (figure 12.4). His look resembles that of a blind man, a visionary who transports us to the past with his voice, who sits facing us without gesture—which itself is a form of gesturing. In his voice he carries the voices of others, most particularly of Alonso. Antonio tells us of the Zapatista uprising; indeed, as he relates it, the Abejas knew the EZLN was an indigenous army struggling for the same causes, in the same condition of oppression, but one they would not join because they did not believe in violence. After a few seconds of silence, in voiceover, he goes on to tell us about the verbal exchange with Alonso on the eve of the massacre: "Había desplazados aquí en esta ermita y un hermano que se llama Alonso Gómez Vázquez, y el me preguntó, 'Toño,' dice—'¿qué?'—'¿estás seguro que nos van a matar?' Ahi comenzó a llorar. Ya nosotros tuvimos que esperar la muerte" [There were refugees here in the small church and a brother named Alonso Gómez Vázquez, and he asked me, "Toño," he says—"what?"—"Are you sure they are going to kill us?" Then he started to cry. We had to await

FIGURE 12.4. Antonio. *A Massacre Foretold*. Courtesy of Nick Higgins and Landsdowne Productions.

death]. Antonio barely moves, barely makes a gesture other than the inflection of martyred Alonso's voice.

Otherwise the interviewees avoid our eyes, with only an accidental touching of our sight. This is the standard, the protocol in testimonial documentaries: never to address the viewers directly, as if the insistence on credibility that would supposedly come from the gaze would betray a mask—indeed, expose the face to destruction. In these documentaries direct eye contact occurs only in the case of Zedillo, whose assurance seems to beg for credibility, and in that of the newscasters who partake, precisely, of a setting that calls for a mask: we know they are reading a teleprompter. By looking to the side, witnesses avoid the smashing of the iconoclast who would scream, "look at the eyes, the face is a mask, it conceals a liar."

In the flow of time there is no time for such a fixing, unlike in still photography, which inevitably calls forth and anticipates the death of the subject in the embalming of the face. Clearly, we can reproduce stills, as I am doing in this essay, and stills may or may not appear in a given film. But when they do, they may serve an authenticating function or even reproducing the semblance of the dead as in the capturing of the photographs of the massacred in the collective tomb in Acteal. And yet the still will inevitably permeate the temporality of film with a remainder of what cannot be wholly mastered. Stills become actors with uncertain meanings that interact with the use of sound and silence to accentuate the sordidness of the events, to infuse nature with melancholy, or to anticipate the emergence of speakers, pilgrims, musicians. For instance, in Lacourse and Patry's use of freeze frames of the victims in the collective tomb of Acteal, one cannot but wonder at the ways in which the capture of stills in cinema furthers the martyrdom of the face. Whereas stills of landscapes or solitary dirt roads offer pauses for meditating on life lived, those of the dead and the living suggest masks that delimit the impenetrability of the faces.

To the stills we must add the use of slow-motion cinematography as a means of identifying and authenticating a landscape and capturing the movement of people: paramilitaries roaming the towns, military weaponry, the sadness of mourning. Stills and slow motion both provide images that penetrate our consciousness, depositing meaning and sensations deep in our unconscious and shaping our habitus. The past will now explore the world with new eyes, or better, with a new sense of touch that affects all the senses, saturating them with haptic qualities.

In viewing films, not only our eyes and ears are touched, but through the various techniques of which stills and slow motion are limit cases, we learn to touch the world with sight and listening. And listening to sound and silence in turn transforms the visual. In relation to the function of the face and speech, let's choose an example of how gestures speak for themselves. In *A Massacre Foretold*, gestures emphasize the ironic tone in which the mayor of Chenalho, Jacinto Arias, accuses the Bishop Samuel Ruiz and his catechists of the Diocese of San Cristobal de las Casas of promoting the violence plaguing the municipality. As his pointing hand lectures us on the truth of the causes of violence in Chenalho, the film captures the posturing that betrays his attitude. Mayor Arias was shortly thereafter arrested for his intellectual participation in the massacre. Now let us contrast this scene with Maria's gestures in Higgins's film. If the inscrutability of the face could lead a viewer to see a mask disguising a liar (admittedly, a forced reading considering the pain her face expresses), Maria's credibility is secured in the constant wringing of her hands, in the nervousness that conveys the agony of having to recount the story one more time. Maria herself was not at the scene of the massacre, but she lost several family members, including her brother Alonso. We learn from Maria that the police kept them from entering Acteal, and she tells of the struggle they faced to get the authorities to return the bodies for a proper burial.

Gestures in the video reveal character, not because of a body language that had to be pierced through to get at the truth, but because the truth itself is on the surface of the image. For the gestures touch the camera and touch us. While being touched by the request to answer questions and the camera's intrusion, those filmed—whether Maria, who speaks as a witness to the atrocity, or the mayor of Chenalho, who speaks as a witness to the political activities of the Tzotzil catechists and Roman Catholic priests—must at once know the media anticipate the effects on the viewer and also remain unconscious, blind to their own gesturing. Gestures as such are mediated and yet spontaneous.

Sean Cubbit has further supported what Christian Metz understood (through the Foucauldian notion of the *dispositif*) as cinema's work of reproducing normalized subjectivities: "I would suggest," writes Cubbit, "that cinema needs to be understood as a machine and an institution that promotes, if it doesn't determine, the erasure of difference through the promotion of a central, all translating, normalizing position for the spectator, rather in the way that perspective gives us a place in front of the picture."[20] The diagnosis of an all-encompassing machine, institution, normalizing position and perspective would seem to further the erasure of difference Cubbit intends to expose. In this theoretical understanding, there seems to be no room for citation, for the use of film stock or, for that matter, any perspective for purposes other than representation.

In early colonial works indigenous painters would commonly deploy perspective as one more signifier rather than as the instrument to record a phenomenal (whether imaginary or real) occurrence in the world. Their use of perspective, for instance, could depict the colonizing gaze of inquisitors and confessors, rather than reproduce the semblance of a specific confessor or inquisitor.[21] In the same vein one may reference or draw on film archives to produce meanings other than those *intended* by the original cinematographer or inherent in the machine. The maleness of the apparatus could be further complicated by the fact that if the machine is an *actant*, it is also *acted* on by those it captures. In Higgins's juxtaposition of the mayor and Maria, we certainly find the competing discourses, on the one hand, of patriarchy as fomented by state institutions, and, on the other hand, of a feminine space that, if we cannot call it feminist, nevertheless carries its own force from within a patriarchal society where men might manifest openness while still reproducing a social order with clearly defined gender roles.

Note that these roles are constantly subjected to negotiation in terms that escape our patriarchal categories. The Zapatistas are known for making gender a central issue in their examination of indigeneity by underscoring that patriarchy is not a determining element of Maya social institutions, just as the regime of *caciques*, the local political bosses that emerged after the conquest, is not. It is not simply a question of contending discourses but of multiple institutions with different histories. Urban middle-class feminists are often criticized for their assumption that the terms of their struggles apply universally, hence shunning the ways in which Maya women might be conducting their own struggles.[22] The Abejas are not unaware of the transformations in the Zapatista communities; they know that patriarchy and gender roles have histories that can be undone.

The dictating mayor of Chenalho who waggles his finger at our face conveys a rhetorical expression of authority that competes with the equally rhetorical gestures of Maria's wringing hands that express genuine vulnerability. By "rhetorical" I do not want to suggest that Maria's expression lacks authenticity; rather, she chooses to caress the camera with her equally genuine timidity before men from outside the community (that is, Higgins and his film crew). By comparison, in the video *Acteal. 10 Años de impunidad, ¿y cuantos más . . . ?* by the Abeja filmmaker José Alfredo Jiménez, Maria does not shy away from making forceful declarative sentences in Tzotzil to the effect: "I declare that it is true that they came to massacre us." By this I want to suggest that the *dispositifs* belong to multiple institutions, and that the apparatus might appear less gender specific, at least less determining, once we remove it from a *visualism* that ignores and hence undermines other senses that in watching the video would include touch along with listening, as one possibility in a series of haptic impressions. Another form of touch involves the use of slow motion accompanied by avant-garde music and noise to convey, for example, the sordidness of paramilitaries surveying villages or the army invading territories. Indeed, we can find the filmmakers incorporating film stock that likely had other intended uses than the *factishes* a particular documentarist, Higgins in this case, produces by citing them.

High theory of the 1960s through the 1980s engaged the apparatus and the *dispositifs* in an effort to unmask the ways in which power was exerted in film, but it was equally invested in tracking forms of resistance in viewers. Laura Marks has argued quite convincingly for a haptic criticism that would enable us "to 'warm up' [in the spirit of Marshal McLuhan's thermostatic lingo] our cultural tendency to take a distance."[23] Marks not only argues against the determinacy of the apparatus, but also offers an approach one might take toward documentaries such that we would no longer seek to subject them to our will. Marks is particularly interested in visual eroticism and the undoing of psychoanalytic perspectives that assume the male gaze as a given in the production and consumption of pornography instead of as one possible reading, even if it is a particular reading so integrated into our common sense, into our *critical* habitus that we have to make an extraordinary effort to see and feel differently. By the same token, we can argue against the notion of the camera as an apparatus that reproduces an imperial eye, and we can resist the pull to generalize a colonialist objectification. We may appeal to the same theorists of the 1960s through the 1980s, in particular, Michel de Certeau, to invoke the oppositional practices of the everyday—including the undoing of the patriarchal and imperial gaze—that may be traced in the touching of the camera by the witnesses giving testimony. For the purpose of tracing instances of quotation, we may benefit from Certeau's dictum, "memory does its work in a *locus* that is not its own," but also from the cultural practices he defines as *"poaching* in countless ways on the *property* of others."[24]

Filming as poaching can be traced to those instances when the documentarists cite the newscasts of addresses to the nation by then-president Zedillo, newscasts that seek to present him in the most authoritarian and patriarchal manner to secure the viewers' complicity. In citing such passages, the documentaries under discussion can and do create a contrary effect: the end is obviously not to confirm Zedillo's (or, for that matter, the newscasters') accounts of the events but to undo the force of his authoritarian posturing by means of an ironic use of the image and voice in a montage that reveals the absurdity and falseness of his communications to the nation. Note that at least in Higgins's work, there is no voiceover drilling a message, but rather a poaching of the archive that *steals* the elements for an oppositional memory. Another instance of citation would be the use of stock footage of the paramilitary, soldiers, and police, not just to represent their presence in the highlands of Chiapas, but to expose them as perpetrators of sordid violence. In one instance we find Faustina, along with her husband, Alonso, and their children, watching a video, pointing at paramilitaries that Lacourse and Patry have turned into a citation through the work of cinematic montage. The slow-motion effect that transforms the handsome smile of a Toztzil into the gesture of an arrogant murderer affects our sense of touch through the retina that receives the face, the composure, and the smile. And it affects our nervous system beyond the reception of a mere image. Faustina points at the video and identifies the paramilitaries. Her authority is drawn from her position of witness to the creation of paramilitary forces but, perhaps even more important, from her historical condition as a refugee who cannot return to the highlands.

The gift of testimony in the documentaries can certainly be destroyed by an iconoclastic gesture that would *kill* the face of the witness in an attempt to silence the voice. But the wager of the filmmaker and the witness resides in the rhetorical force of audiovisual testimony to produce popular history for a long-term struggle against impunity—a struggle that seeks to dismantle the state and its repressive institutions—at least in their current forms.

13 $\equiv$ Exception to the Political

We must stop feeling complacent about the return of the Left in Latin America. The list of left-leaning governments now includes Argentina, Bolivia, Brazil, Ecuador, El Salvador, Nicaragua, Uruguay, and Venezuela, but not yet Mexico—although intellectuals have spoken of a transition to democracy with the 2000 defeat of the Partido Revolucionario Institucional (PRI)—and the ascent of the Left goes on and on. At the turn of the twenty-first century, the socialist specter is haunting Latin America and its nemesis, the United States of America. In reflecting on the new political status quo of the Left, we ought to consider the state as both a repressive force and a protector of capital. It makes little sense to beg the question of a new kind of state (kind, benevolent, democratic) when the state cannot be conceived outside its role of protecting and administering capital, whether in the mode of safeguarding international finance or in the mode of a socialist administration of capital. Cases of state-administered repression and systematic violence against indigenous peoples (who supposedly intend to offend the new leftist states) abound, suggesting that the so-called return of the Left might be nominal at best.

When the new states call for the respect of private property and the Estado de Derecho, they remind us that the new constitutions are precisely that—forms of constituted power that safeguard the interests of a ruling class. If the notion of safeguarding the interests of a ruling class seems homogenizing, modify the indictment to forms of constituted power that put pressure on the wealthy about the need to make the distribution of wealth less extreme. In our complacence we risk losing sight of the wide array of political subjects that often participated in bringing these new governments to power. These political subjects (choose to) remain outside the state in spite of the new constitution's claims of inclusiveness. Their mobilization continues to haunt the designs of new constitutions. The concept of "without history" captures the existence of organizations, indigenous communities, individuals, indeed of multitudes in the process of turning *flesh* into *body*, to borrow coauthors Michael Hardt and Antonio Negri's phrasing in *Multitudes*, that cannot be written into history by either legal recognition or by representation in state apparatuses. In reflecting on these new left governments, we need to understand in what ways these political subjects aim to build forms of government that cannot be identified with the concept of the state and the modes of engaging it—parties, constitutional reform, bodies of law, or even constituent assemblies. The extent to which the state brings about the possibility of its withering should depend on its willingness to undo its ties to capital.

Examining two specific cases, this essay traces the limits of these new or not-so-new kinds of state. I look at the first case through the lens of a political cartoon by the Mexican artist El Fisgón that brings into play an entire tradition of political theory on the "state of emergency" (for instance, the ideas of Carl Schmidt, Giorgio Agamben, Antonio Negri) as well as a whole tradition of reflections on the Paris Commune of 1871 (for instance, the work of Marx, Lenin, and Badiou). I develop the second case after the 2007 speech by Bolivia's vice president, Alvaro García Linera, at the Latin American Studies Association congress in Montreal. García Linera invoked Lenin's call for a state that is no longer a state, calling forth a political tradition that has reflected on what it means to speak of the withering of the state.

These two examples provide the terms to discuss the rule of exception, constituent power, the legacy of the Paris Commune, the aesthetics of insurgency, and the specters of history. The relationship between history and those who remain outside the state needs to be addressed. It is not a question of going way back to earlier thinkers (in particular, to Marx and Lenin) but of considering their theoretical contributions as contemporaneous. The assertion that all history is contemporaneous is a most materialist position. The irreducible fact is that the historical past (a past privileged over the pasts that individuals and collectivities construe through myth, legend, or fiction) does not exist outside documents the historian has constituted as historical evidence in terms of ethical and epistemological choices. One may certainly find historians who claim that their epistemological and ethical choices are absolutes that guarantee knowledge about the past. However, we need to ask them about the *why* of knowing the past, as if it is not to privilege a conception of the present that must be imposed. The guardians of culture and the state rattle their sabers.

Case 1: El Fisgón's Political Cartoon

El Fisgón's political cartoon echoes philosopher Walter Benjamin's dictum in thesis eight of his "Theses on the Philosophy of History": "The tradition of the oppressed teaches us that the state of emergency in which we live is not the exception but the rule."[1] El Fisgón has depicted the current president of Mexico, Felipe Calderón, stating: "Queremos que Oaxaca no sea considerado un estado excepción" [We don't want that Oaxaca be considered a state of exception], with the retort, "Queremos que sea la regla" [We want it to be the rule] (figure 13.1). On Calderón's left arm figures the symbol of the secret extreme-right paramilitary organization El Yunque (The Anvil). The letter "Y" extends downward into a cross. The group was purportedly created to defend the values of Catholicism by any means necessary, including a series of assassinations by front organizations. The rebellion of the Asamblea Popular de los Pueblos de Oaxaca (the APPO)—which started in 2006 during a school-teachers' annual strike (to demand salary increases, materials, better working conditions, and so on) and arguably continues today in a network compris-

FIGURE 13.1.
"Detenciones al por mayor" by El Fisgón. Courtesy of Rafael Barajas Durán.

ing a broad range of activist groups—must be suppressed, handled with the toughest repressive apparatus to prevent its generalization all over the state of Oaxaca and the nation.[2] In years past the Oaxaca government negotiated with the teachers union, but the current governor of Oaxaca, Ulises Ruiz, refused to negotiate with them. This led to the creation of a mass movement that took over governmental buildings, radio stations, and the city's central square, which was blocked off with barricades.

The cartoon lends itself to at least two readings. One reading would expose Calderón's fascist state in turning a state of emergency that would temporally suspend the law (that is, make room for repression) into a permanent situation ["que sea la regla"]. A second reading would place the emphasis on the need to invoke the law to denounce and correct human rights abuses. These two readings call for further consideration since the cartoon gives the impression that the suspension of the law (whether temporarily or permanently) cannot be conceived in terms of the legal frame of the constitution. El Fisgón would lead us to believe that the only alternative for the insurgents is recognition of their rights by the state. Many journalists argued in 2006, at the height of the rebellion and its repression, that the state of exception was de facto lacking the official declaration that would make it de jure. The Mexican Constitution and the Constitution of the State of Oaxaca offer ample mechanisms, which by the way could be easily manipulated by both the federal and state governments, to turn the de facto into a de jure state of exception.

Journalists often cite Agamben's *State of Exception*, but they elide the initial comments at the beginning of the treatise that define the legal nature of Hitler's civil war:

> No sooner did Hitler take power (or, as we should more accurately say, no sooner was power given to him) than on February 28, he proclaimed the Decree for the Protection of the People and the State, which suspended the articles in the Weimar Constitution concerning personal liberties. The decree was never repealed, so that from a juridical standpoint the entire Third Reich can be considered a state of exception that lasted twelve years. In this sense, modern totalitarianism can be defined as the establishment, by means of the state of exception, of a legal civil war that allows for the physical elimination not only of political adversaries but of entire categories of citizens who for some reason cannot be integrated into the political system. Since then, the voluntary creation of a permanent state of emergency (though perhaps not declared in technical terms) has become one of the essential practices of contemporary states, including so-called democratic ones.[3]

The distinction between a state of exception de facto and de jure is inconsequential in Agamben's diagnosis of Hitler's legal civil war and legacy in "the essential practices of contemporary states, including so-called democratic ones."[4]

El Fisgón's ideal reader would not only find an allusion to Walter Benjamin, who characterized his time—the rise of the Nazis—as a moment in which the exception had become the rule, but also to Carl Schmitt, the German philosopher known as one of the main theoreticians of Nazism. Schmitt first developed the theory of exception in 1922 and further revised it in 1934 during the rise of National Socialism. Schmitt's association with Nazism, as that of his contemporary Martin Heidegger, has not kept his critics from considering him one of the most brilliant philosophers of law in the twentieth century. He develops the concept of the state of exception in a small book titled *Political Theology*. The opening line sums up his argument about sovereignty: "Sovereign is he who decides on the exception."[5] Giorgio Agamben has observed that Schmitt's use of the word "decides" seeks to neutralize Benjamin's exposure of violence as the common link between *lawmaking* (constituent power) and *law-preserving* (constituted power) insofar as both are defined as means toward ends. In his "Critique of Violence," Benjamin proposes the concept of pure violence, of revolutionary violence: that by neither making nor preserving the law, but by deposing it, this act "inaugurates a new historical epoch."[6] Schmitt's sovereign may assume dictatorial powers legally to respond to the suspension of the law in insurgencies. Thus he leads violence back to a juridical context. Wouldn't revolution or insurgency, by definition, establish a state of exception, insofar as it stands outside the law, breaks the law, and sidesteps the applicability of the constitution to justify a constituent assembly?

This opposition between Benjamin and Schmitt enables us to characterize the suspension of the law brought forth by both the APPO and the governor of Oaxaca. The APPO embodied (continues to embody at least among some of its participants) an instance of revolutionary violence: in some of its articulations, the APPO seeks neither to assume a role of lawmaking (a reformist position that would remain content with the abdication of the governor of Oaxaca, Ulises Ruiz) nor the role of enforcing the preservation of the law (a call for the recognition of human rights).[7] This neither/nor has not excluded the call to overthrow Ruiz or the exposure of human rights abuses. However, the revolutionary force that characterizes some of its more radical formulations partakes of an unalloyed violence that lacks the means/ends distinction that define lawmaking and law-preserving. In *Teaching Rebellion*, Diana Denham and the CASA Collective have gathered a series of testimonies that enable us to gauge the radical proposals. For instance, in her account, Leyla—an activist from the Comité de Defensa de los Derecho del Pueblo (the Committee for the Defense of the Rights of the People), an organization committed to the construction of

a *poder popular* (popular power)—expresses unalloyed violence in unequivocal terms: "at that time in Oaxaca, the *topiles* represented the people's police
and the APPO represented the government. The empowerment of the people,
what we had always worked for, was really happening."[8]

We may further define the nature of the *topiles* with activist Cuautli's testimony: "The *topiles*, the people's police that served the entire movement, was
formed as part of the APPO Security Commission. Traditionally, the *topiles*
are responsible for security in indigenous communities; its job rotates among
community members. In these communities every man has to be a *topil* for
at least a couple of years as part of his duty to the community. . . . It's part of
usos y costumbres, which are indigenous systems of governance. So the APPO
decided to re-claim that tradition and form our own security system, based
on the customs of Oaxaca's pueblos."[9] The *topiles* constitute a nonprofessional
entity—that is to say, they do not represent a transcendent structure to the
communities in that they form part of a system of rotation that includes all the
male community members. The *topiles* are grounded in the indigenous normative systems and have as their main call the defense of communal claims
against governmental incursions and neoliberal exploitation of resources in
their territories: As Cuautli explained: "We already had a political formation;
we knew about the government plans to exploit natural resources; we know
how the neo-liberal system works."[10] Nothing would be farther from the judicial administration and protection of capitalist regimes of private property.

The community itself conducts the policing in the name of self-defense.
As it is the case with other communal police, such as the Policía Comunitaria in the state of Guerrero, these forms of self-defense are systematically
repressed by state and federal authorities, but at least in Cuautli's description
of the *topiles* in Oaxaca, there is no appeal to the state to recognize their policing efficacy.[11] They exist outside the state, often against the policing by the
state. The *topiles* enforce a system of norms that state and federal constitutions willy-nilly recognize and try to manipulate. Given this legal status, the
national and the state governments infiltrate the communities by promoting
leaders who will respond to their interests in an attempt to corrupt the will of
the communities.

El Fisgón's cartoon, however, assumes an accepted opinion on the legal
framework that would legitimate the declaration of a state of exception in the
Mexican constitution. El Fisgón expresses a position within Mexican society
and among some members of the APPO that would appeal to a legal common
sense that exposes illegality of repression as if the law could not provide the
grounds for state violence. My observation on the diversity of the APPO calls
for one caveat: multitudes that turn, to borrow Hardt and Negri's terms, from

flesh into *body*, always carry in their constitution the force of multiple singularities that cannot be reduced to a state.[12] It hardly makes a difference if the state in question is conceived as including a plurality of nations, if one ends up with a plurality of forms of preserving the regime of law and system of property. If the state is an inevitable reality one faces today, revolutionary violence would seek to dismantle the state—not to reform the state—to construct a new world in which the state would disappear.

We know that most liberal democratic constitutions guarantee the process by means of which the "sovereign" decides on and calls forth the state of emergency—a state of siege, an exception of the law, or extraordinary measures. For the most part sovereignty resides in the legislative powers, but the decision to retain or suspend the exception belongs to the executive power. Consider, for instance, Article 29 of the Mexican Constitution:

> En los casos de invasión, perturbación grave de la paz pública, o de cualquier otro que ponga a la sociedad en grave peligro o conflicto, solamente el Presidente de los Estados Unidos Mexicanos, de acuerdo con los Titulares de las Secretarías de Estado, los Departamentos Administrativos y la Procuraduría General de la República y con aprobación del Congreso de la Unión, y, en los recesos de éste, de la Comisión Permanente, podrá suspender en todo el país o en lugar determinado las garantías que fuesen obstáculo para hacer frente, rápida y fácilmente a la situación; pero deberá hacerlo por un tiempo limitado, por medio de prevenciones generales y sin que la suspensión se contraiga a determinado individuo. Si la suspension tuviese lugar hallándose el Congreso reunido, éste concede las autorizaciones que estime necesarias para que el Ejecutivo haga frente a la situación, pero si se verificase en tiempo de receso, se convocará sin demora al Congreso para que las acuerde.

> [In cases of invasion, severe perturbation of the public peace, or any other event that puts society in severe danger or conflict, only the President of the United States of Mexico, in accord with the Holders of the Secretaries of State, the Administrative Departments, and the Office of the Attorney General of the Republic and with the approval of Congress of the Union and, during its recesses, of the Permanent Commission, will be allowed to suspend in the whole country or a determinate place the guaranties that would be an obstacle to facing the situation, rapidly and easily; but this would be done only for a limited time, by means of general preventives and without contracting the suspension to a determinate individual. If the suspension took place while Congress was in session, this organ concedes the authorizations it deems necessary so that the Executive faces the situation, but if it were verified while in recess, Congress will be convened without delay so that they agree upon them.][13]

The question then would be: What defines a "limited time," hence the possible illegality of a permanent suspension of the law? But once granted, the decision to retain the suspension resides in the executive, even if in consultation with the legislative power.

We also find in Article 39 the expression that sovereignty resides in the people: "La soberania nacional reside esencial y originariamente en el pueblo. Todo poder público dimana del pueblo y se instituye para beneficio de este. El pueblo tiene en todo tiempo el inalienable derecho de alterar o modificar la forma de su gobierno" [National sovereignty resides essentially and originally in the people. All public power emanates from the people and is instituted for its benefit. The people have at all times the inalienable right to alter or modify the form of its government].[14] Article 39 includes the right of the people to form a constituent assembly. As it were, there is an institutionalization of constituent power as an inalienable right. In this regard, constituent power and the rule of exception (for the time needed to formulate the new constitution) would be sanctioned by the constitution. As such, it is a sanctioned suspension of the law. In such cases, constituent power—an *asamblea constituyente* (a constituent assembly)—would be a temporary measure marking the transition to a new constitution and its corresponding constituted power. The implicit assumption to this transition is that the old constitution would remain in effect while the new one comes into force.

But there is no reason for limiting the interpretation of Article 39 to the establishment of a legally sanctioned constituent assembly. Let's recall that in the first Declaración de la Selva Lacandona, on the eve of the 1994 uprising, the Ejercito Zapatista de Liberación Nacional (EZLN, the Zapatista National Revolutionary Army) appeals to Article 39 to legitimate the insurrection. On January 2, 1994, the EZLN published "Ley Revolucionaria" in the *Despertar Mexicano*, the official organ of the EZLN. The "Ley Revolucionaria" established a series of laws to regulate the expropriation of private property, the appropriation of the means of production, and the collective nature of the emergent regime of property. By privileging indigenous communalism, the section on the "Ley Agraria Revolucionaria" [Agrarian Revolutionary Law] offers a model for the new society. As such, the EZLN expresses a brilliant instance of Benjamin's revolutionary violence. One may also wonder the extent to which we may associate the "Ley Revolucionaria" with Lenin's concept of the "withering of the state" and with Evgeny Pashukanis's prescription in *The General Theory of Law and Marxism*. Pashukanis wrote: "The withering away of the categories of bourgeois law will, under these conditions, mean the withering away of law altogether, that is to say the disappearance of the juridical factor from social relations."[15]

The juridical component for Pashukanis is no other than the regulation of capital in commodity exchange. The Zapatista appeal to the sovereignty of the people in Article 39 defines the *Revolución* (the capitalization is theirs) as a state of exception guaranteed by the Mexican Constitution. It is a state of exception intended to give place to the dissolution of both the law and the regime to which it is applicable. The "Ley Revolucionaria" does not call for a transitional state, nor does it propose "a direct transition from bourgeois law to no law," but the regulation of the transition to a regime in which capitalist forms of private property would no longer exist.[16]

Let's examine two articles in the Constitution of the State of Oaxaca that address the suspension of the constitution in cases of rebellion or emergencies:

> Artículo 142. Esta Constitución no perderá su fuerza y vigor aun cuando por alguna rebelión se interrumpa su observancia. En caso de que por un trastorno público se establezca un Gobierno contrario a los principios que ella sanciona, tan luego como el pueblo recobre su libertad, se reestablecerá su observancia, y con arreglo a ella y a las leyes que en su virtud se hubieren expedido, serán juzgados, tanto los que hayan figurado en el Gobierno emanado de la rebelión, como los que hayan cooperado a ella.

> [This constitution will not lose its force and effect even when a rebellion interrupts its observance. In the case of a contrary government to the principles she sanctions on account of a public upheaval, as soon as the people recover their freedom, its observation will be reestablished, and according to it and the laws that in its power were issued, both those who figured in the government that emanated from the rebellion and those who cooperated will be judged.][17]

The article lends itself to the prosecution of all those who participated in the APPO. Beyond the act of rebellion, participants have been imprisoned on false charges of drug trafficking and other common crimes. Article 62, however, opens a whole other set of possible charges on grounds that the rebellion of the APPO poses a state emergency that imperiled the normal conduct of life: "La Legislatura podrá autorizar al Gobernador el uso de facultades extraordinarias, en caso de desastre o para afrontar una emergencia" [The Legislature will be able to authorize the governor the use of extraordinary faculties in the case of disasters or to confront an emergency].[18] By citing these two articles, I want to underscore that the suppression of the APPO and the persecution of its leaders can be argued as constitutional. Little is to be gained by denouncing human rights abuses when the constitution allows for violent repression to face a state of emergency.

The clarification of the tension between constituent power and constituted powers is one of Antonio Negri's salient contributions to political thought. If Negri traces the origins of constituent power to Machiavelli, the concept of constituent assembly is a product of the Enlightenment first implemented in the context of the French and the American revolutions. The establishment of a constituent assembly for drafting new constitutions is a defining trait of post-Enlightenment constitutional theory. Negri, however, seeks to wrench constituent power from the teleological conceptions of the social and the political that privilege transitions to capital narratives. He seeks to dismantle socioeconomic purgatories that would prepare the terrain for socialism and revolution. And this, despite the appearance that *Insurgencies* seems to offer a historical account of the development of the concept of constituent power in Western societies. Is there a tension between the formation of constituent assemblies, the new constitutions that emerge from them, and the recognition of non-Western, indigenous normative systems in places like Bolivia and Chiapas? Do these normative systems need the recognition of the state, or are they a reality the state has to work with?

Understood as a revolutionary force, one would expect that the APPO would place itself outside the law. For the state authorities, the participants in the Oaxaca uprising were criminals to be persecuted, indeed assassinated if necessary to retain the Estado de Derecho. We thus find "law-preserving violence" (even if under the mode of a legal suspension of the law) doing whatever it takes to prevent "unalloyed violence" from abolishing the state and taking power.[19] Agamben has made the following distinction: "And if the connection between pure violence and juridical violence, between the state of exception and revolutionary violence, is thus made so tight that the two players facing each other across the chessboard of history seem always to be moving a single pawn—force of law or pure means—what is nevertheless decisive is that in each case the criterion of their distinction lies in the dissolution of the relation between violence and law."[20] In Agamben's distinction, the constitutional right to establish a constituent assembly, retains the enforcement of the law while the new constitution is drafted. Revolutionary violence, on the other side of the *chessboard of history*, would in the end not aspire to establish a "proletarian" law but an affirmation of life that would lead to the withering of capitalist economic, social, and legal structures. The suspension of the constitution in juridical violence declares a state of exception in which the constitution legalizes the use of force to implement the dissolution of the law in the name of preserving order.

Thus the APPO was subjected to "state terror" in the name of preserving the law. The "single pawn"—that is, the force of law or pure violence, the "state of exception and revolutionary violence"—would seem to resonate in the (re)use of space in the city that was first inscribed with revolutionary slogans: the forum for reflection on the connection between violence and law that the insurgency used as a site of memory was reinscribed with signs celebrating the restoration of the Estado de Derecho after the recuperation of the center of Oaxaca.[21] The distinction between "state terror" that suspends the law in the name of preserving it and unalloyed revolutionary violence in which means and ends correspond should make suspect appeals to the law and human rights, including that most paradoxical principle of the right (force implied) of resistance. If from a human rights perspective it makes sense to appeal to the law—although we should be cautious of the violence of its implementation— one incurs contradiction when one seeks to ground insurrection, rebellion, and revolution in the law. Human rights advocates of yesterday turn into those who violate the law upon assuming the power of the state.

But perhaps it would be more accurate to reinstate the thesis with Benjamin's pure revolutionary violence and leave the language of decision and exception to the sovereign, who, according to Schmitt, "decides whether there is an extreme emergency as well as what must be done to eliminate it." Schmitt further defines this idea by stating that "although [the sovereign] stands outside the normally valid system, he nevertheless belongs to it, for it is he who must decide whether the constitution needs to be suspended in its entirety."[22] If the state remains solidly in place in the process of defining the borderline nature of sovereignty and decision, the Paris Commune of 1871 inaugurated a new revolutionary ethos defined by the political power of the working class that aspires to take power without taking over the state apparatuses. If El Fisgón "cites" Schmitt and invokes a long series of disputes that invoke Benjamin, Taubes, and Agamben, dozens of Web sites have linked the APPO to the 1871 Paris Commune. These interpretations of the APPO as akin to the Paris Commune call for a reflection on the APPO's significance in the *duration* of insurrections and constituent power. If the APPO participates in the changes in the revolutionary duration of the first workers' government, we may ask, in turn, what have been the APPO's contributions to this sediment of insurrectional temporality?

AESTHETICS OF INSURGENCY

Questions of aesthetics, in particular of what we may define as *pure aesthetics* in line with the concept of *pure violence*, pertain to both the participation in the insurgency and the kinds of stories we tell about the communes. The poets singing in the midst of the barricades find their complement in the philosopher-historian who narrates in the mode of satire and farce. One scribbles the walls of the city, while the other keeps at bay the assimilation of the rebellion into the ideology of a new benign state. We ought to imagine Rimbaud, a sixteen-year-old in the midst of the barricades of 1871, and cite him along with Marx's *The Civil War in France*. Rimbaud's letter to his former teacher, Georges Izambard, offers a point of entry for reflecting on the aesthetics, if not also the ethos, of insurrection. Insurgent aesthetics calls for the *smashing* of everything sacred without invoking an end (Benjamin's notion of "pure violence"). Rimbaud wrote:

You are a teacher again. You have told me we owe a duty to Society. . . . You are right, for now. In reality, all you see in your principle is subjective poetry: your obstinacy in reaching the university trough—excuse me—proves this. But you will always end up a self-satisfied man who has done nothing because he wanted to do nothing. Not to mention that your subjective poetry will always be horribly insipid. One day, I hope—many others hope the same thing—I will see objective poetry according to your principle, I will see it more sincerely than you would! I will be a worker: This idea holds me back, when mad anger drives me toward the battle of Paris—where so many workers are dying as I write to you! Work now? Never, never, I am on strike.[23]

This letter provided the surrealist, in particular in André Breton's *Surrealist Manifesto*, with a favorite topoi: Marx and the social are complemented by Rimbaud and the subjective. The subjective in Rimbaud paradoxically calls forth the recognition of an autonomous world of objects in his appeal to objective poetry.

Beyond this letter denouncing escapist poetry in favor of materialist poetry, we can trace Rimbaud's communist vocation in his "communard" poems, in which he expresses his solidarity with the Commune. Take, for instance, the following lines from his "L'Orgie parisienne ou Paris se repeuple" (1871):

> The storm consecrated your supreme poetry;
> The immense stirring of strength succors you;
> Your work boils, death groans, chosen City!
> Amass in your heart the blast of the heavy trumpet.
>
> The Poet will take the sobs of the Infamous
> The hate of the Convicts, the clamor of the damned;
> And his rays of love will scourge the Women.
> His stanza will leap forth, this is for you, bandits![24]

The subaltern poiesis of those poets who brake with the salon, who run among the workers in the barricades, singing their struggle in the struggle itself, exemplifies unalloyed violence. "Sobs," "hate," "clamor," "rays of love" will rebound in a language that incorporates these objects, not unlike other poems by Rimbaud in which the words "rock, iron, coal," turn into living entities that invoke labor and revolution. In the first stanza Rimbaud brings forth the rage of the divine, "the blast of the heavy trumpet," indeed, the poetics of the insurgency itself, "your supreme poetry." Far from a privileged position the subaltern poet, the sixteen-year-old high school student who joined the multitude of insurgents, turning flesh into body in the Paris Commune, have become the poets of the graffiti, of the political stencils, of the songs of protests, of the affirmation of life, who mock all claims to an elitist privileged stand in the Oaxaca commune.[25] There is a continuum between Rimbaud and the poet/artists of the APPO—indeed, we ought to trace a repetition of the spirit of insurgency in which there is endless invention of new forms of expression. Unfortunately, established poets have resented the force of the young poets, of life, and lament the excesses of the APPO.

On the question of insurgent aesthetics, we ought to cite William Kentridge's installation *I am not me, the horse is not mine*, which builds on Russian constructivist motives to explore the aesthetics of the October Revolution.[26] In one panel Kentridge projects excerpts from Nicolai Bukharin's trial by Stalin in 1938. The excerpts are striking because of the repetition of those moments in the trial when Bukharin was accused of duplicity. Bukharin's confessional statements underscore that his duplicity was always equally forceful and committed. Kentridge furthers the question of duplicity with panels that underscore the duality of forms repeating themselves as essential to all illusionist art—Is there art that is *not* illusionist, hence deceptive?—in particular, to his own experimentations with music and space, with time and movement, in which he often looks back at us in a comic mode that exposes the tricks he has produced and chosen to unveil. Kentridge defines his art as an extension of the insurgent aesthetic that we have traced back to Rimbaud's poetry of the barricades.

David Lloyd has insisted, in his "Rage against the Divine," that the pure violence in Benjamin's "Critique of Violence" should be read in terms of the passage where Benjamin speaks of rage as manifestation. Lloyd writes: "The nonmediate function of violence at issue here is illustrated by everyday experience. As regards man, he is impelled by anger, for example, to the most visible outbursts of a violence that is not related as a means to a preconceived end. It is not a means but a manifestation."[27] In Rimbaud's poem we find an instance of rage as *pure violence* but also as a form of *pure beauty*, a *manifestation of creativity and rage without ends*—the aesthetics of insurgency thus embodies the spirit of revolution that cannot be contained in a state. The objective poetry Rimbaud speaks of in his letter to Izambard—where he characterizes subjective poetry as *fadasse*, insipid, trite, lame—manifests its violence in letting objects speak. Whence we *ought* to think aesthetics as a pure domain—the *ought* is not simply a moral injunction but a revolutionary ethos.[28]

The notion of *pure aesthetics* is further illustrated with the practice of satire in Marx's ridicule of the "intellectuals" sympathizing with the workers during the Paris Commune. He wrote: "Some patronizing friends of the working class, while hardly dissembling their disgust even at the few measures they consider as 'socialist,' although there is nothing socialist in them except their tendency, express their satisfaction and try to coax genteel sympathies for the Paris Commune by the great discovery that, after all, workmen are rational

men and whenever in power always resolutely turn their back upon socialist enterprises!"[29] Whereas to coax genteel sympathies for the revolutionaries
could not be farther from the pure violence in Rimbaud's *communard poetry*,
the great discovery that workmen are after all rational men, who in power
would turn their back on socialist enterprises, assumes the sempiternal truths
of capitalism. Marx explains that the socialist enterprises the patronizers had
in mind—that is, the utopian communities of Charles Fourier and Étienne
Cabet—have nothing in common with the new reality that makes possible the
emergence of the commune. The *poetics* of history entails for Marx a revolutionary ethos that curtails narratives that would assimilate the Paris Commune into the logic of the state and capitalism.

Sarcasm is a staple of Marx's historical writing, traced back to the famous opening lines of *The Eighteenth Brumaire of Louis Bonaparte*: "Hegel
remarks somewhere that all great, world-historical facts and personages occur, as it were, twice. He has forgotten to add: the first time as tragedy, the
second as farce."[30] If the story of the two Napoleons points to farce, to such
farcical repetitions we may add the long line of "Bonapartist" authoritarian
regimes in Latin America. Repetition also points in the direction of the continuum of struggles and the recurrence—the eternal return—of revolutionary
movements, rebellions, communes, insurgent aesthetics. As Marx has pointed
out with respect to 1871 Paris Commune, it was "the first revolution in which
the working class was openly acknowledged as the only [class] capable of social initiative, even by the great bulk of the Paris middleclass—shopkeepers,
tradesmen, merchants—the wealthy capitalists alone excepted."[31]

Repetition suggests the ever-present possibility that *first time* may be repeated *forever*, against the history of exterminators, as Marx vividly expressed
it at the end of his "Address of the General Council": "Working men's Paris,
with its Commune, will be for ever celebrated as the glorious harbinger of a
new society. Its martyrs are enshrined in the great heart of the working class.
Its exterminator's history has already nailed to that eternal pillory from which
all prayers of their priests will not avail to redeem them."[32] Rather than mourning the dead and engaging in the ensuing melancholia, perhaps a trait of the
tragic, Marx calls forth farce and a manic call for repetition. For if melancholia is insurmountably linked to the recollection of the lost object, repetition
calls forth the reenactment of the past in *pure transformation* in the embodi-
ments of the now eternal object (the first worker's government) of the Paris
Commune: "But this is communism, 'impossible' communism!"[33] We catch a
glimpse of a smiling, joyous Marx. Laughter we may associate with Nietzsche's
eternal return—here, the eternal possibility of the impossible or the eternal
impossible of the possible.

Beyond Nietzsche, as Gilles Deleuze has pointed out in *Difference and Rep-*

etition, the juxtaposition of recollection and repetition calls forth Sören Kierkegaard's *Repetition*, a book that Schmitt has cited generously to emphasize
his preference for the exception over the general: "The exception explains the
general and itself. And if one wants to study the general correctly, one only
needs to look for a true exception. It reveals everything more clearly than does
the general. Endless talk about the general becomes boring; there are excep-
tions. If they cannot be explained, then the general cannot be explained. The
difficulty is usually not noticed because the general is not thought about with
passion but with comfortable superficiality. The exception, on the other hand,
thinks the general with intense passion."[34]

Schmitt invokes the nineteenth-century theologian, as he refers to Kierkegaard, perhaps to lend support to his definition of the theological grounds
of political thought and his defense of the state: "All significant concepts of the
modern theory of the state are secularized concepts not only because of their
historical development—in which they are transferred from theology to the
theory of the state."[35] But what if Kierkegaard is not read as a theologian, but as
the *one* touched by the religious genius? After all, the exception belongs to the
poet—in particular, to the poet who writes in the transition to the religious exception. The exception would thus correspond to the *now* of the messianic—to
repetition, to the experience of the eternal, which resides outside the law and
dogma, a fortiori, *without* history and the state. In fact, one ought to discuss
the full passage, which has been selectively cited by Schmitt.[36] For Kierkegaard
mocks the general by referring to it as sempiternal truths, which are repeated
to the point of the most boring insipidity. Schmitt misses the language of sarcasm that links Kierkegaard's religious genius to the sensibilities of the farcical
in Marx's historical writing.

And yet, if the exception explains the general, Kierkegaard conceives the
dialectic between the exception and the general in terms of a struggle in which
the exception affirms its right to exist. There is a combat in which the rage
and impatience of the general betrays resentment as well as an amorous pre-
dilection for the exception. The general expects the exception to come home
to roost; Kierkegaard offers as an example the story of the young girl who in
the end enjoys the favor and honor in the stepmother's recognition. Substitute
the stepmother with the state and you will have an anticipation of Schmitt's
reading that favors the return of general, of the law. Kierkegaard's story of the
stepmother's recognition suggests a mock allegory of Hegelian dialectic that
marches the constituent into the constituted without reprieve. In the end, as
manifest in Schmitt's opening lines to the passage from Kierkegaard, Schmitt
calls for the return of law that confirms the rule but is revitalized by the legal
hiatus: "In the exception the power of real life breaks through the crust of a
mechanism that has become torpid by repetition."[37] This sense of repetition

misses the eternal, which can never be confined to the general in a dialectic that always reinstates the rule of the general. The flight of the poetic imagination belongs to the exception not to the insipidity of the general.

WITHERING OF THE LAW, WITHERING OF THE STATE

We may along this line of Kierkegaard's religious genius invoke not theology and the state, but the call for the *now* of the law that is no longer the law as manifest in Saint Paul's *Letter to the Romans*. Agamben offers a productive point of entry to link Saint Paul and the Marxian tradition: "The difficulty Benjamin faces here corresponds to a problem that can be formulated (and it was effectively formulated for the first time in primitive Christianity and then later in the Marxian tradition) in these terms: What becomes of the law after its messianic fulfillment? (This is the controversy that opposes Paul to the Jews of his time.) And what becomes of the law in a society without classes? (This is precisely the debate between [Andrey] Vyshinsky and [Evgeny] Pashukanis.)"[38] It is not inconsequential that Agamben closes his comment by mentioning Vyshinsky, the state prosecutor of Stalin's trials and purges, and Pashukanis, who exposed the ties between law and the commodity exchange of capitalist society. Recall, mentioned earlier, Kentridge's exposure of the farcical and yet sordid nature of the Stalinists' trials in his installation, *I am not me, the horse is not mine*, which reproduces parts of Bukharin's trial. There is perhaps no more lucid articulation (and development of Lenin's theses in *The State and Revolution*) on the withering of the state and the law than in Pashukanis's *The General Theory of Law and Marxism*. Pashukanis's arguments entail the corollary that unless constituent assemblies keep in mind the need to avoid the emergence of proletarian categories of value and capital, they will end up reinstating constituted power and thereby choking the life of the multitude.

The shuffling back and forth to theoreticians of the Russian revolution and their all too often tragic end in the Stalinist purges enables us to explore the question of the state with the rigor demanded by the urgency of the present. If their language, perhaps because of the Stalinist distinction between "base" and "superstructure," makes them sound a bit out of date, if not dogmatic, we still have much to learn from the connection they draw between historical specificity and the disciplines that are created to make sense of the social (that is, political economy and jurisprudence). This follows Marx's maxim: "It is not the consciousness of men that determines their existence, but their social existence that determines their consciousness."[39] As it has been often argued among Marxists, against the Stalinist extension of this maxim to all forms of culture, we *ought* to limit this principle to the institutions of domination, otherwise we would be at pains in explaining how Marx could offer an analysis of capitalist society. If those inclined to sputter anti-Marxist babble stopped for a second to reflect on this proposition, they would understand that the task is to weigh the specificity of each concrete social situation.

Negri draws from Pashukanis his understanding of Lenin's concept of the state as comprising both the repressive forces of violence and "the law that constitutes the specific authoritarian form of the relationship between the State and the organization of labor."[40] As such, "the abolishing of the state as state," in Lenin's *The State and Revolution*, also would entail for Negri the destruction of work—of what Pashukanis exposed as proletarian State capitalism. The 1871 Paris Commune manifested the (im)possibility of an outside-of-history (*without history* as lack and outside) with respect to both the state repressive forces and the legal administration of capital; it constitutes a singularity that promises its repetition in an inexhaustible proliferation of workers' governments. I am here glossing over endless debates among Marxists on the desirability of a "purgatory" phase in the transition from capitalism to communism.

This debate is evident in the discussion of Michel Foucault with the *Maoist* in 1971, exactly one hundred years after the Paris Commune. Note that of all the examples of revolutionary processes they mention, the Paris Commune stands out in their silence about the centennial—and yet it remains in the background when Victor, one of the Maoist activists, raised the question of the transitions to communism:

> Victor: So I would put the following question to you: are you not dreaming up the possibility of going straight from present-day oppression to communism without any transition period . . . during which there is a need for a new type of state apparatus, of which we must define the content? Is it not this which lies behind your systematic refusal of the people's court as a form?

> Foucault: Are you certain that it is merely the *form* of the court that is involved here. I do not know how these things are done in China, but look a bit more closely at the meaning of the spatial arrangement of the court, the arrangement of the people who are part of or before a court. The very least that can be said is that this implies an ideology.[41]

Foucault goes on to specify that the arrangement of the court consists of a table that separates the two litigants from the third party, the judges, who are purportedly neutral. Neutrality is quite foreign to the idea of popular justice: "In the case of popular justice you do not have three elements, you have the masses and their enemies." The masses, argues Foucault, do not "rely on an abstract universal idea of justice, they rely only on their own experience, that of the injuries they have suffered."[42]

Victor does not agree, and builds an argument for a revolutionary state apparatus: "The 'third element' in the case of popular justice is a revolutionary state apparatus—for example, the Red Army in the early stages of the Chinese

Revolution. In what sense is it a 'third element,' a repository of a *law* and of a *truth?* This is what needs to be explained."[43] At the core of the debate resides an argument by Foucault that reminds us of Pashukanis: "The revolution can only take place via the radical elimination of the judicial apparatus, and anything which could reintroduce the penal apparatus, anything which could reintroduce its ideology . . . must be banished."[44] Let this suffice to grasp the tenor of the discussion. For our purposes the questions on form that Foucault raises resonate with how the *topiles* of Oaxaca (and other indigenous communities in Mexico) conceive *Justicia comunitaria*. To some extent, these debates reside in the weight one places on such phrases by Lenin as: "The more democratic the 'state,' which consists of the armed workers, and which is 'no longer a state in the proper sense of the word,' the more rapidly *every form* of the state begins to wither away."[45] Lenin poses two questions that would gauge the seriousness of anarchist proposals: "Must the old state machine be *smashed?* And *what* should be placed in its place?"[46]

While discussing the 1871 Paris Commune, we ought to consider Lenin's April Theses: "The masses must be made to see that the Soviets of Workers' Deputies are the only possible form of revolutionary government, and that therefore our task is, as long as this government yields to the influence of the bourgeoisie, to present a patient, systematic, and persistent explanation of the errors of their tactics, an explanation especially adapted to the practical needs of the masses."[47] In his *Letters on Tactics*, Lenin refined this statement on the need for a transitional state: "Nor can it stray into the swamp of anarchism, for anarchism denies the need for a state and state power in the period of transition from the rule of the bourgeoisie to the rule of the proletariat, whereas I, with a precision that precludes any possibility of misinterpretation, advocate the need for a state in this period, although, in accordance with Marx and the lessons of the Paris Commune, I advocate not the usual parliamentary bourgeois state, but a state without a standing army, without a police opposed to the people, without an officialdom placed above the people."[48]

This is a radically different Lenin from the one that called for a vanguard party in *What Is to Be Done?* The Lenin of the top-down revolution, suspect of voluntarism and spontaneity, gives place to the reading of the Soviets in accordance with Marx and the lessons of the Paris Commune. Lenin calls forth the notion of a nonrepressive government that Marx first envisioned in the commune. Marx wrote: "But the working class cannot simply lay hold of the ready-made state machinery, and wield it for its purposes."[49] Lenin repeats this phrase (almost verbatim but with the difference of the singularity of the event) in *The State and Revolution*: "Marx's idea is that the working class must break up, smash the 'ready-made state machinery,' and not confine itself merely to laying hold of it."[50] But little is to be gained by building a new kind of state that would be charged with the administration of Socialist capital. In brief, the state must be destroyed if the law that regulates work is to be abolished. Can the state abolish itself? If the answer is positive, then the means to this end cannot be the apology of a new kind of state but a reflection on the destruction of the state, even under the temporal existence of a transitional form. In this regard the means would correspond with the ends in the destruction of the state.

However, Lenin's contributions to Marx's reflections on the Paris Commune correspond to the months between February and October 1917. After the triumph of the Bolsheviks, Lenin casts his thoughts on the Paris Commune as relevant to the period that led to the revolution but thereafter became obsolete. "The first issue of *Kommunist* contained a very flattering review by Comrade Bukharin of my pamphlet *The State and Revolution*," Lenin wrote. "But however much I admire the opinion of people like Bukharin, my conscience compels me to say that the *character* of the review reveals a sad and significant fact. Bukharin reads the task of the proletarian revolution from the point of view of the *past* and not of the future."[51] Lenin's judgment on Bukharin in "'Left-Wing' Childishness and the Petty-Bourgeois Mentality" eventually lent the ideological grounds for condemning Bukharin in 1937 during the Stalinist purges. But my point in citing this pamphlet and its connection to the purges is not to provide a historical perspective on Leninism, but rather to treat it as one more contemporary text (that is, according to the principle that all history is contemporaneous) for reflecting on revolutionary violence. Indeed, we may read the April Theses and *The State and Revolution* without privileging Lenin's reconsideration of the ideas proposed in later pamphlets. In reflecting on the question Lenin poses in *The State and Revolution*—"Must the old state machine be *smashed*? And *what* should be placed in its place?"—we need not privilege Lenin's call for large-scale "state capitalism."[52] We face no obligation to define an orthodox Leninism. These observations are particularly relevant when we consider the second case examined in this essay, García Linera's speech at LASA.

In *Logiques des mondes*, Badiou sees the Paris Commune as the first workers' government that remains a possibility in the long *durée*, perhaps as a radical transformation of the common sense of humanity. To speak of humanity might lead us to assume a single *durée* and common sense. We ought to juxtapose this common sense that has been deeply affected by the experience of the Paris Commune to common sense located in (temporal and spatial) cultural and social *elsewheres* that participate in the memory of the same events or that engage these events in the anarcho-communist *durée* from an *elsewhere*. These multiple spaces with their own horizons of universality remain discrete though porous. This suggests interstices, places of "transcritique" (in Kojin Karatani's terms) that should not, however, be subsumed under one unifying world or transcendental subjectivity.[53] One may participate in the memory and duration of the Paris Commune without abdicating the memory and duration of indigenous insurgencies. The Zapatista insurrection of 1994 is one such instance. The association of middle-class revolutionaries (combatants in the guerrillas of the 1970s, with strong ideological links to the anarcho-communism of Ricardo Flores Magón) and Maya communities led to powerful crossings of these durations. The groups comprising the APPO also carry at least two historical memories: the teachers unions and the indigenous groups with long histories of struggle against colonialism. The power of mobilization of the *ayllu* in Bolivia clearly conveys an insurgent duration that remains independent of the history of the Paris Commune.

The revolutionary ethos of pure violence, which one can trace in indigenous uprisings, should lead us to interrogate Schmitt's famous definition of sovereignty: "Sovereign is he who decides on the exception."[54] Examining the Mexican Constitution (as an instance of liberal democratic constitutions), we have noted clauses that define the means by which a state of siege, an exception to the law, or extraordinary measures are decided: the decision resides in the executive power in consultation with the legislative power. We also find the expression that sovereignty resides in the people. The creation of revolutionary governments, at least in the expression of indigenous movements, systematically excludes the establishment of the traditional three powers in liberal constitutions. Revolutions or insurgencies, by definition constitute a state of exception, and, insofar as they counter the law, they stand outside the law, break (with) the (regime of) law, and sidestep the applicability of the constitution to preserve the Estado de Derecho. Even when the Zapatistas cite Article 39 to establish the sovereignty of the people and the right to create a new government, the Mexican Constitution has no place in the "Ley Revolucionaria." We may then complicate the concept of the sovereignty of the people with the Maya Tojolalbal maxim: "ja ma' 'ay ya'tel kujtiki, mandar 'ay kujtik," meaning "the authorities we elect are governed by us." The Zapatistas adopted this maxim in 1994 with the succinct expression "mandar obedeciendo" (to govern obeying).

But then again, what are we to do in the face of a perspective that argues that capital is by nature a regime of means without ends? Can this notion be reconciled with the destruction of the legal foundation of capital? Or is this a subterfuge that reifies globalization and neoliberalism's antistate posturings without acknowledging its ultimate appeal to an Estado de Derecho? What would define the terms of the interaction between that most Western of institutions, the state, and the proliferation of non-Western social entities known as soviets, the Mesoamerican indigenous communities, or the *ayllu* (the ancestral communities defined by territory and genealogical ties) in Bolivia?

CASE 2: ALVARO GARCÍA LINERA'S SPEECH

The vice president of Bolivia, Alvaro García Linera, addressed the 2007 LASA Congress in Montreal to offer an account of the political situation in Bolivia. In the process he conveyed his affinities with Lenin, his view of the necessity of "a state that is not a state." García Linera, to the dismay of some in the audience, reminded us that the state, by definition, holds the monopoly of violence. He also called intellectuals to work on assuming the responsibility of contributing to the common sense that would further the socialist ideals of the MAS (Movimiento al Socialismo). His use of the term "common sense" (*sentido común*) has clear resonances with Gramsci and the need to create a counterhegemonic ideology. Acting on the common sense entails transforming the prevalent cognitions, ethos, and sensibilities of a given community. But, as García Linera put it, the current common sense is articulated by government officials (often with ideologies incompatible with the revolution Evo Morales and García Linera have claimed) that have been incorporated into the regime because of a lack of indigenous intellectuals trained in the hard sciences and finance.

As García Linera said, the new state lacks a cadre of Aymara intellectuals with traditional training in the disciplines of finance, medicine, engineering, and so on (that is, beyond the expertise of anthropologists, historians, and sociologists) able to contribute to the creation of a common sense of the nation that would ground the revolution in socialism. In this regard we have in García Linera's statements another instance of state of exception: an intellectual (in fact, a mathematician) who invokes Lenin from a position of power in the context of neoliberal dogmatic assumptions about the need to weaken the state so it can operate successfully in a globalized world. García Linera has exposed the neoliberal weakening of the state as a *"gran fraude"* (a grand fraud):

> En el fondo el neoliberalismo es keynesiaismo al revés: el estado reduce sus funciones productivas pero agiganta sus funciones regulatorias e intervencionistas para entregar cuanto bien público haya y para disponer cuanto recurso y medio disponga (impuestos, leyes, burocracia, créditos) en beneficio de la inversión extranjera.
>
> Resulta así que el estado ocupa el segundo lugar en cuanto a inversión (600 millones de dólares) y está a punto de igualar a la inversión extranjera sólo que ahora utilizados para favorecer las actividades de entes privados.
>
> [Deep down neoliberalism is an inverted Keynesianism: The state reduces its productive functions but makes enormous its regulating and investor functions

to hand over all public goods and to use all the resources and means it disposes (taxes, laws, bureaucracy, credits) for the benefit of foreign investments.

Consequently the state occupies the second place with respect to investments (six hundred million dollars) and is on the verge of equaling foreign investment to favor the activities of private entities.][55]

García Linera wrote this in 2002, three years before the Morales/García Linera electoral triumph on December 18, 2005. Clearly their government faces the task of undoing the privileges and the protection private sectors enjoyed under the neoliberal state, but the question remains: What is to be done, given that these forces and interests will not disappear overnight? What will be the role of the *ayllus'* power to mobilize and make the Morales/García Linera government assume the responsibility of destroying this inverted Keynesianism?

One answer may reside in the creation of a new kind of leftist state, but this option obviates the power of the opposition and the inevitability of operating from within the established neoliberal power structure. A second answer would point in the direction of an internal dissolution of the state, of a withering in Lenin's terms—that is, of an end in itself and not a passage to an Aymara, a proletarian, or otherwise defined complex of state apparatuses. With respect to this second option that would aspire to the withering of the state, we find a tension between the common sense grounded in the hard sciences and finance that García Linera called intellectuals to promote and the common sense grounded in traditional knowledges that prevails among Aymara *mallku* (the local leader), *jilaqata* (the main authority of the *ayllu*), and *amawt'a* (the holders of wisdom) that led and articulated the mobilizations that brought García Linera and Morales to power. If the concept of "a state that is not a state" responds to Aymara proposals for a new state, these Aymara proposals are self-conscious of the paradoxes involved in entertaining the notion of an Aymara state when the concept of the state is absent in Aymara.

Raúl Zibechi has conceptualized the paradox as follows: "las relaciones sociales no capitalistas y los poderes no estatales que potenciaron el movimineto, pueden entronizar en el poder a fuerzas que pretenden legitimar el estado y expandir el capitalismo" [the noncapitalist and nonstatist social relations that empowered the movement can enthrone in power forces that pretend to legitimate the state and expand capitalism].[56] García Linera's disparaging of the proliferation of Aymara sociologists and anthropologists at the expense of experts in finances and engineers betrays, Zibechi would argue, a deep-seated prejudice against Aymara forms of knowledge, political organization, and aesthetic sensibilities:

En esta dirección, García Linera sostiene que para el buen funcionamiento de la democracia representativa "la existencia de estructuras productivas no capitalistas, de regímenes de intercambio no mercantil, son un obstáculo a la constitución de sujetos no igualados con capacidad de asumir el mercado como fundamento racional de sus comportamientos sociales, incluido el político." Al revés de los que plantea Marx, para quien la comuna rural rusa puede ser la plataforma para la construcción del mundo nuevo, del comunismo, para García Linera este mundo "tradicional" es un obstáculo para el cambio.

[In this sense, García Linera sustains that for the good functioning of representative democracy, "the existence of noncapitalist structures of production, of nonmercantilist regimes of exchange, are an obstacle for the constitution of unequal subjects with the capacity to assume the market as a rational foundation for their social behavior, including the political." Contrary to what Marx argued, for whom the Russian commune can be the platform for the construction of a new world, of communism, for García Linera this "traditional" world is an obstacle for change.][57]

The passage from García Linera's *Estado multinacional*, which characterizes, in a word, the *ayllus*, as an obstacle for change speaks for itself. In his denunciation, Zibechi has in mind Marx's responses to the questions Vera Zasulich posed to him about the analyses in *Capital* that remain ambiguous about the vitality and viability of the Russian commune.

Marx wrote four drafts of the letter to Zasulich, the first being the longest and to my mind the one that offers the elements for theorizing capitalism and the Russian commune as contemporaneous. The contemporaneity of the communes with capital enables them to benefit from modern technology without undergoing the stages that led from the archaic communities to capitalist forms of property in the West. In fact, Marx argues: "Another circumstance favouring the preservation of the Russian commune (by the path of development) is the fact that it is not only contemporaneous with capitalist production but [it] has outlasted the era when this social system appeared intact."[58] Given that for the Russian peasants land was never their private property, the argument for the historical inevitability that would lead from *private property* to *capitalist private property* is not applicable to the Russian commune. However, the United States and Western Europe are undergoing a crisis that will only find its resolution in the "return of modern societies to the 'archaic' type of communal property."[59]

This passage in which "archaic" appears leads to a citation of L. H. Morgan, where the American anthropologist argues that "the 'new system' towards which modern society tends will be A REVIVAL OF SUPERIOR FORM of an archaic social type."[60] The capitalization is by Marx, intended to underscore that if the Washington government subsidized Morgan, "we must not let ourselves to be alarmed at the word 'archaic.'"[61] In citing Marx, I do not intend to argue that the so-called Asiatic Mode of Production should be a defining trait of Marxism. Rather, I believe that Marx offers us the elements for a conceptualization of societies whose histories paradoxically exist *outside* history—that is, that their specific life forms *lack* the built-in historical necessity of the stages that have defined the history of capital.

To my mind, such a conception of societies with singular temporalities, contemporaneous with capital and yet outside capital, offers a most consistent view of historical materialism. It is not, as Dipesh Chakrabarty would put it, the task of elaborating two histories of capital in which History 1 corresponds to the kinds of history we would write on the basis of the abstract categories of Marxism, and History 2 to histories we would write taking into account the analyses of temporalities we would derive from Heidegger. Chakrabarty thereby redefines the terms for writing the good history of capital rather than proposing an alternative to history and capital. Nor is it a question of asserting with Partha Chatterjee that all contemporary societies are modern and that the premodern forms we identify today are the result of modernity. And even less to follow Hardt and Negri's definition of the peasantry as a doomed mode of production.[62] They have apparently chosen to ignore Marx's indictment in the letter to Vera Zasulich of the ever-recurrent death certificate of the Russian commune. In short, it is not a question of another history of capital but of the possibility of conceptualizing societies existing in an *elsewhere* to the modern. These stories will no longer be told according to the criteria that define the discipline of history.[63] In fact, the communities existing in *elsewheres* to modernity have been telling stories for millennia. Our task is not to translate these stories into history by turning them into documents now to be deposited in an archive that erases their specificity.

Reading Marx's letter to Zasulich, one only has to replace "Russian commune" with "*ayllu*" to arrive at an argument that claims that noncapitalist relations can be beneficial—indeed, that they anticipate social structures—for the construction of a new world. This disclaims readings of *Capital* that would argue that capitalism represents a more advanced stage in the evolution of humanity. Thus Zibechi exposes the Marxism of García Linera as bound to the logic of the state and capitalism. The state's monopoly on violence would reveal another facet that goes beyond the function of the police and the army: it proposes a common sense that severs Aymara leaders from the communities by integrating them into the national government.[64] Here, as in the case of Pashukanis, we find the relevance of the debates of yesterday for reflecting on indigenous revolutions. It is not a question that Indians must learn to interpret the world from Marx, Lenin, Pashukanis, Zasulich et al., but that the connections between the state, noncapitalist communes, and constituent assemblies tend to reproduce a limited set of possibilities. It is as if the monopoly on violence that García Linera would claim as vice president would bring forth the normalization of Aymara intellectuals and the pacification of the *ayllus'* power to mobilize.

Would the inclusion of Aymara forms of social organization in the new multicultural and multinational constitution seek to neutralize the *ayllus*? One should expect that having read Zibechi's critique, García Linera would have reconsidered his exclusion of the *ayllus* from the new world the Morales/García Linera government aspire to build. One would have hoped that García Linera would not retain the inevitability of the dominance of the market and the capitalist state, and would draw all the implications of his call for "a state that is no longer a state." But then again García Linera's Leninism might have in mind Lenin's proposals for "state capitalism"—but, if that is the case, the inevitability of state capitalism must remain a "state" secret, otherwise the *ayllu* will mobilize against the regime.

Is pure revolutionary violence possible in a state that (even when aspiring to no longer be a state) retains a legal framework of capitalism—that is, a state that legislates the conditions for the "respect" of private property and the Estado de Derecho? In the frame of the new constitution—the result of intense debates among the diverse participants in the *asamblea constituyente*—the Bolivian nation defines itself as plurinational and recognizes, though in a subordinate position to the national constitution, the normative systems of the *ayllus*. I single out "nation" because the state constitutes a supranational entity that faces the task of marking a transition "to a state that is no longer a state," in García Linera's definition. There is, however, an ironic turn in the evolution of the constitutionally sanctioned *asamblea constituyente* that was put together against the tides of right-wing opposition in the aftermath of the election of Morales and García Linera. The *asamblea constituyente* derives its legitimacy and legality in terms of the long tradition of Western discourses on constituent power that Negri analyzes in *Insurgencies*. The concept of constituent assemblies is a particular product of the Enlightenment that first appeared in the French and American revolutions. These forms of governance today face the challenge of coexisting and being contemporaneous with the communal consensual tradition of the *ayllu*.[65]

The *asamblea constituyente* carries an ironic turn, for Morales and García Linera ride on the tails of Aymara and Quechua popular mobilizations grounded in the territorial and social structures of the *ayllu*—that is, it depends on the authority of *mallku* (political leaders) and *amawt'a* (spiritual leaders), who on the spur of the moment could arguably mobilize *against* the Morales/Linera government.[66] It is also ironic because the *ayllus* and the power of the *mallku* and *amawt'a* hardly need constitutional recognition to be effective political subjects. That is, unless the objective of the new state is to normalize the relationship between the *ayllus* and the state, in an effort to foreclose crisis, rather than in the assumption that the possibility of "a state that no longer is a state" resides on the *ayllus*' power to mobilize. It seems that the commitment to a dispersal of power by the Morales/García Linera state must draw its force to move beyond the state by precisely strengthening the social and political logic of the *ayllus*' inclination to define themselves as societies against the state.

As Zibechi has lucidly put it: "El Manifesto de Achacachi, promulgado el 9 de abril de 2001, debe ser leído a partir de la última página: decenas de sellos de comunidades, subcentrales y sindicatos agrarios, más de 80 firmas de representantes de miles de comuneros y sus familias de la provincia de Omasuyos" [The Achacachi Manifesto, pronounced on April 9, 2001, must be read starting on the last page: the tens of seals form the communities, subcentral offices, and agrarian unions, more than eighty signatures by representatives of thousands of commoners and their families from the province of Omasuyu].[67] For Zibechi, the question of an Aymara "state," which I enclose in quotation marks that reproduce his own use and hesitation to join *Aymara* and *state*, must take into account the seals and signatures of what he likens to a "rompecabezas comunitario" (a communitarian puzzle); the more than eighty signatures would manifest a thick layering of communal leaders in just one district of El Alto, comprising dozens of "barrios-villas-comunidades."

Zibechi likens these politics to the Zapatista maxim of "mandar obedeciendo." Reading the "Manifesto de Achacachi," one cannot but find echoes of the 1871 Paris Commune's workers government (or the APPO, for that matter) that dissolved the judicial system (that is, the police and the army, but also the courts) and refused to take over the state apparatuses even if to define them as proletarian or Aymara. For Zibechi the Achacachi call for *a society against the state* founded in the *ayllus* suggests a concerted effort to avoid the rise of an Aymara fascist state. The political virtue of the *ayllus* consists of the struggles among the different *ayllus*, zones, and territories that prevent the ascent of one entity that would try to hegemonize the rest. One may deplore these struggles as self-defeating fragmentation only if one forgets that all political decision among and within the *ayllus* follow a consensual model that excludes the rule of majorities and representative democracy.[68]

INSURGENCY—FROM THE LATIN *INSURGERE*, "TO RISE UP"

According to the U.S. Department of Defense Joint Publication (JP) 1-02, *Dictionary of Military and Associated Terms*, an insurgency is defined as an "organized movement aimed at the overthrow of a constituted government through use of subversion and armed conflict." We must juxtapose to this apparently transparent definition of ills, the urgency of systematic struggle to take over the state. "Taking over the state" can come in handy when the United States seeks to brand insurgents of their dislike as "terrorist." But the State Department readily deploys the term "insurgent" in the mode of "freedom fighters" who topple regimes of their dislike. This leads to the semantics of empire: what for the oppressed is self-defense, for the oppressor is rebellion; political activism is criminalized; insurgency is turned into terrorism; and so on. Clearly Antonio Negri's *Insurgency* offers a more sophisticated—hence enabling—understanding of insurgency than the definitions by the State Department, perhaps because he is an insurgent himself. If Negri's concept of the multitude is a constant in both the cases of the APPO and of García Linera's speech at LASA, then this concept offers a point of entry into the question of the specter of history. If *Insurgencies* is a history of constituent power, of the sedimentation of previous processes, then we are caught in a single history and the inevitability of being bound by social conditions that determine the revolution—hence the emergence of constituent power. Are we bound to repeat the limits that became manifest in the Russian Revolution? Are we bound by the same categories? Are we falling into a trivial mode that history repeats itself?

In the context of the indigenous movements in Latin America—in particular, in Bolivia, Chiapas, and Ecuador—we find a specific set of patterns and dangers that indigenous movements must anticipate in order to avoid their repetition. Patterns that do not necessarily repeat those we could trace in the Russian Revolution, and yet these temporalities have points in common. In the case of the APPO, it is perhaps clearer the extent to which one can speak of the insurgent duration that was first inaugurated in the Paris Commune of 1871, but we should consider that the memories of Indian movements that can be traced back to ancestral times also interact with other memories that connect the *ayllus* and Indian communities in general to unions, and minimally to the state and the history of capitalism that haunt the indigenous movements.

García Linera's proposal of "a state that is no longer a state" courts paradox in that it presumes an institutionalization of insurgency and revolution. To suggest that there can exist an insurgent state make no sense unless we were to speak of a form of government that no longer fulfills the role of regulating the administration of capital. Minimally, the doctrine of the withering away of the state would entail the following axiom by Pashukanis, which establishes that "the withering away of the categories of bourgeois law" will lead "to the disappearance of the juridical factor from social relations."[69] This axiom entails the premise that if the abolition of the state cannot be done overnight, as it is implied in García Linera's call for "a state that is no longer a state," we ought to envision the creation of a constituent assembly that, beyond its power of drafting a new constitution, would carry the logic that leads to the dissolution of law itself.

Can the new constitution be conceived with the elements that would transform society in ways that would lead to "the disappearance of the juridical factor from social relations"? Would the recognition of the excluded components in the plurinational state amount to more than a pacification of the communities? There is perhaps nothing more symptomatic of a need to reflect on the pacification of the communities than García Linera's reminder to the members of the Sankajahuira that their expropriation and transformation of Victor Hugo Cardenas's house on Lake Tititca into a communal house for elders was not allowed by the new constitution:

> Hay interpretaciones arrojadizas del texto constitucional. El texto constitucional tiene absoluto respeto a la propiedad privada, incluso transcribe la misma frase de la antigua Constitución (de) respeto a la propiedad privada en tanto cumpla una función social; por tanto, nadie puede utilizar la nueva constitución como argumento para agredir la propiedad privada.

> [There are rash interpretations of the constitutional text. The constitutional text has absolute respect for private property; in fact, it transcribes the exact phrasing of the old constitution of respect of private property in as much as it fulfills a social function; therefore, no one can use the new constitution as an argument to assault private property.][70]

García Linera's language leaves no doubt about the function of the constitution as a guarantee of the right to private property. Or is it mere opportunist talk designed to appease the bourgeoisie? In any case, it leaves no room for the supposition that the Cardenas property might go against the juridical norms of the community where it is located. The state and the constitution prevail over the juridic norms of the Sankajahuira. The so-called multination and multi-institutional state remains suspect, if not a ruse, that in the end conceals a modernization of the nation as its ultimate end.

García Linera would thus reiterate the developmentalist view he expressed in *Estado multinacional*: "la existencia de estructuras productivas no capitalistas, de regímenes de intercambio no mercantil, son un obstáculo a la constitución de sujetos no igualados con capacidad de asumir el mercado como fundamento racional de sus comportamientos sociales, incluido el político" [the existence of noncapitalist structures of production, of nonmercantilist regimes of exchange, are an obstacle for the constitution of unequal subjects with the capacity to assume the market as a rational foundation for their social behavior, including the political].[71]

The specter of capitalism and the history of the state that haunt indigenous movements leads to the following questions: To what extent can social movements step out of the logic of the state? Is the concept and practice of indigenous autonomies a form of residing without history—that is, outside the social conditions of capitalism that define the terms under which political economy and legal theory make sense? Is the concept of "a state that no longer is a state" caught in an aporia that binds it to the repetition of the history of constituent power? Does the multitude point to the reconfiguration of the project of constituent power?

This chapter underscores the need to remain within the spirit of Benjamin's revolutionary pure violence, which entails an exception to the political—the manifestation of rage in the conjunction of means and ends. We ought to think of insurgencies as carrying deep transformations in the common sense of a given class, society, historical moment, or culture. Here Raymond Williams's notion of "emergent structures of feeling" might be pertinent.[72] Insurgencies broaden the experience of everyday practices, the transmission of new forms of feeling, the opening of places where art is art, and the politics of representation. If the Paris Commune introduced a deep transformation in the duration of insurgency, the mobilizations of the APPO, the *ayllus*, and the Zapatista uprising carry millennial forms of social organization and knowledge that interact and transform the (im)possible communism that Marx lucidly diagnosed after the 1871 commune: "But this is communism, 'impossible' communism!"[73]

The concept of exception as it is connected to aesthetics of insurgency may thus be productively extended to questions of politics, cognition, and ethics. Exception to the political would signify the suspension of all connections and subordination to parties, representative democracy, and the state. Indigenous mobilizations partake of cognitive forms that connect them to spiritual forces populating the Bolivian highlands, where *wak'as* and *achachilas* punctuate the landscape, or those spirits populating the Lacandon Selva, where Votán-Zapata appears riding his horse with rifle in hand on the horizon of the mountains. The universal claims of human rights would also be suspended in finding them bound to homogenizing impulses that accompany claims to the right of diversity and ethnicity. These claims ultimately lead to the splintering of the movements into individual leaders detached from communities in their participation in state-engineered or NGO-articulated developmental plans. But then again the exception to the political would also question the plurinational or multinational programs originating in the state, political parties, or intellectual elites exterior to the processes generated in the mobilizations.

Thus the paradox of *constituent assemblies* and the new constitutions they draft resides in the impulse to regulate and legitimate the same mobilizations that led to their creation in the first place. As such, García Linera's "state that is no longer a state" remains a state exterior to the logic of the *ayllus*. Ultimately his statement at LASA reenacts Lenin's questions in *The State and Revolu-*

tion: "Must the old state machine be *smashed*? And *what* should be placed in its place?"[74] In responding to these questions, the Morales/García Linera government remains haunted by two specters: on the one hand, if the state is not smashed, the rule of the bourgeoisie will curtail their initiatives; on the other, if they give occasion to an Aymara state, the *ayllus* will mobilize to dismantle initiatives that ignore the consensual politics of the communities and the internal struggles that define the inexorable principle of *society against the state*. The will to suppress this millennial common sense at the root of the *ayllus'* ethos, politics, and cognitive structures, and their power to mobilize the masses, would in turn reenact the violence of conquest and colonization—be it in the mode of the Spanish conquest, neoliberal colonization, or "state capitalism." As long as the *ayllus* (read: soviets, indigenous communities, communes) remain *without* history—both in the sense of lack and outside explored in the essays comprising this book—the force of the law and the state will be kept at bay.

NOTES

Chapter 1. Introduction

1. I can still remember vividly when Ileana Rodríguez arrived at the airport in Washington, D.C., for an interview at the University of Maryland. Rodríguez had resigned from her tenure position at the University of Minnesota to join the Sandinista revolution. She did not get the position for which she interviewed but instead was awarded a Rockefeller Fellowship at Maryland. During the year of Rodríguez's tenure at Maryland, the two of us formed an affinity group along with Javier Sanjinés, Robert Carr, Patricia Seed, and John Beverley that eventually led to LASSG. The story of the group—as well as our debates, conversations, and exchanges with our Indian counterparts—has been chronicled in several publications. See, for instance, the debates on postcolonialism and subaltern studies in Moraña et al., *Coloniality at Large*; Moraña, *Nuevas perspectivas desde*; and Verdesio, *Dispositio/n*, special issue on "Subaltern Studies."

2. The chronicle of these transformations can be traced in many of the essays in Chakrabarty's *Provincializing Europe* and *Habitations of Modernity*; for an explicit essay on the topic, see Chakrabarty's "A Small History of Subaltern Studies" in *Habitations of Modernity*.

3. For an exploration of the concept of "elsewhere," see Rabasa, "Elsewheres."

4. Bellinghausen, "Denuncian hostigamiento contra activistas."

5. Rabinow, *Anthropos Today*, 25.

6. "También vamos a ir viendo de levantar una lucha para demandar que hacemos una nueva Constitución o sea nuevas leyes que tomen en cuenta las demandas del pueblo mexicano como son: techo, tierra, trabajo, alimento, salud, educación, información, cultura, independencia, democracia, justicia, libertad y paz. Una nueva Constitución que reconozca los derechos y libertades del pueblo, y defienda al débil frente al poderoso" [We will also go about seeing how to build a struggle to demand a new Constitution that is of new laws that take into account the demands of the Mexican people such as: roof, land, work, food, health, education, information, culture, independence, democracy, justice, liberty, and peace. A new Constitution that recognizes the rights of the people, and defends the weak against the powerful] (from *Sexta Declaración de la Selva Lacandona*, part 4). We ought to resist reading this call for a new constitution as mere reformist intervention in the continuation of a benevolent leftist state.

7. Marx, "Civil War in France," 233.

8. Ibid.

9. Lenin, *State and Revolution*, 476; emphasis in the original.

10. Jameson, *Singular Modernity*, 29. For a critique of the singular modernity from the perspective of the colonial divide that cannot be reduced to one more instance of a passage to modernity, see Rabasa, "Colonial Divide."

11. Geological formations are one of Marx's preferred metaphors for reflecting on the contemporaneity of the Russian communes: "The history of the decline of primitive communities (it would be a mistake to place them all on the same level; as in geological

formations, these historical forms contain a whole series of primary, secondary, tertiary types, etc.) has still to be written" (Marx, "Drafts of the Letter to Vera Zasulich," 358).

12. In what follows I have benefited from Nancy's proposals in *Creation of the World*.

13. Ibid., 85, emphasis in original.

14. Ibid., 43, emphasis in original.

15. Nandy, "History's Forgotten Doubles," 44; emphasis in the original. I am limiting my observations to Nandy, but the reader could benefit from Vinay Lal's review of debates over Indian history in "Subaltern Studies and Its Critics." Also see Lal, *History of History*.

16. Rabinow, *Anthropos Today*, 35.

Chapter 2. Pre-Columbian Pasts and Indian Presents in Mexican History

This piece was originally published as "Pre-Columbian Pasts and Indian Presents in Mexican History," in a special issue on Subaltern Studies in the Americas, edited by José Rabasa, Javier Sanjinés, and Robert Carr, *Dispositio/n* 46 (1996): 245–70. Copyright © 1996, José Rabasa. All rights reserved. Reprinted by permission of the author.

1. Readers of Gayatri Spivak's essay "Can the Subaltern Speak?" have generally failed to foreground a recommendation to learn how to speak to the subaltern rather than limit the import of her question to an affirmative or negative response. We might all be willing to listen to the subaltern, but how should we know that the subaltern agrees on what we are hearing? The "learn-to-listen" solution invariably ends up in a we/them structure that ultimately betrays an anthropological will to objectivity that obviates dialogue.

2. Personal communication with John Beverley.

3. I return to this question in chapter 11, where I examine speech, script, and time in the Nahuatl writings of Fernando Alvarado Tezozomoc and Domingo Francisco de San Antón Muñón Chimalpahin.

4. Nietzsche, *Use and Abuse of History*, 18.

5. See Boone, "Collecting the Pre-Columbian Past"; Errington, "Progressivist Stories and the Pre-Columbian Past"; and Florescano, "Creation of the Museo Nacional."

6. Another mode of addressing the "imaginary of violence" is the notion of "places of rage" (see Halberstam, "Imagined Violence/Queer Violence").

7. The archaeological dimension is informed by Foucault's work in *The Order of Things, The Archaeology of Knowledge,* and his essay "What Is an Author?" This essay is especially pertinent for comparative study of authority in collecting pre-Columbian pasts. I am indebted to the comparativist approaches in Boon, *Other Tribes, Other Scribes*.

8. Chakravarty, "Marx after Marxism," 16.

9. See Boone, "Aztec Pictorial History of *Codex Mendoza*"; and Berdan, "Imperial Tribute Roll of the *Codex Mendoza*."

10. Brotherston, *Book of the Fourth World*, 67.

11. Berdan, "Imperial Tribute Roll of the *Codex Mendoza*," 57; and see Robertson, *Mexican Manuscript Painting*, 105.

12. Calnek, "Ethnographic Content," in Codex Mendoza, vol. 1: 81–91.

13. Howe, "Relationship of Indigenous and European Styles."

14. Codex Mendoza, vol. 4: 148.

15. Ibid.

16. Ibid.

17. Ibid.

18. Ibid., vol. 4: 34.

19. Ibid.

20. Ibid, vol. 4: 148.

21. Ibid.

22. Ironically, Sigüenza y Góngora's books on Mexican antiquities have been lost. We know of Sigüenza y Góngora's historiography of ancient Mexico from later historians who referred to him as "la autoridad del distinguido anticuario" [the authority of the distinguished antiquarian] (Orosco y Berra, *Historia antigua*, vol. 1: 71), and as "uno de los más beneméritos de la historia de México, porque formó a grandes expensas una copiosa y selecta colección de manuscritos y de pinturas antiguas" [one of the most worthy historians of Mexico, because he formed at great expense a copious and select collection of manuscripts and ancient paintings] (Clavigero, *Historia antigua de México*, vol. 1: 92).

23. Sigüenza y Góngora, *Alboroto y motín de los indios de México*, 123. I follow William G. Bryant's modernized edition of the *Alboroto y motín de los indios de México*. For a paleographic edition, see Irving A. Leonard's 1932 edition. The English version is by Irving Leonard (*Don Carlos de Sigüenza y Góngora*, 256). I have modified his translation when I have felt it necessary. If I abstain from using such terms as "mob" and "riot" in my discussion of the events, I retain those terms in the translations of Sigüenza y Góngora's use of *tumulto* (mob), *motín* (riot), and *alboroto* (disturbance), which are part and parcel of this counterinsurgent discourse. Ranajit Guha in *Elementary Aspects of Peasant Insurgency*, in particular chapters 3 and 4, has discussed the use of these terms as a form of negating the political character of subaltern insurrections. We have become especially sensitive to language in the wake of the 1992 Los Angeles uprising, as the use of the term "riot" has systematically undermined the possibility of conceiving any political motivation beyond the characterization of an irrational mob.

24. Leonard, *Don Carlos de Sigüenza y Góngora*, 256.

25. Sigüenza y Góngora, *Alboroto y motín de los indios de México*, 130.

26. Leonard, *Don Carlos de Sigüenza y Góngora*, 268.

27. See Zárate, *Don Carlos de Sigüenza y Góngora*; Iglesias, "La mexicanidad de Don Carlos de Sigüenza y Góngora"; Paz, *Sor Juana Inés de la Cruz*; Codgell, "Criollos, Gapuchines, y 'plebe tan extremo plebe'"; and Moraña, *Relecturas del Barroco de Indias*.

28. See Guha, *Elementary Aspects of Peasant Insurgencies*, 1–17. Cf. Hobsbawn and Rudé, *Captain Swing*; and Hobsbawn, *Social Bandits and Primitive Rebels*.

29. Sigüenza y Góngora, *Alboroto y motín de los indios de México*, 113.

30. Leonard, *Don Carlos de Sigüenza y Góngora*, 240.

31. Sigüenza y Góngora, *Alboroto y motín de los indios de México*, 123.

32. Leonard, *Don Carlos de Sigüenza y Góngora*, 257.

33. Sigüenza y Góngora, *Alboroto y motín de los indios de México*, 123.

34. I emphasize this last point to counter recent scholarship that has questioned whether there ever was colonialism in the New World (Klor de Alva, "Colonialism and Postcolonialism as (Latin) American Mirages"). If Spanish colonialism in the sixteenth and seventeenth centuries differs from the English or French imperial enterprises of the nineteenth century, it does not follow that there is not much to gain by comparative study from both regional and temporal perspectives.

35. See Pratt, *Imperial Eyes*.

36. Sigüenza y Góngora, *Alboroto y motín de los indios de México*, 124; Leonard, *Don Carlos de Sigüenza y Góngora*, 259.

37. Sigüenza y Góngora, *Alboroto y motín de los indios de México*, 119.

38. Leonard, *Don Carlos de Sigüenza y Góngora*, 251.

39. All interviews, declarations, and communiqués by the EZLN, the Comité Clandestino Revolucionario Indígena, Comandancia General (CCRI-CG), and Subcomandante Marcos have been posted online at the official Web site of the EZLN, http://palabra.ezln.org.mx (accessed on April 20, 2008). Translations into English of EZLN documents are regularly updated at Chiapas 95, http://www.eco.utexas.edu/faculty/Cleaver/chiapas95.html (accessed on May 5, 2008).

40. For a more detailed discussion of this communiqué and the question of translation, see chapter 3 in this book.

41. See Leonard, *Don Carlos de Sigüenza y Góngora*, 136–38.

42. Sigüenza y Góngora, *Alboroto y motín de los indios de México*, 120; and Leonard, *Don Carlos de Sigüenza y Góngora*, 251–52.

43. Sigüenza y Góngora, *Alboroto y motín de los indios de México*, 116; Leonard, *Don Carlos de Sigüenza y Góngora*, 245.

44. Quoted in Saignes, "Borracheras andinas," 102. Translation is mine.

45. Sigüenza y Góngora, *Alboroto y motín de los indios de México*, 134; and Leonard, *Don Carlos de Sigüenza y Góngora*, 274.

46. Sigüenza y Góngora, *Alboroto y motín de los indios de México*, 134; and Leonard, *Don Carlos de Sigüenza y Góngora*, 275.

47. A classic instance is Fernando de Alva Ixtlilxóchitl's description of a group of Indians led to their *repartimiento* (labor draft to perform work for Spaniards) by their governor, Don Juan de Aguilar, Ixtlilxóchitl's grandfather. According to Ixtlilxochitl, they were singing songs to Netzahualcoyotl in which they recalled their noble origins (Ixtlilxóchitl, *Obras históricas*, vol. 2: 267–69). Their nobility should have kept them from the *repartimiento*: "la desdicha ha llegado a tanto que como si fueran maceguales y villanos los llevan a repartir a Tacuba" [the extent of their misfortune is so great that they are taken to Tacuba as a labor draft as if they were *maceguales* and peasants] (ibid., vol. 2: 270, the translation is mine). There is a striking contrast between Ixtlilxóchitl's separation of the *macehualtin* (the commoners) from the indigenous elite to which he belongs and Chimalpahin's use of the term *timacehualtin* (*ti* = we + *macehual* + *tin* = plural) to speak of this condition as all of the Nahua, beginning with himself. See chapter 11 in this book for a discussion of Chimalpahin's writings.

48. Sigüenza y Góngora, *Alboroto y motín de los indios de México*, 134; and Leonard, *Don Carlos de Sigüenza y Góngora*, 275.

49. García, *Tumultos y rebeliones*, 250. The translation is mine.

50. Guha, *Elementary Forms of Peasant Insurgency*, 225.

51. García, *Tumultos y rebeliones*, 248. The translation is mine.

52. Cf. Ross, "Alboroto y motín de México."

53. Sigüenza y Góngora, *Alboroto y motín de los indios de México*, 117.

54. Sigüenza y Góngora, *Alboroto y motín de los indios de México*, 117.

55. Leonard, *Don Carlos de Sigüenza y Góngora*, 246.

56. Sigüenza y Góngora, *Alboroto y motín de los indios de México*, 117; and Leonard, *Don Carlos de Sigüenza y Góngora*, 247.

57. See Sommer, "Resisting the Heat."

Chapter 3. Of Zapatismo

This essay was originally published as "Of Zapatismo: Reflections on the Folkloric and the Impossible in a Subaltern Insurrection," in *The Politics of Culture in the Shadow of Capital*, edited by Lisa Lowe and David Lloyd (Durham, N.C.: Duke University Press), 399–431. Copyright 1997, Duke University Press. All rights reserved. Reprinted by permission of the publisher. *Epigraphs*: Comité Clandestino Revolucionario Indígena, Comandancia General del EZLN (CCRI-CG), "Carta a Zedillo," Chiapas, Mexico, February 10, 1995. All interviews, declarations, and communiqués by the EZLN, the CCRI-CG, and Subcomandante Marcos have been posted online at the official Web site of the EZLN, http://palabra.ezln.org.mx (accessed on April 20, 2008). Translations into English of EZLN documents are regularly updated at Chiapas 95, http://www.eco.utexas.edu/faculty/Cleaver/chiapas95.html (accessed on May 5, 2008). Unless specified, all translations are mine. Marcos, one of the three initial non-Indians within the Zapatista ranks, bears the title of "subcomandante" in contradistinction to the higher-ranking Indian comandantes. From the beginning of the rebellion on January 1, 1994—the same day the North American Free Trade Agreement (NAFTA) was implemented—Marcos has expressed his subordination to the CCRI-CG, composed of Chol, Mam, Tojolabal, Tzeltal, Tzotzil, and Zoque Indians, who are in turn obliged to consult their own communities (see communiqué January 4, 1994). Spivak, "Can the Subaltern Speak?," 295; emphasis in the original. Carlos Monsiváis, "¿Todos somos indios?" *La Jornada*, February 17, 1995.

1. For a sustained formulation of strategies and methods to understand, interpretet, and grasp the politics of popular movements from the perspective of the masses themselves, see Ileto's *Pasyon and Revolution*. Although the subject of this essay is a contemporary insurrection and not a historical event, Ileto's assesment of the failure to understand popular movements applies to the letter: "Social scientists unable to view society in other than equilibrium terms are bound to conclude that these movements are aberrations or the handiwork of crazed minds, alienated individuals, or external agitators. On the other hand, many scholars sympathetic to these movements tend to fit them into a tight evolutionary framework that leads to a disparagement all together of cultural values and traditions as just a lot of baggage from our feudal and colonial past" (Ileto, *Pasyon and Revolution*, 13).

2. One of the beginnings of modern philosophy—in particular of philosophies concerned with current events, *la philosophie de l'actualité* (as the French like to call it)—is Hegel's statement: "Reading the morning paper is a kind of realistic prayer" (quoted in Descombes, *Barometer of Reason*, 3). The Internet, as it were, has opened a new site of "prayer" and made it possible to dismantle the control of information by press agencies. It is worthwhile to remember that only a few years ago the United States pulled out of UNESCO for its insistence (due to what was perceived as overtly political, as maintaining a "third world" bias) on creating an international bank of information (the New International Order). This circulation of information, however, does not exclude forms of control that do or may yet come to exist over e-mail. The circulation via the Internet of Zapatista communiqués published in *La Jornada* has enabled me to read about Chiapas and Mexico on a daily basis and ultimately to write this essay. Beyond a contribution to an understanding of "the now"—after all, as the letter from the CCRI-CG put it, if the EZLN, Zapatismo as we know it today, could very well be exterminated in the next few days, Zapata would endure)—the question would be: In what ways can this essay contribute to Zapatismo?

3. April 10, 1995, communiqué at http://palabra.ezln.org.mx.

4. April 10, 1994, communiqué at http://palabra.ezln.org.mx; ellipsis in the original.

5. Seler, "Wall Paintings of Mitla," 295.

6. See articles in *La Guillotina* 30 (March–April 1995).

7. Gossen, "From Omecs to Zapatistas," 566.

8. Ibid., 566 and 567

9. Camú Urzúa and Tótoro Taulis have written a detailed history of the movement since the early 1980s in *EZLN, el ejercito que salió de la selva*. Their history establishes a connection to earlier guerrilla movements and differentiates the nature of the Zapatistas precisely in terms of the subordination of the Ladinos to the recommendations of the Indian committees. John Ross, in *Rebellion from the Roots*, has written a most detailed and empathetic chronicle of the early days of the insurrection. For an analysis of the socioeconomic causes of the insurrection, see Collier, *Basta!*. This chapter seeks to examine the political discourse of Zapatismo. The sources for this reflection are the communiqués by Marcos and the CCRI-CG as well as the invaluable reports from the *Selva Lacandona* of journalists for *La Jornada*: Hermann Bellinghausen, Elio Henríquez, Epigmenio Ibarra, and Blanche Petrich, just to mention the most prominent and indefatigable. Since this essay was first published in 1996, numerous essays and studies have been published, but arguably the most thorough is Muñoz Ramírez, *EZLN: 20 y 10*, which has been published in updated Spanish and English editions with the titles *El fuego y la palabra* and *The Fire and the Word*.

10. Monsiváis, "¿Todos somos indios?" *La Jornada*, February 17, 1995.

11. I owe this posing of the question to David Lloyd.

12. See Guillermoprieto, "Shadow War"; Romero, *Marcos*; and Trejo Delarbe, *Chiapas*.

13. May 7, 1995, communiqué, at http://palabra.ezln.org.mx.

14. For a testimonial on the significance of the events in Berlin in 1989 and an argument for the relevance of Marx and Communism, see Terray, *Le troisème jour du communisme*. This book in many ways anticipates Jacques Derrida's assessment of the relevance of Marx's concept of revolution and critique and call for a new internationalism as detailed in Derrida's *Specters of Marx*.

15. See María Josefina Saldaña-Portillo's "Irrestible Seduction: Rural Subjectivity under the Sandinista Agricultural Policy," in *Revolutionary Imagination in the Americas*, 109–49. Saldaña-Portillo provides a lucid analysis of why the Sandinistas faced resistance to their program of land reform by the same people it was supposed to benefit.

16. Beverley, "Writing in Reverse," 273. The Latin American Subaltern Studies group has been accused of inviting a new wave of cultural imperialism (in this case of Indian origin but through the U.S. academy) and of ignoring the long tradition of oppositional writing in Latin America. Both observations harbor a misconception about the project. My response is that the Southeast Asian group's work on the category of the subaltern provides an exceptional corpus of texts without parallel elsewhere in the world. In the end, because of the debates within both groups and the temporal and geographic differences, what is of interest in this new circuit of theory are the possible conversations, debates, and shared investigations between scholars working with similar problematics and colonial legacies in different parts of the world.

17. Hardt and Negri, *Labor of Dionysus*, 310.

18. June 8, 1995, communiqué at http://palabra.ezln.org.mx, accessed on December 9, 2009.

19. See Guha and Spivak, *Selected Subaltern Studies*.

20. For definitions of the project of the Latin American Subaltern Studies Group, see the "Founding Statement" and "Introduction: The Politics of Subaltern Studies" in Rabasa, Sanjinés, and Carr, *Subaltern Studies in the Americas*.

21. My critique of Gramsci has many affinities with David Lloyd's critique of Gramsci's view that the history of subaltern groups is episodic and fragmentary. See Lloyd, *Anomalous States*, 127 and passim.

22. Gramsci, *Selections from the Prison Notebooks*, 197.

23. Ibid., 30.

24. This passage from *Gli intellectuali e l'organizzazione della cultura* is quoted in Gramsci, *Selections from the Prison Notebooks*, 326n5.

25. Ibid.

26. On the centrality of negation in subaltern studies, see Guha's *Elementary Aspects of Peasant Insurgency*, 19–76. Guha finds in the following passage by Gramsci a starting point for an understanding of negation in subaltern insurgencies: "Not only do the people have no precise consciousness of its own historical identity, it is not even consciousness of the historical identity or the exact limits of its adversary. The lower classes, historically on the defensive, can only achieve self-awareness via a series of negations, via their consciousness of the identity and class limits of their enemy; but it is precisely this process which has not yet come to the surface, at least not nationally" (ibid., 273). Guha's chapter on "Negation" goes on to document modalities and instances of actual negations in the history of Indian peasant insurgencies. But Guha, from the concluding remarks, seems to suggest an incompatibility of nonmodern social formations with modern political concepts—that is, with "advanced ideas of democracy" (ibid., 76). As we will see in the example of the Zapatistas, we find a *negation* of this teleology that privileges supposedly more developed political forms in the interpretation of subaltern identities. Reynaldo Ileto, in *Pasyon and Revolution*, presents a lucid argument for approaching popular movements in their own terms.

27. Bhadra, "Four Rebels of Eighteen-Fifty-Seven," 173–74.

28. Ibid., 175.

29. Ibid.

30. See Sommer, "Resisting the Heat."

31. Spivak, *Subaltern Studies*, 211.

32. See Womack, *Zapata and the Mexican Revolution*, which is Spivak's source. For other studies of the Zapatistas of 1910 and their legacy, see Knight, *Mexican Revolution*; De la Pena, *Legacy of Promises*; and Warman, *"We Came to Object."* More recently, Samuel Brunk has attributed the "failure" of Zapata to his dependence on urban intellectuals. See Brunk, "Zapata and the City Boys." But this emphasis on the role of "education" has been undermined by JoAnn Martin in a study of the use of historical authenticity in a movement to defend communal land in Buena Vista, Morelos, Mexico. See Martin, "Contesting Authenticity." Both of these articles antecede the Zapatista uprising in Chiapas, but Martin's piece is particularly relevant to the EZLN in the emphasis it places on the future, on contemporary movements rather than on events in the past (see Martin, "Contesting Authenticity," 447).

33. February 9, 1995, communiqué at http://palabra.ezln.org.mx.

34. Barker, *Culture of Violence*, 233.

35. Womack, *Zapata and the Mexican Revolution*, 526.

36. CCRI-CG, "Carta a Zedillo," Chiapas, Mexico, February 10, 1995, at http://palabra.ezln.org.mx (accessed on April 20, 2008).

37. Womack, *Zapata and the Mexican Revolution*, 509.

38. Gramsci, *Selections from the Prison Notebooks*, 196.

39. Although the main ideas as well as the political motivation are Zapata's, the composition of the Plan de Ayala involved other leaders, and the actual writing of the document is attributed to a schoolteacher named Otilio Montaño. Points one to five of the plan denounce President Francisco I. Madero's negotiation with *hacendados* (large landholders) and *científicos* (intellectuals) from the dictatorship of Porfirio Díaz. The remaining ten points call for a reappropriation of lands that had been taken from communities (*pueblos*) and citizens (*ciudadanos*) who held the corresponding titles; justify the expropriation of *latifundia*; define the terms to compensate widows and children of fallen combatants; and establish the criteria for a democratic revolutionary society.

40. "Founding Statement," in Rabasa, Sanjinés, and Carr, *Subaltern Studies in the Americas*, 10.

41. September 22, 1994, communiqué at http://palabra.ezln.org.mx. See Rabasa and Sanjinés, "Introduction," in Rabasa, Sanjinés, and Carr, *Subaltern Studies in the Americas*, v–xi. I discuss this issue in chapter 2.

42. February 9, 1995, communiqué at http://palabra.ezln.org.mx.

43. See Guha, *Elementary Aspects of Peasant Insurgency*, and "Prose of Counter-Insurgency."

44. The press repeats a constant form of counterinsurgency that Lloyd has defined as follows: "Of course from the perspective of dominant history, the subaltern must be represented as violence. 'Must' in two senses: that which cannot be assimilated to the state can be understood only as outside the law, disruptive and discontinuous, unavailable for narration; secondly, the history of the state requires a substrate which is counter to its laws of civility and which it represents as outrageous and violent, in order that the history of domination and criminalization appear as a legitimate process of civilization and the triumph of law" (Lloyd, *Anomalous States*, 127).

45. Trejo Delarbre, *Chiapas: La guerra de las ideas*.

46. Womack, *Zapata and the Mexican Revolution*, 375.

47. Petrich and Henríquez, *La Jornada*, February 4, 1995.

48. Ibid.

49. Tacho quoted in Henríquez and Pérez Silva, "La contraparte 'ha querido engánamos.'" *La Jornada*, June 10, 1995.

50. Ibid.

51. February 3–4, 1994, communiqué at http://palabra.ezln.org.mx.

52. Ibid.

53. May 13, 1995, communiqué at http://palabra.ezln.org.mx.

54. Ibid.

55. February 3–4, 1994, communiqué at http://palabra.ezln.org.mx.

56. Castañeda, *Sorpresas te da la vida*, 44–45.

57. December 3, 1994, communiqué at http://palabra.ezln.org.mx.

58. Romero, *Marcos*, 23.

59. Quoted in Silverstein and Cockburn, "Killers and the Killing," 306.

60. Foucalt, "What Is an Author?"

61. Derrida as quoted in Spivak, "Supplementing Marx," 111.

62. June 9, 1995, communiqué at http://palabra.ezln.org.mx; Marcos's capitalization is in the original.

63. Ibid.

64. Ibid.

65. Hardt and Negri, *Labor of Dionysus*, 307

66. See Spivak, "Supplementing Marx," 115.

67. See Parish and Weidman, *Las casas en Mexico.*

68. Las Casas, "El tratado de las 'Doce Dudas,'" 218; the translation is mine.

69. For a critique of developmentalist discourse as the imaginary of our time, see Escobar, "Imagining of a Post-Development Era?"

70. Benjamin, "Theses on the Philosophy of History," 263.

71. Ibid., 257. Benjamin, "Critique of Violence," 300.

72. Foucault, "What Is an Author?" 120.

73. I have found Walker's critique useful for reading Garcilaso de la Vega's positioning as an Indian writing in a context where there was no place for an Indian author in late-sixteenth-century Spain. See Walker, "Feminist Criticism and the Author." See Rabasa, "'Porque soy Indio.'"

74. Walker, "Feminist Criticism and the Author," 568; emphasis in the original.

75. See Spivak, "Can the Subaltern Speak?" 276 and passim.

76. June 9, 1995, communiqué at http://palabra.ezln.org.mx.

77. See Rabasa, "Aesthetics of Colonial Violence." Since this essay was published in 1996, my book *Writing Violence on the Northern Frontier* has appeared.

78. Foucault, "What Is Enlightenment?"

79. Haraway, "Promises of Monsters."

80. Menchú, *Me llamo Rigoberta Menchú.*

81. February 4–7, 1994, communiqué at http://palabra.ezln.org.mx.

82. Quoted by Spivak, "Can the Subaltern Speak?" 274.

83. See Vera Herrera, "Relojes japoneses."

Chapter 4. Historical and Epistemological Limits in Subaltern Studies

This essay was originally published as "Historical and Epistemological Limits in Subaltern Studies," *Interventions* 1, no. 2 (1999): 255–64. Copyright © 1999, José Rabasa. All rights reserved. Reprinted by permission of the author. *Epigraph*: Don Carlos de Ometochtzin, in *Procesos de indios idólatras.*

1. The Codex Telleriano-Remensis consists of four sections: (1) the series of feasts known as the *veintena*, named after the twenty months of the year in which the feasts were celebrated; (2) the *tonalamatl*, or divinatory calendar; (3) the history of Mexico-Tenochtitlan; (4) a history of the colonial period. Even though the pre-Columbian history continues, it is formally distinct. In fact, formal change marks the historical rupture of the conquest. I return to folio 46r of the Telleriano-Remensis in chapter 10.

2. For a fuller discussion of this communiqué and Benjamin's *jetztzeit*, see chapter 3.

3. See Ramos, *Desencuentros de la modernidad.*

4. This chapter originally responded to a series of queries posed by Robert Young for a special issue of *Interventions* on "Ideologies of the Postcolonial."

5. The lineage Descartes-Kant-Hegel—privileged regardless of assertive or negative purposes (e.g., Foucault, Habermas, Husserl, Lacan)—is but one narrative taken to be the dominant paradigm. Other readings of the history of modernity could favor Baude-

laire, Leibniz, Spinoza, Vico, and Wittgenstein as expressions of modernity that are not derivative from the first narrative, which moreover constitutes an arbitrary list—rather than an alternative narrative—that enables us to take a plural-world approach to modernity. See Descombes, *Barometer of Modern Reason*.

6. Guha, "Not at Home in Empire."

7. For details on the movement, see chapter 3.

8. In formulating the concept of a plurality of worlds, I have benefited from Spinosa and Dreyfus, "Two Kinds of Antiessentialism and Their Consequences"; and Goodman, *Ways of Worldmaking*.

9. For a reconsideration of Benjamin Whorf's views on language and worldview that no longer imply a Romantic understanding of worldview nor a stable concept of language that would supposedly embody such a conception of the world, see Lucy, "Scope of Linguistic Relativism"; and Hill and Mannheim, "Language and Worldview." Also see Whorf, "Relation of Habitual Thought and Behavior to Language."

10. See Spivak, "Politics of Translation," 197.

11. See, for example, Cummins, "From Lies to Truth."

12. See Adams, *William Ockham*; and Panaccio, "Intuition, abstraction et langage mental."

13. For the case of India, see Schwarz, "Laissez-Faire Linguistics."

14. See Certeau, "Ethno-Graphy."

15. See chapter 10 in this book.

16. See, for example, García Martínez, *Los pueblos de indios*; and Stavenhagen, "Clases, colonialismo y aculturación," and *Derecho indígenas*.

17. In chapter 9 and 12, I discuss the massacre, the spirituality of the Las Abejas (The Bees), and documentaries involved in disputing revisionist histories.

18. Guha, "Dominance without Hegemony."

19. Hegel, *Phenomenology of Mind*, 240.

20. In passing, we should underscore the difference between Gloria Anzaldúa's observation in "How to Tame a Wild Tongue" (in *Borderlands*) that Chicano Spanish is a border tongue with its own rules and multiple modalities, and the skewed view of "Spanglish" as a moment in becoming fluid in English, hence monolingual or even bilingual. Needless to say, Chicano Spanish has a life not bound by the desire of recognition from linguistic purists.

Chapter 5. Beyond Representation?

This essay originally appeared as "Beyond Representation? The Impossibility of the Local (Notes on Subaltern Studies in Light of a Rebellion in Tepozatlán, Morelos)," in *The Latin American Subaltern Studies Reader*, edited by Ileana Rodríguez, 191–220. Copyright © 2001, Duke University Press. All rights reserved. Reprinted by permission of the publisher.

1. For accounts of the rebellion, the historical roots, and the new revolutionary politics of the EZLN, see, for example, Barreda et al., *Chiapas*; Le Bot, *Le rêve zapatista*; Ross, *Rebellion from the Roots*; Rojas, *Chiapas*; and Collier, *Basta!* All interviews, declarations, and communiqués by the EZLN, the Comité Clandestino Revolucionario Indigena, Comandancia General (CCRI-CG), and Subcomandante Marcos have been posted online at the official Web site of the EZLN, http://palabra.ezln.org.mx (accessed on April 20, 2008). Translations into English of EZLN documents are regularly updated

at Chiapas 95, http://www.eco.utexas.edu/faculty/Cleaver/chiapas95.html (accessed on May 5, 2008).

2. Hegel as quoted in Descombes, *Barometer of Modern Reason*, 3.

3. John Womack's *Zapata and the Mexican Revolution* is the classic, although somewhat dated, study of the life of Emiliano Zapata and Zapatismo in general.

4. See Lomnitz, "La decadencia en los tiempos de la globalización," 90–91.

5. See García Canclini et al., *De lo local a lo global*.

6. My critique of Gramsci has many affinities with David Lloyd's critique of Gramsci's view that the history of subaltern groups is episodic and fragmentary (see Lloyd, *Anomalous States*, 127 and passim).

7. Gramsci's "The Modern Prince," in his *Selections from the Prison Notebooks*, 197.

8. Gramsci's "On Education" is in ibid., 30.

9. This passage from *Gli intellettuali e l'organizzazione della cultura* is quoted in Gramsci, *Selections from the Prison Notebooks*, 326n5.

10. Ibid.

11. Bhadra, "Four Rebels of Eighteen-Fifty-Seven," 173–74.

12. Guha, "Preface," 35.

13. See "The Modern Prince" in Gramsci, *Selections from the Prison Notebooks*, 196.

14. Bhadra, "Four Rebels of Eighteen-Fifty-Seven," 175.

15. See Spivak, "Subaltern Studies."

16. Ibid., 211.

17. Chatterjee, "More on Modes of Power and the Peasantry," 375 and passim.

18. See Ranger, "Power, Religion, and Community," 221.

19. Beverley, "Writing in Reverse," 273.

20. "Founding Statement," in Rabasa, Sanjinés, and Carr, *Subaltern Studies in the Americas*, 146.

21. Rigoberta Menchú as quoted in ibid.

22. Sommer, "Resisting the Heat," 409.

23. In the conversations at "Larráinzar VI" in September 1995, the government and the EZLN finally agreed on the formats for the discussion of particular issues in specific tables. Five tables have been established and have met in San Cristóbal and San Andrés Sacamch'en de los Pobres, as the Indian people prefer to call the town officially known as Larráinzar. The five groups addressed issues pertaining to (1) community and autonomy: indigenous rights; (2) guaranties of justice for Indians; (3) participation and political representation of Indians; (4) situation, rights, and culture of indigenous women; and (5) access to communication media. For a balance of the first round of the discussions, see the communiqué by the CCRI-CG on October 19, 1995, at http://palabra.ezln.org.mx.

24. For an assessment of the government's hypocrisy and manipulation at the dialogues, see Armando Bartra, "Chiapas: El diálogo sobre el tema indígena. 'No podemos hablar con palabras blandas,'" in the special section "Del Campo," *La Jornada*, November 1, 1995. Articles in *La Jornada* were not available online until April 1996.

25. Garrido, "La resistencia," *La Jornada*, September 22, 1995.

26. Pablo González Casanovas as quoted in *La Jornada*, October 29, 1995.

27. See González Casanovas's article, "Causas de la rebelión in Chiapas," in the special section "Perfil de La Jornada," *La Jornada*, September 5, 1995.

28. See Lomnitz, *Las salidas del laberinto*, 34.

29. See Rojas, *Chiapas*, 17.

30. See Antonio García de León, *La Jornada*, September 20, 1995.

31. See José Antonio Román, "No basta cancelar el campo de golf: CUT," *La Jornada*, April 14, 1996, available online at www.jornada.unam.mx (accessed on December 9, 2009). The translation is mine.

Chapter 6. Negri by Zapata

This essay originally appeared as "Negri by Zapata: Constituent Power and the Limits of Autonomy," in *The Philosophy of Antonio Negri*, volume 1, *Resistance in Practice*, edited by Timothy Murphy and Abdul Mustapha, 163–204. Copyright © 2005, Pluto Press. All rights reserved. Reprinted by permission of the publisher.

1. For an account of the destruction of the mural and the attack of Taniperla and other autonomous *municipios*, see the monthly reports by the Centro de Derechos Humanos Fray Bartolomé de las Casas (CDHFBC), "La disputa por la legitimidad," which includes a reproduction of the mural, and "La legalidad de la injusticia," both of which are available online at http://www.frayba.org.mx/index.php. These two reports cover the events in 1997 and 1998, the years with the highest incidence of systematic violence by the army, the so-called Seguridad Pública (Public Security, a euphemism for the federal police), and Indian paramilitary groups formed by Indians associated with the Partido Revolucionario Institucional (PRI), which ruled Mexico from 1928 to 2000, when it was ousted by the former president Vicente Fox and his conservative Partido de Acción Nacional (PAN). It is important to note that the open military campaigns against autonomous *municipios* and sympathizers of the Zapatistas gave place to low-intensity warfare. Fox often spoke of Chiapas as a pacified territory, a fact that is contradicted by the weekly reports from the CDHFBC and other human rights organization as well as by the denunciation of violence in letters from autonomous municipalities. Fox's removal of the army consisted simply of relocating some of the military camps off the main roads.

2. See Bartra, *Regeneración, 1900–1918*, 533.

3. Flores Magón's anarcho-communist aphorisms on revolution as quoted in ibid., 282.

4. For the language of Convention 169 on Indigenous Peoples and Tribal Peoples (1989), see the Web site of the International Labour Organization, http://www.ilo.org. Relevant documents pertaining to human rights in Chiapas can also be found under "documents" on the Web site of the CDHFBC, http://www.frayba.org.mx/index.php.

5. All interviews, declarations, and communiqués by the EZLN, the Comité Clandestino Revolucionario Indigena, Comandancia General (CCRI-CG), and Subcomandante Marcos have been posted online at the official Web site of the EZLN, http://palabra. ezln.org.mx (accessed on December 9, 2009). Translations into English of EZLN documents are regularly updated at Chiapas 95, http://www.eco.utexas.edu/faculty/Cleaver/chiapas95.html (accessed on May 5, 2008).

6. In the conversations at "Larráinzar VI," in September 1995, the government and the EZLN finally agreed on the formats for the discussion of particular issues in specific tables. Five tables were established and met in San Cristóbal and San Andrés 'Sacamch'en de los Pobres, as the Indian people prefer to call the town officially known as Larráinzar, until the EZLN pulled out in September 1996. The five groups began to address issues pertaining to (1) community and autonomy: indigenous rights; (2) guaranties of justice for Indians; (3) participation and political representation of Indians; (4)

situation, rights, and culture of indigenous women; and (5) access to communication media. For a balance sheet of the first round of the discussions, see the September 10, 1995, communiqué by the CCRI-CG.

7. For the text of Acuerdos de San Andrés and an analysis of the different versions, see Hernández Navarro and Herrera, *Acuerdos de San Andrés*. Also see the publication *San Andrés*, by the Comisión Nacional de Intermediación (CONAI), a commission headed by former bishop of San Cristóbal de las Casas, Samuel Ruiz García.

8. The speeches of the Zapatistas given at different stops of the Zapatour and those addressing Congress have been posted on the Web site of the EZLN, http://palabra.ezln. org.mx. For English translations, see Chiapas 95, http://www.eco.utexas.edu/faculty/ Cleaver/chiapas95.html.

9. Boutmy, *Studies in Constitutional Law*, 250; quoted in Negri, *Insurgencies*, 2.

10. Negri, *Insurgencies*, 14. The passage in Italian reads: "la potenza costitutiva non si conclude mai nel potere, né la multitudine tende a divenire totalità ma ensieme de singularità, multiplicità aperta" (Negri, *Il potere constituente*, 23). I follow Boscagli's translation of *potere* as "power" and *potenza* as "strength."

11. Negri, *Insurgencies*, 10.

12. Ibid., 23.

13. Ibid., 35

14. See Taussig, *Magic of the State*.

15. Although I conceive this indigenous discourse on the West from a theoretical perspective, one should consult the work on 'Ch'ol agrarian discourses of José Alejos García, *Ch'ol/Kaxlan*. In an essay on the relationship between missionaries and Indians in the colonial period, I examine how a *tlacuilo*, an Indian painter/writer trained in the pre-Columbian tradition, invented a pictorial vocabulary in the Codex Telleriano-Remensis to represent and reflect on the colonial order (Rabasa, *Franciscans and Dominicans under the Gaze of Tlacuilo*). The Codex Telleriano-Remensis is the product of a missionary demanding an indigenous history of the power that dominated Indians; as it were, the *tlacuilo* responds to the question: "Tell me the story of how I conquered you." Thus the question occasioned a situation in which the colonial observer ends up being observed. In representing colonial rule, the *tlacuilo* managed to inscribe differences in the Christianity of the Dominican and the Franciscan orders. This classification of the two orders and other semantic spaces pertaining to the culture of conquest entails a discourse that objectifies these European realities without using or getting entangled in the represented forms of thought: that is, the *tlacuilo* sees and conceptualizes the Europeans in terms of indigenous languages and systems of representation. As such, the *tlacuilo's* history has nothing to do with an appropriation of European writing and modes of representation, which would inevitably be subject to the ambivalence of making the *proper*, but with the invention of a pictorial vocabulary to record the new realities from within indigenous systems of writing and thought. Also see Gruzinski, *Mestizo Mind*, for a reading of the translation of Ovidian motifs into an indigenous pictorial vocabulary in the murals in the church of Ixmiquilpan, Hidalgo, Mexico. I further develop these ideas in chapter 10 of this volume.

16. For a critique of the concept of autonomy as plagued with aporias and the need to think in terms of autonomization, see Hamacher, "One 2 Many Multiculturalisms."

17. For a critique of the ways in which North America—i.e., scholars located in the United States—reads Latin American cultural artifacts, most often under the seduction and distinction derived from metropolitan theory, see Neil Larsen's brilliant essays in

Larsen, *North by South*. On the construction of Latin America as an object of study in the United States, see De la Campa, *Latin Americanism*. For a critique of Occidentalism and a definition of transculturation as a mode of subverting Western hegemony, see Coronil, *Magical State*; and Mignolo, *Global Designs*.

18. Susan Buck-Morss, "Hegel and Haiti," has argued that we must trace the origin of the Hegelian dialectic of the master and the slave to articles Hegel read on the Haitian revolution. For Buck-Morss, this reading would enable us to evaluate the contributions made by the Haitian revolution to the development of European political culture and philosophy, and thereby to break from those narratives that attribute all the developments in "universal" culture to European thinkers. Her argument is interesting and to some extent convincing. Buck-Morss's denunciation of the silence the philosophers of the Enlightenment kept regarding slavery would, paradoxically, lend credence to my argument that European thought does not constitute itself in opposition to a non-European "other" but with respect to its own phantoms. This does not mean that we do not find instances in which Europeans posit non-Western "others" as inferior (colonial discourse abounds with such cases), but rather that because of their dismissal of other cultures, the not-European "other" hardly figured or mattered in the development of philosophical thought. Take as a symptom of this utter disregard for other cultures the fact that someone like Michel Foucault could write *The Order of Things* without mentioning "imperialism" once. Again, Foucault might be accused of disregarding questions pertaining to colonialism and European expansionism, but not of shaping the identity of poststructuralism in opposition to the "rest of the world" or some other construct of the like. This observation would not deny the fact that Euro-American civilizations have been extracting and appropriating knowledge from Amerindian cultures starting with Columbus's first voyage. I have argued in *Inventing America* that the new subjectivity of modernity (the split between the subject and the object commonly associated with Descartes) emerges as a result of Columbus's need to codify unknown natural and cultural phenomena that entailed an epistemological mutation that has little or nothing to do with positing the binary European civilization versus Amerindian savagery. Clearly, this is part of the story but not the fundamental aspect of the epistemological mutation. In this chapter I argue that Indian struggles for autonomy and the right to govern themselves according to their normative systems do not partake of a desire to have their life forms recognized according to European models. I also have reservations on the benefit to be derived from thinking in terms of a single universality, which now, according to Buck-Morss, would manifest how non-Europeans have participated in shaping (Western) universality. My preference is for a concept of multiple horizons of universality.

19. See note 15.

20. All Zapatista communiqués have been posted online at http://www.palabra.ezln.org.mx.

21. Negri, *Insurgencies*, 324.

22. For documents pertaining to autonomy, forms of government in Indian communities, access to media, a plan for action, and addresses by Marcos and other members (Comandantes David, Tacho, and Zebedo) of the CCRI–CG, see Hernández Navarro and Vera Herrera, *Acuerdos de San Andrés*.

23. See Hardt and Negri, *Empire*.

24. Virno and Hardt, *Radical Thought in Italy*.

25. See Bartra, *Los herederos de Zapata*.

26. I owe this observation to Javier Sanjinés.

27. Bartra, *Regeneración, 1910–1918*, 16.

28. Ibid., 488.

29. Hardt and Negri, *Empire*, 350.

30. Ibid., 47.

31. "Do You Remember Revolution?" in Virno and Hardt, *Radical Thought in Italy*, 238. The collective signing of this text lays out a theory in which the alternative to violence signifies a more advanced state rather than an instance of lacking the conditions for revolution, as would be argued from a traditional Leninist position: "Struggle and political mediation, struggle and negotiation with institutions—this perspective, in Italy as in Germany, is both possible and necessary, not because of the backwardness of the social conflict but, on the contrary, because of the extreme maturity of its content" (ibid.). In an interview with Carlos Monsiváis, Marcos has made a similar point on political mediation and struggle from the opposite end of the geopolitical spectrum, from the Selva Lacandona, a paradoxical mixture of an area quite remote from the metropolitan centers of the Italian radicals and "the extreme maturity of its content": "No se plantea un asalto al Palacio de Invierno ni el derrocamiento del poder ni el fin del tirano, sino un vuelco, no sólo de los términos político-militares de la primera declaración. . . . Queremos que esta nación asuma legalmente que nos reconoce . . . que diga: 'legalmente reconozco que estos que son diferentes tienen estos derechos y son parte mía'" [We are not planning an assault on the Winter Palace nor the overthrow of power nor the end of the tyrant, but rather a turn, not only of the politico-military terms of our first declaration. We want this nation to legally assume our recognition . . . to say: "I legally recognize that these people who are different have these rights and are part of me"] (Monsiváis, "Marcos, gran interlocutor"). Nevertheless, the question "what is to be done?" remains, even if the answer differs radically from Lenin's call for a hegemonic Communist Party. The need for the vanguard party and the call to hegemonize all sectors of society is questioned by both the Zapatistas and Negri, but one wonders if this refusal does not partake of a paradox, of an aporia, inasmuch as one could speak of both calling for a hegemony of the diverse. The concept of the multitude in Negri entails a subjectivity that would overturn hegemonic programs that sought to reduce the multitude to a concept of the people held together by an encompassing ideology: "The multitude is a multiplicity, a plane of singularities, an open set of relations, which is not homogeneous or identical with itself and bears an indistinct, inclusive relation to those outside of it. The people, in contrast, tends towards identity and homogeneity internally while posing its differences from and excluding what remains outside of it" (Hardt and Negri, *Empire*, 103). Marcos could not be clearer in his interview with Monsiváis: "Pienso que el fin de siglo y de milenio debiera reportar dentro de los movimientos progresistas o de izquierda . . . también un movimiento que plantea el fin de las luchas por la hegemonía" [I think that the end of the century and the millennium should also announce within progressive or leftist movements . . . a movement that proposes the end to all struggles for hegemony] (Monsiváis, "Marcos, gran interlocutor").

32. As of June 4, 2002, President Vicente Fox had not freed the Zapatista political prisioners, a condition by the EZLN for resuming the dialogues with the government. On May 24, 2002, Enlace Civil (at http://www.enlacecivil.org.mx) released a communiqué by "La Voz de Cerro Hueco," an association named after the penitentiary in which they were held in Chiapas, denouncing their liberation as an act of "good will" from the federal government. They insisted that they had served their sentences. They also insisted that they were unjustly imprisoned in the first place and that Indians demand-

ing their rights continue to be harassed and persecuted. They demanded the liberation of political prisioners held in penitentiaries in the states of Tabasco and Queretaro. I am unsure of when Professor Valdez Ruvalcaba was freed and what his sentence was for the subversive, if not terrorist, act (in the paranoid imagination of the state) of painting a mural with the people.

33. On the COBAS and the social centers, see Virno, "Do You Remember the Counterrevolution?" 254. Marcos speaks of the COBAS in "La historia de los espejos," June 9, 1995, available online at http://palabra.ezln.org.mx. See the discussion in chapter 3 in this collection.

34. See Avilés, "Marcos agradece." Also consult the Web site for the Associazione Ya Basta, at http://www.yabasta.it.

35. I derive this information from the description included in the back of the reproduction prepared by the CDHFBC.

36. Carson and Brooks, "Pozol y biopiratería."

37. Lacan, *Seminaire XVII*, 22.

38. Hardt and Negri, *Empire*, 360–61.

39. See Ceceña, "La resistencia como espacio."

40. Morales Padrón, *Teoria y leyes*, 434.

41. For an assessment of pre-Columbian and colonial elements in the normative systems, see Carsen, "Autonomía indígena y usos y costumbres."

42. Spivak, *Critique of Postcolonial Reason*, 1.

43. See chapter 3 in this collection for an earlier discussion of this essay by Spivak.

44. As an instance of this danger entailed in quick responses to Spivak, consider the following passage in her *Death of a Discipline*: "Where on this grid of reading literature as text and/or evidence of the permeability shall we put a graduate student's comment that the subaltern's remark is improbable, because only an academically educated person would know such a comprehensive list of African languages? The least sense of the shifting demographies of Africa would correct this" (*Death of a Discipline*, 17). Does she mean that because Africans are traveling outside their traditional spaces, they have become aware of other African languages? Would this knowledge and the possibility of its articulation be confined to those obvious manifestations of speech whose existence Spivak was not intent on denying? Or is she thinking of someone like the Nigerian doctor played by Chiwetel Ejiofor in Stephen Frears's *Dirty Pretty Things* (2003), a highly educated person but a subaltern nonetheless because of his need to drive a cab and not practice medicine in London? I would also wonder about the kind of education that is imparted in the schools Spivak runs in Manbhum, India. Is the ideal that the students will learn to dwell in two or more worlds, or that they will learn the ways of the West to overcome their subalternity? Here is how she phrases the issue: "Surely I am obliged to rewrite the aporia as a moral dilemma: How is it possible to reconcile what I touch in the field—other people—with what I teach for a living—literary criticism?" (ibid., 36). Spivak's brilliant call for a new comparative literature remains within the one-way street of translating the "other" for metropolitan readers. Her call for learning the languages of the "other" (her term—I would rather use the more neutral "not-European languages") could not be more timely, but I would push the proposal to include a reflection on the ways the "other" translates the projects and concepts "we" bring into the field.

45. Ranajit Guha's oeuvre is very broad, so I will limit myself to citing his classic study *Elementary Aspects of Peasant Insurgency*. My reading of "the subaltern can't speak" as an absurdist moment is informed by White, "Absurdist Moment in Contemporary Lit-

erary Theory." From the perspective of history as discipline, this absurd moment takes the form of the incapacity of the historian to sever her ties to the "disenchanted world" of modernity that the discipline requires: the work of the historian and of subaltern studies would be inevitably linked to the production of subaltern pasts. I insist on the creation of subaltern pasts because these pasts do not exist in an unproblematic empirical state; rather, they are the result of a particular form of thought, regardless of how much one may want to universalize disenchanted modernity as the only valid (in this case epistemologically valid) view of the world. Is the discipline of history inextricably vitiated by an epistemological elitism? Do we exercise discursive violence by the mere fact of wearing the cloak of the historian? Does this mean that we must destroy history as an institution? In this essay I am arguing for the possibility of dwelling in a plurality of worlds and that there exists a porosity between different knowledges (as in *saberes, savoirs*) that gives place to mutual critical exchanges in which neither one of these knowledges would hold an absolute epistemological privilege. Our historian of subaltern studies of India finds herself forced to generalize her own personal biography—that is, her academic elite formation (Oxford and Cambridge, and perhaps today Princeton and the rest) and her family past that would seem to lack any links (at least willingly retained or consciously assumed) to an enchanted world. It is inevitable that we reflect at this point on the parallelisms between this Indian elite and the perspective of the Criollo elite that rose to power after the independence of Latin American countries in the nineteenth century. In both cases the liberation is established in terms that privilege a particular sector: the peasantry and the working class retain their status of exploited labor, but now under the tutelage of a native elite that presumes to care for its well-being (even if under a Marxist banner) and that thus displaces and domesticates the constituent power of the multitude under a definition of the people. The most visible exponent of this tendency is in Chakrabarty, *Provincializing Europe*.

46. For a study of German colonization of Chiapas in the early twentieth century, see García, *Ch'ol/Kaxlan*. Also see Rodolfo Stavehagen's study of transformations in the law that led to the pauperization and exclusion of Indians in Latin America after the wars of independence, *Derechos indígenas*, and the essay in which he elaborates the concept of internal colonialism, "Clases, colonialismo y aculturación."

47. I discuss this in detail in chapter 3 in this book.

48. Bierhorst, *Cantares Mexicanos*, 321. In addition to Bierhorst's introduction, one should consult Serge Gruzinski's reading of the *Cantares* in his *Mestizo Mind*. In passing, I should mention Miguel León Portilla's bitter dismissal of Bierhorst's reading and translation of the *Cantares* in "¿Una nueva interpretación de los Cantares Mexicanos?" I say "bitter" because León Portilla finds his whole work undermined by Bierhorst's assertion that the names of pre-Columbian figures, such as Netzahualcoyotl, are rhetorical and stylistic forms rather than identifications of authors. León Portilla has identified fifteen poets that he feels are authentic examples of pre-Columbian expression. Bierhorst prefers to read the colonial prints rather than identify a pure tradition. The other point that León Portilla attacks is Bierhorst's thesis of the *Cantares* as ghost songs. As can be surmised from my reading of ghostly demarcation, to borrow the title of a book on Derrida, I cannot but take Bierhorst's reading and run with it. The fear expressed by missionaries such as Sahagún and Durán regarding songs in which Indians invoked their ancient leaders—read: warriors—suggests that memories of old haunted their projects; in the end we have ghosts and songs even if there is no historical basis for Bierhorst's ghost songs, as León Portilla asserts. For León Portilla's project of recuperating authen-

tic pre-Columbian expressions and the identification of poets as well as his dismissal of Bierhorst, see, for example, Léon Portilla's *Quince poetas del mundo náhuatl, Literaturas indígenas de México*, and "¿Una nueva interpretación de los Cantares Mexicanos?" (his review of Bierhorst's edition).

49. Chapter 2 in this book examines the production of the pictographic Codex Mendoza, and chapter 11 the question of collective authorship in the work of Fernando Alvarado Tezozomoc and Domingo Francisco San Antón Muñón Chimalpahin Quauhtlehuanitzin, two sixteenth- and early-seventeenth-century Nahua historians.

50. Durán, *Historia de las Indias de la Nueva España*, vol. 2: 27–28.

51. Ibid., vol. 2: 99.

52. Certeau, *Writing of History*, 2.

53. See chapter 2 for the chronicles by Carlos de Sigüenza y Góngora.

54. Communiqué of September 22, 1994, online at http://palabra.ezln.org.mx, accessed on December 9, 2009.

55. In recuperating the oral tradition of Mackandal resides the greatness of Alejo Carpentier's novel *El reino de este mundo* (Kingdom of this World). Compare the place of Mackandal in Carpentier's novelistic treatment of the Haitian revolution with the brief mention of him and the preference for the figure of Toussaint L'Overture in James, *Black Jacobins*.

56. April 10, 1994, communiqué at http://palabra.ezln.org.mx, accessed on December 9, 2009; ellipses in the original.

57. Hardt and Negri, *Labor of Dionysus*, 311.

58. Ibid., xiv, 21.

59. Negri, *Insurgencies*, 305–7; emphasis in the original.

60. Ibid., 308.

61. September 22, 1994, communiqué at http://palabra.ezln.org.mx, accessed on December 9, 2009.

62. Negri, "Specter's Smile," 15. See Derrida, *Specters of Marx*.

63. Negri, *Politics of Subversion*, 47; emphasis in the original.

64. Ibid., 175.

65. Ibid., 59–60; emphasis in the original.

66. Ibid., 70.

67. Negri, "Constituent Republic," 222.

68. Since I first wrote this essay, Subcomandante Marcos wrote "Chiapas: Treceava Estela" (Chiapas: The thirteen wake) in July 2003, an essay on the EZLN Web site consisting of five parts in which he develops the figure of the Caracol, the snail, as a new way of constructing a network of autonomous *municipios* and the creation of forms of self-government that create an alternative to Capital. The concept and the poetics of the Caracoles merit a full essay, and I must limit this note to mentioning that it materializes a political structure that furthers the process of autonomization. The formation of the Caracoles, also known as "Junta de Buen Gobierno" [councils of good government] in Zapatista-controlled territories reinforces the need to conceive autonomy as a process and not as a status that would be granted by the state. In fact, Article 39 of the Mexican Constitution already grants, in the words of Marcos, the right to govern and to govern oneself. Under the Caracoles the Zapatistas no longer expect nor demand the recognition of the government; rather, they call for all Indians to act and exercise their rights as legitimate peoples and first inhabitants. For interpretative essays on the Caracoles, see the dossier "Raices profundas de los Caracoles," in *Revista memoria* (October and

November 2003): 176–77, which includes essays by Armando Bartra, John Holloway, Guillermo Peimbert, Araceli Burguete Cal y Mayor, Hector Díaz-Polanco, Juan Carlos Martínez, Pablo González Casanova, and Alejandro Cerda García. In his article "Caracoles: El realismo mágico y los agujeros en el ozono," John Holloway compares the Caracoles to holes in capitalism. For Holloway, in fact, every instance of a "no" that negates the rule of capital and defines a new form of determining life constitutes a hole. The Zapatistas are one of the largest and most beautiful of the holes contemplated by Holloway. He has systematized his ideas on new forms of revolution in his *Change the World*.

69. Negri, *Insurgencies*, 307.

70. Kant, *Toward Perpetual Peace*, 344.

71. Ibid., 345.

72. Ibid., 347.

73. Ibid.

74. Ibid., 346. My reading of Kant tends to be reductive and fulfills the function of mapping out aporias in the project of autonomization. Kant has been read from within a Lacanian psychoanalytical tradition in ways that have complicated his concept of the ethical subject and the possibility of ethical acts. Here I limit myself to citing an assessment by Alenka Zupančič: "As Kant knew very well, we are all pathological subjects, and this is what eventually led him to the conclusion that no ethical act is really possible in the world" (Zupančič, "Subject of the Law," 52). Even if Kant arrived at the conclusion that there are only pathological subjects and by association states (a Christian, indeed Lutheran, position), his practical philosophy constitutes an effort to ground morals and politics on formal principles.

I am interested in outlining the aporias inherent to the project of autonomy rather than establishing Kant's conclusion as to the impossibility of ethical acts; that is, I am assuming that the belief in its possibility is earnest and fundamental to Kant's project. Slavoj Žižek has reminded us that according to Kant we could very well "follow the law on account of a pathological reason (fear of punishment, narcissistic satisfaction, admiration of peers), while the same act can be a proper moral act if only I perform it out of the pure respect for duty, that is, duty is the sole motive for accomplishing it" (Žižek "Melancholy and the Act," 672). Žižek goes on to present the case of an ethical act that transgresses the law, "a transgression that, in contrast to a simple criminal violation, does not simply violate the legal norm, but redefines what is a legal norm. The moral law does not follow the good—it generates a new shape of what counts as good" (ibid.). Thereby, one can argue with Kant that if revolutionary acts fall outside the law, their motives and the resulting redefinition of the good could be pure ethical acts. Kant, of course, would add that if one is apprehended in the process of carrying out revolutionary illegal acts, one deserves the corresponding punishment for breaking the law. Žižek's example can be thought in terms of the relation between constituent power and constitutional institutionalization. Kant will always adopt a position in which the constituent power of the multitude must in the last instance be subordinated to a constituted power, to a constitutional republicanism.

75. Kant, *Toward Perpetual Peace*, 324.

76. Ibid., 326.

77. For a critique of Kant's racism and imperialism, see Spivak's reading of Kant in "Philosophy" in Spivak, *Critique of Postcolonial Reason*, 1–37.

78. Kant, *Toward Perpetual Peace*, 329–30; emphasis in the original.

79. Ibid., 328; emphasis in the original.

80. Ibid., 322.

81. The current (January 4, 2004) war against Iraq by the United States–led alliance would seemingly contradict the peaceful vocation of empire, but the rationale for a pre-emptive strike as it was articulated by the Bush administration defined the need for war in terms of preserving "universal peace," to borrow this sixteenth-century Spanish legalistic term. The face of the United States today is that of a benevolent empire. Its disregard for the United Nations in going to war without its support and validation would seem to indicate that the United States has been practicing nineteenth- and early-twentieth-century forms of imperialism, but the opposition of major players (France and Germany, in the main) does not seemingly alter the fact that the United States has seen itself—has sought to establish itself—as the military, if not the economic and political, leader of the empire. One could even argue that "empire" is a historical invention of the United States. Unfortunately, these policies do not seem to have changed much under President Barack Obama's administration. The language of "just war" continues to justify the wars in Iraq and Afghanistan as manifest in Obama's acceptance speech of the 2009 Nobel Peace Prize.

82. For arguments on multiculturalism that deploy an ecological perspective on the survival of indigenous cultures, see the essays collected in Taylor, *Multiculturalism*. For a critique of the concept of multiculturalism in these essays, see Hamacher, "One 2 Many Multiculturalisms."

83. Derrida, *Politics of Friendship*, 105; emphasis in the original.

84. Marcos has made this point in a 2001 interview with Carlos Monsiváis: "No es lo mismo que llegue alguien y que diga: 'Vengo a liberarlas a ustedes mujeres oprimidas' a que el propio movimiento que se genera provoque esto en las mujeres indígenas. No es lo mismo que una femenista de ciudad diga: 'las mujeres indígenas tienen derechos' a que las mujeres indígenas digan, como lo acaban de hacer las de Xi' Nich y Las Abejas, en el monumento de Independencia: 'Ademas, tenemos nuestras demandas como género. Nosotras queremos una paz con justicia y dignidad. No queremos la paz del pasado.' Esto ya está ocurriendo y los resultados son irregulares pero creéme las soluciones no vendrán de fuera" [It is not the same that someone arrives and says, "I come to liberate you oppressed women" than that the movement that emerges brings this out among the women. It is not the same that the feminist from the city says, "Indigenous women have rights," than that indigenous women do it as was recently done by the Xi' Nich and Las Abejas at the Independence monument: "In addition, we have our own gender demands. We want a peace with justice and dignity. We do not want the peace of the past." This is already occurring and the results are irregular, but trust me, the solutions don't come from outside] (Monsiváis, "Marcos, gran interlocutor"). In passing, I would like to mention the 2000 film by the Tunisian filmmaker Moufida Tlatli, *La Saison des hommes*, where we find an insightful tension between the Tunisian law of 1956—which liberated Tunisian women to an extent beyond the most advanced Western democracies—and the law of tradition, which continues to bind women in their everyday interactions. The possibility of freedom resides within the community of women; an autistic child who learns to weave symbolizes hope for men. The men, who visit the women on the island once a year, for which event the women diligently prepare, lack any influence and perhaps do not even exert any significant power over their lives.

85. Hernández Navarro and Vera Herrea, *Acuerdos de San Andrés*, 66.

86. The communiqué is cited in ibid., 185.

87. See Chakrabarty, "Time of History."

88. Hegel, *Phenomenology of Mind*, 445; emphasis in the original.

89. Hegel's critique of Kantian formalism is taken as a point of departure in debates over the particularity of new social movements and their aim to transform the nature of universality and hence to redefine hegemony. In such a struggle for hegemony, there is the risk that accomplished transformations of the universal will consolidate a constituted power that undermines the constitutive strength of the multitude that aspires not to hegemony and the stasis achieved by the inclusion of diversity in new definitions of the universal, but to constitutional transformations that enable constituent power and further the materialization of autonomous self-governments. But then again we may understand *stásis* as internal struggle relative to *polémos* as war (see Derrida, *Politics of Friendship*, 90–93 and passim), a distinction that would amount to putting the emphasis not on instituting diversity (in subsuming constituent power in the real, as Hegel would put it) but in opening spaces for the revolutionary potential of the *many* that comprises the multitude. I am thinking here of the essays by Judith Butler, Ernesto Laclau, and Slavoj Žižek in their *Contingency, Hegemony, Universality*. As I have pointed out in this essay, the demand for recognition of indigenous rights does not mean a recognition of the rights themselves as compatible with or as requiring a new definition of universality, but the recognition of the right to self-determination according to their normative systems. This demand does not aim at transforming the universal as defined in contemporary political discourses in the West, which inevitably partakes of a will to hegemonize; rather, it aims at the right to multiple conceptions of universality. The point is not that all norms are equally valid (a flaccid relativism), but rather to propose a conception of normative systems in terms of their own horizons of universality and their own mechanisms for modifying them (a radical relativism).

90. See Kant, "Answer to the Question."

91. Derrida, *Politics of Friendship*, 106.

92. For a development on the traffic of ideologies between Flores Magón and Zapata, see Bartra's introduction in his *Regeneración, 1900–1918*.

93. This horizon of plural-world-dwelling would not involve a privileging of Western discourses but a questioning of the pretense that all modern discourse must originate outside of and impinge upon the discourse of Indian peoples. And let us trivialize the shift I am proposing here by insisting that the anomaly, the radical gesture would consist in imagining Derrida and others reading and discoursing on Indian discourses: The history of Western expansionism abounds with examples of "Derridas" intervening in and speaking for native forms of life.

Chapter 7. The Comparative Frame in Subaltern Studies

This essay originally appeared as "The Comparative Frame in Subaltern Studies," *Postcolonial Studies* 8, no. 4 (2005): 365–80. Copyright © 2005, José Rabasa. All rights reserved. Reprinted by permission of the author.

1. See Guha, "On Some Aspects of the Historiography of Colonial India."

2. For debates on "the multitude" and "the people," see Virno, *Grammar of the Multitude*; and Hardt and Negri, *Labor of Dionysus, Empire*, and *Multitude*. John Beverley has sustained a critique of the concept of the multitude in his *Subalternity and Representation* and *Testimonio*. For the extensive critical literature on Hardt and Negri's *Empire*, see Balakrishnan, *Debating Empire*. As for Antonio Negri's work on the multitude, see his *Insurgencies* and *Savage Anomaly*. Also of interest are the essays in Virno and Hardt, *Radical Thought in Italy*. Inasmuch as the concept of the multitude is linked

to a post-Fordist historical configuration, its applicability outside metropolitan centers would seem to be limited in that it would presume a single history. Having said this, we may also want to consider to what extent post-Fordism in developed countries might not have parallel manifestation in developing countries in which the consumerist and leveling promises of unions and land reform have been undermined by neoliberal policies. Thus, in the context of Mexico and the Zapatistas, the dismantling of communal and *ejido* lands would entail a post-1917 constitution. For a systematic critique of post-Fordism as a universal temporality, see chapter 8 in this book.

3. Marx, "Civil War in France." Lenin, *What Is to Be Done?*. The April Theses is the name given to Lenin's, "Task of the Proletariat in the Present Revolution."

4. Marx, "Civil War in France," 249; emphasis in the original. For the concept of the "withering away" of the state, see Lenin, *State and Revolution*.

5. Marx, "Civil War in France," 206.

6. If I have chosen to concentrate on the work of Ranajit Guha and the South Asian Subaltern Studies Collective, it is because, to my mind, they provide a most productive recent reading of Gramsci. Gramsci was read in Latin America throughout the 1950s, 1960s, and 1970s, mainly to reflect on the place of the intellectual in proletarian struggles. For a most clear reflection on what it meant to be a Gramscian intellectual during those years in Latin America, see Aricó, *La cola del diablo*. As a consequence of the loss of the election of the Sandinistas in Nicaragua and the destruction of the Berlin Wall, several Latinamericanists, including myself, formed the Latin American Subaltern Studies Group with the intent of addressing the issues of what at that time felt like a complete debacle of the left in Nicaragua and elsewhere in Latin America. We were inspired by the work of the South Asian Subaltern Studies Group. For debates within the Latin American Subaltern Studies Group, see Rabasa, Sanjinés, and Carr, *Subaltern Studies in the Americas*; and Rodríguez, *Latin American Subaltern Studies Reader* and *Convergencia de tiempos*. For conversations between Latin American scholars and South Asian counterparts outside the intellectual circuits of the U.S. academy, see Rivera Cusicanqui and Barragán, *Debates postcoloniales*.

7. By this I do not want to suggest that subalterns (or, for that matter, the multitude) are inherently good because of their resilience to be subjected to a political order. Whether conceived as the "subaltern," the "people," or the "multitude," there is nothing inherent to mass movements that would live up to utopian ideals. Paramilitaries terrorizing the countryside, gangsters killing each other, fascist workers subscribing to racist ideologies, fanatics committing massacres and whatnot that could be conceived as "bad" subjects—that is, not of our liking—would seemingly require that we conceive them from within a political telos in which they would realize their folly. Having said this, we should note that there is nothing inherent to these social formations that can be attributed to not-modern forms of life. In fact, paramilitaries, gangs, fascist workers, and fanatics are imbedded in modern social processes. Moreover, the overcoming of "bad" subjects can only be carried out from within and in the idioms of the communities plaguing them. No discourse and campaigns from elite centers against superstition and fanaticism (along with magic and folklore) can avoid the epistemic violence that constitutes them as not modern.

8. Gramsci, *Prison Notebooks*, vol. 2: 49. The Italian passages correspond to Gramsci, *Quaderni del carcere*, vol. 3: 328.

9. Marx, "Civil War in France," 254.

10. Viezzer, *"Si me permiten hablar,"* 184. English translations are mine; however, I have consulted and benefited from Victoria Ortiz's translation of Viezzer's work, *Let Me Speak!*

11. Ibid., 7

12. Ibid., 41. We must add to Domitila's *testimonio*, Jorge Sanjinés's film *El coraje del pueblo* (1971), which documents many of the same events that Barrios de Chúngara mentions in *"Si me permiten hablar."* Sanjinés's film exemplifies a practice in so-called third cinema in which films are produced with the people, in which the people themselves are the actors and the final arbiters of the final cut. Sanjinés has written a theoretical tract with the Grupo Ukamau on what it means to make revolutionary cinema (see Sanjinés, *Teoría y práctica de un cine junto al pueblo*; selections have been translated and published as *Theory and Practice of a Cinema with the People*). This project is clearly defined in terms of Gramsci's call for the creation of a national-popular culture. Today, his proposal might have lost credibility in the aftermath of the destruction of the Soviet Union. Nonetheless, it remains exemplary of cinematic work that attempts to avoid vertical impositions in national liberation struggles.

13. Lenin, *What Is to Be Done?* 74

14. Ibid., 82; emphasis in the original.

15. Gramsci, *Selections from Cultural Writings*, 191; the Italian is from Gramsci, *Quaderni del carcere*, vol. 3: 2,314.

16. Gramsci's vanguardism has been the subject of critique for some time now. See, for instance, Lloyd, *Anomalous States*; and Beverley, *Subalternity and Representation*. Also see my critique in chapter 3 of this book. My point is to draw attention to the comparative frame that informs subaltern studies, rather than to limit my observations to a "flawed" and "dated" Gramsci.

17. Chatterjee, *Politics of the Governed*, 7.

18. Gramsci, *Prison Notebooks*, vol. 2: 51, with the Italian from Gramsci, *Quaderni del carcere*, vol. 1: 331.

19. Gramsci, *Selections from the Prison Notebooks*, 202.

20. Bhadra. "Four Rebels of Eighteen-Fifty-Seven," 173–74.

21. Guha, *Elementary Forms of Peasant Insurgency*, 9–10.

22. Ibid., 10–11.

23. Spivak, "Can the Subaltern Speak?" 280–81. In the section dedicated to Kant under the chapter "Philosophy" in Spivak's *Critique of Postcolonial Reason*, Spivak uses the term "epistemic violation"—that is, "the 'scientific' fabrication of new representations of self and world that would provide alibis for the domination, exploitation, and epistemic violation entailed by the establishment of colony and empire" (ibid., 7). At the conference at the University of California–Santa Barbara on the "Subaltern and the Popular," held on March 8–9, 2004, when this chapter was first presented, Spivak spoke of violation as rape, as "fucking with one's mind."

24. Spivak, *Critique of Postcolonial Reason*, 308.

25. Ibid., 310.

26. I am here working on statements to this fact that she has given at the gathering in Santa Barbara and other conferences. See note 23, earlier.

27. Spivak, *Death of a Discipline*, 39.

28. Gramsci, *Southern Question*, 43, with the Italian from Gramsci, *Alcuni temi della quistioni meridionale*, 739.

29. Gramsci, *Southern Question*, 43, with the Italian from Gramsci, *Alcuni temi della quistioni meridionale*, 740.

30. Gramsci, *Selections from the Prison Notebooks*, 168; with the Italian from Gramsci, *Quaderni del carcere*, vol. 3: 1,612.

31. The Juntas de Buen Gobierno were first instituted in the summer of 2003. For an assessment of their first year, Subcomandante Marcos wrote a series of communiqués titled "Para leer un video" [To read a video]. The term *caracol*, literally "snail," refers to the symbolic political, cognitive, spiritual, and epistemological meanings the structure of sea snails has had in Mesoamerica since precolonial times. All interviews, declarations, and communiqués by the EZLN, the Comité Clandestino Revolucionario Indigena, Comandancia General (CCRI-CG), and Subcomandante Marcos have been posted online at the official Web site of the EZLN, http://palabra.ezln.org.mx (accessed on April 20, 2008). Translations into English of EZLN documents are regularly updated at Chiapas 95, http://www.eco.utexas.edu/faculty/Cleaver/chiapas95.html (accessed on May 5, 2008).

32. Chakrabarty, *Provincializing Europe*, 250–51; emphasis in the original.

33. Ibid., 254–55.

34. Chakrabarty, *Habitations of Modernity*, 34.

35. Ibid., 36.

36. Ibid., 37.

37. See chapter 9 in this collection for elaborated readings of revolutionary spiritualities in Chiapas.

38. The Mexican army destroyed the mural in 1998 in an attempt to stop the formation of the autonomous municipality of Flores Magón. The army to this day occupies the town of Taniperla; however, the autonomous municipal government relocated to La Culebra. I want to thank the authorities of the Junta de Buen Gobierno "Hacia un Nuevo Amanecer" [Towards a New Dawn], the *caracol* to which La Culebra belongs, for granting me permission to use the image of the mural. For a reading of this mural, see chapter 6 in this book.

39. I am here following Jan de Vos, *Una tierra para sembrar sueños*, 381–83. Also see Marcos's communiqué of December 13, 1994, at http://palabra.ezln.org.mx (accessed on December 9, 2009).

Chapter 8. On the History of the History of Peoples *Without* History

This essay originally appeared as "On the History of the History of the Peoples *without* History," *Humboldt Journal of Social Relations* 29, no. 1 (2005): 204–22. Copyright © 2005, José Rabasa. All rights reserved. Reprinted by permission of the author. *Epigraph*: Wolfe, *Europe and the People without History*, 23.

1. See Ankersmith, *History and Tropology*.

2. Hardt and Negri, *Multitude*, 124; emphasis in the original.

3. Gramsci, *Selections from Cultural Writings*, 191, with the Italian from Gramsci, *Quaderni del carcere*, vol. 3: 2,314.

4. Hardt and Negri cite Marx's letter of March 8, 1881, to Vera Zasulich (Hardt and Negri, *Multitude*, 379–80). Also consider Lenin's view of the communes as a model for the Soviets in the April Theses (in "Task of the Proletariat in the Present Revolution") and *State and the Revolution*.

5. Hardt and Negri, *Multitude*, 90.

6. Dabashi, "No soy un subalternista," 50.

7. As Derrida puts it: "*Globalatinization* (essentially Christian, to be sure), this word names a unique event to which a meta-language seems incapable of acceding, although such a language remains, all the same, of the greatest necessity here. For at the same time that we no longer perceive its limits, we know that such a globalization is finite and only projected. What is involved here is a Latinization and rather than globality, a globalization that is running out of breath [*essouffée*], however irresistible and imperial it may be" (Derrida, "Faith and Knowledge," 67). The undoing of the universal naming and categorization—hence erasure of indigenous concepts, of the world with a Latin-derived conceptual framework (note that "globalatinization" absorbs Greco-Abrahamic cultures)—could not merely consist of extending the concepts of history, modernity, and so forth to societies and cultures to which these life forms have been denied. I cannot go into any detail here, but a similar erasure of categories to Dabashi's occurs when scholars insist on proving that Mesoamerican pictorial codices are histories. For instance, Elizabeth Boone, in *Stories in Red and Black*, has classified the main genre of historical pictographic writing as annals, res gestae, and cartographic histories. Boone cites several entries from Alonso de Molina's 1571 *Vocabulario en lengua castellana y mexicana y mexicana y castellana*, where the Franciscan friar translates Nahuatl terms such as *veuetlatolli* as "'historia antigua' [old history], o dichos de viejos [sayings of elders]." In the section from Spanish to Nahuatl, Molina provides several entries for "historia," "historia de lo presente," "historia de dia en dia," "historia de los tiempos antiguos," but also "historiador" and "historial cosa," which suggests that for at least this missionary the denial of history was not really an issue. On the contrary, the reduction of all pictographic writing in the colonial period to "history" suggests the neutralization of forms of knowledge that would have threatened the imposition of Christianity as the sole version of the sacred. *Mere* history would be first invented and then expropriated for the administration of the colonial state. This does not mean that the enterprise was successful, but rather that we should develop strategies of reading that avoid the reduction of pictographic texts to just history and go beyond merely recognizing mythic components. Boone also mentions that for Miguel León Portilla the Nahuatl word for history is *ihtloca*, which Boone translates as "what is said about something or someone" (Boone, *Stories in Red and Black*, 76). No wonder Guha, in *History at the Limit of World-History*, warns us about the poverty of historiography.

8. See Chakrabarty, *Provincializing Europe*, 11–15, 101–6, and passim.

9. Clastres's usage of the terms "Savages" and "Primitives" might strike the reader as dated categories of a former anthropology that defined itself as the study of primitive forms of life, but his work seeks to debunk the prejudices and stereotypes. The primitive as "societies against the state"—to paraphrase the title of his best known book, *La société contre l'état*—has many lessons to teach those of us who are in this book reflecting on political action that no longer aspires to take over the state. Observe that if Hardt and Negri call our attention to this possibility, they do not develop it beyond this statement: "We need to grasp the kind of struggles that Clastres sees and recognize the adequate form in our present age" (Hardt and Negri, *Multitude*, 90). For a most lucid assessment of the new struggles that do not aspire to take over the state, see Halloway, *Change the World without Taking Power*.

10. Among the Spanish chroniclers of the sixteenth century, the clearest exposition of Amerindian societies with different degrees of social evolution is José de Acosta's classification in terms of "savages" (those who wander through the forest with no pattern of

settlement), *behetrías* (small chiefdoms), and "empires" (as in the case of the Mexica and the Inca). For a critique of the long history of the policies and hierarchies that have undermined "savage" peoples in the Americas, see Verdesio, "Forgotten Territorialities."

11. In August 20–28, 2004, Subcomandante Marcos wrote an eight-part communiqué titled "Para leer un video" [To read a video] in which he assessed the accomplishments and the shortcomings of the first year since the implementation of the autonomist Juntas de Buen Gobierno, also known as Caracoles. All interviews, declarations, and communiqués by the EZLN, the Comité Clandestino Revolucionario Indígena, Comandancia General (CCRI-CG), and Subcomandante Marcos have been posted online at the official Web site of the EZLN, http://palabra.ezln.org.mx (accessed on December 9, 2009). Translations into English of EZLN documents are regularly updated at Chiapas 95, http://www.eco.utexas.edu/faculty/Cleaver/chiapas95.html (accessed on May 5, 2008). Also on that Web site are the communiqués that first instituted the Caracoles in August 2003. The term *caracol* (literally, snail) refers to the symbolic political, cognitive, spiritual, and epistemological meanings the structure of sea snails has had in Mesoamerica since precolonial times. Let us note, however, that Marcos reiterates commonplaces that convey the effects of an internalization of denial of history and the attribution of backwardness when he assesses the accomplishments and shortcomings of the first year of the Juntas de Buen Gobierno.

In speaking of the schools in the Caracoles, Marcos tells us that "'Mariya' ya sabe escribir su nombre y te puede contar que los antiguos mexicanos tenían una cultura muy avanzada" ["Mariya" already knows how to write her name and she can tell that the ancient Mexicans had a very advanced culture] (Subcomandante Marcos, "Leer un video: Sexta parte," August 25, 2004). The language of progress, of "advanced culture," can actually backfire in two ways: (1) it could lead to differentiating one's ancestors as advanced with respect to "primitive" contemporary peoples; and (2) it could reintroduce the commonplace that today's Indians are shadows of the great civilization of yesterday whose knowledge was much like that of modern science and thereby invalidating indigenous knowledge today. Marcos furthers this commonplace when he praises those who "levantan escuelas y conocimientos donde antes sólo había ignorancia" [build schools and knowledge where there was only ignorance before] (ibid.). These inconsistencies in Marcos's generally generous evaluation of indigenous cultures *today* repeat the *indigenista* policies that the Mexican state implemented after the Mexican Revolution to integrate the pre-Columbian past as an integral component of the nation's identity and to conduct literacy campaigns that would bring knowledge to ignorant Indians. Minimally, these statements contradict Marcos's insistence of the right Indians have to exist as Indians. These are comments made in passing, perhaps unimportant but perhaps also indicative of a developmentalist mentality that undermines indigenous knowledges.

12. Whereas representative democracies build their authority on a concept of the people that subordinates differences to unity, the Zapatista maxim of "mandar obedeciendo" calls forth the direct participation of all the members of a given community and thereby affirms the diversity of the multitude. If the first privileges constituted power, the latter ensures the prevalence of constituent power (see chapter 6 in this book; and Negri, *Insurgencies*).

13. Marcos communiqué from October 29, 2008, at http://palabra.ezln.org.mx.

14. See the issue, edited by Manuel Callaghan, dedicated to Zapatista discourses and practices in the *Humboldt Journal of Social Relations* 29, no. 1 (2005).

15. Hardt and Negri, *Multitude*, 125–26.

16. Ibid., 126. This effort to define the "challenge for this conception of African modernity" risks reproducing the elements characteristic of the persecutory society that, according to Robert I. Moore, emerged in Europe in the eleventh century and has been a continuous characteristic of European society (and others where it extended its colonial power) ever since. Moore has argued that if there have been societies that persecute all over the world and history, Europe alone developed a persecutory society. He extends his argument to the differentiation between societies with slaves and (European) slave societies, societies with writing and (European) writing societies (Moore, *Formation of a Persecuting Society*).

17. See Bonfil Batalla, *México profundo: Una civilización negada*; also see the English version, Bonfil Batalla, *México Profundo: Reclaiming a Civilization*.

18. See chapters 3 and 6 in this book.

19. Hardt and Negri, *Multitude*, 142.

20. Ibid., 102.

21. Communiqué from October 29, 2008, at http://palabra.ezln.org.mx.

22. Virno, *Grammar of the Multitude*, 99.

23. Ibid., 42.

24. Ibid., 41.

25. See chapter 3 in this book for a discussion of the possibility that indigenous communities participate in post-Fordist social and economic formations as well as in liberatory practices that have emerged; however, the argument here is that the periodization that absolutizes the "new" moment should not necessarily erase indigenous temporalities that were systematically excluded by Fordism.

26. Communiqué from September 15, 1994, at http://palabra.ezln.org.mx.

27. Communiqué from October 2, 2004, at http://palabra.ezln.org.mx. Translated by irlandesa. For many years all the EZLN documents were translated by irlandesa and could be accessed at the official Web site of the EZLN, but they stopped including translation sometime around 2006. See irlandesa's Web site http://zaptranslations.blogspot .com.

Chapter 9. Revolutionary Spiritualities in Chiapas Today

This chapter originally appeared as "Revolutionary Spiritualities in Chiapas Today: Immanent History and the Comparative Frame in Subaltern Studies," in *Race, Colonialism, and Social Transformation in Latin America and the Caribbean*, edited by Jerome Branche, 160–203. Copyright © 2008, University of Florida Press. All rights reserved. Reprinted by permission of the publisher.

1. In chapter 6 in this book, I provide a detailed reading of the mural at Taniperla. See chapter 12 for a discussion of documentaries that seek to curtail revisionist histories of the massacre of Acteal, during which forty-five members of the organization were murdered by paramilitaries trained by the army and police.

2. There is a large literature on the Relaciones Geográficas, but to my mind, Barbara Mundy's *Mapping of New Spain* provides the most exhaustive and detailed study of the maps. Serge Gruzinski has provided a most interesting reading of the map of Cholula in his *Mestizo Mind*. I have benefited greatly from both Mundy and Gruzinski. In the appropriate places I have indicated my differences with their readings.

3. It is worthwhile reminding readers of the demographic collapse in central Mexico during the sixteenth century. As Mundy has pointed out, "At the time of the conquest, Cholula held one of the larger populations outside the Valley of Mexico, holding about

a hundred thousand inhabitants within about eleven or twelve square kilometers; at the time the Relación Geográfica was made, Cholula had perhaps nine thousand people" (Mundy, *Mapping of New Spain*, 127). Mundy bases her numbers on Cortés's description of the Cholula in the Second Letter as well as the estimates of twentieth-century geographers and demographers (Gerhard, *Geografía histórica de la Nueva España*, 117; and Peterson, "Real Cholula," 71).

4. *Relación de Cholula* in Acuña, *Relaciones Geográficas*, vol. 2: 143. In his introduction to the *Relación de Cholula*, Acuña identifies Gabriel de Rojas as an *erasmista* that manifested a highly critical consciousness when he undermines the missionaries' speculation on the mysteries behind the lightnings that destroyed the crosses: "Y, quien considera bien la naturaleza de los rayos, y que en esta ciudad y comarca de ordinario caen muchos, no tendrá a milagro (como algunos historiadores quieren) el haber derribado dos veces aquella cruz, por estar, como está dicho, mas alta que los altos edificios de la ciudad [en] cuarenta varas" [And whoever considers well the nature of lightnings, and that in this city and region there are ordinarily many, will not have for a miracle (as some historians want) that the said cross was destroyed twice, because it stands forty *varas* above the tallest buildings of the city] (ibid., 143). One vara equals 0.83 meters. As Acuña has pointed out in a footnote, the reference was most like to Motolinía's manipulation of the Indians: "Confundiamos a los indios, diciéndoles que por aquellas idolatrías enviaba dios sus rayos" [We confounded the Indians, telling them that God sent the lightning because of their idolatries] (ibid., 143). Whether it is in response to a pious association of the lightning strikes with God's wrath or an equally Erasmian-like rational manipulation of fear, Rojas could have also reflected the Indians' incredulity for such an explanation. After all, Indians had observed the phenomena of lightning for millennia, and given their construction of large temples, they could have very well experienced the connection between height and lightning.

5. Gruzinski, *Mestizo Mind*, 139.

6. *Relación de Cholula* in Acuña, *Relaciones Geográficas*, vol. 2: 132.

7. Ibid., 144–45.

8. Gruzinski, *Mestizo Mind*, 140–41.

9. Mundy, *Mapping of New Spain*, 215–16.

10. I am here borrowing F. R. Ankersmit's definition of background in *History and Tropology*. I have also benefited from John Searle's discussion of "background abilities" in *The Social Construction of Social Reality*. As Searle has pointed out, "background abilities" imply knowledge of basic rules but not that one's actions can be explained as following rules consciously. He provides the example of the baseball player who follows the rules she learned early in her life in the choices she makes but does not actively bring to consciousness. We may extend Searle's point and say that one is never fully conscious of the absolute presuppositions *from which* and *against which* we make sense of the world.

11. Derrida and Stiegler, *Echographies of Television*, 37.

12. I have examined these questions in detailed readings of a page from the Codex Telleriano-Remensis (see Rabasa, *Franciscans and Dominicans under the Gaze of Tlacuilo*, and "Elsewheres").

13. Kirchhoff, Odema Güemes, and Reyes, *Historia Tolteca-Chichimeca*, 181

14. Acuña, *Relaciones Geográficas*, 143.

15. Kirchhoff, Odema Güemes, and Reyes, *Historia Totleca-Chichimeca*, 131.

16. See Swanton, "El texto popoloca de la *Historia Totleca-Chichimeca*."

17. In chapter 7 in this volume, I further elaborate the terms of this critique of the comparative frame in subaltern studies.

18. Gramsci, *Selections from the Prison Notebooks*, 197; and Gramsci, "Alcuni temi della quistioni meridionale," in *Scritti politici*, 810.

19. Ibid.

20. Gramsci, *Selections from the Prison Notebooks*, 199; "Alcuni temi della quistioni meridionale," 811.

21. Gramsci, *Selections from the Prison Notebooks*, 198; "Alcuni temi della quistioni meridionale."

22. Gramsci, *Selections from the Prison Notebooks*, 202; "Alcuni temi della quistioni meridionale," 829.

23. Gramsci, *Selections from the Prison Notebooks*, 168; "Alcuni temi della quistioni meridionale," 767.

24. Note the language of the following passages on folklore and teaching in which Gramsci subjects historical immanence to a transcendental source of meaning: "Folklore should instead be studied as a 'conception of the world and life' implicit to a large extent in determinate (in time and space) strata of society and in opposition (also for the most part implicit, mechanical and objective) to 'official' conceptions of the world (or in a broader sense, the conceptions of the cultural parts of historically determinate societies) that have succeeded one another in historical process. This conception of the world is not elaborated and systematic because, by definition the people (the sum total of the instrumental and subaltern classes of every form of society that has so far existed) cannot possess conceptions which are elaborated, systematic and politically organized and centralized in their albeit contradictory development." He continues: "For the teacher, then, to know 'folklore' means to know what other conceptions of the world and of life are actually active in the intellectual and moral formation of young people, in order to uproot them and replace them with conceptions which are deemed to be superior" (Gramsci, *Selections from Cultural Writings*, 189, 191).

25. See the detailed reading of the mural in chapter 6 in this volume.

26. All interviews, declarations, and communiqués by the EZLN, the Comité Clandestino Revolucionario Indigena, Comandancia General (CCRI-CG), and Subcomandante Marcos have been posted online at the official Web site of the EZLN, http://palabra.ezln.org.mx (accessed on April 20, 2008). Translations into English of EZLN documents are regularly updated at Chiapas 95, http://www.eco.utexas.edu/faculty/Cleaver/chiapas95.html (accessed on May 5, 2008). This communiqué from Marcos is from December 13, 1994.

27. See plates 75 and 76 of the Codex Vaticanus B and plates 56 and 73 of the Codex Borgia.

28. The literature on the role of women in the Zapatista insurrection is enormous. I have found useful Carlsen, "Las mujeres indígenas"; Eber and Kovic, *Women in Chiapas*; Millán, "Chiapas y sus mujeres indígenas" and "Las zapatistas del fin del milenio"; Ortiz, *Never Again a World without Us*; M. Rabasa, "New Social Movements"; Rovira, *Mujeres de maíz*; and Vrijea, "Las mujeres indígenas como sujetos políticos."

29. This communiqué from Marcos is from July 2003, at http://palabra.ezln.org.mx.

30. The struggles of the indigenous in Chiapas have less to do with seeking the recognition of their rights by the state than with the recognition of their right to autonomous regions in which they will conduct their affairs according to their normative systems, the *usos y costumbres* in governmental documents. It is not the recognition of the ratio-

nality of their normative systems but of the right to determine their legality and justice internally. For a discussion of the processes of autonomization in Chiapas, see chapter 6 in this volume.

31. To my knowledge, the most thorough study of Las Abejas is Marco Tavanti, *Las Abejas*. Las Abejas practice a forms of Christianity known as *teología india* (Indian theology), an inter-American movement that seeks to recognize the spirituality of millenarian indigenous religious practices as compatible with Christianity. Its leadership includes Samuel Ruiz, the former bishop of San Cristóbal de las Casas. Whereas liberation theology promoted a form of Christianity that emphasized the commitment of the Catholic Church to social causes of the poor, *teología india* insists on the need to consider ethnicity and language. There are several publications of conference proceedings under the titles of *Teología India* and *Teología India Mayense*. In chapter 12 in this volume I discuss a series of videos that have been produced to counter revisionist histories of the massacre.

32. Chimalpahin Quauhtlehuanitzin, *Codex Chimalpahin*, vol. 2: 172–73.

33. Meier-Weidenbach, personal communication with the author, 1998.

34. These accounts are both in *Esta es nuestra palabra*, 58 and 73.

35. This passage from the Historia de Tlatelolco is in Lockhart, *We People Here*, 313.

36. J. Rodríguez, *Lok'tavanej*, 65.

37. For a discussion of the notion of "without history," see chapters 1, 8, and 10 in this volume.

Chapter 10. *Without* History?

This essay, "*Without* History? Apostasy as a Historical Category," was first presented at the colloquium on "Examining Heretical Thought," held February 7–11, 2006, at the University of California at Berkeley. Copyright © 2006, José Rabasa. All rights reserved. Reprinted by permission of the author.

1. For a facsimile edition and detailed study of Codex Telleriano-Remensis, see Keber, *Codex Telleriano-Remensis*. We ignore the identity of the native painter/scribe. Codex Telleriano-Remensis is a colonial manuscript that consists of four parts: (1) the ceremonies and deities associated with an annual ritual calendar known as the *veintena*; (2) the *Tonalamatl* or divinatory calendar know as the *trecena*; (3) an account of the origins and rise of Mexico-Tenochtitlan; and (4) an account of the colonial order up to 1562.

2. See chapter 1 in this volume for a sustained discussion of "the without" in the context of Nancy's *The Creation of the World*.

3. Tello, *Fragmentos de una historia de la Nueva Galicia*, 389.

4. The most ambitious and thorough study of Mesoamerican historiographical traditions is in Boone, *Stories in Red and Black*. For a critique of Boone's terms, see Navarrete, "Path from Aztlan to Mexico."

5. The literature on Lacan is too wide to even begin citing here. I teach a class on the "colonization of the imaginary" in which we take the title of a book by Serge Gruzinki, *La colonization de l'imaginaire* and pair it with selections from *The Seminar of Jacques Lacan*, in particular, the section on "The Topic of the Imaginary," in *Book 1: Freud's Papers on Technique, 1953–1954*, and "Of the Gaze as *objet Petit a*," in *Book 11: The Four Fundamental Concepts of Psychoanalysis*. The idea is not to apply Lacan but to interrogate the notion that the imaginary could be colonized as a discrete entity independent from knowledge and experience of the real. Such a colonization would entail the total substitution of the background—that is to say, the absolute presuppositions *from*

which and *against which* individuals and societies make sense of the world. I am borrowing this definition from Ankersmit's *History and Tropology*. To my mind, it makes more sense to speak of the incorporation of European life forms into the Mesoamerican background rather than placing the emphasis on occidentalization (see Rabasa, "Elsewhere"). In reading Lacan, I have found useful Evans, *Introductory Dictionary of Lacanian Psychoanalysis*. I am also tempted to relate the concept of *background* to Pierre Bordieu's *habitus*, as developed in his "Postface to Erwin Panofsky, *Gothic Architecture and Scholasticism*." I say "tempted" because I am less bound to the "hard" structuralism of Bordieu and find that the concept could fruitfully be lifted from scholastic philosophy without adopting Bordieu's deterministic sociology. Later on I discuss Alonso de la Vera Cruz's tract *De dominio infidelium et Iure Belli*, in which we find, along with the Thomistic use of the term *habitus*, the concept of *ignorantiam invicibilem*. For a reading of Bordieu's medievalism in his adoption of the term *habitus*, see Holsinger, "Indigenity: Panofsky, Bordieu, and the Archaeology of the *Habitus*."

6. The best-known example is Wolfe, *Europe and the People without History*. Also see my critique in chapter 8 in this volume.

7. Wyclif, *Tractatus de apostasia*, 1

8. Ibid.

9. Ibid., 19.

10. The Lollards were followers of Wyclif, who believed that the meaning of the Bible was plain and convincing in itself.

11. Dziewicki in ibid., xxvii.

12. See Derrida, "Cogito and the History of Madness."

13. Carrillo Cázares, *El debate sobre la guerra chichimeca*, vol. 2: 708–9.

14. Tello, *Crónica miscelánea de la Sancta Provincia de Xalisco*, vol. 2: 147.

15. Tello, *Fragmentos de una historia de la Nueva Galicia*, 404.

16. Ibid., 422.

17. Ibid., 423.

18. Ibid., 431.

19. Ibid., 432.

20. Ibid., 457–58.

21. Ibid., 406.

22. Carrillo Cázares, *El debate sobre la guerra chichimeca*, vol. 2: 708.

23. Ibid., 696.

24. Ibid.

25. Ibid., 701.

26. Ibid., 710.

27. Ibid., 712.

28. See the discussion of these terms in note 3.

29. Tello, *Fragmentos de una historia de la Nueva Galicia*, 413.

30. Ibid., 410.

31. Tello, *Crónica miscelánea de la Sancta Provincia de Xalisco*, vol. 2: 295.

32. Ibid., 312.

33. Tello, *Fragmentos de una historia de la Nueva Galicia*, 321.

34. Ibid., 322.

35. Acazitli, *La relación de la jornada*, in García Icazbalceta, *Colección*, vol. 2: 328.

36. Ibid., vol. 2: 314.

37. Ibid., vol. 2: 317.

38. Ibid., vol. 2: 311–12.

39. Ibid., vol. 2: 311.

40. Ibid., vol. 2: 318.

41. Barlow and Smisor, *Nombre de dios, Durango*, 4–5.

42. Acazitli, *La relación de la jornada*, Garcia Icazbalceta, *Colección*, vol. 2: 307.

43. *Anales de Tlatelolco*, 105.

44. See ibid., 107–14.

45. For alternate readings of this mural, see Gruzinzki, *Mestizo Mind*; Wake, "Sacred Books and Sacred Songs from Former Days"; and Albornoz Bueno, *La memoria del olvido*. By emphasizing the Christian perspective of the *tlacuilo* who painted this mural, I am not suggesting a full-fledged Westernization or even a form of cultural mestizaje, if by this one means an in-between *background*. Rather, I am suggesting the incorporation of the Western techniques and visual quotations of Ovid into a Mesoamerican *background* that ultimately defines their significance.

46. See León-Portilla, *La flecha en el Blanco*. Also see relevant documents in Carrillo Cázares, *El debate sobre la guerra chichimeca*.

47. León-Portilla, *La flecha en el blanco*, 143; and Carillo Cázares, *El debate sobre la guerra chichimeca*, 516. I am including page numbers from both León Portilla's and Carrillo Cázares editions of Tenamaztle's letters. As Carrillo Cázares has pointed out, Leon Portilla's edition has many errors.

48. León-Portilla, *La flecha en el blanco*, 140; and Carillo Cázares, *El debate sobre la guerra chichimeca*, 514.

49. León-Portilla, *La flecha en el blanco*, 140; and Carillo Cázares, *El debate sobre la guerra chichimeca*, 514.

50. León-Portilla, *La flecha en el blanco*, 143; and Carillo Cázares, *El debate sobre la guerra chichimeca*, 516.

51. For a longer discussion of the figure of the noble savage as a form of utopian discourse, see Rabasa, "Utopian Ethnology in Las Casas's *Apologética*." Also see Louis Marin's theorization of utopian discourse in *Utopics*. The noble savage is a utopian figure in the sense that Marin gave to the concept of utopia as form of discourse rather than as the projection of some ideal society: "When talking about a Perfect Island, the Lunar States, or the Austral Continent, utopia talks less about itself or the discourse it has on the island, moon, or lost continent than about the very possibility of uttering such discourse, of the status and contents of its enunciating position and the formal and material rules allowing it to produce some particular expression" (Marin, *Utopics*, 10). Also see my discussion of Las Casas in chapter 11 in this volume.

52. León-Portilla, *La flecha en el blanco*, 144; and Carillo Cázares, *El debate sobre la guerra chichimeca*, 517.

53. León-Portilla, *La flecha en el blanco*, 145; and Carillo Cázares, *El debate sobre la guerra chichimeca*, 517.

54. León-Portilla, *La flecha en el blanco*, 146; and Carillo Cázares, *El debate sobre la guerra chichimeca*, 518.

55. Ibid.

56. Certeau, *Writing of History*, 2.

57. Vera Cruz, *Relectio de dominio infidelium*, 149.

58. Las Casas, *Apologética historia sumaria*, vol. 2: 245.

59. Vera Cruz, *Relectio de dominio infidelium*, 153.

60. Ibid., 379–81.

61. Vera Cruz, *Relectio de dominio infidelium*, 152–53.

62. Ibid., 406–8.

63. Vera Cruz, *Relectio de dominio infidelium*, 163.

64. Ibid., 447.

65. Ibid., 387.

66. Ibid., 437.

67. Ibid., 415.

68. Ibid., 437.

69. Ibid., 397.

70. Ibid., 399.

71. Ibid., 361.

72. Ibid., 409.

Chapter 11. In the Mesoamerican Archive

This chapter was first presented as a keynote address with the title "Reading Tezozomoc and Chimalpahin in the Mesoamerican Institutions of Historical Writing," at the conference on "Colonialism and the Culture of Writing: Language and Cultural Contact in Colonial Discourse Traditions," at the Zentrum für interdisziplinäre Forschung, Universität Bielefeld, June 20–22, 2007. Copyright © 2007, José Rabasa. All rights reserved. Reprinted by permission of the author. *Epigraphs*: Foucault, quoted in Agamben, *Remnants of Auschwitz*, 141. Agamben, *Remnants of Auschwitz*, 145.

1. In *Stories in Red and Black*, Elizabeth Hill Boone has identified three forms of "doing history" in Mesoamerica, which she classifies as annals, cartographic histories, and res gestae. These historical forms, according to Boone, emphasize in different degrees time, space, and genealogy. If Boone's typology offers an understanding of the different formats, there is a danger of erasing the specificity of the Mesoamerican genre. Despite a long-standing tradition in ethnohistory that speaks of annals, I use *xiuhamatl* (book of the years) or *xiuhpohualli* (count of the years). For a critique of Boone's use of European concepts, see Navarrete, "Path from Aztlan to Mexico."

2. I derive the term "Greco-Abrahamic" from Derrida, "Faith and Knowledge." Also see Anidjar, "Secularism."

3. Certeau, "Oppositional Practices of Everyday Life," 40.

4. Certeau, *Practice of Everyday Life*, xii. See Derrida, *Archive Fever*.

5. Agamben, *Remnants of Auschwitz*, 148, 150.

6. Allow me a somewhat long theoretical note that should clarify the impression that I am using the terms "speech" and "voice" as synonyms. "Voice" is hardly a transparent term that would simply correspond to recorded speech, in this case by sixteenth-century Nahuas. The long-term project of tracing Nahuatl voices, of finding ways of identifying them, may be characterized as an ec(h)ography of voice, as the art of tracing the sound, breath, gesture, noise, timbre, and tone manifest in visual forms. I first pointed to this project in Rabasa, "Echografías de la voz en la historiografía nahua." The project, of which this essay is only a beginning, entails reading pauses, unconventional punctuation marks, repetitive words, spaces, lines, and crossings in manuscripts. The parenthesis in ec(h)ography signals the need to reflect on the ecology of voice and, perhaps, also on the economy of voice. I owe this expansion of the term "echography" to Tom Conley and Regina Harrison.

Along with the gestural forms we may trace in manuscripts, the task also calls for an identification of "speech genre," which should not be folded into discursive or literary forms. M. M. Bahktin's essay "The Problem of Speech Genres" offers a good starting guide. By placing *voice* in italics, I want to underscore a distinction from "speech" and its subordination to language. Among the most forceful differentiations between "voice" and "speech" figures in Jean-Luc Nancy's essay "Vox Clamans in Deserto," where he includes laughter, dance, timbre, shouting, tone—in brief, all those aspects of *voicing* that cannot be reduced to a code—that exceed the limits of language and interpretation. Also of interest is Adriana Cavarero's critique of Derrida's *Speech and Phenomena* and his seminal essay "Differance"; the English version first appeared in the translation of *Speech and Phenomena* and later, with slight modifications, in Derrida's *Margins of Philosophy*. However useful Cavarero's reminder of Derrida's critique of *presence* in Edmund Husserl, we should add to her reading the apparently paradoxical notion that Derrida is in fact allowing a distinction between *voice* and *speech* in his critique of Husserl. If Derrida deconstructs Husserl's privileging of *presence* in/of consciousness and intentionality (knowing what one *wants* to say as the telos of speech in communication), Derrida does this by underscoring the involuntary associations, the nondiscursive, the notion of words as gesture—indeed, what I call *voice* and *voicing* in this essay. For all Derrida's denial of the difference between "speech" and "writing" in "Differance," in his long discussion of the silent differentiation between the words *difference* and *differance* in French, a reader of the English or the Spanish translation cannot but be perplexed by his insistence on the unpronounceable *a* given the need for voicing *differance* with a "funny" accent, with the gesture of a twang.

Also note that Derrida closes his essay by invoking Nietzsche: "On the contrary we must *affirm* it—in the sense that Nietzsche brings affirmation into play—with a certain laughter and with a certain dance" (Derrida, *Speech and Phenomena*, 159). He makes this comment right after stating that we must conceive the name of Being without *nostalgia*—that is, "outside the myth of the purely maternal or paternal language belonging to the lost fatherland of thought" (ibid.).

Affirmative deconstruction would proceed to read Tezozomoc and Chimalpahin outside the history of salvation that seemingly circumscribes their Nahuatl narratives to a Christian telos; such a reading would entail *laughter* in that theirs are not to be understood as *history* but rather as chronicles that accumulate *voices* without the repression of *differance*. By underscoring that the stories will be read by future generations of Nahuas, thereby differing their reading *outside* the hermeneutics, that is the history, that apparently bind them to a Christian code of interpretation or their embalming in the museums of the national Mexican identity. The written collected voices are traces of minimally heard voices, which would send us back to the "voicing" of voices belonging to earlier generations going back to the kinds of stories that were told before the advent of Christianity and Spanish contact. It would then not be a case of a denial of *presence* but of irreducible evanescence of an impossible presence for which there should be no nostalgia. The deferral of their significance of their articulation of voice remains within an open horizon of possible *laughter and dance*. Derrida closes "Differance" by invoking Heideggerian hope, by citing "Der Spruch des Anaximander," with brackets that suggest *voicing*, certainly a pausing for effect: "Being / speaks / through every language; / everywhere and always" (ibid., 160). Is this an exposure of logocentrism, of a single history of Being that would have Western metaphysics as its most refined expression, or is it a program that remains painfully logocentric? For an interrogation of singular history in philosophies of the end of philosophy, see Rabasa, "Elsewheres."

7. We count with two editions and translations of the *Chronica Mexicayotl*. Here I cite the English edition by Arthur J. O. Anderson and Susan Schroeder, *Codex Chimalpahin*, vol 1. I have compared her translations with Adrián León's translations in the Spanish edition of Fernando Alvarado Tezozomoc's *Chronica Mexicayotl*. Although I follow Anderson and Schroeder's translation, I have modified it to match the terms of my reading and interpretation. León extracts the title *Chronica Mexicayotl* from the section with the opening lines: "Yscatqui nican ompehua yn Chronica Mexicayotl" (Tezozomoc, *Chronica Mexicayotl*, 11). Schroeder includes Tezozomoc's *Chronica Mexicayotl* in a two-volume collection of papers attributed to Chimalpahin titled *Codex Chimalpahin*. There is a lack of uniformity in the spelling of Chimalpahin's name, hence the differences in entries. Entries are listed in the bibliography under "Chimalpahin," "Chimalpahín," and "Chimalpain." I follow Schroeder, who uses Chimalpahin's spelling of his name in internal self-references. Here, citations of Tezozomoc's *Chronica Mexicayotl* are in the text as Chimalpahin, *Codex Chimalpahin*. When I felt it necessary, I have modified Schroeder's translation.

8. Chimalpahin, *Codex Chimalpahin*, vol. 1: 75. Juan Franco's narrative appears right after a brief section that opens with a heading that states *tlatolpeuhcayotl* ("principio o introduccion de sermon o de platica" [beginning or introduction of sermon or talk] translates Alonso de Molina in his *Vocabulario en lengua castellana y mexicana y mexicana y castellana* [1571]), which is followed by a phrase in Spanish, "aqui comiença La Chronica, y Antiguedad De los Mexicanos" [here begins the chronicle and antiquity of the Mexicans] arguably an intercalation by Chimalpahin, not a heading by Tezozomoc, who begins the account in Nahuatl: "Yzcatqui Nican ompehua yn chronica Mexicayotl" [Behold here begins the Chronicle of things Mexican] (Chimalpahin, *Codex Chimalpahin*, vol. 1: 65). The section attributed to Juan Franco begins with "Yzcatqui nican ompehua nican ycuiliuhtoc yn intlahtollo in Mexica. yn huehuetque" [Behold, here begins, here lies written, the account of Mexico, of the elders], ibid., vol. 1: 68.

9. Chimalpahin, *Codex Chimalpahin*, vol. 1: 65.

10. Ibid., vol. 1: 91.

11. Schroeder, *Chimalpahin and the Kingdom of Chalco*, xvi.

12. Chimalpahin, *Codex Chimalpahin*, vol. 1: 65.

13. Ibid., vol. 1: 63.

14. Ibid.

15. Ibid., vol. 1: 175.

16. Ibid., vol. 1: 61.

17. Agamben, *Time That Remains*, 43.

18. Chimalpahin, *Codex Chimalpahin*, vol. 1: 168–69.

19. Sahagún, *Colloquios y doctrina*, 155, 157, 161.

20. Ibid., folio 37r. León Portilla's edition includes a facsimile of the Nahuatl and Sahagún's translation.

21. Bautista, *Confesionario en lengua mexicana y castellana*, folio 42.

22. Zumárraga, *Doctrina cristiana cierta*, folio 2v.

23. Motolinía, "Carta al Emperador Carlos V, 1555," in *Memoriales o libro de las cosas de la Nueva España*, 411, 412.

24. Zumárraga, *Doctrina cristiana cierta*, folio 2r.

25. Chimalpahin, *Codex Chimalpahin*, vol. 1: 66.

26. Ibid., 54–55.

27. Motolinía, "Carta al Emperador Carlos V, 1555," in *Memoriales o libro de las cosas de la Nueva España*, 412.

28. Chimalpain Cuauhtehuanitzin, *Primer amoxtli libro*, 31; 14.

29. Chimalpáhin, *Las ocho relaciones*, 14.

30. Ibid., 18–19.

31. Ibid., 20.

32. Ibid., 22.

33. Chimalpáhin, *Las ocho relaciones*, 162; 164.

34. Ibid., 172–74.

35. Ibid., 186.

36. Ibid., 196.

37. Las Casas, *De unico vocationis modo*, 113.

38. Chimalpain Cuauhtehuanitzin, *Primer amoxtli libro*, 14.

39. Ibid., 16.

40. Ibid.

41. Chimalpahin Quauhtlehuanitzin, *Annals of His Time*, 26–27. Hereafter cited in text as *Annals of His Time*. I am following the Lockhart, Schroeder, Namala edition, but I have modified their translation when I felt it necessary. They chose to title the work *Annals of His Time*, instead of following the traditional title of *Diario*, arguing on the fact that Chimalpahin does not record personal or subjective impressions. But given the systematic entry of days and at time of hours within the days, I have chosen to retain the traditional title. I have consulted and benefited from Rafael Tena's edition and translation of Domingo Chimalpáhin's *Diario*.

42. Chimalpahin Quauhtlehuanitzin, *Annals of His Time*, 50–51.

43. Chimalpahin, *Codex Chimalpahin*, vol. 2: 182.

44. Ibid., *Annals of His Time*, 180–81.

45. Ibid., 184–85.

46. Ibid., 182–83.

47. Ibid., 182.

48. Ibid.

49. Once more we should address Derrida's critique of Husserl's phenomenology of presence. I cannot go into detail here, but again Derrida's critique works as long as we work on the assumption that experience cannot be thought *without* re-presentation and retention. As I have argued throughout this book, the *without* points to an amphibology that at once entails *a lack* and *an outside*. The *now* in Chimalpahin should be thought of in terms of the metaphor *tonatiuh quallo* and Mesoamerican temporality, and not subsumed under what Derrida calls the privileging of *presence* in Western metaphysics. And this, despite the connections we may draw with the Paulinian *now* of the instant of salvation and Chimalpahin's suspension of time. In both instances it is a flight from time and history—in fact, from representation. In Derrida's reading of Jean-Luc Nancy (Derrida's *On Touching—Jean-Luc Nancy*), we can trace a softening (perhaps it is more apt to speak of a complication) of the *dogmatics* of mediation and representation that defined his early critique of Husserl. Let this suffice for now. This is not the place for elaborating a critique of Derrida's insistence on the inescapability of the dilemma of "re-presentation." See note 6 for a lead.

50. Chimalpahin Quauhtlehuanitzin, *Annals of His Time*, 184–85.

51. Chimalpahin, *Las ocho relaciones*, 272–73.

52. Anidjar, "Secularism," 59.

Chapter 12. On Documentary and Testimony

This essay originally appeared as "On Documentary and Testimony: The Politics of Truth, Revisionist History, and the Massacre of Acteal Chiapas," in *Moving Testimonies: New Documentary Assemblages*, edited by Bhaskar Sarkar and Janet Walker, 173–95. Copyright © 2009, Routledge. All rights reserved. Reprinted by permission of the publisher. *Epigraph*: Vidal-Naquet, "'Inquiry into a Massacre,'" 229.

1. Although Las Abejas shared the reasons for the insurgency and sympathized with the ends of the Ejercito Zapatista de Liberación Nacional (EZLN), they remained independent in their pacifist vocation. The EZLN took arms in 1994 on the eve of the implementation of the North American Free Trade Agreement (NAFTA). After twelve days of struggle a truce was signed between the insurgents and the Mexican state. While in the theater of dialogue all seemed to promise a peaceful negotiation, the army was conducting covert violence against the Zapatista bases and sympathizers. Given the truce and that neither the Mexican army nor the forces of Seguridad Publica could exercise violence directly, these entities trained paramilitaries to conduct low-intensity warfare. Las Abejas organized themselves in 1992 to struggle by peaceful means to transform the social conditions of oppression in which the indigenous people of Chiapas live.

2. In a series of three articles for the October, November, and December 2007 issues of the magazine *Nexos* (issues 358, 350, and 360 are available online at http://www. nexos.com.mx, accessed on April 23, 2008), Hector Aguilar Camín has revived the once-thought-discredited accounts given by the Procuraduria General de la República (General Attorney of the Republic) and Gustavo Hirales. These articles have been echoed in the Mexican press by less known journalists who underscore the professionalism of Aguilar Camín's journalism and historical vocation. These accounts have been refuted by Carlos Montemayor and Herman Bellinghausen in their articles for the Mexican newspaper *La Jornada* (http://www.jornada.unam.mx, April 28, 2008). Bellinghausen published twenty articles from November 5 to 24, 2007, tracing the history of the documentation of violence in Chiapas in numerous articles published in *La Jornada* during 1997 and 1998. Montemayor's articles appeared in the December 17–19, 2007, issues of *La Jornada*. Bellinghausen, like Montemayor, wrote from a committed position to the Zapatista struggles.

3. Named after the PRI, the Priístas are followers of the Partido Revolucionary Institucional (the Institutional Revolutionary Party).

4. Aguilar Camín, "Regreso a Acteal I."

5. Vidal-Naquet, "'Inquiry into a Massacre,'" 228–29.

6. Victoria Sandford and Asale Angel-Ajani, eds., *Engaged Observer: Anthropology, Advocacy, and Activism* (New Brunswick, N.J.: Rutgers University Press, 2006), 5.

7. Aguilar Camín, "Regreso a Acteal III."

8. Two collections of verbal and photographic testimonies have been collected: *Acteal: Una herida abierta, ipuc sc'oplal milel ta* consists of a bilingual collection of photographs, testimonies, memorials for the dead, and essays by anthropologists, human rights activists, Jesuit priests, and prelates. The second testimony, . . . *esta es nuestra palabra . . .* , gathers verbal and photographic snapshots of the witnesses, of life in the refugee camps, and of the community in mourning; the ellipsis in the title captures well the collected fragments of testimonies. The black-and-white photographs by Jutta Meier-Weidenbach and Claudia Ituarte offer an aesthetic celebration of the martyrs and the strength of Las Abejas.

9. Aguilar Camin, "Regreso a Acteal III."

10. Sarlo, *Tiempo pasado*, 23; my translation. For a critique see John Beverley, "Neo-conservative Turn."

11. Sarlo, *Tiempo pasado*, 40.

12. Walker, *Trauma Cinema*, 19.

13. Ibid., 18.

14. Latour, *Pandora's Hope*, 272

15. Ibid., 281.

16. Latour's concept of *factishes* enables us to sidestep the debates over the genre of *testimonio* in Latin American cultural studies. I should be courting paradox when I question the existence of a literary genre of *testimonio* and speak of documentary testimonies as having a dynamic in which the categorization of a statement necessarily involves taking a position regarding its veracity. The term "testimony" cannot be thought outside the category of truth in favor of an ethics of producing stories that respect the face of those rendering testimony. It is not merely a question of truth but of a broad range of speech genres that cannot be contained nor circumscribed by a literary genre. The literature on *testimonio* is immense. I limit myself to noting the collection of essays in Gugelberger, *Real Thing*. The debates over *testimonio* have privileged Rigoberta Menchú's *Me llamo Rigoberta Menchú, y así me nació la conciencia*. During the cultural wars of the 1990s, Menchú's book became a preferred testimonial to debunk. A key text in the conservative onslaught on Menchú's credibility was Stoll, *Rigoberta Menchú and the Story of All Poor People in Guatemala*. For assessments of Stoll, see Arias, *The Rigoberta Menchú Controversy*. The essays in this volume tend to privilege questions of epistemology (Western versus Amerindian) in the discussion of Stoll's exposure of factual inconsistencies. My approach on the phenomenology of the face has close affinities with Sommer's ethics for reading minority writing in her *Proceed with Caution*.

17. Marion, *In Excess*, 126.

18. Ibid., 120.

19. On the concept of "elsewhere" and the undoing of the modern/premodern binary, see Rabasa, "Elsewheres."

20. Cubbit, *Videography*, 78. Also see Cubbit, *Cinema Effect*.

21. See Rabasa, *Franciscans and Dominicans under the Gaze of Tlacuilo*.

22. See Mora, "Decolonizing Politics"; Eber and Kovic, *Women in Chiapas*; Hernández Castillo, *La otra palabra*; and Rovira, *Mujeres de maíz*.

23. Marks, *Touch*, xiii. On the cinematic apparatus criticism, see De Lauretis and Heath, *Cinematic Apparatus*. Marks outlines the limits of haptic subject criticism as follows: "But just as the optical needs the haptic, the haptic must return to the optical. To maintain an optical distance is to die the death of abstraction. But to lose all distance from the world is to die a material death, to become indistinguishable from the rest of the world" (Marks, *Touch*, xvi). In placing the emphasis on the haptic, I am not so much calling forth a form of subject criticism as laying out the haptic component in the relationship between filmmaker, recorded subject, apparatus, and viewer. My observations on touch have benefited from Derrida, *On Touching—Jean Luc Nancy*.

24. Certeau, "Oppositional Practices of Everyday Life," 43; and Certeau, *Practice of Everyday Life*, xii.

Chapter 13. Exception to the Political

All translations from Spanish into English in this chapter are mine.

1. Benjamin, "Theses on the Philosophy of History," 257.

2. For grasping the plurality of voices, organizations, personal experiences of those involved in the rebellion of the APPO, see the testimonials collected in Denham and the CASA Collective, *Teaching Rebellion*. The range of experiences goes from great-grandmothers, who gained consciousness of their oppression and the possibility of changing their conditions and those of their families, to young (and not so young) activists belonging to organizations and movements who for years, if not decades, have been calling for the radical transformation of Oaxaca and the nation, passing through rural and urban teachers who have refused to listen to the corrupt leaders of the Sindicato de Trabajadores del la Educacción (STE). Among the reporters who have documented the rebellion in Oaxaca, Diego Osorno, in his work *Oaxaca Sitiada*, offers a detailed account of the movement and the systematic repression by the state. John Gibler has singled out Osorno, in an environment in which even the best reputed daily newspapers like *La Jornada* have "published scores of paid advertisements formatted almost exactly like news stories reporting the endless string of public works inaugurated by [the governor] Ulises Ruiz—none of these advertisements were identified as such, the only difference was that the headlines were printed in Italics" (Gibler, *Mexico Unconquered*, 155–56). Gibler exposes the schizophrenia of the media by underscoring that "the newspaper *El Milenio* would print editorials denouncing the APPO as a group of violent and radical vandals while the main news story written by their special correspondent, Diego Osorno, would detail the involvement of plainclothes police and state officials in armed attacks against members of the APPO" (ibid., 156).

3. Agamben, *State of Exception*, 2.

4. Let me note that the government of Calderón, in its current war against the drug cartels, operates under a state of emergency de facto without making a formal declaration. This state of emergency that entails a generalized state of impunity was denounced in the Encuentro Nacional Contra la Impunidad (the National Encounter Against Impunity) that gathered in Acteal, Chiapas, during the tenth anniversary of the massacre of Acteal in December 2007. Even though groups with different political orientations were at the gathering, the mobilization was not limited to denouncing and bringing to justice specific individuals; rather, it entailed an interrogation of the Mexican juridical-legal structures and the model of the nation. Hence, the gathering called to dismantle state institutions that monopolize violence while claiming to be democratic (see chapter 12 in this volume). Recently several organizations have convoked an Encuentro Americano Contra la Impunidad using unequivocal language that leaves little hope for official institutions: "la justicia institucional no funciona, favorece la represión de quienes protestan y la impunidad de los que despojan, masacran, desaparecen y violan los derechos más elementales del pueblo" [institutional justice does not work, it favors the repression of those who protest and the impunity of those of who despoil, who massacre, disappear, and violate the most elemental rights of the people]. The article goes on to cite the organizers, stating that justice "no está en las instituciones oficiales, ahí sólo queda la impunidad para los que están arriba y el terror para los que estamos abajo" [is not in the official institutions; there only remains the impunity for those who stand above and terror for those of us who stand below] (in Bellinghausen, "Activistas anun-

cian realización de encuentro nacional contra la impunidad"). Following Article 17 of the Mexican Constitution, the conveners of the encounter demand the right to find other forms of exercising justice on those responsible for a series of serious violations of rights. The tone leaves no doubt about the need to dismantle the state institutions even when appealing to an article in the constitution. The conveners' appeal to the law might make them *right* but also subject to the same regime of law they denounce as safeguarding the *rights* of capital and protecting the impunity of those whom the same laws allow to "stand above."

5. Schmitt, *Political Theology*, 5.

6. Agamben, *State of Exception*, 53–54.

7. According to Osorno, *Oaxaca Sitiada*, the APPO was under the control of the Partido Comunista Mexicano Marxista Leninista (PCMML) and its parallel organization, the Frente Popular Revolucionario (FPR). Osorno introduces his description of these organizations by posing the question: "¿Cómo está estructurado, a grandes rasgos, el grupo que de manera discreta dirigió a la APPO tácticamente? Comienzo a armar el rompecabezas con los apuntes que he tomado, con las entrevistas hechas y los documentos consultados" [In broad strokes, how is the group organized that provided guidance to the APPO in a discreet fashion? I begin to assemble a puzzle with the notes I have taken, with the interviews I have conducted, and with the documents I have consulted] (Osorno, *Oaxaca Sitiada*, 126). Personally, I find the "manera discreta" [in a discreet fashion] a bit manipulative in his assessment of the PCMML's control of the APPO; it is as if he lacked sufficient evidence. Osorno cites interviews to document the affinities the PCMML has with Stalin, whose portrait is often displayed in rallies. Although the interviews with PCMML leaders offer a historicist understanding of social process in which Stalin figures as a key for understanding history, they recognize that the dictatorship of the proletariat and the Gulag "es un debate que se da incluso en el movimiento comunista" [is even a debate within the communist movement] (ibid., 137). Clearly, the recognition of Stalin and the stages he outlined in the development of socialism offers one more instance of the connections between the state and history.

8. Leyla's testimony is in Denham and CASA Collective, *Teaching Rebellion*, 88.

9. Cuautli's testimony is in ibid., 99.

10. Ibid., 100.

11. On the Policía Comunitaria: Sistema de Seguridad y Justicia Comunitaria de la Costa Chica y Montaña de Guerrero, see "Declaración de los Pueblos y Organizaciones durante el Foro Guerrero: Donde se castiga la pobreza y se criminaliza la protesta, 23 de junio 2008," available online at http://www.policiacomunitaria.org/ (accessed on December 8, 2009).

12. See Hardt and Negri, *Multitude*. For a discussion of the problematic nature of "the turning of flesh into body," see Mutman, "Difference, Event, Subject," 154 and passim.

13. Article 29 of the Mexican Constitution; translation mine.

14. Ibid.

15. Pashukanis, *General Theory of Law and Marxism*, 61.

16. Pashukanis, "Marxist Theory of Law and the Construction of Socialism," 194. This is not the place to revisit the debates over the role of the law and the state in the years after the October Revolution, but to underscore the specificities, perhaps originality, of the "Ley Revolucionaria" when compared with Stalinists' statist alternatives. For a summary of the debates and the trials that led to the purge of Pashukanis, see

Milovanovic, "Introduction to the Transaction Edition," in Pashukanis, *General Theory Law and Marxism*.

17. Article 142 of the Constitution of the State of Oaxaca; translation mine.

18. Article 62 of the Constitution of the State of Oaxaca; translation mine.

19. See Benjamin, "Critique of Violence," 300

20. Agamben, *State of Exception*, 62–63.

21. I owe this observation to Alejandro Reyes, who revisited Oaxaca right after the police retook the center of the city.

22. Schmitt, *Political Theology*, 7.

23. Rimbaud, letter to Georges Izambard, May 13, 1871, in *Rimbaud: Complete Works, Selected Letters*, 371.

24. Rimbaud's "L'Orgie parisienne ou Paris se repeuple" is in ibid., 89

25. See myspace for the Asamblea de Artistas Revolucionarios de Oaxaca (ASAR-Oaxaca), at http://www.myspace.com/asaroaxaca. Also see the blogspot for the APPO, at http://todoelpoderalpueblo.blogspot.com. For photographs of the rebellion and the graffiti of the Oaxaca commune, see Leyva, *Memorial de agravios Oaxaca*.

26. See the reproduction of the stills and the video recording in Kentridge, *Five Themes*.

27. Lloyd, "Rage against the Divine," 294.

28. My use of *ought* should resonate with Kant's linking of the judgment of taste to an *ought* with universal implications: "A judgment of taste requires everyone to assent; and whoever declares something to be beautiful holds that everyone *ought* to give his approval to the object at hand and that he too should declare it beautiful" (Kant, *Critique of Judgment*, 86).

29. Marx, *Civil War in France*, 262.

30. Marx, *The Eighteenth Brumaire of Louis Bonaparte*, in *Marx-Engels Reader*, 594.

31. Marx, *Civil War in France*, 214.

32. Marx, "Address of the General Council," in ibid., 233.

33. Ibid., 213.

34. Schmitt, *Political Theology*, 15, citing Kierkegaard, *Repetition*, 217.

35. Schmitt, *Political Theology*, 37.

36. Cf. Schmitt's citation to the full passage in Kierkegaard, *Repetition*, 227. In elaborating Kierkegaard's thoughts, I have benefited from the French translation by Paul-Henri Tisseau and Else-Marie Jacquet-Tisseau in Kierkegaard's *La répétition*, 92–97 and passim.

37. Schmitt, *Political Theology*, 15.

38. Agamben, *Time That Remains*, 63

39. Marx, "Preface," in *Contribution to the Critique of Political Economy*, 21.

40. Negri, as cited by Hardt, "Into the Factory," 33.

41. This interview with Maoist activists is cited in Foucault, *Power/Knowledge*, 8.

42. Ibid.

43. Ibid., 11.

44. Ibid., 16.

45. Lenin, *State and Revolution*, 474; emphasis in the original.

46. Ibid., 476; emphasis in the original.

47. Lenin, "Task of the Proletariat in the Present Revolution" (The April Theses), 23.

48. Lenin, *Letters on Tactics*, 49.

49. Marx, *Civil War in France*, 206.

50. Lenin, *State and Revolution*, 414.

51. Lenin, "'Left-Wing' Childishness and the Petty-Bourgeois Mentality," 352; emphasis in the original.

52. Lenin, *State and Revolution*, 476; emphasis in the original; and Lenin, "'Left-Wing' Childishness and the Petty-Bourgeois Mentality," 349 and passim.

53. See Karatani, *Transcritique*, 1–25.

54. Schmitt, *Political Theology*, 5.

55. García Linera, "El ocaso de un ciclo estatal," 152.

56. Zibechi, *Dispersar el poder*, 165.

57. Ibid., 170.

58. Marx, "Drafts of the Letter to Vera Zasulich," 349.

59. Ibid., 350.

60. Ibid.

61. Ibid.

62. See Chakrabarty, *Provincializing Europe*; Chatterjee, *Politics of the Governed*; and Hardt and Negri, *Multitude*. For earlier discussions of these texts, see chapters 7 and 8.

63. For arguments against writing the past in the mode of history, see Nandy, "Histories Forgotten Doubles"; and Guha, *History at the Limit of World-History*.

64. García Linera repeats this sort of proposal in articles and books that include *Estado multinacional* and "Democracia multinacional y multi-institucional." In the latter, a debate with Jorge Lazarte from 2003, García Linera proposes a multicultural perspective inspired by the theories of Charles Taylor that suggest a hierarchy of cultures that privileges the state as a transcendent entity: "Para el primer tema, el de la multiculturalidad, proponemos la segmentación vertical de las estructuras de poder estatal con niveles diferenciados de competencia política. A escala inferior los municipios con sus actuales atribuciones; a nivel meso o subnacional, regímenes de autonomía por identidad cultural aymara y qheswa, que son las dos identidades indígenas mayores y, en el ámbito superior, un sistema de gobierno general que unifique y sintetice la diversidad cultural del país" [For the first theme, on the multicultural, we propose a vertical segmentation of the structures of state power with differentiated levels of political competence. On the lower scale, the municipalities with their current attributions; on a meso or subnational level, regimes of autonomy with Aymara and Qheswa cultural identity, which are the two major indigenous identities, and, in the higher ambit, a system of general government that unifies and synthesizes the cultural diversity of the country] (García Linera, "Democracia multinacional y multi-institucional").

The verticality of this schema not only establishes the significance of these levels within the state, but defines their significance in terms of political competence. Aymara and Qheswa communities must adopt the languages of the state in order to participate fully, hence legitimately, in the political process. If legal and political competence has forced the Aymaras to operate in a dual power structure that dates back at least to the colonial imposition of an extraneous order, García Linera's proposal reenacts the exigency to address the state in its own language. It lays out a segmentation of the nation that de jure and de facto limits the participation of the lower and middle sectors to their immediate context. Denise Arnold, in "New Cartographies of the Bolivian State," has made a parallel argument for a hierarchical conceptualization of political actors in the context of a mapping that privileges the subordination of communities to transcendental state structures.

65. The Morales/García Linera government finds itself delimited by what Lenin analyzed as "dual power" during the 1917 Revolution: "This dual power is evident in the existence of two governments: one is the main, the real, the actual government of the bourgeoisie, the 'Provisional Government' of Lvov and Co., which holds in its hands all the organs of power; the other is a supplementary and parallel government, a 'controlling' government in the shape of the Petrograd Soviet of Workers' and Soldiers' Deputies, which holds no organs of state power, but directly rests on the support of an obvious and indisputable majority of the people, on the armed workers and soldiers" (Lenin, "Task of the Proletariat in the Present Revolution," 60). The question now is whether Morales and García Linera will give place to a *transitional* government that will empower the communal governments. In "State Crisis and Popular Power," García Linera offers the following scenario: "The two paths, electoral and insurrectional, are not necessarily antagonistic; they could turn out to be complementary. On both, however, the indigenous-popular pole should consolidate its hegemony, providing intellectual and moral leadership of the country's social majorities. There will be neither electoral triumph nor victorious insurrection without wide-ranging, patient work on the unification of the social movements, and a practical education process to realize the political, moral, cultural and organizational leadership of these forces over Bolivia's popular and middle strata" (ibid., 85). Although this article appeared in 2006, it represents García Linera's thought before the electoral triumph of 2005. It anticipates, in what suggests pure Leninism, the dual structure of power that emerges after the election that built on the mobilization of the Aymara communities. And yet it is not clear who will be assigned the task of the "unification of the social movements" and will conduct the "education process."

66. For a reading of popular mobilizations in Bolivia inspired by Negri, see Prada, "Multitud y contrapoder."

67. Zibechi, *Dispersar el poder*, 149; my translation.

68. In addition to Zibechi, consider the following diagnoses by Prada: "El ayllu es una *sociedad contra el estado*, por lo tanto se trata de una sociedad que evita la emergencia del estado por los medios a su alcance. Particularme esto se hace significativo cuando se recurre a los mandos rotativos o a las confederaciones de jefaturas, es decir, jefes de clan" [The ayllu is a *society against the state*, therefore it is a society that avoids the emergence of the state by the means available to it. This becomes particularly significant when it resorts to the revolving authorities or the confederations of leaderships—that is, clan leaders] (Prada, "Multitude y contrapoder," 87). Further on Prada adds: "La cultura es el eterno presente. Antiguas luchas emergen en el presente de forma renovada, viejos conflictos que no se han resuelto, luchas contra el colonialismo, luchas por las tierras, vuelve a reaparecer constante y sistematicamente" [Culture is the eternal present. Ancient struggles emerge in the present in renovated fashions, old conflicts that have not been resolved, struggles against colonialism, struggles for the land, reappear constantly and systematically] (ibid., 92–93). The concept of "society against the State" obviously invokes Pierre Clastres's classic study *La société contre l'état*. See my discussion of Clastres's concept in chapter 8.

69. Pashukanis, *General Theory of Law and Marxism*, 61.

70. García Linera as quoted in "El gobierno dice que invadir casas va contra la CPE," *La Razón*, March 12, 2009.

71. García Linera as quoted by Zibechi, *Dispersar el poder*, 170.

72. Williams, *Marxism and Literature*, 128–35.

73. Marx, *Civil War in France*, 213.

74. Lenin, *State and Revolution*, 476; emphasis in the original.

REFERENCES

Acazitli. *La relación de la jornada que hizo don Francisco de Sandoval Acazitli*. In *Colección de documentar para la historia de México*. Edited by Joaquín García Icazbalceta. 2 vols. Mexico City: Editorial Ponría, 1971.

Acteal: Estrategia de muerte. Directed by Carlos Mendoza. Mexico City: Canal 6 de julio, 1998 (film).

Acteal: 10 años de impunidad, ¿y cuántos más. Directed by José Alfredo Jiménez Vasquez. Acteal: Orgainzación Civil Las Abejas, 2007 (film).

Acteal: Una herida abierta, ipuc sc'oplal milel ta. Tlaquepaque, Jalisco: Instituto Tecnológico y de Estudios Superiores de Occidente, 1998.

Acuña, René, ed. *Relaciones geográficas del siglo XVI*. 10 vols. Mexico City: Universidad Nacional Autónoma de México, 1986.

Adams, Marilyn McCord. *William Ockham*. 2 vols. Notre Dame, Ind.: Notre Dame University Press, 1987.

Agamben, Giorgio. *Homo Sacer: Sovereign Power and Bare Life*. Translated by Daniel Heller-Roazen. Stanford, Calif.: Stanford University Press, 1998.

——. *Remnants of Auschwitz: The Witness and the Archive*. Translated by Daniel Heller-Roazen. New York: Zone Books, 2005.

——. *State of Exception*. Translated by Kevin Attel. Chicago: University of Chicago Press, 2005.

——. *The Time That Remains: A Commentary on the Letter to the Romans*. Translated by Patricia Dailey. Stanford, Calif.: Stanford University Press, 2005.

Aguilar Camín, Héctor. "Regreso a Acteal I: La fractura." *Nexos* 358 (October 2007). Available online at http://www.nexos.com.mx. Accessed on June 25, 2009.

——. "Regreso a Acteal II: El camino de los muertos." *Nexos* 359 (November 2007). Available online at http://www.nexos.com.mx. Accessed on June 25, 2009.

——. "Regreso a Acteal III: El día señalado." *Nexos* 360 (December 2007). Available online at http://www.nexos.com.mx. Accessed on June 25, 2009.

Albornoz Bueno, Alicia. *La memoria del olvido. El lenguaje del Tlacuilo: Glifos y murales de la iglesia de San Miguel Arcángel Ixmiquilpan Hidalgo: Teopan dedicado a Tezcatlipoca*. Pachuca, Mexico: Universidad Autónoma del Estado de Hidalgo, 1994.

Alonso's Dream. Directed by Danièle Lacourse and Yvan Partry. Brooklyn, N.Y.: First Run/Icarus Films, 2000 (film).

Anales de Tlatelolco y Códice de Tlatelolco. Edited and translated by Heinrich Berlin, with a commentary of Codex of Tlatelolco by Robert H. Barlow. Mexico City: Antigua Librería Robredo, 1948.

Anderson, Arthur J. O., and Susan Schroeder, eds. *Codex Chimalpahin*. 2 vols. Vol. 2. Norman: University of Oklahoma Press, 1997.

Anidjar, Gil. "Secularism." *Critical Inquiry* 33 (Autumn 2006): 52–77.

Ankersmit, F. R. *History and Tropology: The Rise and Fall of Metaphor.* Berkeley: University of California Press, 1994.

Anzaldúa, Gloria. "How to Tame a Wild Tongue." In *Borderlands/La Frontera.* San Francisco: Aunt Lute Books, 1987.

Arias, Arturo, ed. *The Rigoberta Menchú Controversy.* Minneapolis: University of Minnesota Press, 2001.

Aricó, José. *La cola del diablo: Itinerario de Gramsci en América Latina.* Buenos Aires: Puntosur Editores, 1988.

Arnold, Denise Y. "New Cartographies of the Bolivian State in the Context of the Constituent Assembly, 2006–2007." In *Race, Colonialism, and Social Transformation in Latin America and the Caribbean.* Edited by Jerome Branch. Gainesville: University Press of Florida, 2008.

Avilés, Jaime. "Marcos agradece a italianos la entrega de una turbina." *La Jornada* 4 (December 2000). Available online at http://www.jornada.unam.mx/.

Badiou, Alain. *Logiques des mondes. L'être et l'énénements, 2.* Paris: Editions du Seuil, 2006.

Bahktin, M. M. "The Problem of Speech Genres." In *Speech Genres and Other Late Essays,* 60–102. Translated by Vern W. McGee. Austin: University of Texas Press, 1990.

Balakrishnan, Gopal, ed. *Debating Empire.* London: Verso, 2003

Barker, Francis. *The Culture of Violence: Essays on Tragedy and History.* Chicago: University of Chicago Press, 1993.

Barlow, R. H., and George T. Smisor, eds. and trans. *Nombre de dios, Durango: Two Documents in Náhuatl Concerning Its Foundation.* Sacramento, Calif.: The House of Tlaloc, 1943.

Barreda, Andrés, et al., eds. *Chiapas.* 4 vols. Mexico City: Instituto de Investigaciones Económicas, Universidad Navional Autónoma de México,1995–97.

Bartra, Armando. *Los herederos de Zapata: Movimientos campesinos posrevolucionarios en México, 1920–1981.* Mexico City: Ediciones Era, 1985.

———. *Regeneración, 1900–1918: La corriente más radical de la revolución de 1910 a través de su periódico de combate.* Mexico City: Hadise, 1972.

Bautista, Juan. *Confesionario en lengua mexicana y castellana.* Santiago de Tlaltelolco: Melchior Ocharte, 1599.

Bellinghausen, Hermann. "Activistas anuncian realización de encuentro nacional contra la impunidad." *La Jornada,* May 28, 2009. Available online at http://www.jornada.unam.mx/. Accessed on December 9, 2009.

———. "Denuncian hostigamiento contra activistas y el Centro Bartolomé de las Casas." *La Jornada,* June 24, 2009. Available online at http://www.jornada.unam.mx/. Accessed on December 9, 2009.

Benjamin, Walter. "Critique of Violence." *Reflections: Essays, Aphorisms, and Autobiographical Writings.* Edited by Peter Demetz, 277–300. Translated by Edmund Jephcott. New York: Schocken, 1986.

———. "Theses on the Philosophy of History." *Illuminations: Essays and Reflections.* Edited by Hannah Arendt, 254–67. Translated by Harry Zohn. New York: Schocken, 1969.

Berdan, Frances F. "The Imperial Tribute Roll of the *Codex Mendoza.*" In *Codex Mendoza.* Edited by Frances F. Berdan and Patricia Rieff Anawalt. 4 vols. Vol. 1, 93–102. Berkeley: University of California Press, 1992.

Beverley, John. *Latinamericanism after 9/11*. Durham, N.C.: Duke University Press, forthcoming.

——. "The Neoconservative Turn in Latin American Literary and Cultural Criticism." *Journal of Latin American Cultural Studies* 17, no. 1 (2008): 65–83.

——. *Subalternity and Representation: Arguments in Cultural Theory*. Durham, N.C.: Duke University Press, 2001.

——. *Testimonio: On the Politics of Truth*. Minneapolis: University of Minnesota Press, 2004.

——. "Writing in Reverse: On the Project of the Latin American Subaltern Studies, Group." Subaltern Studies in the Americas. Special issue of *Dispositio/n* 46 (1994): 271–88. Edited by José Rabasa, Javier Sanjinés, and Robert Carr.

Bhabha, Homi. "Of Mimicry and Man: The Ambivalence of Colonial Discourse." In *The Location of Culture*, 85–92. New York: Routledge, 1994.

Bhadra, Gautam. "Four Rebels of Eighteen-Fifty-Seven." In *Selected Subaltern Studies*. Edited by Ranajit Guha and Gayatri Chakravorty Spivak, 129–75. New York: Oxford University Press, 1988.

Bierhorst, John. *Cantares Mexicanos: Songs of the Aztecs*. Translated and with an introduction by John Bierhorst. Stanford, Calif.: Stanford University Press, 1985.

Bonfil Batalla, Guillermo. *México profundo: Una civilización negada*. Mexico City: Centro de Investigaciones y Estudios Superiones en Antropología Social (CIESAS), 1987.

——. *México Profundo: Reclaiming a Civilization*. Translated by Philip A. Dennis. Austin: University of Texas Press, 1996.

Boon, James A. *Other Tribes, Other Scribes: Symbolic Anthropology in the Comparative Study of Cultures, Histories, Religions, and Texts*. New York: Cambridge University Press, 1982.

Boone, Elizabeth Hill. "The Aztec Pictorial History of *Codex Mendoza*." In *Codex Mendoza*. Edited by Frances F. Berdan and Patricia Rieff Anawalt. 4 vols. Vol. 1, 35–54. Berkeley: University of California Press, 1992.

——, ed. *Collecting the Pre-Columbian Past*. Washington, D.C.: Dumbarton Oaks Research Library and Collection, 1993.

——. "Collecting the Pre-Columbian Past: Historical Trends and the Process of Reception and Use." In *Collecting the Pre-Columbian Past*. Edited by Elizabeth Hill Boone, 315–51. Washington, D.C.: Dumbarton Oaks Research Library and Collection, 1993.

——. *Stories in Red and Black: Pictorial Histories of the Aztecs and Mixtecs*. Austin: University of Texas Press, 2000.

Bordieu, Pierre. "Postface to Erwin Panofsky, *Gothic Architecture and Scholasticism*." Translated by Laurence Petit. In *The Premodern Condition: Medievalism and the Making of Theory*. By Bruce Holsinger, 221–42. Chicago: University of Chicago Press, 2005.

Boutmy, Emile. *Studies in Constitutional Law: France, England, United States*. Translated by E. M. Picey. London: Macmillan, 1981.

Branch, Jerome, ed. *Race, Colonialism, and Social Transformation in Latin America and the Caribbean*. Gainesville: University Press of Florida, 2008.

Brotherston, Gordon. *Book of the Fourth World: Reading the Native Americas through Their Books*. Cambridge: Cambridge University Press, 1992.

Brunk, Samuel. "Zapata and the City Boys: In Search of a Piece of the Revolution." *Hispanic American Historical Review* 73, no. 1 (1993): 33–65.

Buck-Morss, Susan. "Hegel and Haiti." *Critical Inquiry* 26, no. 4 (Summer 2000): 821–65.

Butler, Judith, Ernesto Laclau, and Slavoj Žižek. *Contingency, Hegemony, Universality: Contemporary Dialogues on the Left.* London: Verso, 2000.

Calnek, Edward. "The Ethnographic Content of the Third Part of *Codex Mendoza.*" In *Codex Mendoza.* Edited by Frances F. Berdan and Patricia Rieff Anawalt. 4 vols. Vol. 1, 81–91. Berkeley: University of California Press, 1992.

Carillo Cázares, Alberto. *El debate sobre la guerra chichimeca, 1531–1585: Derecho y política en la Nueva España.* 2 vols. Zamora, Mich., and San Luis Potosí, Mexico: El Colegio de Michoacan and El Colegio de San Luis, 2000.

Carpentier, Alejo. *El reino de este mundo.* Barcelona: Seix Barral, 1967.

Carlsen, Laura. "Autonomía indígena y usos y costumbres: la innovación de la tradition." *Revista Chiapas* 7 (1999). Available online at http://www.revisitachiapas.org/No7/ch7.html. Accessed on December 7, 2009.

———. "Las mujeres indígenas en el movimiento social." *Revisita Chiapas* 8 (2000). Available online at http://www.revisitachiapas.org/No8/ch8.html. Accessed on December 7, 2009.

Carson, Jim, and David Brooks, "Pozol y biopiratería." *La Jornada*, October 7, 2000. Available online at http://www.jornada.unam.mx/. Accessed on December 7, 2009.

Castañeda, Jorge. *Sorpresas te da la vida: Mexico 1994.* Mexico City: Aguilar, 1994.

Casto-Klarén, Sara. "Historiography on the Ground: The Toledo Circle and Guamán Poma." In *The Latin American Subaltern Studies Reader.* Edited by Ileana Rodríguez Rodríguez, 142–71. Durham, N.C.: Duke University Press, 2001.

Cavarero, Adriana. *For More Than One Voice: Towards a Philosophy of Vocal Expression.* Translated by Paul A. Kottman. Stanford, Calif.: Stanford University Press, 2005.

Ceceña, Ana Esther. "La resistencia como espacio de construcción del nuevo mundo." *Revista Chiapas* 7 (2000). Available online at http://www.revisitachiapas.org/No7/ch7.html. Accessed on December 9, 2009.

Centro de Derechos Humanos Fray Bartolomé de las Casas (CDHFBC). "La disputa por la legitimidad. Aniversario de los ataques a los municipios libres." 1999. Available online at http://www.frayba.org.mx/index.php. Accessed on June 25, 2009.

———. "La legalidad de la injusticia." 1998. Available online at http://www.frayba.org.mx/index.php. Accessed on June 25, 2009.

Certeau, Michel de. "Ethno-Graphy: Speech, or the Space of the Other: Jean de Léry." In Michel de Certeau, *The Writing of History.* Translated by Tom Conley, 209–243. New York: Columbia University Press, 1988.

———. "The Oppositional Practices of Everyday Life." *Social Text* 3 (1982): 3–43.

———. *The Practice of Everyday Life.* Translated by Steven Rendall. Berkeley: University of California Press, 1988.

———. *The Writing of History.* Translated by Tom Conley. New York: Columbia University Press, 1988.

Chakrabarty, Dipesh. *Habitations of Modernity: Essays in the Wake of Subaltern Studies.* University of Chicago Press, 2002.

———. "Marx after Marxism: Subaltern History and the Question of Difference." *Polygraph* 6–7 (1993): 10–16.

———. *Provincializing Europe: Postcolonial Thought and Historical Difference.* Princeton, N.J.: Princeton University Press, 2000.

———. "The Time of History and the Times of the Gods." In *The Politics of Culture, in the Shadow of Capital*. Edited by Lisa Lowe and David Lloyd, 35–60. Durham, N.C.: Duke University Press, 1997.

Chatterjee, Partha. "More on Modes of Power and the Peasantry." In *Selected Subaltern Studies*. Edited by Ranajit Guha and Gayatri Chakravorty Spivak, 351–90. New York: Oxford University Press, 1988.

———. *The Politics of the Governed: Reflections on Popular Politics in Most of the World*. New York: Columbia University Press, 2004.

Chiapas 95. EZLN documents in English. Available online at http://www.eco.utexas.edu/faculty/Cleaver/chiapas95.html. Accessed on June 25, 2009.

Chimalpahin Quauhtlehuanitzin, Domingo de San Antón Muñón. *Annals of His Time*. Edited and translated by James Lockhart, Susan Schroeder, and Doris Namala. Stanford, Calif.: Stanford University Press, 2006.

———. *Codex Chimalpahin: Society and Politics in Mexico Tenochtitlan, Tlatelolco, Texcoco, Culhuacan, and Other Nahua Altepetl in Central Mexico*. 2 vols. Edited and translated by Susan Schroeder. Norman: University of Oklahoma Press, 1997

Chimalpáhin, Domingo. *Diario*. Edited and translated by Rafael Tena. Mexico City: Conaculta, 2000.

———. *Las ocho relaciones y el memorial de Colhuacan. Tomo II: Relaciones séptima y octava*. Edited and translated by Rafael Tena. Mexico City: Conaculta, 1998.

Chimalpain Cuauhtehuanitzin, Domingo Francisco de San Antón Muñón. *Primer amoxtli libro, 3ª relación de las différentes histoires originales*. Edited and translated by Víctor M. Castillo F. Mexico City: Universidad Nacional Autónoma de México, 1997.

Clastres, Pierre. *La société contre l'état*. Paris: Minuit, 1974.

Clavigero, Francisco Javier. *Historia antigua de México*. 4 vols. 1780–81. Mexico City: Editorial Porrúa, 1945.

Codex Borgia. *Los tiempos del cielo y de la oscuridad. Oraculos y liturgia. Libro explicativo del llamado Códice Borgia*. Introduction and explanation by Ferdidnan Anders, Maarten Jansen, and Luis Reyes García. Graz, Austria: ADEVA. Mexico City: Fondo de Cultura Económica, 1993.

Codex Mendoza. Edited by Frances F. Berdan and Patricia Rieff Anawalt. 4 vols. Berkeley: University of California Press, 1992.

Codex Vaticanus B. *Manual del Adivino. Libro explicativo del llamado Códice Vaticano B*. Introduction and explanation by Ferdinand Anders and Marten Jansen. Graz, Austria: ADEVA. Mexico City: Fondo de Cultura Económica, 1993.

Codgell, Sam. "Criollos, Gapuchines, y 'plebe tan extremo plebe': Retórica e ideología criollas en *Alboroto y motín de México* de Sigüenza y Góngora." In *Relecturas del Barroco de Indias*. Edited by Mabel Moraña, 245–79. Hanover, N.H.: Ediciones del Norte, 1994.

Collier, George A., with Elizabeth Lowry Quaratiello. *Basta! Land and the Zapatista Rebellion in Chiapas*. Oakland, Calif.: Food First, 1994.

Comisión Nacional de Intermediación (CONAI). *San Andrés: Marco jurídico y normativo del diálogo y negociación*. Mexico City: Serie "Senderos de Paz," Cuaderno No. 2, 1999.

Coronil, Fernando. *The Magical State: Nature, Money, and Modernity in Venezuela*. Chicago: University of Chicago Press, 1997.

Cubbit, Sean. *The Cinema Effect*. Cambridge: Massachusetts Institute of Technology Press, 2004.

———. *Videography: Video Media as Art and Culture*. New York: St. Martin's Press, 1993.

Cummins, Thomas. "From Lies to Truth: Colonial Ekphrasis and the Act of Crosscultural Translation." In *Reframing the Renaissance: Visual Culture in Europe and Latin America, 1450–1650*. Edited by Claire Frarago, 152–74. New Haven, Conn.: Yale University Press, 1995.

Dabashi, Hamid. "No soy un subalternista." In *Convergencia de tiempos: Estudios subalternos/contextos latinoamericanos estado, cultura, subalternidad*. Edited by Ileana Rodríguez, 49–59. Translated by Antonio Calvo Elorrin. Amsterdam: Rodopi, 2001.

Declaración de los Pueblos y Organizaciones durante el Foro Guerrero: Donde se castiga la pobreza y se criminaliza la protesta, 23 de junio 2008. Available online at http://www.policiacomunitaria.org/. Accessed on June 29, 2009.

De la Campa, Román. *Latin Americanism*. Minneapolis: University of Minnesota Press, 1999.

De la Pena, Guillermo. *A Legacy of Promises: Agriculture, Politics, and Ritual in the Morelos Highlands of Mexico*. Austin: University of Texas Press, 1981.

De Lauretis, Teresa, and Stephen Heath, eds. *The Cinematic Apparatus*. London: Macmillan, 1980.

Deleuze, Gilles. *Différence et répétition*. Paris: Presses Universitaires de France, 1968.

Denham, Diana, and CASA Collective, eds. *Teaching Rebellion: Stories from the Grassroots Mobilization in Oaxaca*. Oakland, Calif.: PM Press, 2008.

Derrida, Jacques. *Archive Fever: A Freudian Impression*. Translated by Eric Prenowitz. Chicago: University of Chicago Press, 1996.

———. "Cogito and the History of Madness." In *Writing and Difference*. Translated by Alan Bass. Chicago: University of Chicago Press, 1978.

———. "Faith and Knowledge: The Two Sources of 'Religion' at the Limits of Reason Alone." In *Acts of Religion*. Edited by Gil Anidjar, 42–101. Translated by Samuel Weber. New York: Routledge, 2002.

———. *The Gift of Death*. Translated by David Will. Chicago: University of Chicago Press, 1995.

———. *Margins of Philosophy*. Translated by Alan Bass. Chicago: University of Chicago Press, 1982.

———. *On Touching—Jean Luc Nancy*. Translated by Christine Irizarry. Stanford, Calif.: Stanford University Press, 2005.

———. *Politics of Friendship*. Translated by George Collins. London: Verso, 1997.

———. *Specters of Marx: The State of the Debt, the Work of Mourning, and the New International*. Translated by Peggy Kamuf. New York: Routledge, 1995.

———. *Speech and Phenomena and Other Essays on Husserl's Theory of Signs*. Evanston, Ill.: Northwestern University Press, 1973.

———, and Bernard Stiegler. *Echographies of Television*. Translated by Jennifer Bajorek. Cambridge, Mass.: Polity Press, 2002.

Descombes, Vincent. *The Barometer of Modern Reason: On the Philosophy of Current Events*. Translated by Stephen Adam Schwartz. New York: Oxford University Press, 1993.

Dunlop, R.H.W. *Service and Adventure with the Khakee Ressalah or, Meerut Volunteer Horse, during the Mutinies of 1857–58*. London: R. Bently, 1858.

Durán, Diego. *Historia de las Indias de la Nueva España e islas de Tierra Firme*. 2 vols. Edited by Angel María Garibay K. Mexico City: Editorial Porrúa, 1984 [c. 1581].

Eber, Christine, and Christine Kovic, eds. *Women in Chiapas: Making History in Times of Struggle and Hope*. New York: Routledge, 2003.

Ejercito Zapatista de Liberación Nacional (EZLN). Various documents available online at http://palabra.ezln.org.mx. Accessed on December 8, 2009.

El coraje del pueblo. Directed by Jorge Sanjinés. La RAI Radiotelevisione Italiana, 1971 (film).

"El Gobierno dice que invadir casas va contra la CPE." *La Razón*. March 12, 2009.

Errington, Shelly. "Progressivist Stories and the Pre-Columbian Past: Notes on Mexico and the United States." In *Collecting the Pre-Columbian Past*. Edited by Elizabeth Hill Boone, 209–51. Washington, D.C.: Dumbarton Oaks Research Library and Collection, 1993.

Escobar, Arturo. "Imagining a Post-Development Era? Critical Thought, Development, and Social Movements." *Social Text* 31–32 (1992): 20–56.

. . . *esta es nuestra palabra. . . . Testimonios de Acteal*. San Cristóbal de las Casas, Mexico: Centro de Derechos Humanos "Fray Bartolomé de las Casas," 1998.

Evans, Dylan. *An Introductory Dictionary of Lacanian Psychoanalysis*. London: Routledge, 1996.

Fabian, Johannes. *Time and the Other: How Anthropology Makes Its Object*. New York: Columbia University Press, 1983.

Florescano, Enrique. "The Creation of the Museo Nacional de Antropología of Mexico and Its Scientific, Educational, and Political Purposes." In *Collecting the Pre-Columbian Past*. Edited by Elizabeth Hill Boone, 49–81. Washington, D.C.: Dumbarton Oaks Research Library and Collection, 1993.

———. *Memoria mexicana*. Mexico City: Editorial Joaquín Mortiz, 1987.

Foucault, Michel. *The Archeology of Knowledge*. Translated by A. M. Sheridan Smith. New York: Harper Torchbooks, 1972.

———. *Madness and Civilization*. Translated by Richard Howard. New York: Vintage, 1973.

———. *The Order of Things: An Archeology of the Human Sciences*. New York: Vintage Books, 1973.

———. *Power/Knowledge: Selected Interviews and Other Writings, 1972–1977*. Edited by Colin Gordon. Translated by Colin Gordon et al. New York: Pantheon, 1980.

———. "What Is an Author?" In *The Foucault Reader*. Edited by Paul Rabinow, 101–20. New York: Pantheon, 1984.

———. "What Is Enlightenment? In *The Foucault Reader*. Edited by Paul Rabinow, 32–50. New York: Pantheon, 1984.

García Canclini, Nestor, et al., eds. *De lo local a lo global: Perspectivas desde la antropología*. Mexico City: Universidad Autónoma Metropolitana, 1994.

Garcia Icazbalceta, Joaquin, ed. *Colección de documentors para la historia de México*. 2 vols. Mexico City: Editorial Ponría, 1971.

García Linera, Alvaro. "Democracia multinacional y multi-institucional." Available online at http://aymara.org/listarchives/archivo2003/msg00129.html. Accessed on June 29, 2009.

———. "El ocaso de un ciclo estatal." In *Democratizaciones Plebeyas*. Edited by Raquel Gutiérrez et al., 147–76. La Paz: Muela del Diablo Editores, 2002.

———. *Estado multinacional: Una propuesta democratica y pluralista para la extinción de la exclusión indígena.* La Paz: Editorial Malatesta, 2005.

———. "State Crisis and Popular Power." *New Left Review* 37 (2006): 73–85.

García Martínez, Bernardo, ed. *Los pueblos de indios y las comunidades.* Mexico City: El Colegio de México, 1991.

García, Genaro. *Tumultos y rebeliones acaecidos en México: Documentos inéditos o muy raros para la historia de México.* 36 vols. Vol. 10. Mexico City: Viuda de C. Bouret, 1993.

García, José Alejos. *Ch'ol/Kaxlan: Identidades étnicas y conflicto agrario en el norte de Chiapas, 1914–1940.* Mexico City: Universidad Nacional Autónoma de México, 1999.

Garrido, Luis Javier. "La resistencia." *La Jornada*, September 22, 1995.

Gerhard, Peter. *Geografía histórica de la Nueva España, 1519–1821.* Translated by Stella Mastrangelo. Mexico City: Universidad Nacional Autónoma de México, 1986.

Gibler, John. *Mexico Unconquered: Chronicles of Power and Revolt.* San Francisco: City Lights, 2009.

Goodman, Nelson. *Ways of Worldmaking.* Indianapolis, Ind.: Hackett Publishing, 1978.

Gossen, Gary H. "From Omecs to Zapatistas: A Once and Future History of Souls." *American Anthropologist* 96 (1994): 553–570.

Gramsci, Antonio. "Alcuni temi della quistioni meridionale." In *Scritti politici.* Edited by Paola Spriano. Roma: Editori Riuniti, 1967.

———. *Prison Notebooks.* 2 vols. Edited and with an introduction by Joseph A. Buttigieg. Translated by Joseph A. Buttigieg and Antonio Callari. New York: Columbia University Press, 1992.

———. *Quaderni del carcere.* 4 vols. Critical edition by the Istituto Gramsci under the direction of Valentino Gerratana. Torino: Giulio Einaudi editore, 1975.

———. *Scritti politti.* Edited by Paola Spriano. Rome: Edition Reuniti, 1967.

———. *Selections from Cultural Writings.* Edited by David Forgacs and Geoffrey Nowell-Smith. Translated by William Boelhower. Cambridge: Harvard University Press, 1985.

———. *Selections from the Prison Notebooks.* Edited and translated by Quentin Hoare and Geoffrey Nowell Smith. New York: International Publishers, 1971.

———. *The Southern Question.* Translated and with an introduction by Pasquale Verdicchio. West Lafayette, Ind.: Bordighera, 1995.

Gruzinski, Serge. *The Conquest of Mexico: The Incorporation of Indian Society into the Western World, Sixteenth–Eighteenth Centuries.* Translated by Eileen Corrigan. Cambridge, Mass.: Polity Press, 1993.

———. *The Mestizo Mind: The Intellectual Dynamics of Colonization and Globalization.* Translated by Deke Dusinberre. New York: Routledge, 2002.

Gugelberger, George M., ed. *The Real Thing: Testimonial Discourse and Latin America.* Durham, N.C.: Duke University Press, 1996

Guha, Ranajit. *Dominance without Hegemony: History and Power in Colonial India.* Cambridge: Harvard University Press, 1997.

———. "Domination without Hegemony and Its Historiography." In *Subaltern Studies* 6. Edited by Ranajit Guha, 210–309. Dehli: Oxford University Press, 1989.

———. *Elementary Aspects of Peasant Insurgency in Colonial India.* Delhi: Oxford University Press, 1983.

———. *History at the Limit of World-History.* New York: Columbia University Press, 2002.

——. "Not at Home in Empire." *Critical Inquiry* 23, no. 3 (Spring 1997): 482–93.

——. "On Some Aspects of the Historiography of Colonial India." In *Selected Subaltern Studies*. Edited by Ranajit Guha and Gayatri Chakravorty Spivak, 37–44. New York: Oxford University Press, 1988.

——. "Preface." In *Selected Subaltern Studies*. Edited by Ranajit Guha and Gayatri Chakravorty Spivak, 35–36. New York: Oxford University Press, 1988.

——. "The Prose of Counter-Insurgency." In *Selected Subaltern Studies*. Edited by Ranajit Guha and Gayatri Chakravorty Spivak, 45–86. New York: Oxford University Press, 1988.

——, and Gayatri Chakravorty Spivak, eds. *Selected Subaltern Studies*. New York: Oxford University Press, 1988.

Guillermoprieto, Alma. "The Shadow of War." *The New York Review of Books* 42, no. 4 (1995): 34–43.

Gutiérrez, Raquel, et al., eds. *Democratizaciones Plebeyas*. La Paz: Muela del Diablo Editores, 2002.

Halberstam, Judith. "Imagined Violence/Queer Violence: Representation, Rage, and Resistance." *Social Text* 37 (1993): 187–201.

Hamacher, Werner. "One 2 Many Multiculturalisms." In *Violence, Identity, and Self-determination*. Edited by Hent de Vries amd Samuel Weber, 284–325. Stanford, Calif.: Stanford University Press, 1997.

Hanks, William F. *Converting Words: Maya in the Age of the Cross*. Berkeley: University of California Press, 2010.

Haraway, Donna. "The Promises of Monsters: A Regenerative Politics for Inappropriate/d Others." In *Cultural Studies Reader*. Edited by Lawrence Grossberg, Cary Nelson, and Paula Treichler, 295–337. New York: Routledge, 1992.

Hardt, Michael. "Into the Factory: Negri's Lenin and the Subjective Caesura (1968–73)." In *The Philosophy of Antonio Negri: Resistance in Practice*. Edited by Timothy S. Murphy and Abdul-Karim Mustapha, 7–37. London: Pluto Press, 2005.

Hardt, Michael, and Antonio Negri. *Empire*. Cambridge: Harvard University Press, 2000.

——. *Labor of Dionysus: Communism as Critique of the Capitalist and Socialist State-Forms*. Minneapolis: University of Minnesota Press, 1994.

——. *Multitude: War and Democracy in the Age of Empire*. New York: Penguin Press, 2004.

Hegel, G.W.F. *The Phenomenology of Mind*. Translated by J. B. Baillie. New York: Harper Torchbooks, 1967.

Henríquez, Elio, and Cirio Pérez Silva. "La contraparte 'ha querido engáñamos': *Ramon*; en la selva fundarán otro Tepeyac." *La Jornada*. June 10, 1995.

Hernández Castillo, Rosalva Aída. *La otra palabra: Mujeres y violencia en Chiapas, antes y después de Acteal*. Mexico City: CIESAS, 1998.

Hernández Navarro, Luis, and Ramón Vera Herrera, eds. *Acuerdos de San Andrés*. Mexico City: Ediciones Era, 1998.

Higgins, Nick. *Understanding Chiapas: Modernist Visions and the Invisible Indian*. Austin: University of Texas Press, 2004.

Hill, Jane, and Bruce Mannheim. "Language and World View." *Annual Review of Anthropology* 21 (1992): 381–406.

Hiriales, Gustavo. *Camino a Acteal*. Mexico City: Rayuela Editores, 1998.

Hobsbawn, Eric. *Social Bandits and Primitive Rebels: Studies in Archaic Forms of Social Movement in 19th and 20th centuries*. Glencoe, Ill.: Free Press, 1959.

———, and George Rudé. *Captain Swing: Social History of the Great English Agricultural Uprising of 1830*. New York: Norton, 1975.

Holloway, John. "Caracoles: El realismo mágico y los agujeros en el ozono." *Revista Memoria* 176 (October 2003). Available online at http://memoria.com.mx. Accessed on June 25, 2009.

———. *Change the World without Taking Power: The Meaning of Revolution Today*. London: Pluto Press, 2002.

Holsinger, Bruce. "Indigeneity: Panofsky, Bourdieu, and the Archaeology of the *Habitus*." In Bruce Holsinger, *The Premodern Condition: Medievalism and the Making of Theory*. 94–113. Chicago: University of Chicago Press, 2005.

Howe, Kathleen Steward. "The Relationship of Indigenous and European Styles in the *Codex Mendoza*: An Analysis of Pictorial Style." In *Codex Mendoza*. Edited by Frances F. Berdan and Patricia Rieff Anawalt. 4 vols. Vol. 1, 25–33. Berkeley: University of California Press, 1992.

Iglesia, Rámon. "La mexicanidad de Don Carlos de Sigüenza y Góngora." *El hombre Colón y otros ensayos*. Mexico City: El Colegio de México, 1944.

Ileto, Reynaldo Clemeña. *Pasyon and Revolution: Popular Movements in the Philippines, 1840–1910*. Quezon City, Philippines: Ateneo de Manila University Press, 1979.

Ixtlilxochitl, Fernando Alva. *Obras históricas*. Edited by Edmundo O'Gorman. 2 vols. Mexico City: Universidad Nacional Autónoma de México, 1975–1977.

James, C.L.R. *Black Jacobins: Toussaint L'Ouverture and the San Domingo Revolution*. Second revised edition. New York: Vintage, 1962.

Jameson, Frederic. *A Singular Modernity: Essay on the Ontology of the Present*. London: Verso, 2002.

Kant, Immanuel. "An Answer to the Question: What Is Enlightenment?" In *Emmanuel Kant, Practical Philosophy*. Translated by Mary J. Gregor, 11–22. Cambridge: Cambridge University Press, 1996.

———. *Critique of Judgment*. Translated by Werner S. Pluhar. Indianapolis, Ind.: Hackett Publishing, 1987.

———. *Toward Perpetual Peace: A Philosophical Project*. In *Practical Philosophy*. Translated by Mary J. Gregor, 317–51. Cambridge: Cambridge University Press, 1996.

Karatani, Kojin. *Transcritique: On Kant and Marx*. Translated by Sabu Kohso. Cambridge: Massachusetts Institute of Technology Press, 2005.

Keber, Eloise Quiñones, ed. *Codex Telleriano-Remensis: Ritual, Divination, and History in a Pictorial Aztec Manuscript*. Austin: University of Texas Press, 1996.

Kempis, Thomas á. *Of the Imitation of Christ*. Translated by Abbot Justin McCann. New York: Mentor Edition, 1957.

Kentridge, William. *Five Themes*. Edited by Mark Rosenthal. Essays by Michael Auping et al. Includes videorecording. San Francisco: San Francisco Museum of Modern Art, 2009.

Kierkegaard, Sören. *Fear and Trembling* and *Repetition*. Translated by Howard V. Hong and Edna H. Hong. Princeton, N.J.: Princeton University Press, 1983.

———. *La répétition*. In *Oeuvres complètes*. Vol. 5. Edited by Paul-Henri Tisseau and Else-Marie Jacquet-Tisseau. Paris: Éditions de L'Orante, 1972.

Kirchhoff, Paul, Lina Odema Güemes, and Luis Reyes, eds. *Historia Tolteca-Chichimeca.* Mexico City: INAH-SEP, 1976.

Klor de Alva, J. Jorge. "Colonialism and Postcolonialism as (Latin) American Mirages." *Colonial American Review* 1, nos. 1–2 (1992): 3–23.

Knight, Alan. *The Mexican Revolution.* 2 vols. Cambridge: Cambridge University Press, 1986.

Lacan, Jacques. "Of the Gaze as *objet petit a.*" In *The Seminar of Jacques Lacan, Book 11: The Four Fundamental Concepts of Psychoanalyis.* Edited by Jacques-Alain Miller, 67–119. Translated by Alan Sheridan. New York: W. W. Norton, 1998.

———. *Seminaire XVII: L'envers de la psychanalyse* Paris: Seuil, 1991.

———. "The Topic of the Imaginary." In *The Seminar of Jacques Lacan, Book 1: Freud's Papers on Technique, 1953–1954.* Edited by Jacques-Alain Miller, 73–106. Translated by John Forrester. New York: W. W. Norton, 1991.

Laclau, Ernesto. *Politics and Ideology in Marxist Theory.* London: New Left Books, 1977.

La Guillotina. La Guillotina 30 (March–April 1995).

La Jornada. Available online at http://www.jornada.unam.mx. Accessed on December 9, 2009.

Lal, Vinay. *The History of History: Politics and Scholarship in Modern India.* New York: Oxford University Press, 2001.

———. "Subaltern Studies and Its Critics: Debates over India." *History and Theory* 40, no. 1 (2001): 135–48.

Larsen, Neil. *Reading North by South: On Latin American Literature, Culture, and Politics.* Minneapolis: University of Minnesota Press, 1995.

La saison des hommes. Directed by Moufida Tlatli. Paris: Editions Montparnasse, 2000 (film).

Las Casas, Bartolomé. *Apologética historia sumaria.* Edited by Edmundo O'Gorman. Mexico City: Universidad Nacional Autónoma de México, 1967 [c. 1559].

———. *Brevísima relación de la destrucción de las Indias.* Edited by André Saint-Lu. Madrid: Cátedra, 2001 [1552].

———. *De unico vocationis modo omnium gentium ad veram religionem.* Edited by and translated by Paulino Castañeda Delgado and Antonio García del Moral. In *Obras completas.* Vol. 2. Madrid: Alianza Editorial, 1988 [c. 1534].

———. *El tratado de las "Doce Dudas."* In *Obras completas.* Edited by J. B. Lassegue, O. P. Vol. 11.2. Madrid: Editorial Alianza, 1992 [c. 1566].

Latin American Subaltern Studies Group (LASSG). "Founding Statement." Subaltern Studies in the Americas. Special issue of *Dispositio/n* 46 (1994): 1–11. Edited by José Rabasa, Javier Sanjinés, and Robert Carr.

Latour, Bruno. 1999. *Pandora's Hope: Essays on the Reality of Science Studies.* Cambridge: Harvard University Press, 1999.

———. *We Have Never Been Modern.* Translated by Catherine Porter. Cambridge: Harvard University Press, 1993.

La Voz de Cerro Hueco. Communiqué released on May 24, 2002. Available online at http://www.palabra.org.mx. Accessed on December 9, 2009.

Le Bot, Yvon. *Le rêve zapatista: Sous-commandant Marcos.* Paris: Seuil, 1997.

Lenin, V. I. *Collected Works.* Moscow: Progress Publishers, 1964.

———. *Essential Works of Lenin: "What Is to Be Done?" and Other Writings.* Edited by Henry M. Christman. New York: Dover, 1987.

————. "'Left-Wing' Childishness and the Petty-Bourgeois Mentality." Translated by Clemens Dutt. In Lenin, *Collected Works*, vol. 27, 323–54.

————. *Letters on Tactics*. Translated by Isaacs Bernard. In Lenin, *Collected Works*, vol. 24, 42–54.

————. *The State and Revolution*. Translated by Stepan Apresyan and Jim Riordan. In Lenin, *Collected Works*, vol. 25, 381–492.

————. "The Task of the Proletariat in the Present Revolution" (The April Theses). Translated by Isaacs Bernard. In Lenin, *Collected Works*, vol. 24, 19–26.

————. *What Is to Be Done?*. In Lenin, *Essential Works of Lenin*, 53–175.

León Portilla, Miguel. *Francisco Tenamaztle, primer guerrillero de América, defensor de los derechos humanos*. Second revised edition of *La flecha en el blanco*. Mexico City: Editorial Diana, 2005.

————. *La flecha en el blanco. Francisco Tenamaztle y Bartolomé de las Casas en lucha por los derechos de los indígenas, 1541–1556*. Mexico City: Editorial Diana, 1995.

————. *Literaturas indígenas de México*. Mexico City: Fondo de Cultura Económica, 1992.

————. *Quince poetas del mundo náhuatl*. Mexico City: Editorial Diana, 1994.

————. "¿Una nueva interpretación de los Cantares Mexicanos?" *Estudios de Cultura Náhuatl* 18 (1986): 385–400.

Leonard, Irving A. *Don Carlos de Sigüenza y Góngora: A Mexican Savant of the Seventeenth Century*. Berkeley: University of California Press, 1929.

Leyva, Rubén. *Memorial de agravios Oaxaca, México, 2006*. Oaxaca: Marabú Ediciones, 2006.

Lloyd, David. *Anomalous States: Irish Writing and the Post-colonial Moment*. Durham, N.C.: Duke University Press, 1993.

————. *Ireland after History*. Notre Dame: University of Notre Dame Press, 1999.

————. "Rage against the Divine." *South Atlantic Quarterly* 106, no. 2 (Spring 2007): 345–72.

Lockhart, James. *We People Here: Nahuatl Accounts of the Conquest of Mexico*. Berkeley: University of California Press, 1998.

Lomnitz, Claudio. "La decadencia en los tiempos de la globalización." In *De lo local a lo global: Perspectivas desde la antropología*. Edited by Nestor García Canclini et al., 88–101. Mexico City: Universidad Autónoma Metropolitana, 1994.

————. *Las salidas del laberinto*. Translated by Cinna Lomnitz. Mexico City: Joaquín Mortiz, 1995.

Luhmann, Niklas. *Observations on Modernity*. Translated by William Whobrey. Stanford, Calif.: Stanford University Press, 1998.

Lucy, John. "The Scope of Linguistic Relativity." In *Rethinking Linguistic Relativity*. Edited by John J. Gumperz and Stephen C. Levinson, 37–69. Cambridge: Cambridge University Press, 1996.

A Massacre Foretold. Directed by Nick Higgins. Glasgow: Landsdowne Productions 2007 (film).

Marin, Louis. *Utopics: Spatial Play*. Translated by Robert A. Vollrath. Atlantic Heights, N.J.: Humanities Press, 1984.

Marion, Jean-Luc. *In Excess: Studies of Saturated Phenomena*. Translated by Robyn Horner and Vincent Berraud. New York: Fordham University Press, 2002.

Marks, Laura V. *Touch: Sensuous Theory and Multisensory Media*. Minneapolis: University of Minnesota Press, 2002.

Martin, JoAnn. "Contesting Authenticity: Battles over the Representation of History in Morelos, Mexico." *Ethnohistory* 40, no. 3 (Summer 1993): 438–65.

Marx, Karl. "The Civil War in France." In *The First International and After: Political Writings*. Vol. 3. Edited by David Fernbach, 187–268. New York: Penguin, 1974.

———. *A Contribution to the Critique of Political Economy*. Edited by Maurice Dobb. Translated by S. W. Ryazanskaya. London: Lawrence & Wishart. Moscow: Progress Publishers, 1970.

———. "Drafts of the Letter to Vera Zasulich." In Karl Marx and Friedrich Engels, *Collected Works*. Vol. 24, 346–71. London: Lawrence & Wishart and Progress Publishers, 1989.

———. *The First International and After: Political Writings*. Vol. 3. Edited by David Fernbach. New York: Penguin, 1974.

———, and Friedrich Engels. *Collected Works*. 24 vols. London: Lawrence & Wishart. Moscow: Progress Publishers, 1989.

———. *The Marx-Engels Reader*. Edited by Robert C. Tucker. New York: Norton, 1978.

Menchú, Rigoberta. *Me llamo Rigoberta Menchú, y así me nació la conciencia*. Edited by Elizabeth Burgos-Delray. Mexico City: Siglo XXI, 1985.

Mignolo, Walter D. *Global Designs, Local Histories*. Princeton, N.J.: Princeton University Press, 2000.

Millán, Márgara. "Chiapas y sus mujeres indígenas: De su diversidad y resistencia." *Revista Chiapas* 4 (1997). Available online at http://www.revistachiapas.org/No4/ch4.html. Accessed on December 7, 2009.

———. "Las zapatistas del fin del milenio: Hacia políticas de autorepresentación de las mujeres indígenas." *Revista Chiapas* 3 (1996). Available online at http://www.revistachiapas.org/No3/ch3.html. Accessed on June 25, 2009.

Molina, Alonso de. *Vocabulario en lengua castellana y mexicana y mexicana y castellana*. Edited by Miguel León Portilla. Facsimile edition. Mexico City: Editorial Porrúa, 1992 [1571].

Monsiváis, Carlos. "Marcos, gran interlocutor." *La Jornada*. January 8, 2001. Also available online at http://www.jornada.unam.mx. Accessed on December 9, 2009.

———. "¿Todos somos indios?" *La Journada*. February 17, 1995.

Moore, Robert I. *The Formation of a Persecuting Society*. Oxford: Blackwell, 1990.

Mora, Mariana. "Decolonizing Politics: Zapatista Autonomy in an Era of Neoliberal Governance and Low Intensity Conflict." Ph.D. dissertation. Department of Anthropology. University of Texas at Austin, 2007.

Morales Padrón, Francisco. *Teoría y leyes de la conquista*. Madrid: Ediciones Cultura Hispánica del Centro Iberoamericano de Cooperación, 1979.

Moraña, Mabel, et al., eds. *Coloniality at Large: Latin America and the Postcolonial Debate*. Durham, N.C.: Duke University Press, 2008.

Moraña, Mabel, ed. *Nuevas perspectivas desde/Sobre América Latina: El desafío de los estudios culturales*. Santiago: Editorial Cuarto Propio, 2000.

———. *Relecturas del Barroco de Indias*. Hanover, N.H.: Ediciones del Norte, 1994.

Motolinía, Toribio de Benavente. *Memoriales o libro de las cosas de la Nueva España*. Edited by Edmundo O'Gorman. Mexico City: Universidad Nacional Autónoma de México, 1971.

Mundy, Barbara. *The Mapping of New Spain: Indigenous Cartography and the Maps of the Relaciones Geográficas*. Chicago: University of Chicago Press, 1996.

Muñoz Ramírez, Gloria. *EZLN: 20 y 10, el fuego y la palabra*. Mexico City: Ediciones La Jornada, 2003.

———. *El fuego y la palabra: Una historia del EZLN*. San Francisco: City Lights, 2008.

———. *The Fire and the Word: A History of the EZLN*. San Francisco: City Lights, 2008.

Murphy, Timothy S., and Abdul-Karim Mustapha, eds. *The Philosophy of Antonio Negri: Resistance in Practice*. London: Pluto Press, 2005.

———. *The Philosophy of Antonio Negri: Revolution in Theory*. London: Pluto Press, 2007.

Mutman, Mahmut. "Difference, Event, Subject: Antonio Negri's Political Theory of Postmodern Metaphysics." In *The Philosophy of Antonio Negri: Revolution in Theory*. Edited by Timothy S. Murphy and Abdul-Karim Mustapha, 143–68. London: Pluto Press, 2007.

Nancy, Jean-Luc. *The Creation of the World or Globalization*. Translated by François Raffoul and David Pettigrew. Albany, N.Y.: SUNY Press, 2007.

———. "Vox Clamans in Deserto." In *Multiple Arts: The Muses II*. Translated by Simon Sparks, 38–49. Stanford, Calif.: Stanford University Press, 2006.

Nandy, Ashis. "History's Forgotten Doubles." *History and Theory* 34, no. 2 (1995): 44–66.

Navarrete, Federico. "The Path from Aztlan to Mexico: On Visual Narration in Meso-american Codices." *Res* 37 (2000): 31–48.

Negri, Antonio. "Constituent Republic." Translated by Ed Emory. In *Radical Thought in Italy: A Potential Politics*. Edited by Paolo Virno and Michael Hardt, 213–21. Minneapolis: University of Minnesota Press, 1996.

———. *Il potere costituente*. Carnago, Italy: SugarCo, 1992.

———. *Insurgencies: Constituent Power and the Modern State*. Translated by Maurizia Boscagli. Minneapolis: University of Minnesota Press, 1999.

———. *The Politics of Subversion*. Translated by James Newell. Oxford: Polity Press, 1989.

———. *The Savage Anomaly: The Power of Spinoza's Metaphysics and Politics*. Translated by Michael Hardt. Minneapolis: University of Minnesota Press, 1991.

———. "The Specter's Smile." In *Ghostly Demarcations: A Symposium on Jacques Derrida's Specters of Marx*. Edited by Michael Springer, 5–16. London: Verso, 1999.

Nietszche, Friedrich. *The Use and Abuse of History*. Translated by Adrian Collins. Indianapolis, Ind.: Library of Liberal Arts, Bob Merrill, 1979.

Orozco y Berra, Manuel. *Historia antigua y de la conquista de México*. 4 vols. Mexico City: Tipografía de G. A. Esteva, 1880.

Ortiz, Teresa. *Never Again a World without Us: Voices of Mayan Women in Chiapas, Mexico*. Washington, D.C.: Epica, 2001.

Osorno, Diego. *Oaxaca Sitiada: La primera insurrección del siglo XXI*. Mexico City: Grijalbo, 2007.

Panaccio, Claude. "Intuition, abstraction et langage mental dans la théorie occamiste de la connaissance." *Revue de métaphysique et de morale* 97, no. 1 (1992): 61–81.

Pandey, Gyanendra. *Routine Violence: Nations, Fragments, Histories*. Stanford, Calif.: Stanford University Press, 2006.

Parish, Helen, and Harold E. Weidman. *Las Casas en Mexico. Historia y obra desconocidos*. Mexico City: Fondo de Cultura Económica, 1992.

Pashukanis, Evgeny Bronislavovich. *The General Theory of Law and Marxism*. New Brunswick, N.J.: Transaction Publishers, 2002.

———. "The Marxist Theory of Law and the Construction of Socialism." In *Pashukanis: Selected Writings on Marxism and Law*. Edited by Piers Beirne and Robert Sharlet. New York: Academic Press, 1980 [1927].

Paz, Octavio. *Sor Juana Inés de la Cruz, o, las trampas de la fe*. Barcelona: Seix Barral, 1982.

Peterson, David A. "The Real Cholula." *Notas mesoamericanas* 10 (1987): 71–117.

Prada, Raúl. "Multitud y contrapoder." In *Democratizaciones Plebeyas*. Edited by Raquel Gutiérrez et al., 75–146. La Paz: Muela del Diablo Editores, 2002.

Pratt, Mary Louise. *Imperial Eyes: Travel Narrative and Transculturation*. New York: Routledge, 1992.

Procesos de indios idólatras y hechiceros. Vol. 3, 53–78. Mexico City: Publicaciones del Archivo General de la Nación, 1912.

Procuraduría General de la República. *El libro blanco sobre Acteal*. Mexico City: Procuraduría General de la República, 1998.

Rabasa, José. "Aesthetics of Colonial Violence: The Massacre of Acoma in Gaspar de Villagrá's *Historia de la nueva México*." *College Literature* 20, no. 3 (1993): 96–114.

———. "Allegories of Atlas." In *Inventing America: Spanish Historiography and the Formation of Eurocentrism*, 180–209. Norman: University of Oklahoma Press, 1993.

———. "The Colonial Divide." *Journal of Medieval and Early Modern Studies* 37, no. 3 (Fall 2007): 511–29. Special issue on "Medieval/Renaissance: Rethinking Periodization." Edited by Jennifer Summit and David Wallace.

———. "Ecografías de la voz en la historiografía Nahua." *Historia y Grafia* 25 (2006): 105–51.

———. "Elsewheres: Radical Relativism and the Frontiers of Empire." *Qui Parle* 16, no. 1 (2006): 71–94.

———. *Franciscans and Dominicans under the Gaze of Tlacuilo: Plural-World Dwelling in an Indian Pictorial Codex*. Morrison Library Inaugural Address Series 14. Berkeley: Doe Library, University of California at Berkeley, 1998.

———. *Inventing America: Spanish Historiography and the Formation of Eurocentrism*. Norman: University of Oklahoma Press, 1993.

———. "'Porque soy Indio': Subjectivity in *La Florida del Inca*." *Poetics Today* 16, no. 2 (1995): 78–108.

———. "Utopian Ethnology in Las Casas's *Apologética*." In *1492–1992: Re/Discovering Colonial Writing*. Edited by Ren Jara and Nicholas Spadaccini. Hispanic Issues 4. Minneapolis: The Prisma Institute, 1989.

———. *Writing Violence on the Northern Frontier: The Historiography of Sixteenth-century New Mexico and Florida and the Legacy of Conquest*. Durham, N.C.: Duke University Press, 2000.

Rabasa, José, Javier Sanjinés, and Robert Carr, eds. *Subaltern Studies in the Americas*. Special issue of *Dispositio/n* 46 (1994).

Rabasa, Magali. "New Social Movements—New Testimonio: Latin American Women and the Negotiation of Identity in Representation." Undergraduate honors thesis for the International Studies Program. University of Oregon, 2004.

Rabinow, Paul. *Anthropos Today: Reflections on Modern Equipment*. Princeton, N.J.: Princeton University Press, 2003.

Rama, Ángel. *La ciudad letrada*. Hanover, N.H.: Ediciones del Norte, 1984.

———. *The Lettered City*. Edited and translated by John Charles Chasteen. Durham, N.C.: Duke University Press, 1996.

Ramos, Julio. *Desencuentros de la modernidad: Literatura y política en el siglo XIX*. Mexico City: Fondo de Cultura Económica, 1989.

Ranger, Terence. "Power, Religion, and Community: The Matobo Case." In *Subaltern Studies 7*. Edited by Partha Chatterjee and Gyanendra Pandey, 221–46. Delhi: Oxford University Press, 1993.

Revista Memoria. Available online at http://memoria.com.mx. Accessed on June 25, 2009.

Rimbaud, Arthur. *Rimbaud: Complete Works, Selected Letters: A Bilingual Edition*. Translated by Wallace Fowlie. Updated and revised by Seth Widden. Chicago: University of Chicago Press, 2005.

Rivera Cusicanqui, Silvia, and Rossana Barragán, eds. *Debates postcoloniales: Una introducción a los estudios de la subalternidad*. La Paz: Editorial historias, 1997.

Robertson, Donald. *Mexican Manuscript Painting of the Early Colonial Period: The Metropolitan School*. New Haven, Conn.: Yale University Press, 1959.

Rodríguez, Ileana Rodríguez, ed. *Convergencia de Tiempos*. Amsterdam: Rodopi, 2002.

——, ed. *The Latin American Subaltern Studies Reader*. Durham, N.C.: Duke University Press, 2001.

Rodríguez, José Angel. *Lok'tavanej, cazador de imágenes*. N.p.: La Casa de las Imágenes/Conaculta-Fonca, 2002.

Rojas, Rosa. *Chiapas: La paz violenta*. Mexico City: La Jornada Ediciones, 1995

Román, José Antonio. "No basta cancelar el campo de golf: CUT." *La Jornada*, April 14, 1996. Available online at www.jornada.unam.mx. Accessed on December 9, 2009.

Romero, César. *Marcos: ¿Un profesional de la esperanza?* Mexico City: Editorial Planeta, 1994.

Ross, John. *Rebellion from the Roots: Indian Uprising in Chiapas*. Monroe, Me.: Common Courage Press, 1995.

Ross, Kathleen. "Alboroto y motín de México." *Hispanic Review* 55 (1988): 181–90.

——. *The Baroque Narrative of Carlos de Sigüenza y Góngora*. Cambridge: Cambridge University Press, 1993.

Rovira, Guiomar. *Mujeres de maíz*. Mexico City: Biblioteca Era, 1997.

Sahagún, Bernardino de. *Coloquios y doctrina con los doce frailes de San Francisco enviados por el papa Adriano VI y por el emperador Carlos V, conviertieron a los indios de la Nueva España. En lengua mexicana y española*. Fascimile. Edited and translated by Miguel León Portilla. Mexico City: Universidad Nacional Autonoma de México, 1986.

——. *Florentine Codex: General History of the Thing of New Spain*, 13 parts. Edited and translated by Charles E. Dibble and Arthur J. O. Anderson. Salt Lake City: University of Utah; Santa Fe: Museum of New Mexico, 1950–82.

Saignes, Thierry. "Borracheras andinas: ¿Por qué los indios ebrios hablan en español?" *Revista Andina* 7, no. 1 (1989): 83–123.

Saldaña-Portillo, María Josefina. *The Revolutionary Imagination in the Americas and the Age of Development*. Durham, N.C.: Duke University Press, 2003.

Sanford, Victoria. "Introduction." In *Engaged Observer: Anthropology, Advocacy, and Activism*. Edited by Victoria Sanford and Asale Angel-Ajani. New Brunswick, N.J.: Rutgers University Press, 2006.

Sanjinés, Jorge. *Teoría y práctica de un cine junto al pueblo*. Mexico City: Siglo Veintiuno, 1976.

——. *Theory and Practice of a Cinema with the People*. Translated by Richard Schaaf. Willimantic, Conn.: Curbstone Press, 1989.

Sarlo, Beatriz. *Tiempo pasado: Cultura de la memoria y giro subjectivo, Una discusión*. Buenos Aires: Siglo Veintiuno, 2005.

Schmitt, Carl. *Political Theology: Four Chapters on the Concept of Sovereignty*. Translated by George Schwab. Chicago: University of Chicago Press, 2005.

Schroeder, Susan. *Chimalpahin and the Kingdoms of Chalco*. Tucson: University of Arizona Press, 1991.

Schwarz, Henry. "Laissez-Faire Linguistics: Grammar and the Codes of Empire." *Critical Inquiry* 23 (Summer 1997): 509–35.

Searle, John R. *The Construction of Social Reality*. New York: The Free Press, 1995.

Seler, Eduard. "Wall Paintings of Mitla: A Mexican Picture Writing in Fresco." In *Eduard Seler: Collected Works in Mesoamerican Linguistics and Archaeology*. 4 vols. Translated by Charles P. Bowditch. Vol. 1, 247–324. Culver City, Calif.: Labyrinthos, 1990–93.

Sen, S. N. *Eighteen-Fifty-Seven*. Foreword by Maulana Abul Kalam Azad. Delhi: Publications Division, Ministry of Information and Broadcasting, Government of India, 1957.

Sigüenza y Góngora, Carlos. *Alboroto y motín de los indios de México. Seis obras*. Edited by William G. Bryant. Caracas, Venezuela: Biblioteca Ayacucho, 1984.

———. *Alboroto y motín de los indios de México, 30 de agosto de 1692*. Edited by Irving A. Leonard. Mexico City: Talleres Gráficos del Museo Nacional de Arqueología, Historia y Etnografía, 1932.

Silverstein, Ken, and Alexander Cockburn. "The Killers and the Killing." *The Nation* 260, no. 9 (1995): 306–11.

Sommer, Doris. *Proceed with Caution, When Engaged by Minority Writing in the Americas*. Cambridge: Harvard University Press, 1999.

———. "Resisting the Heat: Menchú, Morrison, and Incompetent Readers." In *Cultures of U.S. Imperialism*. Edited by Amy Kaplan and Donald E. Pease, 407–32. Durham, N.C.: Duke University Press, 1993.

Spinosa, Charles, and Hubert Dreyfus. "Two Kinds of Antiessentialism and Their Consequences." *Critical Inquiry* 22 (Summer 1996): 735–63.

Spivak, Gayatri Chakravorty. "Can the Subaltern Speak?" In *Marxism and the Interpretation of Cultures*. Edited by Cary Nelson and Lawrence Grossberg, 271–313. Urbana: University of Illinois Press, 1988.

———. *A Critique of Postcolonial Reason: Toward a History of the Vanishing Present*. Cambridge: Harvard University Press, 1999.

———. *Death of a Discipline*. New York: Columbia University Press, 2003.

———. "The Politics of Translation." In Gayatri Chakravorty Spivak, *Outside in the Teaching Machine*, 179–200. New York: Routledge, 1993.

———. "Subaltern Studies: Deconstructing Historiography." In Gayatri Chakravorty Spivak, *In Other Worlds: Essays in Cultural Politics*, 197–221. New York: Routledge, 1988.

———. "Supplementing Marx." In *Whither Marxism?: Global Crises in International Perspective*. Edited by Bernd Magnus and Stephen Cullenberg, 109–19. New York: Routledge, 1995.

Stavenhagen, Rodolfo. "Clases, colonialismo y aculturación." *America Latina* 6, no. 4 (1963): 63–104.

———. *Derechos indígenas y derechos humanos en América Latina*. Mexico City: El Colegio de México and Instituto Interamericano de Derechos Humanos, 1988.

Stoll, David. *Rigoberta Menchú and the Story of All Poor Guatemalans*. Boulder, Colo.: Westview Press, 1999.

Swanton, Michael. 2001. "El texto popoloca de la *Historia tolteca-chichimeca*." *Relaciones* 86, no. 22 (2001): 114–29.

Taussig, Michael. *Magic of the State*. New York: Routledge, 1997.

Tavanti, Marco. *Las Abejas: Pacifist Resistance and Syncretic Identities in a Globalizing Chiapas*. New York: Routledge, 2003.

Taylor, Charles. *Multiculturalism: Examining the Politics of Recognition*. Edited and introduction by Amy Gutman. Princeton, N.J.: Princeton University Press, 1994.

Tello, Antonio. *Crónica miscelánea de la Sancta Provincia de Xalisco. Libro Segundo*. 2 vols. Guadalajara: Gobierno del Estado de Jalisco. Universidad de Guadalajara, Instituto Nacional de Antropología e Historia (INAH) and Instituto Jaliscience de Antropología e Historia (IJAH), 1968 [1653].

———. *Fragmentos de una historia de la Nueva Galicia*. In *Colección de documentos para la historia de Mexico*. Edited by Joaquín García Icazbalceta, vol. 2, 375–438. Facsimile edition. Mexico City: Editorial Porrúa, 1971 [1858–66].

Teología India Mayense: Memorias, experiencias y reflexiones de encuentros teológicos regionales. Mexico City: ABYA-YALA, 1993.

Teología India: Primer encuentro taller latinoamericano. Mexico City: CENAMI; and Quito: ABYA-YALA, 1991.

Terray, Emmanuel. *Le troisième jour du communisme*. Arles, France: Actes Sud, 1992.

Tezozomoc, Fernando Alvarado. *Chronica Mexicayotl*. Edited and translated by Adrián León. Mexico City: Universidad Nacional Autónoma de México, 1992 [1949].

"*Towards the Mountain*": *Chiapas: Prayer for the Weavers*. Directed by Judith Gleason. New York: Filmmakers Library, 1999 (film).

Trejo Delarbre, Raúl, ed. *Chiapas: La guerra de las ideas*. Mexico City: Editorial Diana, 1994.

Urzúa, Camú, and Tótoro Taulis. *EZLN, el ejercito que salió de la selva*. Mexico City: Grupo Editorial Planeta, 1994.

Vera Herrera, Ramón. "Relojes japoneses." *Ojarasca* 44 (1995): 20–25.

Vera Cruz, Alonso de la. *Relectio de dominio infidelium & justo bello. Relectio edita per Reverendum Patrem Alfonsum a Vera Cruce, Sacrae theologiae magistrum, Augustinianae familiae priorem, et cathedrae primariae eiusdem facultatis in Academia Mexicana regentem*. In *The Writings of Alonso de la Vera Cruz*. Vol. 2. Edited and translated by Ernest J. Burrus, S. J. Rome: Jesuit Historical Institute, 1968 [1553–54].

Verdesio, Gustavo. "Forgotten Territorialities: The Materiality of Indigenous Pasts." *Nepantla* 2, no. 1 (2001): 85–114.

———, ed. Special issue on Subaltern Studies. *Dispositio/n* 52 (2005).

Vidal-Naquet, Pierre. *Assassins of Memory: Essays on the Denial of the Holocaust*. Translated by Jeffrey Mehlman. New York: Columbia University Press, 1992.

———. "'Inquiry into a Massacre' by Amnon Kapeliouk." In *The Jews: History, Memory, and the Present*. Edited and translated by David Ames Curtis, 228–33. New York: Columbia University Press, 1996.

Viezzer, Moema. "*Si me permiten hablar . . .*": *Testimonio de Domitila una mujer de las minas de Bolivia*. Second revised edition. Mexico City: Siglo XXI, 1978.

———. *Let Me Speak! Testimony of Domitila, a Woman of the Bolivian Mines*. Translated by Victoria Ortiz. New York: Monthly Review Press, 1978.

Virno, Paolo. *A Grammar of the Multitude: For an Analysis of Contemporary Forms of Life.* Translated by Isabella Berloletti et al. Los Angeles: Semiotext(e), 2004.

———. "Do You Remember Counterrevolution?" Translated by Michael Hardt. In *Radical Thought in Italy: A Potential Politics.* Edited by Paolo Virno and Michael Hardt, 241–59. Minneapolis: University of Minnesota Press, 1996.

———, and Michael Hardt, eds. *Radical Thought in Italy: A Potential Politics.* Minneapolis: University of Minnesota Press, 1996.

Vos, Jan de. *Una tierra para sembrar sueños: Historia reciente de la Selva Lacandona, 1950–2000.* Mexico City: Fondo de Cultura Económica, 2002.

Vrijea, María Jaidopulu. "Las mujeres indígenas como sujetos políticos." *Revista Chiapas* 9 (2000). Available online at http://www.revistachiapas.org/No9/ch9.html. Accessed on June 25, 2009.

Walker, Cheryl. "Feminist Criticism and the Author." *Critical Inquiry* 16 (Spring 1990): 551–71.

Walker, Janet. *Trauma Cinema: Documenting Incest and the Holocaust.* Berkeley: University of California Press, 2005.

Wake, Eleanor. "Sacred Books and Sacred Songs from Former Days: Sourcing the Mural Paintings at San Miguel Arcángel Ixmiquilpan." *Estudios de Cultura Nahuatl* 31 (2000): 95–121.

Warman, Arturo. *"We Came to Object": The Peasants of Morelos and the National State.* Translated by Stephen K. Ault. Baltimore, Md.: Johns Hopkins University Press, 1980.

Williams, Raymond. *Marxism and Literature.* Oxford: Oxford University Press, 1977.

White, Hayden. "The Absurdist Moment in Contemporary Literary Theory." In Hayden White, *Tropics of Discourse,* 261–82. Baltimore, Md.: Johns Hopkins University Press, 1978.

Whorf, Benjamin. "The Relation of Habitual Thought and Behavior to Language." In *Language, Thought, and Reality.* Edited by John Carroll, 134–59. Cambridge: Technology Press of the Massachusetts Institute of Technology, 1956.

Wolfe, Eric. *Europe and the People without History.* Berkeley: University of California Press, 1982.

Womack, John. *Zapata and the Mexican Revolution.* Harmondsworth, England: Penguin, 1972.

Wyclif, John. *Tractatus de apostasia.* Edited and with an introduction by Michael Henry Dziewicki. New York: Johnson, 1966 [1889].

Young, Robert, ed. "Ideologies of the Postcolonial." Special inaugural issues of *Interventions: International Journal of Postcolonial Studies* 1, nos. 1–2 (1999).

Zárate, Julio. *Don Carlos de Sigüenza y Góngora.* Mexico City: Vargas Rea, 1950.

Zibechi, Raúl. *Dispersar el poder: Los movimientos como poderes antiestatales.* Buenos Aires: Tinta Limón, 2006.

Žižek, Slavoj. "Melancholy and the Act." *Critical Inquiry* 26 (Summer 2000): 657–81.

Zumárraga, Juan de. *Doctrina cristiana cierta y verdadera para gente sin erudicion y letras: En que contiene el catecismo o informacion pa indios con todo lo principal y necessario que el cristiano deue sabery obrar. Impressa en Mexico por mandado del Reverendissimo señor Don fray Juan de Çumarraga: Primer Obispo de Mexico.* Mexico: 1546.

Zupančič, Alenka. "The Subject of the Law." In *Cogito and the Unconscious.* Edited by Slavoj Žižek, 41–73. Durham, N.C.: Duke University Press, 1998.

INDEX

Note: page numbers in italics refer to figures.

Las Abejas (The Bees): and plurality of worlds, 239; reconstitution of as community of martyrs, 232; relationship to Zapatistas, 240, 245, 317n1; religious practice, 310n31; *testimonio* on Acteal massacre, 165–70, *167. See also* Acteal massacre

Acazitli, don Francisco de Sandoval, 185–88, 197

Acosta, José de, 228, 305n10

Acteal: 10 Años de impunidad (Jiménez, 2007), 230, 231, 238, 240, 249

Acteal: Estrategia de muerte (Mendoza, 1998), 231, 238, 240

Acteal: Una herida abierta, ipuc sc'oplal milel ta, 317n8

Acteal massacre (1997), 71; attackers, 230; burial of victims, 231; calls for justice, as effort to dismantle state institutions, 230, 235; government response to, 232–33; international press attention for, 233; monthly celebration of martyrdom, 169, 230, 233; and politics of truth, 234–38; revisionist account of, 231, 232–35, 237, 240; as state crime, 238; tenth anniversary of, 230–31; testimonies on, 317n8; *testimonio* of Las Abejas on, 165–70, *167,* 317n8; victims of, 230. *See also* documentaries on Acteal massacre

Acuerdos de San Andrés (1996): and autonomization process, 117, 118; and constitutionalization of indigenous autonomies, 119–20, 123; and EZLN suspension of dialogue, 94–95, 295n32; Indian participation in drafting of, 100; and limits of constituent power, 113; provisions of, 94

"Address of the General Council" (Marx), 264

aesthetics of insurgency, 261–66, 279

Agamben, Georgio, 173, 205, 207–8, 228, 254, 255, 260, 266

Aguilar Camín, Hector, 232, 233–34, 317n2

El Ahuizote, 93

Alboroto y motín de los indios de México (Sigüenza y Góngora): on anticolonial agenda in Tlaxcala riot, 29–31, 33–34; on cause of Tlaxcala riot, 30, 31, 33, 34; critical views on, 27–28; description of, 26–27; fear of Indian irrationality in, 30; historical memory of Indians implicit in, 34, 36; on Indian elite views on Indian subalterns, 33; on Indian idolatry and magic, 33–34; on interracial alliances in Tlaxcala riot, 28–29; on mobilization strategies in Tlaxcala riot, 30; non-Western rationalities implicit in, 36; on rejection of Catholicism in Tlaxcala riot, 29, 32; on role of rumor in Tlaxcala riot, 29–31; on role of Spanish lower classes in Tlaxcala riot, 29–31; on role of women in Tlaxcala riot, 29, 31, 32; on strategic frightening of Spaniards preceding Tlaxcala riot, 31; subaltern insurgency in,

19, 26; subalternity of Indians in, 35–36; on subaltern nature of Tlaxcala riot, 33

Almazán, German, 86–87

Alonso (documentary subject), 241–42, 244, 245, 247, 250

Alonso's Dream (Lacourse and Patry, 2000), 231, 238, 239, 240, 241–42, *243,* 247, 250

alphabet: eucharistic understanding of, 211; fetishizing of, 20; Nahua appropriation of, 206; native scribes' fascination with, 156

Alvarado, Pedro de (Tonatiuh), 174

Alvarado Huanitzin, don Diego de, 212

Anenecuilcans: endurance of, 47; land claims of, 47–48

Anidjar, Gil, 228

annalist tradition, and Mesoamerican historical writing, 205

Annals of His Time (Chimalpahin), 225

anticolonial agenda, in Tlaxcala riot of 1692, 29–31, 33–34

antiquarian historiography: characterization of indigenous culture, 18–19; in New Spain, 26

Antonio (documentary subject), 244, 245–46, *246*

Anunciación, Domingo de la, 221

Anzaldúa, Gloria, 290n20

Apologética historia sumaria (Las Casas), 193

aporia of spontaneity and vanguardism: and comparative frame, 128, 129; in Gramsci, 125–30; in South Asian Subaltern Studies Collective, 130–33; Zapatistas and, 134

apostasy: Chichimec Rebellion of 1541 as, 178–79, 181; forced conversions and, 202; historical dimension of, 176–77; silencing of, 196–98; Spanish colonial rule as effort to prevent, 201; as state imposed from outside, 177; Vera Cruz on, 203–4; Wyclif on, 176–77

apostates: contamination of other Indians by, 182–83, 184; as outside history, 172

apostles, as agents of historical incorporation, 172–73

APPO. *See* Asamblea Popular de los Pueblos de Oaxaca

"The April Theses" (Lenin), 101, 125, 130, 268, 269

archive(s): Derrida on, 207; and Mesoamerican historical tradition, 210–11, 227, 229; *vs.* testimony, 205

asamblea constituyente of Bolivia, 275

Asamblea Popular de los Pueblos de Oaxaca (APPO): control of, 320n7; historical memories of, 270; legality of repression of, 259, 260; media and, 319n2; and Paris Commune, 261, 277; plurality of voices in, 319n2; poet/artists of, 262–63; as proposal of alternative forms of government, 5; rebellion by,

253–54; and revolutionary violence, 255–56; *topiles and*, 256

Associazione Ya Basta, 102

Aubrey, Andres, 245

auctor-witness: Agamben on, 207–8, 228; Tezozomoc as, 210–11

author: as *auctor*-witness, 207–8; death of, Marcos and, 58

author function, 54, 58

autonomist projects: limits of, 96; Zapatistas and, 309n30

autonomization process: aporias within, 120–21; constitutionalization of autonomies and, 119–20; deconstruction and, 118; Kant on, 113–16; Marcos on, 298n68; need to think in terms of, 96, 98; Negri on, 112–13; singularities and, 146–47; and *Vida y sueños de la cañada Perla* mural, 112–13; Zapatistas and, 138, 146–47

autonomous government, and destruction of capital, 113

autonomous Indian communities, government recognition of right to, 94

autonomy, framing of, within Western legal discourse, 119–20

ayllus: and insurgent duration of, 270; role in Bolivian revolution, 272–76, 279–80, 323n65, 323n68

Aymara: García Linera (Alvaro) on, 271; role in Bolivian revolution, 272–76

Azevedo, Comandante, 163

Badiou, Alain, 269

Bahktin, M. M., 314n6

baptism, 16th-century debates on, 215–16

Barlow, R. H., 189

Barrios de Chúngara, Domitila, 127–28

Barthes, Roland, 58

Bartra, Armando, 101

El Barzón, 84

Basu, Ramram, 141

Bautista, don Juan, 211, 215, 225

Bellinghausen, Hermann, 7, 317n2

Benavente Motolinía, Toribio de, 26

Bengali historiography, Guha on, 139, 141

Benjamin, Walter, 57, 66, 253, 255, 261, 263, 266

Berlin wall, fall of as failure of socialism, 41

Beverley, John, 18, 83, 84

Bhadra, Gautam, 44, 131

Bierhorst, John, 107, 297n48

Bolivia, socialist state in, 271–76, 277–78, 279–80, 322n64, 323n65

Boone, Elizabeth Hill, 20, 305n7, 313n1

Boutmy, Emile, 96

Breton, André, 262

Brevísima relación de la destrucción de las Indias (Las Casas), 184, 193, 197

Brotherson, Gordon, 20

Buck-Morss, Susan, 294n18

Bukharin, Nicolai, 263, 269

Bush administration, and just war, 300n81

Butler, Judith, 301n89

Calderón, Felipe, 253, 253–54

Calderón, state of emergency in, 319n4

Callaghan, Manuel, 143

Canal 6 de julio, 231

Canañas, Lucio, 100

Cantares Mexicanos, 107, 297n48

"Can the Subaltern Speak?" (Spivak), 4, 66, 81, 105–6, 282n1

capitalism, possibility of discourse outside of, 3

Caracoles. *See* Juntas de Buen Gobierno

Castañeda, Gabriel de, 185

Castañeda, Jorge, 53

categorical imperative: and limits of constituent power, 114; and progress of history, 115

CCRI-CG. *See* Comité Clandestino Revolucionario Indígena, Comandancia General

CDHFBC. *See* Centro de Derecho Humanos Fray Bartolomé de las Casas

centri sociali, 102

Centro de Derecho Humanos Fray Bartolomé de las Casas (CDHFBC), 7, 165–66

Certeau, Michel de, 109, 196, 206–7, 249–50

Chakrabarty, Dipesh: on comparative frame in subaltern studies, 135; and constituent power of multitude, 297n45; on Guha, 141; on multiple histories of capital, 134–35, 274; on subaltern history, 20; and subaltern studies, 4

Change the World without Taking Power (Holloway), 6

Chatterjee, Partha, 82, 130, 140, 274

Checo (Sergio Valdez Ruvalcaba), 102–3

Chiapas: La guerra de las ideas (Delarbre), 49–50

Chiapas: La paz violenta (Rojas), 87

"Chiapas: La Treceava Estela (premier parte)", 163–65

Chiapas: Prayer for the Weavers (Gleason; 1999), 231, 239, 240–41

"Chiapas: Treceava Estela" (Chiapas: The thirteen wake; Marcos), 298n68

Chichimec Rebellion of 1541: as apostasy, 178–79, 181; Codex Telleriano-Remensis on, *188–89*, *188–90*; Indians fighting for Spanish in, 185–90, *188–89*; justification for, 180, 183–84; justifications for Spanish dominion, 199–200; justifications for war of extermination, 182–84, 202–3; monumentalization of, 194–96, *195*; as nativistic, 177, 178–80; Spanish demands for surrender, 181–82, 186; Tenamaztle's plea following, 191–94; war of extermination against, 184–85, 202–3; as without history, 198. *See also* Mixton War of 1541

Chichimecs, Spanish views on, 199–200

Chimalpahin Quahtlehuanitzin, Domingo de San Antón Muñón: and annalist tradition, 205; as *auctor*-witness, 228; biography of, 210, 221; Christian identity of, 206–7; comparative method of, 210, 218, 219–20; deconstructive reading of, 314n6; definition of task, 209–10; on historicity of indigenous peoples, 173; incorporation of Christian time into Mesoamerican time, 220–21, 228; inscribing of Mesoamerican history into Christian history, 228; and memory as archive, 207, 227, 229; and Mesoamerican historical tradition, 228; multiplicity of voices in, 208; preservation of speech forms in, 228; relationship to Tezozomoc, 208; situation of events in Christian history, 218–19, 220; on social class, 284n47; spiritual practice, 224; theology of, 221–23; work of, as hybrid cultural form, 206–7; work of, as response to colonial expropriation of past, 205. *See also Diario*

Chinese revolution, as revolution conducted with peasantry, 138

Ch'ol/Kaxlan (Alejos Garcia), 293n15

Cholula, demographic collapse, 16th-century, 307n3

Cholula map, in Historia Tolteca-Chichimeca, *150*; as background for Cholula map, in Relación Geográfica, 154, 155–56, 170; immanent history in, 157; production of, 149

Cholula map, in Relación Geográfica (1851), *150*; coexistence of modern and nonmodern culture in, 149–53; immanent history in, 148–57, 170, 171; production of, 149

Christian God, coexistence with other gods, in Indian consciousness, 152

Christianity, secular dimension of, 228

Chronica Mexicayotl (Tezozomoc): as archive, 210–11; Chimalpahin in, 209–10; multiplicity of voices in, 208–9; non-Western perspectives in, 209, 212; provenance, 211, 218; resurrection trope in, 209, 211

The Civil War in France (Marx), 261

class-consciousness, pre-capitalist subalterns and, 82

class struggle, and peoples without history, 142–43

Clastres, Pierre, 139, 142, 200, 305n9

COBAS (*comitati di base*), 102

Codex Borgia, 162

Codex Féjérváry, 20–21, 23

Codex Mendoza, *21*; description of, 20; as example of writing violence, 19; functions within Indian society, 22; and indigenous pictographic writing, 22; interpretative commentary on, 22–24; as justification for *encomienda*, 24–27, 35; privileging of antiquarian historiography, 18; provenance, 20–21

Codex Telleriano-Remensis, *64, 65*; assertion of multiple worlds in, 62, *63*, 71–72; description of, 289n1, 310n1; and framing of dominant system, 71; and issue of translation, 68; Mixton War depicted on, 62–64, *63*; plural worlds of, 69; and recognition through translation, 72–73; and relativity of modern, 70; representation in, 293n15; and Spanish desire to understand Indian culture, 70; subversion in, 72

Codex Telleriano-Remensis, folio 46r: Chichimec Rebellion of 1541 on, 177, *188–89*, 188–90; description of, 174; space without history in, 172; transition to history in, 174

coexisting universalities, plurality of, 121, 301n89

Coex Vaticanus B, 162

"Cogito and the History of Madness" (Derrida), 178

Colegio de Santa Cruz de Tlatelolco, 214, 221

collectivism, of Leyes Revolucionarias, 6

colonial history, flattening of, resisting tendency toward, 66–67

colonialism: and creation social classes, 2; and epistemic violence, 131–32; historical location of, 104–5; indigenous condemnations of, 32; internal, enlightenment binary and, 70; Kant on, 116–17; rationalizations for conquest, 10, 59

colonialist discourse: appropriation of indigenous culture, 18; coexistence of multiple worlds in, 69–70; conceptualization of indigenous culture as antiquity, 18–19; and creation of intermediary subjects, 73; delimiting of subaltern insurgencies, 28; intellectual elite as collaborators in, 17–18; need for inventory of forms of, 45, 56–57, 60; presupposition of space outside history in, 13–14

colonial violence, aesthetic of, 59

Coloquios y doctrina cristiano (Sahagún), 214–15

comitati di base (COBAS), 102

Comité Clandestino Revolucionario Indígena, Comandancia General (Clandestine Indigenous Revolutionary Committee, General Command; CCRI-CG): addressing of government prejudices by, 84; and author-function, 54; avoidance of vanguardism, 163; on constitutionalization of indigenous autonomies, 120; decision to rebel, 52; on endurance of Zapata's legacy, 47; folkloric understanding of revolutionary agency, 37–39; insistence on Indian leadership, 49–50; internationalism of, 42, 56; Marcos's subordination to, 52; on Mexican tradition of revolt, 46–47

Comité de Defensa de los Derecho del Pueblo (the Committee for the Defense of the Rights of the People), 255–56

common sense: and *durée* from *elsewhere*, 269–70; as folklore of philosophy, 79–80; García Linera (Alvaro) on, 271, 272, 280; Gramsci on, 43–44, 79–80; insurgencies and, 279; need for inventory of tropes of, 57; role in peasant rebellion, 44, 80

communalism: emphasis on, in new politics, 85; Ley Agraria Revolucionaria and, 258; Marxist definitions of, 82; in *Vida y sueños de la cañada Perla* mural, 102–3

communalism, indigenous: conversion into individual holdings, 139; multiculturalism's inability to encompass, 2, 4–5; ongoing adaptations in, 8; survival of, 2, 10; and transition to communism, 139; in Zapatistas, 39

communism: Hart on, 101–2; Negri on, 76, 101–2, 110, 111; transition to, 266–71

communitarianism: concept of justice in, 268; in Vera Cruz, 199, 202

community histories: inability of history to homogenize, 12; promise of liberation from history in, 9–10

comparative frame in subaltern studies: assumption of singular history, 133–34; critique of, 125; and erasure of historical difference, 175; implicit teleology of, 135, 157–61, 175; possibility of escaping, 161; project envisioned by, 131; ubiquity of, 124; Zapatistas and, 134. *See also* teleological reasoning

Concilio of 1585, 183, 184

Concilio Tercero, 193

Confesionario breve en lengua mexicana y cai castellana (Molina), 215

Confesionario en lengua mexicana y castellana (Bautista), 215

Confesionario mayor en lengua mexicana y castellana (Molina), 215

Conquest of Mexico (Gruzinski), 20

Consejo de Unidad Tepozteca (CUT), 89

consensus: emphasis on, in new politics, 85; emphasis on, in Zapatista government, 164–65

constituent power: and creativity of rebellion, 104; democracy as, 110–11; framing of, within Western legal discourse, 119–20; historical immanence and, 163–65; Kant on, 113–16; limits of, 113–17; in Mexican constitution, 258–59; Negri on, 55–56, 96–97, 99–100, 110–11, 113–15, 259–60, 277; Zapatistas and, 113, 117–18

constituent subjectivities, 41

Consulta Nacional e Internacional (National and International Consultation; 1995), 85
Contingency, Hegemony, Universality (Butler, Laclau, and Žižek), 301n89
Convention 169 of Indigenous and Tribal Peoples (1989), 94
El coraje del pueblo (film), 303n12
Cortés, Hernán, 34, 214
Council of the Indies, Tenamaztle's case before, 191–94, 196–98
creativity: Judeo-Christian tradition of, and limits of constituent power, 114–15; of rebellion, constituent power and, 104
Critique of Postcolonial Reason (Spivak), 132, 303n23
"Critique of Violence" (Benjamin), 255, 263
Cronica miscelanea de la Sancta Provincia de Xalisco (Tello), 179
IV Guerra mundial, Zapatistas on, 145–46
Cuautli (activist), 256
Cubbit, Sean, 248
cunning of history, 72
CUT. *See* Consejo de Unidad Tepozteca

Dabashi, Hamid, 140, 141, 143
David, Comandante, 51, 60, 84, 120, 163
Davila, Pedrarias, 181
Death of a Discipline (Spivak), 105, 132–33, 296n44
Declaración de la Selva Lacandona, 6, 39, 258
decolonization: original genealogies of, 10; of present, impossibility of, 206
deconstruction: and autonomization, 118; indefinite perfectibility of, 118, 121–22; and problems of testimony, 236. *See also* Derrida, Jacques
Deleuze, Gilles, 132, 264–65
de los Ríos, José, 90
De Man, Henri, 126, 157
De Man, Paul, 236
"Democracia multinacional y multi-institucional" (García Linera), 322n64
democracy: as constituent power, 110–11; Derrida on, 118; Negri on, 110
demonstration of May 1, 1995, 41
Denham, Diana, 255–56, 319n2
Derrida, Jacques: on archiving, 207; critique of Husserl's phenomenology of presence, 314n6, 316n6; on democracy, 118; on exappropriation, 154, 168; on globalatinization, 305n7; on incalculable nature of justice, 54–55; on indefinite perfectibility of deconstruction, 121–22; Negri on, 111; on paradox of apostate discourse, 177–78; on voice *vs.* speech, 314n6
Descartes, René, 45, 289n5
Descripción breve del Perú (Lizarraga), 32
Despertar Mexicano, 6, 258
De unico vocationis modo omnium gentium ad veram religiornem (Las Casas), 194, 197
De Vos, Jan, 161–62
Diario (Chimalpahin): description of, 223–25; on eclipse of June, 1611, 225–27; and Mesoamerican historical tradition, 223–24; rewriting of European knowledge in, 227
Diego de Durán, Fray, 18, 26
"Differance" (Derrida), 314n6
Difference and Repetition (Deleuze), 264–65
dignity, Zapatista demands for, 51–52

disciplinary breakdown, in Western constructions of Otherness, 82
dispositifs, in film, 248–49
disremembering, 236
Doctrina cristiana breve y compendiosa por vía del diálogo entre un maestro y un discípulo sacada en lengua mexicana y castellana (Anunciación), 221
Doctrina mas cierta y verdadera para gente sin erudicion (Zumárraga), 215–16
documentaries, testimonial: conventions of, 246, 318n16; as political interventions, 234; and politics of truth, 234–38
documentaries on Acteal massacre, 230–31, 238–48; gender issues in, 248; gesture in, 247–48; and politics of truth, 234–38; stills and slow motion in, 246–47, 250; time in, 245, 246. *See also Acteal: 10 Años de impunidad; Acteal: Estrategia de muerte; Alonso's Dream; Chiapas: Prayer for the Weavers; A Massacre Foretold; "Towards the Mountain"*
dominant discourse: assumption of, as illusion, 71–73; need for epistemology curtailing appropriation by, 42
Dominicans: debates on baptism, 215–16; doctrine of, 224; favored method of evangelization, 221–22
double-consciousness, *vs.* coexistence of two cultures, 152
"Do You Remember Revolution?", 102, 295n31
drunkenness, 32. *See also pulque*
Dunlop, R. H. W., 44, 81
Durán, Diego, 26, 108–9, 205, 228
Durito, 41, 55
Dziewicki, Michael Henry, 177

eclipse of June, 1611, 225–27
Eighteen Fifty-Seven (Sen), 44, 81
The Eighteenth Brumaire of Louis Bonaparte (Marx), 139, 264
Ejercito Zapatista de Liberación Nacional (Zapatista Army of National Liberation; EZLN): Acteal massacre and, 232, 233; address to Mexican congress, 95; calls for radical democracy, 42, 55; conditions for renewal of dialogue, 94–95; and endurance of Anenecuilcans, 47; government military action against, 54; histories of, as denial of contemporary relevance, 7; and Mexican constitution, efforts to change, 8, 94, 281n6; and Mexican tradition of revolt, 46–47; as political prisoners, 94–95, 295n32; press mischaracterizations of, 49, 53–54, 288n44; as proposal of alternative state, 5; as revolutionary organization, 53; and revolutionary violence, 258; subaltern politics of, as inspiration for new politics, 85. *See also* Declaración de la Selva Lacandona; *entries under* Zapatista; Leyes Revolucionaria; *Sexta declaración de la Selva Lacandona*
Elementary Aspects of Peasant Insurgency in Colonial India (Guha), 4, 28, 34–35, 131, 140, 287n26, 296n45
elite discourse, revisioning of insurgencies outside of, 35
emergency. *See* exception, state of
emergent subjectivities, 41
empire: emergence of, 100; reiteration of hegemony of exclusion, 146–47
Empire (Hardt and Negri), 100, 101–2
encomienda: Codex Mendoza as justification for, 24–27, 35; and New Laws of 1542, 104

Encuentro Americano Contra la Impunidad (American Encounter Against Impunity), 7, 319n4

Encuentro Nacional Contra la Impunidad (National Encounter Against Impunity), 230, 319n4

Engels, Friedrich, 10

enlightened de-enlightenment, 44, 60, 80; coexisting multiple worlds and, 69–73; necessity of, in subaltern studies, 66

Enlightenment: binary emerging from, 70; concept of history, *vs.* pre-Enlightenment forms, 141; constituent assemblies as product of, 259; distinguishing binary of from early Spanish forms, 105–6; and emergence of ethnography, 70; Gramsci as representative of, 129; and invalidation of indigenous spaces, 70; and peoples-with-and-without-history binary, 139; silence of toward slavery, 294n18

epistemic violence: abandonment of nativistic discourses as, 134, 160–61; campaigns against subaltern beliefs as, 302n7; colonialism and, 131–32; Indians' refusal to internalize, 160; subjugation of indigenous knowledges as, 59

epistemology: need for unappropriable form of, 57; and silences in subaltern discourse, 83, 84

essentialism, strategic, coexisting multiple worlds and, 68

Estado mulinacional (García Linera), 273, 278, 322n64

. . . esta es nuestra palabra . . . , 165–70, *167*, 317n8. *See also* Las Abejas (The Bees), *testimonio* on Acteal massacre

Esther, Comandante, 95, 163

ethnography, emergence of, enlightenment and, 70

Euro-American thought, indigenous experience of without hierarchical relation, 98–99

evidence, and establishment of historical truth, 15

exception, state of: and aesthetics of insurgency, 265–66, 279; dialectic with general, 265; El Fisgón on, *253*, 253–55; García Linera (Alvaro) and, 271; legality of, 254, 256–61; theory of, 254–55; as without history, 265

expropriation of modern life forms by indigenous peoples, 154–55

EZLN. *See* Ejercito Zapatista de Liberación Nacional

EZLN, el ejercito que salió de la selva (Urzúa and Taulis), 286n9

Fabian, Johannes, 142

factishes, 236–37, 242, 318n16

fact *vs.* fetish, 236

Faustina (documentary subject), 242, *243*, 250

film: *dispositifs* in, 248–49; haptic criticism of, 249–50, 318n23; as poaching, 250; reproducing of normalized subjectivities, 248; resistance in viewers, 249; revolutionary, 303n12. *See also* documentaries, testimonial; documentaries on Acteal massacre

El Fisgón, 252, *253*, 253–55, 256, 261

La flecha en el blanco (León Portilla), 196

Florentine Codex, 22

Florescano, Enrique, 20

Flores Magón, Ricardo, 270; call for direct action, 137; ideology of, 93, 100, 101, 109, 114, 117; in *Vida y sueños de la cañada Perla* mural, 92–94, 100–102, 122, 136–37, 161, 163

folklore: binary relationship with history, establishment of, 140–41; as component of Tepoztlán rebellion, 85; outsiders' curiosity about, 87; reduction of Indian cultures to, 70; role in peasant rebellion, 80; tendency to caricature, 85–87; use of for transformation of peasantry, 43, 79, 126, 129, 138–39, 157, 309n24. *See also* idolatry and magic

folkloric: and communist, 79; and compatibility of modern and nonmodern culture, 76, 79; Gramsci's blindness to, 40, 42–44, 57, 71, 78, 79–80, 129, 309n24; Indian spaces as, 70–71; role in new politics, 85; role in peasant rebellion, 44

folkloric understanding of revolutionary agency, in EZLN, 37–39

The Formation of a Persecuting Society (Moore), 178

Foucault, Michel: and author function, 54, 58; on culture of conquest, 60; on discourse without authors, 205, 207; on *dispositif*, 248; Foucauldian perspective on subaltern studies, 42; *Madness and Civilization*, 177–78; and non-European Other, 294n18; Spivak critique of, 60–61, 132; on withering of the state, 267–68

Fox, Vicente, 95, 292n1, 295n32

FPR. *See* Frente Popular Revolucionario

Franciscans: and debate on baptism, 215–16; historicist conception of God, 216

Francisco Tenamaztle, primer guerrillero de América, defensor de los derechos humanos (León Portilla), 196

Franco, Alonso, 208–9

Frente Popular Revolucionario (FPR), 320n7

Fuerzas de Liberación Nacional (National Liberation Forces), 46–47

García Linera, Álvero, 5, 252, 270–80, 322n64, 323n65

Garcilaso de la Vega, 173

gaze, return of, indigenous depictions of colonial institutions as, 12

The General Theory of Law and Marxism (Pashukanis), 6, 258, 266–67

ghost dances, 107

Gleason, Judith, 231. *See also Chiapas: Prayer for the Weavers*; "Towards the Mountain"

global: intertwining with local, 77; lack of symbolic elements to institutionalize an alternative community, 77

global anthropology, and abandonment of otherness, 144–45

globalatinization, 141, 305n7

globalization: changes in structure of press's feeling toward, 77; local as site of resistance to, 88–89; logic of invincibility of, 85–86; mobilization against, 85; singularities as challenge to, 143–44. *See also* transnational interests

González Casanovas, Pablo, 85, 88

Gossen, Gary, 39

A Grammar for the Multitude (Virno), 146

Gramsci, Antonio: blindness to folkloric, 40, 42–44, 57, 71, 78, 79–80, 129, 309n24; Cartesian epistemology in, 44–45; on common sense, 43–44, 79–80; conceptions of Culture, critiques of, 79; on documentations of subaltern struggle, 47–48; on education, 43, 79; on hegemony, 79; on historical immanence, 158–61, 171, 309n24; on instinct, 130–31, 158; intellectual vanguardism of, 46; privileging of Western culture, 79; refusal to historicize,

10–11; on spontaneity, 126–27, 133, 157–59; on subalterns, 78–79, 83–84, 287n26; on subalterns' need
for theory, 130, 158, 171; teleological reasoning in,
124–31, 133, 138–39, 157–59; vanguardism of, 124,
125–26, 157, 303n16
Grupo KS, 86, 90
Gruzinski, Serge, 20, 151, 152, 297n48
Guha, Ranajit: on Bengali historiography, 139, 141;
and binary thought of Spivak, 105, 296n45; call
for subaltern studies, 125; on colonial anxiety, 67;
on colonialist rhetorical strategies, 28; on dominance without hegemony, 72; Gramsci and, 403n6;
on historiography's subordination of subalterns,
140; on negation in subaltern studies, 287n26; on
rhetoric of counterinsurgency, 49; on subaltern rebellion, 33, 34–35; and subaltern studies, 3, 4; teleological reasoning in, 131; on writing in reverse, 57
La Guillotina, 38–39

Habitations of Modernity (Chakrabarty), 134
hacienda system, 139
haptic criticism, of film, 249–50, 318n23
Haraway, Donna, 60
Hardt, Michael: on Chinese revolution, 138; on communism, 101–2; on democracy, 110; on disappearance of peasantry, 139, 145; on emergence of
Empire, 100; on emergence of multitude, 146; on
human rights organizations, 117; on peasantry
as doomed mode of production, 274; prejudice
against peasants, 139; on transformation of flesh
into body, 252, 256–57; vanguardism in, 145
harmony and equilibrium, emphasis on, in indigenous practice, 39
Hegel, Georg W. F.: critique of Kant, 121, 301n89; and
"cunning of history," 72; dialectic of master and
slaves, 72, 73, 98, 103, 294n18; and dominant philosophical paradigm, 289n5; Guha on, 140; and *la
philosophie de l'actualité*, 75
"Hegel and Haiti" (Buck-Morss), 294n18
hegemonic discourse, transformation of, in recognition of Indian rights, 118–19, 301n89
hegemony: Gramsci on, 79; of the West, guerrilla efforts to overturn, 143–44
hegemony of the diverse: emergence of, 84–85; impossibility of the local and, 88–89; Zapatismo
as, 78
Heidegger, Martin, 67, 135, 254–55
hierarchical relation, possibility of intercultural experience without, 98–99
Higgins, Nick, 230. *See also A Massacre Foretold*
Hinojosa, Ortiz de, 182–83, 183–84
Historia de la Nueva Galicia (Tello), 180–82
*Historia de las Indias de la Nueva España e islas de
Tierra Firme* (Durán), 18, 26, 108–9, 205
Historia de Tlatelolco (1528), 169–70
Historia Tolteca-Chichimeca: as bilingual text, 156–
57; as oral text, 156–57; production of, 157. *See also*
Cholula map, in Historia Tolteca-Chichimeca
historical immanence: and constituent power, 163–
65; as contemporaneity of multiple pasts, 12;
Gramsci on, 158–61, 171, 309n24. *See also* modern
and nonmodern culture, compatibility of; multiple worlds, coexisting
historical memory of Indians: in *Alboroto y motín*

de los indios de México, 34, 36; need for recuperation of, 56–57
historical necessity, possibility of escape from, 9–10
historicity of indigenous peoples, as problematic
concept, 173
historiography: Indian subalternists' transformation
of, 45, 81, 83; internationalization of, 46, 82; of pre-
Columbian Mesoamerica, archaeology of, 19; subordination and subsumation of subalterns, 140
history: appropriation of, by Spanish, 26; articulation of subaltern-state relationship, 199; as effort
to neutralize subaltern insurgency, 141; Enlightenment and, 141; evidentiary criteria and, 15; as
foreclosing of alternative spaces, 9–10; homogenization of the past by, 12; lack of, *vs.* space outside of, 14; pre-Columbian past, coopting of, 2; as
progress, Kant on, 115; promise of liberation in life
histories of individuals and communities, 9–10;
redefining direction of, 16; specter of, 9–12; as tool
of state, 15; as Western invention, 141; Zapatista
views on, 57. *See also* immanent history; Mesoamerican historical writing; without history
history, as discipline: epistemological and ethical
choices in, 252; epistemological elitism in, 297n45
history, revisionist: in Acteal massacre, 231, 232–35;
as effort to establish new standard of truth, 15
history, single: Indian resistance to, 171; interrupting
narratives that result in, 5, 16; *vs.* multiple, 133–35;
subsumation of Indian documents into, 175, 305n7
history, unappropriable, need for, 57. *See also* writing in reverse
History at the Limits of World-History (Guha), 140
history of people without history, as history of struggle against the state, 139
"History's Forgotten Doubles" (Nandy), 14
Holloway, John, 6
"How to Tame a Wild Tongue" (Anzaldúa), 290n20
Hugo, Comandante, 109
huhuexiuhtlapohualli, 219
Huitzilopochtli, 34, 209, 217, 221, 222, 223
human rights: constitutionalization of indigenous
autonomies and, 119; and insurgency state of exception, 279; Kant on, 114; legitimacy and power
of, 7–8; Mexican government refusal to recognize,
8; Zapatista reliance on, 7

Ibarra, Miguel, 180, 192
idealization of pre-Columbian past, as denigration
of historical Indians, 17–19
"Ideologies of the Postcolonial" (Young), 66
ideology of progress, critique of, 43
idolatry and magic: *Alboroto y motín* on, 33–34; exclusion from global anthropology model, 145; in
Tlaxcala riot of 1692, 33–34. *See also* folklore
ignoratiam invincibilem, 199, 200
Ik'al, 162
Ik'al Zapata, 162
Ileto, Reynaldo Clemeña, 285n1
imaginary, colonization of, 310n5
immanent history: in Las Abejas *testimonio* of Acteal
massacre, 165–70; Historia Tolteca-Chichimeca
Cholula map as, 157; Relación Geográfica Cholula
map as, 148–57, 170, 171; subordination of to transcendental narrative, 158; *Vida y sueños de la ca-*

ñada Perla mural as, 161; in Zapatista political forms, 163–65, 170

impossibility of the local: and emerging hegemony of the diverse, 88–89; in subaltern movements, 77; in Tepoztlán uprising, 88

the impossible: as horizon of alternative rationalities, 39; role in new politics, 85; Zapatista discourse as, 97–98; Zapatista goals as, 76. *See also* folklore; folkloric

Indian exclusion, interpretation of as outside history, 142–43

"An Indian Historiography of India" (Guha), 139

Indian resistance: legacy of, 106–10; subaltern studies' approach to, 17

Indian rights, hegemonic discourse and, 118–19

Indian spaces, as magical (folkloric) spaces, 70–71

Indian subalternity, *in Alboroto y motín de los indios de México*, 35–36

Indian subaltern studies group: evolution of subaltern concept in, 80–81; postcolonial subject position of, 45, 81

Indigenous and Tribal Peoples (1989), 94

indigenous autonomies outside history, possibility of, 278–80

indigenous culture: appropriation by colonialist discourse, 18; and binary narrative of conquest, 72; conceptualization of as antiquity, 18–19; narrative frames inscribing, 1–2; ongoing practice of, 2; reduction to folklore, 70; Spanish desire to understand, 70; survival of, in clandestine forms, 18

indigenous discourse: forcing recognition of, 166; inaccessibility to modern European thought, 135; inevitable subalternization of, 61; necessity of abandoning to resist oppression, 134; possibility of, 134; possibility of coexistence with modern discourse, 134, 160–61

indigenous documents, Spanish recognition of historical nature of, 174–75

indigenous history: as beyond writing, 107–8; colonial efforts to coopt, 108–9; subordination to Spanish historiography, 19

indigenous insurgencies: revolutionary violence and, 270; and specter of history, 277; and traditional liberal government, 270

indigenous knowledge: appropriation by transnational corporations, 103; destruction of in colonialism, 132

indigenous law, Spanish codification of, 70

indigenous Mexico, endurance of, 47

indigenous normative systems, as term, 104

indigenous peoples: compatibility of modern and nonmodern discourse in, 134; experience of Euro-American thought without hierarchical relation, 98–99; failure to internalize normative discourses, 14; historicity of, as problematic concept, 173; suffering under leftist governments, 251

indigenous social structures, as model for construction of new world, 274–76

indigenous spirit, of Zapatista revolution, 6, 8–9

indios ladinos, 182, 201, 203–4

individual and community histories: inability of history to homogenize, 12; promise of liberation from history in, 9–10

instinct, Gramsci on, 130–31, 158

Insurgencies (Negri), 97, 99–100, 110, 260

insurgency: aesthetics of, 261–66; and binary construct of conquest, 72; definition of, 276–77; and framing of dominant system, 71; imaginary of, Zapata and, 109; in Latin America, traditional readings of political program, 34–35; as proposed alternative forms of government, 5; revisioning of outside of elite discourse, 35. *See also* indigenous insurgencies; revolution; subaltern insurgency

Insurgency (Negri), 277

insurgency, duration of: modern and indigenous as contemporaneous, 11; Paris Commune and, 11, 270, 277, 279; Zapatista revolution and, 9

insurrection, fear of generated by subaltern world, 67, 73

intellectuals: as collaborators in colonialist discourse, 17–18; dissolution of as privileged agent, 89; epistemic violence against indigenous peoples, 147; inadequacy of as representatives of subaltern groups, 82–83, 84; indigenous, and defining of autonomization process, 120; Mexican, necessity of confronting racism, 84; and plurality of worlds in subaltern subjects, 67; role in subalternization process, 89; role of, 44, 59, 60, 80, 126–27, 127–28; subjugation of indigenous population in New Spain, 26; and vanguardism, 59

Interamerican Commission on Human Rights, 165–66

International Labor Organization, 94

interracial alliances, in Tlaxcala riot of 1692, 28–29

Inventing America (Rabasa), 294n18

Iraq War, just war theory and, 300n81

itihasa, status of, 140–41

Ixmiquilpan (Hidalgo) Augustinian church, mural in, 190–91, *191*

Ixtlixochitl, Fernando de Alva, 173, 211, 216–18, 284n47

Jameson, Frederic, on periodization, 12

Jaramillo, Rubén, 100

Jiménez, José Alfredo, 230. *See also Acteal: 10 Años de impunidad*

La Jornada, 50, 85, 101, 319n2

Judeo-Christian tradition of creativity, and limits of constituent power, 114–15

Juntas de Buen Gobierno (Caracoles), 134, 142, 163–64, 298n68, 304n32, 306n11

justice: incalculable nature of, 54–55; for indigenous peoples, history of calls for, 56; popular, Foucault on, 267

just war theory: Iraq War and, 300n81; and legality of Spanish conquest, 200–202, 203; and wars of extermination, 182–84, 202–3

Kant, Immanuel: on colonialism, 116–17; and dominant philosophical paradigm, 289n5; and plurality of coexisting universalities, 121, 301n89; and possibility of ethical actions, 299n74; and project of autonomization, 299n74; on project of autonomy, 113–16

Kentridge, William, 263, 266

Kierkegaard, Sören, 67, 265

knowledges, indigenous, subjugation of as epistemic violence, 59

Labor of Dionysus (Hardt and Negri), 110
Lacan, Jacques, 175, 310n5
Laclau, Ernesto, 42–43, 79, 301n89
Lacourse, Danièle, 231. *See also Alonso's Dream*
Larráinzar VI talks, 74, 291n23, 292n6
LASA. *See* Latin American Studies Association
Las Casas, Bartolomé de: atrocities related by, 184; on baptism, 215–16; calls for justice by, 56; on conversion of Indians, 221–22; on noble savage, 222; on Spanish dominion, 198–200; Tenamaztle case and, 191–94, 196–98
LASSG. *See* Latin American Subaltern Studies Group
Latin, teaching of, to Indians, 69
Latin American studies, introduction of subaltern studies to, 3–4
Latin American Studies Association (LASA), García Linera speech before, 252, 271, 279–80
Latin American Subaltern Studies: accusations of cultural imperialism against, 286n16; agenda of, 17–20, 42, 44; evolution of subaltern concept in, 81–83; need for epistemology curtailing appropriation by dominant discourse, 42; questioning of intellectuals as representatives of subaltern groups, 82–83; on subaltern, groups included in, 48
Latin American Subaltern Studies Group (LASSG): establishment of, 3–4, 281n1, 403n6; Founding Statement, 48, 83, 84
Latour, Bruno, 236–37, 242, 318n16
law, withering of, 266–71, 277–78
leadership: in peasant rebellions, 44, 80–81, 126; spontaneity and, 158; of Zapatistas, 51
leadership, indigenous: CCRI-CG's insistence on, 49–50; impossibility of, 54
leadership of women: in indigenous rebellions, 48; in Zapatista movement, 52
Left: failure to represent the peoples' interests, 41; success in Latin America, as illusory, 251–52
"Left-Wing Childishness and the Petty-Bourgeois Mentality" (Lenin), 10–11, 269
Lenin, Vladimir: "The April Theses," 101, 125, 130, 268, 269; on armed struggle, 102; on dual power during Russian revolution, 323n65; "Left-Wing Childishness and the Petty-Bourgeois Mentality," 10–11, 269; *Letters on Tactics*, 268; on Paris Commune, 269; on role of intellectuals, 128; *The State and Revolution*, 10, 268, 269, 279–80; vanguardism of, 10; *What Is To Be Done?*, 10, 101, 125, 128, 268; on withering of state, 10–11, 266–69
León Portilla, Miguel, 191, 196–97, 297n48
Letters on Tactics (Lenin), 268
Ley Agraria Revolucionaria (EZLN), 6, 258
Leyes Revolucionaria (EZLN): collectivist nature of, 6; and constituent power in Mexican Constitution, 258–59; as outside traditional liberal government, 270
Leyla (activist), 255–56
literature, Gramsci on role of, 129
Lloyd, David, 263, 288n44
local: impossibility of, 77; as relational term, 77; as site of resistance to transnational interests, 88–89
Logiques des mondes (Badiou), 269
Lord Ik' (Black Lord), 109, 111
los Rios, Pedro de, 63–64

Mächler, Stefan, 235
Madness and Civilization (Foucault), 177–78
Manifesto de Achacachi, 276
Maoist, 267
Mao Zedong, 138
Marcos, Subcomandante: addressing of government prejudices by, 84; assessment of Juntas de Buen Gobierno, 304n32; and author-function, 54, 58; on autonomization process, 298n68; avoidance of vanguardism, 163; on Caracoles, 163–64, 171, 306n11; as caudillo, 54; on causes of Zapatista revolution, 50–51; "Chiapas: Treceava Estela," 298n68; on constitutionalization of indigenous autonomies, 120; cry of Enough! (órale!) from, 30–31, 48; on destruction of the state, 114–15; efforts to reduce Zapatista movement to, 53–54; efforts to unmask, 49–50; elements of popular culture in, 137; government unmasking of, 54; on historical immanence and constituent power, 163–65; and imaginary of insurrection, 109; as intellectual, 60; on intellectuals, role of, 59; multiple subject positions of, 57–59; on neoliberalism's inability to accept singularities, 143; privileging of, in interpretations of Zapatista movement, 40; on reform of Article 27, 50; on revolution, necessity of, 55; and revolutionaries as illegals, 94; on revolutionary nature of Zapatista movement, 53; and revolutionary spirituality, 161–62; role of in Zapatista movement, 52; and semiotic identities of Zapata, 99, 100; subordination to CCRI-CG, 52; support of Italian labor movement, 41; teleological reasoning in, 306n11; and theorization of the concrete, 101; unlearning of privilege in, 67; on violence, 295n31; on women's rights, 300n84; and Zapatour, 95
Margins of Philosophy (Derrida), 314n6
Maria (documentary subject), 245, 247, 248, 249
Marion, Jean-Luc, 237
Marks, Laura, 249, 318n23
Martínez, Carlos, 231, 242, 244, 245. *See also Tierra Sagrada en Zona de conflicto*
Martínez Busto, Blanca, 245
Marx, Karl: on archaic forms of communalism, 10; Chakrabarty on, 135; *The Civil War in France*, 261; on contemporaneity of Russian communes, 281n11; on Paris Commune, 11, 125, 134, 136–37, 264, 279; and poetics of history, 263–64; prejudice against peasants, 139; refusal to historicize, 10–11; on repetition in history, 264; satire and sarcasm in, 263–64; on social existence and consciousness, 266; on spontaneity, 126–27; on transition from formal to real subsumption of labor to Capital, 112; on transition to communism, 268; on viability of Russian commune, 273–74
Marxism: on spontaneity, 132; Western, continuation of imperialism and neocolonialism in, 82
MAS (Movimiento al Socialismo), 271
A Massacre Foretold (Higgins, 2007), 230, 231, 238–40, 242–46, 244, 247–50
Matrícula de Tributos, 20
Meier-Wiedenbach, Jutta, 165, 167, *167*, 168, 170, 317n8
Me llamo Rigoberta Menchú (Menchú), 318n16
Memorial de los indios de nombre de dios, Durango, acerca de sus servicios al rey (c. 1563), 186
Memoria mexicana (Florescano), 20
memory: assassination of, in revisionist histories,

237; in colonized peoples, 206; in Mesoamerican historical writing, 207, 227, 229. *See also* historical memory of Indians

Menchú, Rigoberta, 60, 83, 318n16

Mendoza, Antonio de, 174, 178, 180, 181–82, 185–86

Mendoza, Carlos, 231. *See also Acteal: Estrategia de muerte*

Mendoza Huitznahuatlailotlac Imauyantzin, D. Diego de, 189–90

Mesoamerican gods, Spanish characterizations of, 212–14

Mesoamerican historical writing: and circumscription of Mesoamerican history into messianic time, 228; forms of, 313n1; incorporation of Christian time into Mesoamerican time, 220–21, 228; inscribing of Mesoamerican history into Christian history in, 212–18, 228; memory in, 207, 227, 229; rewriting of European knowledge in, 227; and trope of resurrection, 205, 209, 211. *See also* Chimalpahin Quauhtlehuanitzin, Domingo de San Antón Muñón; Tezozomoc, Hernando Alvarado

mestizaje: *vs.* coexistence of two cultures, 152; ideology of, and denial of Indian roots, 48–49

Mestizo Mind (Gruzinski), 297n48

Metz, Christian, 248

Mexican Constitution: Article 4, 8, 94, 95–96; Article 17, 7–8; Article 27, 46, 49–50; Article 29, 257–58; Article 39, 6, 7–8, 88, 270, 298n68; Article 115, 88; constituent power in, 258–59; desire to change, and tension between constituent power and will to control, 96; restitution of communal holdings in, 139; state of emergency provisions in, 257–58, 270; Zapatista efforts to change, 8, 94, 281n6

Mexican government: attitude of, and peace negotiations, 84; inability to understand Zapatista revolution, 40–41; as incapable of speech, 66; low-level warfare against Indian communities, 102, 292n1; military action against Zapatistas, 54; necessity of confronting racism, 84; recognition of Indian right to self-determination, 94; refusal to recognize human rights discourse, 8; and Tepoztlán rebellion, 88; Zapatista characterization of as outlaw state, 75

Mixton War of 1541: in Codex Telleriano-Remensis, 62–64, 63, 70; death toll, 185; and fear of insurrection, 67, 73; as moment of contestation, 70. *See also* Chichimec Rebellion of 1541

mobilization strategies, in Tlaxcala riot of 1692, 30

modern, definition of, conceptions of state and, 176

modern and nonmodern culture, compatibility of, 2–3; in Las Abejas, 170; folkloric and, 76, 79; and grip of comparative frame, 161; and indigenous expropriation of modern life forms, 154–55; indigenous subalterns' ability to accept, 152–53; possibility of, 130, 148, 160; project of understanding, 37; and reason, conceptions of, 45–46; in *Relación Geográfica* map of Cholula, 149–53, 156; subaltern movements and, 57; in Tepoztlán rebellion, 88; in Zapatista discourse, 39–40, 76, 100, 134, 137, 138, 285n2. *See also* historical immanence; multiple worlds, coexisting

modernity: abandonment of otherness, 144–45; colonial legacy, need for inventory of, 60; as comparativist, 5–6, 160; contemporaneity of nonmodern with, 2–3; dating origin of, 158; foreclosing alternative spaces, 9–10; inaccessibility of indigenous discourse to, 135; possibility of discourse outside of, 3

"The Modern Prince" (Gramsci), 43, 79, 80–81

Molina, Alonso de, 215, 225, 305n7

Monsiváis, Carlos, 37, 39–40, 41, 295n31, 300n84

Montaño, Otilio, 288n39

Montemayor, Carlos, 317n2

Moore, Robert I., 178, 307n16

Las moradas (Santa Teresa), 224

Morales, Evo, 5, 271, 275–76, 280, 323n65

Morgan, L. H., 273

Morrison, Toni, 236

Moteuccoma, doña Francisca de, 212

Motolinía, 215–16, 217, 221, 223, 228

Movimiento al Socialismo (MAS), 5, 271

multiculturalism: inability to encompass indigenous communalism, 2, 4–5; *vs.* plural worlds, 164–65

multiple worlds, coexisting: in Codex Telleriano-Remensis, 62, 63, 71–72; in colonial discourse, 69–70; and enlightened de-enlightenment, 69–73; Indian assertion of, 62–66; and issue of translation, 68–69; *vs.* multiculturalism, 164–65; necessity of subaltern dwelling in, 66, 67–69; porosity between, 68, 297n45; possibility of, 297n45, 301n89, 301n93; of Tzotzil, 239; Zapatistas and, 65–66, 69, 73, 164, 171. *See also* modern and nonmodern culture, compatibility of

multitude: emergence of, 146; and epistemic violence of subaltern category, 125; and erasure of singularities, 146; Negri on, 146, 295n31; *vs.* the people, 125; and specter of history, 277

Multitude (Hardt and Negri), 138, 139, 252

Mundy, Barbara, 152, 307n3

Municipio Autónomo Ricardo Flores Magón, government attacks on, 92, 95

Muñoz, José, 236

murmur, in Tlaxcala riot of 1692, 31

naguales, Zapatista use of, 39

Nahua history, Spanish interest in, 107

Nancy, Jean-Luc, 13–14, 314n6, 316n6

Nandy, Ashis, 14

National Public Radio (NPR), report on Tepoztlán rebellion, 85–87, 89

nation-state, weakening of, and emergence of empire, 100

native elite, formation of, 297n45

natural right of social foundation, and limits of constituent power, 114

Nazi rule, and state of exception, 254–55

Negri, Antonio: on autonomization process, 112–13; on Chinese revolution, 138; on communism, 76, 101–2, 110, 111; on constituent power, 55–56, 96–97, 99–100, 110–11, 113–15, 259–60, 277; on constituent subjectives, 41; on democracy, 110; on destruction of state, 112, 114–15; on disappearance of peasantry, 139, 145; on empire, 117; Flores Magón's revolutionary program and, 100; on human rights organizations, 117; jailing of, 102; on law and the state, 267; and limits of rationality, 113; metaphysics of, 110–11; on multitude, 146, 295n31; parallelisms with Zapatismo, 96–113; on peasantry as doomed mode of production, 274; prejudice against peasants, 139; on reinvention of revolution, 102, 111; on resistance preceding power, 103–4; on socialized workers,

111–12; on subversion, 112; on tension between constituent power and will to control, 96; thinking, in non-Western categories, 99, 122; on transformation of flesh into body, 252, 256–57; vanguardism in, 145; on violence, 102, 111, 112

neoliberalism: changes in structure of press's feeling toward, 77; inability to accept singularities, 143; mobilization against, 85; subaltern studies as response to, 4; war against humanity by, 145–46; weakening of state in, 271–72

nepantla, colonial discourse and, 73

New Laws of 1542, 25, 104, 194

new politics: EZLN politics as inspiration for, 85; increasing momentum of, 84–85; program of, 85; Tepoztlán rebellion and, 88

New Spain, antiquarian historiography in, 26

newspapers: accounts of Tepoztlán rebellion as mirrors of outside world, 77; reification of local as universal, 75

Nietzsche, Friedrich, 18–19

noble savage: in Chimalpahin, 222–23; in Las Casas, 222

Nochistlan, 180, 194–96, *195*

noise, strategic deployment of, in Tlaxcala riot of 1692, 34

nonmodern: contemporaneity with modern, 2–3; recharacterization of premodern societies as, 5; as term, 5, 148, 176. *See also* modern and nonmodern culture, compatibility of

non-Western rationalities: *in Alboroto y motín de los indios de México*, 36; in Zapatismo, 39–40, 285n2

Notes on Italian History (Gramsci), 42–43, 78–79, 80

NPR. *See* National Public Radio

Nuño de Guzmán, 192, 194–96, 197, 203

Oaxaca Constitution, emergency powers in, 259

Oaxaca Sitiada (Osorno), 319n2

Obama, Barack, and just war, 300n81

Occidentalism, limitations of, 98, 100

Ockham, William of, 68–69

Octava relación (Chimalpahin), 227

Olmos, Andrés de, 26

Ometochtzin, don Carlos de, 62, 68, 69, 71

Oñate, Juan de, 192, 194–96

"On Education" (Gramsci), 43, 79

The Order of Things (Foucault), 294n18

"L'Orgie parisienne ou Paris se repeuple" (Rimbaud), 262

The Origin of the Family. Private Property, and the State (Engels), 10

PAN. *See* Partido de Acción Nacional

"Para leer un video" (Marcos), 306n11

paramilitary groups: attacks by, 292n1; government denial of connection with, 232; government involvement with, 234, 238; naming of participants by Las Abejas members, 241–42, 250; oppression by, 242–44

Paris Commune of 1871: duration of, and indigenous insurgencies, 11, 270, 277, 279; Lenin on, 269; Marx on, 11, 125, 134, 136–37, 264, 279; as new revolutionary ethos, 261, 264; and (im)possibility of without history, 267; and withering of state, 268

Partido Comunista Mexicano Marxista Leninista (PCMML), 320n7

Partido de Acción Nacional (PAN), 292n1

Partido Liberal Mexicano, 93

Partido Revolucionario Institucional (PRI): corruption of, 165; lack of reason in, 71; loss in 2000 elections, 251; paramilitary arms of, 292n1

Pashukanis, Evgeny, 6, 258, 266–67, 274

past, as presence that faces us, 11–12

Pasyon and Revolution (Ileto), 285n1

patriarchy, Zapatista rejection of, 248–49

Patry, Yvan, 231. *See also Alonso's Dream*

Paul (apostle), 266

Paz, Octavio, 28

PCMML. *See* Partido Comunista Mexicano Marxista Leninista

peasant rebellion: leadership in, 44, 80–81, 126; role of common sense in, 44

the people, *vs.* the multitude, 125

peoples-with-and-without-history binary: efforts to overcome, as subsumption by modernity, 143–45, 159–60; interpreting without as outside history, 142–43; origin of, 139; overcoming of, 139–41; resolution of into single history, 175

periodization, and identification of multiple coexisting life histories, 12

perspective, pictorial: Nahua appropriation of, 206; as signifier, 248

Petrich, Blanche, 50

Pez, Don Andrés, 27

Phenomenology of Mind (Hegel), 121

Philip II (king of Spain), 56

photographs: in Las Abejas *testimonio* of Acteal massacre, 166–70, *167*; Indian understanding of power of, 168–69; as technology for conquering colonialism, 169

pictographic texts: centrality to Nahua world, 68; of Chichimec Rebellion of 1541, *188–89*, 188–90; photographs and, 169; reduction of to "history," 175, 305n7; sorting of Real and Imaginary elements in, 175; Spanish recognition of translatability of, 174–75; and univocal content, 24

Plan de Ayala, 48, 56, 288n39

plurality of worlds. *See* multiple worlds, coexisting

poaching: De Certeau on, 207, 250; filming as, 250

Political Theology (Schmitt), 254–55

Politics and Ideology in Marxist Theory (Laclau), 42–43, 79

politics of citizenship, Tepoztlán rebellion and, 75

Politics of Friendship (Derrida), 118

politics of recognition, effectiveness of, 67

The Politics of Subversion (Negri), 111–12

politics of truth, Acteal massacre and, 234–38

Poniatowska, Elena, 165

popular culture, tendency to dismiss as folklore, 85–87

Portilla, Miguel León, 305n7

possibilities of hearing, proliferation of, 58

post-Fordism, singularities and, 146

postmodern theory, subaltern studies and, 42

poststructuralism: continuation of imperialism and neocolonialism in, 82; critique of the subject, 67

pozol, 103

Pratt, Mary Louise, 29

pre-Columbian past: as beyond writing, 107–8; colonialist efforts to deny present reality of, 1–2; ide-

alization of, as denigration of historical Indians, 17–19; republican efforts to coopt, 2
premodern, as term, 5, 148, 176
PRI. *See* Partido Revolucionario Institucional
Priístas, 232, 233, 317n3
Prison Notebooks (Gramsci), 78, 138
"The Problem of Speech Genres" (Bahktin), 314n6
progress, as direction of history, 70
"The Prose of Counter-Insurgency" (Guha), 28
Provincializing Europe (Chakrabarty), 134, 297n45
pulque: as cause of Tlaxcala riot of 1692, 30, 31; increased consumption of, under Spanish colonial rule, 32–33

Quauhtzin, D. Martin, 189–90
Quest International, 103
Quetzalcoatl, 137, 161–62

Rabinow, Paul, 7
"Rage against the Divine" (Lloyd), 263
Ramona, Comandante, 52, 84, 163
Ramos, Julio, 66
Ranger, Terence, 82
reason: colonialist discourse on lack of in indigenous forms, 59; Kant on evolution of, 115; limits of, Negri and, 113; reification of, necessity of avoiding, 45–46; Zapatista discourse as beyond, 100, 113
recognition, through translation, 72–73
Regeneración, 93, 101
"Regreso a Acteal" (Aguilar Camín), 232
Relación de Cholula (Acuña), 308n4
"Relación del doctor Hernando de Robles sobre la Guerra de los chichimecas," 182–83
Relación Geográfica. *See* Cholula map, in Relación Geográfica (1851)
Relectio de dominio infidelium & justo bello (Vera Cruz), 201
repartimiento, noble classes and, 284n47
repetition, and recurrence of revolutionary movements, 264
republican period, coopting of pre-Columbian past by, 2
Requerimiento, 71, 72, 181, 197, 214
resistance models, effectiveness of, 67
resistance preceding power, 103–4, 113
respect, ethic of: Mexican government's learning of, 84; and new politics, 84–85; and subaltern discourse, 83, 84
resurrection, as trope in Mesoamerican historical writing, 205, 209, 211
retrocedere, 176, 201
revisioning of insurgencies outside of elite discourse, 35
revolution: indigenous right to, 56; Kant on, 114; necessity of, Marcos on, 55; need to recuperate memory of, 56–57; role of folklore in, 44; role of intellectual work in, 44. *See also* insurgency
revolutionary spirituality, 170–71; among Las Abejas, 165–70; in *Vida y sueños de la cañada Perla* mural, 161–63
revolutionary thought: impact of 20th century events on, 1; tension between constituent power and will to control in, 96
revolutionary violence: APPO and, 255–56; Benjamin on, 255; EZLN and, 258; and indigenous uprisings, 270; Lenin on, 269; Lloyd (David) on, 263; need for, 279; retention of capitalism framework and, 275; and withering of state, 257
Rimbaud, Arthur, 261–63
Rivera, Librado, 93
Robertson, Donald, 20
Rodríguez, Ileana, 281n1
Rodríguez Castañeda, Lazaro, 88, 90–91
Rojas, Gabriel, 149, 151, 152–53, 155–56, 308n4
Rojas, Rosa, 87
Rolando, Mayor, 40–41, 51
Romo, Pablo, 165
Ruiz, Samuel, 40, 50, 245, 247, 310n31
Ruiz, Ulises, 254, 255, 319n2
rumor, role in Tlaxcala riot of 1692, 29–31
Russian revolution, and withering of the state, 266

Sahagún, Bernardino de, 22, 26, 68–69, 72, 107, 214, 215, 224
La Saison des hommes (film), 300n84
Salinas de Gortari, Carlos, 46, 49–50
San Cristóbal de las Cassas, assault of, 109
Sandinistas, defeat in 1990 elections, 41, 403n6
Sanjinés, Jorge, 303n12
Sarlo, Beatriz, 235–36
Schmitt, Carl, 255, 261, 265, 270
Schroeder, Susan, 210
Searle, John, 308n10
Seguridad Pública (Public Security), and Acteal massacre, 230
Seler, Eduard, 38
self-determination, right of, government recognition of, 94
Sen, S. N., 44, 81
Séptima relación (Chimalpahin), 219–20
Sermonario (Bautista), 225
Service and Adventure with the Khakee Ressalah (Dunlop), 44, 81
Sexta declaración de la Selva Lacandona, 8–9, 281n6
Sigüenza y Góngora, Carlos de: critical views on, 27–28; description of Tlaxcala riot of 1692, 27, 109; fear of insurgency, 28; lost works of, 283n22; racism of, 19, 28; rescue of national archives, 27; Tezozomoc and, 211. *See also Alboroto y motín de los indios de México*
"Si me permiten hablar. . ." (Barrios de Chúngara), 127–28
Sindicato de Trabajadores del la Educacción (STE), 319n2
singularities: and autonomization process, 146–47; multitude as erasure of, 146; neoliberalism's inability to accept, 143
Society against the State (Clastres), 200
Sommer, Doris, 35, 83, 84
South Asian Subaltern Studies Collective: Gramsci and, 403n6; ideas present at origin of, 130–33; teleological reasoning in, 131
The Southern Question (Gramsci), 133, 139
soviets of mass intellectuality, 112–13
Spanish colonial rule: binary of, *vs.* Enlightenment binary, 105–6; Chimalpahin's criticisms of, 224; codification of indigenous laws and customs, 70; as colonialism, 283n34; desire to understand Indian culture, 70; disinclination to claim historical exclusivity, 70; as dominance without hegemony,

72; as effort to prevent apostasy, 201; fear of rebellion, 107; increased consumption of *pulque* under, 32–33; Indian negotiation of place in, 185–88, 189–90, 191–94; interest in Nahua history, 107; legality of, 201; protections against appropriations of Indian lands, 105; recognition of historical nature of indigenous documents, 174–75; Vera Cruz on, 201–2. *See also* Tlaxcala riot of 1692

Spanish conquest: and Franciscans' historicist conception of God, 216; legality of, 200–202, 203

Specters of Marx (Derrida), 111

speech, *vs.* voice, 313n6

Speech and Phenomena (Derrida), 314n6

Spivak, Gayatri Chakravorty: binary thought in, 105–6; critique of Foucault and Deleuze, 60–61, 132; critique of Indian subaltern studies, 82; danger of quick response to, 296n44; on epistemic violence, 132, 303n23; on Guha, 140; on historical location of colonialism, 104–5; on internationalization of historiography, 46; metalepsis in, 105; on subaltern speech, 4, 66, 81, 105–6, 132, 282n1; teleological thinking in, 132–33; on unlearning of privilege, 37, 39

spontaneity: and conscious leadership, 158; critique of, 125; Gramsci on, 126–27, 133, 157–59; Lenin on, 128; Marxism on, 132. *See also* aporia of spontaneity and vanguardism

state: new politics and, 85; possibility of discourse outside of, 3; protection of capital as *sine qua non* of, 251; Zapatista avoidance of, 142

state, destruction of: Acteal massacre calls for justice as effort toward, 230; Negri on, 112; Zapatistas on, 112

state, withering of: in Bolivia, 272; García Linera on, 252; Lenin on, 10–11, 266–69; and redirection of history, 16; and willingness to undo ties to capital, 252; and withering of law, 266–71, 277–78; in Zapatista revolution, 6, 8, 281n6

The State and Revolution (Lenin), 10, 268, 269, 279–80

"State Crisis and Popular Power" (García Linera), 323n65

state of emergency. *See* exception, state of

State of Exception (Agamben), 254

STE. *See* Sindicato de Trabajadores del la Educacción

Stories in Red and Black (Boone), 305n7, 313n1

subaltern(s): choice to remain outside history, 4–5; and class-consciousness, 82; fear of insurrection engendered by, 67, 73; groups included in, 48; history of transformations in concept, 78–84, 89; impossibility of speaking, 4, 60–61, 66, 81, 105–6, 132, 282n1, 296n4; lack of historical self-awareness in, 80–81, 126; lack of inherent goodness, 302n7; production of as object of knowledge, 45; recovery of place in history, 45, 81, 84; as relational term, 77

subaltern discourse: silences in, 83, 84; *vs.* subaltern studies, 60

subaltern insurgency: in *Alboroto y motín*, 19, 26; delimiting of in colonial discourse, 28; history as effort to neutralize, 141

subalternity, ethics of reading, need for, 58

subaltern studies: agenda of, 45–46, 56–57; avoidance of teleological reasoning in, 125; and colonial discourse, need for inventory of forms of, 45, 56–57, 60; and conceptualization of multiple possibilities

of creative political action, 80; contributions of, 3, 5; and culture of conquest, 60; definition of intellectual work in, 80; early *vs.* later forms of, 4; historical and epistemological limits in, 66–73; on inadequacy of progressive models of the 1960s, 41; introduction to Latin American studies, 3–4; negation in, 287n26; nonvanguardist union of political movements as utopian horizon of, 46; and postmodern theory, 42; and reason, conceptions of, 45–46; rejection of Cartesian epistemology, 45; revisioning of insurgencies outside of elite discourse, 35; *vs.* subaltern discourse, 60; on Tlaxcala riot of 1692, 28; as unlearning of privilege, 67; vanguardism in, 78

subaltern subjects, constitution through dominance and coercion, 42

subsumption of labor to Capital, transition from formal to real, 112

subversion: as destruction of violence, 112; Negri on, 112

Surrealist Manifesto (Breton), 262

Swanton, Michael, 156–57

Tacho, Comandante, 51, 55, 60, 84, 120, 163, 239

Tagore, Rabindranath, 140

Taniperla, mural in. *See Vida y sueños de la cañada Perla* (mural)

Taylor, Charles, 322n64

Teaching Rebellion (Denham and CASA Collective), 255–56, 319n2

teleological reasoning: avoidance of, in subaltern studies, 125; in comparative frame in subaltern studies, 135; in Gramsci, 124–31, 133, 138–39, 157–59; in Marcos, 306n11; in South Asian Subaltern Studies Collective, 131; in Tezozomoc, 173, 216–18, 223. *See also* comparative frame in subaltern studies

teleology, of modernity, 5–6

Tello, Antonio, 179, 180–82, 184–85, 203–4

Tena, Rafael, 225

Tenamaztle, Francisco: case at Council of the Indies, 191–94, 196–98; in Chichimec Rebellion of 1541, 178, 180–81, 190; monumentalization of, 194–96, 195; as without history, 196–98, 202–3

Tepoztlán, feast of the Virgin of the Nativity, 87–88

Tepoztlán rebellion (1995): cause of, 76; compatibility of modern and nonmodern culture in, 88; and concept of subaltern, 77–78; constitutionality of municipio libre, 88; and emergent hegemony of the diverse, 84; folklore as component of, 85; impossibility of the local in, 88; installation of new government, 76–77, 88; as localization of global issues, 76; and new politics, 88; newspaper accounts of, as reflection of outside world, 77; NPR report on, 85–87, 89; renunciation of municipio libre status, 90; as subaltern struggle, 75; Tepoztlán elections following, 90–91; violence and injustices surrounding, 89–90

Tercera relación (Chimalpahin), 222

Teresa de Avila, Saint, 200, 223–24

terrorist, as term, 276–77

testimonial documentaries: conventions of, 246, 318n16; as political interventions, 234; and politics of truth, 234–38

testimony: Las Abejas *testimonio* on Acteal massacre, 165–70, 167; *vs.* archive, 205; epistemological limits of, 235–36; as genre, 318n16; and politics of truth, 234–38

Tezozomoc, Hernando Alvarado, *213*; and annalist tradition, 205; as *auctor*-witness, 210–11, 228; biography of, 221; Christian identity of, 206–7; comparative method of, 210; deconstructive reading of, 314n6; definition of task, 209–10; inscribing of Mesoamerican history into Christian history, 212–18, 228; and memory as archive, 207, 229; and Mesoamerican historical tradition, 228; preservation of speech forms in, 228; relationship to Chimalpahin, 208; teleological reasoning in, 173, 216–18, 223; work of, as hybrid cultural form, 206–7; work of, as response to colonial expropriation of past, 205. *See also Chronica Mexicayotl*

theory, dialectical relation with movements outside of historico-philosophical outlooks, 80

"Theses on the Philosophy of History" (Benjamin), 253

Thomas de Kempis, 200–201

Tierra Sagrada en Zona de conflicto (Martínez, 2000), 231, 242

Time and the Other (Fabian), 142

Tlacochalca, 219

tlacuilos (painter-writers), 20, 62; characterization of, in Codex Mendoza, 23, 26, 35; resistance by, 35; role of, post-conquest, 19, 22

Tlatli, Moufida, 300n84

Tlaxcala riot of 1692: anticolonial agenda in, 29–31, 33–34; causes of, 30, 31, 33, 34; delimiting of in colonial discourse, 28; Indian idolatry and magic in, 33–34; interracial alliances in, 28–29; mobilization strategies in, 30; rejection of Catholicism, 29, 32; role of rumor in, 29–31; role of Spanish lower classes in, 29–30; role of women in, 29, 31, 32; Sigüenza y Góngora's description of, 27; strategic deployment of noise in, 34; strategic frightening of Spaniards preceding, 31; subaltern nature of, 33; subaltern studies perspective on, 28

Tojolabal world, as hybrid world, 67–68

tonalamatl, 38, 64–65

topiles, 256, 268

totalitarianism, and state of exception, 254–55

Tovar, Juan de, 26, 228

Toward Perpetual Peace: A Philosophical Project (Kant), 114

"Towards the Mountain" (Gleason, 1999), 231, 239, 240

Tractatus de apostasia (Wyclif), 176–77

transcendental theory of foundation, and limits of constituent power, 113–14

translation: coexisting multiple worlds and, 68–69; recognition through, 72–73

transnational interests: appropriation of indigenous knowledge, 103; local as site of resistance to, 88–89; logic of invincibility of, 85–86; Tepoztlán rebellion (1995) and, 76

Trinidad, Comandante: addressing of government prejudices by, 84; and colonial forms of writing violence, 60; and enlightened de-enlightenment, 71; and framing of dominant system, 71; and government monopoly on rationality, 67; hybrid world of, 67–68; and multiple worlds, coexistence of, 65–66, 69, 73; negotiations with government, 52, 61; and problem of translation, 68; and theorization, 163; visibility of, 51

Tzotzil, understanding of video technology, 231

UNAM. *See* Universidad Nacional Autónoma de México

UNESCO, U.S. withdrawal from, 75–76, 285n2

Universidad Nacional Autónoma de México (UNAM), 38–39, 84–85

University of Minnesota, 103

Urzúa, Camú, 286n9

The Use and Abuse of History (Nietzsche), 18–19

usos y costumbres: and alienation of Indians, 104; demands for recognition of, 104; and elections of 1997 in Tepoztlán, 90–91; history of, 104; as protection for Indians, 104; Spanish codification of, 70; *topiles* and, 256

Valdez Ruvalcaba, Sergio (Checo), 102–3

vanguardism: of Gramsci, 124, 125–26, 157, 303n16; intellectual elite and, 59; of Negri, 145; in subaltern studies, 78; Zapatista avoidance of, 163. *See also* aporia of spontaneity and vanguardism

vanguard party, need for, 295n31

Vásquez, Genaro, 100

Velasco, D. Luis de, 189, 191

Velasquez Tlacotzin, don Juan, 212

Vera Cruz, Alonso de la, 197, 198–202, 203–4

Vicente (documentary subject), 244, *244*, 245

Vidal-Naquet, Pierre, 230, 233

Vida y sueños de la cañada Perla (mural), 92–93; aporias within, 120–21, 122; and autonomization process, 112–13; description of, 92–93; destruction of, 103, 304n38; as embodiment of communalism, 100–101; immanent history in, 161; recurrence of liberatory impulses in, 104; revolutionary spirituality in, 161–63; right to self-determination expressed in, 117; symbolism of, 100–101, 136–37, 161–63

Viezzers, Moena, 127, 128

violence: colonial, aesthetic of, 59; colonialist discourse on, 59; García Linera (Alvaro) on, 271; Marcos on, 295n31; Negri on, 102, 111, 112; subversion as destruction of, 112; Zapatistas views on, 57–58. *See also* epistemic violence; revolutionary violence; writing violence

Virno, Paolo, 100, 146

Vitoria, Francisco, 197, 200

Vocabulario en lengua castellana y mexicana y mexicana y castellana (Molina), 305n7

voice: identification of, 313n6; *vs.* speech, 313n6

Votán Zapata, 38, 106–7, 109–10, 137, 161–62

"Vox Clamans in Deserto" (Nancy), 314n6

Vyshinsky, Andrey, 266

Walker, Cheryll, 58

Walker, Janet, 236

war of extermination against Chichimecs, 184–85, 203; justifications for, 182–84, 202–3

warriors, Indian, fighting for Spanish: in Chichimec Rebellion of 1541, 185–90, *188*–89; indigenous pictorial descriptions of, *188*–89, 188–91, *191*

Western discourses: possibility of discourse outside of, 3; thinking, in non-Western categories, 122

West–non-West binary opposition: coexistence of, 97; and constituent power, 100; and European philosophy, 294n18; limitations of Western and non-Western identity in, 98

"What Is an Author" (Foucault), 58

What Is To Be Done? (Lenin), 10, 101, 125, 128, 268

The Wilkomirski Affair (Mächler), 235

Williams, Raymond, 279

without history: as amphibology, 172; as challenge to hegemony of modern, 143–44, 171; in Codex Telleriano-Remensis, 172; conceptualization of society existing as, 274–76; efforts to deny, 5; guerrilla efforts to expand, 143–44; indigenous choice of, as option in colonial period, 203–4; indigenous peoples' place in, 14; interpreting exclusion from history as, 142–43; leftist governments and, 252; Paris Commune and, 267; possibility of discourse in, 3; possibility of indigenous autonomies in, 278–80; possibility of remaining within, 14–15; presupposition of, in concept of history, 13–14; role in forestalling history, 16; state of exception and, 265; subalterns' choice to remain in, 4–5; Tenamaztle as, 196–98; writing of history as production of, 12, 15; Zapatistas and, 14, 198

Wolf, Eric, 138

Womack, John, 46, 47

women: leadership in indigenous rebellion, 48; leadership in Zapatista movement, 52; participation in Zapatista movement, 52; role in Tlaxcala riot of 1692, 29, 31, 32

women's issues: constitutionalization of indigenous autonomies and, 119; Marcos on, 300n84; in *Vida y sueños de la cañada Perla* mural, 100–101; Zapatista interest in, 52, 89, 95

writing, as technology for conquering colonialism, 169

writing in reverse, 28, 57

writing violence in colonialist discourse, 17–18; and construction of other forms as devoid of reason, 59, 285n1; instances of, 19; maintaining the possibility of the impossible within, 59; need for inventory of forms of, 45

Wyclif, Johannes, 176–77

xiuhamatl, 205

xiuhpohualli, 224, 225

Young, Robert, 66

El Yungue (The Anvil), 253

Zabedo, Comandante, 120

Zapata, Emiliano: and aporias in Zapatista revolution, 122; endurance of legacy, 47; and imaginary of insurrection, 109; land claims of, 47, 105; repossessions of haciendas and factories, 93; semiotic identities of, 99, 100, 104; in *Vida y sueños de la cañada Perla* mural, 92, 93, 100–101, 136, 161–62; and Votán Zapata, 38, 106–7, 137, 161–62

Zapata revolt of 1910: Flores Magón and, 92–94; repossessions of haciendas and factories, 93, 137, 139; utopian element in, 48

Zapatismo: as new vanguard, 78; non-Western rationalities in, 39–40, 285n2; parallelisms with Negri, 96–113

Zapatista Army of National Liberation. *See* Ejercito Zapatista de Liberación Nacional

Zapatista discourse: as beyond rationality, 100, 113; compatibility of modern and nonmodern culture in, 39–40, 76, 100, 134, 137, 138, 285n2; and emergent hegemony of the diverse, 84–85; and enlightened de-enlightenment, 69; interpretations of, privileging of Marcos in, 40; as learning process, 84, 88–89; as otherness, 97–98; tension between constituent power and will to control in, 96

Zapatista goals: impossibility of, 58; and necessity of revolution, 54–55

Zapatista movement: efforts to explain away, 53; founding of, 67; histories of, 286n9; women's participation in, 52

Zapatista political forms, immanent history in, 163–65, 170

Zapatista revolution: as anti-capitalist revolution, 7, 8; and aporia of spontaneity and vanguardism, 126; aporias within, 122; as articulation of indigenous life forms, 117–18; and autonomization process, 138; call for, as outside history, 14; causes of, 50–51; and constituent power, 117–18, 258–59; development of new forms of, 102; goals of, 55–56; government's inability to understand, 40–41; impossibility of, 40, 54; indigenous spirit of, 6, 8–9; intellectuals' views on, 127; internationalization of, 76, 117, 143; as new mode of revolution, 9; and Paris Commune duration, 270; political practice of, 6; as proposal of alternative government form, 5; withering of state in, 6

Zapatistas: autonomization process and, 146–47, 309n30; avoidance of vanguardism, 163; awareness of global politics, 50–51; claims of sovereignty, 197; communalism of, 306n12; and comparative frame in subaltern studies, 134; and concept of subaltern, 77–78; and constituent power, 113; demands for dignity, 51–52; on destruction of state, 112, 114–15; efforts to infantilize, 49–50; folkloric understanding of revolutionary agency, 37–39; groups supporting, 48; influence of Flores Magón on, 93–94; *mandar obedeciendo* maxim of, 76, 136, 142, 270, 276, 306n12; and multiple worlds, coexisting, 65–66, 69, 73, 164, 171; on neoliberal war against humanity, 145–46; parallels with Marxist projects, 137; and patriarchy, rejection of, 248–49; and plurality of worlds, 239; relationship to Las Abejas, 240, 245, 317n1; self-conscious subalternity of, 40; and state, avoidance of, 142; view of history, 47, 57–58; views on violence, 57–58; as without history, 198. *See also* Comité Clandestino Revolucionario Indígena, Comandancia General; Ejercito Zapatista de Liberación Nacional

Zasulich, Vera, 273, 274

Zedillo Ponce de León, Ernesto: Acteal massacre and, 233, 235, 238, 239, 246, 250; and Indian rights, 95; Tepoztlán rebellion and, 90

Zibechi, Raúl, 272–73, 274, 276

Žižek, Slavoj, 299n74, 301n89

Zumárraga, Juan de, 215–16